REPORTS FROM HELL

REPORTS FROM HELL

CHAS SMITH

Rare Bird Books
Los Angeles, Calif.

THIS IS A GENUINE RARE BIRD BOOK

Rare Bird Books
453 South Spring Street, Suite 302
Los Angeles, CA 90013
rarebirdbooks.com

FIRST HARDCOVER EDITION

Set in Dante
Printed in the United States

10 9 8 7 6 5 4 3 2 1

Library of Congress Cataloging-in-Publication Data

Names: Smith, Chas, 1957- author.
Title: Reports from hell / Chas Smith.
Description: Los Angeles : Rare Bird Books, 2020
Identifiers: LCCN 2020013233 | ISBN 9781644280751 (hardback)
Subjects: LCSH: Smith, Chas, 1957—Travel—Yemen (Republic) | Qaida (Organization) | Surfing—Yemen (Republic) | Yemen (Republic)—Description and travel.
Classification: LCC DS247.Y42 S65 2020 | DDC 953.305/3—dc23
LC record available at https://lccn.loc.gov/2020013233

To Circe Wallace, Maria Bangu, Chrystina Woody
and your almost endless patience.

PART ONE

PROLOGUE

Miami, Yesterday

I'M STANDING IN THE RIGHT WING OF A Baz LUHRMANN–DESIGNED theater behind a luxurious velvet red curtain with General David Petraeus, who happens to be telling me about Syria, and I'm nodding along but mostly thinking that he is not as short as everyone says. His biceps, knotted little balls sticking out of a shiny gray polo shirt, pull most of my focus. His skin is that waxy, shiny, taut thing that happens to people who work out compulsively in subscription gyms—but he seems normal, at least height-wise. Maybe even above average. Everyone had said he was really short. Like, exceptionally short.

On stage, a hedgefund manager is talking about shorting Warren Buffett's company, Berkshire Hathaway. Or actually he's saying that he would never short Warren Buffett while also saying that Berkshire Hathaway's stock will lose at least 15 percent of its value when Buffett steps down as chairman and that he is basically two hundred and thirty years old and might step down any day, so it sounds to me like he is talking about shorting Warren Buffett.

The room is filled with other hedgefund managers scribbling furious notes as titans of finance, political insiders, professors, doctors, and billionaires discuss the state of the world at a very exclusive, invite-only financial conference in Miami's just-opened Faena Hotel. There is a $20 million penthouse up top and a $20 million Damien Hirst–gilded wooly mammoth in hurricane-proof glass out front.

And General David Petraeus is sharing with me that Syria will likely never again unify, but he's doing so in a small-talky sort of way. After the brave man calling bullshit on Buffett's empire is finished, I'm supposed to interview the general onstage about current events in the Middle East and how they affect international marketplaces. I'm also supposed to be calling him "general" but he's not a general anymore unless "general" is like "doctor" and you get to keep the title even after being unceremoniously shown the door and retiring to save whatever face you used to have.

Either way, he earned it.

After graduating from West Point, he'd served in Haiti and Bosnia before being promoted to general and heading off to Iraq, distinguishing himself in both combat and the nation-building that followed. After, it was off to command the US forces in Afghanistan then retired from the military and became the director of the Central Intelligence Agency. That's where he had a steamy affair with his biographer, Paula Broadwell, and lost everything except his handle.

Of course, I'm not supposed to ask him about the affair, but really, and I say this even as a famous-in-some-circles surf journalist, who cares? The appetites and foibles of powerful men are as interesting and unpredictable as American Treasury Bonds, which I just learned about two speakers ago and which are neither interesting nor unpredictable. The narcissism that it takes to climb to the top—the drive, ambition, self-obsession, and the self-belief—is an utterly knowable phenomenon.

His voice is quiet yet authoritative. He delivers easily digestible, easy-to-understand drips of Middle Eastern insight that I imagine rack-rate conference-goers crave, though he isn't looking at me but rather studying the printed notes in his hand instead. They are the questions I'm supposed to ask him once we go out onstage, ones submitted in advance, but I was drunk when I wrote them a week ago, so I can't remember what they are. I try to steal a glance, but the only one I can see reads, "Oil?"

He has transitioned now and says something about Hezbollah's interference in regional stability and I accidently snort. He stops suddenly and fixes me in his steely eyes. They're piercing, almost like a bird's, and I wish he would stop looking at me again.

To break the tension, I say, "Oh. I've spent some time with Hezbollah." The stare intensifies and I want him to go back to looking at my drunken questions while patronizingly walking me through the current state of Syria's union but add, "They kidnapped me and my best friend, Josh. Or not really *kidnapped*, but they did blind us, stick pistols to our temples, drive around for a bit, throw us in a blood-smeared dungeon, interrogate us, and then feed us a delicious dinner."

He cocks his head slightly and now I'm stuck, so I just start rolling out the story.

"Okay, so do you remember when Al Gore launched his television channel Current TV in the mid-2000s? I can't think of why he did it or who his partners were, but anyhow, along with my best friends Josh and Nate, we were sent over by Current to Lebanon in 2006 to cover the Israeli invasion because, well..." and I pause trying to do the math. His expression hasn't changed. "...right after 9/11 we were the first people to ever surf mainland Yemen and while we were there sort of stumbled onto the headwaters of violent anti-state radicalism…or, wait, we found that the second time we were in Yemen, riding motorcycles through Osama bin Laden's ancestral village, which we were only doing to get to India and this madrassa where that ideology had metastasized but got all screwed up because Josh saved me from a life spent trying to be famous and decided we needed to kidnap a monkey in Bombay and take it to Pakistan first…or not kidnap but somehow *procure* a monkey in Bombay and take it to Pakistan because in Pakistan he would be truly revered and live a better life but…sorry, that was right after Lebanon."

My mouth kept moving and the words kept coming out, even though they all sound patently ridiculous even to me, even though I lived them. Like, what the hell was Al Gore thinking when he launched a premium cable network channel in the mid-2000s? Especially one built off user-generated content? Hadn't he foreseen the Internet and/or invented it?

In any case, a producer at Current had read some of our adventure stories, reached out and asked us if we'd consider doing a bit for them, possibly a series or host a segment. "Pods" is what they called them, and they were basically YouTube videos for cable television before YouTube videos existed. Tensions between Hezbollah and Israel had just started to flare with Hezbollah snagging two Israeli soldiers and Israel threatening full-scale invasion. We told him that the only thing we were interested in was the impending war. They agreed at once and Josh and I were thrilled because we had signed a development deal at Fremantle Media the year before as they had also wanted to make a show about our adventures, partying with terrorists, etc., but things had taken a very ugly turn and devolved into a show about us going to Timbuktu in order to discover new musical acts.

We gave them an ultimatum—either let us go and cover a real war or let us out of our deal—which seemed a fine scenario, all things considered, and it worked like a charm. They balked, insisting that the musical acts of Timbuktu would shine if we would only give the concept a chance, but they understood our bloodlust. We recruited our other best friend, Nate, who had just finished his master's degree at American University of Beirut in political studies, and found ourselves on an airplane to Amman, Jordan, just two weeks later, right after Israeli bombs had rendered Beirut International useless.

"...so we found a cab driver in Amman who agreed to drive us into Syria," I continue to tell the general, "then we headed over the border to Beirut even though the border had been totally bombed out. But the driver started to get cold feet as we got farther and farther away from Amman because he said our giant shiny Mylar surfboard coffin strapped to the cab's roof would look like missiles or something nasty to the Israeli jets that were running around-the-clock sorties..."

Now General David Petraeus is really staring at me.

Going all the way back to Yemen, Bombay, and Amman to get to the damned Hezbollah kidnapping story was misguided in retrospect, but as I was thinking about it again, why had we brought surfboards with us in the first place? I mean, obviously to surf, but the war happened in the summer and the Mediterranean that laps Lebanon's coastline is as flat as a pancake from late spring to late autumn. The only possibility of surf, which we had gotten pretty good on a few different occasions, was middle winter, when the seasonal storms were violent enough to whip the sea into little head-high nuggets. We'd had some honest-to-goodness fun sessions in Lebanon, though I pry my mind away from remembering them so I don't spin General David Petraeus out any further.

"...but that guy had a brother or cousin or brother-in-law in Syria who agreed to finish the job, so we bundled into his cab and he was furious about the surfboards but also had a small Chinese or Korean van. You know the ones, right? I'm sure they were all over Iraq when you were there. Those super micro vans that they love to stuff forty adult males into throughout the Middle East. Yeah?"

General David Petraeus dips his head slightly in agreement, though his eyes have lost none of their intensity.

"Well, he called that in and figured we would put the damned surfboards inside the van and away from prying Israeli pilot eyes once we arrived at the border, which was a total junk show when we did. It was crowded with all sorts of displaced people and so bombed out and smoldering that his small Japanese van wheels had an impossible time and we had to get out and lift the damned van and our surfboards and the driver over the bigger craters. We were sweating like crazy, and I had an awful haircut then that made me look exactly like Ellen DeGeneres but we made it, somehow, to Beirut where our first stop was Europcar, where we rented an Audi A4 because we figured that was the only right way to cover a war..."

He thinks I'm an idiot. I can tell he thinks I'm an idiot because I'm telling him about an Audi A4 and I would think I was an idiot too. He's a decorated veteran who cut his teeth in Iraq, took towns under fire while bravely sitting shotgun in a Humvee with his jaw set and his eyes birdlike, scanning the horizon. I mean, I guess he's short, though not *that* short. A Humvee is the sort of car General David Petraeus drives, though. Humvees or maybe Dodge Durangos. Something big and American. But it's true. We had rented an Audi A4 because we figured that was the real way to cover a war, Anderson Cooper and the rest of them be damned. We would have rented a Porsche 911 if they had had one. It really was crazy that Europcar was open at all, much less renting cars, to say nothing of renting them to us. It was still in the very early days of the Israeli bombing campaign and I don't think they had even sent troops across the border yet, but it was still a war, and what in the world were we doing there? Why did those Lebanese Europcar employees think we were there? They certainly didn't ask too many questions, though we would later supplement our Audi A4 with two motor scooters because we realized quickly, and should have realized in the small Japanese van, that bomb-cratered roads are an absolute pain in the ass. We wanted the scooters to be motorcycles, cool James Dean café racers, but we couldn't find any and had to settle for ugly Chinese toys.

"…and Josh and I were on our scooters because we had just ridden them from Beirut to Damascus to deliver our MiniDV tapes to our editor back in the States, who was a lunatic, and we had spent our entire budget on champagne and children's Halloween costumes, but since the airport was all bombed out in Beirut, and since Israeli intelligence was snooping on every piece of mail coming out of Lebanon, it was our only play. The thing was supposed to be 'current' after all.

"Man, that was a savage run. Israeli drones strafed us as we throttled across the Beqaa at midnight. You could hear them coming. Hear them like giant mosquitos looking for blood…oh, and Hezbollah had gotten ahold of us on that run too but let us go because they assumed the Israeli Air Force would take care of the job for them. But we made it, dropped the tapes, slept for a few hours, had Bloody Marys in Damascus's brand-new Four Seasons, then made it back to Beirut right when we saw a huge bomb explode in the Dahieh and decided we had to scooter in and check it out…"

I feel a tap on my shoulder and swing around to see the stage manager, a kind, middle-aged Puerto Rican or possibly Cuban wearing a navy-blue H&M suit, looking at me very apologetically. "I'm so sorry, but it's time for you and the general..." He motions toward the stage.

Wow. I sure had gone off the rails there despite not wanting to begin, savoring the utter absurdity as I relived it again. General Petraeus is less into it. His eyes have transitioned from birdlike to politely interested to mildly shocked to mostly addled to dead as doornails, either because his Middle Eastern life is far more fabulous than my own, what with his leading troops into combat, knowing every secret in the CIA's vault, and sexting a biographer with an epically shiny, Botox-enhanced forehead, or because my Middle Eastern life makes no sense at all. In fact, it makes such non-sense that it forces everyone from Fremantle to the general public to General Petraeus into a catatonic, what-the-hell-are-you-on-about-I-literally-have-zero-handle-on-your-references state. *Or* because my Middle Eastern life makes his look like a dull, uninspired sitcom where the punchlines are telegraphed, the lessons are canned, and the laughter is too. A tableau of suppositions and formulae connected to reality by only the most boring strands.

In this particular case, it may be a combo of all three. I follow him onto the stage muttering, "...so then we were kidnapped by Hezbollah and I wrote about it in a surf book that mostly dealt with life on Oahu's North Shore from the perspective of a surf journalist raised in Coos Bay, Oregon..." but he doesn't hear me because he's in conference mode, soaking in hedge-fund applause while the master of ceremonies details all of his decorations and then introduces the surf journalist who will be interviewing him. We both sink into the plush chairs that have been set up for us—General Petraeus sitting ramrod straight and me all bendy and fidgety. The conference's founder thought it would be funny to throw a screwball at the audience. Something they wouldn't expect.

I'm supposed to be the screwball, but I've also seen General Petraeus's Global War on Terror from more angles than he has. I have seen it spreading across a Yemen, Syria, Lebanon, Somalia, Egypt, Jordan, Iraq, India, Pakistan, and Afghanistan that no longer exist. I have seen and experienced a world vanished forever by an epic explosion, and as General Petraeus starts to drone on about Saudi Arabia being our great ally and a great investment opportunity, I put my Tom Ford sunglasses on, slouch deeply in my chair, and stare into the burning klieg light.

CHAPTER 1

Yemen, Early 2000s

Sweat is pouring into my eyes though, I don't rub them—mostly because my fingers are covered in goat fat, but also mostly because I don't want to miss a thing. We fly past a bearded man selling a selection of floral bras and full-bottomed panties from a wooden pushcart, past a boy clutching an exotically curved knife that's close to as big as he is tightly to his belly, past a nonplussed skeletal dog gnawing on a shark head, past a ninja whose head whips around as she presses against a wall just inches away from where our Land Cruiser is now screeching around a corner into a tight alley littered with green qat shoots and torn plastic baggies all the colors of the Yemeni plastic baggie rainbow. Light green, light pink, light blue, and clear.

I start singing the chorus of the Aerosmith smash "Don't Want to Miss a Thing" at the top of my lungs, the video of which features Liv Tyler, Steven Tyler's daughter. It had been on constant rotation on all the Lebanese music video stations up in Sana'a, along with Sean Paul's "Get Busy," Jennifer Lopez's "Jenny from the Block,"

Vanessa Carlton's "A Thousand Miles," and Nelly's "Dilemma" feat. Kelly Rowland.

Nobody joins.

"How much for Steven Tyler?" I scream.

Nobody answers.

Major Ghamdan al-Shoefy hammers the gas and we rocket forward. I'm sitting directly behind him and grab his headrest to stabilize. My Spy sunglasses, which had been holding my hair up, fly backward off my head, and now my hair whips my wide-open eyes, causing even more pain, but I don't close them. Instead I belt out, "...'cause I don't want to miss a thing!" once again.

Josh, Midwestern handsome with piercing blue eyes framed gorgeously by a rich, auburn, Mandy Moore–esque haircut streaked with blond, rides shotgun, one hand on the dashboard, one hand hovering over the pistol Major Ghamdan keeps wedged in the bench seat's gap. I know he wants to grab it. I know it is taking every ounce of his willpower not to grab it and sit where the window should be, waving the pistol in the air while grimacing like Mad Max, or better yet, climb up to the roof, where our surfboards are, and lie on top of them, legs swinging this way and that while lining up our target like Frank Bullitt, still grimacing.

Nate, who happens to look exactly like Steve McQueen playing Frank Bullitt if Frank Bullitt wore a bleached fauxhawk, is typically stoic, staring out his open window in the back seat next to me. Stoic or determined. Those are the only two emotions he exudes, and they look the exact same. The only time I've ever seen him anything other than stoic or determined was when I talked too loudly in the hallway of our shared house right after college one early evening and he bellowed, "Charlie!" as if he were a grouchy dad who worked night shifts. It made me so angry that I dumped his family-size bottle of orange juice down the sink to teach him a proper lesson.

Cole, cheek full of qat, is poking at his cuticles with a tiny branch and entirely disinterested from the bitch seat. He's wearing the same outfit that he was when I met him for the first time six days ago in front of the Sana'a Arabic school, which is notable for having turned young Johnny Walker Lindh into the "American Taliban." He's rocking a Jean-Paul Gaultier pirate mélange with baggy shorts, a rakishly buttoned paisley button-up, green-tinted sunglasses, and an orange horse-and-carriage-motif'd Hermès scarf topping it all off. It's a good look overall, suiting his élan perfectly.

Johnny Walker Lindh. I chuckle to myself, remembering when ex–President George Herbert Walker Bush, father of current President George Walker Bush, described him as "some misguided Marin County hot-tubber" after he was caught fighting on the wrong side of the Global War on Terror in Afghanistan, and I begin wondering how Senior would describe us, when…BAM!

We smash through a giant divot that causes our Land Cruiser to lurch, and all of us bonk our heads on its ceiling—save for Major Ghamdan, who seems glued to his seat. Cole, in his sassiest English, moans, "Ugh, Major Ghamdan…could you, like, cool it a little?" despite Major Ghamdan not speaking English, much less the sassy varietal, and Cole speaking refined Sana'ani Arabic perfectly.

Josh has used the unexpected bounce to actually grab the pistol and pull it into his lap. Nate has used it to shift into an extra stoic forward-leaning position. I find my Spy sunglasses, which were just behind my neck.

Major Ghamdan takes the next hard left onto a street that seems too crowded for us. It's bigger than the alley but packed with locals out for a sunset shop. Men in calf-length, sarong-like skirts and wedged sandals admiring Russian-made Kalashnikovs, men in floor-length gowns and wedged sandals perusing tables with bejeweled cell phone cases, men with hiked-up skirts squatting on wedged sandals underneath umbrellas cleaning their teeth with small sticks. Not one of them changes expression as we fly by. Not one of them even seems surprised.

Josh catches a glimpse of the black Toyota Hilux we've been looking for racing down a parallel side street choked with sun-bleached signs advertising "Bower Horse" energy drink—"Bower" since Arabic doesn't have a corresponding "P" sound—and shouts, "There!" while pointing with his non-pistol hand. Major Ghamdan snaps his head that way and cranks the wheel hard to the left down another alley with signs advertising banana milk.

Not three minutes ago, the same black Toyota Hilux had pulled up next to us at a busy intersection after we had finished a goat, giant flatbread, rice, and sweet tea dinner, rolled down one of its black windows, and…

BANG!

BANG!

BANG!

BANG!

…four gunshots either across our bow or accidental misses into Aden's thick humidity. Major Ghamdan had turned his head slowly in their direction and muttered the two Arabic words that kept the West awake at night: "al" and "Qaeda." The Foundation, the Leaders, the Base. However it's translated from Arabic to English, the Islamic fundamentalist outfit achieved instant renown after one fateful September 11 day. Everyone in the world knew al-Qaeda. Everyone in the entire world. As a branding exercise, this is wildly impressive.

The Hilux sped away. Major Ghamdan followed. So now we're in a car chase, blowing through stoplights and Adeni policemen wearing all-white uniforms with black spats and black berets. Blowing past accidentally organic mango smoothie stands and upholstery stalls decorated with various rococo fabrics. Blowing past clusters of men drinking tea from white plastic shot glasses. Hitting one of them square in the shoulder, sending one white plastic shot glass flying into the air, and its owner sprawling.

The prudent thing, I suppose, would have been to flee in the opposite direction, but the Global War on Terror is still fresh. President George W. Bush had only first used the words "war on terror" five days after the September 11 attack, but how does a nation go to war against an idea or a method? What are the rules of engagement? Where is the battlefield? It is magically ill-defined, and Major Ghamdan knows better than to waste the opportunity for a grand, unhinged time. He knows that he is piloting a Land Cruiser filled with white Americans and knows, instinctively, that he can do whatever the hell he wants. The world is his oyster because, for this historical moment, it is *our* oyster, and he wants to race through a crowded city running down the bad guys. But who hasn't dreamed of Hollywood car chases? *French Connection*, *Italian Job*, *Bullitt*?

They are the true universal language. Car chases are our modern lingua franca.

The Call to Prayer rises up all around us, beginning with one lonely muezzin before turning into an absolute cacophony of "Allahu akbars" coming from all directions at once, cascading down on us like the walls and signs and dusty mountains that rise vertically in the distance, but religious duty doesn't temper Major Ghamdan's resolve. He has the Hilux in his sights now, just five cars ahead, weaving in and out of micro vans, flatbed trucks, off-brand Chinese cars, and small motorcycles loaded with entire multiple-wife families. Horns honk, the Call to Prayer drones, my eyes hurt. Out of nowhere, a technical cuts across our path, one of the all-too-common vehicles seen in movies about terrorists. A pickup truck, usually Toyota, with a machine gun affixed to its bed by a long metal post that allows its operator a clear line of sight. It slams on its brakes, nearly spilling its load of dusty soldiers onto the street.

Major Ghamdan swerves to miss it, and we end up sliding 180 degrees, pointing in the opposite direction, facing a donkey that gives us a sexy whistle through its shockingly white teeth. The Major slams the steering wheel with the palms of his hands, furious, swings his door open and bull charges into the street, arms raised over head, gesticulating and shouting, to confront the equally incensed soldiers now jumping out of the bed of their truck. They are wearing nighttime camo uniforms with white piping. Major Ghamdan is pairing a freshly pressed skirt with a new, still-creased T-shirt featuring a picture of a very cute fish.

"But, seriously, how much for Steven Tyler?" I ask again as the stifling wet heat settles back in.

Nate says, "Three."

Josh thinks for a moment, then says, "Nunce."

Cole isn't allowed to play yet.

CHAPTER 2

Surfer magazine's Dana Point bureau was only vaguely aware of Yemen prior to Josh's and my stopping by unannounced one summer afternoon in 2002. It had been just under a year since a crew of Saudis, Egyptians, Emiratis, and an almost-sympathetic Lebanese nerd hijacked four American Airlines and United Airlines flights, smashing them into New York's World Trade Center towers, the Pentagon, and a Pennsylvania field, ultimately marking the deadliest American day since Pearl Harbor.

My phone began ringing off the hook very much too early on the morning of Tuesday, September 11, 2001. I rubbed my eyes, answered annoyed, and greeted my mother, who was beside herself with grief and furious at me for spending the past year defending Muslims, even radicalized ones—*especially* radicalized ones—to anyone who would listen.

I didn't understand what she was talking about at the start. Planes hit what? Why? Who?

She told me it was terrorism. Islamic terrorism.

I had done six months in Egypt as part of a university undergraduate study abroad program and become enchanted by an idea, a reality, a way of life. As clichéd or tacky as it is to become inspired by the Hegelian "other," it had grabbed me. Egypt, fundamentalist Islam, exoticism, all of it—I dove in headfirst. "They actually believe…" I would tell anyone who would listen to my experience when I came home. "They actually believe. They're willing to go all the damned way."

"You were wrong," she said through tears. "You were wrong, and look now. Who could do this? What kind of people could do this?" She was usually coolheaded, and I was tired and confused. What was going on? She was even more furious that I was snoozing while the world burned. I flipped on the television and witnessed the unfolding coverage while she continued to demand answers. I didn't have any, and I didn't try and argue, didn't try to advance fundamentalist Islam as the grand alternative discourse to vacant Western humanism, because watching the gates of hell open live, watching news organizations piece together that it was not an accident but a deliberate act, a deliberate act carried out in the name of Islam, was heartrending. It was horrific, and for those first few minutes I hated Muslims too and regretted every life choice I had made up until that point. I didn't have the intelligence to put the horror into any sort of context, so I just sat long after my mom hung up and stared at the horror with my head in my hands.

The television rambled on, heating my self-loathing. The whole thing felt otherworldly, like it wasn't really happening. I wasn't actively listening but heard the name "Osama bin Laden" mentioned once, then twice, then nonstop as it began to materialize that he and his al-Qaeda were the number-one suspects. The same man and network responsible for bombing the United States embassies in Kenya and Tanzania in 1998 and bombing the USS *Cole* in Aden, Yemen, two years later.

He was a striking figure, tall and angular. Not necessarily menacing, with a knowing half-grin dancing on his lips and eyes that laughed. He wore a pillow on his head just like Uncle Dave, and there was something darkly compelling about the man. Something undeniably magnetic. Some bizarre calm.

Journalists and news anchors dug in, and a skeletal narrative began to form. A construction magnate grandfather born on the Hadramawt coast of southern Yemen who had emigrated to Saudi Arabia. A family deeply connected with Saudi royalty. Wealth, access, rigid belief. Bin Laden had fought the Soviets in Afghanistan, formed al-Qaeda in Sudan, and dabbled in the Yugoslav wars. It was an interesting life by any stretch, though the only words that stuck in my head were "Yemen" and "Hadramawt."

Maybe it was because of my father. Along with *Lawrence of Arabia,* he had also introduced me to *National Geographic*, and his favorite features were always about Yemen. I don't know what specifically attracted him. The history? Maybe. It might have been the Queen of Sheba's kingdom or its striking, lightly trafficked beauty. All I remember is that when issues featuring Yemen came, he would point out the pictures and we would study together. Houses that looked like they were made from gingerbread. Trees that appeared to grow upside down and bled red blood when cut. Men with stern faces and curved knives on their belts. Women who looked like ninjas, dressed all in head-to-toe black with a menacing slit for the eyes.

Yemen and Hadramawt.

I pulled down an old *Lonely Planet Middle East Travel Guide* off my homemade cinder block-and-plywood bookshelf, the same one that I had taken to Egypt a year prior, and flipped to the Yemen section. It was thin, almost nonexistent, but featured some of the same pictures that I remembered from my youth. Upside-down trees and gingerbread houses. I studied the map, the way it dominated southern Arabia, the way it almost kissed Africa, and found the Hadramawt region halfway toward Oman. I traced my finger along its coast.

The apocalypse continued to play on the television. Burning fires and terror. Confusion and utter heartbreak. Closed skies and political paralysis. I was still completely disgusted with Arabs and Islam and also with myself for falling so head over heels for the people and the religion now responsible for shifting the world off its axis. When I couldn't take it anymore, I shuffled out the door, through the Hawaiian-themed Lanai garden, and down the street toward Josh's bungalow.

He was home, packing his stodgy bag, ready to head off to UCLA for the day. I told him his Islamic studies classes were likely canceled. He looked at me, confused, and I told him what was transpiring, as he didn't have a television and also regularly preached the dangers of modern technology.

Josh didn't seem surprised. We both slumped on the couch and chatted until the sun went down. He had a long view, had just come home from Pakistan and seen the agitation, and at the end he simply said, "This is the way history works, bro. Convulsions and spasms. To imagine any different, to imagine that we are somehow removed from the long bend, is ludicrous."

He was not necessarily callous, but he was analytical, and it comforted me, allowing the pieces to reorder. Muslims weren't bad. History is filled with terror, horror, death, and destruction. I thought about that for a minute, then said, "But what do you know about Hadramawt in Yemen?"

He sauntered to his vintage midcentury modern bookshelf, featuring some sort of reclaimed wood, and pulled down an oversized atlas that he had "borrowed" from UCLA's library, opened it to the pages featuring Yemen, and we both stared at the yellowing pages.

"What ocean is that?" I asked him.

"Indian."

"Like, same Indian that bakes all those perfect Indonesian waves?"

"Same."

"Hmmmmm."

The next few weeks spooled out as expected. President George W. Bush had ordered a thundering explosion of the Taliban in Afghanistan as initial payback, snagging Johnny Walker Lindh in the rubble, and was making the case for a second front in Iraq while kicking various tires from Mauritania to the Philippines. War had been declared on terror, wherever terror made a home—wherever terror drank its tea or prayed to Allah. The world was united, coalitions built, internal security apparatuses bolstered, personal freedoms put on hold, and balled-up fists shaken at television cameras. "We will not let the terrorists win!"

"Yemen?" *Surfer*'s silver-haired executive editor Sam George asked while squinting back and forth from me to Josh then Josh to me. "Isn't that where Osama bin Laden is from?"

"Exactly." I nodded, happy that he was at least somewhat versed in terror's new and evolving narrative.

"Well, isn't it dangerous?"

"Extremely, but look here…" I motioned toward Josh, who hauled the same oversized atlas out of his briefcase and slammed it onto Mr. George's desk, flipping the pages until arriving at the Arabian Peninsula.

"So…" he said, drawing a finger up the coast from Aden to the border with Oman, "…the mainland coast should catch the same Indian ocean swell as the Maldives. There are all sorts of ancient accounts detailing shipwrecks and rough water here…"

He pointed to a giant bite near Oman. "Obviously there are waves, somewhere, and its modern exploration has been extraordinarily limited. Very few Westerners have been outside the major cities. Certainly no surfers."

A starburst bounced off Mr. George's dangly earring as he tilted his head to take in the map. Studying the undulations and exotically named towns being kissed by the Arabian Sea as he sought further clarification, he asked, "But, like, how dangerous?"

"It's the most heavily armed nation on Earth, per capita, with no central control, famous for kidnapping foreigners and its own government's troops alike," I told him. "It's where the USS *Cole* was bombed right before 9/11. Where Osama bin Laden found his true followers, who Mohammed himself also happened to praise in the hadiths, and has a particularly virulent faction of al-Qaeda growing unchecked in all the areas we'll be reconnoitering."

"Could you take a pro with you?" Mr. George asked, studying us both for the first time. "Someone who can really surf?"

Josh leaned back in his chair, shaking his head back and forth. "Out of the question."

"We're uniquely skilled," I added. "It would be impossible for some damned pro surfer to move the way we do in these lands, and we can't be responsible for his safety."

"Simply not possible," Josh emphasized again while twiddling his thumbs and looking up at the ceiling.

"Anyhow…" I interjected "…this is about finding surf, obviously, and surfing it competently, which, don't worry about that because we do, but it's mostly about interpreting our brave new world. What is this Age of Terror? What does it actually mean to go to war against it? How can we live in it? What new fun can be had in the margins? You must understand that. This trip will actually be meaningful."

"Radical Islamic fundamentalism is the new alternative discourse," Josh added.

I looked over at him and nodded. It really was, and for both of us. I'd had a brief crisis of faith when my mother called me on 9/11, but what's a best friend for if not this? If not to drag a best friend back from the precipice of sensibility and guide him back to the path of true, harsh, dogmatic belief, where "gray" is less a color than a sin?

In truth, genuine, sacrificial belief made much more sense than anything to us. We had been raised in different households but both as Christians, serious Church every Sunday, Bible before bed, not smoking or swearing or drinking or carousing Christians, and had met at a bible college with the same values. We weren't "fundamentalists," per se, as the word had become so loaded as to only be used in order to garner some visceral reaction, but we were believers, and other believers out trying to burn the world down based on faith was understandable and felt exciting. This radical Islamic fundamentalism was the most potent idea of our lifetime, and not to be there on the ground where it was bubbling from the earth, dancing with it, playing with it, splashing in it, was a possibility worse than kidnapping, sickness, or death. Walt Whitman's vision of a secular paradise on Earth had gone up in flames. *This*, whatever this actually was, was the future, and it was happening right now.

"*Surfer* magazine's readership demands a firsthand view of the new revolution. Booties on the ground," I closed, while Sam George confusedly rubbed his clean-shaven chin.

We left with the promise that a $3,000 check would be mailed in the next week or so for a feature to be published upon our return. We'd need a photographer, airline tickets, visas, special permission passes to travel through the all various tribal areas, guns, surfboards, money, a needle, and some thread.

"How are we going to get our visas?" I asked Josh as we walked toward his older Nissan pickup.

"Let's call Nate," he responded.

"What about a photographer?"

"Our man's already embedded. He's one of the best young Arabic language scholars around and just so happens to be studying in Yemen's capital."

Josh was right. Nate secured our visas within ten days. He had never surfed a day in his life, having been born and raised in landlocked Bolivia as the child of missionaries, but he could sort through seemingly overwhelming problems via his proprietary combination of steady determination and inscrutable international-speak. He had been forced to perform in a folk music troupe with his two brothers and three sisters, singing Spanish songs to the churches his family visited when they came back to the United States on furlough, and therefore had been embarrassed more in his first fifteen years of life than the average man is over a lifetime.

He didn't care about bucking societal norms, asking awkward questions, doing whatever it took. He was used to simply pressing ahead and not taking no for an answer, pressing, pushing, slowly but steadily, wearing down opposition like an Old Testament prophet. After I dumped all his orange juice down the sink to teach him a lesson about telling me what to do, he offered to give me a haircut. I sat on the porch as he snipped and realized he didn't care about emotional ups and downs. About whims. He cared about an almost extinct form of brotherhood and in never giving up.

Yemeni visas were not being given out to Americans like candy—mostly they were not being given out at all—but Nate had determinedly emailed a local Yemeni FedEx affiliate and was sent up the chain all the way to Yemen's ex-president's son, who happened to own Yemen's FedEx franchises. He told us to fly into

Sana'a and everything would be worked out no problem. He had gone to university in America, apparently, and had windsurfed at some point and therefore understood the importance of our mission, or so he thought.

In my experience, windsurfers are generally very strange folk who don't understand much of anything.

I took care of our money by convincing the failing surf brand Ocean Pacific that our *Surfer* feature about Yemen would give it credibility in this new Age of Terror and was given another $3,000 dollars—then went and got free sunglasses and T-shirts from Spy, free shoes from a brand named Savier that had Evangelical overtones, free surfboards from JC in Costa Mesa by way of Hawaii, and free surf traction from a start-up called StickGrip.

"What are we going to do with all these sunglasses?" Josh asked with six months to go until our scheduled departure. "I don't think $6,000 minus airfare, camera, and film will be enough to surf check Yemen for three months."

"We're going to wear them and look cool. Also, are you kidding me? $6,000 is an absolute fortune. I think we might even have *too* much money."

To be fair, I had never gotten near $6,000 at one time in my entire life, and so it did feel like an infinite sum. But Josh had grown up in rural Minnesota and started a construction company with his brother when he was twelve years old, smashing nails in subzero temperatures, and so he understood real costs. He took care of our other money by applying for a UCLA study grant and promising to enroll in the same Yemeni Arabic language school as our theoretical photographer.

We spent the rest of the time practicing our surf skills in Manhattan Beach, right off the pier—a.k.a. California's dirtiest and most worthless wave. A wave that could even take competent surfers and erode their ability down to adult learner level. Josh, Nate, and I bobbed in the tiny filth, paddling for closeouts, praising each other's terrible bottom turns and Nate's determined paddling when we weren't otherwise talking about fundamentalism, parsing Qu'ranic verses over Americanos, and dreaming about the adventure to come.

CHAPTER 3

"Giving Steven Tyler a zero is both rude and uncalled for..." I tell Josh as we wind our way through Aden's Sheikh Othman neighborhood, back toward Elephant Bay and our "resort" overlooking the eponymous elephant's trunk. Half-finished cinder block buildings jockey with half-finished cinder block walls, both plastered with faded posters of President Ali Abdullah Saleh promising something, or declaring some promise met, in swooping font. Men in skullcaps loll in doorways. Boys skip through diesel-scented traffic, chomping on Chiclets, chasing a mostly deflated red balloon. Four minarets from a giant mosque hover in the distant haze.

"...he's a rock legend and objectively pretty."

"Pretty if you think Julia Roberts is pretty," Josh retorts.

I had, in fact, struggled with Julia Roberts for years, finding her absolutely stunning at times (*Sleeping with the Enemy*) and finding her utterly without charm at others (*My Best Friend's Wedding*), and I stop to wonder how I feel about her at this moment in her latest film, *The Mexican*.

Cole leans forward, into the momentary stalemate. "So, Major Ghamdan, what was up with all that craziness?"

A sly smile parts his lips. I can see it in the rearview mirror, playing on his perma five-o'clock-shadowed face before disappearing just as quickly. He grumbles some long string of Arabic of which I gather ten or so words.

"Did he just say he was angry because those al-Qaeda bros were mixed juice?" I ask.

"No, he said that they were a problem," Josh and Cole correct me at the same time.

"A problem? Why are they a problem? Aren't we the problem? Does he not have any small sympathy for his people's cause?" I ask. After all, this is why we're here, or partially why: to come face to face with our new reality. To see, feel, taste, and smell what it's like to surf through al-Qaeda country, and while it is nice that our presence is noted, I need more.

Cole shrugs and makes a cheeky face, then sticks another qat shoot in his mouth.

Josh says, "He has no sympathy at all, and they're not his people. The Major is dissipated, looking for kicks, and I've punctured every other one of his creepy plans. He's been bugging me about getting booze or hookers all the way down from Sana'a. The chase was the first appropriate thing this asshole has done yet. Maybe there's hope."

Major Ghamdan al-Shoefy was not Josh's idea at all. Haitham Alaini, son of Yemen's ex-Prime Minister, owner of Yemen's FedEx franchises, Nate's epic discovery via cold-call email, had absolutely insisted we take him when we met at his estate in Sana'a three days prior, demanding, "He's my best man, guys, and I'll only feel comfortable if you have him along."

We had to oblige because, true to his word, Haitham had secured not only our visas but offered up a Land Cruiser for as long as we needed and a sailboat waiting on the Red Sea even though I told him repeatedly that the Red Sea has no surf. Most importantly, he had gotten us permission slips to travel throughout the entire country.

They were called *tasrih* and reflected both the central government's complete lack of control outside the capital and its attempt to play off tribal alliances. Yemeni soldiers may put on national military uniforms like all normal uneducated folk belonging to a nation-state should, but tribe is the only thing that truly matters here, and checkpoints are where this dance plays out. A tasrih is required to get through, but whichever tribe is manning the checkpoint didn't necessarily have to honor it. A high-level slip—from the president, for instance—could be traded in by the tribe for favors like a bridge or paved road, however.

Major Ghamdan was a well-respected military man with all that gravitas and tenor, part of Haitham's tribe, a loyal and honorable servant who also had promises of bridges and paved roads from President Ali Abdullah Saleh in his literal pocket, a fine woodland camo featuring various insignia. Haitham explained he would get us through the myriad checkpoints, tribal allegiance be damned, and we wouldn't even need to buy guns.

This directly confronted Josh's primary urge above all else to seek danger wherever and whenever possible. I had long held that his impulses were a simple knee-jerk reaction to his childhood before he started a construction company with his brother, to when his playwright sister forced him to attend musical theater performances and learn all the lyrics to *A Little Night Music* and *Into the Woods*. Or maybe it was a reaction to when his playwright sister got married in a Renaissance faire–themed wedding and forced Josh to dress up like an earnest young page in green tights and green tunic.

Self-learning was paramount in his Minnesota home. School was optional, but he had read the complete works of Rudyard

Kipling and Ludwig Wittgenstein by the time he was ten. His father didn't put parameters on what he read or how he interpreted it as long as it wasn't lazy or contrived, and then he'd head out into the woods, dreaming of adventure. Troy, his older brother, would follow along and make him climb trees, jump off cliffs, rub dirt in any wound. The torture wasn't idyllic. It was no *Walden Pond*–esque business, but it hardened the little nerd right up and gave him an unquenchable desire to prove his toughness perpetually.

"Is this about your green tunic?" I ask him.

"What?" Josh says, clearly getting annoyed, the humid heat plus missed gunshots plus my questioning his desire for confrontation no doubt affecting him. "And whatever you're on about, no. Steven Tyler is, objectively, an ugly woman, however you want to parse that, unless you think Julia Roberts smoked it in *Runaway Bride*."

"Unfair!" She didn't and he knows it. "Richard Gere is a universal ten and absolutely crushes any movie he's ever been in, including *Runaway Bride* and not limited to *Internal Affairs*, but I'll grant you it was not Julia's finest moment."

"He's a Buddhist," Nate says. "He gets a *cepher*."

Cepher being zero in Arabic.

"You don't even speak Arabic!" I yell over Cole at Nate. "These bastards don't have indefinite articles, and Richard Gere is an American hero. We would all be so lucky to look like him at eighty-five."

"Richard Gere is a total ten," Cole croons.

"That's why you're not allowed to play yet," Josh says. "And Arabic does too have indefinite articles..." He turns toward me. "They put the 'al' in al-Qaeda."

"That's definite, bro," I contend. "*The* Leaders."

"Ugh..." Cole sighs. "Whoever translated that deserves to be beheaded."

CHAPTER 4

THE SUN FINALLY SLIPS BEHIND THE JAGGED MOUNTAINS THAT GUARD Aden's rear flank as we turn past the lonely guard booth and into the Elephant Bay's almost manicured grounds illuminated by garden lights. The night is hot and still. Car horns can be heard wailing in the distance. Bathtub-temperature waves lap the sand a hundred yards in front, the cicadas hollering in the trees.

Aden would definitely *not* have surf, Josh and I had assumed during the initial planning stages, because it was tucked too far behind Africa's horn, which would effectively shadow any wave from sneaking through, but when we had arrived four hours earlier, the first thing we saw were waves. Real waves, even—waist high and running down the line. Better than any wave that has ever washed up in Manhattan Beach, California.

Neither of us could believe it, and we spent the afternoon laughing, surfing, and laughing some more while Cole posted up under an almost palapa and took photos. It was a dream. We were surfing in Yemen, and though I knew these waves wouldn't be enough for our *Surfer* magazine feature, I figured if there are waves here, tucked too far behind Africa's horn, then the rest of the country must be a veritable cornucopia and we would be the first in history to ever surf it, just like Yuri Gagarin was the first in history to ever touch space. Just like Sir Edmund Hillary was the first in history to stand on the roof of the world. Who would imagine boys from Coos Bay, Oregon; Bemidji, Minnesota; Camiri, Bolivia; and wherever the hell Cole was from being the first to do anything? All those *National Geographic* copies spread out on the living room floor, all those hours watching Indiana Jones and taking notes while the rain fell ceaselessly outside. All those damned rednecks spitting mint-flavored Skoal on my notebooks scribbled with drawings of Indiana Jones discovering the lost ark.

"Our names are going to be etched in the anals of history!" I shouted mid-surf.

"It's annals, bro," Josh corrected.

The fact that there was surf out the front required we stay the night at an astronomical seventy-five bucks per room, regardless of the fact that our budget was already severely compromised. Major Ghamdan had insisted we eat a feast at a road stop gas station/diner on the way down from Sana'a. Chicken following chicken following chicken following local Yemeni delicacy called saltah and a very heavy bill. Josh gave him a serious lecture afterward that we weren't made of money and weren't suckers. Major Ghamdan issued a knowing look, then took us to buy a small fortune's worth of good qat, a new T-shirt featuring a picture of a very cute fish for himself, and a full tank of premium gas for the Land Cruiser before driving straight to the most expensive resort in Aden that happened to have surf.

We park opposite a white two-story building that looks like it was built in the late seventies, but this is ostensibly where British officers drank their gin and tonics when Aden was part of their empire some fifty years ago, the only one to be managed directly by London. I wonder about exoticism back then. Was Aden exotic, or alongside India, Cameroon, and Canada did it feel like a little spicier version of home?

Major Ghamdan turns to me and makes one more halfhearted plea for either booze or hookers, thinking he's found a sympathetic ear for his vice, offering to take us into town again and show us an even better time, but I tell him no while Josh stands behind me shaking his head extra paternally. He shrugs and shuffles off into the night while we shuffle to our "sea view" room to watch Lebanese music videos and continue arguing about Richard Gere.

"Do you think those guys were really al-Qaeda?" I ask as we pass an almost ice machine spewing out hot air.

"Either al-Qaeda or some Yemenis just out looking for a good time," Nate responds.

"But is there a difference? I mean, all these delineations between 'terrorist' and 'non-terrorist' are easy back home. What do they mean here? Like, if I saw a pack of white bros cruising through town with damned surfboards on top of their Land Cruiser I would have shot at them too, purely on principle. If we're here hunting belief, true belief, alongside waves, how are we ever supposed to properly engage? Or is getting shot at the engagement? Is that the only honest dialogue?"

"Ugh..." Cole moans "...I would have shot at Major Ghamdan. His cute fish shirt is just one step too far."

We make it to our door, flip on the TV, and find CNN's International Edition broadcasting a story about the US–led forces continuing to search for Saddam Hussein in Iraq. He has somehow slipped out of their grasp, much like the weapons of mass destruction they also haven't found. Bush administration officials are confident that he will be apprehended soon, though, and that democracy is taking firm root in the middle of the Middle East.

I change the channel, and we fall asleep to a very expressive Lebanese woman riding a white stallion, singing about her "*habibi*," and wake up after what feels like seconds to the Call to Prayer smashing through our open windows before the sun is up. "I'm gonna start a franchise named 'Allahu Snackbar' someday and it is going to specialize in serving annoyance…" Cole says, pulling a qat-stained pillow over his sweaty head.

Josh, Nate, and I go for a sunrise dip, but the magic of these tiny waist waves has already worn off. We're itching to get a move on, hoping to make it to a little town we've pinpointed on the map called Bi'r Ali some 600 kilometers up the road. The drawing of Yemen's coastline depicts the town as being surrounded by multiple jagged coves and spits, and we figure it's our first best shot at proper surf. In order to do it in one day, though, we'll have to leave soon, but Major Ghamdan is nowhere to be found. We check his room, check the lobby, check the restaurant with a ceiling fan that almost works, check the hammock strung between one date palm and nothing else, before eventually getting too hot and retreating to the water.

Three hours later he waltzes around the corner and comes to the sand, looking the very picture of cool, out of his cute fish tee/skirt combo and back in the military uniform he was wearing when we first met him at Haitham's house, plus mirrored aviators.

"What's up, Maverick?" Cole bellows from underneath the palm-frond parasol he's fashioned.

Major Ghamdan tilts his head knowingly then motions us all over, pulling a small book from his back pocket once we arrive. "*Shoof shoof…*" he says, flipping it open and showing us pictures that he must just have had developed. They feature him in his wifebeater/skirt combo and two nondescript women dressed like chubby Midwestern boys in swim T-shirts and calf-length trunks.

One is wearing a Spy baseball hat. Picture after picture of them lounging against each other, them eating plates of fruit, them in the water, swimming where we just surfed with a bright moon illuminating what the flash doesn't. Major Ghamdan slides his aviators down his nose as he flips and grunts, "Oooooh. Veddy nice…veddy, veddy nice."

Josh flies right off the handle as Major Ghamdan reaches the middle of the book and the "veddy nices" become more sensual. "This is not 'veddy nice.' *This* is gross and *that* is my hat in the picture there. Did you give them my hat?"

Major Ghamdan doesn't answer, nor does he seem to care that Josh is apoplectic. He looks at me and raises his eyebrows suggestively while pointing with a limp index finger at one of the women. "*Shoof shoof.* Veddy nice."

"Shoof" means "look" in Arabic, and I'm not instinctively cruel like Josh, so I tell him that she seems veddy nice. Encouraged, he presses toward me, angling the book away from the others and shows me a special set of pictures. One of the women is wearing a floor-length silk nightgown and half-sitting awkwardly on the bed. The other is wearing Josh's Spy shirt.

Josh is marching around in a rage, cursing about his Spy hat despite my having never seen him wear a baseball hat in all the years I've known him, or any other sort of hat, for that matter. He was all the way physically fit and could have been a sporting type but years of on and off homeschool had wreaked havoc on any sort of natural flow with organized athletics.

"Your hat is covered in hooker sauce now," Cole tells him.

"So gross…" Josh mutters. "So, so, so, so gross."

"Okay, enough!" I interject after one too many nightgown pictures. "Josh, you've never worn a baseball hat in your life and we're burning daylight here. We've got to get to Bi'r Ali and stat.

There's gonna be absolutely epic surf. I have a feeling about this. An *instinct*, man."

Major Ghamdan suddenly turns very serious and launches into an extended Arabic monologue of which I gather ten words or so.

"Is he saying they sell mixed juice there?" I ask.

"No, he's saying there is a problem," Josh and Cole say at the same time. "Something happening in the Shabwah and we should just post up here..."

"...but over my dead body," Josh adds while glaring at Major Ghamdan. "There is absolutely no way we are going to sit in Aden while this bastard goes a-whoring."

Instinctively cruel, but also correct this time.

I agree and pound Major Ghamdan with my rusty Egyptian Arabic, joining in Josh's UCLA Arabic and Cole's sassy English, informing him that it is absolutely not possible to stay in Aden, that we are on an important mission for the most important surf magazine in the world, and does he even know what that means? Does he even know the pressure we're under? If we fail, this will come back on *his* head. He eventually caves, and we reboard the Land Cruiser as the sun reaches its smoldering peak.

Everything feels good as we peel out of Aden, heading first through the Abyan, then into the great Shabwah province. I remember reading about it before leaving—about the turmoil and its perpetual inability to be brought under heel. It was "one of the ones we should look out for," but surf was waiting, and so was the Global War on Terror. The Arabian Sea passes on our right. Rocky, gray desert on our left. The two-lane highway, freshly paved, shimmering ahead like a yellow brick road.

We motor through a town named Zinjibar that gets Josh all turned on even though it looks like every other small Yemeni town we've passed since leaving Aden: dust-colored and unfinished, but crackling with energy. He explains it must be named after Zanzibar and was certainly important during the third century's aromatics trade and that "Zanzibar" means "coast of the dark-skinned" in Persian.

I smile at my favorite autodidact and remember the very first time we ever met. There I was, sitting on the stoop of my all boys' dorm, poring over a dog-eared copy of Camus's *The Plague*, when his late-eighties Nissan pickup came screeching to a halt. He leaned out the window and shouted, "Who wants to go surfing in Mexico?"

We had never formally met, but I raised my hand then looked around awkwardly in case he was talking to someone else. There was only one other student there, the boy who led worship in chapel while wearing jean shorts. He was sitting on a bench, crooning earnest acoustic praise songs to a blonde freshman who lived in the all girls' dorm down the way. It was something about being able to sing of "your" love forever, aimed theoretically at Jesus but confusing in the moment. There was no way Josh meant that guy. He had an ankle tattoo of a Christian fish and wore jean shorts even when he wasn't leading worship.

I scrambled to my room, grabbed my very much too thin Rockin' Fig potato chip surfboard, tossed it into his truck's bed, slid into the passenger seat, and off he sped toward Tijuana. Mexico was so close, yet still it felt like a proper mission. We made normal small talk as we passed through Orange County into San Diego—which classes we were taking, books we loved, my time studying in Egypt, his recent travels around India and Pakistan—and as we drove south we also began discovering deeper truths. Namely that both of us revolted violently against any accepted academic narrative—any block of thinking that not only demanded fidelity but assumed it.

We also shared a deep starvation for adventure, a ravenous hunger, and decided as we came near *La Misión*, there on Baja's

Pacific shore, that it would be more adventurous to hitchhike than drive, so we parked his truck, stashed our surfboards on the beach, went back up to the road, and stuck our thumbs out.

It wasn't long before an old Chevy pickup rounded the bend. The driver, a fortyish-year-old man with decent stubble and a straw hat, had his twelvish-year-old son roll down his window and ask what we needed. We told him, in our best broken Spanish, that we were looking for a ride to Ensenada some thirtyish kilometers down the coast. He motioned with his head for us to hop in the bed, and off we went, just like brave explorers.

After a few minutes, we took a sharp left off the main road and started climbing a dirt track through boulders and around dry brush. Deeper and deeper we went, passing grazing goats and cement shacks before arriving, half an hour later, at a clearing. Another truck was parked there near another cement shack. The sun had dipped all the way down, and the last few shadows were doing their final dance before retreating for the night.

We were clearly not in Ensenada, had clearly never even been going to Ensenada. The driver opened his door. His son followed and then motioned for Josh and I to get out of the truck. We did, less proud but still hopeful that some great adventure was unfolding before us.

Another man holding something in his hand got out of the other truck near the cement shack and made his way over to us. Josh and I stood there, and after the two drivers had a short chat, our driver's son explained that he was buying the truck from the other man and needed us to cosign.

We looked at each other. Cosign?

The boy said, "Yes." A very staid, white, urban demand—but we did. Signed our names on the empty reserved lines, then climbed back into the bed of the truck, which turned around and ambled back down the hill.

An hour later, it was pitch black. The driver dropped us off exactly where he had picked us up and said something to his son, who translated for us, "Don't hitchhike here. It's dangerous."

And like that, their taillights disappeared into the darkness.

That night, lying on the damp sand underneath the stars on top of my sleeping bag, having drunk two defiant mini Kahlua bottles each, we decided to push further next time. To always push further.

"Speaking of aromatics…" Cole says from his heat-induced slump. "Ghamdan, pull over at the qat souq." Major Ghamdan acquiesces and turns down a little dirt road between two dust-colored buildings with rebar poking the sky and stops in an open square littered with plastic baggies, two-liter bottles of Canada Dry ginger ale, candy wrappers, and dried qat stems. Five men sit on wooden pallets underneath a roof that has no walls. One has his leg tied up like a camel in order to assist his lounging, using the tension expertly.

We all lumber out and approach the one in an off-yellow turban. He observes us casually, not surprised to find four white Americans on his coast of the dark-skinned wearing last year's Ocean Pacific samples too gauche for even Kmart. He puffs air into one cheek, points to it with a dirty finger, and slightly widens his black eyes. The Yemeni sign for "Do you chew?"

I give him an exaggerated *aiwa*—the way Egyptians say yes—and he peels back the black-and-white-checked keffiyeh at his feet, revealing the mound of hedge trimmings that dominate Yemeni life. Everything orbits around qat here. The workday has qat breaks given in lieu of lunch breaks. The houses too, with the most important feature being large rooms on the highest floor, or best floor, with a low couch running along each wall, piled with many ornate cushions called the *mafraj*, where men lounge chewing for endless hours. The main meal of the day, served at lunch, features a dish called saltah, designed to give enough energy so only one would have to be eaten each day, making more time for chewing. It is a thick, khaki stew topped with some sort of cheese substitute. Josh hated it, which meant that Nate ordered extra whenever and wherever he could.

Qat grows at the same elevation as coffee, mostly in the north of the country, but can be found in every town no matter how remote, despite needing to be chewed within twenty-four hours of being picked. The Yemenis are logistics masters when it comes to their preferred drug. True problem-solvers, really.

Cole selects a bundle and rubs the small leaves in his hand, making a frowny face, and we move on to the next seller, where the process is repeated, and we move on the next seller, the man who has his leg tied up like a camel, whose qat is Cole approved. He tries to negotiate the price in sassy English until Josh takes over and we spend another small fortune.

Back in the Land Cruiser we divvy it up and begin filling our cheeks one tender shoot at a time. The sunlight gets brighter as we chew, the rugged desert more beautifully rugged, the sea cataract-inducing shinier, the road a gossamer shimmer leading us into the very heart of the Global War on Terror.

The thoughts bouncing around in my head feel born of pure genius.

"Okay, bros..." I say while gawking at a branch completely pinned, "...when I get home I'm going to launch a new business that's whole mission will be to rate the top fast-food burger places' best burger offerings, and I'm totally serious." Everyone in the Land Cruiser bobs their heads in agreement, recognizing the obvious white space in the market for something like this. Even Major Ghamdan, whose cheek looks like Dizzy Gillespie's.

I continue, "I'm going to dig deep with all the standards, the Jumbo Jacks versus Big Macs versus Whoppers, but also all the specialty sandwiches, like the western bacon cheeseburgers and the jalapeño cheeseburgers. It's going to be a total game changer. For the first time in history there will be an accepted standard, and I can't imagine it won't raise the fast-food burger across the board. The chains won't be able to hide behind poorly executed concepts anymore."

Everyone agrees that it's a good idea and probably a great one. Even Major Ghamdan.

Three hours later, after fully parsing the lyrics to "Jenny from the Block" and attempting to nail down the true meaning of Mark 9:23–25 and discussing Oliver North's haircut, we pull up to a checkpoint featuring a barrel filled with cement and a red, white, and black Yemen flag planted in its guts, an extremely bent metal pole running across half the road, a spike strip running across the other half, and four Yemeni soldiers in naval camo lounging next to a cinder block shed. Three of them also have very chic burgundy berets.

Major Ghamdan slows to a stop. One of the burgundy berets slowly lifts himself off the dusty ground and meanders to his door, leaving a well-worn Kalashnikov behind. He exchanges militaristic pleasantries with Major Ghamdan before the conversation takes a darker turn. I come close to asking Josh and Cole if they're talking about mixed juice but stop myself and think about how little surfboard wax we've brought. Two bars? Four bars? Whatever it was, it wasn't enough, and I was going to have to institute a rationing program once I had everyone's attention, but why are we still at this checkpoint?

Providing instant clarification, Major Ghamdan spins around grimly and mumbles something about trouble, terrorists, an attack, kidnapped government troops. It would be impossible for us to continue down the coastal road. We'll have to go back to Aden. There is no other option.

Josh and I get very fussy at the mention of Aden. Cheek filled with hedge trimmings, I muster every ounce of Egyptian Arabic rage I know and blurt out, "*La, la, la, la, la. Inta wehesh awi!*" or "No, no, no, no, no. You are a very bad man!" while Josh levels a more sensible attack in UCLA Arabic, which I'm certain is equally misunderstood.

Major Ghamdan just looks at us with no expression. We both swing our doors open and go plead with the checkpoint master, pointing up at our surfboards, telling him that it's essential we continue down the coast. He studies us for a minute, looks at our cheeks, then puffs air into one of his and points with slightly widened eyes.

"Yes, we chew…" I say. "I'm Yemeni." It was a trick that worked wonders during my time studying in Egypt. I could laugh myself out of any problematic situation simply by saying, "I'm Egyptian." I got out of illegally climbing the pyramids at three in the morning, getting arrested in the subway station, and loitering outside the Muslim Brotherhood's headquarters all by claiming to be a tall, blond, Oregonian Egyptian.

When Josh and I were there together a few months later on a circumnavigation of Egypt, Jordan, and Syria, he didn't find it funny or valuable—but again, he's instinctively cruel; doesn't like shallow, cheap personality tricks; and doesn't value charm as highly as he should.

We didn't necessarily butt heads, but we did work differently. Josh would force his will on a situation, driving people to act or react toward his stated goal by daring them to come up with a better plan. I would just try to bewitch people with my undeniable charisma. It was a near perfect combination in tandem but would blow right out when both of us honestly felt our path would deliver results and/or when I got snowed by a local with more undeniable charisma than me.

"*Inta Yemeni*?" the checkpoint master says.

"*Aiwa*," I say while smiling.

Something inside him cracks, and he roams over to his compatriots and has an animated discussion before roaming back to Major Ghamdan and explaining something. I watch his hands make a path in the air. Turning left, turning right, going around a roundabout. I watch Major Ghamdan take in the information and then load back up.

"We're heading to a town called Ataq for the night. It's about 150 kilometers inland, but we won't have to return to Aden and Mr. Burgundy Beret says there's a road from Ataq that goes straight to Bi'r Ali that we can take tomorrow," Cole translates.

Josh protests slightly. We're going to miss 50 kilometers of coast, but the surf we'd seen since leaving Aden hadn't been overly impressive anyway. Mostly it was dumpy, unremarkable beach break, but the fact that we get to move forward is a net positive.

"It'll be an emprise..." Cole says. "...like Sir Gawain and the Green Knight or James Frey's misery-lit epic *A Thousand Little Pieces*."

"What's *A Thousand Little Pieces*?" Josh asks.

"Oh, how have you not read it yet?" Cole starts to launch into the explanation. "It is an absolutely fabulous book about a man going through addiction. A phenomenon. The best first-person narrative nonfiction of the decade. Just beyond."

"No," Josh replies. "I hate addiction memoirs. You know that. I will absolutely not read it."

"Why?" I demand to know. "Isn't addiction sort of fun and exciting?"

"Don't encourage him," Josh says.

"You are such a prude," Cole hisses right before reaching the Hour of Solomon, the time in the qat chew when conversation comes to a halt. When genius ideas percolate internally and no one says a thing.

I mentally finalize my hamburger consultancy and begin the first brush strokes on a plan to launch a water pipe catering business focusing exclusively on private university frat houses as I quietly munch my qat stash down to bare twigs. Outside, the sun sinks low. Our paved road has long disappeared as we wind up mountain then down mountain, dust filling the Land Cruiser cabin, dust coating Spy sunglasses, and roll past ancient rivers that had cut their way through red stone before disappearing forever.

We arrive in Ataq just in time to score the best chicken and giant flatbread dinner yet in an empty restaurant playing *The Best of Mecca* on an overhead television. Pilgrim after pilgrim all dressed in white circumambulating the black box hiding a black stone that Father Abraham planted with an extra sultry muezzin calling the action. Close-ups, pull-backs, star wipes, sweet filters.

The man making the giant flatbread doesn't seem surprised that we're here, which is something of a marvel. Back home in the United States, every Arab or vaguely Arab-looking person is regarded with austere suspicion, like he is hiding a suicide bomber vest underneath his blazer. Like she is concealing some ugly contraband underneath her hijab. Our clearly American ensembles aren't getting a second glance even though American forces are busily enacting the president's stated goal of planting democracy in the Middle East. Even though he has declared that it is America's holy mission to spread our democracy to these backward Muslims.

I wonder if this bro wants democracy. He goes about his business, keeping his forearms wet using an old coffee tin filled with water so they don't burn as he plasters family-sized-pizza balls of dough on the inside of a fire-heated metal drum.

We eat like Americans, too, stuffing our faces until we can stuff no more and making fun of each other for having small, dribbly penises thanks to the lengthy qat chew. The effects are temporary but shocking for any male first-time participant. Qat shrinks the penis and makes it dribble. The Eurasian Journal of Medicine conducted a study related to qat and erectile dysfunction but concluded that Yemen's ED problems were due to "psychological problems," so we remain unconcerned, enjoying the rare opportunity to make penis jokes without sounding unintentionally sexual.

After an orange Fanta dessert, we wander the dusty streets, passing a disco mosque with so much green neon tubing on its corners and minaret it fills the town with a Michael Jackson *Thriller* light. We find a minimart and buy Nujoom candy bars and Snickers knockoffs made from local Yemeni ingredients in Yemen and way better than Snickers, then retreat to the town's only hotel to find more Lebanese music videos and lounge like indulgent, small, dribbly-penised American buttholes.

Yemeni hotels, especially in very out-of-the-way places like Ataq, surprised me each and every time. Who was traveling here? Why? And did whoever was traveling love largeish rooms with random twin beds scattered here and there? Every out-of-the-way Yemeni hotel had random twin beds scattered here and there. Sometimes comfortable, always random.

"How much for an Enrique Iglesias, Shania Twain meatsa-meatsa?" I ask the room.

Josh says two. Nate says three. Cole says ten.

Josh says, "That's why you're not allowed to play, Cole..." while replacing his contact lenses with heavy, black-framed Coke bottle glasses.

"Cole's number is closer to the truth than either of you," I say loudly. Both Enrique Iglesias and Shania Twain are iconic.

"Neither of them are iconic," Nate grumbles, incorrectly.

We fall asleep to Shakira shaking it underneath her clothes and wake up to "Blurry" by Puddle of Mudd.

"What the hell is this racket?" I ask, still bleary-eyed. "It's absolute torture."

"Puddle of Mudd, bro," Josh says.

"They're big in Bolivia," Nate adds.

I pull myself out of bed, rinse my face, then ask if anyone wants breakfast. Everyone does, and we muster our resolve, then head downstairs to see what sort of delicious sour yogurt and hot bean combination is on offer, elbowing each other while Josh and I laugh uncontrollably about Nate's dad going to Amsterdam.

Right after we had turned inland toward Ataq, right before the Hour of Solomon, Nate had innocently mentioned that his dad had been offered a speaking opportunity in Amsterdam. Josh responded "bummer" without missing a beat, and the two of us laughed until our sides split.

I don't know why it was so funny, but it is to everyone except Cole, Nate, and Major Ghamdan, who had to pick me up off the floor of the chicken and giant flatbread restaurant last night because I was on the floor crying, holding my stomach, tears streaming out of my eyes.

Amsterdam is a bummer, honestly, and I'm asking grouchy Nate why that's not the funniest thing he's ever heard when we reach the bottom of the stairs and see the lobby packed wall to wall with Yemeni government troops all dusty, tired, red-eyed. Slouched here and there still chewing last night's qat or drinking fresh tea. Twitchy, paranoid, clearly exhausted and possibly traumatized.

Last night it was empty and the town was empty. Did they get stuck at the checkpoint like us? Where did they all come from? I ask an important-looking man with gold epaulettes standing nearest me drinking fresh tea, "What's happen now? Why so much army?"

Thankfully Cole is there to translate the meat of his answer. Supposedly, al-Qaeda had been alerted to our presence in town and had come to come finish what the blacked-out Hilux in Aden had started. The government troops rallied and met them 12 kilometers outside of town. There had been sixteen al-Qaeda. The government troops had killed them all, losing none of their own.

The whole story sounds fantastic, and I bounce between Cole's face and the important-looking man's trying to discern some joke or exaggeration, but neither betray any sort of giggle. It's all explained matter-of-factly without flourish or wild detail, and the important-looking man isn't looking for praise or any sort of compensation, which gives it an air of real truth.

I don't know how to feel. Thankful, of course, that these boys would put their lives on the line for a monumental surf trip. Guilty, too, that these boys would put their lives on the line for a surf trip, however monumental. But not that guilty. Adventure may not be on Maslow's Hierarchy of Needs, but it's universally understood at some very basic level, especially here. There has never been a question that riding waves means something. There's never even a moment's confusion as to the value of our mission.

"Well, at least we're not in Amsterdam…" Josh says, breaking the silence, and I spit my tea out in a convulsion. Nate is not amused. "But seriously. Did these bros just fight off an entire al-Qaeda… what's sixteen men called in military terms?" I ask, looking at Josh. "A phalanx?"

"No, it's not a phalanx. I think it'd be a squad," he responds.

"Platoon," Cole says.

Nate is still mad.

"Well, let's get on the road," I say. "Bi'r Ali is totally pumping right now. Barrels. We're gonna bag the cover shot today. I feel it in my bones."

We tell Major Ghamdan that it's time to move out, and for the first time he looks shaken, his eyes darting. The important man, perceiving that we are about to leave, protests vigorously, explaining that it is too dangerous out there. We shouldn't leave, but we brush off his concerns and push past him and through the door and out onto the empty streets, then sit in the Land Cruiser like kids after church waiting for parents: annoyed and fiddly.

I continue to press Nate to the very precipice of an angry break, asking if his dad enjoyed Amsterdam's famed red-light district and what he did there until Major Ghamdan comes out after a few minutes shaking his head but resigned to whatever lies ahead.

I want to know how long it will take to get to Bi'r Ali.

He grunts, "*Inshallah.*"

Good Muslims believe "inshallah" with all of their hearts. "If God wills…" God is in control and he will do what he sees fit. It's why Egyptian cab drivers drive with no brakes while reading the newspaper. Why Jordanian boat drivers smirk when their boats sprout leaks. What is man that his preparation or care will alter history's trajectory?

It is as good an answer as any, the proper answer for Muslims and Calvinists alike, and he fires the engine as we backtrack through the same terrain we'd conquered last evening. It looks Martian in the harsh morning light. Stark, beautiful, tinged with depression.

"Too bad your dad didn't have Major Ghamdan with him in Amsterdam. He would have liked it. He would have done very well there—and speaking of which, how much for Marcus Schenkenberg?"

CHAPTER 5

THE GAME HAD BEEN INVENTED A HANDFUL OF YEARS EARLIER AND honed into a most perfect way to gauge both general and specific appeal. "How much?" could be asked about any man or woman. The answer, a number between zero and ten, referred to how many nights during a double business week, or ten days with weekends off, would be spent with that man or woman. It was a contract of sorts, both unbreakable and unchangeable once stated. Intimacy was implied but the details never discussed, seeing as we were Christian gentlemen, and the contract was also morally okayed by God personally.

Its apparent simplicity belies intense complexity. Inked contracts run concurrently, for example, so participants have to be aware of personal scheduling, overall stamina, and the natural human desire for variety. The ten-day business week does not exist in a vacuum either. Work, parties, and the variances of daily life must be factored in.

The "meatsa-meatsa" or "two-for-one" is one of the real art forms, like curating a wonderful dinner party where each guest plays off the strengths of the others or makes up for the weaknesses of others. It takes a master to throw good numbers here. A black belt so in control of his facilities that he knows both parties will leave satisfied every night of the contract and he'll have energy for the other contracts plus the variances of daily life.

It's why new players are encouraged to watch from the sidelines for a few weeks before participating and why Cole keeps making the rookie mistake of giving every option a ten. There's just no way to sustain that sort of activity, no matter how debauched.

"How much for Marcus Schenkenberg?" I repeat, since nobody answers the first time.

"Zero," Josh says. "And nobody here gets as excited by tall men as you, so whatever number you throw, he's yours."

"Okay, fine. Then how much for Laura Bush?" I ask.

"I'm gonna go with six," Josh offers. "She reads a mean bedtime story."

Cole starts to say ten but Josh cuts him off.

Nate is looking out the window at the sea that's glowing off to the right, pretending he doesn't hear.

"Night Capper!" I shout. "¿Cuánto cuesta de Laura Bush?"

"Two..." he mumbles without turning toward me.

"Man, you are GROUCHY today. Josh is right. Laura Bush is very good at reading bedtime stories and it really seems like you could use one right now."

He doesn't respond.

We make it through the checkpoint with no problem, having dropped down the final mountain right before lunch—we picked up some bread, cheese, yogurt, boxes of mango drink—and then continue to press toward Bi'r Ali, which should be close now. The straight beachy coast is finding more variety—small coves bitten out, some craggy black rock formations. Josh and I keep our eyes glued to the water, looking for any possibility of swell.

The road cuts slightly inland then pops back to the water again directly at Bi'r Ali. I climb out of the window as Major Ghamdan drives, taking it in as the oven-hot air whips my face. The town is beautiful, perched on a handsome little bay. It looks like the set of an orientalist Spaghetti Western with squatty whitewashed buildings featuring exotically curved blue windows and two homes that look as if they were built from gingerbread, complete with white icing around the windows. A mosque.

Major Ghamdan pulls off onto the only road and winds down to the water's edge. Small, wooden fishing boats have been pulled onto the rocky beach. A few fishermen chewing qat laze on nets that have been stacked underneath an overhang.

We park, and Josh and I try to get to the highest vantage point, brushing away flies that are swarming in the fish scent. There are no waves, or none we can see. It appears as if the seafloor slopes too gradually, or maybe there is just no swell at the moment.

"Bummer," I say. "We are not going to get barrels today. I don't feel it anymore. You think it's too shallow here to break? There has to be a channel somewhere. You think we should stay a few days and see if it changes?"

"Let's go over there." Josh points to a large hill in the water connected to the mainland with a tiny strip of sand. "We can climb to the top and get a good look of this entire coast, then figure out our plan."

We tell Major Ghamdan, who shrugs lazily, and we heap back in, driving the Land Cruiser down the beach to the base of the hill. The water is gorgeously turquoise, the sky sandy and hot. A few Yemeni families are actually enjoying the perfect beach day, and we notice them as we get closer to the hill. The children chase each other with sticks, the little girls in burkinis, one of the little boys in a red David Beckham Manchester United jersey. The Yemeni woman is a very rare sighting in public, usually shrouded in head-to-toe black. Extremely modest. It's amazing to see them enjoying a summer's day, though I don't know if "enjoying" is the right word. Women are such a vital part of Yemeni culture, but as a Western interloper, there's no way into their lives as a male. It would be the absolute height of inappropriateness, flying in the face of culture and religion, to try to chat up a woman, no matter how innocent the intentions, and so they hover on the fringes filled with intense unknowability.

At its base, it looks like a castle, and we all get out and stare at its imaginary turrets and towers before beginning our climb. Josh leads, followed by me, Cole, and Nate. Major Ghamdan grabs his Kalashnikov and picks up the rear.

"This place was a big trading stop in the first century," Josh says between breaths.

It's not a hard climb but it is tiring, fighting against the sand that makes up the base. "What'd they trade?" I exhale. "Coffee?"

"Nope, that's all the west side. Over here it was frankincense and other beautiful things that made the ancients stink less."

"Yemenis should have gotten into the green tea business rather than coffee…" Cole says. "It has all the caffeine and doesn't stain the teeth. God knows each and every single one of them needs a serious teeth whitening."

Cole's assertion confuses me, seeing as his own teeth are falling out of his head, more or less, thanks to his ceaseless qat habit.

"Wait…" Josh says as we stop for a rest three-quarters of the way up, underneath a small rock overhang. "…green tea doesn't have caffeine."

Cole makes a cheeky face. "It sure does, Mr. First Century Aromatics Scholar. It has as much caffeine as coffee."

Now Josh is mad. He stomps a Swedish-military-surplus-booted foot, nearly sliding down the hill, and says, "Is this like the hot drink industrial complex lying every direction as it suits them? First green tea had zero caffeine, black tea had all the caffeine, and coffee was the caffeine standard by which all hot drinks could be measured. Then green tea had a little bit as the energy drink and health drink market surged. Now it has *all* the caffeine? What?"

"Green tea puts the 'Bower' in a 'Bower Horse,'" Cole says while pulling out his camera, but Josh isn't taking it.

"So is caffeine even real? And is its correlation to wakefulness just totally made up?"

Nate, who has been silent the whole march, says, "I think it's like the health benefits of eggs," which effectively ends the debate.

Major Ghamdan has been listening passively off to the side. Letting our banal chatter wash over him like the waves we aren't surfing. I don't know how much he understands and am wondering what his position on caffeine is when he suddenly rises out of his squat and comes over with a particularly mischievous look in his eye, Kalashnikov slung over shoulder.

"*Izzayak, ya bey…*" or "What's up, king?" I ask him in butchered colloquial Egyptian Arabic.

"*Shoof shoof.*" He responds while winking and unshouldering his rifle. It's a good-looking classic sort, with a nicely oiled wooden stock and a sensually curved magazine. Kalashnikovs are everywhere here, with Yemen being the most heavily armed nation on Earth per capita, but there is an ultra-serious caste system when it comes to the iconic rifle. Chinese-made ones are the untouchables and mocked. American-made AKs are merchant class. They're functional and fine, but they're not Russian-made Brahmins. A Chinese Kalashnikov could be purchased in any corner gun shop for forty dollars. An AK would run eighty. However, a Russian-forged, real-life, Mikhail Kalashnikov could spike all the way past five hundred.

Major Ghamdan says *"shoof shoof"* again, this time directing it toward Josh, wanting to make sure that he has everyone's attention, then buries the nicely oiled wood stock into his shoulder, tilts his head slightly, closes one eye and…

BANG!

BANG!

BANG!

BANG!

He squeezes off four rounds in rapid succession.

It startles all of us, and as the gunpowder scent washes over, Cole says, "What the hell, Ghamdan? My ear is, like, right here."

Major Ghamdan just laughs and squeezes off three more rounds.

BANG!

BANG!

BANG!

Nate now has his fingers in his ears, which is probably a good move, but then again, he also pinches his nose when he jumps into water. Josh's face is filled with horror, and I don't know why until looking down at the beach. The family we'd just driven past, the family enjoying a Yemeni beach day, is scrambling like ants. Ninja high-stepping away from the ocean. The skirted man keeps his head low and follows closely behind her. The two children have dropped their sticks, running to the water. A lone burkini swims toward the horizon.

"Is Major Ghamdan shooting at that family?" I ask Josh.

His horror has morphed into a shocked laugh. "I think so. This guy is completely something else."

I don't really know if Major Ghamdan is actually shooting at them, but he's shooting so near them that the difference is purely academic. He is also completely enjoying himself, smirking as broadly as one can until a smirk is officially recategorized as a smile.

BANG!

BANG!

And like that he reshoulders his weapon and looks at us, bored. Like nothing happened.

"Did you just shoot at that family?" Josh asks him.

Major Ghamdan doesn't move.

Josh breaks into a full-bellied laugh, looking at Nate, Cole, and then me. "What an absolute butthole thing to do. This guy is unbelievable. He totally just shot at that family down there. That's literally crazy."

Major Ghamdan retreats back to his squat, waiting for us to decide what to do next, but there really is no surf, or at least no surf as far as we can see in front of us, so we slide back down the hill in order to find a boat to cruise us around in the very off chance that waves are hitting the backside of our sniper castle.

Waves do not hit the backside of our sniper castle. They do not hit the next cove over. They do not hit the cove past that either. They do not hit a sandbar we spot far out to sea. We've come to a place cursed with no waves, and the longer we fruitlessly hunt for them in the heat of the day, the better Major Ghamdan's entertainment seems. That family did scamper fast in curious fashion, and while Josh was right about shooting at them being an absolute butthole thing to do, it was wildy entertaining. It felt very American. Not in the sense of what "American" actually is but what it should be. Liberty. Freedom. The second amendment exercised in the pursuit of happiness. Democracy taking hold in the Middle East.

"Do Yemenis regularly shoot at each other?" I ask Cole, after finishing our boat ride from a nice man who cradled a black submachine gun and getting back in the Land Cruiser. "Is it sporting fun here?"

"No, they don't regularly shoot each other. Major Ghamdan is just a MAJOR pain in the ass."

Josh cranks his neck toward the back seat. "What've I been saying?"

Nate is still grumpy about the Amsterdam incident, I think, and keeping his participation in any conversation, especially ones threatening a gross turn, to an absolute minimum. Josh transitions to being frustrated with the way Major Ghamdan is driving through the sand.

We'd insisted on driving farther up the beach since the main road wouldn't give us a good vantage point. Major Ghamdan agreed at once and just as quickly ran afoul of Josh. Again. He doesn't deflate the tires beforehand and tries to drive in a straight line instead of wiggling the steering wheel back and forth. Josh keeps yelling at him, trying to demonstrate what to do, gripping an imaginary steering wheel and shaking it vigorously back and forth, but Major Ghamdan doesn't pay attention and continues in a straight line until we hit an extra soft, extra deep patch of sand and get impossibly stuck. Major Ghamdan's first instinct is to mash the gas pedal to the floor without shifting to four low, which sends Josh into absolute paroxysms. "GHAMDAN! WHAT ARE YOU THINKING? DO THEY NOT HAVE NOT HAVE SAND IN MARIB?"

We all get out and Josh, Nate, and I start unburying the tires with the nose of Nate's surfboard, since I contend he's never getting barreled anyway, while Cole trails off and takes pictures of giant dead crabs. It is as hot as hell, honest to goodness hell, and hard work. When we finally achieve probable success, Josh refuses to return the wheel to Major Ghamdan and defiantly sits in the driver's seat, slams the door shut, and eases the Land Cruiser out of its pit.

Everyone is elated, except for Cole, who is now only a dot on the horizon, taking pictures of sticks that look like Mother Theresa.

Nate and I let out exhausted cheers while Major Ghamdan goes over to the driver's door to take over once again. Josh refuses, informing Major Ghamdan that he grew up in Minnesota, where thick snow is a part of life, and that driving through thick snow and thick sand is basically the same thing. I don't know if Major Ghamdan picks up the actual gist of Josh's UCLA Arabic argument, which is becoming more and more incensed. He slams the hood of the Land Cruiser with his palm, eyes flashing with rage, but Josh adamantly stays in the driver's seat, revving the engine.

On the third loud roar Major Ghamdan has had enough and backs away from the driver's side door, positioning himself directly in front of the Land Cruiser. Josh revs the engine. Major Ghamdan shouts something about mixed juice. Josh eases out the clutch and starts moving forward. Major Ghamdan reaches back into the waistband of his skirt, his cute fish T-shirt delicately tucked into it, and pulls out a pistol, aiming squarely at the windshield. Josh keeps moving forward, then punches it. Major Ghamdan's eyes widen for a brief moment as he weighs the cost of shooting Josh versus getting out of the way and decides on the latter. Nate and I watch his shoulders slump, then watch Josh sink our Land Cruiser into the deepest sand ever, knowing instantly that we'll spend the next three hours digging it back out. Three hours if we're lucky.

Josh swings the door open, laughing uncontrollably. Bent over laughing. Nate sighs under his breath, but a smirk dances on his lips. He loves when people act in character, and Josh taking control then getting us extra stuck is in character. I break character, unfortunately, and get irked. It's hot as hell, and the thought of digging the Land Cruiser out again feels crushing. It feels life-altering. I should find it as amusing as Major Ghamdan shooting at an innocent Yemeni family but can't. Major Ghamdan puts his pistol back into the waistband of his skirt and Cole takes a picture of a strange gull he insists looks exactly like Michael Bolton.

We spend that night stuck in the sand, where we are hungry, exhausted, surfless, and filled with existential angst at letting Sam George down.

Nobody cares that Major Ghamdan thought about shooting Josh today or at least pretended to. Nobody cares about him actually sport shooting at a Yemeni family enjoying a beach day. We are all too far gone. Too exhausted to even joke or rate Laura Dern, we fall asleep around the unburied but still unmoved Land Cruiser as a blinding moon climbs high into the sky. I dream that I hear the Call to Prayer.

CHAPTER 6

We all wake at first light, starving, thirsty. There is sand clinging to my teeth and buried in my ears and turning my hair a dusty yellow that I almost like when examining it in the Land Cruiser's side mirror. I look very Lawrence of Arabia after his march across the Sun's Anvil. After he went and saved a fallen Arab comrade whom none of the other Arab comrades cared about.

Yesterday's tension is fully evaporated, and without a word, Major Ghamdan gets behind the wheel. We lug into our assigned seats and he drives off like Josh taught him the day before, guiding the Land Cruiser through deep sand, shallower sand, then back to the main road. Coffee would taste fantastic. Tea would be fantastic too, but the desire for waves bigger than waist high takes precedence and we drive for thirty minutes in silence, eyes glued to the coastline, until Josh spots another roadside minimart.

The cinder block shed-lettes are oases of deliciousness and spread randomly throughout the country, often in unexpected places. This one has booming ocean views, its own technical without wheels, and a minaret with two bullhorns tied to its top.

"Jossy hungry," Josh says.

"Shocking." Nate smirks again, enjoying Josh both staying in character by being perpetually hungry and also by using a diminutive nickname in the third person.

"Are you not hungry, Nate? You couldn't go for a nice, ripe banana right now? A nice, healthy, potassium-filled banana?" I ask him.

"No," he says in his patently low, mostly inaudible voice.

Nate hates bananas and is the only person I have ever met in my life with such a predilection. He claims even the smell makes him vomit, but I think mostly he is turned off by the phallic nature and thinks that men who eat bananas look like they are giving blowjobs. This is a dubious position to hold considering he gave Steven Tyler three nights out of ten.

"You're going to get cramps if we don't stop and get a banana, Nate," Josh turns around to tell him then instructs Major Ghamdan to pull over. "It's really important that none of us get cramps. Even if you're not hungry."

"Potatoes have more potassium than bananas," Nate replies.

"That's a lie propagated by your Bolivian government and absolutely not true," I bark. "We discussed this yesterday. It's why they don't hand out potatoes at the end of marathons but do hand out bananas."

We had, in fact, spent most of the drive from Ataq to Bi'r Ali arguing the relative potassium levels between bananas and potatoes with Nate holding firm, even in the face of a mountain of evidence suggesting otherwise, like my mention of marathons and also that they don't serve potatoes at swim meets or soccer games.

"Maybe you could just get a banana milk. Then you don't have to worry about the sexual overtones but still get your potassium," Josh helpfully suggests as we come to a stop and head into the store.

"I told you, the smell makes me vomit."

Our snacking had started appropriately enough, buying water and some fruit or crackers in case we became stranded somewhere, but had evolved into an artistically gluttonous expression. First there was the rediscovery of Canada Dry ginger ale to accompany the qat chew. Yemenis love the soda more than any other, and rightly so. Then we added strawberry Fanta, mango juices, banana milk, Nujoom candy bars, chocolate biscuits, some Yemeni version of Twix, hot tea with sweetened condensed milk, chips, crackers, some Yemeni version of Pringles, and ice cream bars. We leave with a veritable feast and dig in straight away.

The banana milk tastes like heaven as we turn back on the road. Frosty and satisfying. I tell Nate he's truly missing out then focus on the coastline, which is showing real signs of life. Mixed up, un-surfable waves are bashing off the increasingly rugged shore, but the energy is there. Real energy. And it's stunningly beautiful—water every shade of Pantone color wheel blue, birds flying and diving for fish, the spray from the waves creating magical little rainbows. It feels tropical. Hypnotically tropical. The sort of tropical that snares Germans, Danes, and Poles in poorly built Mediterranean island hotels.

Al Mukalla will be the next major stop, and although I've just eaten two candy bars, a bag of chips, a banana milk, then another banana milk, I'm excited for lunch. The city is capital of the Hadramawt, the region that gifted us Osama bin Laden, and I have an even better feeling about its potential than I had had about Bi'r Ali's, which I had pestered Josh with last night.

He had wanted to camp for a few more days in the shadow of the make-believe castle and take another fishing boat farther up the coast, where we couldn't see from the road, truly exploring the various coves. I had demanded we move on toward Mukalla.

"I have a feeling, man. We're going to score. We're going to find our waves."

Really, one night of camping had been enough for me, and I was going through music-video withdrawals. I figured we'd at least stay a night in Mukalla, waves or no, and maybe even two if the town showed any promise. I kept up a low-grade campaign denigrating Bi'r Ali and praising Mukalla until Josh and Nate became chafed enough to move out. Cole missed his chance to weigh in, as the giant dead crabs had become a major fixation.

I stare out the window, watching the water, the birds, the goats, small scrubby trees and brush, and the slow increase in population density as we hit the outskirts of suburban Mukalla, and right then I see it.

"Josh!" I shout, hitting Cole across the face as I point. "Look! Is that…working?"

Major Ghamdan eases the Land Cruiser off the road, and we all sit and strain our eyes out to sea, Cole rubbing his nose. I hold my breath until the next set comes in, and sure enough it seems as if there's a chunk of reef that jacks the swell into a racy left and a solid right. A proper A-frame.

Josh and I fling our doors open and slide down a dusty slope and out onto a rock jutting into the water. The wave is breaking a hundred yards out and is definitely big enough, though it's difficult to judge its exact size.

"We found it! I told you!" I shout right in his face.

He isn't so sure, but we scramble back up to the car, pull our giant shiny Mylar surfboard coffin down from the roof, screw in our fins, wax our boards, and slide scoot back down, this time skirting to the left of the jutting rock and into the water.

It is a perfectly refreshing temperature, not the bathtub of Aden or Bi'r Ali. Josh and I paddle slowly, right next to each other, peering into the water trying to figure out how shallow the reef is, if there are any big fish or bigger sharks. I can see an endless supply of purple sea urchins, my fingers passing right above their spines.

Nerve-racked and shaky, we make it out to what we think is the channel, watching a few waves pass before moving into position. I look back toward shore and see Cole positioned on the rock, camera ready. Nate is on the beach, holding his board, preparing himself. The hillside on the other side of the road is beginning to fill with Yemenis chewing their qat and perched very high up like mountain goats, wondering what this early afternoon entertainment means. Wondering about this new Caucasian extravagance in their ancient land.

CHAPTER 7

"Did I hit that one section okay?" I ask the Land Cruiser as Major Ghamdan peels out toward Mukalla proper. The two-lane road is now clogged with donkeys, camels, a few longhorn bulls, cement mixers, schoolchildren wearing green uniforms, and giant ceramic palm trees as we move closer to the city center. "I probably wasn't high enough on the wave, but did it almost look passably good?"

I glance around, waiting for someone to dismiss my modesty and deliver a powerful compliment. Waiting for Josh, Nate, or especially Cole to say, "No way, man. That turn was super sick, totally legit, epic." And, if it was Cole, then an added, "...and I nailed the shot."

In my mind's eye, I hit the section perfectly and probably looked very much like a pro surfer. Knees bent just right, arms not flailing, spray being sent skyward, shooting off my deeply buried rail. I can imagine the image on an impressionable kid's wall. Him gazing at it, thinking, "Someday I'm going to surf like that."

No one says anything, so I mumble, "Waapow," and mimic how I imagine the turn looked.

The wave was everything I had ever dreamed, ever hoped, ever prayed it would be. Fun, fast, almost big or at least overhead with an easy roll-in section in a picturesque amphitheater where more and more Yemeni spectators gathered the longer we surfed. They watched passively, and when we were finished after a few hours, they shuffled off to their lives. I wasn't expecting to give autographs, but I was disappointed that their interest in what we were doing was coupled with an almost pure indifference.

"I'm starving," Josh exclaims, breaking the sun-induced, saltwater-crusted silence. I can hear Nate smirking. "Ya Major Ghamdan. *Dajaj*?" Josh asks. "Hey, Major Ghamdan. Chicken?"

Major Ghamdan grunts.

"We're going to have to get a hotel too…" I add. "We definitely have to surf back there for at least a few days." Dreams of covers and double-paged spreads dance in my head. Dreams of surf fame.

We swing around a corner and the city of Al Mukalla spreads out before us, glimmering white, nestled at the foot of a naked gray and brown mountain range that has literal turrets as opposed to the figurative turrets of Bi'r Ali. Ancient guard towers run along its entire spine. It's an Orientalist dream, and I know, without even making it all the way in, that it is my favorite city on Earth.

"This is my favorite city on Earth," I announce loudly.

No one says anything but I don't care. It is.

Major Ghamdan pilots the Land Cruiser around the first roundabout, across a Tiber-sized river flowing out to sea, then up the corniche fronting a beautiful harbor that features two half-exposed sunken ships, toward a large white mosque with green piping and an extra bulbous minaret. There is a large white hotel next door with Persian-looking windows also outlined in green.

We park and pile into the early afternoon heat and the most delicious smell snags us all.

"What is that?" Josh says, sniffing the air.

"Follow your nose, bro. It always knows," Nate tells him through yet another smirk.

"Well, I don't know about you, Mr. Extreme Abstinence. We've got to find it," Josh shoots back.

We walk past the hotel and into an open-air market. Men in skirts sell fish, greens, fruit, and what appears to be freshly fried fish balls and bread mashed up with overripe bananas and drizzled with sweetened condensed milk. I don't see any ninjas at all. Not one woman. Mukalla appears to be a town made up entirely of men and their sons.

"How good does that look?" I say, eyeing Nate suggestively, pointing to the banana mush. He rolls his eyes while Cole gets distracted by a freshly severed goat head and maunders away.

Josh orders double of everything plus three Canada Dry, and we sit down on a picnic table set up underneath a homemade sunshade, waving at flies, sipping the second-best thing that's ever come from the Great White North after Bob and Doug McKenzie. I still can't believe we found a wave that no one had ever surfed in the history of mankind. A real, honest-to-goodness discovery à la Sir Edmund Hillary and Dr. David Livingstone. A proper first that no man or woman had ever even attempted à la Yuri Gagarin. Pride of accomplishment pulses through my veins along with Canada Dry and I wonder if the National Geographic Society will be reaching out sooner rather than later. Oh, sure, surfing is an empty, utterly silly pursuit—but isn't any human accomplishment outside Pythagoras' theorem and Jonas Salk's anti-polio vaccine? I mean, what's the actual point of flying into space, chasing waterfalls, or climbing tall mountains? Isn't it all just a laugh at the end?

And while I'm trying to insert myself into Western civilization's proudest moments, Major Ghamdan quick-steps around the corner, Kalashnikov slung over his shoulder and pistol jammed into his skirt's waistband, all agitated and sweaty. "Come," he says in rare and angry English, keeping his eyes swiveling around the square. "Come. We go."

"Where?" Josh asks. "We just ordered a delicious feast."

"We go now," Major Ghamdan says again and lifts me up by my collared T-shirt.

"Hey, watch the Op, guy. It's a sample from their yesteryear collection. One of a kind, man," I whine.

He either doesn't like my joke or doesn't hear it and makes sure we all get up despite the halfhearted protest of the fried fish ball chef. He marches us over to where Cole is taking close up pictures of the goat's teeth and pushes us out in front of him, through a crowd that has seemed to swell.

"OMG, what's your deal, Major Ghamdan?" Cole asks.

Josh translates reluctantly.

"Too much beards," Major Ghamdan says in quiet Arabic, eyes darting.

"Oh, come on. It's the same as anywhere we've been. Anywhere from Morocco to Mecca. You people are Muslims. Remember? You enjoy growing beards," Cole says, rolling his eyes.

Major Ghamdan keeps shoving us toward the Land Cruiser and looking over his shoulder at the same time. I follow his line of vision and observe the tight knot of men in white, floor-length wedding dresses, white knitted skullcaps, and bushy black beards standing out front of the mosque. They are watching back—sternly, but not necessarily menacing. Or maybe menacing, but nothing that can't be diffused with a quick "*Ana* Yemeni" crack. It gets them every time. "*Mish mushakkal!*" I yell toward them. "Ana Yemeni!"

No one breaks a smile, so I yell it again.

"It's 'mish *mushkella*,' bro." Josh whispers. "'Mushakkal' means 'mixed.' And what they call their juices."

"Oh, I know..." I snap back. *Mushkella* and *mushakkal* get me every time.

Major Ghamdan shoves us into the Land Cruiser, swings behind the steering wheel, and evasively maneuvers away from the corniche, taking his first right then speeding up the river.

"Okay, okay, okay..." Josh tells him. "We're very hungry and need to stay here at least one night. Our mission demands it. You can go if you're scared, but we're not leaving."

Major Ghamdan grunts, then pulls over in front of a sign picturing a bucking horse that must be a hotel. Through two open doors I can see the front desk and a chubby Indian watching something on TV. I read the script out loud like a slow Arab would, sounding each squiggle slowly, "a-l K-h-a-i-l. Al Khail. What's a 'khail?'"

"Horse," Josh and Cole say at the same time.

Major Ghamdan tells us to wait and gets out of the car and starts punching his little Nokia brick with one angry digit, then puts it up to his ear and screams into it with a barrage of guttural nonsense just like all Arab men do when they talk on the phone, so it's impossible to tell if he's angry or just being an Arab.

"Oooooh, dajaj!" Josh says, pointing through the windshield to a rotisserie machine spinning deliciously bronzed chickens. We all spill out like preschoolers and find a table on the essentially Parisian patio, the sun blocked by a giant tamarind, and order, but instead of Canada Dry we get Royal Crown Cola. Yemenis love obscure sodas from different eras more than any people on Earth. Major Ghamdan seems oblivious, marching up and down the river screaming into his mini phone, apparently getting intel.

"How does this hot, hot desert have such a huge river?" I ask. "Why aren't there all kinds of oasis-esque trees growing everywhere and not just above our heads?"

"I think they just cut a big ol' channel up from the ocean to give the tiny river girth and gravitas," Cole says.

I study it deeply for the first time and realize he's right. "Well, even better," I say while stuffing my face with the best rotisserie chicken I've ever eaten. A rotisserie chicken that puts Boston Market to absolute shame. "They care about aesthetics here. They want a river walk for happy citizens just like San Antonio, Texas. I'm going to look for an apartment. Screw going home."

The idea of "home" had even faded into a hazy mist. I couldn't remember why "home" mattered at all or why Odysseus was so intent on getting there in his Odyssey. Home was flat, dull, constricted. All things are possible away, or at least probable. Why didn't Odysseus just live with Circe on her isle? Wasn't a woman who could turn men into swine much more compelling than his wife and all her damned suitors? Why are road narratives always about heading home? Home is where dreams die. The road is where they take flight.

Major Ghamdan returns when we're nearly finished with our meal and tells us that we have to leave directly. He's still shifty, though not as shifty as he was near the mosque. We tell him absolutely not. We're going to stay in town for a few days, at least. If his own boozing, whoring, sinful ways are weighing on his conscious in front of his fundamentalist brethren, then that's something he must carry and carry alone.

He looks at us incredulously for a few moments, eyes bouncing from one to the other to the other, then sighs. His shoulders collapse, defeated. A look of pure pride spreads across Josh's face. First he had entirely curtailed Major Ghamdan's wanton spending.

Now we had all dictated where we could go. "Okay…" he says after killing the last of his Royal Crown, "back to the mosque and that hotel across the street."

Major Ghamdan instantly reanimates, barking a string of guttural protests while gesticulating wildly. Josh stands his ground, insisting that the hotel by the mosque is where we want to stay and where we will stay, until I pull the rug out from under him.

"Okay, okay, okay, fine, Major Ghamdan. We stay at The Horse." I tell him in my best Egyptian Arabic while patting his shoulder. "Everything's fine. The whole world is fine. I'm Yemeni."

Josh shoots a devil glare through me, and it was rude to undermine him in front of Major Ghamdan, but also there is no telling if the mosque-adjacent hotel has television. The front desk at al-Khail definitely did, though, which bodes well for the rooms. Music videos are as essential as water. Josh knows it, and I can't let his lust for danger cloud his better judgment.

"It's fine…" I turn to him, dishing up the same paternal tone I had just served Major Ghamdan. "…the whole world is fine."

They both stand shoulder to shoulder, burning internally.

CHAPTER 8

We treat Al Mukalla over the next ten days the way sloppy Germans, Danes, and Poles treat Majorca, ambling around in the heat of the day between shops that sell ice cream and internet cafés, driving out to the wave for a surf, driving back for a massive chicken lunch, driving out to the wave for an evening surf, driving back for a dinner of fried fish balls and banana mush next to the mosque.

Major Ghamdan mostly stayed in his room as far as I could tell and seemed resigned to whatever would happen, throwing up his hands and letting God decide our fate, really and truly getting into the "inshallah" spirit the way all good Muslims and Calvinists do.

Irate younger men would approach semi-regularly, especially after evening prayers, eyes burning, and tell us that George Bush is a dog. Yemen was severely punished by George Sr. for holding the position that Arab nations should not intervene in the business between Iraq and Kuwait during the first Gulf War, and even more severely punished by Kuwait and her neighbors as thousands of working Yemenis were expelled without warning.

George Jr. had just taken Baghdad in the second Gulf War not two months ago as the Global War on Terror found a new theater and was saber-rattling through the rest of the region, demanding that nations were either for us or against us, and if they were against us—well, things would not go well.

Depending on our collective mood we would either argue back that the Bush family was a proud American legacy or agree, and either way the conversations would end with warm proclamations of friendship and hand-holding beneath the starry skies of Mukalla, a striking town that grows better with experience.

The way the light bathes it in the day, the way heat radiates off every surface at night. The mix of Indian, British, Persian, Indonesian, and East African influences. Architecture, food, and dress harkening to the days when it was a center of the trading world. Osama bin Laden's family chose their region well, and my desire to live in the Hadramawt grew unchecked.

Most nights belonged to music videos or accidentally CNN's international version. The Horse did indeed have televisions and not one but two music video channels from Saudi Arabia and from Lebanon, which worked brilliantly when one switched to Live from Mecca programming unless they both switched to it at the same time. It blew my expectations out of the water, and even though Josh would semi-regularly reference how epic the hotel by the mosque was and how it was also closer to fried fish balls, we all feasted on Stone Temple Pilots, Ricky Martin, Alicia Keys, Incubus, Uncle Cracker, Nelly Furtado, and Enrique Iglesias with equal relish—especially the Enrique Iglesias video featuring Jennifer Love Hewitt and Mickey Rourke in an epic ballad that brought me near tears every time it played, particularly when Enrique Iglesias looked deep into Jennifer Love Hewitt's eyes and said, "I can be your hero, baby. I can kiss away the pain."

And then we'd go eat.

One evening, as we traipsed back to our hotel from fried fish balls, a group of young men followed us into a small, empty corridor and unsheathed their *jambiyas*, flashing the curved steel and yelling that we were Americans. Josh lowered his shoulder and ran at them like a corn-fed University of Michigan fullback. They tossed their weapons into a nearby bush and took off sprinting, and the whole scene felt wonderful, harkening back to a simpler, less litigious time when back-alley street fights between rival hoods were commonplace.

"When you're a jet you're a jet all the way!" I shouted as they rounded the corner, Josh hot on their wedge-sandaled heels.

Another evening, as we sauntered back, we saw a massive crowd out front of the shopfront where we bought our morning coffees. A sea of turbaned heads sitting cross-legged on a piece of Astroturf rolled out for the occasion. As we got nearer, we saw they were all watching a tiny rabbit-eared television, and as we got nearer still saw the television was showing a pro surf contest from Hawaii the year earlier.

I couldn't believe it. Here in Al Mukalla—a thousand miles from the nearest semblance of surf culture and ten thousand miles from Oahu's North Shore—a few hundred men were silently basking in the Pastime of Kings. I elbowed one wearing a particularly neat turban-skirt combination, pointed at the television, and told him that's what we did, what those men were doing on the television, riding tables on the ocean exactly like them. His eyes widened and I almost invited him to watch us live the next day but thankfully caught myself, realizing that while we indeed rode tables on the ocean exactly like the men on television, our surfing looked very different. So different, in fact, that it might have been confused as a separate water game altogether. One not so graceful or exciting.

Still, the entire scene was so gorgeously surreal it made me positively giddy for days afterward.

And then, one hot morning, it is time to move on.

We have been in the country for just over a month, have experienced the highlands with gorgeously terraced qat plantations, mist-shrouded crags, gingerbread houses, deep valleys, quaint towns, and bustling cities. And also the guns, skirts, ninjas, banana milk, and rotisserie chicken, of course.

Ahead is the lightly tamed hinterland. The paved portion of our journey will conclude in a hundred or so kilometers and we'll be alone in a mountainous coastal desert or maybe a rain forest. Josh has said the monsoonal flow hits the coast where Yemen touches Oman, but it is difficult for me to believe him. Even if I stretch my imagination all the way out, I can picture neither rain nor forest. We are in dry lands, and wild, untamed dry lands await. Dry lands that even the heartiest Yemeni has never seen. That nobody has ever seen.

We buy qat from Mukalla's qat *souq* before leaving, and though it's early, it also guarantees the quality of our purchase. Cole had already been a sommelier before we arrived, but a sommelier unburdened by price. It took a hot minute, but we figured out the game, and it serves us now. We begin chewing as Major Ghamdan points the Land Cruiser northeast and continue chewing through an almost fun wave we discover right past an oil facility 30 kilometers past Al Mukalla owned by a Canada-based firm. We surf for an hour, cheeks filled with qat, at an almost very fun beach break we dub "Oh, Canada" afterward. Naming each break we discover is very important in the moment, not that any other surfer on Earth will ever follow. Still, very important. When watching a movie about Everest or Half Dome or whatever, the nomenclatures are set to memory. I know the "Hillary Step" without having climbed a day in my life. I know "Monster Offwidth" thanks to the madman Alex Honnold. Names mean something even when they don't.

We have the honor and privilege of naming every break we surf, since we are the first to surf them, and I dutifully scribble their names in my notebook, gazing at it with pride as the list grows longer. After "Oh, Canada" I draw a maple leaf. Cole leans, studying my work, and says, "I like weed too."

"How much for a Cheech and Chong meatsa-meatsa?" I ask him.

"Oooooh, a total ten."

"Gross, Cole," Josh says without looking back.

And then, like that, the road ends. We stop for a moment and study a dirt path that crawls up the horizon and disappears around a giant boulder planted into an even bigger mountain, rugged and wild. A lazy checkpoint attendee casually strolls over, takes the *tasrih*, studies it for a moment, pokes his head in the car, examines us all in the same way we'd now been examined fifty or so times at each of the fifty or so checkpoints we'd passed through so far, puffs air into one cheek, points to it with a crooked finger, and slightly widens his dark brown eyes.

"*Aiwa*," I say. "*Ana*..." but Josh cuts me off before I can say "Yemeni."

Major Ghamdan presses the pedal and we crunch forward into the even greater unknown.

I lose track of time as the magic of our surroundings overwhelms me. We climb mountains pocked with caves and ease down their backsides. We cut across wadis and large open expanses of sand. Josh takes the wheel while Major Ghamdan snoozes, his burgundy beret pulled over his eyes. Dust fills the Land Cruiser's cabin, coating us all in a fine layer that accents our already robust tans.

When night finally conquers day, the sky explodes with stars, more stars than I have ever seen in my life—galaxies of stars, a whole universe of stars—and we all lie on our backs and watch satellites crisscrossing, some of them likely beaming music videos back to Earth.

"How do you say 'stars' in Arabic?" I ask.

"*Nujoom*," Josh and Cole say in their usual unison.

I wake in the middle of the night absolutely starving. We'd purchased enough supplies for a few days—bread, candy bars, banana milk, a jar of peanut butter—and I dig in, dipping a few of the candy bars into the peanut butter and washing it down with two boxes of banana milk. I would have felt a little bad, taxing our not-altogether-robust resources, except I'm the skinniest of the group and suffer from skinny man's disease. A true and self-diagnosable medical condition, I tell everyone, that makes me hungry for candy and shaky if I don't eat candy. Neither Josh, Nate, nor Cole could possibly understand the burden I carry.

And we're all up early, as soon as the sun pokes over the mountains, hammering us with its heat. We eat some candy bars, except for Nate because there isn't enough, and climb back into the Land Cruiser without a word. Up and down, across and over. Kidneys starting to revolt. We stop at a few waves and surf. One requires so much paddling that we name it "Paddlewheel." One has a rock outcropping that looks like Bill Cosby so we name it "Sweaters."

Just before noon, we hit our first hinterland checkpoint. Its soldiers lounge in the shade of a few scrubby brushes, the raggedy nondescript trees, the guard shack, and the shadow their black, white, and red Yemeni flag casts. An important superior with military shirt unbuttoned revealing a sparkling white wifebeater approaches, and he and Major Ghamdan carry on a lengthy, serious conversation with much gesticulating and head shaking.

Cole leans forward, trying to pick it up, and I ask, "What are they talking about?"

"Pirates," he answers.

We all get out, and the superior explains to us that pirates had come ashore at the nearest village and are busy sacking the town. There is absolutely no way he can let us though. We try all the tricks we had learned, absolving him of responsibility, promising that we won't blame the government for our possible demise, demanding that surf history needs this moment, before retreating to the patchy shade of another nearby nondescript scraggly tree in order to reassess our options.

While waiting, throwing pebbles at a plastic bag crucified on a bush, a truck comes rushing up in a cloud of dust. It is the first car we've seen in the past fifteen hours, at least. As it nears the checkpoint then stops, I can see clearly that it is being piloted by two United States Special Forces operatives. Regardless of these being early days in the Global War on Terror, their uniform is already iconic: tight green T-shirts, bulging biceps, overgrown beards, dusty baseball caps flipped backward, wraparound sunglasses, and dirty black-and-white checked keffiyehs acting as fashionable neck warmers in the thousand-degree heat.

I watch them argue vigorously with the same commandant who told us about the pirates, but they too are rebuffed and retreat a little farther back than we did, staying in their car with the air-conditioning pumping. I don't know if they see us since their wraparound sunglasses really do the trick, but I wonder what they think. I'm basically naked at this point, only wearing an increasingly worn pair of Op trunks and a pair of Spy sunglasses.

"I bet they wish they had Spy sunglasses," I tell Josh. "It would be very on brand. Aren't you happy we have them rather than too much money?"

He doesn't answer.

After thirty minutes of rock throwing and arguing the proper numbers on Anastacia, a particularly difficult one to nail down seeing as she was never big in America but was in Bolivia and evidently Lebanon, the commandant ambles over casually, buttoning up his military shirt, and tells us we can head through. We load up without asking questions, thank him profusely, and creep past a bunched-up spike strip pulled off to the side.

The Special Forces truck comes roaring up hot and we can see the commandant step in their way, arms raised, as they slide to a halt. We watch them arguing maniacally through the back window as our Land Cruiser climbs up and over the next hill, arms swinging, heads thrown back then thrown forward, and it's the last we ever see them, even hearing weeks later that they had been frustrated at every turn and left the country without achieving any sort of goal.

Special Forces were, more and more, becoming the sharp end of the Global War on Terror. Their abilities to move stealthily in and out of tricky situations combined with a Chuck Norris–meets-MacGyver skillset made them an easy sell to both purse-string-holding politicians and the general American public, and while their value is undeniable, there is something about watching them operate outside the wire that made me question our supposed tactical advantage.

That afternoon we eat our chicken lunch in the freshly sacked town, bullet holes still smoking in the whitewashed walls. The proprietor shrugs and tells us the pirate sacks happen so often that nobody cares. They generally go after other smugglers or insurgents trying to snag televisions, golf carts, and pallets of Chocodiles and Twinkies headed illegally across the Empty Quarter into Saudi Arabia. No big deal.

We find an epic left breaking off a shipwrecked tanker later in the evening that we name "Tetanuses" because the takeoff backwashes into a gaping black hole ringed with rusty, jagged, menacing metal.

CHAPTER 9

"Have any of you bros ever been to a Rainforest Café?" I ask as we stand on a high cliff, staring out to sea, watching lines of swell marching toward shore. "I went once with my family when I was a kid but we couldn't afford to eat, so I just wandered in between tables dreaming of someday ordering Amazon Fajitas and making animatronic boa constrictors jealous, but this is better."

Josh was right. There is a rain forest where Yemen touches Oman. Everything is misty green, lush, healthy. Alive. Thick gray clouds block the sun overhead and threaten rain. The red dirt shows clear evidence of a recent shower. Three wild camels dawdle past, disinterested. Josh is trying to find a way to make it down the cliff.

The fact that we are standing in rain forest, staring at surf with wild camels on the Arabian Peninsula while Josh plans a world-class free solo would feel more surreal if we had not just returned from a magical island that floats nearer to Somalia than Yemen not ten days ago.

After the freshly sacked town and shipwreck, we had pushed up the coast and through a roadside stop where the locals touched our blond hair and gazed into our blue eyes, proclaiming we were the first white people they had ever seen in Al Ghaydah, the capital city of Al Mahrah. It was a sprawling, dusty commercial center that felt very much like Luke Skywalker's Tatooine would if Tatooine was coastal and not populated with grouchy uncles intent on keeping important secrets from their nephews. Its locals spoke a unique language not related to Arabic and which predated Islam's hot run, and their camels, much sought after, were the fastest on Earth.

We fell into our now refined art of living. Music videos, looking for surf, surfing, eating, snacking, and wandering. Major Ghamdan had given up on us entirely at this point, maybe hoping we'd get kidnapped and out of his life for good. Cole had mostly given up too, hanging back in various rooms, chewing qat, and packing then repacking his bag.

One hot evening, we wandered into town for dinner, found a "meat" restaurant, and ate at a picnic table across the street from a mosque. Chinese lanterns were inexplicably hung across the road. Halfway through our meal, a handsome man wearing clean slacks and a blue button-up approached apologetically and asked where we were from. We told him America and he broke into perfect English. We spent the next hour talking about life in Yemen, life in America, and the troubles in Iraq. It was the first non-televised English we had heard outside of our own conversations in weeks.

I said, "Well, he sure was nice..." as we wandered back to our hotel after he left.

Josh snorted. "He was a spy."

"Yeah. He was," Nate agreed.

"What are you bros talking about?" I demanded to know, incensed. "Just because some nice Yemeni man wants to have a conversation with us in our native tongue doesn't mean he's a spy. You are both buttholes and rude and have treated every single person in this country very rudely, including Major Ghamdan al-Shoefy." It wasn't true, of course. Mingling with the locals had been some of our greatest times. Getting long, drawn-out stories while sipping tea, chewing qat, eating chicken, and chatting. There were no Western tourists here, so nothing to cater to them. No fast-talking hustlers with pockets full of knickknacks and greasy charm. Yemeni locals weren't looking for conversation. They would eye us warily and things would begin slowly, but once we got to talking it was a veritable feast of insight. One we all appreciated.

"Oh, don't even get me started on Major Ghamdan..." Josh said, clearly piqued. "If I hadn't manhandled him from the beginning, we'd probably still be in Aden with unattractive companions and a hundred thousand dollars in debt."

Nate tried to diffuse the rising temperature by rolling out grandfatherly advice. "Hey, guys, we're a long way from home and tensions are high. Let's just keep that in mind."

We spent the rest of the night arguing about nice folk in Middle Eastern backwaters not necessarily needing to be covert operators. About how curiosity is a virtue and English is the lingua franca, which he could have easily learned through a combination of watching CNN and music videos alone.

"I have a master's degree in applied linguistics. This is my area of expertise, bro," I spat at Josh while puncturing the hot air with a defiant finger.

He glared back at me and said, "I thought Hollywood car chases were our lingua franca."

We sat there in stony silence until Maroon 5's "She Will Be Loved" transitioned to Hoobastank's "The Reason" and Nate, continuing to play peacemaker, asked, "Is Maroon 5 or Hoobastank going to have the more culturally significant career arc?"

Josh said "Maroon 5" and I said "Hoobastank" at exactly the same time, and we fell into stony silence once again.

The next morning was twice as hot as all previous mornings, yet the chill between Josh and I remained. We dressed without saying a word then went downstairs for some breakfast. Al Ghaydah stirred to life around us, men in skirts pushing through the humidity to work, a bricklayer squatting next to a half-finished wall, adding a layer of mud to the tallest portion like icing.

We were drinking a second cup of thick Arabic when I swore I heard a snippet of Spanish. I listened carefully and swore I heard a snippet more, turning to Nate this time and asking, "You hear your native tongue, Simone de Bolívar?"

"No," he grumbled. Spanish had been Nate's first language well before he learned English, and there was nothing he hated more than when Josh and I started tossing Spanish puns.

"Simón de Beauvoir was very hot," Josh added. "You are lucky that your country was named after him."

"Yeah. Real lucky," Nate said without even cracking half a smile.

"Oh, come on..." I said. "That's funny. You have to admit that Simón Bolívar and Simone de Beauvoir are a funny mash. Only the completely illiterate wouldn't catch the humor. Are you completely illiterate, Nate?"

"Yes," he grunted. "I'm completely illiterate."

"No, you're not, Nate," Josh said. "You can read the speeches of Ronald Reggaeton with the greatest of ease."

Nate frowned.

I laughed, and it felt good to be back on the same side as Josh: pushing Nate into angrier and angrier places.

And then we all heard it. Very clear Spanish coming from a small portable radio set up in front of a middle-aged, nondescript Yemeni sitting drinking coffee at a table two down from ours. It was a Spanish news feed, and Nate listened for a while before greeting him in Spanish.

He looked up, mostly unsurprised, and responded in kind, then moved to where we were. He and Nate went back and forth rapid fire with many rolled Rs and many swallowed consonants, straddling the line between voiced bilabial plosives and voiced labiodental fricatives.

After ten minutes, he looked at his watch and excused himself, giving Nate a hearty handshake and hurrying into the street then around a corner, nearly getting clipped by a flatbed truck hauling oil drums.

"Talk about a spy," I said.

"That bro wasn't a spy," Nate responded.

Josh backed him up.

"You two are impossible!" I felt my blood beginning to boil once again. "If we stumble on an English speaker he's a spy, even though English is a damned global language, but if we stumble on a Spanish speaker then he's just a normal old worker bee, even though Spanish is exclusively spoken in salsa-dancing countries?"

"He is a camel veterinarian…" Nate said after my rant ended. "He is from Al Ghaydah originally but did all his studying in Cuba."

"You're saying that's not fishy?" I looked to Josh for support.

"Not fishy, bro. South Yemen was communist from the early 1970s all the way up to reunification in the early 1990s. There was lots of movement between here, Cuba, and Moscow."

"Well, ain't that just a geographical oddity," I said, after soaking it in for a few moments, truly impressed.

"Speaking of geographical oddities…" Josh interjected. "Should we go to Soqotra? I was talking to the money changer yesterday. He had been out there for work and said the ocean is 'rougher' middle summer. Obviously 'rougher' can mean anything, but I would hate to miss it if that swell is seasonally specific."

Soqotra was an island that belonged to Yemen though was closer to Somalia and had a reputation for wildness. Its trees were said to bleed and its lizards were said to be legless. Its isolation has long fascinated scientists, as up to one-third of life on the island is endemic. English anthropologist George Wynn Brereton Huntingford went to study birds in the mid-1960s and called it "the most alien-looking place on Earth."

We all decided that the border push could wait and informed Major Ghamdan of our plans. He seemed all too eager and we raced back to Mukalla in a record two days, resurfing a few of the waves we had just discovered and sleeping on the naked dirt. He stood on the tarmac as we loaded into a small propeller plane, waving manically as our flight pulled away.

Soqotra made mainland Yemen with its gingerbread houses, druggy hedge trimmings, creeping ninjas, bold-skirted men, disco mosques, al-Qaeda street racers, pirate sackers, nice English speakers (no matter what Josh and Nate said), nicer Spanish speakers, curved knives on exotic leather belts, and professional-surf-watching townsfolk seem positively normal.

Our flight landed in the evening, and we lugged our giant shiny Mylar surfboard coffin to the only hotel, which was made entirely of rocks in the main city of Hadibu. Not stone. Not finely hewed anything. Big, head-sized, rough rocks half-mortared with loose gravel. The wind howled that first night and every night thereafter, but always offshore, no matter which corner of the island we found ourselves, which meant the island itself generated the wind from its center. We didn't sleep a wink, instead falling into possessed semi-conscious states as a substitute.

We found a local who owned one of the two cars on the island, and he took us to the other side, where we ended up in another rock fishing village that happened to have a decent wave directly out the front. We hooted, hollered, and paddled out, surfing as best we could while trying not to get blown fa out to sea. The villagers gathered on the shore and cheered like we were good.

When we were through splashing, they gathered around us and praised Allah. The village elder, a handsome man with serious eyes and a full white beard, took my surfboard in his hands and danced on the rocks while we clapped along, thrusting a gnarled fist to the sky in pure joy.

The surfboard was decorated with a giant sticker of the Argentinian revolutionary Che Guevara, which should have been an embarrassing emblem of trendy nineties fashion but wasn't to me. I actually believed. We all did. Not in Che's lo-fi communist shtick, per se, but in the pursuit of belief above all else. In doggedly stalking hard ideology instead of money, comfort, popularity, or party invites. When Josh had told *Surfer*'s silver-haired executive editor Sam George that "radical Islamic fundamentalism is the new alternative discourse," he was speaking for all of us and not kidding. Los Angeles could keep its cool and New York could keep its tawdry cocaine. The entire Western world could keep its scientific rationalism. We wanted to swim in real belief. We wanted to be with honest believers, with people willing to sacrifice everything for conviction.

After the beach celebration, they slaughtered a goat and cooked us a feast featuring a big bowl of goat milk. The last time they'd had this much fun, they told us, was twenty some years ago when a Soviet submarine surfaced and its crew piled out onto the rocky shore to play beach volleyball. Unlike us, the Russians had played in their underwear. It would have been more surprising except for the newly learned business about South Yemen being communist.

"Russians…" I said. "If they ain't wearing Adidas then they're hanging around some beach in their underwear. Am I right?" Then asked Cole to translate it to the villagers, hoping they'd find it as amusing an observation as I did. They laughed but it seemed more polite than genuine. Still, it was fascinating hearing about life on this bizarre little island so close to Yemen and yet so far.

We stayed in the village schoolhouse that night, wind howling, none of us sleeping but instead gazing at the old chalkboard with a roughly drawn map of either Egypt or Bulgaria, and surfed out the front in the morning. It was fun but small and we wondered what possibilities lay up the coast so we went for an hour hike and discovered another wave that was even better so surfed it all day before retreating to the schoolhouse for another vampire night.

The next day, starving and showing the first signs of real madness, we wondered if there was perhaps a wave even farther up the coast, so we went for a two-hour hike and discovered seven pristine coves, each one better than the next. Perfect lefts peeling off gorgeous points. Turquoise water barreling emptily like it had been forever over pure white sand, all guarded by peaks Josh had dubbed "Little Diphtheria."

After surfing waves beyond all of our dreams, we sprinted back to the village and somehow wrangled the other only car on the island to give us a ride back to Hadibu, where we stocked up on supplies: Nujoom candy bars, peanut butter, ramen noodles, banana milk boxes, tea, canned tuna, water, canned beans, and oatmeal.

On our way back, we noticed mist-crowned mountains in the island's very center. Mystical mountains, legendary mountains, mountains that belonged in epic Hollywood fantasies. Josh, Nate, and Cole thought they must be Black Doom from the Black Lands of Mordor. I had never read any Lord of the Rings so insisted Pamela Anderson and Carmen Electra lived up there, conducting all manner of secret business, conjuring the winds that blew off shore in every direction, and maybe using Marcus Schenkenberg in some dark ritual. The mystical mountains were known as Pam and Carmen thereafter, and like that, we arrived at the fishing village and traced our steps to our own private heaven.

We'd surf in the morning then retreat to the rocky cliffs that kept our world hidden, trying to find shelter from the relentless sun. I had Fyodor Dostoyevsky's *Notes from Underground* with me, and I'd lie in the dirt under outcroppings and feel reality slip. We'd surf again in the evening, then cook a dinner of canned beans and canned tuna before not falling asleep in a circular stone fisherman's structure that didn't have a roof. The stars would dance overhead and I'd marvel at them while eating everyone's candy bars and all the peanut butter.

At the end, we were left with two packets of tea, one package of ramen noodles, a scoop of sugar, and half a bottle of water. We had arranged one of the two cars to come and get us in a week, and the driver showed up just in time, hiking all the way to where we were crawling around like animals.

As we surfed our goodbye surf, the driver made a pot of sugary tea with the last of our water. We were so starving when we paddled in that we made sugary tea ramen. I thought it was a culinary stroke of genius and imagined opening a ramen tea café when we returned, but Nate puked on the way back to Hadibu, and so I temporarily shelved the idea.

CHAPTER 10

Major Ghamdan picked us up at Mukalla airport and seemed shocked when we fell down the propeller plane's sizzling metal steps. We hadn't gone native in the traditional sense—none of us wore a skirt, carried a *jambiya*, or had converted to Islam—but we were a sight. Skinny as rails, brown as dirt, blond as Laplanders, and in retrospect, just as crazy.

I studied my reflection in the Land Cruiser's rearview mirror as we returned up the desolate coast and made our way to the Yemen-Oman border. My eyes didn't belong to me. They were bluer, redder, more narrow. My pupils were so pinned that I was having trouble finding them. Maybe they were David Spade's eyes.

"Do my eyes look like David Spade's?" I asked Cole, trying to push my Spy sunglasses into my hair, which had become a saltwater helmet long ago.

"Duh," he responded. "You're chewing qat."

I had forgotten I was chewing qat. We all felt absolutely invincible and were let through every checkpoint with brisk waves of the hand. The soldiers knew they didn't need to worry about us. They knew we were dusted with Teflon.

But now I'm slightly worried about Josh, as he puts one of his feet on a moss-covered rock in the middle of a sneaky rain forest with the gray Indian Ocean beautifully corduroyed some three hundred feet straight down.

"Remember when you tried to climb that electrical tower in Whittier and got shocked off it then couldn't remember anything for the rest of the day?" I shout at him.

"If you want him to stop just go try and climb down yourself..." Nate whispers. "You know how much it hurts his feelings when he can't be the only one doing tough-guy stuff."

Cole has found four more wild camels and is taking close-ups of their soft feet with a pink cardigan wrapped around his head like a turban.

"Do camels have cloven hooves?" I ask Nate.

He looks at me with fatherly disappointment. "No."

"But do they chew cud?" I ask

"Yes."

"Okay, wait, so they don't have cloven hooves and they do chew cud. I forgot if that means they're clean or unclean, per Rabbinical law."

"Camels are unclean," he says, adding one more layer of fatherly disappointment. "Did you not learn anything in Old Testament history, guy?"

Nate and I had, indeed, shared an Old Testament history and literature class with a semi-friend named Matt Bissonette, who much to our surprise would later insert himself into the very middle of the Global War on Terror by claiming to have killed Osama bin Laden. Who knew a small Christian university could deliver such spunk?

"Let's go back down the coast a little and find an easier access point..." I shout at Josh. "There's no way we'll be able to get our boards down there unless we fling them off the cliff and there's no way we'll be able to climb back up with them."

Josh, annoyed at either my lack of pluck or my lack of belief in his physical abilities, comes high-stepping back and pitches a rock above my head, nearly hitting one of the camels.

"Good thing you didn't hit and kill it, bro. It's unclean. The locals wouldn't have been able to feast on its impossibly gamey yet unbelievably greasy meat."

"Oh, yes, they would have," Josh says. "Halal is better than kosher, and camel meat is on the menu."

"Yeah," says Nate, somehow even more disappointed.

"That is absolutely not better," I interject. "Camels are the greatest animals on Earth, biological marvels, and eating them would be both a sin and gross. Damn you both."

Josh and Nate both shrug. We climb back into the Land Cruiser, broadening our conversation on religious dietary restrictions, and Major Ghamdan blows a plume of smoke out the window while offering us cigarettes. He must have taken up smoking while we were on Soqotra, and it's a nice gesture. It almost seems as if he likes us. A 180-degree shift from the antagonistic relationship that had been established a few months ago. Maybe the fact that we still hadn't died even though he had given up protecting us impressed his corrupted but still Islamic heart. A wonderful expansion of his newfound inshallah spirit.

We decline, of course, since we are wholesome, and drive away from the coast over Josh's half-hearted protest, because I insist on heading through Osama bin Laden's father's village near Tarim in wadi Hadramawt, Yemen's almost dead center. This time we skirt Oman, then head west through the vast empty quarter. It's paved up here due to increasingly robust oil exploration and proper desert.

Conventional wisdom had long held that Yemen didn't have any oil, a concept openly mocked by Yemenis. They'd point to Saudi Arabia to the north, Oman to the east, and the UAE, Kuwait, Bahrain, and Qatar all sharing their peninsula, all oil rich, and laugh, knowing they must have plenty. Knowing that the oil companies are scared of them, and the more conspiratorial knowing that Saudi Arabia wants to keep them down.

The desert is hot, endless, alien, but it also feels more like home than home now. I can't even imagine that place now with its…rules? And…regulations? And…expected ways of acting and lack of adventure and small-minded boredom? We stay silent as the sun slips low, filling our world with dusty red light, and pull into a faceless desert town with the ubiquitous largeish rooms with random twin beds scattered here and there across the street from a disco mosque, and I fall into the deepest sleep.

Morning comes too soon, and though I am still exhausted, I can't return to a murky snooze. After eyeballing the flies socializing on the ceiling, I get up and fiddle with the TV I was too tired to fiddle with last night. Before I find any music videos, the door bursts open and Major Ghamdan marches into the room freshly showered, five o'clock shadow radiating health, with the same mischievous look in his eye he had in Aden, running from al-Qaeda, and in Bi'r Ali, shooting at a family enjoying their beach day all those months ago.

He heads straight to Josh's bed and stands above Josh, who has now woken and grabbed his Coke bottle glasses off the nightstand. Major Ghamdan looks at me and then Nate, who is now also awake, then Cole, who is still asleep, hovers his crooked finger over the middle of Josh's bed, presumably at Josh's midsection, gives one mischievous wink, and says, *"Shoof, shoof."*

I have absolutely no idea what he's on about. Josh pushes up to his elbows and squints through his Coke bottles up at Major

Ghamdan, who points again, winks again, and says, *"Shoof, shoof"* again.

It suddenly dawns on me that he is trying to maybe point out Josh's potential morning wood, though the sheet is so bunched up that even if Josh did indeed suffer from that common issue it would be impossible to tell if he was suffering from it at this moment.

"Shoof, shoof," Major Ghamdan says again, adding a tongue click to his wink.

Josh falls back and groans, then grunts, "Leave," and Major Ghamdan skips out the door.

During breakfast downstairs, he giddily offers to take us to his house in Marib for a few days of fun. We would drive around, shoot guns, and feast in the qat plantations—basically a version of everything we'd been doing every single day up to this point, except not in Marib, not in Yemen's most notoriously brutal town famous for kidnapping whole phalanxes of government troops just for fun. Famous for being dubbed "The al-Qaeda Town of Yemen." Famous for big, strong, extra-violent people who lay claim to the Queen of Sheba over Ethiopia's muted outcry.

We agree at once, and Josh is most excited of all, despite the fact that he had just been sexually assaulted, seeing that Marib is the most dangerous town on the peninsula. We're so thrilled that we blast through Osama bin Laden's family village, not stopping by the gift shop, and marathon straight to Marib's outskirts, pulling into a gas station the very next day in the heat of the mid-afternoon.

Major Ghamdan fills up the Land Cruiser, positively over the moon that we're so close. We buy plenty of snacks for the final ten minutes of road. Right when we're ready to pull out, a jacked-up technical bounces out of the desert and blocks our exit. Another comes hot after it, almost slamming into the passenger door, the high-caliber machine gun affixed to its bed wobbling back and forth.

Men file out of each and saunter around the Land Cruiser very aggressively, shoulders thrown back, chests puffed out. They are clearly angry and look mean. These are not skinny, bored kids, but grown men. The biggest men I'd seen in Yemen. Big by any measure, and farcically scary.

These are Major Ghamdan's people, Maribites, but he looks like a little runt compared to this crew. Like the Big Friendly Giant looked compared to Fleshlumpeater, Bonecruncher, Childchewer, and Meatdripper. Their five o'clock shadows are steel wool. Their biceps bulge underneath pale yellow gowns. Some wear baggy suit jackets that could double as two-person tents. Their jambiyas are menacing. Their Kalashnikovs look extra-used.

Major Ghamdan grabs his own Kalashnikov, opens the door, and approaches semi-cautiously while they launch into a cacophony of invectives, pointing at us, raising palms to the sky, their teeth pulled into snarls and cheeks filled with qat.

Marib loves its reputation, and I imagine that fathers raise their sons to be tougher than all the kids around, teach their kids to kidnap government troops before the age of eight. To roll into other Yemeni towns, stealing wives and other wives, leaving only a cloud of Drakkar Noir–scented dust behind.

"We're fucked," Josh says. "We're proper fucked."

I can see the tension spreading across his face for the first time in my life. Real tension. Cole is staring straight out the window and has turned slightly pale. Nate's expression has gone from stoic to determined. I'm still naked, save my Op trunks, and too addled to appreciate the stakes.

"These bros just want to party," I tell Josh. "Let's crack some fresh banana milk and dance to 'Get Busy.' 'Shake that thing, Miss Kana Kana…'"

He doesn't respond.

"Shake that thing, Miss Annabella..."

Nobody smiles.

"Come on. Sean Paul is the greatest voice of our generation."

Silence, and I give up.

After too long, Major Ghamdan walks back to the Land Cruiser followed by Bloodbottler, who sticks his oversized head through the window and glares at each of us one at a time. At Josh, at Nate, at Cole, at me. He says something else to Major Ghamdan, who dips his head then slides behind the wheel, and we pull out of the gas station following one of the trucks; the other, with a bed-mounted machine gun, drops behind us.

We drive through dusty, nondescript streets with dull buildings and past a dry orange farm. I keep mumbling the lyrics to "Get Busy" but feel Josh's annoyance radiating. This is his favorite moment of the adventure, maybe his favorite moment of his life. We're in legitimate danger, being driven who knows where by two trucks' worth of infamous men, and I'm trying to turn it into a cheap laugh instead of soaking in the adrenalized waft of imminent death.

To make matters worse, my joke isn't funny. Sean Paul *is*, unironically, the greatest voice of our generation.

A group of boys lean against a guard shack smashing balled-up fists into open hands as we pass, and then the lead truck stops in front of a high sheet-metal gate, its paint a faded red, white, and black. Two military men come out a small side door and don't look happy at all. Following a brief discussion, they head back inside and the metal gate opens, revealing an old American West meets Soviet-era bunker. Two technicals are parked to the side, painted Yemeni military beige. I wait for a tumbleweed to roll past scored to Ennio Morricone but played on a traditional Middle Eastern oud.

Major Ghamdan definitely does not seem himself as he gets out, subtly motioning for us to wait in the car. For the first time, we listen. He straightens up, walks over as purposefully as he can, and salutes the commander who comes out and does not look happy at all. Then the fuse ignites. The Maribites shout and point. Major Ghamdan and the commander gesticulate back. The two soldiers who opened the gate shrink into the growing shadows.

It is an honest miracle that Yemenis can have such vigorous arguments and not shoot each other in the face. Each one of the men in front of us has, at the very least, a Kalashnikov and pistol. A few might have briefcase machine guns. There might be a rocket launcher in their truck, and there is definitely a high-caliber machine gun bolted to its bed.

They argue wildly. I can't imagine the commander wants any part of this. It's his men the Maribites normally kidnap and ransom back to the government. It's why his two men here are now shrinking into the bunker and slowly closing its door. Major Ghamdan is not backing down. The commander, in an act of ill-advised camaraderie, stands shoulder to shoulder with him, barking viciously.

On and on it goes, and we sit silently in the Land Cruiser. I'm still too addled to imagine anything bad actually happening, still feeling the Teflon on my skin, but the faces of Josh, Nate, and Cole say something different. Or at least the faces of Josh and Cole. Nate's has returned to stoic.

The sun is low now, adding its Satanic red glow to an already bad scene, but on and on the argument goes until, like that, it's over. The Marabites look furious. Rage-filled. Like they are ready to explode. They each move back to their trucks but don't get in, standing there, arms crossed, all burning holes in our now vulnerable Land Cruiser. The same Land Cruiser that had just invincibly gone to the very edge of Yemen then almost back.

Major Ghamdan comes back, and it's the first time I've seen him sheepish. He didn't care about feasting and chewing our money away, about seeking hookers and booze in one of the most virulently Islamic countries on Earth, about shooting at picnicking families or sexually assaulting Josh, but now he is a hung dog.

"I'm sorry," he says in a cracking voice that sounds on the verge of tears. "We can't stay in Marib tonight but we can go to the ruins."

We all nod.

Marib was the capital of the Sabaean kingdom, which sorted out irrigation in an impossibly dry region and trade, dominating the important Middle Eastern frankincense business for a thousand years. Its kings built glorious temples and palaces. Many scholars and all tough Marabites believe Saba is one and the same as Sheba, famously ruled by the Queen of Sheba, who notably seduced Israel's King Solomon with her intelligence and charm.

Sometime before the birth of Mohammad, Marib's dams failed and other scholars suggest that this failure led to the Arabian Peninsula slipping into backwater status, accidentally missing Christianity's expansion and paving the way for Mohammad's Islam.

We gad around the ruins, three Christians and Cole, while Major Ghamdan twitches, looking over his Kalashnikov shoulder behind us. It is interesting, but even though I love Indiana Jones with all my heart, none of us are archeologists.

"Look at that…thing," I say to Josh, pointing at a rectangular spire that doesn't mean anything to me.

"Yeah…cool," he responds, despondent.

CHAPTER 11

"JUMP!" I SCREAM AT NATE, WHO IS STANDING ON THE TEAK DECK OF THE most beautiful yacht I've ever seen. A yacht more beautiful than the one in Jay-Z's "Big Pimpin'" music video because it has sails, lines, fishing tackle, air tanks, and a compressor. The sheet glass Red Sea spreads out before him as flat as I knew it'd be but entirely more gorgeous. I'm treading water. Josh is somewhere below me, trying to spear a fish. Cole is under a white umbrella, on a white beanbag chair, nursing a bottle of Hennessy.

Nate pinches his nose and plunges through the surface into a world exploding with color. Neon green, hot pink, electric blue, and impossibly clear. Yemen hovers somewhere to our left, Eritrea to our right, a smattering of volcanic islands used by pirates and smugglers all around.

Captain Maurico, an Italian by way of Eritrea whose hobby is scuttling boats and collecting the insurance before then salvaging them, leans his head out of the cabin and hollers, "Lunch will be soon."

I can already taste the freshly caught *pesce crudo* singed with lemon and dusted with salt.

Depression had sunk in after Marib, after failing to die there or at least even eat dinner, and after three months of failing to die in Aden, Zinjibar, Ataq, Bi'r Ali, Mukalla, Qusay'ir, Sayhut, Qishn, Al Ghaydah, Thamud, or Seiyun—not that death was what anyone except Josh was seeking. The vastness of our Yemeni circumambulation—what we had seen, smelled, tasted, surfed, done—was simply too difficult to process, so we moped around Sana'a without direction.

But Haitham al-Aini was right all that time ago. He knew a ten-day sail on the surf-less Red Sea was exactly what we'd need at the end, so off we shuttled to the coastal plain on Yemen's west and pushed out onto his boat. He had business in Dubai so couldn't join but said we'd be well taken care of by Captain Maurico.

And we were. We dove shipwrecks, swam, read, lounged, played soccer with Yemeni military stationed on otherwise lonely islands, ate fresh fish, and drank chilled Canada Dry while Cole continued to drink Hennessy. We laughed about everything we had just experienced, everything we had just done. We recounted moments one by one and buried them deep in our hearts.

Then, like that, the fun ended. We drug our Mylar surfboard coffins to Sana'a International to fly back to Los Angeles via Dubai this time, which Haitham insisted we visit, rerouting our flights away from Moscow. "Dubai is the future, guys..." he said, knowingly. "You absolutely have to see it. Amazing. Truly amazing."

He wasn't wrong, per se. Early-2000 Dubai felt like *Blade Runner* might if written and directed by trust-funded Saudi Arabian boys who loved robot porn. Shiny, future-shaped skyscrapers grew out of the blank desert by the hundreds, by the thousands. Shiny Mercedes shuttled locals and other assorted Kuwaitis, Bahrainis, Qataris, and Saudis from one air-conditioned haven to another. Pakistani laborers were shuttled in windowless jail buses to finish a cluster of islands off the coast that, together, created the shape of a palm tree.

We ate at Dubai's first-ever sushi restaurant, all pristine and white, and we arrogantly vibed the trust-funded Emirati boys around us—not because Los Angeles had many sushi restaurants, but because we had been to Yemen and were wild, tan, and free. We had eaten goat on Soqotra and *pesce crudo* on the Red Sea.

We had lived. Truly lived.

Eventually one of the Emirati boys approached us and we talked about how much better Yemen was than Dubai and how it had better surf too. Lightly impressed, he invited us onto his boat the next day to wakeboard.

"We'll be there," Josh told him.

He had Minnesota-bred confidence in his lake skills, and I was also confident he would make us look good, as a group.

The next day was scorching hot and humid. True to his word, the boy—whose name sounded very much like "Ride the Bus"—and his friends were prepped and ready to go with their brand-new, properly kitted Ski Nautique. Nate's run was unremarkable, as was mine, but with Josh batting cleanup I didn't worry. He knew the wake game. He had 10,000 lakes buried deep in his heart.

And he did not disappoint, grasping the rope and whipping in fakey straight away. A couple straight airs over the wake, then a 180, then a 360, and I looked around at our hosts nodding dismissively and feeling proud. Feeling brave, tough, enlightened, tan, skilled. Like Lawrence of Arabia, Sir Wilfred Thesiger, Henry de Monfreid, Sir Richard Burton, Bertram Thomas, and Indiana Jones.

Then Josh really wound up and threw some tweaked off-axis thing high and furious, landing hard in the flats and disappearing in a burst of whitewash.

Ride the Bus looped the boat back around and picked him up, clearly impressed, asking, "Are you a professional?"

Josh smiled then took a seat next to me.

"I think I broke my foot," he whispered between small talk.

I continued nodding dismissively.

On the flight home, it swelled to balloon size. The Emirates stewardess—a cute thing from Ireland done up in Orientalist fantasy—felt pity and told Josh that he shouldn't be embarrassed, that many people suffer from swelling joints when stuck on longer flights and maybe he should wear compression socks next time. Maybe that would help. Josh tried to explain to her that his foot wasn't just swollen. He had broken it throwing some tweaked off-axis wakeboard thing in Dubai after surfing Yemen for three months.

She didn't believe him.

I nodded dismissively.

PART TWO

CHAPTER 1

Lebanon, mid-2000s

We returned home as conquering heroes, iconic explorers, one-of-a-kind visionaries who recognized radical Islamic fundamentalism as the most potent idea of our lifetime, our parents' lifetime too, and went out to meet it on surfboards hand-shaped in Costa Mesa. The first to ever do, the only to ever do. Absorbing and synthesizing the razor's edge state of the world in a brand-new, entirely unexpected way because it was equal parts earth-shaking and fun. It was both wonderfully unexpected yet impossible to categorize.

Or at least that's how I saw it.

Now, I probably should have figured out that this overarching narrative wasn't exactly "on brand" for "The Bible of the Sport" *Surfer* magazine. Managing editor Sam George bought us as tweed-jacket-with-leather-elbow-patches academic bros and was looking for a serious take on this post-9/11 world with a hefty dash of surf mixed in. When his staff hovered over the light board in their Dana Point offices, loupes pressed to eyes, bending over our slides, alternately hmmm-ing and tilting their heads while other editors read Josh's story about the adventure and frowned, I should have perceived that our rollicking good time in the world's most dangerous country didn't tell the expected story.

But I didn't.

The photographs turned out better than I thought they would. Sure, the surf action was suspect, but I had convinced myself that, in context, it was physical art because that context was rusty shipwrecks, mist-shrouded mountains, giant dead crabs, and sticks that looked like Mother Theresa. Skirted men, proud ninjas, stone villages never before captured on film. Kalashnikovs, heavy caliber machine guns, terrorists, and other terrorists—i.e., Yemenis—holding guns, chewing qat, looking vaguely menacing in Osama bin Laden's homeland. The Global War on Terror made flesh.

And it was fun. Spending three months in the breadbasket of terror with the best people, best food, and best tans had been the greatest time ever, but it wasn't supposed to be. It was supposed to be a mostly serious, ham-fisted, traditional surf adventure narrative, and cleanly sensible à la Joseph Campbell's hero's journey.

But it wasn't.

The editors and managing editors scrunched up their noses as Josh and I stepped all over each other's explanations of the power of alternative discourses, the lazy decadence of Western hegemonic thought, the perpetual value in looking at both sides now and refusing to stuff anything into the box where it belongs.

Then they all rubbed their chins.

I didn't care and didn't stop to imagine why anyone would have a problem with our honest reckoning, even as the dust from the World Trade Center was still settling in Manhattan. Bulldozing through those frowns, scrunched noses, and rubbed chins exactly like I had in my high school literature class when I wrote an essay on

Oliver North's autobiographical book *Under Fire* being the pinnacle of important paradigm shifts in American literature even though my teacher was a dyed-in-the-wool communist and Oliver North was not an "author." Exactly like I had during my master's degree program where I insisted on doing a linguistic analysis of Anton LaVey's *Satanic Bible* even though I was studying at a Christian university and Anton LaVey's *Satanic Bible* has zero scholarly merit and somehow less linguistic value.

I failed both papers, and failed badly, but didn't care and didn't stop to imagine why. The burning fringes, the bizarre juxtapositions, the alternative discourse was endlessly fascinating, and radical Islamic fundamentalism was the hottest fire I'd ever felt. It was dangerous, electric, alive, and metastasizing at that very moment. Warping, changing, consuming, and challenging what we'd been taught as self-evident: that once Communism bit the dust, free-market, liberal democracies would be the only coherent show in town, and every nation would hop on that sweet train.

Josh and I rammed some semi-neutered version through *Surfer* editorial staff, our Yemen feature came out, and I ran down to the grocery store to buy that issue, imagining we had just become famous. Imagining the general public would see right through *Surfer* editorial staff small-mindedness and embrace the ride.

It looked good, or good enough. We had a blurb on the cover and a full eight pages inside, though all the pictures had been shrunken to thumbnail size and Josh's words were missing the most salient bits but still. There we were, in *Surfer* magazine, hundreds of thousands reading, hundreds of thousands seeing this bold new vision, and I wondered if that would be the last time I'd ever be able to walk around in public again without being recognized.

It wasn't, if you can believe it, but I was high on the representational possibilities, on this new, brave world, a place where belief was tantamount. Our gambit had worked in real practical terms. We had published a story juxtaposing surfing and radical Islamic fundamentalism, and I wondered what else might be possible.

Thankfully my "job" provided ample time for mind wandering. I had applied for an English-as-a-second-language adjunct teaching position at Los Angeles City College before we took off for Yemen and somehow snagged it while we were there. Upon return, I spent my "working" hours telling Armenian grandmothers that the best part of English was its lack of actual rules and they didn't have to worry about "passing" because grades are meaningless, then running to the staff lounge computer and searching airline ticket prices anywhere in the world that radical Islamic fundamentalism flowered. To Tehran so we could snowboard with the Revolutionary Guard, Grozny so we could snowboard with the radical Chechen separatists, Afghanistan so we could snowboard with the embattled Taliban, Pakistan so we could surf with Taliban who were not yet embattled, or Beirut so we could skateboard with Hezbollah. Getting right into the dead center of it all, the heart of belief and action using a decidedly asinine medium. Oh, not asinine to me. I dreamed of all the untracked mountains, all the unridden waves, and felt it was the most honest reason to go anywhere. Much more honest than some political charade, capitalistic play, or academic *fait accompli*.

Skateboarding with Hezbollah seemed particularly compelling, as the Shia militants had started to dial up their campaign against Israel, declaring that the Palestinian Intifada was also their fight, snagging Israeli soldiers tiptoeing too close to the border, and lobbing rockets into northern Israel.

As fate would have it, Nate had flown to Lebanon weeks after we returned home, chasing a graduate degree in political studies from the American University of Beirut but spending most of his time in a Hezbollah boxing gym. Their taciturn dispositions jibed well with his stoicism, and he soon moved to a spartan flat in their neighborhood and did bag work in between courses on Islamic political thought and communalism in the Middle East.

Yes, we needed to go skateboarding with Hezbollah, and I texted this to Josh straight away. Thankfully he had stayed in Los Angeles, tripling down on unorthodoxy in his UCLA Islamic Studies doctorate and becoming an academic *enfant terrible*, authoring papers rocking the established canon, leaving famous professors scratching their heads at the handsome boy with the Mandy Moore–esque haircut who had invaded their stodgy ranks while scrambling to counter his radical destruction of the established canon.

He responded within minutes: "Ha ha ha. None of us skate and you kick mongo."

But he'd always been slow in perceiving the breadth of my genius. We didn't really "surf" either in the traditional sense of the word, or at least skilled sense. I quickly pitched the germ of a story to *Vice* magazine, a free "edgy" heroin lifestyle publication out of Canada, while he was in class and while I was supposed to be teaching one and received a reply minutes later:

"Intrigued. Would like to hear more."

I spent the evening with Josh, spinning an outline of where we would go, who we would see, and what we would do. He talked, I typed, and two weeks after that we were both on an Aeroflot flight to Beirut via Moscow. Unfortunately, Cole was not with us. He had stayed in Yemen, losing his mind in a qat den haze while dating a girl from the Japanese consulate, crocheting tea cozies, and translating the collected works of Karl Lagerfeld into ancient Sabaean, but Nate had a classmate who had a camera, this time, and off we went to meet him with a whole two thousand Canadian heroin dollars in our shared pocket plus four Sector 9 skateboards, three pairs of Joven sunglasses, and a bundle of T-shirts from Seven2, which was Ocean Pacific's last gasp at cracking the elusive Kmart market.

And thus began a florid, manic, three-year rip.

The story came out, and while we still weren't getting stopped on the street, the addiction had its claws fully set. Three months later we were surfing in Somalia, getting chased and shot at by wild-eyed Islamo-pirates. Two months after that, we were hunting for illegal Islamo-arms dealers while surfing in Syria, then back to Beirut, up to Azerbaijan, down to Egypt, over to Morocco, back to Syria, over to Pakistan, into Colombia for its radicalized Druze population, down to Syria, and then back to Beirut. Surfing, snowboarding, surfing, "skating." Sitting with mullahs, Qur'anic students, tribal leaders, and terrorists, discussing and debating the virtues of radicalization. Writing them all for various magazines whose editors had stopped scrunching their noses and started calling for more.

There was something visceral about what we were doing. Something compelling. Even *Paper* magazine, widely respected in bleeding edge circles for breaking the next trans supermodel and most fabulous it-it club kid did a feature on us, declaring that we were the boy band of radical Islamic terrorism, ramming our smirking mugs and fiery defenses of belief, a belief worth fighting over, a belief worth dying over.

Strange days, indeed.

At the same time, I had become the most popular teacher at Los Angeles City College. Each semester would begin, and I'd tell my Armenian grandmothers, who had been followed by Russian taxi drivers, Thai bakers, Ukrainian hairdressers, Korean masseuses, Mexican contractors, and Guatemalan busboys, that if they really wanted to learn English they should drop out of my class and take another, but if they wanted a guaranteed "A" they should stay. The *only* caveat was they weren't allowed to tell the administration that I'd be gone for at least a month every semester, traveling to the Middle East.

For the working Los Angeles poor trying to supplement meager incomes with student aid, this was the best deal ever, and my classes were swelled to standing room only, students stretching from wall to wall, dragging desks from other classrooms that contained an appropriate number of learners.

Administrators would walk by and dip their heads through the door, confused. I'd roar, combatively, that my class was an oasis for the tired, the poor, the huddled masses yearning to be free and that I would never turn a student away. In my heart, I wondered how long it would take for the administration to question the 120 "As" being given every semester to the most wonderfully kind but decidedly not "academically sound" cast.

And while we still weren't getting stopped on the street, Hollywood had come knocking. I now know the entertainment machine has a ravenous appetite for random nonsense, but our *mise en scène* was also working. Josh and I had lunch with Brian Grazer, the famous partner of Ron Howard and producer of *Splash*, *Apollo 13*, *8 Mile*, and *The Nutty Professor* to name but a fraction. His people reached out, desperate to set a date. Josh and I showed up late and salt crusted from an ill-advised Topanga surf where we'd gotten in a splash fight with a notorious grumpy local. Brian, hair coiffed into a perfect spike, peppered us with questions about what we were doing and what life was like playing with terrorists. He'd lean forward in his chair as we answered, antsy legs bouncing slightly, eyes wide. After we'd thanked him for lunch, he chased us out to ask if 50 Cent's G-Unit brand was cool and if he should wear it.

We told him no.

Next came Fremantle media, a Santa Monica–based production company that wanted to sign me and Josh to a development deal. They were hypnotized by what was being described as "our fun thing with terrorists" and wanted to create a show around it.

Josh was skeptical. Skeptical that they really understood what we were doing. Skeptical that it would translate to a broadcast television audience. Skeptical that we could ever be even halfway sellable on screen or remotely understandable.

His doubt infuriated me.

"Of course we'll crush it!" I'd scream at him over the barbeque chicken pizza dipped in ranch dressing that I'd just discovered in Pasadena. "Look at us. Look at what we're doing. We're basically almost famous! We've spent the afternoon with the al-Aqsa Martyrs' Brigade leader, for crying out loud. We've been chased around Syria and Somalia. We've surfed in Yemen, for pity's sake. We're born stars, out getting amongst it in ways nobody has ever dreamed—no journalist, no *médecin sans frontières*, no soldier—and this is our moment."

"But I think being on camera is a real thing, a real…I don't know if it's a skill, but it's something," he'd offer back meekly. "Plus, I don't know if our making an apology for radical Islamic fundamentalism is going to be a big hit with a mainstream American audience."

Even still, my confidence was at an all-time high. Hadn't we proven that people care through our endless magazine articles? Hadn't we revealed our hidden skill? Plus, I had just gotten an epic haircut. Longer and a bit shaggy, but not too shaggy. I felt progressive, chic, and smart. For the first time in my life, I felt smart.

So I'd drag him to twice-weekly meetings in Fremantle's Santa Monica offices. Things went well at first. They'd ask us what we'd want to do. We'd tell them. Algeria, Chechnya, Iraq, Afghanistan, Iran, Somalia, Yemen. Surfing or whatever. Insurance issues came up and their pitches to us devolved further and further until the last ugly turn, almost a year after we signed, where the show would be about us searching for folk music in Timbuktu. Literally Timbuktu, there in Mali, Africa, but most commonly used as shorthand for "far away." As in Timbuktu to Kalamazoo. Folk music. Probably even world music. In truth, I probably should have smelled the pivot coming since Fremantle's only hit was *American Idol.*

And for the first time since al-Qaeda had declared war on the West, I felt defeated. Were we really going to go to Timbuktu? Was there any radical Islamic fundamentalism in Timbuktu? Was there terrorism of any kind close to Timbuktu? How "locked in" to our development deal were we?

I made Josh call our entertainment lawyer, a Hollywood heavy, principal in the Gay Mafia, serious mover and shaker named Erik who worked for us pro bono because he too had been swept away in our glorious pastiche of belief, terrorism, surfing, danger, and music videos. It was quite obviously ridiculous, absurd, but, at the same time, something fundamentally more. *Vice* was busily changing their whole "journalism" model to reflect what we were doing after its founders tagged along on a trip to Beirut; Brian Grazer was kicking around vague movie plots; Fremantle was trying to derail it all but just because they didn't understand that we had to be in the middle of it.

Not *near* it. Not *adjacent* to it.

In it.

Thankfully Erik didn't have to do any more pro bono work, as radical Islamic fundamentalism swung in and saved us from aimless lives once again. In a still disputed move, on July 12, 2006, Hezbollah fighters either crossed the border into Israel and snagged two Israeli soldiers or snagged them tiptoeing into Lebanon and dragged them across. Israel sent five other soldiers in to rescue them and they were promptly killed. Hezbollah demanded the release of its own prisoners held in Israel by the Israeli government, and all hell broke loose. For the first time in years, Israel unleashed a hail of bombs north, destroying Beirut's airport and major infrastructure within minutes.

And it was on. A real, old-fashioned war within the broader Global War on Terror pitting Hezbollah and its fierce, unbending vision of Islamic governance against Israel and its equally fierce, unbending vision of modernity. This was an apex moment in our arc, and not being there on the ground was unthinkable.

We told Fremantle we absolutely had to go cover it. The vice president of programming and the other vice president of programming raised their voices, really trying to sell Timbuktu—but in the end they realized we were possessed, and so they freed us.

"Al Gore!" I shouted at Josh as we drove east on the 10 Freeway toward Los Angeles.

"What?" he shouted back.

We were in my 1977 MG Midget convertible. The top didn't go up and the muffler had just fallen off.

"Al Gore! Some producers reached out to me a few weeks ago about his weird new television-meets-internet media thing called Current TV! I told them we were locked up in a development deal, but I'm going to pitch them right when I get home! We absolutely have to go cover this war!"

CHAPTER 2

"What's this bro's problem?" I'm mumbling through my sweaty Ellen DeGeneres haircut at Josh, who's sitting shotgun in the microvan we'd been transferred to an hour ago from the yellow Chevrolet Caprice we'd been in since Amman, Jordan. "Why aren't we moving?"

Josh shakes his head, annoyed. "He's saying that he won't take us if we keep the surfboards on the roof. He says they look like missiles and if Israeli jets spot us, they'll take us out."

"Well, ain't that a *mishmish*." I whistle while looking at Nate. "Ain't that just a real mishmish."

Nate loosens his black pencil tie slightly, looking back at me quizzically and asks, "An apricot?"

I had meant "peach," but same difference.

"We need the surfboards," I say. "It's nonnegotiable, so what's our play here?"

In truth, we didn't need the surfboards at all. We had surfed in Lebanon a handful of times already over the past few years, up near Tripoli in the north, just outside Tyre in the south, and all around Beirut but always in the winter. Lebanon, like Italy, the south of France, and Barcelona, hugs the Mediterranean, which requires violent storms in order to create any semblance of surf—and violent storms only occur in the winter. Summer is gorgeous, warm, sensual, and flat as a pancake, but it didn't matter. There is always the odd chance that waves might break, and if they do, and if I don't have a surfboard, it will be the cruelest torture.

The driver grunts then climbs out of his door and lights a cigarette. He's theoretically braver than his brother or cousin or brother-in-law, the one who owns the yellow Chevrolet Caprice, the one who turned out to be a chicken.

We'd found him outside Queen Alia International Airport in Amman, a city we all despised for being boring and stable. He'd been lounging under an artificial date palm at the edge of the hot parking lot, and we told him we needed a lift to Beirut. His eyes lit with money signs. Amman to Beirut was just over a 300-kilometer trip and usually took four hours, up through Syria on the M5, cutting west just outside Damascus on the 1, past the border, through the Beqaa, over the Mount Lebanon mountain range, down into Beirut. A hefty fare by any measure. A nice wad of cash. A wartime economy bump.

We would have just flown into Beirut, but its airport had been bombed defunct in the first day of the war. Large smoking craters in the middle of runways. Windows blown out of terminals. Aeroflot didn't have any good deals flying into Damascus, plus it was quicker to get Syrian visas at the border rather than sending our passports to the consulate in Washington, DC, so Amman it was.

And while we all found the Hashemite Kingdom terribly droll, quickness was a commodity more valuable than exotic danger at the present time. As soon as we'd gotten home from Fremantle, I'd emailed Current TV telling them it was their lucky day, that they had a most rare opportunity to get us headed into a war but that they had to act immediately. They responded right away, wondering if we had camera experience, editing experience, or producing experience.

"OF COURSE!" I punched back, even though we had none of those.

"Can you send a reel?" they inquired.

"THERE'S NO TIME!" and I nearly broke the "N" key from a very chubby older-model MacBook. "THIS WAR COULD END AT ANY MOMENT!"

I was worried it really would end at any moment and that we'd miss the whole thing. Israel was throwing its entire mighty mite strength at a political party/terrorist organization that didn't have an air force or a navy. Lebanon, as a country, was split in theoretically equal thirds between Christians, Sunnis, and Shia, and I didn't imagine the Christians and Sunnis were too happy taking a shellacking on behalf of their fellow Shia after all fighting each other for fifteen years in one of history's most brutal civil wars.

"JOSH!" I screeched over my shoulder. "Can we film, edit, produce five-to-twelve-minute segments on the road, and somehow get them to Current's San Francisco offices from the middle of war-gutted Lebanon?"

"I'm sure we can sort out a camera..." he said while making an extra strong pot of coffee in my kitchen, "...and probably figure out how to point it at each other, I suppose. And I just met a woman named Mimi at the Roosevelt a few nights ago. She told me that she had run away from home as a child and run to Andy Warhol's factory, where she had learned the art of filmmaking from the foot of the man who said, 'Everyone will be famous for fifteen minutes.' And then...I couldn't really follow her. Apparently many award-winning documentaries, trips to the Alps and various other projects. It all sounded dubious, but while we were sitting there, a never-ending stream of producers, executive producers, content creators, directors, writers, show runners, and those who had development deals with major, major studios came up to trade her air kisses. Not that any of that means anything. I was also on my second vodka soda."

We were lightweights back then.

"CALL HER!" I screamed, reaching hysteria. "We're gonna bag this! We're not only gonna get to go surf in a war, we're gonna get famous for at least fifteen minutes but probably a lot more. This is finally our moment. This is where it all comes together. Fuck Timbuktu!"

"There's no summer surf in Lebanon, bro," Josh responded. "Remember?"

Two days later we were on a plane to Amman, Jordan. We snagged Nate, who, as fate would have it, had just come back from Lebanon, and he instantly secured an ex-classmate's apartment bordering Hezbollah's neighborhood, an area that was getting hit by Israeli bombs every night, and doubled up by enlisting one of his old friends who was currently in a Los Angeles film school as our cameraman. He would have to fly out fifty hours later, as he had film school finals, but it was better than nothing and better than us. Mimi, Josh's contact from the Roosevelt, had promised that if we got her film she'd turn it into art, and that, mixed with boisterous all caps emails to Al Gore, got us $15,000 wired within forty-eight hours.

Everything was working seamlessly, without the slightest hiccup, until we neared Syria and our tough guy started to get fidgety, telling us that Israel had been pounding the crossing between Syria and Lebanon and he didn't feel safe taking us into the country but did have a brother or cousin or brother-in-law living in Syria that would do it no problem and started dialing him on a tiny Nokia.

We were naturally incensed, having negotiated our deal, and there was no way he could back out of it now. Absolutely no way at all. I didn't believe the brother or cousin or brother-in-law actually existed, either, and burning hours on the border was not an option. We'd done that sort of business enough in our "Global War on Terror" years and there could be a giant shift in this actual war at any moment, some seismic happening that we could not afford to miss. This was, after all, our first war—our first real declared war—within the broader, endless Global War on Terror, and I didn't want to be late.

I continued browbeating our driver with Josh looking back from the front seat, alternately amused and befuddled. It was usually his job to rudely harass locals trying as hard as they could to help us, Nate's job to be paternally dismissive, and my job to keep the mood light while semi-carefully stealing snacks when people weren't looking.

My Arabic had, thankfully, improved slightly, and I kept up an almost sensible barrage of insults until we reached the border, he stopped the car, pulled our shiny Mylar surfboard coffin off his roof, and handed it to a man sitting next to a microvan underneath a scrubby tree.

Lo and behold, the brother or cousin or brother-in-law was real and had a Johnny-Ringo-from-*Tombstone* air about him. Strong jawline. Keffiyeh wrapped loosely around his neck like a bandana. Moustache that exuded strength under fire. He took the coffin without saying a word, lugged it over, strapped it to the top of his van, and bid us to enter with a subtle tilt of the head.

We waved goodbye to our old driver and it seemed as if he harbored no ill will from me calling him "a very bad little girl, a very naughty bad little girl" over and over. Even I had to admit we had been upgraded. Not only was the van roomier than the Caprice, but his windows had nice curtains—thick burgundy drapes that lent an air of luxury.

We drove along without incident until we were fewer than 20 kilometers from the Syria-Lebanon border, when our new driver became intransigent, seemingly without provocation.

"We need our boards," I say again, even though we don't. "We're going to find a miraculous swell and surf the war," I add, even though we aren't.

The driver mutters something while looking at his phone. Josh translates, "He's saying there are reports of Israeli jets hitting the border right now. One of his buddies is there."

"We're missing it…" I groan. "We're missing the war. Tell him we'll stick the boards inside the van, how's that?"

Miraculously *that* is an acceptable solution, and we're back on the road in five minutes flat, pressed against the van's burgundy drapes while the shiny Mylar surfboard coffin gets comfortable between us.

We'd been shot at by pistols, uzis, briefcase uzis, shotguns, Kalashnikovs, and heavy caliber machine guns but had never been bombed, which somehow seemed less menacing. Couldn't jets be heard screaming overhead? Couldn't bombs be heard whistling though the air? Bombs seemed like the most easily dodged ordnance and the least personal.

Ten minutes later we see our first real signifiers of war. Vehicles of every make and model clogging the single lane heading out of Lebanon, flatbed trucks crammed with people clutching dusty luggage. Bigger trucks jammed with blue plastic barrels filled with who knows. Cars with men riding on top of concaving roofs, dusty children hanging out of windows. Wives walking alongside holding bunches of carrots in plastic bags.

None of them seem overly bummed. An almost festival atmosphere permeates, Lebanese "habibi" hits floating through the stifling hot air, shouted conversations between friends and neighbors. Children laughing. We are even more joyful since we are headed into Lebanon, not out, so our path is completely clear. Not one other car to slow us down. Not one unnecessary pause and it stays that way until we read no man's land.

The border between Syria and Lebanon includes a 10-kilometer buffer—Syrian soldiers on one end, Lebanese soldiers on the other. A geographically handsome strip of land featuring red dirt, rolling hills, and clear, higher elevation air. Real estate that would make any California developer lust over potential. It has a gold rush quality, and I can easily imagine a prospector-themed amusement park doing well. Something a little like Knott's Berry Farm, but instead of Snoopy as the mascot it would be Ol' Hassan, the grumpy claim-jumping militant.

We've passed through it a baker's dozen times and are used to the Syrian seriousness first modeled by Hafez al-Assad and then aped by his eldest son Bashar, who speaks with the most fragile lisp on one side. The Lebanese arrogance born of having better music videos, better food, better Mediterranean-fronting day clubs on the other.

I want to begrudge the Lebanese their arrogance but simply can't. Their Mediterranean-fronting day clubs rival the best of Europe, with delicate, seasonally appropriate cocktails and satisfying cuisine. I want to mock the Syrian sincerity but also can't. Their bureaucracy is a humming machine. A "secret policeman around every corner, government employee in every kitchen" dynamo.

Our driver pulls into the entirely empty military installation and we drain from his van, sauntering into the generic cement building featuring painted Persian-esque "windows" on the walls and bold "Syrian Arabic Republic" painted elsewhere. The room, usually teeming with fathers, mothers, and children, is empty. We stand for a few minutes at a half window, rudely clearing our throats until a Syrian military man ambles out from his smoky office and asks why we are going into Lebanon. Didn't we know now was not the time? Hadn't we heard that the Lebanese were getting pummeled?

We tell him we had heard, that's why we are here. We're war journalists now, carrying out an important mission, informing the people of America what is really happening on the ground as humble servants of Al Gore. He shrugs dutifully and stamps our passports with Syrian exit visas. It isn't what I expected, to be honest. I thought real wars upended life. I thought that wartime humans reverted to a basic form of anarchy.

We file back to the microvan and continue pressing toward our destination, seeing the first physical signs of war. Massive bomb craters, some still smoking, some half filled with still-smoking semitrucks and cars twisted like burned pretzels. It's difficult for me to understand why the drivers hadn't heard the screaming jets and whistling bombs and gotten the hell away from trouble.

The closer to Lebanon we get, the more craters we see, until they are clipping and then obliterating the road leading out. Thick, jagged chunks of concrete forming grotesque miniature Matterhorns. The masses shouting and pushing their vehicles over them. Clearing paths off to the side. And then they clipped our road. Red dirt mixing in with the brokenness.

We drip out of the microvan for the first real crater once we hear the axle grinding then catching, helping push it over the next real crater when it becomes clear that the microengine and microwheels don't have what it takes. We lift the whole damned thing into the air in the third crater, making me truly understand

and appreciate miniature vans for the first time in my life. Very practical things. Moveable little squat machines.

I'm sweating through my plain white V-neck T-shirt, and my thighs are burning underneath my 7 for All Mankind jeans featuring slight ankle flare by the time we arrive at the Lebanese end of no man's land. I'm proud of the jeans, having just discovered designer denim and finally jettisoning surf fashion. That godforsaken industry could keep its big-logoed Spy, Globe, StickGrip, Joven, Ocean Pacific, Seven2. We are serious now, not needing surf dollars to fund our exploits, and we're on the verge of major fame. It's time to look the part, and I look through my Versace sunglasses with rococo golden suns adorning the arms at Josh as he wedges out of the microvan, looking the part in black women's Dickies and a black T-shirt. He'd gone perpetual black on black before it was cool for non-goth kids. I look at Nate in his white button-up soaked through with sweat like my V-neck and his loosened black pencil tie and black pants, pressing after Josh. He'd adopted that as his uniform at some point during his graduate degree and wore nothing else, but it suited him. I bend around the surfboard bag and follow underneath the oversized red and white flag featuring a massive green cedar in the middle.

The Lebanese border agents don't appear particularly rattled as they take our passports and ask after our business. We tell them we're war journalists, and I make sure to dip my Versaces for emphasis. They rifle through the pages, flipping back and forth, studying Somali stamps, Yemeni stamps, and the multitude of Lebanese stamps, apply one more, and we all turn around, climb back into the microvan, and start to jabber excitedly about what we should do first.

"We should get to the apartment and see if it's still standing," Nate says.

"But we've got to get a car before anything else, and also, Jossy hungry," Josh parries.

Nate sighs.

"Hey, Nate…" I clamor from the back, "…do you think that shawarma place is open? And do you think the apartment has TV?"

He doesn't hear me because the surfboard coffin is burying my head.

"Chicken shawarma!" I repeat, louder.

Josh hears me this time and says, "Mmmmm. Shawarma."

Our driver has sped up noticeably now, and we fly past fresh craters just off the road. Smoldering cars and trucks twisted and grotesque guide us up toward the mountain range separating Lebanon's verdant Beqaa Valley from its coastal strip. He periodically thrusts his head out the window, listening, looking into the sky. His radio is on loud, crackling, and I can hear the names of southern Lebanese towns.

"They're really hitting the south!" Nate says above the din.

"We need to get down there ASAP!" I holler back.

"Hungry!" Josh adds.

The sun has almost dipped into the Mediterranean by the time we reach Beirut's outskirts, painted a dark red as the light filters through smoke. The city looks the same—the same Burger Kings, same billboards advertising jewelry featuring puckered-mouthed sensual beauties, same Europcar rental place that we'd used before.

"Pull over!" Josh tells the driver, who seems relieved to be getting rid of us. Before even seeing if it is open, he hops out, runs to the passenger side, slides the door open, and starts tugging at our surfboard coffin.

I guess this is our stop no matter what.

Josh grabs his passport and heads into the office. I gather our bags into a small pile while Nate pays our man his fare. He's in such a hurry that he doesn't even try to haggle for more, just takes his wad of US dollars mixed with Jordanian pounds and skedaddles into the sunset.

"There's absolutely no way they're renting cars," I tell Nate, feeling 100 percent certain that we will have to get very creative in acquiring a vehicle.

"I don't know. The civil war didn't end that long ago. I think the Lebanese are generally more comfortable with risk."

"Yeah, but this is Europcar," I remind him, "owned by the notoriously sissy French. They love nothing more than rolling over. I bet the clerks have received orders directly from Paris to hide under the customer service counter and only peek around when the Gauloises run low."

Josh comes bouncing out smiling before Nate can respond, and says, "I upgraded us to an Audi."

"What? I'm shocked. Honestly shocked. They're renting Audis?"

"Yeah," Josh says. "It's only an A4, but it was either that or a Pajero for their 'luxury' vehicle selection, and while I know Nate would have preferred the Pajero, I made an executive call."

"The Pajero does have four-wheel drive," Nate deadpans, purposefully ignoring Josh's Spanish joke. Mitsubishi's mid-sized SUV is ubiquitous throughout the Middle East, including Yemen, and Nate had mistakenly told us that in his native Bolivia, "*pajero*" meant "masturbator."

"Well, epic," I say, really feeling the glow of our concurrent successes and only slightly bad for needlessly denigrating France. It was rare to stack so many in a row and especially in the modern Middle East, where confused God's unknowable will is a way of life.

We'd spent countless hours in smoky back rooms waiting for this general or that terrorist to sign off on this or that step. We'd become masters of outwaiting men with no real sense of time, persisting up various chains of command, making lemonade out of lemons, but this adventure seemed positively blessed. Our Aeroflot flight made it to Amman, we've found a taxi driver to take us all the way to Beirut, we didn't have any visa issues in Syria or Lebanon, and now we have an extremely low-mile, gunmetal-gray Audi. "Let's get the coffin on the roof and head south. We've got a war to cover here. Time to make Al Gore proud."

Josh helps me lug it up while Nate fishes nylon straps from its side pocket and slides them through the open rear passenger doors, cinching them down like we had to roofs in Yemen, in Somalia, in Syria, and in Lebanon on seven separate occasions. I snag the other strap, slide it through the front driver's side door and front passenger door, tug it tight, and finish it with a nice shoelace bow.

Even though this is Nate's city, where he came to study, where he boxed with Hezbollah, where he fell in love with two sisters—one who shaved her head and made progressive art, the other who wore a hijab and worked with Palestinian refugees—it had become such a regular feature in our last three years that I knew more hot Beirut nightspots than I did in LA.

"You think BO 18 is open during this war?" I ask Nate as soon as we get on the main road heading through downtown.

He twists his head to answer. "I hope so. It stayed open every night during the Cedar Revolution."

"But wasn't the Cedar Revolution just a street party? Like a giant Electric Daisy Carnival featuring anti-Syria interventionist DJs?" I ask, wondering if I had fundamentally misunderstood the Cedar Revolution while it was happening.

"Yes," he answers simply.

BO 18 is a fantastic club, no doubt, in an underground graveyard with a giant helicopter pad roof that opens each night when the party hits full tilt, revelers dancing on coffins beneath the stars, but it has the stupidest name of any club on Earth. BO 18 stood for

Be Over Eighteen, Lebanon's legal drinking age—or at least that's what I had heard.

Beirut zips past us, strange but intact. It's always strange, not in an off-putting way, but layered in surreal tulle, having played host to that incredibly violent, drawn-out civil war in a region famous for them followed by a multi-million-person demonstration that left no dead and quickly achieved all of its goals.

Hovering over us now is the darkened hulk of the Holiday Inn, which had been the center of the green line during that civil war. Snipers from all sides—Christian Phalangists, Palestinian Liberation Organization, early rendition Hezbollah—would hide up in its suites and pepper those scrambling for cover below, hitting whichever side represented the current, shifting enemy. Alliances were formed, broken, reformed, rebroken, but the green line didn't move more than fifteen feet in either direction for all those fifteen years, and at the end of the war the Christians agreed to give up 5 percent of their official stated population numbers, dropping them from 55 to 50 percent, even though they were probably much closer to thirty-five, and that was being generous. Muslims just had more babies than Christians no matter if they were Sunni Muslims or Shia Muslims, whether they were native born or had run up from Israel during the various other wars.

Bridges, freshly destroyed from Israeli sorties, set off the newer Emirati- and Saudi-funded properties downtown. All this destruction, figuratively yesterday and literally yesterday, gives Beirut its magic, its undeniable magnetism. That and the French occupation, which gives it best-in-class baguettes, smoky-eyed supermodels, and fashion designers who use layered tulle for their progressively chic collections.

The common refrain is that the Middle East is always hell, always pulling apart at the seams, but that is a tired, lazy song. From

1200 to 1900, Europe was either a disease-ridden backwater or a complete bloodbath. Meanwhile the Ottomans ruled over one of the largest empires in history, stretching from Morocco all the way to Iran, across the entire region. The only wars were with Italian city-states and Eastern European hovels, and only then to keep its soldiers sharp. There were major advances in medicine, science, and engineering. There was gorgeous art, beautiful literature, awe-inspiring architecture, fantastic cuisine, and dance and music folding various elements from North African, Mediterranean, Arabian, and Persian cultures.

After 700 years of stabbing each other in the eyeballs, Europeans finally got decent and immediately began lecturing everyone else on how to live, and thus the tune begins. "The Middle East is always hell, always pulling apart at the seams, always fighting like the tribal savages they are. Fighting exactly like they are fighting right now, Muslims pitted against other Muslims. Muslims pitted against Christians. Muslims pitted against their most ancient enemy: the Jews."

This last falsehood is particularly egregious. Ingrained, systemic trouble between Jewish populations living in the Middle East and their Muslim neighbors only began in 1948, with the establishment of the state of Israel on lands previously occupied by Palestinians. When swaths of Spain were rolled under the Ottoman flag in the sixteenth century, the peninsula's Jewish inhabitants happily stayed with their new Muslim rulers because Spanish Christians loved rounding them up and setting them on fire.

We loosely debate heading to our apartment or heading south, where the action is, but it's all half-hearted and mostly in vain because there is only one real option. We must head toward shawarma, another gift from the Ottomans claimed hardest by the Egyptians but made better than anywhere on Earth at Barbar, right in the middle of Beirut. The ubiquitous spit-carved meat sandwich is so good here that it bustles from very early in the morning to very early in the morning, twenty-four hours a day, seven days a week, and has since its founding in 1979. Four years after the civil war started, eleven years before its end. Lebanese are proud that Barbar never closed once, even in the darkest, bloodiest days, because all Lebanese from Christian Phalangists to Palestinian Liberation Organization to early rendition Hezbollah needed the tender meats—the succulent, garlic-drenched tender meats folded into miniature flattened French baguettes—exactly like we need them now.

Josh pilots the Audi through the crowded streets. Men sit outside smoking shisha, listening to crackling full-volume radio reports from the field. Women huddle around tea tables beneath bright fluorescent lights, listening to crackling full-volume radio reports from the field. Hezbollah has its detractors here in central Beirut, where intellectual Christians, Sunnis, and Shias mingle. Nate's American University of Beirut is a stone's throw away, but this major Israeli incursion seems both asymmetric and odd. The tit for tat has been going along the border for a decade. Why did the hostilities escalate so quickly and destructively this time? What is Israel's endgame? Will they actually send troops across in a full invasion, or just continue to bomb the south and strategic targets like the airport and main bridges? Will they start hitting Christian and Sunni neighborhoods too, in order to put maximum pressure on the Lebanese government to cut a deal they would be unable to actually cut?

These are the questions suburban natives are asking while Josh, Nate, and I chew silently, lounging against our surfboard coffin, studying them with bright red eyeballs. Obviously, I don't know the answers, and it does seem like a weird fight for Israel to pick. Hezbollah is serious and disciplined, well backed and well trained by patron Iran. Those boys won't be cowed by a few bombs, or at least that was my impression when I got busted kicking mongo in front of their super-secret police building.

After Josh goes back for seconds we get down to hard business. Apartment or south?

In a rare moment of food-born comradery, we all agree at once: south.

The crackling full-volume radio reports outside Barbar and the flickering BBC reports inside suggest it is all picking up. That the whole southern half of the country is getting hammered. Low-resolution video footage shows red flashes and white tracers against a grainy black backdrop.

We decide to point toward Nabatieh, a predominately Shia town some 70 kilometers inland and south. It was mentioned by name more than anywhere else, and so we speed down empty streets past the freshly destroyed airport that had been named Rafik Hariri International Airport, after the influential prime minister who ruled over the fractured country from 1992 to 1998 and then again from 2000 until his resignation in 2004, when he flew to Saudi Arabia and claimed that Iran was unduly influencing Lebanon's politics through their relationship with Hezbollah. He was one of the richer men in Lebanon thanks to a construction firm he had formed up in Saudi Arabia used for major Saudi royal family projects.

In 2005 he was assassinated by a massive truck bomb detonated in the heart of Beirut. Four Hezbollah operatives were held responsible, which led to the Cedar Revolution, Syria's ouster from the country, and likely Israel's current power move.

"Look, there's Wafik Hawiwi Intewnational..." Nate says at the first sign. He loved mimicking Rafik almost as much as he loved seeing Josh agitated. Hariri apparently couldn't pronounce his "Rs" and it tickled Nate to no end whenever archival footage of the man played on television.

It's odd to see the airport completely darkened and difficult to imagine how Lebanese of all stripes, not just painted Team Hezbollah yellow and green, didn't take the attack personally. The ostensible reason given by the Israeli Defense Forces for the wide-scale destruction of bridges, border crossings, and Wafik Hawiwi Intewnational hours after the Israeli soldiers going missing was to stop their transport around the country. Also, Ehud Barak, Israel's prime minister, made it known that all of Lebanon would be held responsible for the actions of those few bad apples.

A large SUV flies by, heading north with a giant T and V taped to its hood and its doors. We all start snickering about the sissy newsman headed north instead of south, like us. In an SUV heavily branded TV instead of a sleek Audi, like us. Very clearly lame, like CNN's Anderson Cooper, who on last report was having trouble getting into Lebanon and was currently reporting from the Israeli side of the border in his helmet and flak jacket.

We had spent much of the dead time between Amman and Beirut chuckling about the aesthetics of covering war. Not Hemingway's Spanish Civil War, World War II, or Vietnam coverage, but the modern embedded reporter. Helmets and flak jackets, puffy microphones and shifty eyes that I always imagined were completely manufactured. None of us had ever covered a real declared war before, but we'd all been in radically pear-shaped situations, shot at, shot around, detained for questioning by non-governmental organizations, i.e., declared terrorist groups, and been to Somalia. A damned helmet and flak jacket don't help. They are very hot in already hot climates and are impossible to pull off with any sort of style unless the wearer is in some branch of the military or paramilitary, wears no shirt, has a pack of smokes tucked into the band of his helmet, and replaces all his shifty-eyed stares with devil-may-care sneers.

Worst of all, the heavy "TV war journalist" branding completely destroys any ability to blend in and get a real story. Accoutrement for the sake of accoutrement makes a complete mockery of Henry Crabb Robinson, Martha Gellhorn, and Michael Herr. It's a silly, narcissistic affectation that draws attention to the journalist instead of the conflict—and at that very moment an ugly whipping sound shatters our luxurious Audi interior.

Flap, flap, flap, flap.

"Nate…" I scream. "Did you not cinch the damned surfboard coffin down properly? Is that what that is? Are we somehow rookies again?" He doesn't hear me because he is already sitting there where the window should be, grimacing and pulling the straps as tight as he can while Josh accelerates then slides around a bomb divot.

It totally isn't Nate's fault. Both he and Josh tie exceptional knots. I was the one who took care of the front with a nice enough shoelace bow.

Josh drifts around another fresh bomb divot then drives right though one, sliding the Audi's chassis across the broken asphalt and creating an ugly grinding sound that makes me laugh so hard I can taste the succulent garlic Barbar shawarma for the second time. It's gross but also very funny, and I really don't know what Europcar was thinking renting Audis, or even Masturbators, during a war.

Most of the lights are off as we hit the coast heading toward Sidon, the roads choked with trucks, taxis, motor scooters, and motorcycles sitting lonely. The billboards featuring models with plenty of duct tape applied to where the cleavage should be advertise to no one. This is Hezbollah country here, and the decadence of the Christian north, just 30 kilometers back, is not welcome. There, smoky-eyed, scantily clothed models showcase all manners of sensuality. Sensual dishwashers, sensual perfume, sensual chocolate. Scantily clothed models with shirtless, clean-shaven men as their props. Here some of the same images are used but they are all doctored to reflect conservative social mores, and the only men that appear are bearded and severe, usually martyrs.

Another TV SUV rips north, flying so quickly that it is a blur of light and dust, and I only catch the TV tape on the back window as it disappears into the night.

"Why're these war journalist bastards so damned chicken? It's not like you can't hear the bombs coming and go hide," I tell Nate. "Speaking of, where's our cameraman?"

We had a Handycam with us and had been passing it back and forth so far, looking directly into the lens, pointing at bomb craters, and saying vaguely sarcastic things about war and human suffering. It didn't feel great. Anytime the camera turned on and was pointed at me, I could feel my face, the muscles twitching, my tongue moving, the words coming out stilted as opposed to well-timed and funny like they were in real life, but I was sure that I'd ease into a natural camaraderie with the camera. I was born to be a star and just needed a bit more practice, and for sure, I looked good. My hair was just the right amount of sweaty and falling over my Versace sunglasses with just the right amount of flair.

"He was supposed to leave two days after we did, that's when his finals ended and when his ticket is booked, so he is theoretically getting ready to head out," Nate responds.

His name was also Josh and we were really throwing him to the wolves. He had never traveled outside of the well-developed West, and we gave him minimal instruction.

Fly to Amman. Figure out how to get to Beirut. We'll meet you there.

Nate had only texted him to say we had arrived and to hurry. We are covering a war here, damn it, and Cameraman Josh's trial by fire is necessary. Plus, we have the Handycam, and along with growing into stars, I have no doubt we'll make excellent soundmen and cameramen too, or good enough for Al Gore by any stretch.

Just past Sidon, which seems a complete ghost town, we cut up into the hills, winding toward Nabatieh. Ten or so kilometers out, we hear our first bomb hitting the ground. Dull thumps that reverberate through the spine and my heart flutters. We all look at each other slack-jawed, and Josh pulls over and slides to a stop at an overlook. A valley drops sharply in front of us and a rock-strewn hill gradually climbs toward the starry sky behind us.

With the engine cut, a sickening silence fills the air. We all get out and sit on the Audi's hood, listening with newborn ears and seeing with newborn eyes.

Thump.

Thump, thump, thump, thump.

The ridge on the other side of the valley is getting hit—and hard. Flashes of red precede each thump, and the destructive force is mesmerizing. Picturing being right there underneath the hits is absolutely terrifying. How do humans survive such things? How does anything survive?

Suddenly I'm aware that I don't hear any jets and I don't hear any bombs whistling to the ground. Sickening silence until the thumps rattle the earth, and I whisper, "Wait. Where's the sound of the jets? Where's the whistling of the bombs?"

Josh whispers, "I think the jets fly too high to be heard, and do bombs whistle?"

In that very moment I realize that my entire vision of war had been stitched together from slow-motion World War II documentaries and *Apocalypse Now*. Mostly I'd been imagining slow-moving propeller bombers flying at relatively low altitude dropping slow-motion bombs while a gravelly voiced narrator describes how German forces had been pushed from some town sounding like the name of a fancy cheese to another town sounding like the name of a fancy cheese. Or Martin Sheen's laconic drawl.

Suddenly I'm aware that we're the only vehicle here, no more than 10 kilometers from where the earth is being punched, we have a Mylar surfboard coffin strapped to the roof, and for sure Israel's vaunted Air Force has satellite imagery piercing the darkness with that nighttime vision technology, showing three figures standing next to a vehicle bathed in Desert Storm green with some oblong shiny thing on its roof.

Shit.

We all get the same idea at the same time and without a word between us untie the surfboard coffin straps, drag it down, and slide it under the car before tiptoeing into the rock-strewn hill behind us and lying out flat on our stomachs behind three neighboring boulders.

Josh sets the camera on one and keeps recording.

And we watch modern warfare playing out in a tableau before us. It all seems so wildly impersonal and so unfair. So heartless. There was no angry-faced man wagging a gun, no apparent escalation, no sense or even nonsense to be talked.

One moment, silence. The next moment, a fiery red ball on the horizon. It is terrifying in its impersonality.

After a few hours, during a fifteen-minute break in the action, we sneak back to the car, take the boards out of the bag and shove them inside, fold the Mylar surfboard coffin and jam it in the trunk, put the Audi in neutral, and push it back until we're on the road, then hop inside.

Josh coasts without the engine on, manhandling the steering wheel in order to navigate the curves until we reach the bottom, and then he fires the engine. We sit at an intersection, debating whether we should race north like those TV SUVs before us or creep slowly toward Nabatieh—but, again, there is only one real option. We can't let Anderson Cooper win, so we creep toward Nabatieh.

There's no way we're going to die tonight. We're coated in Teflon. Untouchable, though slightly shaken if not stirred.

CHAPTER 3

The next few days blended into an exhausting blur. We'd chase destruction wherever it was happening, which happened to be more and more places. Random little towns in the south, bridges and overpasses in the north, the oil refinery on the coast spewing black smoke for days and staining my white V-neck a pallid gray. I paddled out next to the refinery even though there wasn't a wave in sight. Surfing just felt like the right thing to do, all things considered.

Israel seemed to be frustrated that the first shock and awe didn't bring Lebanon to its knees and was intent on making the country's diverse population feel the weight of war, but the whole enterprise seemed to backfire. Hezbollah had dug in, and the group's pluckiness even earned the grudging respect of Christians and Sunnis who, were normally very much at odds with their Shia enemy.

We'd scamper around, up with the first light with almost no time for music videos. Just one, maybe two while Josh put his contact lenses in and Nate made grumpy coffee in our apartment's kitchen. If we were lucky, we'd catch a short run of American or

European artists like Sean Paul or Nickelback instead of mournful Lebanese hits.

"How much for Chad Kroeger?" I asked one morning at five.

"Mmmm, yeah, veddy nice," Josh answered, blinking his contact into place. "I can't go any less than ten."

Nate shot him an ugly look from the kitchen and muttered, "What the hell, guy? You're blowing the scale this early?"

But Josh was right. Chad Kroeger had never looked better than he did right then in an apocalyptic glow, giving him an undeniable rock star sheen. Nickelback's latest video, "Rockstar," was peak Nickelback without even showing the band, but I knew, thanks to my traditional airplane *US Weekly*, that Chad Kroeger's hair was cut into a sharp, bleached bob. His moustache plus goatee were very on point. His choker necklace tight but not sado-masochistically tight and his black T-shirt leaving very little to the imagination. Josh's numbers made sense, and while I couldn't go higher than a four, I understood.

It was a small wonder that music videos were still being broadcast, seeing as Israel was trying to demoralize the entire population. It also seemed surprising that our apartment was still standing. It was close enough to Hezbollah's Burj al-Barajneh neighborhood on the south side of town, where the pounding bombs a few kilometers away would have kept us awake if we hadn't been absolutely drop-dead exhausted.

In the morning we'd head into the Bourj, some of the only Western journalists able to do so thanks to Nate and his boxing pals. He had steadily and determinedly built his Hezbollah Rolodex during his two years studying at the American University of Beirut and living Burj al-Barajneh adjacent. They didn't necessarily trust him, nor were they happy to see us, but he was at least a known quantity, and after many phone calls and much passport examining, we'd get through to the organization's operational heart. It had been turned into rubble, more or less, but Hezbollah's television station was still broadcasting even though the building had been sheared in half, its social services still operating and its foot soldiers still resisting.

We took our war journalism seriously then retreated into Beirut's fabulous culinary scene late every night, spending our Al Gore dollars like the world was ending, because it was. Gemmayze, the hip neighborhood that *Travel + Leisure* magazine had dubbed the "SoHo of Beirut" just a year earlier, lived up to its billing and featured a handful of patisseries, coffee spots, bars, and lounges. Our favorite, the steakhouse, served note-perfect filet mignon with some sort of burgundy jus, and we'd feast while drinking bottles of red wine before finally retreating to our front-row apartment.

Cameraman Josh somehow made it all the way from Los Angeles to Amman to Beirut forty-eight hours after us with the help of a Syrian named Dany. We met him at the main taxi station, and he was smiling ear to ear, looking exactly like Dave Grohl. Same hair, slightly shagged and flipped out, same eyes, same smile. So much like Dave Grohl that he told us he had once gone to a Foo Fighters concert and had been pulled out of the crowd by security, taken backstage, and introduced to Dave Grohl, who looked into that mirror with a shocked expression while the security guards laughed and laughed.

Dany's one request was that Cameraman Josh find his girlfriend, who worked in a restaurant just north of town called "Bobby's," and deliver her a wad of old American dollars. That night, after interviewing and filming a Palestinian man who had set up a theater program for kids whose homes had been destroyed, we went looking.

Dany had given Cameraman Josh an address, but the numbers were smudged, and so we spent a few hours driving around the neighborhood before seeing a car, waving it over, and asking its driver if they knew where Bobby's was. He looked very confused and repeated "Bobby's?" before turning to his passenger, conversing with him, then turning back with a wide smile and saying, "You guys are going to Bay-bees?"

He quickly described how to get to "Bay-bees," then winked. We thanked him and found "Babes" within minutes.

"Bobby's and Bay-bees are not very similar to Babes," Josh remarked.

"Stop being so punctilious."

"Oh, man…" Nate said as Josh guided the Audi into one of the twenty empty parking spots, looking extra grim. "I think this is a super nightclub."

It had been explained on our maiden voyage that Beirut has nightclubs and also super nightclubs. The nightclubs were what might be expected. Music, dancing, bottle service. The super nightclubs were a mystery but theoretically contained music, pole dancing, prostitution, and bottle service, though were somehow not strip clubs. We had driven past many, over the years, brashly advertised as super nightclubs, and had never once stopped. There were enough thrills on the radical Islamic fundamentalist side of town to keep us well occupied, but now we had to go. Dany had done Cameraman Josh a great favor, getting him to the border, and in this crazy wartime environment we both owed him and the rules we normally operated under had to be suspended.

God would understand.

I straightened my V-neck T-shirt, freshly stained with the rubble pit that used to be Hezbollah's neighborhood. We had snuck the camera in there before filming heartwarming children's theater and captured fantastic hidden footage. Nate tightened his tie and Josh quickly cleaned his square-toed Swedish military boots while Cameraman Josh stood smiling like Dave Grohl.

"Well, what are you waiting for, Dave Grohl?" I said. "Let's get in there."

None of us had ever dawned a strip club's door before, and my heart was pounding harder than it was when I had realized bombs couldn't be heard falling, jets couldn't be heard flying, and our Mylar surfboard coffin really did look like a bundle of missiles.

What's the etiquette in a strip club? What's the protocol? Is eye contact expected or uncool? Is tipping required and how much? Must bills be placed into the string of a G-string or is there sometimes a basket? Are lap dances fait accompli?

None of us knew, so discussing it was pointless. We all pushed passed a bored security guard, Cameraman Josh leading the way, into a small, completely empty room with a bar in the corner and a silver pole in the other corner. Two Russian-looking girls sat slumped against a mirrored wall. I thought they might be asleep.

We all stood in the middle of that small, completely empty room with dumb masks plastered on as faces. Josh made the first move and strutted over to the bar then came back with four warm Lebanese Almaza beers.

"Enjoy them, bros," he said. "They cost thirty dollars each."

"I think that's how it works in super nightclubs," Nate responded. "You buy the girls very expensive drinks."

I wondered how he knew.

We continued to stand in the middle of that small, completely empty room with dumber masks plastered on our faces, wincing as we sipped warm Lebanese beer and wincing more when one of the Russian-looking girls shook to life, stumbled to the pole, and started wiggling. She was fully clothed in loose-fitting pants, a nice enough blouse and clunky heels, and there was nothing overtly sexual about her wiggles other than the fact she was clutching a pole, but she did keep all of us fixed in her gaze. Bouncing from my eyes to Josh's eyes to Nate's eyes to Cameraman Josh's eyes then back to mine.

This super nightclub was the most uncomfortable, difficult-to-navigate place I'd ever been, and by the looks on Josh and Nate's faces, the most uncomfortable, confusing place they'd ever been too. After what felt like an eternity, Nate elbowed Cameraman Josh and said, "Ask one of the girls if Dany's girlfriend is working tonight." He shook his Dave Grohl shag slightly, snapped out of his stupor, and, without having to be told again, stumbled to the corner where the two who weren't dancing continued to slump.

After a few moments, he returned to us sporting a proudly informed look and reported, "They said she was working and would be out in a minute."

After an eternity of nursing our warm Lebanese beers all the way down to their even warmer bottoms, a very sad, fully clothed, Russian-looking girl entered the room from a door I hadn't seen earlier and came up to us with eyes as dead as doornails. There was nothing noteworthy about her. Her hair was some sort of blonde. She had a body with two arms and two legs. Cameraman Josh launched into a warmhearted explanation about how he had never traveled the Middle East before, much less into a war, and Dany had saved him.

Did she know Dany? She nodded.

It was a long story with far too many details but well-meaning, and eventually it led to Cameraman Josh pulling out Dany's wad of old American dollars, extra-small heads of Thomas Jefferson and Benjamin Franklin, and handing it over to her.

She seemed unimpressed, bored even, shrugged, and retreated to the secret door from whence she came. That was it and almost unsatisfying, but our duty had been done, our ledger wiped clean, and that felt like another in our string of successes.

"But should we get a dance, however you do it?" I asked Josh as we nodded graciously to the bartender while placing our empty bottles on his bar.

"Hell, no," Nate responded, even though I wasn't asking him, and like that we were free, though slightly agitated. The outside air tasted sweet and hot, and we talked about what fresh destruction might be happening and if we should go chase it, though the thought of getting into the Audi and driving to austere lands being pounded heavily from above didn't quite seem the thing to do.

We all stood around the empty lot knowing we should get in but also knowing once we did our path would be set and we'd spend yet another evening laying in the dirt watching Israel continue to advance while continuing not to make one ounce of apparent difference in the overall narrative.

Modern war was weird.

"What if we hit the casino instead?" Josh offered out of nowhere.

It was truly a brilliant idea. We had driven by the massive red sign just off the main freeway that read "casino" so many times but had never stopped. Gambling was akin to extramarital sex, which was akin to going to strip clubs in all our lives, including Cameraman Josh's, but we'd freshly broken the seal, and even though we hadn't seen one flash of flesh, our dirty impulses were awake and we were craving more. Maybe it was the same phenomenon that drove chaste Midwestern boys into vile Saigon brothels during the Vietnam situation or a generation earlier moved chaste New York boys into Neapolitan brothels. War is hell, or so they say, and the various circles thereof, including lust, greed, and especially gluttony thanks to our nonstop steakhouse ventures, were just too tempting.

I didn't even have to ask what game we were going to play. We'd play roulette and put the rest of our Al Gore money on black because red seemed like something Anderson Cooper would do and he still wasn't in Lebanon, though we'd watched his reports live from Haifa in Israel just across the border when those retaliatory Hezbollah bottle rockets hit, and he looked sincere.

Josh insisted on driving yet again, and spun out of the parking lot, winding through the side streets, climbing onto the main coastal road and flooring it, launching us forward as fast and furious as Germany's fourth-favorite automobile could take us.

Lights climbed from the Mediterranean on our right up to the hills toward the stars on our left. Christians lived up there, and many Sunni and Shia had fled up there too, assuming Israel wouldn't drop bombs on their one-time ally.

During the civil war, the Israeli military, led by future Prime Minister Ariel Sharon, surrounded the Palestinian refugee camps Sabra and Shatila just south of the city center. Christian Phalangists went on a twenty-four-hour killing spree, slaughtering thousands of Palestinian and Shia men, women, and children. The enemy of my enemy is my friend business. Then again, the Israeli Defense Forces were very serious in proving their point that all of Lebanon was responsible for Hezbollah's actions thus far, so I couldn't imagine the mountain dwellers were entirely comfortable.

Nate fiddled with the radio dial, finding mournful Nancy Ajram ballads then a BBC report in Arabic detailing the day's trauma before Josh, who had been paying attention to the radio and not his driving, cut across all lanes and exited, parking in a mostly empty lot. We all gave each other our best *Ocean's Eleven* winks, and I wondered if Josh was Danny Ocean or if I was Danny Ocean, though I assumed it was probably me. That meant Josh was probably the Brad Pitt character and Nate was Matt Damon, while Cameraman Josh was still Dave Grohl. We marched shoulder to shoulder toward the massive white box building and the swooping red font that read "casino."

We walked through the sliding-glass doors into an extremely well-lit grocery store, aisles and aisles of prepackaged food and bread stretching as far as the eye could see. Apparently this was a complex that included a grocery store, casino, and probably a hotel. We walked up the fruit aisle, down the baking aisle, up the crackers and cookies aisle, down the pasta and sauce aisle, all the while looking for the entrance to the casino part of the complex.

Up the yogurt aisle, down the salami aisle. But still nothing.

My first instinct when lost is to ask straight away. Both Josh and Nate like to use their wits to sort through navigational trouble, but I had grown up doubting my own sense of direction so severely that I couldn't ask "Which way to…?" quickly enough.

I found an employee with a nice red vest putting bread onto a shelf and asked, "*Wayn* casino?"

He stared at me with big brown eyes, confused, maybe even shell-shocked from this war we were all living through, and so I repeated myself slowly and politely.

"*Wayn* casino *minfudluck*?" *Where's the casino, please?*

He looked very confused. "*Hina*," he said, meaning "here."

I smiled while shrugging my shoulders and tried again. "*Aiwa, aiwa…wayn hina*?" Of course I knew it was here, but *where* here?

Now I really had him flummoxed, and he shuffled off to get his manager. Josh, Nate, Cameraman Josh, and I stood there in the bread aisle excited to get this all going. Nothing feels worse than purposing to sin then not being able to. After a few moments, our friend returned with an English-speaking manager.

"Can I help?" he asked.

"Yes," I answered. "We were just looking for the casino."

Now he too looked confused. "The casino?"

"Yes," I repeated. "The casino. We are here covering the war and excited to blow off some steam playing blackjack."

"Blackjack?" he repeated, and then a funny look spread across his face. "This is the casino here. You are in it."

"Or roulette."

He didn't respond, and the awkward truth dawned on all of us at the same time.

The grocery store was named "Casino."

We thanked him, found the ice cream aisle, bought a box of Lebanese Dew Bite bars, and drove to the apartment feeling frustrated but saved. We had been to a super nightclub and a casino on the same night without needing to ask God's forgiveness for our wayward behavior in the morning, and I had a nagging feeling that had something to do with our Teflon coating, even though we were all soundly Protestant, firmly believing in His grace and not our works.

That night, Israel put on the biggest show yet, hammering at ten-minute intervals for eight straight hours just a few kilometers away. We set the cameras up on our balcony and tried to artistically capture the beat while eating Dew Bites and singing along to Justin Timberlake's "SexyBack," which was playing every fourth video.

CHAPTER 4

And then we officially had too many tapes. A shoulder bag's worth, which meant a real problem on our hands. Al Gore's people hadn't quite expected live coverage from the theater but did want something vaguely current, seeing that their business model was putting the internet on television and the channel's name was Current. We had poked lots of fun of real news media, their helmets, their flak jackets, their duct-taped SUVs, but we had no idea how they actually did their jobs. I had taken live television being beamed into my living room from the most far-flung corners of the Earth for granted my whole life. I had watched two Desert Storms live, but how did they do it? Generators and satellites?

We had eaten and drank our generator and satellite money in the form of steak and red wine, but we absolutely had to get our footage back to Mimi, who was waiting in Los Angeles to cut, edit, and forward it along to Current's San Francisco offices—right across the street from AT&T ballpark, where the Giants played their awful brand of baseball.

What did real war journalists do? Helicopter and airplanes?

That last option might work, but Beirut's airport was still worthless and going back to Amman was out of the question, would take too long, and might make it impossible for us to get back in. Mailing it was out of the question, as Israel was in charge of the post and severely restricting coverage. The whole war had escalated severely, and we couldn't gamble on getting lucky with a brave enough cab driver a second time.

Damascus was the only option. It was only a few hours away, give or take the bombed bridges. Its airport was operating and its DHL offices open. It was decided that Josh and I would buy motorcycles and make the run while Cameraman Josh and Nate would stay behind and continue documenting Beirut's day-to-day.

We spent the morning looking for proper motorcycles that reflected our obvious *je ne sais quoi* but couldn't find any no matter how hard we looked. The proper motorcycle shops were shuttered and there was only one in the hills selling anything close, but those were motor scooters.

One white. One black. Even though the white one was faster than the black one, it was clear what the situation had to be. I would take the white one, because I wearing white V-neck T-shirts, and Josh would have to take the black one because he wore all black.

We were stuck on something we'd never ride back home but tried to talk it up like we were on Vespas and in a ska gang. But we weren't on Vespas or in a ska gang, and our scooters were dumb. Still, they could be lifted over bomb craters with ease, and that was what mostly mattered. Plus, our scooters could get over 100 kilometers per gallon. With the refineries bombed and the borders closed, getting gas in Lebanon had become a major chore. Rumors would spread like wildfire about which gas stations around greater Beirut were open, which ones had mile-long lines, and which ones could be staked out and pounced on. Our scooters could easily get us to Damascus, where we could much more easily refill.

After waving goodbye to Nate and Cameraman Josh, we scooted up into the hills, hot and bathed in that quintessential Lebanese light. Warm yellows, golds, the sky a cloudless blue. The faint roar of Israeli jets running recon overhead. It would have been perfection, except, you know—motor scooters.

For the first few kilometers we wore helmets, but it was positively too lame, so we threw them off the side of the road near a church and kept zipping around the hairpin turns with the wind in our hair and bugs on our Versaces. The Christian mountains leaned in on us and sultry models suggested we buy parfum or dishwashers.

Then, around one last twist, we saw the Beqaa Valley stretching out before us, green and crackling with energy. Plumes of smoke rose in the distance, as Israel was hitting it, and hitting it hard, around the clock.

The valley is one of the more archeologically significant areas in Lebanon. During Roman times it was a fertile grain-growing region. The city of Baalbek, just east of the river that cuts north to south, has two of the largest Roman temple ruins. During the civil war it was a fertile cannabis and opium poppy growing region, hash and heroin providing the various militias with much-needed cash for perpetual armaments.

The valley's population is mostly Shia, and it was Beqaa clerics, agitated by Israel's 1982 invasion, who got together and formed the Party of God—or Hezbollah—in order to slap back. Twenty-four years later, the two have locked horns once again. Overwhelming military might on one side, clenched-jaw determination on the other.

As we wound down to the valley floor, burnt-out, freshly bombed trucks replacing sexy billboards, the gold and green

Hezbollah flags became more and more ubiquitous. They're surprisingly good, aesthetically, with the Arabic "L" of "Allah" holding a slightly tilted Kalashnikov. Photos of Hezbollah martyrs were attached to every streetlight and giant wheat-pasted posters of Hezbollah's leader, Hassan Nasrallah, encouraged the residents in their shared fight.

The streets were absolutely destroyed here and we had to tug our motor scooters over, around, and through messes. It was hard, sweaty work, but we looked ridiculous and would laugh at each other, especially when we tried to do sweet little jumps using concrete hunks as ramps.

A few residents would appear from darkened doorways and watch us toil, our absurd dance not tickling them like it did us. I got confused when we reached a large intersection, doubting Josh's sense of direction too, and asked one of the angry men which was the right way to Damascus.

He stood there shaking his head, refusing to answer when three other men in leather jackets and Don Johnson beards came out of nowhere and grabbed our arms, snatched the keys out of our motor scooters, and pushed us down a side street into what looked like a money exchange kiosk.

I was frustrated by their Arab grabbiness and wondered what all this dumb business was about before it dawned on me. These were Hezbollah operatives. The Don Johnson beards should have given it right away, ditto the leather jackets in the dead heat of summer, but I was distracted by feeling lost. Hezbollah operatives love nothing more than shaving their beards down to the perfect five o'clock shadow and pairing those beards with leather jackets.

Even though their leader, Hassan Nasrallah, had gone for the prototypical bushy beard cleric motif, the foot soldiers generally opted for that 1980s *Miami Vice* stubble, and I don't know why they wore leather jackets, but they always did. Often burgundy, too—not just black. It was a good look, though, all things considered, and Josh and I should have been truly circumspect, but we had both been in so much self-inflicted Middle Eastern trouble that it was impossible to take this current predicament seriously. I had been arrested for climbing the pyramids in Cairo and also for sprinting in Cairo's subway station so that I could slide on the dust. He had been arrested for sneaking across the border into Kashmir. We had both been in trouble in Yemen, Somalia, Azerbaijan, and Djibouti, and with Hezbollah, mostly me for kicking mongo, I think, and this felt like another one of those silly yell fights even when they threw us in the kiosk and declared that we were Israeli special forces helping the Israeli Air Force pick their targets.

These men had lost their homes, their compatriots, maybe even their children and wives, and there Josh and I sat with a bag full of tapes, a Handycam, odd attitudes, and no TV duct tape anywhere.

The hours ticked by and the shadows outside became longer. There was no breaking their absolute insistence that we were spies no matter how much of our footage they watched, no matter how many times they flipped through our passports examining our Yemeni, Somali, Syrian stamps, no matter how much we insisted that we were desperately trying to produce even-handed coverage of the war for Al Gore's television channel back home in the United States and that those tapes would likely convince the American public of the wanton destruction and possibly turn the tide, forcing an Israeli withdrawal.

I watched some of the footage over their shoulder, and while none of it looked overtly spy-ish, the quality was a bit worse than I had hoped. My hair looked okay and my white V-neck stylish, but my face really was a dumb mask. My tongue sounded paralyzed and the words coming out of my mouth were fifth-grade level at best.

I sounded like an idiotic surfer.

Night fell with no end to the stalemate in sight. Our Hezbollah captors had started to get edgy, looking outside and listening then coming back in. One was perpetually on the phone with what sounded like Hezbollah HQ. The other told us that Israel had just started running drones at night that were specifically targeting motor scooters. He ran out quickly, at one point, and pushed ours under an overhang.

Then, four long hours after first getting pulled into the kiosk, the one who had mostly been on the phone told us we were free to go and returned our motor scooter keys, camera, passports, all of our tapes. The one who had told us about the Israeli drone smirked slightly, and I wondered if this was their plan all along. Hold us until night then let Israel take us out.

If true, I had to give them credit as it was a very on-brand, faith-based strategy. If we were innocent and made it to Damascus along a demon road, then our innocent blood wouldn't be on their hands. If we were guilty and got exploded by an Israeli drone, then our guilty blood would be smeared along the already broken demon road, not needing to be mopped up. I suppose I didn't consider the possibility of us being guilty and making it because why the hell would anyone videotape potential targets then mail them from Damascus?

Josh and I thanked them and laughed about getting hit, mimicking a little drone bomb landing on our heads. They laughed back, and then we were off, maxing out our throttles until we reached an abandoned gas station on the town's outskirts, where we stopped to call Nate and tell him about our day's adventure.

He wanted to know if the Hezbollah operatives had been angry or merely curious.

"Oh, yeah..." Josh said. "They were majorly mad."

And then I heard it—clearly, distinctly—like a lawnmower in the sky. Buzzing in a high-pitched octave. It definitely wasn't a jet. The rare times I'd heard those, they roared crazy loud and sometimes created sonic booms for fun, or maybe intimidation, rattling the fillings in my teeth.

This was different.

I pointed to the sky. Josh paused the call, heard it himself, then said, "Oh, frick."

"The drones are out…" I said, as if he didn't know.

He dutifully reported the information to Nate, hung up, and we looked at each other grinning ear to ear.

We should have been scared. We should have been scared about the whole damned day, but our detention had just felt like more Arab nonsense, and this new threat felt like a video game.

We were going to put our Teflon to a serious test.

The road across the Beqaa was relatively straight. Our motor scooters didn't go very fast, but even Ducati Monsters would have trouble outrunning a drone, or so I imagined. This would be like John Henry versus the machine. A true test of wills.

Without another word, we ignited our engines, rolled back our throttles, put our heads down, and flew as fast as our miniature steeds would carry us. The night had cooled. The air felt fantastic, and we were truly living. I don't think I'd ever been that invigorated. Not running from al-Qaeda in Yemen, not surfing never-before-surfed waves, not submitting a class roster featuring eighty-seven "A" grades to the Los Angeles City College academic office. It made me understand why people play Russian roulette. Why people rob banks. We were playing loose and fast with a losing hand—but we knew, somehow, we positively *knew* we'd win.

Seven hours later we rolled into Damascus completely exhausted. We'd heard the drones until we had reached the Syrian border and the sound disappeared. The soldier there took our passports and looked at us like we were insane but stamped them and let us through. Thirty kilometers later we were stopped by three truckloads of Syrian soldiers who were furious, demanding paperwork we didn't have for our motor scooters, wondering who we were and where we thought we were going.

We told them that we had left Beirut that morning, been detained by Hezbollah all afternoon, and had made the run across the Beqaa that very night. They didn't believe us at first, but at some point the wildness in our eyes convinced them.

The soldiers piled out of the truck, laughing, and lined up to shake our hands.

CHAPTER 5

"You kidding me?" Josh is screaming into a payphone right outside the Burj al-Barajneh. "You've got to make it. It's getting hit hard right now. No? Okay. Well, we've got to do it. We have to go in."

He slams the receiver into its hook, looks at me with fiery red eyes but then softens them. "Nate can't make it. He's on the other side of town and says all the roads are blocked."

"I'm so pissed!" I growl to the heavens, imagining Nate enjoying an espresso on ice somewhere and rudely not motivating for the monster scoop of our young lives.

BOOM!

The ground under our feet shakes as another bomb bites the earth. A mushroom cloud rises from the middle of the Bourj, turning the noontime sunlight a hazy, sickly yellow. Up until that point the Israeli Defense Forces had only been working the neighborhood over at night, and had been dropping leaflets in the day that warned citizens holding on that their neighborhood would be catching fire. This broad daylight offensive seems a clear raising of the stakes, an undeniable escalation, and I can't believe we had arrived in time to catch it.

We had gotten to Damascus at an ungodly hour, slept for a few minutes, made it to the DHL as it opened, sent our tapes to Mimi in Los Angeles, headed to Damascus's legitimately epic Four Seasons to drink a Bloody Mary, then headed back to Beirut before most brunch restaurants began service.

On the way, in no man's land, we found a small roadside stall selling what was labeled "Strong Beer" and had a bear on the can. We purchased two. I could only drink a sip of mine, as it tasted like rubbing alcohol and I didn't really know how to drink. Josh cleaned his out, wincing the entire time. It was the second time he bested me in a drinking contest.

The first time was when we were fresh out of college, living a few blocks away from each other in the quiet little town of South Pasadena. We got into a big debate about who could drink more alcohol. Neither of us were "drinkers," by any stretch of the imagination, but I had seen Josh get chatty at a few parties after he'd had a few glasses of champagne and considered him a lightweight, making much fun of him as a result. I also considered myself a heavyweight, imagining that drunkenness was just a state of mind.

There was only one way to settle it. We would have a competition to decide once and for all who could hold his booze better—and, as an extension, who was the tougher man. We marched to the grocery store and bought two six-packs of Rolling Rock beer then marched straight back to Josh's bungalow.

Rolling Rock was clearly not considered a "tough man" beer. It was, in fact, considered a "sorority girl" beer, but we didn't know any better and popped the tops of our first, clinking the glass necks, ready to dominate in this test of wills.

It was difficult getting that first one down, but I persisted onto the second, and by the third I knew that this day belonged to me, which was confirmed by the fourth. But then things started to go sideways. The joy that had been bubbling in my stomach turned almost instantly to nausea.

Five Rolling Rock beers was what it took to bring me low. I crawled the few blocks from Josh's bungalow to my apartment puking the entire way and couldn't get out of bed for a full forty-eight hours. I don't know how Josh fared, we didn't talk about it much after, but he didn't have to crawl and puke. My taste for beer was compromised from that moment on, and I rarely saw Josh drink beer either, though I figured it was for aesthetic reasons.

We made it through the Syrian checkpoint and the Lebanese checkpoint without issue and rolled into Beirut's southern Hezbollah neighborhoods just as the daylight bombs began falling. This was our moment, and we knew it. We were going to capture the war as it was happening. Not the aftermath, not from hundreds of miles away, but from the war's very middle. Our cell phone had died hours ago but there was a bank of payphones at a gas station at the entrance of the Bourj. We stopped and called Nate so he could facilitate our access, but he couldn't, or wouldn't.

Josh and I are now standing, looking at each other, sleep-deprived with the taste of Strong Beer still vaguely present, thinking about what to do. But there's only one option. This is the monster scoop of our young lives. This is what is going to make us famous. More than fame, fortune, glory, this is how we've been wired. Adventure lies before us, and if we don't accept its invitation, then who are we? The flinch would dog us both for the rest of our lives, and so without a word we remount our motor scooters and turn right, heading into the neighborhood—dust in our lungs, dust in our eyes, dust on my Versaces. We roll down the hill, past the

Palestinian refugee camp and a whole block of red dirt, riding the brakes, me in front, Josh slightly behind.

Halfway, Josh screams, "Dude, we're gonna get roasted!"

I look back and scream, "We've got to go in."

"We gotta go in? Okay."

My conviction is not necessarily born of bravery or journalistic sincerity at that very moment, nor even a hunger for fame. It's something far less refined. It's a simple desire to make Anderson Cooper look like a sissy.

I cut in and race past two blocks of shuttered storefronts. There is no one around, not one person, and the streets are filled with smoke and debris, shattered glass, twisted cars, and it is hot. Crazy hot. Steamy, thick, and still.

Now that we're here, I'm confused. Should we go straight, take a left? Right? I've got to make a call, since I'm leading the way, but am terrible with directions and had just gotten us detained by Hezbollah not even twenty-four hours ago thanks to my indecision.

I stop to let Josh guide us, grinning stupidly as he passes, and the second he does, a bomb smacks half a block in front of us. In a three-year run filled with surreal moments, this one reigns supreme. It's an utter bump to the system. The deafening boom is one thing, and semi-expected, but the concussion or blast wave is a complete shock.

It is only listed as tertiary damage in the "International Guide to Bomb-Induced Injury," after actually getting hit directly or sprayed with shrapnel, but ahead of burns, getting crushed, and respiratory meltdown.

When a bomb explodes, there is an initial rush of air outward, followed by a sucking of air back in toward the blast site. A very quick combination of overpressure then underpressure. It impacts ears, hair cells, lungs, and guts as the air goes crazy. It feels like a massive punch in the stomach while the oxygen is being pumped from my body. I can't breathe, and when the air comes sucking out it causes my vocal chords to vibrate so I hear a strange groan that I'm not making but am making while watching the metal roll-up doors shuttering storefronts blow out then get sucked in while my motor scooter pops an uncontrolled wheelie.

Getting bombed is a singular experience, though not recommended. It feels infinite though only lasts a few seconds, and the second my motor scooter stops wheelie-ing involuntarily, I hear Josh shout, "Go, go, go, go!" as if through cotton balls stuffed in my ears.

Since the blast wave has already twisted my motor scooter 180 degrees, all I have to do is hammer the throttle, and that's what I do, heading back around the corner and up the hill, retreading ground we had just trod.

We stop at the top, looking at each other with wide and crazy eyes. Josh, who has had the Handycam on the entire time, points it back to where we just were, at the smoke mushroom slowly rising and the devastation in its wake, trying to narrate, "So, all right..." before I cut him off all breathless, excited, saying, "We were right there. We almost got nailed!" pointing at the smoke mushroom as if it is our pièce de résistance because it is.

We just got bombed. We literally just got bombed.

Josh, undeterred, continues, "We were in the concussion zone on that last hit, this is the Bourj..." squaring Hezbollah's neighborhood in the camera's viewfinder before swinging right and saying, "They're also hitting super close to the Palestinian refugee camp..." at which point I cut in again, hustling out a "*Yalla*...we have to go...let's go."

I had seen a lurking shadow pop out between rubble-strewn buildings and seen it lower what looked like a rifle in our direction. A proper rifle, and while it all feels like a dream and my ears are filled with cotton and my guts are filled with trauma and it might actually be a dream, Josh responded immediately. "We have to go? Let's go."

We both kick our motor scooters onward while the lurking shadow becomes clear, a thick man wearing full camouflage. He points his rifle, a Kalashnikov, in our direction and...

Pop!

Pop!

Pop!

Pop!

He's shooting at us and there's no doubt about it because we're close enough to see his eyes, and they're resolute. But he's missing, or I hope he's missing. Don't they say the gunshots you hear won't hurt you? I'm hearing each one and feeling good and also hearing Josh shouting, *"Ana sahafi! Ana sahafi!"* or, "I'm a journalist! I'm a journalist!"

The shooting doesn't stop. Shots pop around us as we round the next bend, full bore, but since Josh has the camera and is still trying to film, riding one-handed, he crashes, and crashes badly. Skidding into the middle of the road all akimbo. It does not look fun, and I spin back toward him to help get his motor scooter started again but my 7 For All Mankind bootcut jeans get caught around a peg on my own bike and rip.

Shit. I look down and see that my right leg has gone from bootcut to bell-bottom. Not something I am going for. Not something I've ever even liked, but this forced stylistic error will have to wait. Josh needs my help. I whip around, getting to him as quickly as I can and trying to help him start his motor scooter. It just won't work. No matter how many times he presses the ignition button, no matter how many times he turns the key and twists the throttle, there is just nothing.

I'm so intent on getting it started that I don't recognize that people are moving in until it's too late and my arms are grabbed and I'm being pulled away from my task. I look over incensed and see a Palestinian twenty-something waving a pistol in my face while four others circle around.

One hops on Josh's motor scooter. One drags me at gunpoint to mine. Two others force us to sit on the back and then follow as we start getting chauffeured back where we came from. Back to the Palestinian refugee camp.

I'm trying to process what's happening. Trying to figure out why these younger Palestinians have grabbed us and what their intentions are. Everything is so hot and I'm sitting on the back of a motor scooter, sort of clutching the waist of a younger Palestinian. Why am I doing that? It was bad enough to be driving motor scooters instead of motorcycles, but it was completely unforgivable to be riding nuts to butt on one. Absolutely shockingly embarrassing and there is no way playing through here will lead to any good. Definitely not stylistically.

Josh is behind me, I think, and I look back to make sure. Yes, he's behind me, and I see a well-muscled older Palestinian in full camouflage and a beret standing off to the side of the road. That seems better than riding nuts to butt on a motor scooter.

Why am I riding nuts to butt on my own motor scooter, especially when it's my nuts to unknown butt?

I jump off, but the well-muscled older Palestinian in full camouflage half-catches me, surprised. Josh jumps off right behind me and the younger Palestinians start motioning toward us and screaming like banshees. A crowd begins to gather around us; none of its members look too happy. I'm looking at mothers waving shoes at me. Fathers clawing at my Ellen DeGeneres hair.

Why are they doing that?

The well-muscled older Palestinian, clearly outnumbered and still surprised, grabs Josh and I by our scruffs and carries us to a shuttered storefront, quickly opening it, shoving us inside, and slamming the metal roller door behind us. We stand looking at each other. Sweaty, breathing, laughing.

"What the hell is happening?" I ask.

"I think we're in real trouble," he responds, eyes smiling.

Dust floats in the strips of light coming in from the boarded-up windows until the roller door opens again and the well-muscled older Palestinian scoots in and slams it shut behind him.

He is sweating but not laughing. He is shaking his head slowly. He is not happy, but there is something kind about his demeanor. Something almost fatherly.

"There is a crowd outside that wants to kill you," he says matter-of-factly after catching his breath, in proper, clear Arabic. "They believe you were calling in targets for the Israeli planes and want you to pay for it, but you will wait here, and when everyone goes away, then you can go home."

This is the second time within twenty-four hours that we have been accused of calling in Israeli bombs, and I wonder, do the Israeli Defense Forces really have men and women on the ground this deep into Lebanon calling strikes? Actually driving around providing coordinates to pilots while sitting in the concussion zone just to make sure they get it right? It seems fantastical but it's apparently the going narrative, and far stranger things have been proven true.

The well-muscled Palestinian pulls two chairs up for us and we slump into them. I suddenly feel completely enervated but at peace. My 7 For All Mankind jeans are super lame, but we'll be out of this spot soon and I can sew them back together or something.

He even rustles us up two cold bottles of juice from a refrigerator that is magically still working.

We make small talk with him for a few minutes. He is in the Palestinian Liberation Organization, responsible for guarding the entrance to the refugee camp, serious about his mission. He tells us not to worry, that we just have to wait for emotions to cool, that we'll be gone soon. I don't know why he trusts us. I don't know why he cares. He should kick us to the mob on principle and let them rip our arms from our torsos, probably.

We tell a few stories about living near Hollywood, our favorite Yemeni restaurants, the poor construction of Syrian socks until his phone rings and he excuses himself to take it in another room. Josh and I sip our cold juices and sigh. Our situation isn't quite as absurdly funny as it just was, but we're going to be okay. I know we're going to be okay even if we have to sit in this room and sip juice for a few hours.

When our well-muscled Palestinian returns from his call a few moments later, his face looks gray.

"Hezbollah has called for you," he says, looking truly depressed. "There's nothing I can do."

I don't know what that means, that Hezbollah has called for us, and don't know what happens next. While I'm thinking about it, the metal roller door flies open, and I can see the mob out front has grown. Hundreds of women, men, and children shaking fists and waving shoes. Screaming, yelling, cursing, and when they get a sight of us it turns into a roar.

The Hezbollah operatives, Don Johnson beards dialed to perfection, slam the door behind them. One marches up to Josh and slaps the juice from his hand. It hits the ground and shatters. I'm mid sip and he slaps it from my hand too. It shatters more severely.

Uh oh.

There is a very uncomfortable rising of the temperature. A turn that feels properly dangerous. He demands that we strip to our underwear while his colleagues check us for recording devices, transmission devices, or whatever it is that spies use, then he orders us to redress.

Josh and I are standing shoulder to shoulder, like dumb kindergarteners lining up for snack, when he rushes over, rage shooting like daggers out of his eyes, grabs the bottom of my V-neck, and pulls it over the back of my head.

It is remarkably effective, blocking light and pulling my head down into an uncomfortable bent position. I assume the same has been done to Josh, though I don't know for sure, and before I can ponder any more I'm being pushed forward. Pushed into the sunlight. I hear the mob in my ear, feel their hands clawing at me, but I can also feel that I'm being protected. That Hezbollah, for whatever reason, doesn't want to feed us to a pack of Palestinians yet.

A heavy hand lands on the top of my head. I duck while my shins hit metal and I know I'm getting into a car. I sit and feel the vinyl slide beneath me, or maybe it's very smooth leather. Either way I slide until I hit another person then feel cold metal slammed into my temple.

It's a gun. I can't see anything, marveling how my whiteish Fruit of the Loom V-neck is so effective at blocking my vision, but I know it's a gun. Bodies press against mine. Then some guttural Arabic echoes and we begin moving.

Somehow I know it's a Mercedes. Maybe I can see through my shirt and my mind is just not processing quickly enough, because I also know the body pressed against mine is holding a Kalashnikov but I don't know how it can fit. I don't know if Josh is here. I don't know anything except that I am breathing heavily and sweating and that my Fruit of the Loom V-neck is over my head.

Shit.

Shit.

Shit.

Maybe it's Hanes. I remember going to Target to get two six-packs of white V-necks, my new look, before we left for Amman but can't remember if I bought Fruit of the Loom or Hanes. Michael Jordan advertises for Hanes. I loved him as a kid, but would that have affected my purchasing decision a decade later? Is that how advertising works? Is a white Hanes V-neck pulled over my head because I loved Michael Jordan as a kid?

Time stands still. All I can hear is my breath. All I can feel is the pistol and the Kalashnikov, I'm almost 100 percent certain, being bumped awkwardly against knees. We're driving fast. Taking corners fast. Tires squealing. Shouts from inside the car. The smell of diesel, smoke, dirt, dust. The reek of paranoia everywhere. Sweat and paranoia, and not just from me. The car is absolutely filled with paranoia. And sweat.

And then we lurch to a stop. I feel my arm pulled from the surreal adrenaline inside to the just-plain-scorching-hot outside. I try to stretch my back but there is no time for stretching, apparently, as my arm is now being pulled forward and I'm in the same awkward hunch that I was placed in before.

I shuffle as best as I can, not being able to see, and have you ever done corporate team-building exercises where one in the group must put on a blindfold and the others in the group must guide her around?

I don't think I have, but understand the tension here as I'm shuffling forward, being pulled by the arm, but can't see where I'm going. I need to trust. What if there is something in my way? What if I trip? It is uncomfortable. I just need to trust. I want to be moving faster but also am not a psychic, plus I'm tripping over my damned new bell-bottom, when I feel it. The hardest blow I've ever experienced. A thump so severe that it knocks the wind out of me for the second time and makes me stumble like an invalid, almost tripping over my newly bell-bottomed 7 For All Mankinds.

What does 7 For All Mankind mean? Does it make sense? In fifth grade I got the courage to ask one of the cuter girls in class what I was supposed to guess about her jeans. She stared at me and said, "Nothing," before rolling her eyes and walking away.

Ugh.

My spine hurts. It had to be a kick. I just got kicked by a boot. Kicked by a boot right in my bottom. It hurts worse than any other bottom strike, and let me tell you, I'm no tourist here. My parents believed in spanking, and I caught more than a few with a wooden spoon, and sometimes with a metal spoon after my bottom had broken the wooden spoon, but wow. Hezbollah knows how to kick a bottom, and they kick it straight up some stairs then down some stairs into an extra dark space to where I am suddenly flung.

I hear a metal door rolling up. I hear muffled Arabic voices. I hear another metal door slam shut. I'm forced to sit down on something soft, and have no idea if I am alone, if Josh has been boot spanked too, or if this is the end, but I'm pretty sure it is.

This is the beginning of actual torture, and I begin imagining how many fingernails pulled out by pliers it will take for me to say…what? That I hate Lebanese music videos filmed in front of dramatically lit ruins? That I can't stand Nancy Ajram?

Other than that, I have nothing to cop to. How much worse is a potential torturous interrogation when there is nothing to cop to? Does it just go on and on and on and on ad nauseam? I picture George Clooney in *Syriana* getting his fingernails pulled out by pliers and remember hearing that he broke his neck filming the scene. He broke his neck filming a scene about torture, so how much worse will actual torture be?

Ugh.

It's dark. I know it's dark, and I can't hear anything or see anything or smell anything other than my own sweat, dust, must, stink, must. I can also hear my breath, but it is slowing because I've been sitting on something soft for a full minute. A full two minutes. A full three minutes.

I keep my T-shirt over my head. I keep sitting there on whatever it is without daring to remove it because I only know it is dark and I am going to have my neck broken at any moment, if I'm lucky. What if I take my T-shirt's base off of my head and there is someone standing there to boot spank my face? What if the Don Johnsons are standing around in a semicircle just waiting to tee off?

In truth, it shouldn't matter. My nose is beyond crooked from having a friend in Papua New Guinea smash it with a log while we were hunting for fire ants and fifteen years later having a gang of teenaged South Pasadena ne'er-do-wells set upon it after I delivered some ill-conceived "your mom" joke, but this is certainly more serious and more like George Clooney in *Syriana*. I almost got bombed, was accused of guiding those bombs, got taken by Palestinian kids, found myself momentarily liberated from an angry mob by the Palestinian Liberation Organization, and then got kidnapped by Hezbollah.

This is serious.

My mind starts wandering about the worst-case scenario after torture. Getting held for years? Shuttled around the country? Shipped to Iran? Used as a bargaining chip? When we first went to Yemen, kidnapping was a real possibility but something none of us cared about. Rumor was that it happened often to foreigners but would only last for a few weeks until the kidnappees demands were met, which were usually for new roads or schools. The kidnappers would then be returned well-fed and speaking some very okay Arabic, or so it was told.

This is very much different, and I think of all those brave women and men who spent years upon years in captivity. The Iran Hostage crisis. All those stupid ones too, the ones who knowingly and purposefully pushed the envelope. For the first time since 9/11 I feel bad for my mother and father. Will the rest of their lives consist of wondering about me? It had better not. I hope they know that this is all my choice. I hope they are able to laugh it off. There's no way they're going to be able to laugh it off.

"How thoughtful..." Josh's voice cuts through my spiraling thoughts. "They gave us Hezbollah dresses for their Hezbollah dance."

I almost can't believe he's here with me, and relief washes over me like a warm bath. I slowly reach toward the back of my head, loosen my V-neck's hem, and release it, allowing it to fall down and billow around me.

I blink furiously and take in our surroundings, our dark blood-smeared dungeon with one blood-smeared mattress pushed into the corner that I'm sitting on and slats of light cutting through the edges of a small, metal, jail-like door.

Josh is sitting, legs crossed, directly across from me on his own blood-smeared mattress and admiring the billow of his T-shirt. Sweat and tension blasted our tops into extra-large baby doll dresses, perfect for a Courtney Love cosplay. He looks over at me with a wide, comforting smile washing over his face. I want to puke, though I can't help but smile back because he's twisting it like he's a supermodel. Really admiring it. I twist my shirt around and see that it is in fact a Hanes.

Michael Jordan has really done a number on me.

We whisper back and forth for a minute until a voice rockets through the metal door in Arabic.

"Quiet! Shut up! Bush is a dog!"

"*Aiwa?*" I shout back, though halfheartedly. "Yes?"

The insults continue. Bush has done this, that, and the other thing. Bush is responsible for children deaths, mass destruction, carnage.

"Okay…which Bush?" Josh asks, seeking clarification.

The insults stop and silence fills the dungeon.

"Are we toast?" I ask Josh.

"No way," he replies. "I was more worried with the whole PLO thing. These Hezbollah bros are something we know. We can figure this out."

He looks completely amused, and the fact we're together gives me small hope, but much like strip-club etiquette, I don't know how these things are supposed to go down. We can hear bombs hitting nearby, intermittently, but nothing else. It is surprisingly quiet.

We sit for a few hours, alternatively wondering if Nate is capturing the destruction of Beirut from the other side of town and halfheartedly backing the George W. Bush administration, whom it turns out our captors are furious at. I don't like what he's doing either with regards to his Middle Eastern policy, but always hated Americans who rolled over when traveling. This is our president, whether we like it or not, and totally undermining him will look both weak and weird to men entirely committed to a cause.

Our door clinks and clanks and eventually opens. Three Don Johnsons rush in, grab us both, pull our T-shirts back over our heads, and we repeat the process, getting rushed upstairs, blind, across some downgrade, blind, into a waiting car, blind, gunmetal slammed into temple, blind. We drive what feels like extra-fast circles then stop, are pulled out of the car, march somewhere new and dark but I don't hear any metal and I'm forced to sit on…a couch? Something soft but at appropriate sitting level.

Our Hezbollah dresses are ripped off our heads and we are on a couch, in a living room with two Qu'ranic transcriptions on the wall, a clock featuring the Kaaba and an audience of older, bushy-bearded men looking stern.

In front of us, sitting on a chair backward, is a younger man. Clean-shaven, well-dressed, with some of the most evil eyes I've ever seen. They reek pure terror. Murderer eyes. Rapist eyes. Uncomfortable eyes. "I'm sorry we had to detain you," he says in the creepiest, most perfect English I've ever heard. "We just need to ask you a few questions," he adds before asking us what we were doing.

We tell him about filming for Al Gore, or rather Al Gore's Internet-esque television station.

He chuckles. "But why in the Bourj?"

We tell him, "To get the true, honest story of what's happening."

He chuckles again. "Hmmmm. Tell me, what do you think of Jennie Garth in the television show *Beverly Hills, 90210*? Is she not the most beautiful woman in America?"

Josh and I look at each other, momentarily knocked off our game. We will defend George W. Bush because it looks worse not to. We will die for Christianity because we actually believe. But Jennie Garth? *Beverly Hills, 90210* had not been on air for six years, and while I watched many of those early episodes, I could not definitely say which actress owned the zeitgeist. Definitely not the ones playing Donna Martin or Shannen Doherty. Probably Valerie Malone played by Tiffani Amber Thiessen, but that is deep cut *Beverly Hills, 90210*, and if I'm really going to be honest, Luke Perry's Dylan McKay really stole the entire show appearance-wise.

Josh looks at me confused, as he has never seen any of them, and so I'm stuck answering for the both of us.

"She's very beautiful, and yes," I say, instantly hating myself. Not that she's not very beautiful, as she clearly is, but she's not even the most beautiful actress on *Beverly Hills, 90210*, not to mention America.

I should have said Halle Berry, and now I really hate myself for pulling that punch.

Our interrogation continues and the hours twist by on that Kaaba clock. The elders, still sitting around stern-faced, take turns flipping through our passports. We are asked multiple times what we are doing, and we mention Al Gore multiple times. Our interrogator returns to Jennie Garth. I agree again, this time adding that she is the most beautiful woman in America, not just on television, and I hate myself all the more.

At some break, Josh reads one of the Qur'anic transcriptions on the wall and the room grows silent. They are impressed that he can pick his way through the fancy calligraphy and even more impressed when he provides a nuanced understanding of what the verse means, how it was applied in Mohammed's day, and how it should be applied to our own.

Our interrogator even sits back and rubs his chin, his evil eyes still nightmarish but a little softer. It may be a turning point. The next few hours continue with many of the same questions as before, but I no longer fear fingernail pulling. Unless they're just softening us up. Unless this is the "good cop" routine and the "bad cop" is just behind the door.

I still have no idea where we are, though I assume it's somewhere in south Beirut. Bombs drop periodically and sound very close, but nobody in the room flinches. Nobody pauses. One finally knocks the lights out, and one of the elders gets up to light candles.

A younger man knocks on the door after five or six hours and hands plastic bags through it to another even younger man, who appears from out of a corner then comes into the room, dutifully studying me and Josh. Standing there, hands at his sides, wearing very tight jeans, really taking us in.

I think about the state of my own jeans and am profoundly disappointed. It is not the look I want. I don't want to be wearing bell-bottoms, and now I'm wearing bell-bottoms *and* a baby doll dress. I look like a well-to-do girl from Connecticut who snuck off to Woodstock.

The baby doll dress wasn't my fault. That Hanes T-shirt fit well before the sweat and stress and stretching. The bell-bottoms are, though, and it makes me rethink the bootcut entirely. I was all in on bootcut, my look of choice, but now that I see how easily they've been turned into bell-bottoms I'm sad and disgusted with myself.

Imagine if this takes a hard turn and we do end up getting tortured. Imagine how horrible I'll feel, blood gushing out on my bell-bottoms. Blood spurting all over my bell-bottoms. The afterschool special warning kids off of misguided surf adventures airing on Al Gore's Current TV, will feature Josh and me. He will be getting tortured in straight-legged black jeans, and I will be getting tortured in the next room looking like Benny Andersson from ABBA.

An elder takes the bags, sets them down, then unfurls a large, very thin piece of plastic over the rug. Everyone in the room stands up, stretches, and moves to the center of the room, sitting barefoot and cross-legged in a circle. We are invited to sit on the floor too, and a veritable feast of bread and cheese is laid out on the floor next to their collection of freshly pedicured feet.

The cleanliness of the feet here is an honest wonder of the Islamic world. Most men wear sandals all the time, which makes sense considering that if they're good Muslims they must perform prayers five times a day, which includes washing the hands up to the elbows and the feet up to the ankle bones. It is no wonder, then, that their bare feet all look freshly pedicured, a stark contrast to the unfortunately stinky feet freshly pulled from steamy Swedish surplus military boots and sockless white low-top Converse belonging to me and Josh.

Josh had told me a funny story on our first trip to Yemen about an Arab doctor who observed and wrote about the Crusader invasion sometime in the 1100s. Disease decimated the brave Christian knights from today's Germany, England, and France. This doctor watched their disgusting habits, and being a kind man, said, "You'd live longer if you bathed." According to Josh, the Crusaders mocked him and said, "Bathe? We're not Mohammedans!" then went ahead and proceeded to die some more.

It was a funny story then, but it rang particularly true now. We are gross compared to our dinner hosts, but then we also have better taste in women, which also makes sense considering we don't duct tape our billboards.

Our interrogator is eating and staring at us with still evil eyes. Josh and I start eating and I quickly realize how starving I am. Completely famished. So hungry that I'm wolfing down bread and cheese but not so hungry that I'm not calculating what this turn means. Are they softening us up before the torture? Being kind before a mercifully quick kill? What's the angle here?

The easy kill or hosing us down and sticking us in a refrigerated room with a looping "Best of Jennie Garth" video. Radical Islamic fundamentalists are being hosed down then stuck in refrigerated rooms in Guantanamo Bay and forced to listen to "Dirrty" by Christina Aguilera feat. Redman at full volume right now, but if I'm honest I'd rather listen to that than the Slipknot, System of a Down, Insane Clown Posse business that most Marines actually choose to listen to. Maybe cultural misunderstandings make for incomplete torture.

Bombs hit close during our meal, and still no one flinches. They sit and eat in the candlelight while the ground quakes furiously and the air heaves. It is a beautiful tableau, if I'm honest, or maybe I have Stockholm Syndrome. Talk is kept to a minimum during the meal and a feeling of dread begins creeping in as I see it all winding down, because something has to happen. We've got to be moved somewhere, whether back to the dungeon, another safe house, or off to Iran. I know from watching movies that captors have to move captees around a lot, especially in the first few days. So where are we off to next?

Right when I'm thinking about Iran, the door bursts open and a younger man in a tracksuit comes in, breathlessly. His tracksuit is such a fine look and I further hate my bell-bottoms and begin to hope that I'll eventually get some new pants in the next few years of captivity. The younger man in a tracksuit approaches our evil-eyed interrogator and whispers something in his ear. He nods subtly, with a slightly pained look on his face, and talks to one of the elders, who also nods subtly and leaves with three other elders.

And then our interrogator tells Josh and I, "We are finished. We have gotten your motor scooters back from the Palestinians." He makes the same slightly pained look again. "But one of the tires is damaged. We have also retrieved your camera and tapes. We will review the tapes thoroughly then deliver them to you."

I look at Josh. Josh looks at me. Before we can say anything, we are beckoned outdoors. Our motor scooters sit there in the dark. One of the elders is down on his knees, fiddling with Josh's front tire.

He stands and shakes his head, saying "broken" in Arabic.

I look closer and see it's flat.

The elders each come up and hug us one by one. Our interrogator hands us the keys. We walk over to the motor scooters, start them, then ease them backward, giving us enough room to clear a wall then head into an alley.

I glance over my shoulder one more time before twisting the throttle. They are all still standing there in a clump, like parents and older siblings sending younger siblings off to college, both wistful and proud.

I have no idea where we are, but after a few random corners, we see an entrance to the main freeway running through southern Beirut into the city center. We ease down the empty ramp and ride shoulder to shoulder for a few kilometers on the empty road, Josh's flapping flat tire the only other sound besides the whine of our engines.

CHAPTER 6

We crept back to Amman seven days later, at the official end of the war. The UN had voted, with Israeli and Lebanese approval, for a resolution that declared Hezbollah would disarm and that Israel would withdraw forces from Southern Lebanon. While both Hezbollah and Israel claimed victory, the feeling on the ground in Lebanon and in press was that Hezbollah had won, especially since Israel did withdraw forces and Hezbollah did not disarm. They not only withstood an overwhelming air assault but a full ground invasion as well. We had been to the south and seen the front on a few occasions, but it was an almost impossible task with land mines everywhere and shifting lines. The Israeli Defense Forces got bogged down, undervaluing Hezbollah's will and the rest of the country's fractured population's willingness to get behind their usual enemy.

The fact that Israel started bombing the Christian hills and the Sunni north didn't help its cause. We were in those Christian hills one night while bombs were thumping close, but the Christians didn't care. War had canceled work, school, and normal life, and in turn a massive rave was happening in the street under the stars, the bomb explosions barely audible over the deep bass drops.

That entire week I was looking over my shoulder, convinced that Hezbollah HQ would realize the error of their ways and come scoop us up, like cats that let injured mice free for a few seconds before re-pouncing. Either that or they wanted to observe our comings and goings so they could scoop us up along with Nate and Cameraman Josh and the slow dancers at Babes, not that we had any plans to return there.

Why had they let us go? Josh had theories, one of which was that the elders were there to listen to our Arabic. The fact that I spoke some bizarre mash of Egyptian and Yemeni colloquial, the fact that Josh spoke stilted academic Arabic mixed with Yemeni colloquial, proved to them that we weren't American Intelligence, who learn their Arabic in Monterey, California, and all speak it the same way. Also, historically, Hezbollah hasn't been in the kidnapping business outside of Israeli soldiers that can be used for prisoner swaps. Being Shia, they had a greater religious duty to protect our lives if we were not guilty, or rather *because* we were not guilty. And to top it off, we were able to discuss belief with them in an honest way. We were believers too.

Still, I knew we wouldn't have been afforded the same grace had the sandal been on the other foot. Had we, for instance, been Arab and Muslim and creeping around some American military site, had we been suspiciously loitering during an attack, we would certainly have been shipped off to Guantanamo for our Christina Aguilera sound bath.

That the United States of America was more ruthlessly unforgiving than one of the founding members on its list of Designated Foreign Terrorist Organization didn't surprise me, but...I don't know. It made me feel lost. Adrift.

We had embarked on this adventure into the very heart of radical Islamic fundamentalism and come face to face with it, surfed with it, shot with it, shot at it, had it shoot at us, and done it all for years now, yet I couldn't say that I was any closer to its deeper truths and meanings. To how it could or should be woven into a broader, Western life. Between al-Qaeda, the al-Aqsa Martyrs' Brigade, proto-al-Shabaab Somalis, the Muslim Brotherhood, the Taliban, and Hezbollah, we had tugged and pulled, screamed and smashed heads over belief, but to what end? Outside our stories which, I suppose, humanized "the other," had we done anything meaningful?

The world had never been more black and white or more polarized. Radical Islamic fundamentalists were blasting holes in Madrid, London, Moscow, Amsterdam. In Baghdad, Kabul, Peshawar, Cairo, and boring old Amman. They were getting blasted back in Baghdad, Kabul, Peshawar, Riyadh, Beirut, and every other Middle Eastern suburb as anti-terrorism task forces grabbed more money, more power, and more surveillance state control.

It was good versus evil, but who was good and who was evil? Being gray and weird was not a popular position, but what choice did we have? What choice did I have? Having fun in the margins, refusing to abide by a manufactured narrative has its downside.

We dragged our drained bones off the plane at LAX, and after three weeks of being war journalists I respected the craft both more and less. More because of the hours war journalists put in. Less because treating those hours as "work" is ridiculous. War is a party, or at least our war was. Feeling the heart always hammering. Tasting every second. Really and truly living as opposed to just passing time. Human suffering is real and tragic, but humans also love war and there is simply no denying this fact, as disgusting as it may be.

The next day Josh and I woke up early, still spent but kinetically wired, hovering in that strange mental island that jet lag gifts, and drove to Mimi's house to see what had already aired on Al Gore's Current TV and what was in the pipeline. She answered the door after multiple knocks in a Hermès wrap, smoking a cigarette from an ivory cigarette holder, oversized Chanel sunglasses hiding her eyes, and sighed, "Darlings, great to see you. How did it go? I just got back from Nice late last night and saw a note from DHL that I have a package from the Middle East. How exciting."

Nothing had been done, nothing at all. No edited footage. No aired "pods."

Nothing. And I had a sneaking suspicion that what we captured, minus what Hezbollah was still "reviewing," wouldn't tell much of a story. It was a frustrating turn, but Mimi was too fabulous to be angry with, and she promised that she would make it up to us. Still, we had just lived like young, steak-eating, Audi-driving kings in a warzone and delivered nothing.

Passive-aggressive phone calls started flooding in from San Francisco as Josh and I tried to find someone with enough technical skill to edit. Eventually it was decided that the Current staff would take care of that work and we would all have to go to San Francisco to provide interstitial commentary before the Lebanon War was a forgotten relic.

I'd cut my Ellen DeGeneres into a misguided Brian Grazer–esque spike and was wearing a surf-branded Army-style jacket as we drove north. We had watched the tapes we had, and there were some real moments in there. When a missile zoomed right over the Audi and slammed into a garage, for example, or the day we spent with the Palestinian man who had set up a theater program for kids whose homes had been destroyed. Plus, true to their word, Hezbollah had mailed the tapes we had on us before our capture back to Los Angeles. A neat little package with neat little writing addressed to Mr. Josh and Mr. Charly.

When I opened it and saw four miniDV tapes, I could barely believe it. When I raced them to Josh's then raced out to find a miniDV player, my jaw was on the floor. There it was, footage of us driving down the hill, driving into the neighborhood, bombs hitting, smoke everywhere, guttural grunts from me, us speeding up the hill while getting shot, Josh yelling *"Ana sahafi! Ana sahafi!"* and finally Josh's tumble.

The Palestinians who had initially grabbed us even left the camera running when they stuffed it into Josh's motor scooter's seat compartment. The video is black for fifteen minutes then comes into the light, set sideways on a table. Their hands come in and out of frame, digging through our camera bag, pulling apart receipts for strong beer. Their voices can be heard too.

One asks, "What happened to the Americans?"

Another answers, "We killed them." It was surreal listening to talk of our own demise, and I hoped it would be enough to placate Al Gore's understandable rage.

Hezbollah had tracked it down, watched it, and mailed it mostly uncut back to the United States of America. There was a gap in the middle, a substantial cut, but whatever was missing was more than made up for by what we had. No one had ever claimed they killed Anderson Cooper on video.

Our time in Current TV's studio was less inspiring. They set us up on tiered boxes in some stylish room with cool neon graffiti on the walls and had Josh say, "I'm Josh. I'm working on my PhD in Islamic Studies. My areas of interest are Pakistan, Yemen, and Somalia," followed by Nate saying, "I'm Nate. I grew up in Bolivia. My specialty is radical Shia politics. I've edited a book on Hezbollah and I've had tea with some of the wealthiest men in the Middle East," before I smashed it out of the park, saying, "Hi, I'm Charlie. I've danced salsa with cocaine bandits in Colombia, surfed across the border into Mexico, and have a master's degree in applied linguistics." It felt wooden coming out of my mouth, and for the first time in my life, I began to doubt my preordained path toward fame. It was a brief flash soon extinguished by willful determination, but a flash nonetheless.

Our pods aired a month later on a cable tier none of us had. I watched a few at my neighbor's house, and while they weren't perfect, they were…something. Compelling? Different? Interesting? Something. Josh was too busy to care and Nate had just gotten a job in Baghdad as a contracted liaison between the United States Army and the international press corps, putting his Lebanon War experience to quick, sensible work.

I ruminated on how we could get better and what our next step should be when, one early fall evening, Josh casually told me while we ate tacos at a taco stand that he had stumbled upon the headwaters of violent anti-state radicalism that led to our current Global War on Terror. That there was a spring bubbling in rural Yemen that flowed to Indonesia then India. It lit a fuse in my addled brain.

We had been nibbling around the buffet table, sampling various ideologies from al-Qaeda, the al-Aqsa Martyrs' Brigade, proto-al-Shabaab Somalis, the Muslim Brotherhood, the Taliban, and Hezbollah, but it had become a shapeless mash. A tangled mess. The headwaters of violent anti-state radicalism sounded pure, though. Like it would provide the one, distilled, applicable principle I was looking for but couldn't quite put my finger on. A storyline that would make easy sense. The final puzzle piece we all needed.

Josh rolled out how the *en vogue* scholastic narrative was missing key readings of certain obscure Arabic texts and other things I didn't quite comprehend because I was already thinking how we'd look on this true adventure. What we'd wear, who we'd sell the story to, how we should film it, and who we should write it for.

Mostly I was thinking about how quickly we could get back on the road.

My phone rang first thing in the morning. I answered, "Hello?" all thick headed and dumb.

"Darling…" the voice on the other end breathed. "It's Mimi. I was out with a very famous European producer, from Cannes I think, and was telling him about you, Josh, and Nate's fabulous trip with Hezbollah. He loved it and says he needs to do something with you. Do you have anything for me? I could get it funded tomorrow."

I couldn't stop myself and said, "Well, Nate is on his way to Baghdad, so he's going to have to sit this one out, but Josh was just telling me last night that he has discovered the illusive headwaters of violent anti-state radicalism or something like that. From what I can tell it's like the Fountain of Youth. Academics have been looking for it for years but looking in all the wrong places. Josh reckons he has it, so we're going to go bathe."

"Violent anti-state radicalism sounds just divine, darling. Absolutely perfect—but what is it exactly?" she breathed.

"From what I could gather, it's where modern terrorism came from, and these headwaters are in rural Yemen, so it must be Islamic."

"I'll have your money tomorrow. This simply sounds wonderful."

I rushed to Los Angeles City College after hanging up, and told my 230 students that it was their lucky day. I would be gone soon, probably for three weeks, and they would all be receiving A's.

A cheer rose from the room.

I called Josh straight after and said, "Pack your bags, bro. We're headed to Yemen."

"What? When? How?" he answered.

"Mimi's got a budget." Before he could get a word in, I continued, "A two-part docuseries. We start in Yemen looking for the spring that feeds the headwaters of modern radical Islamic terrorism, or whatever you said last night, then go to India to actually drink from it."

Josh's end of the phone remained silent.

PART THREE

CHAPTER 1

Yemen, Late 2000s

Unlike Jesus, who got lifted straight to heaven forty days after his resurrection, the world knows exactly where Muhammad's body is buried. Underneath a forest-green dome in the middle of the Prophet's Mosque in the middle of Medina, which happens to be near the middle of current-day Saudi Arabia. A minor sixteen-hour drive from Yemen's capital Sana'a. A mere eight hours from Riyadh, Saudi Arabia's capital, where the country's most important music video channel broadcasts when not playing *The Best of Mecca* programming.

Abu al-Qasim Muhammad ibn 'Abd Allah ibn 'Abd al-Muttalib ibn Hashim, founder of the fastest-growing religion in the world multiple years running, died on June 8, 632, some sixtyish years old, and was interred in the mosque he had built adjacent to his home, where he rests to this day.

His birth is slightly more mysterious. Islamic tradition holds that his father belonged to the powerful Banu Hashim clan of Mecca and had light shooting out of his forehead like a unicorn, a trait as desirable to the women of his day as it is to the little girls of our own. He attracted many hopeful brides, but Amina, said to be a direct descendent from Ishmael, the father of the Arabs, beat all comers and won his hand.

Muhammad was conceived shortly after their union. His father left immediately with a merchant caravan and died before his birth. When he was six, his mother also died, leaving him an orphan in the care of his paternal grandfather, who died, then on to his uncle.

Not much is known about young Muhammad. He worked as a shepherd in order to earn his keep and in his teens accompanied various merchant caravans, once going all the way to Syria. Early Islamic histories suggest that on that journey he met a gnostic or maybe Nestorian monk who foretold his future life as a prophet. His merchant bros considered him an honorable young man and nicknamed him Al-Amin—the one you can trust.

In his early twenties, Muhammad took the goods of a wealthy forty-year-old widow north and returned with a handsome profit. Her name was Khadijah, and she was so impressed that she married the young orphan, giving him a nice big Mecca house and four daughters. She also birthed two sons who both died in infancy.

It was a time of great prosperity for Mecca, with trade booming and the town becoming a force, but Muhammad was disturbed by the robust idolatry and general naughty behavior, and he began hanging out in a nearby mountain cave fasting and meditating. It was here, in the year 610, that he was visited by the archangel Jibril, or Gabriel, who told him to "read." Muhammad told him, "I can't." Then Jibril hugged him and gave him the first revelation.

Muhammad was so shaken by the experience that he did not share it widely. His wife took him to see her cousin, who confirmed that they were indeed messages from Allah, or God, and then died a few days later. He received a number of revelations over the next ten years covering all manner of subjects from dining habits to the proper way to pray, and he slowly began sharing the messages with this tribe. These were written and collected, later becoming the Qu'ran. Over the next decade, a handful believed Muhammad's declarations, but these people were persecuted as Muhammad's monotheistic teachings countered tradition and damaged commerce. Mecca's most important tribe, the Quraysh, banned trade with him and his followers. His wife died, his uncle died, and his emboldened opponents tried to assassinate him, making for a real bummer decade.

In 622, Muhammad had had enough and he gathered his few hundred followers and migrated to an oasis town north of Medina named Yathrib. Its leaders had invited him to help settle a dispute that had been ripping the town apart. He wisely solved their reoccurring problem involving an eye-for-an-eye blood feud, and his numbers began to swell.

Mecca was none too happy with this power shift, and small fights between the two soon led to three major battles. The Muslims, or "submitters" to Allah, won the first, lost the second, and persevered through a siege on the third. The two sides signed a treaty giving them freedom to move about unmolested around the Peninsula, though it was soon breached by Meccan allies.

Two years later, rightly pissed, Muhammad marched on Mecca, gathering tribe after tribe on his way, and he entered the city without bloodshed. It took only three more years to consolidate power on the rest of the Arabian Peninsula.

And then Muhammad returned to Yathrib, which had been renamed Medina, or "City of the Prophet," where he died and was laid to rest in his mosque, which got a dome upgrade a few centuries later and painted forest green a few centuries after that. I have no doubt that the funeral was a beautiful affair with much shoulder-patting and tear-drying, but succession questions arose immediately. Who was supposed to take over?

Most of the faithful determined that the community should choose their next leader. A smaller clique thought it was only right for someone in Muhammad's family to take the reins, suggesting Ali, married to Muhammad's daughter Fatimah, as the obvious choice, and thus began the Sunni-Shia split.

The Sunnis, from the Arabic word for *tradition*, prevailed initially, and Muhammad's father-in-law Abu Bakr quickly consolidated power, becoming Islam's first ruler or "caliph" and leading a series of wars to grow the base and quell any dissention. He expanded the territory over his two-year run until he fell gravely ill. Wanting to avoid the messy issue of succession after Muhammad's death, he appointed Umar, who was killed by a Persian with carpentry, artistic, and engineering skills. A Renaissance man before the Renaissance. An Elon Musk sort before Elon Musk upped things from micro dose to macro.

Before dying, though, Umar blew out the walls, expanding Islam's reach through most of Persia, greater modern-day Turkey, the Levant, and pockets of north Africa. In slightly over forty years since Muhammad's death, Islam gripped a third of the known world.

Uthman came next, elected by a six-person committee, and he added Armenia, Afghanistan, and the rest of Persia to the fold. He too was assassinated, this time by brutal beating, his wife getting her fingers cut off in the process of trying to protect him, and then Ali was cajoled into taking the caliphate but also inherited a fraying solidarity and war. He too was assassinated, while praying in a mosque near Baghdad, and all hell really broke proper loose.

The Shia, those who held that Ali should have been selected in the first place, split from the dominant Sunni, then split again into Seveners, Twelvers, Seven-Eleveners, etc. The Sunni, while unified on the surface and counting 90 percent more adherents, all fractured in their own special ways.

The first four caliphs were called the Rashidun, or Rightly Guided. Next came the Umayyads (Sunni 661–750), based in Damascus. Then there were the Abassids (Sunni 750–1258, 1261–1517), straight out of Baghdad, but they had to deal with parallel caliphate power grabs by the Fatimids (Ismaili-Shia 909–1171) based out of Tunisia and the Mamluks (Sunni 1261–1517) from Cairo. The Almohads (Sunni 1130–1269), calling Morocco home, claimed ownership of Muhammad's vision for a hundred years in there before we finally arrive at the Ottomans (Sunni) in 1517, a mere 885 years after Muhammad's death.

The Ottomans started their strangulation slowly, claiming the caliphate as early as the 1300s then moving its seat to modern-day Istanbul in the 1400s, and finally turning into both a dominant political and dominant religious demarcation in the 1700s with no other legitimate claims to the throne.

Their territory stretched west all the way across north Africa and up into Spain. East through modern Turkey, Iran, Afghanistan, and Pakistan. North to the Caucuses and south to Yemen. It was a fine time, a rich time, as most of the world's trade flowed right through this Middle East and the Ottomans were there to skim the cream, frustrating Europeans and Russians who had all finally crawled out of their caves. In a number of major wars and smaller skirmishes later, the Ottoman rulers were forced to deal with the white devil.

While the Turks were fiddling around on the northern and western borders of their empire, a man named Muhammad ibn Abd-al-Wahhab was quietly born in mostly forgotten Arabia. His family, scholars and judges in the Islamic courts, had young Muhammad educated in the Hanbali school of Islamic jurisprudence. He was a good student, memorizing the Qu'ran and going on pilgrimage to Mecca and Medina, where he became increasingly frustrated with the decadence he witnessed, just like his namesake—particularly the veneration of saints.

The driving power of Islam is belief in the oneness of God, and Muhammad saw the worship of various holy men impinging on this. He set about denouncing any sort of extracurricular praise, claiming that Muslims who practiced any deviation in any of the strictest readings of Islamic law were not only sinning but entirely outside of the fold, the same as Christian or Jewish infidels, which included the illiterate Bedu, Shia, and the Ottomans themselves.

His radical conservative take was not appreciated by the rulers of his home region of Najd, and he was expelled, moving near Riyadh to the settlement of Diriyah, where he formed an alliance with its emir Muhammad bin Saud. The two agreed to purge the deviants and bring the Peninsula back to the true principles of Islam.

By providing a specific religious direction, Wahhab gave the Sauds a reason to expand the territory—and expand the territory they did. After Muhammad ibn Saud died in 1765, his son Abdul Aziz bin Muhammad Al Saud took over, sacking Shia towns in Iraq, massacring thousands of people and destroying Shia shrines in the name of purity. He also took Mecca from the Ottomans in 1802, ten years after Wahhab's death. He ordered the men to destroy the shrines there too, even attempting to burn the Prophet's tomb and its striking forest-green dome but somehow failed, possibly due to the density and relative incombustibility of stone.

In any case, the Saud family passed the leadership from father to son, without incident, and their puritanical vision of Islam, Wahhabism as it came to be called, was a defining characteristic of their rule. They fought a series of decisive, consolidating wars through the 1800s, leaving the unrelenting vision of Islam in their wake.

In the early 1900s, the plucky Sauds earned the admirations of the British, who made a deal with Abdul-Aziz Al Saud to fight the Ottomans during World War I, making the House of Saud a British Protectorate, eventually leading to the official establishment of the Kingdom of Saudi Arabia a few years later.

Right before World War I, an enterprising but poor young Yemeni emigrated from his small Hadramawt village to the city of Jeddah on Arabia's Red Sea coast and worked as a porter before starting a construction business that did very well. He was befriended by Saudi Arabia's first king, Abdul-Aziz Al Saud, who awarded him exclusive contracts for the renovations of the new kingdom's mosques. It was thus that Muhammad ibn Sau bin Awad bin Laden grew incredibly rich, wooing twenty-two wives who bore him fifty-four children.

The seventeenth son, a bright and fervent boy named Osama, was raised with the devout Wahhabi code as his guidepost. He went to secondary school in Jeddah and then to King Abdulaziz University, where he earned a degree in engineering before heading to Afghanistan to fight the infidel Russians, who were now called Soviets. After expelling them and their underwear and Adidas from the country, he formed a group called al-Qaeda, which translates into English as The Foundation, The Leaders, The Base.

And there we have the history of modern Islamic terrorism that led to our current Global War on Terror. Or what Josh calls "violent anti-state radicalism."

CHAPTER 2

"No, it's not..." Josh says, looking up at me from one knee, but his words are muffled by the gold-and-white-checked keffiyeh wrapped tightly around his head and so I think he said, "Wow, it's hot." I stare at him, incensed, but my eyes are hidden behind a pair of Ray-Ban Wayfarers, so he doesn't see how angrily squinty I am. My Lebanese Versaces had been a good call for the war, but I felt this adventure to the stream that feeds the headwaters of radical Islamic terrorism needed something a little less fabulous.

It is totally not hot. It is, in fact, freezing cold.

I pull my own red-and-white-checked keffiyeh down below my mouth and yell, "What are you talking about? It's freezing cold!"

He pauses what he's doing and scrutinizes me, confused.

"I'm freezing!" I yell again.

"Oh," he responds. "I am too. But, also, what you just rolled out as the history of violent anti-state radicalism is not accurate, and we've talked about this. A lot."

"Wait. Which part isn't accurate?"

"Well, the Almohads never did anything even halfway noteworthy, for one, and are not thought of as a legitimate caliphate.

Al-Qaeda has never been translated as 'The Leaders.' Seriously, not ever. I don't know where you keep getting that. Mecca and Medina were never more than 'trading hubs' of trifling significance. The primary sources simply don't support the reading that they were robust towns. All trade was moving up the Red Sea, not on stupid illiterate camels driven by prophets. It's an utter sham propagated to satisfy Marxist reductive demand that money produces religion, not true belief. But, most importantly, Wahhab is not the ideological center of international jihad. Deoband is, with its headwaters bubbling up right in Yemen, or that's what we're here to prove. Remember?"

A brisk wind whips across our now exposed faces and my teeth begin to chatter. I'm straddling my tiny 90cc Chinese motorbike, Josh is puttering around with the carburetor of his tiny 75cc Chinese motorbike. We both wish they were subcontinental Royal Enfields instead, burying the shame of riding motor scooters in Lebanon, but apparently, and as a great surprise to us, Yemenis don't enjoy big, throaty bikes or even dodgy British-by-way-of-India ones. My tiny 90cc and Josh's tinnier 75cc were as big and as throaty as we could find. We flipped the handlebars upside-down and called them café racers anyhow, and now we are somewhere past Rumah back in Yemen's Empty Quarter.

I tug my incredibly chic Japanese motorcycle jacket tighter, trying to block out the icy wind that has somehow found a way through not only the perfectly stiff black leather exterior but also the gorgeous red satin interior, and glance past Josh, who is still jabbering about how fake the Almohad caliphate was at Tony, our new cameraman, who is filming yet another camel.

Josh and I vigorously debated bringing another camera on this trip, even though our budget was for making a documentary. He had not enjoyed the *Vice* experience, the Fremantle meetings, or dealing with Al Gore's Current TV. All he wanted was to have the adventure, discover the secret, ride, shoot, get in trouble, and have the experience wrapped only in our hearts. On the other hand, I felt strongly that without representing our fabulous lives, we'd be letting the world down.

"If a tree falls in the forest and nobody sees it on broadcast television, or in the theater, then what's the damned point?" I bullied Josh once again, and being a best friend in the truest sense of the words, he gave in, likely wishing all the same that instead of using Saddam Hussein's gold toilets and smarming four-star generals, Nate was here to cast the deciding "no camera" vote.

Two weeks later we were on a Sana'a-bound flight ready to reach the headwaters of modern radical Islamic terrorism that led to our current Global War on Terror, planning on circumambulating the entire country for the second time in order to find its various streams. Sitting between us was an enthusiastically pro-marijuana thirty-year-old cameraman named Tony who had worked on a few music documentaries and also had directed a short about house cats.

He was provided by Mimi and may not have known where he was going. She also fronted us an advance that Josh and I used to buy brand-new, rare Japanese leather motorcycle jackets. Mine black with a red satin interior—very Marlon Brando in *The Wild One*. Josh's gunmetal gray and double-breasted with a high leather collar that belonged more to *Das Boot*. Lessons had been learned in Lebanon. Serious lessons. If this run was fated to end in torturous death—a real possibility—then I'd go down proud.

CHAPTER 3

Josh pulls his Das Boot as tight as I am trying to pull my Wild One, and I can tell the glacial wind is getting to him too despite his growing up in rural northern Minnesota, despite his jacket being designed to protect its wearer from the frigid North Atlantic, not just the whips and chains of rival gangs, like mine.

"So how is Wahhabism not what we're chasing here?" I shout. "How is it not the headwaters of modern radical Islamic terrorism that led to our current Global War on Terror?" A giant semitruck roars past, caravanned between two technicals overflowing with Yemeni troops in chic new desert camo.

Last time we were here it was an untamed sandy wilderness. This time there are real roads, asphalted roads, and real semitrucks roaring who knows what to who knows where. The Global War on Terror had gutted oil production with improvised explosive devices and suicide bombers ripping giant holes in Vice President Dick Cheney's dreams of energy dominance, and Yemen, previously thought to be oil free, was now puking black gold, its tribes seemingly purchased and compliant—or at least for the time being.

"What?" Josh shouts back. "You are talking at Nate volume!"

"I am not!" I belt, quietly missing Nate's patently low, mostly inaudible voice and dour attitude. "But if I am, it's because my throat is parched for those delicious headwaters of modern radical Islamic terrorism that led to our current Global War on Terror."

Josh frowns. "I wish you'd stop calling it that because it really sells it short. What we're after is the grandpappy of all transnational radical ideologies. The oldest, most durable factory of anti-state violent rebellion. The ideology that dandled on its knee every radical from Barbary pirates to Baader-Meinhof. The tiny little school that in three centuries has brought the British Empire, the French Republic, the Soviet Union, and finally the American ideal of freedom and crushed them each like a soda can—and it all begins here. Or that's my theory."

"Oh..." I shout, only hearing the words "Baader-Meinhof" above the wind and picturing the phenomenal stylings of the group that terrorized West Germany through the 1970s. "...and did you fix it yet?"

"I think so..." he hollers, climbing onto the seat and giving it three good kicks. It buzzes to life and he throttles it a few times while blue smoke fills the air. It sounds like a no-frills, older-model Honda Civic.

"Okay!" Josh hoots. "Let's go find some lunch. Jossy hungry!"

"Tony!" I scream. He points his video camera from the camel to me and I wave him off. "We're hitting the road again! Tell Mohamed we're going to find a restaurant in Thamud!" He nods, and his brown corduroy pants scamper to the super microvan, where Mohamed al-Behlooly is sitting like a saint in a striking gray gown and skullcap combination paired with a perfectly baggy blazer, his green jambiya setting it all off nicely.

We had called Haitham Alaini, the son of Yemen's ex-president and the owner of the country's FedEx franchises. He was the man who made our exploration possible. Since we had survived our first Yemen blitz, Haitham decided we didn't need Major Ghamdan al-Shoefy, who looked very wistful when we hugged him both hello and goodbye upon arrival, but we *were* going to need a chase vehicle where Tony could ride and film, plus our surfboards in their shiny Mylar coffin that we brought again, just in case, so he offered up a very respected elder from his tribe, Mr. Mohamed al-Behlooly, who worked in security at Sana'a International Airport and turned out to be a saint. The un-Ghamdan. He never forced his will, never ordered feasts, never pressured for illicit company, never sexually assaulted Josh, never questioned where we needed to go or why. He would get us through sticky checkpoints with his beatific smile alone, pulling intransigent guards aside and winning them over with grace.

He was the only Yemeni I'd ever met who didn't carry a gun, which meant he never shot at sunbathing families. More importantly, it meant that Josh *could* carry a gun, and Sana'a's gun market was our very first stop. Josh purchased a Brazilian-made Taurus 9mm and kept it stuffed in his waistband.

Now, Mohamed al-Behlooly looks our way, smile spreading ear to ear, melting me afresh, and slips behind the steering wheel. Tony hops in behind him and slides the door shut. I fire up my bike and we all inch onto the road toward food and, hopefully, some mission-critical enlightenment.

The first turn feels good, crisp, as my little toy bites into the corner. 90ccs, full out, is surprisingly quick, and makes me forget all about those Lebanese motor scooters, though I was rude to force 75ccs of bad carburetor onto Josh, but we all have roles to play, and mine is to be an asshole.

I take the second corner too fast and almost fly off the road. Yemenis had laid proper asphalt through their lightly tamed hinterland but clearly don't know a thing about grading, an art I'd never appreciated before now. I look back over my shoulder and see Josh navigate it better, though still wobble, and see Mohamed al-Behlooly behind him navigate it perfectly.

We've done over a thousand kilometers already and have another thousand to go right into the true headwaters of modern radical Islamic terrorism that led to our current Global War on Terror that I somehow have confused. I swore we were looking for Wahhabis. Like, would have bet money on it.

I don't slow down on the third corner nor accelerate out. I keep a safe, even speed, and the dusty town of Thamud squatting underneath a slate-gray sky rises before me. A lone minaret scrapes the clouds. A herd of goats is being guided past a wall that has been half buried with sand. The boy following behind, periodically whacking the ground with a stick, seems disinterested in his line of work.

We all pull off the main road in front of a square building with an empty gas-fired rotisserie machine out front, park, walk through the open door, and find a seat on the plastic-covered floor in the far corner. Josh and I unwrap our heads while Mohamed al-Behlooly lounges up against a cushion. Tony's brown corduroy pants make that annoying swishing sound as he crosses his legs.

Inside there are four or five other men laconically picking at goat bones and digging fingerfuls of white and yellow rice from a wide, stainless-steel dish. They observe us without care, gawking like four-year-olds. Keeping their eyes fixed while their hands move to and from their mouths.

Tony's brown corduroy pants swish again.

"I'm going to get saltah if the only other option is goat…" I tell Josh.

He shakes his head disapprovingly.

A Yemeni wearing a white skirt rolled to mid-thigh brings us our own dish of white and yellow rice, and I ask if they have chicken. He says, *"La."* No. Josh orders "meat," i.e., goat, and I shake my head disapprovingly while ordering saltah. We both order Canada Dry and order one for Tony, too, who is reviewing the footage he took yesterday of some kids laughing at him.

"So…" I turn to Josh, lounging upon my own cushion. "Not Wahhabis?"

"No, damn it."

"But…okay. I'm confused. Tell me one more time what we're actually looking for here and I promise I'll remember. I also promise I'll stop referring to the original Abu al-Qasim Muhammad ibn 'Abd Allah ibn 'Abd al-Muttalib ibn Hashim's father as a unicorn, but seriously, he was. And babes loved him for his sexy forehead light."

"You're going to get us all fatwa'd with your nonsense," Josh sighs.

"I'm the Oprah Winfrey of fatwas," I tell him, then mimic tossing fatwas to everyone in the restaurant including Mohamed al-Behlooly, even though he is a saint, and the four or five men still staring at us like preschoolers. "You get a fatwa, you get a fatwa, you get a fatwa, you get a fatwa, you get a fatwa…"

Josh shakes his head and begins. "Okay, everyone thinks that Abu Wahhab, the imam to the Sauds or whatever, is where this new, aggressive exporting of Islamic radicalism with an aggressive bent came from, right? When the Hashemites take over after World War I, then the Wahhabs get their control, but they are very inward-looking, very specific. They just want everything clean. They want Mecca, they want Medina, and they want everyone to be good—not venerating saints, not reading illicit texts. It's all very boring. But before their rise to power, when the Wahhabis were still just literally six dudes with one camel in a tent in the middle of the Arabian Peninsula, Deoband was having a full-on anti-colonial intellectual revolution."

"Where's Deoband again?" I cut in while reaching for a fingerful of rice that is wonderfully light and silky, per the norm. Yemenis are all secret rice masters. China would do well to stop sending tiny motorbikes and start sending their chefs so they can learn the secret art of fluff.

"Like a couple hours north of Delhi..." Josh says, too pre-occupied to reach for his own fingerful. He's missing out, but I'm not about to derail story time. I really should be clear as to our mission too. I really did think we were chasing Wahhabis.

"So, anyhow, an Islamic university was established there in the late 1800s. The English had been in India since the 1600s, first as a private trade deal called the East India Company that slowly grew and basically took over. The East India Company ran India like the Wild West. There were all these huge territories administrated by one fella who had raised a private army. He's judge, jury, executioner, and army, and he's only really beholden to the bottom line—to making money for the growing British Empire."

I nod, actually following along.

"Okay..." Josh continues. "Now, in 1857 we have the Sepoy Mutiny. There's hundreds of names for it today—the First War for Indian Independence is how it has been restyled—but it was a proper mutiny against the East India Company, and it's where this rumor spread that the shell casings of the British were dipped in pork, meaning the Muslims wouldn't go to paradise, and Muslims were the vast majority of the north. It wasn't true, just a nasty rumor, but stuff went truly crazy. A lot of death and destruction. The Hindus, who made up the majority of the south, watched the Muslims rebel, and this really leveraged their thing of, like, 'Oh, you can't trust those Muslims. Those guys are nuts. They're not loyal subjects like we are.'"

"Damn tattletales..." I mutter, but Josh doesn't hear me and continues unobstructed.

"During the East India Company years, almost one hundred percent of the British guys, or maybe eighty percent, go local, marry locals, have local kids, get very invested in the jam. Then the Sepoy Mutiny happens and a lot of people get massacred, a lot of British get massacred in really horrible ways, and that's when the East India Company ends and then the crown takes it over.

"Back in England, Queen Victoria is ruling and society has turned very strict and ordered. The Victorian ideas came with new deputies and officers who sought separation between the English and the local population. It was like, 'No, no, no, you marry from home, you don't associate with *them*.' I mean, the East India Company was racist in a real, I don't know, however racism works when you're married to a local and have local children. Like, it's racism, but a strange racism."

I keep nodding, understanding.

"Victorian racism was a full-on remove, and the Hindus loved it," Josh says. "They were like, 'Yes. This is what we were telling you about. This is caste. This is how we do it. This is perfect. It's those Muslims who told you that everyone's equal and you all have to wash your hands and feet and pray together, those are the weirdos. Those are the guys you have to hate.'"

Our Canada Drys arrive at the exact time that a swelling of affection for our egalitarian Muslim brothers rises through my chest, and in this moment, I don't know if I can love them any more than right now. They are the best folk on Earth, and I turn my unceasing nod warmly toward our waiter, who returns it with a smile of his own, flashing a mini qat ball in the process. I want to tell him, "We're all people of the book. You, me, Josh, Mohamed al-Behlooly—except probably not Tony though, I don't vouch for him," but can't remember how to say people in Arabic. I look at Josh, after a sweet sip of ginger perfection, thoroughly enjoying the bubbly kick, giving him permission to continue.

"So Deboand started sometime right around then and there are two parallel institutions. There's Aligarh and there's Deoband. And Deoband, from day one, had these Yemeni scholars from Hadramawt and..." Josh stops, seeing my face turn into a confused frown.

"What the hell is an Aligarh?"

"Okay, this is like, stuff where I haven't finished all the research, but nobody, literally nobody else has followed this," he answers. "So the part where written history stops, in British Raj India there are two major institutions for training Muslims. One is Aligarh, which is south of Delhi, and it's huge and blatantly collaborationist. It's funded by the British, and the leader is this orphan who was raised up to be fabulously wealthy and train all these Muslims to be good little Britishers. It's the Goofus and Gallant thing, where Deoband is much smaller—Aligarh has ten thousand students and Deoband has a mere thousand—but Deoband, from the outset, has all these Yemeni scholars and Afghan, Indonesian, and Yemeni students. It is completely international from the word go."

Josh loves to regularly reference Goofus and Gallant, like anyone in the world knows who they are. Like anyone outside bizarre homeschooled Christian kids from the mid-1980s. I even had to look them up the first time he mentioned them in conversation. Goofus and Gallant, by way of explanation, are two young characters who appeared in the *Highlights for Children* magazine. Goofus is a rude bastard. Gallant is always honorable and wise. I assume I'm the Goofus in our relationship and assume

Josh is the Gallant, but I have zero idea which is supposed to be the Goofus and which is supposed to be the Gallant between Deoband and Aligarh.

"Wait..." I stop Josh, seeking clarification. "Which is Goofus and which is Gallant?"

Josh looks at me like I'm a complete idiot. "Deoband was super punk rock and Aligarh was as if Ned Flanders and Eddie Haskell had an Indian Muslim baby." And I feel good about my own position vis á vis his preferred metaphor, understanding Ned Flanders' place in culture implicitly. Unless... he thinks I'm Gallant.

"Am I Gallant?"

"No," Josh says.

"Fantastic," and I enjoy another fingerful of rice and a sip of Canada Dry, the two pairing better than any forbidden wine and cheese. "So what does that have to do with our Wahhabis?"

"They're not *our* Wahhabis..." Josh rolls his eyes. "And, directly to the point, whereas the Wahhabis are fully stultified, like, 'The gates to Ishtar are closed. The Hadith and the Sunna and the Qur'an, that's all locked up.' That's all they got. That's all they want or care about. In contrast, these Deobandis were like, 'What? This is a whole new world. There's this huge Christian force that we have to deal with on an intellectual level.' They were the ones who really made this ideology of, 'You don't comply with colonialism in any form. You fight it in every way you can. You import fighters, you export fighters. This is a worldwide war.'

"So the Afghans were shipping over their sons from the northwest frontier province in the late 1800s. I mean, they were running a very specific deal, ideologically consistent with the modern Taliban, out of the Khyber area in the 1870s. Guys who were like 'No, no, no, and no. We're not having any of it. We're not having your money, we're not having your buildings. We'll knock off your guns, and we'll kill you.' And that was all running through Deoband, and to me that's one hundred percent al-Qaeda, because if they were Wahhabi they would just say, 'You stay there and we'll stay here and everything's cool.' But it's like the real bee in the Deoband bonnet to go after the infidel wherever he is."

I get it, completely, and shake my head, frustrated with myself for ever thinking Saudi Wahhabis could have done anything interesting. Could have done anything that mirrored true belief instead of reflecting decadent junk.

"I'm telling you..." Josh continues, "...there's no Wahhabi who is anything other than just sleepy. I think it's been proven that any Saudi who is actually involved in our modern version of this terrorism has always spent time in India, Pakistan, Afghanistan, or Yemen. You never get a pure Arab terrorist. They never come straight out of Saudi Arabia. They don't even come straight out of Egypt or Syria. They always go through this Deobandi thing that takes them through Afghanistan, Pakistan, and Yemen, and it all started here, in Yemen. Deoband started when li'l Yemenis sat down with some Pakis and cooked up doctrinal dynamite and then recruited nut job Pathans to go carry it out. And boy, have they."

"Fucking Saudis," I say as my saltah gets dropped at my awkwardly half-folded legs. Awkward since I got straight onto Helmut Lang skinny jeans after our dinner date with Hezbollah, vowing never again to be caught in a pair of unfortunate jeans as long as I live. Promising to never completely blow it again.

Josh, undistracted, moves on. "Speculation now, I've found scholars and writers out of Deoband with a certain last name, and from the very beginning, and this family is Hadrami, out of Seiyun. The guy we were supposed to meet in Mukalla, remember? The bookseller who somehow had big holdings in Indonesia? He was one of them. It seems like they run their family business here and

Indonesia and send their scholarly bros off to Deoband to foment revolution. Nobody in academia has figured this out yet. This is what we're hunting, and the main thing we needed to sort out was if that last name is like the last name 'Patel' in India or 'Smith' in America. And we've sorted out that it's not, which is already huge, because it means that one specific Yemeni family is not only involved but directing everything we see happening today in regards to radical Islamic thinking, which is the only anti-state radicalism that has ever worked transnationally."

"Oh, yeah, I remember that bookseller bro," I say, even though I don't at all.

"No, you don't," Josh says. "We never met him. He was in Indonesia, but we seriously should have waited around for him to come back. We've got one more shot: a phone number for a possible family member in Seiyun that the Islamic scholar gave us when we were eating fish balls. From every historical record I've been able to find, Seiyun is the real seat of the family. But maybe I'm wrong. Maybe this is one big ol' wild hair. If we can't find the bro in Seiyun, we might be cooked."

"Is it wild hare or wild hair?" I ask. Josh is really the one who should have gotten a master's degree in applied linguistics. He knows the etymology of every folk utterance in the English language.

"Hair," he says.

"Yeah, I know, but which? H-A-I-R or H-A-R-E?" I spell them out for clarity. "It's gotta be H-A-R-E. There's no such thing as a wild H-A-I-R unless it was coined by Robyn Davidson. She's got a nutty frizz going."

"It's H-A-I-R," Josh says, "referring to a horse hair that gets a fungus then wiggles by itself. And who's Robyn Davidson?"

"She's some Australian author who rode a camel across Australia then wrote a bestseller and also married Salman Rushdie,"

I inform him, proud that I know something he doesn't. "Speaking of Salman Rushdie..." I continue almost burning my mouth on my percolating saltah. "He's going to be very jealous of all your fatwas. He only got one."

Josh takes a bite of his unbelievably gamey yet impossibly greasy goat. "Thanks, bro."

CHAPTER 4

We linger in the warmth of the restaurant for as long as it takes my saltah to cool down, which is a very long time, reinvigorating Josh's distaste for Yemen's national dish. Tony doesn't seem to mind, as he's deep down all the lifestyle footage he's filmed thus far. Mohamed al-Behlooly doesn't seem to mind about anything at all, smiling beatifically even as I was tossing out fatwas.

Eventually I stand, stretch, and shout, "*Yalla bina*!" an Arabic colloquialism for "Let's go!" that is only used in Egypt and maybe not even there. It's maybe the sort of linguistic mash that got us out of trouble with Hezbollah. Maybe not.

Josh pulls himself up and heads to the sink to wash his goat hands with powdered laundry detergent. Tony flips the camera's pop-out screen closed and puts it back in the bag. Mohamed al-Behlooly floats to his feet. I call him over to have him rewrap my head. Nobody wraps a keffiyeh like an Arab man, and nobody wraps a full head keffiyeh like Mohamed al-Behlooly. It is snug, but not too tight. Warm, but not hot. It effortlessly holds up to naked 90cc aggression. I put my Ray-Ban Wayfarers on, sliding them into the perfect eye opening he left, and catch a glimpse of myself in a mirror next to the "Kaaba of the Month" calendar. I look great, like a Hollywood version of a bad 1980s terrorist. Like the Libyans in *Back to the Future* should have.

Josh comes over from the sink and has Mohamed al-Behlooly wrap his head too before we head outside, where Tony has the camera out of the bag again and is filming a clump of feral cats lounging in the sun next to a faded poster of Ali Abdullah Saleh, the president of Yemen, promising something in a swooping font. One of the cats has a banana milk straw in its mouth that looks like a cigarette. Tony is mesmerized by Yemen, by the gingerbread houses, by the bearded men in the bustling women's lingerie business and the ubiquitous curved knives. By the amount of guns everywhere and the rare slinking ninjas with their Dizzy Gillespie cheeks filled with hedge trimmings, and the disco mosque and rainbow plastic bag trees and skirts and gowns. By the camels and goats and the rolling calls to prayer and the four-year-olds piloting tiny Chinese motorbikes loaded down with entire families.

He keeps the camera turned on every exotic corner—which is every corner in Yemen—though that doesn't make for the action-driven *Indiana Jones*–esque mystery-meets-drama I had envisioned.

"Tony!" I try to scream through my keffiyeh. "Stop filming damned cats and let's get on the road!" He looks over eagerly, flashes a thumbs up, and follows Mohamed al-Behlooly to the van. It's not his fault, I suppose, that every single bush, child, and blowing plastic bag is more dynamic than me or Josh.

We both kick our bikes to life at the same time, pulling out and leaving Thamud behind in a cloud of Josh's blue smoke. It feels good as we bend away, chasing the empty horizon, and I'm warm, the saltah doing its trick from deep within me. If we have no unexpected trouble, by evening we'll hit the proper wadi

Hadramawt, Osama bin Laden's father's ancestral home. The place we blew through last time with hardly a glance in order to get almost killed in Marib, where in retrospect we should have stuck around a bit longer. Folk etymologists translate the word "Hadramawt" as "death has come."

It's one of the oldest continually inhabited places in the world, having first been settled by Noah's grandsons. It's mentioned by name in the Book of Genesis, in ancient Greek accounts, and in the Qur'an. Tarim, considered the intellectual heart of the Hadramawt, is said to have more direct descendants of the Prophet Mohamed than anywhere else.

The frankincense business is still a going concern, and we pass the scrubby Boswellia trees that drool a semi-precious sap as we buzz along toward the wadi. It has been traded on the Arabian Peninsula for over six thousand years and is what gave the Hadramawt its early importance. The Mediterranean ancients used frankincense for religious ceremonies and embalming rituals. Early Europeans used it to mask their stink. Yemen was once named Arabia Felix, or Happy Arabia, because of its virtual monopoly on those scrubby trees. Yemenis say camels were first domesticated here for the sole purpose of carrying it overland through the peninsula, though Josh very much disagrees with that reading. Yemenis also chew it like gum.

Honey is also big business here and we pass the jujube trees that give the Sidr varietal such value as we buzz closer still. It is wildly expensive and tastes like perfume. Like Chanel No. 5 mixed with Dior's Dune. The Saudis are so in love with it that they drive their blacked-out GMC Yukons and gilded Mercedes G Wagons down and leave them, returning with broken old mini Chinese flatbed pickups loaded with golden nectar. The value of the honey, cultivated the same way for thousands upon thousands of years, mocks the standard trappings—i.e., fancy cars—of the nouveau riche.

More gnarled trees and shrubs appear and the dusty flatness shows real life. Dry riverbeds cut through bigger than biggish boulder formations, and then after another long straightaway we hit towering folds of land painted red and orange by a past-its-peak sun. We run the bikes around a series of non-graded hairpins, cutting between them. Josh speeds up behind me and blows past, toying with my conservativism. I hammer the throttle and catch up. We drive shoulder to shoulder, sliding around each turn. This is award-winning cinematography right here, but I know that Tony, riding next to Mohamed al-Behlooly in the van somewhere behind us, is not filming. I know that the camera is firmly in his lap, battery being saved for the next funny-looking goat herd. The pieces are going to come together, though. I just know it. We just have to stick to the plan, to our mission, and perform so well that Tony will have no other choice but to capture our glory. Then we'll be invited to the *Vanity Fair* Oscar party and things will develop properly.

The folds are angular now, awe-inducing sheer walls reaching toward the sky. Table-topped mountain ridges on both sides pocked with caves and who knows what other mysteries. And then we see the green river that cuts through the meat of the Hadramawt, giving the villages their lifeblood. It is festooned with fat trees and shrubs that have gorged on this water, cleaving to some of the driest lands for millennia. Small farms appear with their ancient grain crops dancing in a light breeze. Wooden plows lie in the fields.

We follow the river down to the farming town of Alsowm, where we pull off at a gas pump next to a mosque so Mohamed al-Behlooly can take the opportunity to fill up and we can decide our next move. There is still plenty of daylight left, and we could easily make it to Tarim, a mere 40 kilometers down the way, but I insist on staying here because it is named "Alsowm," which sounds a lot like "Awesome."

"If you want to stay in 'Awesome' so badly, we should at least push up to the next town—or maybe it's the town after that, but anyhow—it's called 'Qasam,' and with the swallowed 'Q' it sounds more like 'Awesome,'" Josh tells me while I survey our possibilities. I see what must be a guest house but don't see any satellite dishes. Pulling the plug on the day too early with no possibility for music videos would be an absolute disaster for morale.

"Okay, okay…" I cave. "Let's go check out Qasam, but if it is not awesome, then let's just go to Tarim." It's an entirely sensible plan and I feel good about it. Plus, it would be an added bonus to meet one of the Prophet Muhammad's actual relatives. I wonder how they know that they're related, though? My dad told me, once, that we are eleventh cousins to Queen Elizabeth of England. I chewed on that for years, telling many junior high friends that I was basically next in line for the throne. Later, I thought, "How the hell does my dad know that sort of thing?" He wasn't into genealogy, nor was anyone else in his family. So where did this eleventh-cousin business come from? Could any Arab claim Muhammad as a relative? They all claim damn Ishmael, Father Abraham's son, as their own.

"Why don't more Arabs name their sons Ishmael?" I ask Josh, suddenly curious. "Wouldn't they want to pump up that lineage too? I mean, 'Ish' is a pretty sweet nickname, and he's number one. Also, lots of Jewish folk name their sons Isaac."

"There's an entire Shia sect named Ismail," he says, looking coolly over my shoulder at Tony, who has magically found a mangy dog dancing the foxtrot to film.

"So do the Shia claim Ishmael harder?"

"Yes," Josh answers. "And you should continue this conversation with Nate. He's the bro who's Shia-curious."

He is right. Nate's specialty is radical Shia politics, and to be fair, we had all discussed this much. If we were going to be Muslims,

Josh would be straight mainline Sunni, Nate would be some sort of Hezbollah-infused Shia, and I'd belong to one of the mystic Sufi sects—the weirdest of the weird who can't keep anything straight but come at you from the heart. Like the Mevlevi order who invented the "whirling dervish" where they spin for hours, heads back, arms outstretched, until they see Allah.

I attended a whirling dervish in Cairo, when I studied there, and was absolutely captivated. The way their skirts billowed. The way their neat fezzes stayed on their heads. The way they spun around, arms outstretched, skirts billowing, for hours upon hours without ever appearing dizzy.

"It was absolutely epic," I told Josh when I returned from my Cairo studies. "It was art."

"Yeah," he responded. "Art for heterodox Turks."

It crushed me that I had been accidentally drawn to some nasty Ottoman thing. Even though Ottoman sophistication made the rest of the world look like the dirty hovel it was from around the thirteenth to seventeenth centuries, it got decadent toward the end. Bloated and hollow. Ottoman soldiers in Damascus were the ones who raped my hero Lawrence of Arabia, or at least according to his diary. They were the ones who killed the practical reality of a caliphate.

"But the whirling dervish..." I parried. "It was mesmerizing, and the fact that they use all this spinning to see God, I mean, come on. That's next level."

"Next level for social-justice-loving United Nations interns," he responded, absolutely crushing me further. "Those dervishes have been recognized as a piece of 'Intangible Cultural Heritage' by the United Nations Educational, Scientific, and Cultural Organization. UNESCO loves nothing more than heterodox Turks."

And I know Josh is right. Anything UNESCO touches automatically makes it boring and snoozy, dresses it up in zip-off travel pants even if it began as the most fabulous thing ever. Damn UNESCO. Damn it straight to hell.

Thankfully Mohamed al-Behlooly has finished filling up the microvan and Tony's fox-trotting dog has been chased off by a thundering technical because it's time to leave "Awesome" and head for even more linguistically appropriate "Awesome." And if there are no decent lodging options there, then it'll be off to the Prophet Muhammad's eleventh cousin's hotel in Tarim, featuring "Hips Don't Lie" by Shakira, "Fergalicious" by Fergie, and "Stars Are Blind" by Paris Hilton, rated PH for Paris Hilton. I generally don't like reggae influences in my music but couldn't help being swept off my feet by Paris Hilton's black lingerie in her newest hit dominating the airwaves. It is an absolute smash, and if the robust Yemeni lingerie trade wouldn't take advantage of this star turn then they were unforgivably blowing it.

CHAPTER 5

"Fuck you, it is NOT!" I scream at Josh, genuinely frustrated with him for the third or fourth time in my life. "Nougat is absolutely and completely not a fucking PROCESS of making the stuff inside Nujoom. It is a real damned thing. It IS the stuff inside Nujoom or Snickers or Milky Way."

"Absolutely wrong," Josh sneers back in a way that I've never seen him sneer before. "It is a process, a way of making something, and nothing beyond that. There are no specific ingredients to a nougat. It's just a way of mixing various items together."

My blood boils. For once I know I'm right—beyond right, even—and not only that, this is important. Islamic history, the headwaters of violent anti-state radicalism, and our own self-radicalization be damned. Nougat is something we live with every day, and not only in our candy bars. Nougat is in See's Candy, albeit the ones people take a bite of and then leave. Nougat is served on the streets in Damascus, a tasty *digestif* after all that tabbouleh and baba ghanoush. Nougat is very popular with the Armenian students that I'm not teaching English as a Second Language to at

Los Angeles City College back home. They bring me box after box when they receive their A's for doing absolutely nothing other than not tattling. They sometimes bring me Armenian brandy, too.

I push back from the plastic table, glaring at Josh, almost knocking our Arabic coffees to the ground in the process. We made it to Tarim directly after the sun set. Qasam had not been very Qasam, and we didn't slow, following the river through Einat, Alqaria, Qahir, and Algoz before coasting in under the just-laid darkness. A large minaret glowed neon green from its tiered windows, and the Call to Prayer rose into the sky, greeting us.

It wasn't as cold as it had been in the Empty Quarter, and the locals, who were out shopping or loitering in their various skirt/blazer/jambiya combinations, hustled to their mosques, virtually deserting the streets. I have been in many Islamic countries now, but nowhere are they as observant as Yemen. In Egypt, the Call wails and is promptly ignored, unless it is Friday morning. In Syria, it is ignored except during Ramadan. In Lebanon, it is ignored altogether unless one happens to be in the Shia south. Yemenis run to mosque during at least three of the day's five calls, abandoning whatever transaction they might be in the middle of, coming back only when finished. We had been left twiddling our thumbs, many times, with a half-mixed mango, strawberry sauce *mushakkal* in the blender while the juice maker scampered off to do his ablutions.

Yemen is extremely observant. The Hadramawt is considered *extremely* extremely observant by Yemeni standards, and Tarim is the most religiously important town in the Hadramawt. It could likely be argued that it is the most serious Islamic town anywhere outside Mecca and Medina.

The monolithic grasp that Islam, real Islam, has on the country is refreshing after our latest run in Lebanon. The interlocking puzzle pieces of Maronite, Eastern Orthodox, Alawite, Druze, Armenian,

Melkite, Shia, Chaldean, and Sunni is enough to rattle even the healthiest brain. Here it is only Islam, though split amongst Shafi'i Sunnis, Zaidi, Ja'fari, and I'm sure a few more that I haven't learned yet.

We found a hotel—a newer, duller, two-story cement building painted brick red—on the outskirts, ate a quick dinner across the street, and retired to rest our kidneys after another long day on the road. It took me three short minutes to sort our music videos, and we settled into our chosen twin beds, though I pushed Tony's to the farthest corner when he went to the bathroom. Somewhere between Nelly Furtado feat. Timbaland's "Promiscuous" and Jessica Simpson's "A Public Affair," an advertisement played showing a Saudi man with an impossibly soft face give a Mars candy bar to his equally soft-faced son. I lifted myself onto an elbow and said, "First, how much for a Timbaland, Jessica Simpson meatsa?"

Josh looked over at me with his Coke bottles and said, "Hmmm. That's a rough one."

Tony piped up from far, far away. "Why can't it be a Nelly Furtado and Jessica Simpson ménage?"

"That's why you're not allowed to play," Josh and I responded at the same time.

I added, "Plus, it's a meatsa-meatsa, not a tacky ménage à trois." Then I turned back to Josh and asked, "So?"

"Well, I'll go three," he answered after some more thought. "I like that gross nougat in Mars better than I like Timbaland."

I agreed immediately that Timbaland made any music video he touched worse and would certainly not add anything special in the bedroom, but Josh's denunciation of Mars bars in general and nougat specifically was surprising.

"What are you talking about? I'm not the biggest nougat fan, but it gives our modern candy an important base, thus making it an important food."

"It's not a food, it's a process," Josh answered, and we argued until we fell asleep, woke up, continued arguing, walked into the city center arguing, found a breakfast spot arguing, and then argued through our hot bean breakfast and are continuing to argue, passionately and seriously, through our Arabic coffee.

"Okay…" I hiss, "…if nougat is a process then why isn't there any such thing as a savory nougat? It is a thing, made from nuts, sugar or maybe honey, and sweet. It is always sweet. If nougat was a process, then you could make it from kale and soy sauce, or potatoes and paprika, or Ritz crackers and lemon juice. Plus, nougat is not a verb. If it was a process, the word would also be a verb. You can't nougat something. Pull your fucking head out, man."

"You are wrong, and ignorantly so." Josh is seething. "For nougat to be a thing then it would have to have specific ingredients. It doesn't. It can be made using walnuts, hazelnuts, almonds, probably cashews or any nut, plus any sweetener. Sugar, honey, Equal, corn syrup. It's a way of mixing nuts and a sweetener. A process."

A gaggle of Islamic scholars pass on their way to one of Tarim's many Islamic schools. I don't know which varietal. They are dressed in white, with full white skullcaps and long, full beards. They study us, expressionless.

"Guys." Tony comes running over, breathlessly. He had been wandering around with Mohamed al-Behlooly filming God only knows what. "This is seriously the most amazing place I've ever seen in my life. There are these tall, thick buildings, almost like skyscrapers, made entirely of earth. Whole blocks of them, with their tops painted sky blue. I have no idea how they built them or how they're still standing, but they are, and they're being used just like they were normal apartment buildings with laundry strung between windows and kids running around chasing metal hoops. There's a huge white mosque and its…what's the pointy thing called?"

"Minaret," Josh says.

"Yeah, its minaret is the biggest one I've ever seen and made out of earth too. It has to be a couple hundred feet tall and the mosque is incredible looking. The alleys between the buildings are so small and wind around endlessly. They're selling all these trinkets in there that look religious or something. There's even an otherworldly palace and graveyards everywhere. It feels like we've gone back to some ancient time. It's incredible, absolutely incredible…"

Tony stops to catch his breath and I use the opportunity to press my advantage. "Tell Josh that nougat is a thing, Tony. Tell him it's not a process. Tell him there is no such thing as a broccoli and grilled cheese nougat."

Tony looks confused and Josh uses the opportunity to press his advantage. "Tell Charlie that he's being shrill and absurd. Of course there is no such thing as broccoli and grilled cheese nougat. We've established that it is sweet but can be made from any variety of nuts and sweeteners. See those date palms right there?"

Josh points to a grove of dark green date palms that grow at the base of a mudbrick skyscraper neighborhood climbing a nearby cliff. It is impossible to tell where the buildings end and the cliff begins, a proper architectural marvel and unlike anywhere else and the whole scene is shadowed by an even bigger, more impressive tabletop mountain painted every color of brown from syrup to coffee with its own nest of mudbrick skyscrapers at its base, some painted sky blue, some painted baby blue.

"Yes, I see those date palms," I snort. "I have both eyes and common sense."

"Well, dates are sweet and a very popular sweetener here in the Middle East used for all manner of sweetening," Josh continues. "You could make a very good nougat, I'd imagine, using dates."

My Ray-Bay Wayfarers are steaming up. "Yes, you can fucking make nougat using dates. The fucking *thing* nougat."

"The *process* nougat," Josh parries. "If you can make it out of dates and you can make it out of honey, then it is a process."

"This is just crazy. Josh is purposely flaunting the most simple definition of a thing that has ever existed. It's madness."

I'm shaking my head vigorously and Tony still looks confused, saying, "I really don't know how you can be talking about this when there are such incredible things to film around here. I feel we could stay here for a month and still not run out of material."

Josh guffaws. I snicker.

Josh says, "Hey, Tony, this is all a UNESCO World Heritage site. It's something I can enjoy at home while looking at it on my computer, like other places I never want to go. See Dubrovnik, Croatia."

"Yeah, Tony," I add. "The UN completely kooks everything they touch, including mystical Islamic dances that should, in theory, be cool. This place sucks thanks to the damn Security Council or whichever United Nations organization decides what should be World Heritage Sites."

"It's the United Nations Educational, Scientific, and Cultural Organization, bro," Josh says, very paternally, reaching near Nate levels. "That's the organization that decides."

"Well, thankfully they haven't categorized nougat as 'world heritage' because then it would suck too but it would still suck as a *thing* and not suck as a *process*," I tell him.

Tony's confusion has turned to disheartenment, and he shuffles off, droopy-headed, swishing his brown corduroy pants while pulling his video camera out of his video camera bag. We let him go film whatever absolutely incredible shit catches his eye even though he may as well just pull it off of his home computer and save the hassle.

"Look," Josh says, softening an almost imperceptible amount. "Preindustrial nougat was really hard to make so it was, *maybe*, an actual thing, but now any machine can make it. There's no art left. No skill. It's just the process. The thing has been stripped away and left behind except for here in Yemen, where they continue to do everything like it has always been done, because this is who they are. Some ancient people who choose not to change because why? Like, why do they all still chew frankincense instead of gum? It doesn't taste super good; it is a bit funky, but it doesn't matter to them. They chew frankincense because they've always chewed frankincense. It's what they do, same as carrying bizarre knives, munching hedge trimmings, and building architecturally outstanding towers so the women and men can have different internal staircases. Why? Because it's Yemen."

"Look at Tony..." I interrupt my clear victory and point at Tony, who seems to be panning down from the tabletop cliff, across a minaret, and to a goat that is chewing on a long reed while standing in a broken pushcart.

Josh sighs.

CHAPTER 6

We sit at a small café, drinking more Arabic coffee while waiting for Tony to finish whatever it is he thinks he's doing. I have hope that in spite of our cameraman's instincts we'll have epic footage after we're done. Josh and I had rigged our bikes with lipstick cameras attached to the handlebars, the wires running down the metal tubing on our bikes connecting them to recording devices that we planted underneath our seats. This road footage would be epic, no doubt, and completely understandable—even context free.

Seiyun, our last best shot to find a member of the Aydarus family and get him to spill all the secrets about the true headwaters of modern radical Islamic terrorism that led to our current Global War on Terror, is only thirty or so kilometers down the river so we're in no real hurry. The number of historically significant little towns packed into the wadi Hadramawt is truly something. Between Tarim and Seiyun there is Thibi, famous for a Biblical ancestor of the same name; Alghuraf, which houses many of the pre-Islamic al Kathari tribe; Taribah, where honest scientists claim true ghosts whisper during prayers; and Bowr, which is not the home of Bower Horse, though it should be.

It'll take us thirty minutes, even if Josh's motorcycle acts up more than once. We could walk the distance in half a day so we enjoy sitting in the stony, angry silence born of the Great Nougat Debate, which I clearly won since nougat is a thing not a process. A position Josh tacitly agreed to by admitting that Yemenis make a thing called nougat in their gorgeously ancient ways. Nobody would ever make a banana leaf and chocolate chip cookie nougat, and Josh knows it.

Eventually we wander over to the qat souq and buy some, keeping it secret from Tony, despite the fact that it'll be impossible to properly chew while riding motorcycles. We debate briefly, and both unnecessarily defensively, the merits of retreating to our hotel and chewing the day away while watching "Ain't No Other Man" by Christina Aguilera but actually have a little work to do if we're going to make this discovery of the stream that feeds the headwaters of modern radical Islamic terrorism that led to our current Global War on Terror happen so decide against it.

"Does the last name Aguilera have Moroccan roots?" I ask Josh as we start stuffing our cheeks with hedge trimmings as quickly as we can. "It sounds like something that should come out of the Caliphate of Córdoba."

"So the Caliphate of Córdoba is even more worthless than the Almohads…" Josh answers between bites of leafy green bitterness. We had learned how to pick a good qat bundle out of a bunch, learned its value and how to negotiate its seller down to the proper, honest price.

"Even still, I think Aguilera is purely Mexican."

"How does my cheek look? Am I getting there?" he asks, pointing at his cheek.

We'd tried with everything in us to reach the Dizzy Gillespie fabulousness of Yemeni local qat chewing ever since our first experience, though we hadn't come anywhere close. I'd catch a glimpse of my own cheek in the rearview mirror or hotel bathroom mirror and be thoroughly deflated each time. My cheek, filled with qat, or so I thought, was deflated too, and lame. No different, really, than my normal cheek after eating one of Carl's Jr.'s Bacon Western Cheeseburgers.

Josh, thankfully, had also never mastered the art, and his qat cheek was even less of a thing than mine since his cheeks trended toward puffy, especially when he was drinking mango juice. He had become wildly allergic to the vitamin C–rich fruit after a stint in Pakistan where he ate mangoes around the clock in order to stave off tropical diseases. He ate so many that he had forced a revolt in his body, showcased by such swelling that a doctor should have been brought in immediately. Nate and I just laughed that first Yemen run when Josh's eyes would puff closed after a fresh mango juice. Nate especially.

And I would be laughing now, except holding qat without letting it slip down the mouth and into the throat is an art. We could both chew. We could both get robustly chatty then enter the Hour of Solomon with no problem, but our qat cheeks were both embarrassing A cups that we were always trying to remedy.

"It looks good," I tell him, before asking, "how does mine look?"

"Great," he responds. "You're really getting it."

An immense warmth floods my body and I mentally block the steady qat stream escaping my cheek and running down my throat. Maybe I'll actually finally conquer the art. Maybe here, surrounded by United Nations Education and whatever buildings, is the time that I officially and really become a Yemeni, the only nationalistic anything I've ever wanted to be besides Australian when I was six years old.

"Yeah?" I rub my cheek with my hand. "Sick. I feel it. It's growing nicely."

After thirty or so minutes, and with qat balls that feel like they won't break down, we rally Tony, who is scampering across an open square chasing some kid doing tricks on his motorcycle: lying down and driving it with his feet, then standing up and surfing it back in the same direction. That sort of unfortunate, showoffy business.

"Damn it, Tony…" I mutter.

"Let's get to Seiyun so we can start being serious here!" Josh shouts.

Tony comes jogging over with Mohamed al-Behlooly right after him. My jagged nerves are soothed by even one look at his saintlike face. He is always in the flow, never hurried, never frustrated, always peacefully going along while getting along. The closest expression of Zen on the entire Arabian Peninsula.

We all stroll back to our hotel and toss our bags on top of the shiny Mylar surfboard coffin in Mohamed al-Behlooly's microvan. Tony climbs into the passenger seat and shoots his camera lens with a blast of pressurized air from what looks like an Easy Cheese can. Josh snaps Das Boot to the top then flips his collar up. I leave Wild One half unzipped. The air is warmer here than it was in the Empty Quarter, and I'm looking forward to riding with the wind in my hair until I see Mohamed al-Behlooly wrap Josh's head, which causes me to get mine wrapped too, just in case it's not *that* warm.

Our bikes fire up right away, a happier surprise each time, and we ease out. A smaller road takes us to the main road, which takes us to the river, and we drive along it for a moment, passing more small farms and date palms before dropping into a narrow valley with a sheer, naked cliff on one side and a steep but verdant hill on the other.

The silence would be nice and the scenery would be stunning, but I can't enjoy either as I feel my qat ball shrinking. I try to readjust it, moving it forward in my cheek with my tongue, but only manage to further break it up and lose more down my throat. I wonder if it is good for me, like spinach, or bad for me, like chewing tobacco. I wonder how hard it would be to bring qat seeds back to California and plant them. I wonder what the US Customs and Border Patrol agents would do if they found them. It's classified as a Schedule 1 drug in the United States. A "substance or chemical with no currently accepted medical uses and a high potential for abuse." The same as heroin. I wonder if the US Customs and Border Patrol would know how qat seeds look. How do qat seeds look?

I'm really puzzling over this last one when I see a thick wall of mudbrick skyscrapers rising up in the distance. They are twice as tall as any in Tarim, many are painted white from midway to top, and they're densely packed together, surrounded by what looks to be an old rock wall.

I follow Josh off the road, through a gate crowded with small taxis and people selling bejeweled cell phone cases, down a narrow street, and into an open square with what looks like a shrine in its middle. We park next to a herd of goats lounging in the shade, unwrap our heads, and stare up in honest wonder. I have never seen anything like this, anything quite so impressive.

The buildings are proper skyscrapers, leaning slightly this way or that, with small windows cut out randomly from bottom to top and covered by white curtains. Air-conditioning units have been mashed through the mudbrick walls at various points.

"This is the Manhattan of the Desert, bro," Josh says with a smirk. "Shibam."

"Wait, it's really named Shibam? Like, Sha-bam!" I ask.

"Yeah. Shibam. Except it's past Seiyun, so we must have missed the turnoff somewhere."

"And they really call it the Manhattan of the Desert?"

"Don't you remember Cole talking about it? He would not shut up. He'd go on and on about how incredible it was then got bummed when we blew right though it because we wanted to get to Marib. Remember how much that socially awkward LA architect who claimed she was Swiss talked up Coachella? I have the same general feeling about Shibam."

"Let's go find a slice of pizza and talk about how much our rent has raised and how cool it would be to be stay-at-home dads."

"It's not the Brooklyn of the Desert," Josh corrects me. "It's the Manhattan of the Desert."

Tony comes up fiddling with his camera, ogling straight up, eyes big as saucers, mouth agape, and he can barely whisper, "Where are we?" through his clear amazement.

"Shi-BAM!" Josh says. "And I got it wrong. I don't think Tarim is a UNESCO World Heritage site, but I know Shibam is."

"Well, hell," I groan. "That means we could have enjoyed it back there a little more, and now we have to shit on this place."

"It's cool..." Josh says. "Cole wouldn't shut up about Tarim either. It's an honorary UNESCO World Heritage site as far as I'm concerned."

Tony's head keeps swiveling. He asks, "When was this place built? What was it for?"

Josh answers, "Sometime in the third or fourth century. They built skyscrapers to be protected from Bedouin attacks, or that's what Cole said when he wasn't shutting up about it."

A group of Yemeni tourists come through the square, necks craned, taking pictures with bejeweled cell phones and older cameras. Josh and I retreat to a small table set up underneath an overhang and order tea while Tony scrambles off to explore. Local tourism in a place like Yemen always makes me feel a happy glow. Witnessing that the desire to gawk, stare, and document is not just German, not just American, but human—and it is honestly wonderful.

"I wish it wasn't so cool," I tell Josh after Tony has rounded the corner. "It's really hard to shit on."

"So is Coachella, bro."

"You kidding? Coachella is the easiest thing to shit on..."

"I was kidding," Josh says.

We sit in silence for a few moments, watching more Yemeni tourists round the corner, necks craned, standing in the same spot to take pictures of their cultural masterpiece. A few stray cats saunter by disinterested. One of the nearby shade goats burps. My qat ball has entirely disintegrated. Josh looks like he's fighting the inevitable end of his, though his cheek still shows some puff. Maybe he has figured out the secret.

"Did you figure out the secret?" I ask him, pointing to my air-puffed cheek with eyes slightly widened, Yemeni style.

"I thought I had," he answers dejectedly, "but I'm losing it all right now."

I shake my head. "We'll never be addicts at this lousy rate."

CHAPTER 7

We watch Tony run by filming a little boy on a school bike before running back, ten minutes later, filming a man pushing a samovar on wheels, then back again, ten minutes later, disappointed that his camera ran out of batteries when he was filming a worker hanging from the side of a skyscraper, patching a hole with mud and plaster. He heads for the van to grab a fresh one, but I yell, "Too bad, Tony. Fate has spoken, and your day is officially over. Shibam!"

He looks genuinely sad, and I wonder how much longer it will be before he recruits Mohamed al-Behlooly into a mutinous rebellion and the two of them picnic through the Hadramawt, enjoying the sights, sounds, and smells.

Mohamed al-Behlooly walks over at that moment from where he was chatting with a retiree in the shade. My jagged nerves are soothed once again. Mohamed al-Behlooly would never participate in Tony's bloodthirsty nonsense. He knows what's important. He senses that Josh and I are his people and that we're onto something here.

Josh tells him that we overshot Seiyun, so we're going to double back. He smiles while nodding, then asks if we want our heads wrapped. I say no first, this time firm in my decision no matter what Josh does. Thankfully he doesn't want his wrapped either.

We kick the bikes to life and limp between towering ancient history in first gear, out through the gate and onto the main road, retracing our tracks up the river for 20 kilometers until we see a huge white square building with turrets, battlements, and what appears to be a keep. It must be a castle, or palace, or Fundamentalist Latter-Day Saints temple. The offshoot nutty Warren Jeffs ones that live in unincorporated Arizona and marry many young girls. That's what it looks most like, and I have no idea how we missed Seiyun this last time through.

We turn off the road and drive toward it, parking in its shadow. Besides the castle / palace / Mormon temple, Seiyun feels much more like the Yemen that I know and love than either Tarim or Shibam. Toyota Hiluxes park without rhyme or reason. Old, half-finished cement buildings fight for space with older mud-brick buildings and newer, half-finished cement buildings. The streetlights advertise President Ali Abdullah Saleh. A rusted scaffolding surrounds a piece of air. There is a store that sells ladders and one that sells bags of cement. The air smells like diesel smoke and rotisserie chicken. I breathe deeply, then exhale. "Ahhhh, Yemen."

Spotting a juice cart, I hurry over with Josh hot on my heels. The vendor, wearing a sharp floor-length skirt with a teal short-sleeved button-up and red-and-white-checked keffiyeh, does both straight mango and *mushakkals*. I study Josh, order two *mushakkals* so he won't get swollen eyes, then ask, "Okay, fella, what's our plan here?"

Josh is in serious mode. Any time there is a real honest-to-goodness mission, he revels in it, especially if it is virtually impossible, like free soloing down a sheer rock cliff in order to surf off a Yemeni rain forest, jamming across a Lebanese valley while Israeli drones hover overhead, sitting in a room filled with Hezbollah elders trying to find our soft spot, or finding one particular family in a sea of other particular families in an ancient Yemeni town in the dead center of the Wadi Hadramawt.

Josh takes a sip of his *mushakkal* and says, "Well, first thing, I'm going to try the number that the Mukalla Islamic scholar guy gave us."

"An Islamic scholar gave us a phone number?" I ask, very confused, while taking a sip of my own *mushakkal*. It's an extra good one with extra strawberry sauce.

"Yes," Josh says. "We were eating fish balls, and he came up after prayers to chat. You told him that you rode tables on his ocean and were Yemeni."

"Oh, yeah," I say, and even though I have absolutely no memory of this, it sounds like something I'd say.

We wander into the dusty throng—men buying spices, men buying perfume, men buying older magazines, men fixing motorcycles, men drinking tea—until we find an internet café and step inside, where men are probably looking at porn while hiding in cubicles.

A chubby Saudi wearing a sparkling white thobe and red-and-white-checked keffiyeh folded like the foil swans used for old-timey leftovers is sitting by the door, fiddling with a tiny Hello Kitty cell phone.

"Why don't we have more Saudis on the cover of *Wiener Mélange*?" I ask Josh.

A few years ago, we had dreamt up a surefire hit. A magazine featuring solely wieners. Men with classically gauche taste doing classically gauche things but who imagine they are absolutely crushing it. Like, men who drive slammed, blacked-out Porsche

Cayennes and have huge wristwatches, or men who know all the lyrics to "Baby Got Back." Past imaginary covers have featured Brett Ratner and Robin Thicke.

"Because they're all so hideously misshapen and bizarre looking that I don't know if they're suited for it," Josh answers while tossing a few Yemeni rials on the counter and heading to the small wooden phone booth in the back. "I mean, Al-Waleed bin Talal doesn't even qualify as a wiener. He's just too weird, and he is as close to a legit wiener as a famous Saudi gets, I reckon. Other than that, they are uniformly total antisocial perverts in their steez."

Al-Waleed bin Talal is the grandson of Abdul-Aziz al Saud, Saudi Arabia's first king, and one of the world's richest men, and as much as I would like to have a Saudi on the cover, Josh is right. A Kuwaiti would work better.

Josh lifts the receiver and pulls a wrinkled piece of paper out of his pocket, punching the Arabic numbers into the Arabic phone. The other patrons casually observe us, except for the Saudi by the door, who is speaking at the top of his lungs to whoever is on the other end of his Hello Kitty.

I look back at Josh and surprise has washed his face. "Oh… umm, *salam alaikum*," he says, then starts stuttering through some formal Arabic that I don't fully understand. I can hear times, places, pleasantries, and then he hangs up, and says, "Whoa."

"Who was that?" I ask.

"It was him. I sort of can't believe it. He's agreed to meet us tonight at a hotel that's right outside of town."

"Well, here we go then." I clap my hands victoriously. "Did you get the address? Let's go grab Mohamed al-Behlooly and Tony and get all ready." I look at my watch and see that it's just past two in the afternoon. We'll definitely have to eat first, and then what? "How should we kill the hours until tonight?"

We'd mangled our qat chew already by starting too early and ending too early. There's no real way to catch that dragon again. Seiyun seems pleasantly Yemeni but without charming structures or restaurants. There is the giant Fundamentalist Latter-Day Saints Temple, but that doesn't look like a good time at all.

"Let's just go find that hotel and get a room," Josh finally says. "A room with music videos."

"Oh, yeah. Perfect," I respond, not knowing what I was thinking. "But what is that big white temple or whatever?"

"That's the Kathari Palace. The Katharis used to rule all of the Hadramawt back in the day but got smacked by their rivals the Qu'aitis before the British showed up, then they did a deal with the Brits. You know the prime minister of East Timor, the one who had to resign this summer? His name is Mari Alkatiri. Al-Kathari. These Hadrami bros love heading anywhere near Indonesia."

We wander through knots of parked taxis and Toyota Hiluxes before finding Tony at the gates of the palace, predictably filming a man making keys with an old machine that needs to be foot pumped. Mohamed al-Behlooly is standing off to the side, blessing the entire scene with his grace and virtue.

"It's game time," I yell at Tony, who looks disappointed—again.

"Any way we could go film around this temple?"

"It's a palace," I snap. "And no. We have a very important interview coming up—the *raison d'être* for this leg of the adventure—and we have to prepare."

"Great," he says, disappointment turning to enthusiasm. "You got a hold of him? This is really great. Fantastic. We sort of need that for the climax, or at least some rising action. Where are we filming? Here? Now? Could we set up in front of the temple—I mean, palace?"

"No," Josh answers. "Tonight at some hotel outside of town. Gather your things."

Tony's enthusiasm turns back to disappointment, and he goes to collect his camera bag from near the foot-pumping key maker.

"I can't believe damn Tony thinks we need rising action. He clearly doesn't know anything at all about filmmaking," I seethe under my breath at Josh, who is too polite to respond.

We go back to our tiny Chinese motorbikes and extricate them from a sea of other tiny Chinese motorbikes. I feel proper warm for the first time since we cut inland from Hawf a week ago and think about losing Wild One, but my T-shirt is from the Brian Setzer Orchestra's "Christmas Rocks" tour and is not the message I want to send. Not that I care what Yemenis think about my celebration of Christmas, seeing as I don't put my light under a bushel, but the Brian Setzer Orchestra's "Christmas Rocks" tour doesn't seem quite…hard enough. Especially when I'm standing next to Josh in his tattered black Public Image Ltd. shirt. PIL was a very good call. All the fun of the Sex Pistols with none of the poseur baggage.

CHAPTER 8

THE SUN SET TWO HOURS AGO, AND THE FAMILY'S REPRESENTATIVE IS supposed to be here any second. He suggested a hotel that has turned out to be very nice, decorated white with green neon piping, almost like a disco mosque, with healthy date palms surrounding a thick St. Augustine lawn. There's an actual swimming pool that has either been lit a soothing green to match the neon piping or is simply green. The rooms are ample, with fewer twin beds almost organized, and a lobby with clocks showing that it is 8:00 p.m. in Dubai, which is on Gulf Standard Time; 5:00 p.m. in London, which is on Greenwich Mean Time; and 7:00 p.m. in Jeddah, which is on Arabian Standard Time. The same as Seiyun. The same as all of Yemen.

We check in and hang in the room while Tony mopes around, frustrated that our "preparation" consists only of watching music videos, even though we've caught a magical run of the Pussycat Dolls, Dixie Chicks, the Pussycat Dolls again, and much to Josh's happy surprise, Daughtry.

"How much for Daughtry right now, here, in Seiyun?" I ask as we lounge in bed while Tony cleans his camera.

"Two," Josh says after careful deliberation. "I like him as much as I like Simply Red and Eros Ramazzotti."

"I win with an easy five," I reply.

With that, Tony stops what he's doing, grunts, gets up, and leaves. I have no idea where. Maybe to the lobby to check the time in Dubai again. He has been annoyed for a few days. Maybe me opening the door to Daughtry, one-time *American Idol* finalist and fake "rocker," five nights out of ten is simply his breaking point.

It confused me that Josh didn't give Daughtry more, seeing that he loves Chad Kroeger from Nickelback. Even I can't quite figure out Josh's Nickelback thing but, at the end, "to each his own" is the ethos that has ordered our steps from day one.

"It absolutely has not," Josh snorts.

"What has not?" I ask while studying Justin Timberlake's "SexyBack," thinking it's strange that the wavy-haired member of a boy band would be the one to bring it back and not the slick-haired one with the razor-sharp pencil beard, but then I realize I'm getting NSYNC and the Backstreet Boys confused.

"'To each his own' has never been our ethos," Josh says. "In fact, it could easily be argued that 'to each his own' is only your ethos, and only when it directly pertains to you. So, accurately, it would be 'to Charlie his own.'"

"Well, now you're just being pedantic," I say as Justin Timberlake gives way to Lebanese superstar Wael Kfoury, bumming me out thoroughly. He's worked himself into an absolute frenzy of toothless romance, eyes closed and crooning in a very high register while clutching his chest, "Habibi, habib, haaaabbbbiiibiiii..."

I turn the channel but get mired in a slough of *The Best of Mecca*. The incredible white mass moving slowly around the domineering black box is mesmerizing, and maybe I've actually crossed over. Maybe this in an important step in my evolution. It's all starting to make sense to me. I understand why multiple entire channels are solely dedicated to around-the-clock coverage and reruns. It's hypnotic.

"You got all your questions sorted?" I ask Josh.

"No," he says. And then our room's phone rings.

I answer and the desk man tells us we have a guest. I thank him profusely, then turn to Josh and say, "It's go time."

We both roll off our bed, and he goes straight for Das Boot, which makes me go straight for Wild One. It was warm this afternoon, but Josh is probably right. It might be cold outside now, and even if it isn't, I don't want the stream that feeds the headwaters of modern radical Islamic terrorism that led to our current Global War on Terror to be unnecessarily confused by the Brian Setzer Orchestra "Christmas Rocks" tour, because it's honestly confusing to me too and I wouldn't be able to provide real clarity.

Josh and I would have said goodbye to Tony, but he's off exploring the one-of-a-kind nighttime songbirds of interior Yemen, no doubt. Being a buzzkill. We take his camera anyhow to capture the first bit of cinematographic glory yet.

"How do you turn it on?" I ask Josh.

"You think I know?" he fires back.

"Touché."

In the lobby sits a neatly dressed man in one of the leather recliners. We introduce ourselves, and he is shy but reserved, sporting a clean moustache instead of a nice beard and wearing a gray suit instead of a skirt/knife combination.

He knows some English and uses it quietly, politely. Josh counters with both polite English and stilted, academic Arabic rolled out slowly and deliberately. I add the pizzazz, calling him "king" and telling him that I too am a Yemeni.

We eventually decide to retreat to the swimming pool. There are chairs up there and the night is warm. Date palms sway ever so slightly in a light breeze. Nighttime songbirds croon their magical, rarely heard songs. The pool glows like it was touched by either Claude Monet or Édouard Manet. I can never remember which painted what.

I set the camera up on the table and hopefully press play as Josh begins with simple inquires. Does he have a wife and children? Does he live here in Seiyun? Has he traveled at all? And he adds simple, honest praises. Seiyun is beautiful. Yemen is fantastic. The pool here makes Seiyun a serious consideration for future family vacations as soon as either Josh or I make a family.

And then, like a forensic expert, he digs in. Does he have family in Indonesia? How many of them have gone to Deoband, India? How many have come back to Yemen? Where do they go after that? Is he aware of the current dull narrative, that Wahhabism is considered "radical"? How silly is that? Deoband is much better. Much more radical. Isn't it?

Our new friend's eyes change as the questions about Deoband hit. He instantly becomes not exactly suspect, but circumspect. Answers clipped. Back stiff. Eyes shifting quickly from Josh to me and back to Josh. It doesn't signal anything in and of itself. These are tense times. The Global War on Terror has got its teeth in two countries that arguably had very little to do with the 9/11 attacks. The Taliban in Afghanistan, however distasteful to liberal democracies of the West, had made an ideological safe space for aggressive Islam and were busy actualizing one of the most severe visions of Qur'anic governance since the early 1700s. They may have been hosting Osama bin Laden as part of a moral code that predates Islam, but since when have religious ideals and hospitality been the bar for war? And Iraq? Saddam Hussein was only ever an opulent despot. He didn't have the creativity, will, nor guts to bring the battle to the Great Satan.

Targets were necessary in order to give the American people their rightly desired sense for justice. And targets were found. But they were arbitrary, unaffiliated, and to a gray-suited, mustachioed Yemeni in the dead center of the Hadramawt, Osama bin Laden's ancestral homeland, with Osama bin Laden's ancestral village fewer that 40 kilometers away as bombs fall from Coalition Forces sky in Afghanistan and Iraq, what could he feel? What could he say?

Or that's what I would be thinking if I were in his black-tasseled loafers. In any event, his voice has lowered and his Arabic has quickened so much that I can't make out the gist of his explanation. Josh is leaning in close, though—nodding, asking, nodding and asking.

On it goes for another thirty minutes and then he pulls his dainty little cell phone out of his suitcoat pocket and listens for a few moments before apologizing, getting up, and abruptly disappearing into the disco green night. Like that, the interview is over.

"What was that?" I ask Josh. "Did we find it?"

"That was the boring surveyor of the family but also confirmation. Yes. We found it," he answers.

"Boring how?"

"Did you see his moustache?" he responds all incredulously. "But, also, yeah. It's legit. This is a thing."

I can tell from the look on his face that he has actually cracked it. He has actually found the headwaters of violent anti-state radicalism, shattering conventional wisdom held in both the halls of academia and the cloistered backrooms of international politics and destroying the Swiss cheese narrative that had been cobbled together from blatant misreadings of secondary texts and refusals to ever actually get beyond the wire. He has upset the apple cart in a radical, earth-shattering way, but what to do with it? Where to go?

Josh sits there quietly for a few long minutes, and I let him, hopefully allowing him to synthesize his thoughts. At least enough so that he can explain again why it matters and what we have done.

After a respectful five more minutes, I press for clarification. "So that was really *really* it?"

"Yes..." Josh says again. "But there's seriously nothing to do with it. We are actually beyond the wire with no structure or institution backing us at all. Imagine that Indiana Jones had found the lost Ark all by himself. What could he have done? How would he have gotten it out of Egypt or wherever he was? Without external infrastructure, discoveries simply exist in their own right. The hustle to make this a movie or TV show or whatever is fun, I'll give you that, but the honest truth of radicalism is its mundane nature. We both grew up fundamentalists. Did it ever feel spicy to you? And what we found here is exactly the same thing.

"Mr. Aydruz there was a boring surveyor, an engineer, supporting boring shipping and trade bros funneling money and students to and around Indonesia back to boring Islamic scholars at a boring school in, literally, the most boring region in all of India and maybe the world. They are serious about their Qur'anic discipline, but none of it signifies as anything other than boring. What comes out of their readings and teachings, though, fires an exponentially more potent, physical, dynamic, creative, radical form of Islamic fundamentalism than the world has ever seen. This moment—here, now—measures up against any rebellion at any time, in any place. And this is where it all begins, though nobody knows that for a fact—except for us. We're like kids who toilet paper the principal's house under cover of darkness and never cop to it: the joy is simply in the doing. Everything else is a distraction."

I smile broadly and understand exactly what he's saying, but I'm not ready to give up on our cinematic explosion yet. I know much better than Josh does in these matters, but tonight we don't need anything more than the fundamentals. Anything more than the radical truth.

"You just discovered the true headwaters of violent anti-state radicalism. What are you doing next?" I ask him as the cicada song rises up all around us. The light dances on the swimming pool.

Josh raises both fists triumphantly and shouts, "I'm going to Marib!"

CHAPTER 9

We wake up at first light, just after early morning Call to Prayer finishes ringing, pack Mohamed al-Behlooly's van, and have him wrap our heads since the chill is back. Josh buttons Das Boot to the very top. I leave a little bit of T-shirt showing underneath Wild One's red satin because it is a white V-neck now and I feel pretty good about the overall look. I put my Ray-Ban Wayfarers on despite their only being half necessary, and we kick our bikes to life.

A whiny, tiny buzz fills the air, and while I still wish we were on Royal Enfields, we've driven to the edge of Yemen and almost back on these tiny Chinese motorbikes with flipped handlebars and they've both wormed their way into my heart. Especially mine, since it has fifteen more cubic centimeters than Josh's and has never had any problems.

And we're on the road with early morning sun splashing the Hadramawt, filling it with a particular glory. We zip along past farms, date palms, mudbrick houses perched on the most precarious rocks, donkeys pulling carts filled with oranges, then turn farther inland, where the geography mirrors the Empty Quarter—sand, sand, sand—before stopping for lunch in the Al Abr District.

Trucks and surprisingly modern tourist-style buses promising A/C and toilets park around a lone three-story building rising up out of the flatness. The trucks I understand. The tourist-style buses? It looks exactly like the Titty Twister from the Quentin Tarantino and Robert Rodriguez masterpiece *From Dusk till Dawn* starring Quentin Tarantino and George Clooney. We park amidst the madness and walk into the crowd.

It's Yemen heaven. Every Yemeni snack is displayed in a large foyer, featuring Nujoom and every other Yemeni candy bar, Pringles and every other Yemeni chip, and all the banana milk brands, including a few that I've never seen before. The side features a classic restaurant serving chicken and "meat" and saltah.

We find a place on the floor, and before anything else Josh turns to me and says, "Please don't order saltah."

"Oh, don't worry…" I tell him. "A quick chicken and rice chased by Nujoom and banana milk and we'll be back on the road straight away."

Tony looks depressed.

I ask, "Why are you depressed, Tony?"

"I wish we could have stayed in Tarim or Shibam a few days longer…" he responds. "I've never seen anything like that."

"You can go see them at home on your computer," Josh says. "They're UNESCO World Heritage sites, or at least one of them is."

"Yeah, Tony. Don't be a buzzkill," I add. "This Yemeni Titty Twister up here, wherever *here* is, has probably never been seen by another Amero-European. Something is afoot. These tourist-style buses mean something, but you're all hung up on significance. Live a little."

He goes back to being depressed.

After lunch we eat our Nujooms, drink our banana milks, refire our bikes, and continue hammering toward Marib, dreaming of finally staying a night or maybe even two in the only town that defeated us last time. It hadn't changed, of course. More and more government troops have been kidnapped, and an almost full hot war has been brewing between the aggressive outlaw town and Yemen's capital, but we have changed. This is our second time around this block. We can handle ourselves. We can even handle ourselves and Tony's artistic ambling. Mohamed al-Behlooly, saint that he is, didn't even throw up an objection when we told him we were planning on staying in Marib before heading back to Sana'a then home. He just smiled and nodded, per his norm.

We had this, we have this, and everyone knows it. We're Teflon.

The sun is past its peak but burning hot when the blacked-out truck comes ripping up behind me and swerves viciously into my path. We are a few kilometers outside of Marib, and I would assume the driver is drunk except we are in Yemen. I'm somewhere north of 140 kilometers per hour, pushing the very limit of Chinese toy-bike engineering, like we have been the entire time, and I almost lose control, downshifting and braking at the same time while dragging a black motorcycle booted foot on the ground. The truck sits next to me for a minute and I wonder what's happening, wonder if he is going to come back for a second brush, when it rockets forward toward Josh.

The blacked-out truck—a Toyota and fancy, I now see—with big fog lights attached to a blacked-out roll bar very much like Marty McFly's Toyota Xtra Cab in *Back to the Future* takes a clean angle at Josh. Somehow he senses them coming up and moves over but they keep coming, pushing him entirely off the road and into the sand at full speed. I expect he's going to die, but the Minnesota boy buried deep within him takes over and he rises to a slight crouch while expertly navigating the whoops.

Marty McFly matches Josh's speed for an eternal moment, refusing to let him back onto the road, then finds another gear and rockets over the horizon. Josh eases back onto the road and I catch up with him. We both look at each other the same exact way we looked at each other after our delicious Hezbollah dinner.

Here, in Yemen, his motorcycle almost instantly loses power and he pulls off the road underneath some leafy trees. I pull off too. We unwrap our heads, look at each other, laugh, then get down on our knees, trying to sort out what went wrong with his machine. Mohamed al-Behlooly pulls in a few moments later. I don't know if they saw the action or if it was actually real until Tony spills out, eyes as wide as I've ever seen them, even wider than when he was studying UNESCO World Heritage–certified wonders of the world, and simply says, "Whoa. That was intense. Where'd they go?"

I hadn't thought about that yet, and Josh shrugs while continuing to fiddle with his very hot engine.

"Maybe they went to get some snacks," I tell Tony.

Mohamed al-Behlooly, pacing in front of his van, looks nervous for the first time.

But we're good. We've already passed the Marib test, right?

"It's a fouled spark plug," Josh says while removing it like a hot potato. I like the phrase "fouled spark plug" almost as much as I like the phrase "fouled anchor," and I breathe a sigh of relief, knowing that it's all easily fixable.

We both stand up tall and stretch our backs. I unzip Wild One a lot but then zip it back up a little more, deciding that half a white V-neck with grease smudges here and there is perfect. Tony heads back to the van while Mohamed al-Behlooly continues to pace. And just like that another car comes speeding up, sliding to a halt right where we're parked. It's not nearly as impressive as Marty McFly's Toyota. It's small and gray with some Arabic scrawl stickered to the windshield. It's not impressive at all, in fact, but its doors open and eight Yemenis spill out, stern-faced and surrounding us without word. Clearly from Marib, as they are all well-built and furious. Another truck pulls up behind the car, its bed filled with eight other Maribi and the cab filled with nobody knows.

"Izzayak," I say in my Egyptian colloquial.

They stay silent.

"Kayf halek?" I say in butchered Lebanese.

"Where are you from?" the sternest asks in crisp, proper Arabic.

I look at Josh for direction and he stays silent, staring back with a menacing scowl.

When I'm about to say "California" I hear the word "Lubnan" come floating over my shoulder from Mohamed al-Behlooly. He is standing there, beatific smile wiped away.

Lebanon.

The fact that we are both dishwater blonds with blue eyes would theoretically make his claim absurd and easily refutable, but Lebanon is the home of dishwater blonds with blue eyes thanks to its proximity to Europe, the Crusades, and its robust French population.

"Lubnan?" the leader of this Yemeni gang asks. *"Weyn?" Where.*

Josh takes the bait and says, "Beirut."

"Weyn fi Beirut?" the leader asks, his eyes squinting in clear disbelief.

"Gmayze," Josh says, dropping the street that had our favorite steak restaurant, where we ate every other night during the war and where I fanned out on Kate Seelye from National Public Radio.

The Marabi Bad News Crew shuffles around us, poking at our bikes, upgraded with lipstick cameras attached to the handlebars with wires running down the metal tubing connecting them to recording devices planted underneath our seats that, in this light, look exactly like bombs. They're eyeing Mohamed al-Behlooly suspiciously, and thankfully Tony has retreated to the van and is keeping his head well down. They pepper Josh and me with a few more questions and our wacky Arabic holds up to their scrutiny of admittedly bizarre Lebanon, and after an interminable five minutes they get back in their small car and drive off.

Mohamed al-Behlooly looks like a trillion pounds have been lifted from his shoulders. I never knew that his Zen felt the weight of trouble, but it clearly does, and he hurries us along, hovering while Josh un-fouls his spark plug. He reinserts it, I throw up a quick prayer, and…

BUZZZZZZZZ!

It works. We're both back, which is an immense relief since riding through Marib's first checkpoint nuts to butt would have lacked the proper dramatic appeal. We both straddle our micro-steeds, give a couple quick flicks of the throttle, and power forward, Mohamed al-Behlooly and Tony somewhere in our dust.

I can see Marib now rising in the distance like forbidden fruit, but before I can even imagine its taste, another car from out of nowhere is hugging my elbow and another Maribi is leaning out the passenger window screaming, "Where you from?" this time in inflected but almost proper English.

I shrug and try to outrun him, but he's there again.

"Where you from?" he shouts even louder and even less inflected.

I pretend I don't understand his gibberish despite every self-respecting Lebanese knowing English. He has to in order to understand all his music video programming, because Britney Spears matters and she mostly matters in English. There's no time to reach a satisfying conclusion, anyhow, as the Black Gate of Marib hovers ominously before us. This time the giant metal crossbar is down and there's already a mob of cars and trucks and technicals pooled around it trying to get through. A few Yemeni soldiers stand out front of their barracks dressed in newish digital desert camo, their cheeks full of qat.

Josh and I both slow to a reasonable speed then stop. The car of English-speaking Maribis does too, except they pair their stop with full-throated yells out the window.

"AMERICAN! AMERICAN! AMERICAN!"

Uh-oh. We totally are.

I'm very hot now. It feels like the sun has dialed up the action by a good twenty or so percent, and I feel the sweat pulsing, feel it dripping beneath Wild One and soaking my V-neck. I look out of the corner of my eye at Josh, who is stone-faced and, I'm sure, internally joyous. I look at the crowd that has gathered, and this is everything I initially dreamed of when forcing Josh to bastardize his genius for popularity. A crowd beaming at me, wanting me, hanging on to what's going to happen next. And I'll admit it feels pretty good. I should be terrified at this point. Mortified. Things never end well in Yemen for normal folk, much less non-Lebanese interlocutors, but we've got a crowd. One thousand eyeballs stuck to us at the very advent of gaming "likes" and "views." One thousand real eyeballs. Staring at me, at us, even though I wish they were staring at us from the other side of a screen.

Beggars can't be choosers, and we start to inch to the checkpoint with the shouts continuing and the crowd now swelling. More eyeballs. More heat.

"AMRIKI! AMRIKI! AMRIKI!"

The intensity continues to rise as the shouts turn angry Arabic mixed in with heavy gesticulation. A hand comes flying out of the air, making some strong point, and almost knocks my Ray-Ban Wayfarers. A few more soldiers dip their heads out of the barracks and study the developing scene. The look on their faces is not reassuring as they study what is developing before them and no doubt think about all of their brethren who have been kidnapped here just for fun. Phalanxes of them. Famous sheiks, local politicians, and foreign workers too.

Josh and I continue inching, and then my bike sputters and dies. I quickly untwist the gas cap and peer inside. It is bone dry. I look at Josh, shrug, and start pushing it very slowly. I look back over at the barracks, which now has ten soldiers standing outside nervously fiddling with their Kalashnikovs and see Mohamed al-Behlooly there in their midst, gesticulating as heavily as anyone. Pointing at the metal crossbar, at us, at the crowd, at us.

I catch his eye and motion that my bike is out of gas. He gives up on the soldiers for a moment and presses through the sweaty mob to us. His face is serious, but unlike the soldiers, he doesn't look nervous. He seems serenely in control. I explain the problem directly. He blinks his eyes then moves into the mass before coming back once again, laying a warm but not sweaty hand on my shoulder.

The crowd is just loud now, and I can't pick out any specific words from the din. I don't know if the gathered are barking about us or if there was some preexisting problem that we stumbled into and proceeded to exacerbate.

Mohamed al-Behlooly guides us to a corner and tells us to wait. Miraculously there's a snack seller set up with fresh mangos, some crackers, and warm boxes of banana milk. Josh and I each snag one and lay some rials down on his wood box. He doesn't move except to gently roll his giant qat ball in his cheek.

"The US killed a bro they said was al-Qaeda right here just a little while back," Josh says in between sips. "With a drone, no less. They all got super pissed."

"Oh."

Mohamed al-Behlooly is now back with the soldiers, explaining who knows what. That the Lebanese in leather jackets on Chinese toy motorcycles needed to get through to see the ruins? That we were archeologists? I honestly should have studied archeology as opposed to applied linguistics, damn it.

It's louder now. Hotter. My banana milk still tastes good, even warm. Josh and I sit there watching the scene, being watched back. It feels like death is actually imminent, but there's also absolutely nothing we can do about it, so worry has vanished. I've reached peak "inshallah."

If this is the end, this is the end.

Suddenly, Mohamed al-Behlooly jumps down from the barracks and pushes over to where he parked the van. I see Tony sitting ramrod straight in the passenger seat. He starts it up and starts driving slowly into the mob. A few men pound the hood with their hands. A few more look to the soldiers, who are now actively screaming back.

The metal crossbar rises up and the van passes under, infuriating the mob further. Josh and I finish our banana milks then push our bikes through behind it. Angry eyes and open mouths surround us. We are in the middle of pure rage. A sea of throbbing rage. Another mob is on the other side of the crossbar, and we push our bikes underneath a corrugated metal overhang. A chicken is roasting on a nearby charcoal grill. Flies make aggressive swoops.

I feel a tug on my elbow. I look down and see a kid standing there, maybe thirteen, with a Kalashnikov slung loosely over his shoulder and a mini qat ball in his cheek. He is holding a red plastic gas can and moves his head slightly without expression. I untwist the gas cap. He pulls out a yellow spout, places it in the dry hole, and turns the can upside down. The smell of low-grade gasoline wafts into my nostrils.

When the can is empty, he tips it back, replaces the yellow spout, and melts back into the mob. Mohamed al-Behlooly is now yelling at individuals in the mob from the van's driver's seat. Motioning to the road ahead with an empty palm, motioning back to us, motioning up to God. He begins moving forward while yelling. Josh and I kick our bikes to life. Both sputter for too long but finally catch and we ease over to Mohamed al-Behlooly, slowly gathering speed until the mob is in our mirror. We wind through town, and I don't take anything in. Not the gun market, not the goat carcass being hung from a rafter by its rear legs, not the half-finished new mosque, not even the ruins, however meaningless they might have been. And like that we are through Marib for the second time without truly enjoying it but also enjoying it fully, getting a real taste of what it does best. And it's not until we stop for dinner two hours later in a small café outside of Sana'a that my heart slows to its normal rhythm.

Mohamed al-Behlooly is glowing like a saint again, smiling his saintlike smile. Tony is completely silent. Josh and I order "meat," because that is the only thing they have, and also Canada Dry Colas since they don't have ginger ale.

"Well, it's a good thing we didn't die today, huh, Tony?" I continue chuckling while leaning against a plastic-wrapped cushion, switching my gaze between him and Josh. "Mimi would have been really mad if this grand adventure, our cinematic masterpiece, ended midway. She would have been extremely upset to have such pure gold but no proper closure. Getting smoked in Marib would have been too clichéd. Too expected."

"It's been totally done to death," Josh agrees as our "meat" arrives.

Tony stays completely silent.

I look at Josh then Tony, then back at Josh so Tony knows, and say, "We're Teflon. Nothing can hurt us."

Josh responds, "I've been meaning to tell you forever. Teflon is mostly used as a non-stick surface on cooking pans. I think you mean Kevlar. *That's* the stuff they use for bulletproof vests."

POSTSCRIPT

CHAPTER 1

Djibouti, Today

"WAIT. I REALLY DON'T UNDERSTAND. WHY WERE YOU KIDNAPPING A monkey again?" Nate twists around on his baking hot wooden barstool underneath a thatched roof covering the outdoor bar of Kempinksi's Djibouti Palace.

The bartender, a kind-faced Djiboutian woman with a loose scarf covering her head, is listening, waiting until I finish whatever it is I'm going to say before kicking the blender to life again.

Nate is looking at me and the back of his white button-up is drenched in sweat, though the front looks remarkably dry. The half-Windsor knot of his pencil black tie is slightly loosened as a subtle nod toward the extreme temperature, but that's all. His two-year run in Baghdad as a liaison between the United States Army and the international press had served him well. He chased that gig by cofounding a high-end design-build firm that operated out of Kabul and Sana'a with Josh, who gave up on being Islamic Studies' *enfant terrible* and decided that what Kabul and Sana'a needed was a high-end design-build firm.

He and Nate spent years on daily flights, shuffling back and forth between Kabul and Sana'a before the whole region blew up in a new fiery ball. Nate mostly keeps his work secret now and refuses to respond to direct questions, so it's mostly impossible to know what he does with his days. The only thing I know, for a fact, is that he attends Elton John's annual Oscar party each and every year. Josh is back in Los Angeles, collaborating with Jay-Z and Beyoncé on something I'm equally confused about. And I quit my job at Los Angeles City College to become a full-time surf journalist. A literal and honest surf journalist. The fact that such a thing exists is absurd enough. The fact that I do it pushes it right overboard.

"Because, bro," I say between sips of still-cold piña colada that I insisted we all order since the outdoor bar has a thatched roof. "Josh was right and you were right. Being on camera is true hell and we were never meant to be famous in any sort of actory way. Our trajectory was never supposed to be tied to being famous. That's the simple truth, and I understand it now. Sorry for making us pursue cellulite stardom all these years. It wasn't a well-thought-out plan."

Josh snorts from his barstool.

Nate says, "Celluloid."

We had flown to Bombay just a few short months after returning from Yemen triumphant, though completely exhausted and filthy. Mimi had watched the footage and was excited to keep pressing.

"You've discovered something so fabulous, darlings..." she breathed heavily the day we arrived home, exhausted and dirty. "We're leaving as soon as I get the rest of our budget to...where? Where is that fabulous school where they teach the radical Islamic terrorism?"

"Deoband, India," Josh replied.

"Absolutely gorgeous, and I'll come too. India is marvelous, and this Deoband sounds very chic."

We were too tired to argue.

So there we all were, night one, in the bar, a monsoon rain pouring outside with our Punjabi bartender towering above us when Mimi told Tony to pull his camera out and get some real descriptive interviews. The bartender was in a Sikh motorbike gang, very tall and handsome, and looked on, interest piqued.

Josh nominated me to start, and Tony swished his brown corduroy pants over to his camera bag, set it up, and turned it on me and said "speeding" while clapping his hands in front of the lens.

Something happened in my heart when I saw that little red light come on. Something deep and profound that I can't quite explain. I just knew, in that moment, that I hated being on camera. I hated it in Lebanon, I hated it in Yemen, I hated it in Bombay. Hated everything about it. Hated the way it made me feel, hated the way I looked afterward, hated the way my voice sounded. And for the first time in my life, I thought, "Those cultures that believe the camera steals your soul are right."

I looked at Josh for help. Tony swung the camera his direction and I was momentarily off the hook. Josh fiddled with his rings for a minute, explaining some deep-cut seventeenth-century Islamic nugget before excusing himself for a cigarette.

Tony pointed the camera toward an ornate picture frame, and I wasn't at all upset with him. It was very beautiful.

That night, after Josh and I got back to our room, I sank, emotionally, and moaned, "This fucking sucks."

Josh laughed. "After just one take? Come on. We went all the way through Lebanon, twice, with cameras, and now Yemen without you pitching a fit. You'll smash it tomorrow. It's what you want to do."

It wasn't anymore, that dream evaporating in a millisecond and leaving nothing behind, but how could I tell Josh that? I had wrangled us into ugly relationships with *Vice*, Fremantle, Al Gore, and now Mimi, all in the hopes of a cinematic capturing of the lives we led instead of just enjoying them ourselves like he had wanted all along.

I headed over to the TV and magically found a Lebanese music video station. "But I won't," I told him dejectedly. "I know this time for a fact, I won't. I have a horrible sinking feeling in my gut that I won't be able to ever look good on camera. Not tonight. Not tomorrow. Not ever."

Josh laughed again. "On the plus side, it looks like we'll be paying out of pocket for Mimi and Tony the whole time. That's fun."

Mimi had "accidentally" forgotten her credit card back home but was "getting it FedExed straight away." Tony wore brown corduroy pants. And the "film's budget" seemed like it might have been spent on drapes for a Beverly Hills apartment.

"This is a disaster," I moaned again, falling onto the bed. The first actual disaster of our run together, which up to that point had featured a weeklong hospital stay replete with IV bag after IV bag into my veins, which were shutting at an alarming rate; our theoretical lives being threatened by a sword-wielding Somali; hookers that we didn't pay for or want secretly destroying our personal property; getting told we were awful at skateboarding by a Hezbollah officer so unversed in skateboarding that his honest assessment would ping until this very moment; and almost dying astride spray-painted Chinese motorcycle toys.

"Is this how all those damned Disneyland employees who call themselves actors feel?" I asked the ceiling. "A delusion of possibility that, carried by its own momentum, propels a man or woman to the ripe old age of forty still believing he or she can be someone who matters?"

Leih Beydary had given way to some older, seemingly wealthy woman crooning passionately alongside a tuxedoed orchestra in front of some dramatically lit ruins.

"This is shit," I continued to mutter. "Absolute shit."

Josh smirked at the TV then looked at me. "Wait, are you saying this trip is shit? Seriously, help me understand. Why are you so bent out of shape here? I'm sure if it's what you want you can totally figure out how to be good on camera. Look at...Ben Affleck."

"Yeah, look at him," I said. "He basically carried *Good Will Hunting,* but I don't want to be an actor anyhow. I just knew in my heart of hearts that this thing, what we do, whatever you want to call it, would get carried along via visual representation. But when Tony's camera turned on today, it was like peering into a succubus. Or...what is the girl demon that sucks your soul?"

"A succubus," Josh said. "The man demon is an incubus—just like that super sick band."

"Maybe I've got Incubus sucking my soul, but I don't know if I can come back from the way that felt. I hate to keep coming back around to damned feelings here, but—son of a bitch—I've spent our entire run, through Yemen, Lebanon, Syria, Somalia, Yemen, India, building for this way to represent what we do in a way that actually looks how it feels. But today, something snapped."

"Yeah," Josh laughed. "But I think you so quickly forgot the amazing company we have along for the ride. That makes it worthwhile."

I grunted and laid my head down on a starchy pillow. It was too early in the evening for sleep, considering the thick jet lag on the horizon, and I knew I was just giving in to the sirens calling me toward rocky shores, but it was better than thinking about Incubus anymore. Josh was right. He had been right all along. I closed my eyes and drifted into the blackness. Maybe sleep would change the predicament. Maybe sleep would give me some new insight into how to carry this thing. Maybe sleep would…

I woke up exactly at 2:15 in the morning, the red digital numbers of the bedside hotel clock shining like a beacon beaming the address of hell. The dread had not only not abated, it was strangling me. It had its hands around my throat choking my will. I stared at the ceiling, the dark cracks that ran away from the overhead light, a spider in the corner catching malaria for snack. What were we going to do? What on Earth could we possibly do?

"We're going to steal a monkey."

Josh's voice cut into my despair so clearly that I thought I was only imagining it.

"What?"

"We're going to steal a monkey, or get a monkey, and take it to an epic monkey temple up past Deoband that I heard of last time I was here. A place where the monkey will live a life that other monkeys only dream. That's what we're going to do."

CHAPTER 2

"I STILL DON'T GET IT," NATE RESPONDS, TWISTING BACK AND FIXING JOSH, who has just lit a cigarette and ordered three more piña coladas for the group, in his stiff stare. Cole has just wobbled around the corner too, wearing a green dashiki, white Birkenstocks, oversized Fashion Nova X sunglasses, and he's gripping a bottle of white wine by its neck. He has either spent the last year in Addis Ababa, Ethiopia, or Grozny, Chechnya, no one is quite sure. He hollers, "Garçon, more white wine!" into the air before starting some yoga routine.

"Oh, don't be so purposefully difficult here," Josh says, turning his attention from Cole back to Nate. "Obviously the monkeys in India live hellish lives, but there's a Hanuman temple up near Karachi, one of the earliest, I think, with a prehistoric Hanuman carved by nature or that's what they say. Our monkey would have gotten to live amongst Muslims with better built-in hygiene and cleaner food. Our monkey would honestly go from depressed to elated. It was all in our hands. We could have been better conservationists than Jane Goodall, the Crocodile Hunter, and Burl Ives combined. We would have made them all look like foolish, selfish humanists, and as a bonus, our monkey would never have had to eat burfi again."

"What's burfi?" Nate asks.

"It's sort of like nougat," Josh answers.

I almost spit piña colada on the both of them.

"Just kidding." Josh almost chokes. "It tastes like hell. Some sort of mix they make from incense, rose water, and plastic Shiva trinkets."

"But why a monkey?" Nate asks again. "What about finishing the mission to Deoband?"

"NATE!" Josh bellows. "What's there not to understand? We had already found what we needed to find in Yemen and didn't need to go to Deoband. Plus, Charlie had had an emotional breakthrough and needed tender loving care."

"Well, what did Mimi and Tony think?" he parries.

"I couldn't have cared less," I cut in. "They represented *Vice*'s Shane Smith, *American Idol*, Brian Grazer, Al Gore, Sector 9 skateboards and all my horrible, unforgivable youthful dalliances."

Josh and I spent the entire day trying to track one down, and as we moved into darker and darker corners we realized that the government had passed a recent law making possession of a monkey far worse than possession of heroin or shoulder-propelled rocket launchers. Finally, though, in some dark Bombay alley, we found a man who said he could get us what we needed. We paid half up front while his eyes shifted and we were supposed to meet him at the train station with the other half. There was a Hindu festival happening and it was impossible to get seats, but we had worked some magic and scored four to Delhi that evening.

We went back to the hotel, packed our stuff, gathered Mimi and Tony, and headed to the central Victoria Terminus train station. Josh went to the meeting spot. I put Mimi and Tony on the train then hung out of the door, gazing dead-eyed into the cavernous crowd. It was a monsoon downpour and hot. I was texting back and forth with Josh, who was texting back and forth with our monkey dealer. He kept responding that he would have our monkey soon but with no real assurances as to when.

I started panicking when the train started inching away from the station and was just about ready to made an executive decision to tell Josh to abort when he came sprinting around the corner and caught the train's corner at the very last second, holding a bundle under his arm.

"So you really got a monkey?"

I twist my barstool back and forth so violently that my surfboard, leaning up against it, falls over. Djibouti has no surf, not even a small hint. "It might have been a monkey, but it also might have been a giant squirrel. I didn't have time to do an inspection because as soon as we got back to our cabin and peeked inside, the thing jumped into my face, pulled my hair, and sprinted into the corridor."

"It was totally a monkey," Josh says. "A big monkey."

We searched the train for the next six or seven hours then sat in silence, a sensation of utter defeat hovering thick and angry above our heads like monsoonal clouds. We arrived in Delhi the next evening, beyond depressed. Mimi and Tony wanted to go see the Taj Mahal, and we told them that they should. Josh and I went to the train station after they left, bought tickets, and rode the train nonstop for over 2,000 kilometers, almost bumping into Burma at the end.

"You just left them without warning?" Nate asks. "That seems like an asshole thing to do, even for you." He is looking right at me.

"It was," Josh responds. "But, also, I like Indian trains almost as much as I like sailboats."

"And," I add "the farther we got, the better we felt. It was like the biblical Jonah in reverse. Like we were getting rewarded for running away from misguided narcissism. Day after day on that train, drinking tea from little unfired clay cups and smashing them on the tracks, eating curry, watching a mind-bogglingly vast, beautiful, complicated, ancient, exotic, mystical country sweep by the open window, hanging off the back, getting blond hair blown out by gorgeous humidity, climbing into cars packed with lounging locals and watching Bollywood music videos over their shoulders. By the time we arrived to Guwahati I couldn't feel my face anymore, and that felt absolutely wonderful."

"Then, a few mornings after we arrived, twenty bombs went off in the city and we were back amongst our element."

"Oh, yeah, that was nuts, but it wasn't racial Islamic fundamentalist terror-related, was it?" I ask Josh.

"Nope," he says in between smartly switching from piña colada to vodka soda and ordering one for each of us. "I think they blamed some hardcore Hindu nationalist anti-immigrant group."

I nod, looking at the bartender who is looking at a bottle of Stolichnaya, before continuing, "In any case, I felt perfectly self-radicalized in the moment."

We stop talking for a minute and stare across the placid haze toward Yemen. We can't see it, of course, but we can feel it. We can taste it, are already sorting out how to get there or get there to us, even though a robust Saudi blockade floats directly in the way. Even though the country has been in a full state of war for a year.

The press reports, all buried and meager, point to an Islamic rebellion in opposition to the central government by an Iran-backed group called the Houthis. The Saudis, in their role as benevolent regional peacemakers and bulwark against evil Iran, are trying to choke resources for the rebels by blockading Yemen's coast and bombing Yemeni hospitals.

Conflict has gripped the country, with pitched street battles being fought in Aden, Mukalla, Al Ghaydah, and the regions north of Sana'a. It looks like a real war, but it also just looks like Yemen.

The root of these troubles comes straight from Riyadh and tied around the wedge-sandaled cankles of an upstart prince, Mohammed bin Salman, who is making a move for the Saudi throne. He is Saudi Arabia's defense minister and using the "war" to distract from interior economic problems, using some of the billions of dollars of weapons the country stockpiles and buying billions of dollars more from great friend the United States of America all while consolidating power.

Yemen is an easy target. A poor country without billions of dollars to spend on anything, a reenergized al-Qaeda, and a robust inshallah spirit. The world won't care, and so bin Salman can do as he wishes, flexing, distracting, consolidating.

"What if we swim across the Bab al-Mandab?" I ask, never wanting to get out of the water. It is so hot, but the air is much hotter, and I figure we could leisurely float the ninety or so miles without worry.

"The Bab is one of the roughest patches of water on Earth. There have been as many shipwrecks there as any place. It's fully gnarly," Josh says. "I don't think we'd have much luck swimming it. I think we'd die pretty quick."

I frown back. He also says that we pissed away all our beginner's luck by doing stupid shit in our twenties and thirties, and he is probably right, because we are in Djibouti, arguably the worst country, though with a nice Kempinski, trying to extract an epic sailboat from Yemen across a Saudi blockade in our forties, and things are not looking good, though I really hate to believe it. Does beginner's luck die?

Shit. It probably does.

The boat is beautiful, though. A ketch named *Kari* that had belonged to a family whose father wanted to "make the world a classroom" for the two children. They sailed through the Mediterranean, down the Red Sea, learning all the way, until they arrived in Aden and someone figured out the world is a shitty classroom, abandoning it there.

Aden's harbormaster told Josh and Nate that he would give it to them if they could only get it out. They spent weeks scrubbing its hull, re-rigging its lining, patching its sails, getting it ready for the greatest mission yet. One that would include me but not include cameras. The morning they planned on finishing preparation and getting underway, they went running on the harbor, the way they had for the past ten days, waving at the Yemeni policemen in their barracks as they passed. When they got to the end of their route, the Yemeni policemen had been exploded by a massive car bomb. Others were popping off all over Aden and the most recent civil war had officially begun. Josh, Nate, and another wonderful edition named Andrew barely got out of the country with their own skin still attached to their bones, much less a sailboat still in need of a few hours' work.

Nobody expected the troubles to last but here we are, a whole year later. The boat still in Aden, us in Djibouti, and a Saudi blockade keeping us apart.

"If we can't get Yemeni visas from the consulate here, then we're going to have to find a tug to somehow bring it through the blockade," he says. "Then once it gets here we'll make sure that sitting in a war zone for the last year didn't cause any damage and off we go. Egypt, here we come!"

Nate whistles.

"What does that whistle signify, fella?" Josh asks, faux seriously.

"Oh, nothing," Nate deadpans. "What did the monkey signify?"

"Well, finally a good question." Josh smiles. "Here's how I see it: Our lives are like those fancy, special, limited-edition Monopoly collectors' sets. You know, the ones they do for specific cities or events? Yeah, they have those artistic, unique game pieces cast in brass. Like Learjets and Nike sneakers. Our unique, brass game pieces are surfboards, motor scooters, motorcycles, a Qur'an, a monkey, and now a sailboat. What does it all mean? They all signify something, but I have absolutely no idea what."

"And Camus thought he knew something about the absurd," I say while knocking my surfboard down again. "We're officially self-radical. David Petraeus and all those US war bastards can go fuck themselves."

"FUCK THEMSELVES!" Cole shouts mid-downward dog. "Garçon! Wine!"

"Give King David his due," Nate says, before adding, "Did I ever tell you the story of his glasses?"

"I'm sure you did..." I reply, "...but shocking I can't remember. Tell it to me again."

Nate smirks but won't pass up the opportunity to tell a good story, respecting his missionary kid heritage.

"So when I was there, the *Washington Post* did an exclusive interview with the general in his office. Now, he was waxing on and on and on, like he does, but he had a pair of those granny glasses on while he was reading various reports. What are they called? Those half glasses?"

"Half-frame reading glasses?" Josh offers.

"Sure, those," Nate continues. "Anyhow, he made a joke about it in the middle of the interview. Something like, 'I hope you don't think I'm a grandma with my glasses.' Well, the story came out a few days later and included a picture of him in those half-frame reading glasses. He was absolutely furious and ordered his aides to get the picture removed. They told him it was no big deal but he made a giant fuss and insisted if it wasn't removed the *Washington Post* would never get another interview."

Josh and I both laugh at the absurd narcissism.

"I bet those glasses were made in Saudi Arabia. That bro is in the shiek's pocket," I say. "And speaking of pockets, where would be the best place to raise kids, in the whole entire world?"

Josh answers directly, not even pausing, thoughts on the matter fully formed. "Not in the United States. Somewhere without a wild security apparatus. In a fragile state. Yemen."

"What about the Old World?" I wonder.

"Not Europe," Josh says at the same exact time.

"Germany," I counter.

"They are worse than America in terms of full-on, around-the-clock surveillance, or at least they want to be," Josh says while Cole continues his vinyasa, flowing into warrior pose.

"But they are so wonderfully decadent and corrupt. Couldn't you just teach your kids to skate underneath all the ridiculousness?" I ask.

"Efficient states are the enemy," he says.

"TIMBUKTU!" Cole bellows.

"Somalia?" I ask, ignoring him. "I don't want to live in Somalia or Somaliland."

"Maybe the best place would be the tiny freaks of shell company nations. The Caymans or some such," he says. "Places where the powerful don't want scrutiny and the locals are penniless."

"I knew it!" I exclaim. "Finally, you are seeing the light. Island lifestyle time!"

I'd been preaching that an island lifestyle with never-buttoned shirts, always-cuffed pants, white nubuck shoes, and tanned feet shoved into their innards was the ideal way to exist, always drawing dismissive guffaws from both Josh and Nate. Cole, I think, agreed with me, though never made his position known and is now drinking his bottle of wine while doing a sun salutation.

Josh changes his mind about the Caymans right away. "No, it can't be the islands. Money means a place can switch to surveillance on a dime. It has to be somewhere like Yemen. Or maybe just real Yemen. Corruption equals freedom, and these people are truly free. What could be a better gift, in this mad world, than giving your kids the almost disappeared gift of freedom?"

"Josh wants to move to Belgium or somewhere the Belgians colonized," Nate offers.

"What, is that true?" I look at Nate, incredulously. Josh had always been completely dismissive of the Belgian's efforts in Africa.

"He's developed a taste for Chimay in Kabul." Nate nods. "He really goes for it on a fun occasion."

I'm incredulous. Not believing. Not being able to imagine Josh drinking some thick ale. The taste of Rolling Rock still torturing my soul.

"That's gross," I say. "Beer is gross, and especially that Trappist Belgian stuff."

"You're wrong, bro." Josh leans back on his barstool, smug. "With Congolese food, it's meant to be. Colonial connection. Congo food is pretty spicy..."

Nate nods a paternal "I-told-you-so" toward me.

Cole screams, "The only thing I care about is a buttery, full-bodied California Chardonnay..." from plank position.

"Gross," Josh, Nate, and I say at the same time.

"Speaking of..." I say. "How much for Sarah Jessica Parker as Carrie Bradshaw?"

"Six," Josh says.

"Three," Nate says.

"Four," Cole says, now sitting in the lotus position, eyes closed or maybe closed as his Cardi B brand sunglasses hide his eyes.

We all commend Cole on his prudent offer before I win the contract by throwing up a seven, then asking, "What about a Mr. Big and Aleksandr Petrovsky meatsa-meatsa?"

"I really hate when you get on to some horrible, decadent television series," Josh says. "I've seen approximately five minutes of one episode. It's lowbrow titillation and unrealistic materialism. *Baywatch* for a female audience. Eight, though, for Mikhail Baryshnikov."

"Two," Nate says.

"I always found John Corbett's Aiden to be the most charming of her boyfriends," Cole whispers sensually after a thoughtful pause, which frustrates me into silence. John Corbett's Aiden is a monument to everything I hate in the American male.

Nate orders yet another round, and I raise the remnants of my hurricane glass in a toast. "Here's to us, war reporters. Us conflict reporters. Us foreign correspondents, and all those who have gone before. We've dug into the dark recesses of dangerous intrigue. We've shined our lights on the war of our age, the Global War on Terror, and between our singular works have brought clarity and understanding."

Everyone except Cole clinks glasses then drains the last bits of island lifestyle from their bottoms.

"Do you really call yourself a war reporter?" Cole asks after a moment, now in a totally wild pigeon pose.

I laugh, deeply, almost spilling my drink, sliding my Tom Ford sunglasses almost entirely off the bridge of my nose and say, "No. I call myself a surf journalist. A self-radicalized anti-state violent surf journalist."

Unprecedented Acclaim for CHARLES FRAZIER*'s*

COLD MOUNTAIN

"Charles Frazier's feeling for the Southern landscape is reverential and beautifully composed. He has written an astonishing first novel." —Alfred Kazin, *The New York Review of Books*

"A great read—a stirring Civil War tale told with epic sweep [and] loaded with vivid historical detail." —*People*

"Strikingly beautiful. . . . In its vivid evocation of a time and place, its steady storytelling momentum, and its unabashed affirmation of a fiction that takes moral choice seriously, *Cold Mountain* calls to mind *Snow Falling on Cedars.*" —*Newsday*

"An exciting work of fiction." —*Washington Post Book World*

"Heartbreakingly beautiful . . . elegantly told and convincing down to the last haunting detail." —John Berendt, author of *Midnight in the Garden of Good and Evil*

"The best Civil War novel since Michael Shaara's *The Killer Angels*. . . . [It] deserves any and all prizes that might be lying about." —Kaye Gibbons

"In prose filled with grace notes and trenchant asides, he has reset much of the *Odyssey* in 19th-century America, near the end of the Civil War. . . . A wealth of finely realized supporting characters. . . . A memorable book."

—*The New York Times Book Review*

"Magnificent—in every conceivable aspect. . . . One of the great accomplishments in American literature." —Rick Bass

"A richly rewarding first novel. . . . Wonderfully convincing, finely detailed." —*Christian Science Monitor*

"This novel's landscape is finely drawn, full of dark beauty and presentiment, and so are its characters." —*The New Yorker*

"Measured and graceful . . . savor it. You'll find the characters living in your head for a long time."
—*Milwaukee Journal-Sentinel*

"This is one of the best books I've read in a long time, and I cried when it was over. It's simply a miracle." —Larry Brown

"*Cold Mountain* is a book with epic sweep, a war-time love story that refuses to give way to tired sentiment."
—*Los Angeles Times*

"A superb novel—thrilling, richly detailed and powerful. I was spellbound." —Frank Conroy

"A remarkable first novel, a romance of love, of friendship, of family, of land. Frazier has inhaled the spirit of the age and breathes it into the reader's being." —*The Times* (London)

"At once spare and eloquent. . . . Interspersed with so many moments of sadness, the many moments of compassion seem entirely convincing and are very affecting. . . . The understatement . . . is almost shattering." —Ann Beattie

"The most enthralling first novel I have read in a long time."
—Willie Morris

CHARLES FRAZIER

COLD MOUNTAIN

Charles Frazier grew up in the mountains of North Carolina. He now lives in Raleigh with his wife and daughter, where they raise horses. *Cold Mountain* is his first novel.

COLD MOUNTAIN

A NOVEL

BY

CHARLES FRAZIER

VINTAGE CONTEMPORARIES

Vintage Books

A Division of Random House, Inc.

New York

VINTAGE CONTEMPORARIES EDITION, AUGUST 1998

Published in the United States by Vintage Books, a division of Random House, Inc., New York. Published in Canada by Vintage Canada, a division of Random House of Canada Limited, Toronto. Originally published in hardcover in the United States by The Atlantic Monthly Press, New York, in 1997.

The 1847 Macrae map of the Southern Blue Ridge Mountains is courtesy of the Department of Cultural Resources, Division of Archives and History, Raleigh, North Carolina.

Library of Congress Cataloging-in-Publication Data
Frazier, Charles, 1950–
Cold mountain / Charles Frazier.—Vintage Books ed.
p. cm.
ISBN 0-375-70075-7
1. United States—History—Civil War, 1861–1865—Fiction.
I. Title.
[PS3556.R3599C6 1998]
813′.54—dc21 98-11053
CIP

Random House Web address: www.randomhouse.com

Printed in the United States of America
10 9 8 7 6 5 4 3

—for Katherine and Annie

It is difficult to believe in the dreadful but quiet war of organic beings, going on in the peaceful woods, & smiling fields.

—Darwin, 1839 journal entry

Men ask the way to Cold Mountain.
Cold Mountain: there's no through trail.

—Han-shan

MAP

OF THE
SOUTHERN BLUE RIDGE
MOUNTAINS

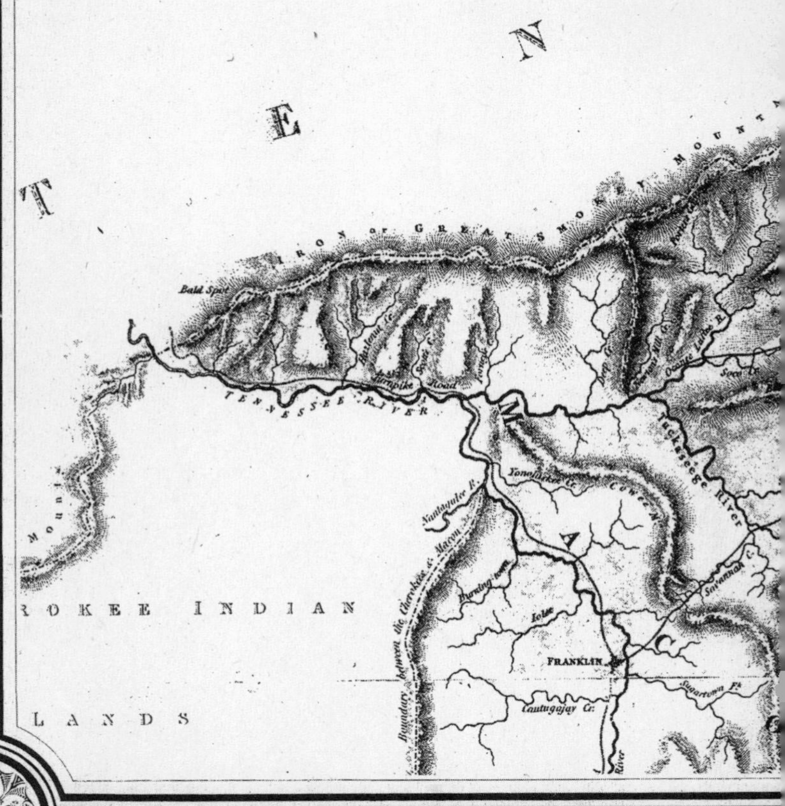

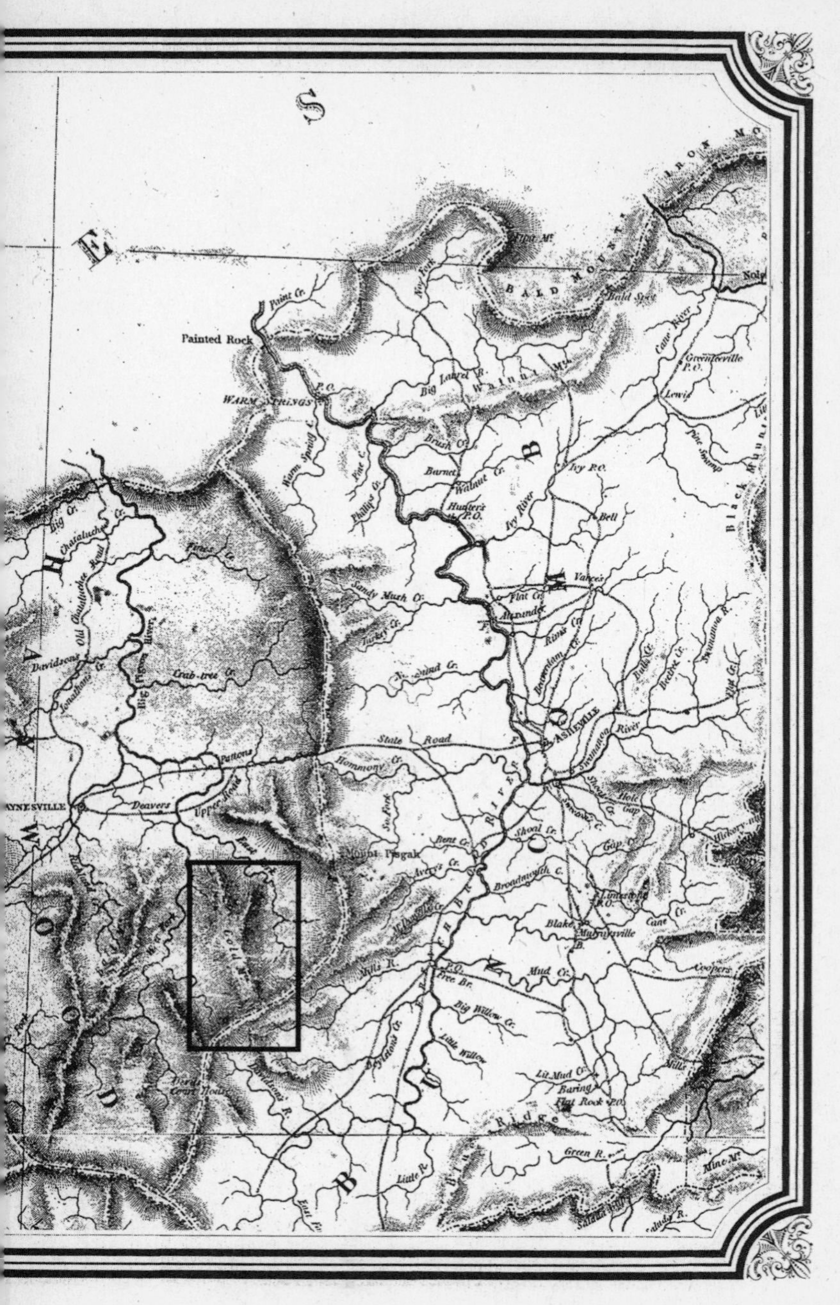
Painted Rock
WARM SPRINGS
P.O.
BALD MOUNTAIN
Walnut Mt.
Big Laurel B.
Brush Cr.
Barnet
Walnut Cr.
Hunter's P.O.
Ivy River
Ivy P.O.
Bell
Vance's
Flat Cr.
Alexander
Sandy Mush Cr.
Turkey Cr.
Big Cr.
Chataluchee Cr.
Old Chataluchee Road
Davidsons
Jonathan's Cr.
Big Pigeon River
Crab-tree Cr.
Pattons
State Road
Hommony Cr.
Deavers
Upper Road
ASHEVILLE
Swannanoa River
Mount Pisgah
Avery's Cr.
Shoal Cr.
Broadnax Cr.
Limestone P.O.
Blake
Cane Cr.
Mills R.
P.O.
Free Br.
Mud Cr.
Coopers
Big Willow Cr.
Little Willow
Lit. Mud Cr.
Baring
Flat Rock P.O.
Ridge
Green R.
Little R.
Mine Mt.
Cane River
Greenleeville P.O.
Lewis
Pine Swamp
Black Mountains
Bald Spot
Nola
Hickory-nut Gap
Cold Mt.
Saluda R.

COLD
MOUNTAIN

the shadow of a crow

At the first gesture of morning, flies began stirring. Inman's eyes and the long wound at his neck drew them, and the sound of their wings and the touch of their feet were soon more potent than a yardful of roosters in rousing a man to wake. So he came to yet one more day in the hospital ward. He flapped the flies away with his hands and looked across the foot of his bed to an open triple-hung window. Ordinarily he could see to the red road and the oak tree and the low brick wall. And beyond them to a sweep of fields and flat piney woods that stretched to the western horizon. The view was a long one for the flatlands, the hospital having been built on the only swell within eyeshot. But it was too early yet for a vista. The window might as well have been painted grey.

Had it not been too dim, Inman would have read to pass the time until breakfast, for the book he was reading had the effect of settling his mind. But he had burned up the last of his own candles reading to bring sleep the night before, and lamp oil was too scarce to be striking the hospital's lights for mere diversion. So he rose and dressed and sat in a ladderback chair, putting the

gloomy room of beds and their broken occupants behind him. He flapped again at the flies and looked out the window at the first smear of foggy dawn and waited for the world to begin shaping up outside.

The window was tall as a door, and he had imagined many times that it would open onto some other place and let him walk through and be there. During his first weeks in the hospital, he had been hardly able to move his head, and all that kept his mind occupied had been watching out the window and picturing the old green places he recollected from home. Childhood places. The damp creek bank where Indian pipes grew. The corner of a meadow favored by brown-and-black caterpillars in the fall. A hickory limb that overhung the lane, and from which he often watched his father driving cows down to the barn at dusk. They would pass underneath him, and then he would close his eyes and listen as the cupping sound of their hooves in the dirt grew fainter and fainter until it vanished into the calls of katydids and peepers. The window apparently wanted only to take his thoughts back. Which was fine with him, for he had seen the metal face of the age and had been so stunned by it that when he thought into the future, all he could vision was a world from which everything he counted important had been banished or had willingly fled.

By now he had stared at the window all through a late summer so hot and wet that the air both day and night felt like breathing through a dishrag, so damp it caused fresh sheets to sour under him and tiny black mushrooms to grow overnight from the limp pages of the book on his bedside table. Inman suspected that after such long examination, the grey window had finally said about all it had to say. That morning, though, it surprised him, for it brought to mind a lost memory of sitting in school, a similar tall window beside him framing a scene of pastures and low green ridges terracing up to the vast hump of Cold Mountain. It was September. The hayfield beyond the beaten dirt of the school playground stood pant-waist high, and the

heads of grasses were turning yellow from need of cutting. The teacher was a round little man, hairless and pink of face. He owned but one rusty black suit of clothes and a pair of old overlarge dress boots that curled up at the toes and were so worn down that the heels were wedgelike. He stood at the front of the room rocking on the points. He talked at length through the morning about history, teaching the older students of grand wars fought in ancient England.

After a time of actively not listening, the young Inman had taken his hat from under the desk and held it by its brim. He flipped his wrist, and the hat skimmed out the window and caught an updraft and soared. It landed far out across the playground at the edge of the hayfield and rested there black as the shadow of a crow squatted on the ground. The teacher saw what Inman had done and told him to go get it and to come back and take his whipping. The man had a big paddleboard with holes augered in it, and he liked to use it. Inman never did know what seized him at that moment, but he stepped out the door and set the hat on his head at a dapper rake and walked away, never to return.

The memory passed on as the light from the window rose toward day. The man in the bed next to Inman's sat and drew his crutches to him. As he did every morning, the man went to the window and spit repeatedly and with great effort until his clogged lungs were clear. He ran a comb through his black hair, which hung lank below his jaw and was cut square around. He tucked the long front pieces of hair behind his ears and put on his spectacles of smoked glass, which he wore even in the dim of morning, his eyes apparently too weak for the wannest form of light. Then, still in his nightshirt, he went to his table and began working at a pile of papers. He seldom spoke more than a word or two at a time, and Inman had learned little more of him than that his name was Balis and that before the war he had been to school at Chapel Hill, where he had attempted to master Greek. All his waking time was now spent trying to render ancient

scribble from a fat little book into plain writing anyone could read. He sat hunched at his table with his face inches from his work and squirmed in his chair, looking to find a comfortable position for his leg. His right foot had been taken off by grape at Cold Harbor, and the stub seemed not to want to heal and had rotted inch by inch from the ankle up. His amputations had now proceeded past the knee, and he smelled all the time like last year's ham.

For a while there was only the sound of Balis's pen scratching, pages turning. Then others in the room began to stir and cough, a few to moan. Eventually the light swelled so that all the lines of the varnished beadboard walls stood clear, and Inman could cock back on the chair's hind legs and count the flies on the ceiling. He made it to be sixty-three.

As Inman's view through the window solidified, the dark trunks of the oak trees showed themselves first, then the patchy lawn, and finally the red road. He was waiting for the blind man to come. He had attended to the man's movements for some weeks, and now that he had healed enough to be numbered among the walking, Inman was determined to go out to the cart and speak to the man, for Inman figured him to have been living with a wound for a long time.

Inman had taken his own during the fighting outside Petersburg. When his two nearest companions pulled away his clothes and looked at his neck, they had said him a solemn farewell in expectation of his death. We'll meet again in a better world, they said. But he lived as far as the field hospital, and there the doctors had taken a similar attitude. He was classed among the dying and put aside on a cot to do so. But he failed at it. After two days, space being short, they sent him on to a regular hospital in his own state. All through the mess of the field hospital and the long grim train ride south in a boxcar filled with wounded, he had agreed with his friends and the doctors. He thought he would die. About all he could remember of the trip was the heat and the odors of blood and of shit, for many of the wounded had

the flux. Those with the strength to do so had knocked holes in the sides of the wood boxcars with the butts of rifles and rode with their heads thrust out like crated poultry to catch the breeze.

At the hospital, the doctors looked at him and said there was not much they could do. He might live or he might not. They gave him but a grey rag and a little basin to clean his own wound. Those first few days, when he broke consciousness enough to do it, he wiped at his neck with the rag until the water in the basin was the color of the comb on a turkey-cock. But mainly the wound had wanted to clean itself. Before it started scabbing, it spit out a number of things: a collar button and a piece of wool collar from the shirt he had been wearing when he was hit, a shard of soft grey metal as big as a quarter dollar piece, and, unaccountably, something that closely resembled a peach pit. That last he set on the nightstand and studied for some days. He could never settle his mind on whether it was a part of him or not. He finally threw it out the window but then had troubling dreams that it had taken root and grown, like Jack's bean, into something monstrous.

His neck had eventually decided to heal. But during the weeks when he could neither turn his head nor hold up a book to read, Inman had lain every day watching the blind man. The man would arrive alone shortly after dawn, pushing his cart up the road, doing it about as well as any man who could see. He would set up his business under an oak tree across the road, lighting a fire in a ring of stones and boiling peanuts over it in an iron pot. He would sit all day on a stool with his back to the brick wall, selling peanuts and newspapers to those at the hospital whole enough to walk. Unless someone came to buy something, he rested as still as a stuffed man with his hands together in his lap.

That summer, Inman had viewed the world as if it were a picture framed by the molding around the window. Long stretches of time often passed when, for all the change in the

scene, it might as well have been an old painting of a road, a wall, a tree, a cart, a blind man. Inman had sometimes counted off slow numbers in his head to see how long it would be before anything of significance altered. It was a game and he had rules for it. A bird flying by did not count. Someone walking down the road did. Major weather changes did—the sun coming out, fresh rain—but shadows of passing clouds did not. Some days he'd get up in the thousands before there was any allowable alteration in the elements of the picture. He believed the scene would never leave his mind—wall, blind man, tree, cart, road—no matter how far on he lived. He imagined himself an old man thinking about it. Those pieces together seemed to offer some meaning, though he did not know what and suspected he never would.

Inman watched the window as he ate his breakfast of boiled oats and butter, and shortly he saw the blind man come trudging up the road, his back humped against the weight of the cart he pushed, little twin clouds of dust rising from beneath the turning cartwheels. When the blind man had his fire going and his peanuts boiling, Inman put his plate on the windowsill and went outside and with the shuffling step of an old man crossed the lawn to the road.

The blind man was square and solid in shoulder and hip, and his britches were cinched at the waist with a great leather belt, wide as a razor strop. He went hatless, even in the heat, and his cropped hair was thick and grey, coarse-textured as the bristles to a hemp brush. He sat with his head tipped down and appeared to be somewhat in a muse, but he raised up as Inman approached, like he was really looking. His eyelids, though, were dead as shoe leather and were sunken into puckered cups where his eyeballs had been.

Without pausing even for salutation Inman said, Who put out your pair of eyes?

The blind man had a friendly smile on his face and he said, Nobody. I never had any.

That took Inman aback, for his imagination had worked in

the belief that they had been plucked out in some desperate and bloody dispute, some brute fraction. Every vile deed he had witnessed lately had been at the hand of a human agent, so he had about forgot that there was a whole other order of misfortune.

—Why did you never have any? Inman said.

—Just happened that way.

—Well, Inman said. You're mighty calm. Especially for a man that most would say has taken the little end of the horn all his life.

The blind man said, It might have been worse had I ever been given a glimpse of the world and then lost it.

—Maybe, Inman said. Though what would you pay right now to have your eyeballs back for ten minutes? Plenty, I bet.

The man studied on the question. He worked his tongue around the corner of his mouth. He said, I'd not give an Indian-head cent. I fear it might turn me hateful.

—It's done it to me, Inman said. There's plenty I wish I'd never seen.

—That's not the way I meant it. You said ten minutes. It's having a thing and the loss I'm talking about.

The blind man twisted a square of newsprint up into a cone and then dipped with a riddly spoon into the pot and filled the cone with wet peanuts. He handed it to Inman and said, Come on, cite me one instance where you wished you were blind.

Where to begin? Inman wondered. Malvern Hill. Sharpsburg. Petersburg. Any would do admirably as example of unwelcome visions. But Fredericksburg was a day particularly lodged in his mind. So he sat with his back to the oak and halved the wet peanut shells and thumbed the meats out into his mouth and told the blind man his tale, beginning with how the fog had lifted that morning to reveal a vast army marching uphill toward a stone wall, a sunken road. Inman's regiment was called to join the men already behind the wall, and they had quickly formed up alongside the big white house at the top of Maryes Heights. Lee and Longstreet and befeathered Stuart stood right there

on the lawn before the porch, taking turns glassing the far side of the river and talking. Longstreet had a grey shawl of wool draped about his shoulders. Compared to the other two men, Longstreet looked like a stout hog drover. But from what Inman had seen of Lee's way of thinking, he'd any day rather have Longstreet backing him in a fight. Dull as Longstreet looked, he had a mind that constantly sought ground configured so a man could hunker down and do a world of killing from a position of relative safety. And that day at Fredericksburg was all in the form of fighting that Lee mistrusted and that Longstreet welcomed.

After Inman's regiment had formed up, they dropped over the brow of the hill and into the withering fire of the Federals. They stopped once to touch off a volley, and then they ran down to the sunken road behind the stone wall. On the way a ball brushed the skin of Inman's wrist and felt like the tongue of a cat licking, doing no damage, only making a little abraded stripe.

When they got to the road, Inman could see they were in a fine spot. Those already there had trenched along the tightly built wall so that you could stand up comfortably and still be in its shelter. The Federals had to come uphill at the wall across acres and acres of open ground. So delightful was the spot that one man jumped onto the wall and hollered out, You are all committing a mistake. You hear? A dire mistake! Balls whistled all about the man, and he jumped back down into the ditch behind the wall and danced a jig.

It was a cold day and the mud of the road was near frozen to the condition of slurry. Some of the men were barefoot. Many wore homemade uniforms in the mute colors that plant dyes make. The Federals were arrayed on the field before them, all newly outfitted. Bright and shiny in factory-made uniforms, new boots. When the Federals charged, the men behind the wall held their fire and taunted them and one called out, Come on closer, I want them boots. And they let the Federals come as near as twenty paces before shooting them down. The

men behind the wall were firing at such close range that one man remarked on what a shame it was that they had paper cartridges, for if they had the separate makings—powder, ball, and wadding—they could tamp in thrifty little loads and thus save on powder.

When he was squatted down loading, Inman could hear the firing, but also the slap of balls into meat. A man near Inman grew so excited, or perhaps so weary, that he forgot to pull the ramrod from the barrel. He fired it off and it struck a Federal in the chest. The man fell backward, and the rod stood from his body and quavered about with the last of his breathing as if he had been pierced by an unfletched arrow.

The Federals kept on marching by the thousands at the wall all through the day, climbing the hill to be shot down. There were three or four brick houses scattered out through the field, and after a time the Federals crowded up behind them in such numbers that they looked like the long blue shadows of houses at sunrise. Periodically they were driven from behind the houses by their own cavalry, who beat at them with the flats of their sabers like schoolteachers paddling truants. Then they ran toward the wall leaning forward with their shoulders hunched, a posture that reminded many witnesses that day of men seeking headway against a hard blowing rain. The Federals kept on coming long past the point where all the pleasure of whipping them vanished. Inman just got to hating them for their clodpated determination to die.

The fighting was in the way of a dream, one where your foes are ranked against you countless and mighty. And you so weak. And yet they fall and keep falling until they are crushed. Inman had fired until his right arm was weary from working the ramrod, his jaws sore from biting the ends off the paper cartridges. His rifle became so hot that the powder would sometimes flash before he could ram home the ball. At the end of the day the faces of the men around him were caked with blown-back powder so that they were various shades of blue, and they put Inman

in mind of a great ape with a bulbous colorful ass he had seen in a traveling show once.

They had fought throughout the day under the eyes of Lee and Longstreet. The men behind the wall had only to crank their necks around and there the big men were, right above them looking on. The two generals spent the afternoon up on the hill coining fine phrases like a pair of wags. Longstreet said his men in the sunken road were in such a position that if you marched every man in the Army of the Potomac across that field, his men would kill them before they got to the wall. And he said the Federals fell that long afternoon as steady as rain dripping down from the eaves of a house.

Old Lee, not to be outdone, said it's a good thing war is so terrible or else we'd get to liking it too much. As with everything Marse Robert said, the men repeated that flight of wit over and over, passing it along from man to man, as if God amighty Himself had spoken. When the report reached Inman's end of the wall he just shook his head. Even back then, early in the war, his opinion differed considerably from Lee's, for it appeared to him that we like fighting plenty, and the more terrible it is the better. And he suspected that Lee liked it most of all and would, if given his preference, general them right through the gates of death itself. What troubled Inman most, though, was that Lee made it clear he looked on war as an instrument for clarifying God's obscure will. Lee seemed to think battle—among all acts man might commit—stood outranked in sacredness only by prayer and Bible reading. Inman worried that following such logic would soon lead one to declare the victor of every brawl and dogfight as God's certified champion. Those thoughts were unspeakable among the ranks, as were his feelings that he did not enlist to take on a Marse, even one as solemn and noble-looking as Lee was that day on Maryes Heights.

Late in the afternoon the Federals quit coming and the shooting tapered off. Thousands of men lay dead and dying on the sloping field below the wall, and by dark the ones who could

move had heaped up corpses to make shelter. All that night the aurora flamed and shimmered lurid colors across the sky to the north. Such a rare event was seen as an omen by the men up and down the line, and they vied to see who could most convincingly render its meaning down into plain speech. Somewhere above them on the hill a fiddle struck up the sad chords of Lorena. The wounded Federals moaned and keened and hummed between gritted teeth on the frozen field and some called out the names of loved ones.

To this accompaniment, the poorly shod of Inman's party climbed over the wall to yank the boots off the dead. Though his own boots were in fair shape, Inman made a late-night foray onto the field simply to see what the day's effort had accomplished.The Federals were thick on the ground, lying all about in bloody heaps, bodies disassembled in every style the mind could imagine. A man walking next to Inman looked out upon the scene and said, If I had my way everything north of the Potomac would resemble that right down to the last particular. Inman's only thought looking on the enemy was, Go home. Some of the dead had papers pinned to their clothing to say who they had been, and the rest were just anonymous. Inman saw one man squat to yank the boots off a body lying flat on its back, but as the man lifted a foot and pulled, the dead man sat up and said something in an Irish accent so thick the only understandable word was Shit.

Later, many hours after midnight, Inman looked into one of the houses scattered about the field. A light shone out from an open door at its gable end. An old woman sat inside, her hair in a wild tangle, face stricken. A lit candle stub stood beside her on a table. Corpses on her doorstep. Others inside, dead in the attitude of crawling to shelter. The woman staring crazed past the threshold, past Inman's face, as if she saw nothing. Inman walked through the house and out the back door and saw a man killing a group of badly wounded Federals by striking them in the head with a hammer. The Federals had been arranged in an

order, with their heads all pointing one way, and the man moved briskly down the row, making a clear effort to let one strike apiece do. Not angry, just moving from one to one like a man with a job of work to get done. He whistled, almost under his breath, the tune of Cora Ellen. He might have been shot had one of the fine-minded officers caught him, but he was tired and wished to be shut of a few more enemies at little risk to himself. Inman would always remember that, as the man came to the end of the row, the first light of dawn came up on his face.

The blind man had sat wordless throughout Inman's tale. But when Inman was finished, the man said, You need to put that away from you.

—I'd not differ with you there, Inman said.

But what Inman did not tell the blind man was that no matter how he tried, the field that night would not leave him but had instead provided him with a recurring dream, one that had visited him over and over during his time in the hospital. In the dream, the aurora blazed and the scattered bloody pieces—arms, heads, legs, trunks—slowly drew together and re-formed themselves into monstrous bodies of mismatched parts. They limped and reeled and lunged about the dark battlefield like blind sots on their faulty legs. They jounced off one another, butting bloody cleft heads in their stupor. They waved their assorted arms in the air, and few of the hands made convincing pairs. Some spoke the names of their women. Some sang snatches of song over and over. Others stood to the side and looked off into the dark and urgently called their dogs.

One figure, whose wounds were so dreadful that he more resembled meat than man, tried to rise but could not. He flopped and then lay still but for the turning of his head. From the ground he craned his neck and looked at Inman with dead eyes and spoke Inman's name in a low voice. Every morning after that dream, Inman awoke in a mood as dark as the blackest crow that ever flew.

Inman returned to the ward, tired from his walk. Balis sat

goggled in the dim room and scratched with his quill at the papers. Inman got into bed thinking to nap away the rest of the morning, but he could not make his mind rest, so he took up his book to read. What he had was the third part of Bartram's *Travels*. He had pulled it from a box of books donated by ladies of the capital eager for the intellectual as well as physical improvement of the patients. Apparently, the book had been given away because it had lost its front cover, so Inman, in an effort toward symmetry, had torn the back cover off as well, leaving only the leather spine. He kept the book tied into a scroll with a piece of twine.

It was not a book that required following from front to back, and Inman simply opened it at random, as he had done night after night in the hospital to read until he was calm enough for sleep. The doings of that kind lone wanderer—called Flower Gatherer by the Cherokee in honor of his satchels full with plants and his attention all given to the growth of wild living things—never failed to ease his thoughts. The passage he turned to that morning became a favorite, and the first sentence that fell under his eye was this:

> Continued yet ascending until I gained the top of an elevated rocky ridge, when appeared before me a gap or opening between other yet more lofty ascents, through which continued as the rough rocky road led me, close by the winding banks of a large rapid brook, which at length turning to the left, pouring down rocky precipices, glided off through dark groves and high forests, conveying streams of fertility and pleasure to the fields below.

Such images made Inman happy, as did the following pages wherein Bartram, ecstatic, journeyed on to the Vale of Cowee deep in the mountains, breathlessly describing a world of scarp and crag, ridge after ridge fading off blue into the distance, chanting at length as he went the names of all the plants that

came under his gaze as if reciting the ingredients of a powerful potion. After a time, though, Inman found that he had left the book and was simply forming the topography of home in his head. Cold Mountain, all its ridges and coves and watercourses. Pigeon River, Little East Fork, Sorrell Cove, Deep Gap, Fire Scald Ridge. He knew their names and said them to himself like the words of spells and incantations to ward off the things one fears most.

Some days later Inman walked from the hospital into town. His neck hurt as if a red cord running from it to the balls of his feet were yanked quivering tight at each step. But his legs felt strong, and that worried him. As soon as he was fit to fight, they would ship him right back to Virginia. Nevertheless, he was glad to be a man of leisure as long as he was careful not to look too vigorous in front of a doctor.

Money had come from home and a portion of back pay had been handed out, so he walked about the streets and shopped in the red-brick and white-frame shops. At a tailor's he found a black suitcoat of tightly woven wool that fit him perfectly, despite having been cut to the measure of a man who had died during its making. The tailor sold it at a bargain, and Inman put it right on and wore it out the door. At a general mercantile he bought a stiff pair of indigo denim britches, a cream-colored wool shirt, two pairs of socks, a clasp knife, a sheath knife, a little pot and cup, and all the loads and round tins of caps for his pistol that they had in stock. These were wrapped together in brown paper, and he carried the bundle away with a finger hooked in the crossed twine. At a hatmaker's, he bought a black slouch hat with a grey ribbon band; then, back out on the street, he took off his greasy old one and skimmed it away to land among the bean rows of somebody's garden. They might find use for it as scarecrow attire. He set the new hat on his head and went to a cobbler's, where he found a good pair of stout boots

that were a close fit. His old ones he left sitting curled and withered and caved in on the floor. At a stationer's, he bought a pen with a gold nib and a bottle of ink and a few sheets of writing paper. By the time he was done shopping, he had spent a pile of near-worthless paper money big enough to kindle a fire from green wood.

Tired, he stopped at an inn near the domed capitol and sat at a table under a tree. He drank a cup of brew said by the tavern keeper to be coffee brought in through the blockade, though from the look of the grounds it was mostly chicory and burnt corn grits with little more than the dust of actual coffee beans. The metal table was rusting in a powdery orange rind around its edges, and Inman had to take care not to scrub the sleeves of his new coat against the decay as he returned his coffee cup to its saucer. He sat a bit formally, back straight, fisted hands resting on his thigh tops. To an observer standing out in the center of the road looking back toward the tables in the shade of the oak tree, he would have looked stern and uncomfortable in his black coat, the white dressing twisted about his neck like a tight cravat. He might have been mistaken for a man sitting suspended during a long daguerreotype exposure, a subject who had become dazed and disoriented as the clock ticked away and the slow plate soaked up his image and fixed for all time a portion of his soul.

Inman was thinking of the blind man. He had bought a copy of the *Standard* from him that morning as he had done every morning lately. Inman pitied the blind man now that he knew how his blindness had come about, for how did you find someone to hate for a thing that just was? What would be the cost of not having an enemy? Who could you strike for retribution other than yourself?

Inman drank all but the dregs of his coffee and then took up his paper, hoping that something in it would engage him and turn his thoughts elsewhere. He tried to read a piece on how badly things stood outside Petersburg, but he couldn't get a grip

on it. And anyway, he knew about all there was to say on that topic. When he got to the third page, he found a notice from the state government to deserters and outliers and their families. They would be hunted down. Their names would be put on a list, and the Home Guard would be on alert in every county, patrolling night and day. Then Inman read a story buried at the bottom of a page in the paper's middle. It told that out in the borderlands of the state's western mountains, Thomas and his Cherokee troops had fought numerous skirmishes with Federals. They had been accused of taking scalps. The paper opined that though the practice might be barbarous, it would serve as harsh warning that invasion carried a stiff price.

Inman put the paper down and thought about Cherokee boys scalping Federals. It was humorous in a way, those pale mill workers coming down so confident to steal land and yet losing the tops of their heads out in the woods. Inman knew many Cherokee of the age to be fighting under Thomas, and he wondered if Swimmer was among them. He had met Swimmer the summer they were both sixteen. Inman had been given the happy job of escorting a few heifers to graze the last grass of summer in the high balds on Balsam Mountain. He had taken a packhorse loaded with cooking tools, side meat, meal, fishing gear, a shotgun, quilts, and a square of waxed canvas for tent. He expected solitude and self-reliance. But when he got to the bald there was a regular party going on. A dozen or so men from Cataloochee had made camp at the crest of the ridge and had been there for a week or better, lazing in the cool air of the uplands and joying in the freeing distance from hearth and home. It was a fine place, there on the bald. They had sweeping views to east and west, good pasturage for the cattle, trout streams nearby. Inman joined the men, and for several days they cooked enormous meals of fried corn bread and trout and stews of game animals over a large fire that they kept burning knee-high day and night. They washed the food down with every manner of corn

liquor and apple brandy and thick mead so that many in the group laid up drunk from one dawn to the next.

Soon, a band of Cherokee from Cove Creek had come up the other side of the divide with a rawboned herd of spotted cows of no singular breed. The Indians made their camp a short distance away and then cut tall pines and crafted goals from them and marked off boundaries for their vicious ball game. Swimmer, an odd big-handed boy with wide-set eyes, came over and invited the Catalooch party to play, hinting darkly that men sometimes died in the game. Inman and others took up the challenge. They cut and split green saplings to make their own ball racquets, strung them with strips of hide and bootlace.

The two groups camped side by side for two weeks, the younger men playing the ball game most of the day, gambling heavily on the outcomes. It was a contest with no fixed time of play and few rules so that they just ran about slamming into each other and hacking with the racquets as if with clubs until one team reached a set number of points scored by striking the goalposts with the ball. They'd play most of the day and then spend half the night drinking and telling tales at fireside, eating great heaps of little speckled trout, fried crisp, bones and all.

There in the highlands, clear weather held for much of the time. The air lacked its usual haze, and the view stretched on and on across rows of blue mountains, each paler than the last until the final ranks were indistinguishable from sky. It was as if all the world might be composed of nothing but valley and ridge. During a pause in the play, Swimmer had looked out at the landforms and said he believed Cold Mountain to be the chief mountain of the world. Inman asked how he knew that to be true, and Swimmer had swept his hand across the horizon to where Cold Mountain stood and said, Do you see a bigger'n?

Mornings on the high bald were crisp, with fog lying in the valleys so that the peaks rose from it disconnected like steep blue islands scattered across a pale sea. Inman would awake, still

part drunk, and walk off down in a cove to fish with Swimmer for an hour or two before returning for the beginning of the game. They would sit by the rushing creek, stickbait and rockbait on their hooks. Swimmer would talk seamlessly in a low voice so that it merged with the sound of the water. He told tales of animals and how they came to be as they are. Possum with bare tail, squirrel with fuzzy tail. Buck with antlers. Painter with tooth and claw. Uktena with coil and fang. Tales that explained how the world came about and where it is heading. Swimmer also told of spells he was learning for making desired ends come to pass. He told of ways to produce misfortune, sickness, death, how to return evil by way of fire, how to protect the lone traveler on the road at night, and how to make the road seem short. A number of the spells had to do with the spirit. Swimmer knew a few ways to kill the soul of an enemy and many ways to protect your own. His spells portrayed the spirit as a frail thing, constantly under attack and in need of strength, always threatening to die inside you. Inman found this notion dismal indeed, since he had been taught by sermon and hymn to hold as truth that the soul of man never dies.

Inman sat through the tales and spells, watching the rill in the water where current fell against his dipped line, Swimmer's voice a rush of sound, soothing as creek noise. When they had caught a sackful of little trout, they would quit and go back and then spend the day swatting at each other with the ball sticks, shoving and shouldering and coming to blows.

After many days wet weather set in, and none too soon, for on both sides they were all worn out, hung over, and beat up. There were broken fingers and noses, sundry flesh rents. All were mottled ankle to hip with blue and green bruises from the racquets. The Catalooch party had lost to the Indians everything they could do without and some things they couldn't—fry pans and dutch ovens, sacks of meal, fishing poles, rifles and pistols. Inman himself had lost an entire cow, a fact he could not figure how to explain to his father. He had bet it away piece by piece,

point by point. Saying in the heat of play, I'll wager the tenderloin of that heifer on this next point. Or, Every rib on the left side of my betting cow says we win. As the two camps parted ways, Inman's heifer was still walking, but various of the Cherokee had claim to its many partitions.

As recompense and memento, though, Swimmer had given Inman a fine ball racquet of hickory with bat whiskers twisted into the squirrel-skin lacing. Swimmer claimed it would power its user with the speed and deception of the bat. It was decorated with the feathers of swallows and hawks and herons, and, as Swimmer explained it, the characters of those animals too would transfer to Inman—wheeling grace, soar and stoop, grim single-mindedness. Not all of that had come to pass, but Inman hoped Swimmer was not out fighting Federals but living in a bark hut by a rushing stream.

From inside the tavern came the sounds of a fiddle being tuned, various plucks and tentative bowings, then a slow and groping attempt at Aura Lee, interrupted every few notes by unplanned squeaks and howls. Nevertheless the beautiful and familiar tune was impervious to poor performance, and Inman thought how painfully young it sounded, as if the pattern of its notes allowed no room to imagine a future clouded and tangled and diminished.

He raised his coffee cup to his lips and found it cold and nearly empty, and he put it down. He stared into it and watched the dark grounds sink in the remaining quarter inch of liquid. The black flecks swirled, found a pattern, and settled. He thought briefly of divination, seeking the future in the arrangement of coffee grounds, tea leaves, hog entrails, shapes of clouds. As if pattern told something worth knowing. He jostled the cup to break the spell and looked out along the street. Beyond a row of young trees rose the capitol, an impressive domed pile of stone blocks. It was only a scant shade darker than the high clouds through which the sun shone as a grey disc already declining to the west. In the haze the capitol seemed to rise im-

possibly high, its bulk large as a medieval tower in a dream of siege. Curtains blew out of open office windows and waggled in the breeze. Above the dome, a dark circle of vultures swirled in the oyster sky, their long wimple feathers just visible at their blunt wing ends. As Inman watched, the birds did not strike a wingbeat but nonetheless climbed gradually, riding a rising column of air, circling higher and higher until they were little dashes of black on the sky.

In his mind, Inman likened the swirling paths of vulture flight to the coffee grounds seeking pattern in his cup. Anyone could be oracle for the random ways things fall against each other. It was simple enough to tell fortunes if a man dedicated himself to the idea that the future will inevitably be worse than the past and that time is a path leading nowhere but a place of deep and persistent threat. The way Inman saw it, if a thing like Fredericksburg was to be used as a marker of current position, then many years hence, at the rate we're going, we'll be eating one another raw.

And, too, Inman guessed Swimmer's spells were right in saying a man's spirit could be torn apart and cease and yet his body keep on living. They could take death blows independently. He was himself a case in point, and perhaps not a rare one, for his spirit, it seemed, had been about burned out of him but he was yet walking. Feeling empty, however, as the core of a big blackgum tree. Feeling strange as well, for his recent experience had led him to fear that the mere existence of the Henry repeating rifle or the éprouvette mortar made all talk of spirit immediately antique. His spirit, he feared, had been blasted away so that he had become lonesome and estranged from all around him as a sad old heron standing pointless watch in the mudflats of a pond lacking frogs. It seemed a poor swap to find that the only way one might keep from fearing death was to act numb and set apart as if dead already, with nothing much left of yourself but a hut of bones.

As Inman sat brooding and pining for his lost self, one of Swimmer's creekside stories rushed into his memory with a great urgency and attractiveness. Swimmer claimed that above the blue vault of heaven there was a forest inhabited by a celestial race. Men could not go there to stay and live, but in that high land the dead spirit could be reborn. Swimmer described it as a far and inaccessible region, but he said the highest mountains lifted their dark summits into its lower reaches. Signs and wonders both large and small did sometimes make transit from that world to our own. Animals, Swimmer said, were its primary messengers. Inman had pointed out to Swimmer that he had climbed Cold Mountain to its top, and Pisgah and Mount Sterling as well. Mountains did not get much higher than those, and Inman had seen no upper realm from their summits.

—There's more to it than just the climbing, Swimmer had said. Though Inman could not recall whether Swimmer had told him what else might be involved in reaching that healing realm, Cold Mountain nevertheless soared in his mind as a place where all his scattered forces might gather. Inman did not consider himself to be a superstitious person, but he did believe that there is a world invisible to us. He no longer thought of that world as heaven, nor did he still think that we get to go there when we die. Those teachings had been burned away. But he could not abide by a universe composed only of what he could see, especially when it was so frequently foul. So he held to the idea of another world, a better place, and he figured he might as well consider Cold Mountain to be the location of it as anywhere.

Inman took his new coat off and draped it across his chairback. He commenced working on a letter. It was long, and as the afternoon passed he drank several more cups of coffee and darkened a number of pages front and back with ink. He found himself telling things he did not want to tell about the fighting. At one point he wrote:

> The ground was awash with blood and we could see where the blood had flown onto the rocks and the marks of bloody hands on tree trunks. . . .

Then he stopped and wadded up his efforts and started again on a fresh sheet and this was part of what he wrote:

> I am coming home one way or another, and I do not know how things might stand between us. I first thought to tell in this letter what I have done and seen so that you might judge me before I return. But I decided it would need a page as broad as the blue sky to write that tale, and I have not the will or the energy. Do you recall that night before Christmas four years ago when I took you in my lap in the kitchen by the stove and you told me you would forever like to sit there and rest your head on my shoulder? Now it is a bitter surety in my heart that if you knew what I have seen and done, it would make you fear to do such again.

Inman sat back and looked across the capitol lawn. A woman in a white dress carrying a small wrapped parcel hurried across the grass. A black carriage went by on the street between the capitol and the red stone church. A wind stirred up dust in the roadway, and Inman noticed that the afternoon was far advanced, the light falling at a slant that spoke of autumn coming. He felt the breeze work its way through a fold in the bandage and touch the wound at his neck, which began aching in the moving air.

Inman stood and doubled up the letter and then put his hand above his collar and fingered the scabbed slash. The doctors now claimed he was healing quickly, but he still felt he could poke a stick in there and push it out the other side with no more resistance offered than might a rotted pumpkin. It still hurt to

talk and to eat and, sometimes, to breathe. Troubling as well were the deep pains on humid days from the hip wound he had taken at Malvern Hill years ago. All in all, his wounds gave him just reason to doubt that he would ever heal up and feel whole and of a piece again. But on the walk down the street to post the letter and then back out to the hospital, his legs felt surprisingly sturdy and willing.

When he reached his ward, Inman saw immediately that Balis was not at his table. His bed was empty. His dark goggles rested atop his pile of papers. Inman asked after him and was told that he had died in the afternoon, a quiet death. He had looked grey and had moved from his table to the bed. He had turned on his side and faced the wall and died as if falling asleep.

Inman went to the papers and riffled through them. The top of the first page said Fragments, and the word was underscored three times. The work seemed a confusing mess. The handwriting was spidery, thin and angular. There were more strikeovers and cross-hatchings than plain writing. And what could be made out clear was just a line here and there, sometimes not even a sentence but just a shattered-off piece of one. A sentiment that struck Inman's eye as he leafed through the pages was this: "We mark some days as fair, some as foul, because we do not see that the character of every day is identical."

Inman believed he would rather die than subscribe to that, and it made him sad to think that Balis had spent his last days studying on the words of a fool. But then he came upon a line that seemed to have more sense to it. It was this: "The comeliest order on earth is but a heap of random sweepings." That, Inman decided, he could consent to. He tapped the pages against the desktop to square their edges and then he set them down in their place.

After supper, Inman checked the packs under his bed. To the blanket and waxed-cloth groundsheet already in his knapsack he added the cup and little pot, the sheath knife. The haversack had for some time been filled with dried biscuit, some

cornmeal, a chunk of salt pork, a little dried beef that he had bought off the hospital staff.

He sat at the window and watched the close of day. Sunset was troubling. Low grey clouds massed at the flat horizon, but as the sun fell to earthline it found an opening in the clouds and shot a beam of light the color of hot hickory coals straight upward. The light was tubular and hard-edged as the barrel of a rifle and stood reared up into the sky for a full five minutes before winking out abruptly. Nature, Inman was fully aware, sometimes calls attention to its special features and recommends them for interpretation. This sign, though, as best he could tell, spoke of nothing but strife, danger, grief. Of those he needed no reminder, so he judged the show a great waste of effort. He got in bed and pulled up the covers. Tired from his day of walking about town, Inman read only a short time before falling asleep while it was yet grey dusk.

He awakened sometime deep in the night. The room was black, and the only sounds were those of men breathing and snoring and shifting about in their beds. There was only faint light from the window, and he could see the bright beacon of Jupiter declining to the western horizon. Wind came in the windows, and the pages of dead Balis fluttered on the table and a few of them curled back and half stood so that they caught the faint window light through their backsides and glowed like runtish ghosts come haunting.

Inman rose and dressed in his new clothes. He added his Bartram scroll to the knapsack; then he strapped on his packs and went to the tall open window and looked out. It was the dark of the new moon. Ribbons of fog moved low on the ground though the sky was clear overhead. He set his foot on the sill and stepped out the window.

the ground beneath her hands

Ada sat on the porch of the house that was now hers, a portable writing desk balanced across her lap. She wet the nib of a pen in ink and wrote:

> This you must know: that despite your long absence, such is the light in which I view the happy relation existing between us, that I will never conceal a single thought from you. Let such fears not trouble you. Know that I consider it a mutual duty, that we owe to each other, to communicate in a spirit of the utmost frankness and candor. Let it ever be done with unlocked hearts.

She blew the paper to dry it and then scanned over what she had written with a critical eye. She mistrusted her handwriting, for no matter how she tried, she had never mastered the flowing whorls and arcs of fine penmanship. The characters her hand insisted on forming were instead blocky and dense as runes. Even more than the penmanship, she disliked the tenor of the letter. She balled up the paper and tossed it into a boxwood bush.

Aloud she said, That is just the way people talk and has nothing to do with the real matter at hand.

She looked off across the yard to the kitchen garden where the beans and squash and tomatoes bore vegetables hardly bigger than her thumb despite the fullness of the growing season. Many of the leaves were eaten away to their veins by bugs and worms. Standing thick in the rows and towering over the vegetables were weeds that Ada could not name and had neither the energy nor the heart to fight. Beyond the failed garden stretched the old cornfield, now grown up shoulder high in poke and sumac. Above the fields and pastures, the mountains were just becoming visible as the morning fog burned away. Their pale outlines stood at the horizon, more like the ghosts of mountains than the actual things.

Ada sat waiting for them to reveal themselves clearly. Her thinking was that it would be a comfort to see something that was as it should be, for otherwise her mind troubled itself with the thought that everything else in her sight was marked by neglect. Since her father's funeral, Ada had hardly turned her hand around the farm. She had at least milked the cow, which Monroe had named Waldo with disregard for gender, and fed the horse, Ralph, but she had not done much more, for she did not know how to do much more. She had left the chickens to fend for themselves and they had gotten skinny and skittish. The hens had abandoned the little chicken house and roosted in trees and dropped their eggs wherever the mood struck them. They vexed Ada with their inability to settle on nesting places. She had to investigate every cranny of the yard to find the eggs, and lately she believed they had taken on a strange taste since the hens' diet had changed from table scraps to bugs.

Cookery had become a pressing issue for Ada. She was perpetually hungry, having eaten little through the summer but milk, fried eggs, salads, and plates of miniature tomatoes from the untended plants that had grown wild and bushy with suckers. Even butter had proved beyond her means, for the milk she

had tried to churn never firmed up beyond the consistency of runny clabber. She wanted a bowl of chicken and dumplings and a peach pie but had not a clue how one might arrive at them.

Ada cast one more look to the far mountains, still faint and pale, and then she rose and went in search of eggs. She checked the weeds along the fence by the lane, parted the long grass at the base of the pear tree in the side yard, rattled among the clutter of the back porch, ran her hands along the dusty shelves in the toolshed. She found nothing.

She recalled that a red hen had sometimes lately taken to hanging about the big boxwoods at either side of the front steps. She went to the bush that she had thrown the letter into and tried to part the dense leafage and peer inside, but she could see nothing in the dim center. She folded her skirts tightly about her legs, and on hands and knees she worked her way inside the boxwood. Its branches scratched at her forearms and face and neck as she pushed forward. The ground beneath her hands was dry and littered with chicken feathers and old chicken shit and the hard dead leaves of the bush. Inside, there was a hollow place. The thick outer growth of leaves was just a husk enclosing a space like a tiny room.

Ada sat up in it and looked about on the ground and in the branches for eggs but found only a broken shell, dried yolk the color of rust in one jag-edged cup. She fitted herself between two limbs and rested with her back against the trunk. The boxwood bower smelled of dust and of the sharpness and bitterness of chickens. Its light was dim, and it reminded her of childhood play in caves made by draping sheets over tables or by tenting carpets over clotheslines. Best of all were the tunnels she and her cousin Lucy dug deep into haystacks on her uncle's farm. They had spent entire rainy afternoons snug and dry as denned foxes, whispering secrets to each other.

It was with a familiar delicious tingle of pleasure, a tightening in her breathing, that she realized she was now similarly hidden away, that anyone walking from the gate to the porch would

never know she was there. If one of the ladies from the church made an obligatory visit to see about her welfare, she could sit motionless as they called her name and knocked at the door. She would not come out until long after she had heard the gate latch clack shut. But she expected no one to call. The visits had tapered off in the face of her indifference to them.

Ada looked up with some disappointment to the faint lacework of pale blue sky visible through the leaves. She wished rain were falling so she would feel even more protected as it rustled the leaves overhead. The occasional drop that might find its way through, plopping a tiny crater into the dust, would only emphasize that though inside she remained dry, outside rain fell wholesale. Ada wished never to leave this fine shelter, for when she considered the pass she had lately reached, she wondered how a human being could be raised more impractically for the demands of an exposed life.

She had grown up in Charleston and at Monroe's insistence had been educated beyond the point considered wise for females. She had become a knowledgeable companion for him, a lively and attentive daughter. She was filled with opinions on art and politics and literature, and ready to argue the merits of her positions. But what actual talents could she claim? What gifts? A fair command of French and Latin. A hint of Greek. A passable hand at fine needlework. A competency at the piano, though no brilliance. The ability to render landscape and still life with accuracy in either pencil or watercolor. And she was well read.

Those were the abilities to be marked down in her favor. None of them seemed exactly to the point when faced with the hard fact that she now found herself in possession of close to three hundred acres of steep and bottom, a house, a barn, outbuildings, but no idea what to do with them. It gave her pleasure to play on the piano, but not enough to compensate for her recent realization that she could not weed a row of young bean plants without pulling half of them out along with the ragweed.

A certain amount of resentment came upon her when she

thought that a measure of applied knowledge in the area of food production and preparation would stand her in better stead at that particular time than any fine understanding of the principles of perspective in painting. All her life, though, her father had kept her back from the hardness of work. As long as she could remember he had hired adequate help, sometimes freed blacks, sometimes unlanded whites of good character, sometimes slaves, in which case the wages were paid directly to the owner. For most of the six years of their mission to the mountains, Monroe had employed a white man and his part-Cherokee wife to run the place, leaving Ada with little to do other than devise a weekly menu. She had therefore been free, as always, to occupy her time with reading and needlework, drawing and music.

But now the hired people were gone. The man had been lukewarm toward secession and counted himself lucky to be too old to volunteer in the first years of the war. But that spring, with the armies in Virginia desperately shorthanded, he had begun to worry that he might soon be conscripted. So, shortly after Monroe died, he and his wife had taken off unannounced and headed over the mountains to cross the lines into territory held by the Federals, leaving Ada to make do on her own.

Since then, she had discovered herself to be frighteningly ill-prepared in the craft of subsistence, living alone on a farm that her father had run rather as an idea than a livelihood. Monroe never developed much interest in the many tiresome areas of agriculture. He had held the opinion that if he could afford to buy feed corn and meal, why bother growing more than they could eat as roasting ears? If he could buy bacon and chops, why be drawn into the more inconvenient details of pork? Ada once heard him instruct the hired man to buy a dozen or so sheep and put them into the pasture below the front yard to mix in with the milk cow. The man had objected, pointing out to Monroe that cows and sheep do not do well pastured together. The man asked, Why do you want sheep? The wool? Meat?

Monroe's answer had been, For the atmosphere.

But it was hard to live on atmosphere, and so the boxwood appeared to offer about all the feeling of protection Ada could soon expect. She decided she would not quit the shrub until she could count off, at minimum, three convincing reasons to do so. But after several minutes' thought she could only come up with one: she did not particularly wish to die within the boxwood.

At that moment, though, the red hen came bursting through the leaves, her wings partially opened and trailing in the dust. She hopped onto a limb near Ada's head and sounded off with an agitated gabble. Immediately behind her came the big black-and-gold rooster that always frightened Ada a little with his ferocity. He was intent on treading the hen but pulled up short, startled when he saw Ada in so unexpected a place. The rooster cocked his head at an angle and fixed a shining black eye on her. He took a step back and scratched at the ground. He was close enough for Ada to note the dirt lodged between the scales on his yellow legs. The amber spurs looked long as a finger. The golden helmet of feathers at his head and neck fluffed and swelled and in their glossiness seemed almost macassared. He shook himself to settle them back into place. The black of his body had a blue-green sheen like oil on water. His yellow beak opened and closed.

If he weighed a hundred and fifty pounds he'd kill me where I sit without a doubt, Ada thought.

She shifted about onto her knees and waved her hands and said, Shoo! When she did, the rooster launched himself at her face, twisting in the air so that he arrived spurs first, wings flogging away. Ada threw up a hand to fend him off and was cut across the wrist by a spur. Her blow knocked the bird to the ground, but he rose and came at her again, wings fanning. As she scrambled crablike to get out from under the bush, the rooster dug at her with a spur and hung it up in the folds of her skirt. She burst from the bush with a great thrash and rose to run, the rooster still attached to her skirt at knee level. The bird pecked

at her calves and struck again and again with the spur of his free leg and beat at her with his wings. Ada hit at it with open-handed blows until it fell away, and then she ran to the porch and into the house.

She sank into an armchair and examined her wounds. There was a smear of blood at her wrist. She wiped it away and with relief saw that she was little more than scraped. She looked at her skirt and found it dusty and smeared with chicken droppings and rent in three places, and then she drew it up and looked to her legs. They were marked variously by scratches and nips, none of them deep enough to draw blood. Her face and neck stung from scratches taken when she scrabbled out of the bush. She patted at her hair and found it moiled all about her head. This is the place I have reached, she thought. I am living in a new world where these are the fruits of even looking for eggs.

She rose from the chair and climbed the steps to her room and removed her clothes. At her marble-topped washstand, she poured water from the pitcher into the basin and washed off with a piece of lavender soap and a cloth. She ran her fingers through her hair to rake out the boxwood leaves and then just let it fall loose below her shoulders. She had abandoned both of the current hairstyles—either gathered all around and swept into two big rolls that hung from the sides of a woman's head like the ears of a hound, or pulled tight to the scalp and bunned at the back like a mud-tailed horse. She no longer had need or patience for such updos. She could go about looking like a madwoman in a bookplate and it didn't matter, for she sometimes went up to a week or ten days without seeing another soul.

She went to her chest of drawers for clean underdress and found none, laundry having been neglected for some time. She put on linens she drew from near the bottom of the dirty clothes pile, theorizing that perhaps time had made them fresher than the ones she had just taken off. She topped them with a somewhat clean dress and wondered how she might get through the hours until bedtime. When had things altered so that she no

longer thought of how to pass the day pleasantly or profitably and began to think merely of how to pass the day?

Her will to do was near gone. All she had accomplished of note in the months since Monroe's death was to sort through his things, his clothes and papers. Even that had been a trial, for she had a strange and fearful feeling about her father's room and had not been able to enter it until many days after the funeral. But during that time she had often stood at the door and looked in as people are drawn to stand at the lip of a cliff and look down. Water had stood in a pitcher at his washstand until it went away of its own accord. When she had finally drawn together the nerve to do it, she went in and sat on the bed, weeping as she folded the well-made white shirts, the black suitcoats and pants for storage. She sorted and labeled and boxed Monroe's papers, his sermons and botanical notes and commonplace journals. Each little task had brought with it a new round of mourning and a string of empty days that eventually ran together until now she had arrived at such a state that the inevitable answer to the question, What have you accomplished this day? was, Nothing.

Ada took a book from her bedside table and went into the upper hall and sat in the stuffed chair she had pulled from Monroe's bedroom and situated to catch the good light from the hall window. She had spent much of the past three damp months sitting in the chair reading, a quilt wrapped around her to hold back the chill of the house even in July. The books she had drawn from the shelves that summer had been varied and haphazard, little but recent novels, whatever she happened to pick up from Monroe's study. Trifles like *Sword and Gown* by Lawrence and many others of its type. She could read such books and a day later not know what they had been about. When she had read more notable books, the harsh fates of their doomed heroines served only to deepen her gloom. For a time, every book she plucked from the shelves frightened her, their contents all concerning mistakes made by wretched dark-haired

women so that they ended their days punished, exiled, and alien. She had gone straight from *The Mill on the Floss* to a slim and troubling tale by Hawthorne on somewhat the same theme. Monroe had apparently not finished it, for the pages were uncut beyond the third chapter. She guessed Monroe would have thought the book unnecessarily grim, but to Ada it seemed good practice for her coming world. No matter what the book, though, the characters all seemed to lead fuller lives than she did.

At first, all she liked about the reading spot was the comfortable chair and the good light, but over the months she came to appreciate that the window's view offered some relief against the strain of such bleak stories, for when she looked up from the page, her eyes swept across the fields and rose on waves of foggy ridges to the blue bulk of Cold Mountain. The prospect from the reading chair confronted her with all the major shapes and colors of her current position. Through the summer, the landscape's most frequent mood had been dim and gloomy. The damp air coming through the window was rich with the fragrance of rot and growth, and to the eye it had much the same shimmering dense quality as looking across a great distance through a telescope. The burden of moisture in the air worked on perception as optics of poor quality do, distorting, expanding, and diminishing distance and altitude, altering the sense of mass moment by moment. Through the window, Ada had been given a tutorial in all the forms of visible moisture—light haze, dense valley fogs, tatters of cloud hanging like rags on the shoulders of Cold Mountain, grey rain falling straight down in streaks all day as if old twine hung from the heavens.

Liking this clouded, humped land, she found, was an altogether more difficult and subtler thing than appreciating the calm voice of Charleston during an evening walk along the Battery with Fort Sumter off in the distance, the great white houses at one's back, palmettos rattling their leaves in a sea breeze. In

comparison, the words this canted landscape spoke were less hushed, harsher. The coves and ridges and peaks seemed closed and baffling, a good place to hide.

The book before Ada this day was another one of her father's, a tale of frontier adventure by Simms, a Charlestonian and a friend of Monroe's that Ada had met on a number of occasions when he was in town from his plantation on the Edisto. She had been put in mind of Simms because she had not long ago received a letter from a Charleston acquaintance which described in passing his great anguish at the recent death of his wife. Naught but opiates saved him from madness, her friend had written, and it was a clause that Ada could not put from her thoughts.

She began to read, but stirring though the story's events were, she could not get food off her mind. Since the search for eggs had not gone in her favor, she had not yet eaten breakfast, though the day was coming up on midmorning. After only a few pages, she put the book into a pocket and went down to the kitchen and prowled through the pantry for something she could turn into a meal. She spent nearly two hours firing up the oven and trying to raise a loaf of wheat bread with saleratus, the only leavening she could find. When the loaf came from the oven, though, it resembled a great poorly made biscuit; its crust was of a crackerlike texture, and the remainder was sodden and tasted of uncooked flour. Ada nibbled at a piece and then gave up and threw it out into the yard for the chickens to peck at. For dinner she ate only a plate of the little tomatoes and cucumbers, sliced and dribbled with vinegar and sprinkled with salt. For all the satisfaction they gave her, she might have just breathed air.

Ada left her dirty plate and fork on the table. She took a shawl from where it lay balled on the sofa and shook it out and wrapped it about her shoulders. She went to the porch and stood looking. The sky was cloudless, though hazed so that the blue looked faded and thin. She could see the black and gold rooster down near the barn. He scratched at the ground and pecked

where he had scratched and then paced about fiercely. Ada left the house and went to the gate and out into the lane. It had carried so little traffic of late that the ridge down the center had grown a tall ruff of asters and foxtails. The fencerows at roadside were lined with tiny yellow and orange blossoms, and Ada went and touched one to watch it snap apart and throw its seeds.

—Snapweed, she said aloud, happy that there was something she could put a name to, even if it was one of her own devising.

She walked down the lane a mile, and then she passed out of Black Cove and turned onto the river road. As she went she picked a bouquet of wildflowers—whatever caught her eye—fleabane, angelica, tickseed, heal-all. At the river, she turned upstream to go to the church. The road was the community thoroughfare and was rutted with wagon tracks and had sunken below grade from hard use. Low spots were churned into a black muddy bog from the passing of horses and cows and pigs, and at such places footpaths had been worn alongside the road by walkers seeking to avoid sinking up to their boot tops. Along the roadside the trees hung heavy with the green burden of leaves approaching the end of the season. They appeared tired of growth, drooping, though not from drought, for the summer had been wet and the black river alongside the road ran deep and smooth.

In fifteen minutes Ada reached the little chapel that had been in Monroe's charge. Compared to the fine stone churches of Charleston, it was hardly more formal in its architecture than a bird trap, but its proportions—the pitch of its gable roof, the relations of its length and width and height, the placement of its simple steeple—were decidedly spare and elegant. Monroe had developed a great deal of affection for the chapel, its strict geometry according well with the plain impulses of his later years. Often as he and Ada had walked toward the chapel from the river he said, This is the way God speaks in this particular vernacular.

Ada climbed the hill and went to the burial ground behind the church and stood before Monroe's plot. The black dirt had not yet grown a thick stand of grass. There was still no marker, Ada having rejected the local styles—either a flat river rock or an oak plank with the name and dates scratched faintly on the surface. She had instead ordered a carved granite headstone from the county seat, but it was slow in coming. She put the flowers on the ground at the head of the grave and picked up the previous bundle, now wilted and soggy.

The day Monroe had died was in May. Late that afternoon, Ada had prepared to go out for a time with a box of watercolors and a piece of paper to paint the newly opened blossoms on a rhododendron by the lower creek. As she left the house, she stopped to speak to Monroe, who sat reading a book in a striped canvas campaign chair under the pear tree. He seemed tired and said that he doubted he had vitality even to finish the page he was on before he dropped off to sleep, but he asked her to wake him when she returned, for he did not want to lie sleeping into the damp of evening. Too, he said, he feared he was just beyond the age at which he could rise unassisted from so low a chair.

Ada was away less than an hour. As she walked from the fields into the yard, she saw that Monroe lay in complete repose. His mouth was open and she thought he might be snoring and that over supper she would tease him for leaving himself exposed in so undignified a posture. She walked up to wake him, but as she approached she could see that his eyes were open, the book fallen into the grass. She ran the last three steps and put her hand to his shoulder to shake him, but at a touch she knew he was dead, for the flesh under her hand was so completely inert.

Ada went as fast as she could for help, running some and walking some over the shortcut trail that crossed the ridge and descended to the river road near the Swangers' homestead. By

that route they were the nearest neighbors. They were members of her father's congregation, and Ada had known them from her earliest days in the mountains. She reached their house breathless and crying. Before Esco Swanger could hitch his team to a buggy and return with Ada by the roundabout way of the road, a rain blew in from the west. When they got back to the cove, darkness was falling and Monroe was wet as a trout and there were dogwood petals on his face. The watercolor Ada had dropped under the pear tree was an abstract splatter of pink and green.

She had spent that night in the Swangers' house, lying wide awake and dry eyed, thinking for a long time that she wished she could have gone before Monroe, though she knew in her heart that nature has a preference for a particular order: parents die, then children die. But it was a harsh design, offering little relief from pain, for being in accord with it means that the fortunate find themselves orphaned.

Two days later, Ada had buried Monroe on the knoll above the Little East Fork of the Pigeon River. The morning was bright, and a temperate wind swept down off Cold Mountain, and all the world quivered in it. There was scant humidity in the air for a change and all the colors and edges of things seemed crisp beyond the natural. Forty people, dressed in black, nearly filled the little chapel. The coffin rested on sawhorses before the pulpit, the lid off. Monroe's face had collapsed upon itself since his death. Gravity working on slack skin had hollowed out his cheeks and eye sockets, and his nose seemed sharper and longer than in life. There was the pale shine of eyewhite where one lid had lifted a crack.

Ada, a hand cupped to her mouth, leaned and spoke softly to a man across the aisle from her. He rose and jingled in his pockets for change and drew out two brownies. He went and set one on each of Monroe's eyes, for just to have covered the opening one would have looked strange and piratical.

The funeral service had been improvisational since no other

ordained minister of their faith lived within traveling distance, and all the ministers of the various types of local Baptists had declined to participate in retribution for Monroe's failure to believe in a God with severe limitations on His patience and mercy. Monroe had in fact preached that God was not at all such a one as ourselves, not one to be temperamentally inclined to tread ragefully upon us until our blood flew up and stained all His white raiment, but rather that He looked on both the best and worst of mankind with weary, bemused pity.

So they had to make do with words from a few men of the church. One after the other they had shuffled to the pulpit and stood with their chins tucked against their chests in order to avoid looking directly at the congregation, especially at Ada, who sat on the front pew of the women's side. Her mourning dress, dyed the day before greenish-black like the feathers of a drake's head, was still fragrant from the process. Her face white as a stripped tendon in her cold grief.

The men talked awkwardly of what they called Monroe's great learning and his other fine qualities. Of how since his coming from Charleston he had shed on the community a glowing light. They told of his small acts of kindness and the sage advice that he dispensed. Esco Swanger had been one of the speakers, a shade more articulate than the rest, though no less nervous. He spoke of Ada and her terrible loss, of how she would be missed when she returned to her home in Charleston.

Then, later, they stood at graveside as the coffin was lowered on ropes by the six men of the congregation who had carried the box from the chapel. With the coffin snugged down in its hole, another of the men led a final prayer, remarking of Monroe's vigor, his untiring service to the church and the community, the troubling suddenness with which he had faltered and fallen into death's eternal slumber. He seemed to find in those simple events a message for all concerning the shifty nature of life, how God intended it as a lesson.

They had all stood and watched as the grave was filled, but

halfway through Ada had to turn her head and look away toward the bend of the river to be able to stand the moment. When the grave was tamped and mounded up, they all turned and walked away. Sally Swanger had taken Ada by the elbow and steered her down the hill.

—You stay with us until you can fix up things for going back to Charleston, she said.

Ada stopped and looked at her. I will not be returning to Charleston immediately, she said.

—They Lord, Mrs. Swanger said. Where are you going?

—Black Cove, Ada said. I will be staying here, at least for a time.

Mrs. Swanger stared, then caught herself. How will you make it? she said.

—I am not entirely sure, Ada said.

—You're not going up to that big dark house by yourself today. Take dinner with us and stay until you're ready to leave.

—I would be obliged, Ada said. She had stayed on with the Swangers three days and then returned to the empty house, frightened and alone. After three months, the fright had somewhat faded, but Ada reckoned that to be little comfort since her new life seemed only a foreview of herself as an old woman, awash in solitude and the feeling of diminishing capabilities.

Ada turned from the grave plot and walked down the hill to the road and decided as she reached it to keep on walking upriver and over the shortcut back into Black Cove. Aside from being quicker, that route had the advantage of taking her by the post office. And, too, she would pass the Swanger place, where they might offer some dinner.

She walked along and met an old woman driving a red hog and a pair of turkeys before her, cutting at them with a willow switch when they strayed. Then a man caught up with her from behind and passed. He was stooped, walking fast, carrying a

shovel out before him. A mound of hot coals smoked in the blade of it. The man grinned and without pausing said over his shoulder that he'd let his fire go out and had gone to borrow some. Then Ada came upon a man with a heavy croker sack hanging pendant from a chestnut limb. Three crows sat high in the tree and watched down and said not a word in judgment. The man was bigly made and he beat at the sack with a broken-off hoe handle, laying into it so that the dust flew. He talked at the sack, cursing it, as if it were the chief impediment to his living a life of ease and content. There was the sound of dull blows, his breathing and his muttering, the gritting of his feet finding hold in the dirt from which to strike another lick at the sack. Ada studied him as she passed, and then she stopped and went back and asked him what he was doing. Beating the shells off beans, he said. And he made it clear that he was of the mind that every little bean in there was a thing to hate. He'd plowed and planted in hate. Trained the vines up poles and weeded the rows in hate and watched the blossoms set and the pods form and fill in hate. He had picked beans cursing every one his fingers touched, flinging them off into a withy basket as if filth clung to his hands. Beating was the only part of the process, even down to the eating of them, that he cared for.

By the time Ada reached the mill, the day's haze had not yet burned away, but she had become too warm for her shawl. She removed it and rolled it to carry under her arm. The mill wheel was turning, spilling its load of water into the tailrace, spraying and splattering. When Ada set her hand to the doorframe, the whole building vibrated with the turning of mill wheel and gears and drive shaft and grindstones. She stuck her head in the door and raised her voice loud enough to be heard over the creak and groan of the machinery. Mr. Peek? she said.

The room smelled of dried corn, old wood, the mossy mill-race, falling water. The inside was dim, and what light did come in the two little windows and the door fell in beams through an atmosphere thick with the dust of ground corn. The miller

stepped from behind the grindstones. He brushed his hands together and more dust flew. When he came into the light of the door, Ada could see that his hair and eyebrows and eyelashes and the hair of his arms were frosted pale grey with corn dust.

—Come for mail? he said.

—If there is any.

The miller went into the post office, a tiny shed-roofed extension cobbled onto the gristmill. He came out with a letter and looked at it, turning it front and back. Ada stuck it into the book in her pocket, the Simms, and walked on up the road to the Swanger place.

She found Esco by the barn. He was bent over trying to cotter a cartwheel with a peg he had whittled from a locust branch, driving it in with a hand sledge. As Ada walked to him from the road, he stood and set down the sledge and leaned forward against the cart, gripping the topboard two-fisted. There appeared to be no great odds between the color and hardness of his hands and the boards. He had sweated through his shirt, and as Ada came near, she drew in his smell, which was that of wet pottery. Esco was tall and thin with a tiny head and a great shock of dry grey hair which roached up to a point like the crest on a titmouse.

He welcomed the excuse to quit working and walked Ada to the house, passing through the fence gate into the yard. Esco had used the fence for hitching rack, and the pointed tops of the palings had been cribbed away to splintered nubs by bored horses. The yard was bare, swept clean, with not a bush or flower bed as ornament, only a half-dozen big oak trees and a covered well, a novelty in that country of moving water, for the place they had chosen to live in was called No Creek Cove. The house was large and had once been painted white, but the paint was flaking off in patches as big as a hand so that currently it could fairly be said to resemble a dapple mare, though one day soon it would just be grey.

Sally sat on the porch threading beans on strings to make

leatherbritches, and five long strings of pods already hung above her from the porch rafters to dry. She was shaped round in every feature and her skin was as lucent and shiny as a tallow candle and her greying hair was hennaed to the color of the stripe down a mule's back. Esco pushed an empty straight chair to Ada and then he went inside and brought out another for himself. He started snapping beans. Nothing was said of dinner, and Ada looked to the pale sky. With some disappointment she saw that the bright spot where the sun stood indicated midafternoon. The Swangers would have long since eaten.

They sat together quietly for a minute, the only sounds the snap of beans and the hiss of Sally pulling thread through them with a needle and, from inside the house, the mantel clock ticking with the sound of a knuckle knocking on a box. Esco and Sally worked together comfortably, hands sometimes touching as they simultaneously reached into the bean basket. They were both quiet and slow in their movements, gentle toward each other, and they touched each pod as if it were a thing requiring great tenderness. Though not a childless couple, they had retained an air of romance to their marriage as the barren often do. They seemed never to have quite brought their courting to a proper close. Ada thought them sweet partners, but she saw nothing remarkable about their ease together. Having lived all her life with a widower, she had no true model in her mind of what marriage might be like, what toll the daily round might exact.

Their first talk was of the war, of how the prospects seemed grim, the Federals just over the mountains to the north, and things growing desperate in Virginia if the newspaper accounts of trench warfare in Petersburg were to be believed. Neither Esco nor Sally understood the war in any but the vaguest way, knowing for certain only two things: that they generally disapproved of it, and that Esco had reached an age when he required some help about the farm. For those and many other reasons, they would be glad to see the war done and their boys come

walking up the road. Ada asked if there was any news from either of the boys, the two Swanger sons being off to the fighting. But they'd heard not a word in many months and knew not even what state they were in.

The Swangers had opposed the war from the start and had until recently remained generally sympathetic with the Federals, as had many in the mountains. But Esco had grown bitter with both sides, fearing them about equally now that the Federals were ranked up just over the big mountains to the north. He worried that they would soon come looking for food, take what they want, and leave a man with nothing. He'd been in to the county seat recently, and it was all over town that Kirk and his bluecoats had already started raiding up near the state line. Came down on a family and looted their farm at grey dawn, stole every animal they could find and every bit of portable food they could carry, and set fire to the corncrib in parting.

—Them's the liberators, Esco said. And our own bunch is as bad or worse. Teague and his Home Guard roaring around like a band of marauders. Setting their own laws as suits them, and them nothing but trash looking for a way to stay out of the army.

He'd heard the Guard had rousted a family out into their yard at dinnertime. Owenses from down about Iron Duff. Teague claimed they were known to be lovers of the Federals and suspected members of the Red String Band and that whatever hoard of treasure they had must fall forfeit. First they took the house apart and then they prodded around in the yard with their sabers to see if they could find soft dirt from fresh digging. They slapped the man some, and later his wife. Then they hanged a pair of bird dogs each by each, and when that failed to get the man's attention, they tied the woman's thumbs together behind her back and hoisted her up by them with a cord thrown over a tree limb. Hauled on it till her toes just touched the ground. But the man still wouldn't say word one, so they took her down and set the corner of a rail fence on her thumbs, but that didn't faze the man either.

The children were wailing and the woman was down on the ground with her thumbs still under the fence corner screaming how she knew her man had hid the silver service and the hoard of gold pieces they had remaining after the hard times of the war. She didn't know where he'd buried it, she just knew he had. She first begged him to tell, then she begged the Guard to have mercy. Then, when Owens still refused to talk, she begged them to kill him first so she could at least have the satisfaction of watching.

About that time one of the Guard, a white-headed boy called Birch, said he believed they maybe should stop and leave, but Teague leveled a pistol at him and said, I'll not be told how to treat the likes of Bill Owens and his wife and the young'uns. I'll go to the Federals before I'll live in a country where I can't deal out to such people what they deserve.

—In the end, Esco concluded, they didn't kill nobody and they didn't find the silver. Just lost interest and headed off down the road. The wife left Owens on the spot. Came to town with the children and is living with her brother and telling the tale to whoever'll listen.

Esco sat for a time leaned forward in the chair with his forearms on his knees and his hands hanging loose from their wrists. He seemed to be studying the porch boards or gauging the wear of his boot leather. Ada knew from experience that, were he outside, he would spit between his feet and then stare at the spot in evident fascination.

—This war's something else, he said in a minute. Every man's sweat has a price for it. Big flatland cotton men steal it every day, but I think sometime maybe they'll wish they'd chopped their own damn cotton. I just want my boys home and out hoeing the bottomland while I sit on the porch and holler Good job every time that clock strikes the half hour.

Sally nodded and said, Uh-huh, and that seemed to close the topic.

They moved on to other matters, Ada listening with interest as Esco and Sally listed the old signs they had noted of a hard winter coming. Grey squirrels rattling in hickory trees, frantic to hoard more and more nuts. Wax thick on the wild crabapples. Wide bands of black on caterpillars. Yarrow crushed between the hands smelling sharp as falling snow. Hawthorns loaded with red haws burning bright as blood.

—Other signs too, Esco said. Bad ones.

He had been keeping a tally of omens and portents from around the county. A mule was said to have given birth near Cataloochee, a pig to have been born with human hands at Balsam. A man at Cove Creek claimed to have slaughtered a sheep, and among its internals no heart was found. Hunters on Big Laurel swore that an owl made utterments like those of a human, and though they found no agreement on its message, all confirmed that as the owl spoke, there appeared to be two moons in the sky. For three years running there had been uncommon raving of wolves in the winter, weak harvest of grain in summer. They all pointed to evil times. Esco's thinking was that though they had so far been isolated from the general meanness of the war, its cess might soon spill through the low gaps and pour in to foul them all.

There was a pause, and then Sally said, Have you set on a course yet?

—No, Ada said.

—You're not yet ready to return home? Sally asked.

—Home? Ada said, momentarily confused, for she had felt all summer that she had none.

—Charleston, Sally said.

—No. I'm not yet ready, Ada said.

—Have you heard from Charleston?

—Not yet, Ada said. But I suspect that the letter I just picked up from Mr. Peek may clarify the matter of funds. It appears to be from my father's solicitor.

—Pull it out and see what it says, Esco said.

—I cannot bring myself to look. And, in truth, all it will tell me is whether I have money to live. It will not tell me where I might find myself a year farther on or what I might be doing with myself. Those are the questions that worry me most.

Esco rubbed his hands together and grinned. I might be the only man in the county that can help you there, he said. It's claimed that if you take a mirror and look backwards into a well, you'll see your future down in the water.

So in short order Ada found herself bent backward over the mossy well lip, canted in a pose with little to recommend it in the way of dignity or comfort, back arched, hips forward, legs spraddled for balance. She held a hand mirror above her face, angled to catch the surface of the water below.

Ada had agreed to the well-viewing as a variety of experiment in local custom and as a tonic for her gloom. Her thoughts had been broody and morbid and excessively retrospective for so long that she welcomed the chance to run counter to that flow, to cast forward and think about the future, even though she expected to see nothing but water at the bottom of the well.

She shifted her feet to find better grip on the packed dirt of the yard and then tried to look into the mirror. The white sky above was skimmed over with backlit haze, bright as a pearl or as a silver mirror itself. The dark foliage of oaks all around the edges framed the sky, duplicating the wooden frame of the mirror into which Ada peered, examining its picture of the well depths behind her to see what might lie ahead in her life. The bright round of well water at the end of the black shaft was another mirror. It cast back the shine of sky and was furred around the edges here and there with sprigs of fern growing between stones.

Ada tried to focus her attention on the hand mirror, but the bright sky beyond kept drawing her eye away. She was dazzled by light and shade, by the confusing duplication of reflections

and of frames. All coming from too many directions for the mind to take account of. The various images bounced against each other until she felt a desperate vertigo, as if she could at any moment pitch backward and plunge head first down the well shaft and drown there, the sky far above her, her last vision but a bright circle set in the dark, no bigger than a full moon.

Her head spun and she reached with her free hand and held to the stonework of the well. And then just for a moment things steadied, and there indeed seemed to be a picture in the mirror. It was like a poorly executed calotype. Vague in its details, low in contrast, grainy. What she saw was a wheel of bright light, a fringe of foliage all around. Perhaps a suggestion of a road through a corridor of trees, an incline. At the center of the light, a black silhouette of a figure moved as if walking, but the image was too vague to tell if it approached or walked away. But wherever it was bound, something in its posture suggested firm resolution. Am I meant to follow, or should I wait its coming? Ada wondered.

Then dizziness swept over her again. Her knees gave way and she slumped to the ground. Everything whirled about her for a second. Her ears rang and her whole mind was filled with lines from the hymn Wayfaring Stranger. She thought she might faint, but suddenly the spinning world caught and held still. She looked to see if anyone had noticed her fall, but Sally and Esco were engaged in their work to the exclusion of all else. Ada picked herself up and walked to the porch.

—See anything? Esco said.

—Not exactly, Ada said.

Sally gave her a sharp look, started to go back to stringing beans, then changed her mind and said, You look white-eyed. Are you not well?

Ada tried to listen but could not focus her thoughts on Sally's voice. In her mind she still saw the dark figure, and the brave phrases of the hymn sang on in her ears: "Traveling

through this world below. No toil, no sick nor danger, in that fair land to which I go." She was sure the figure was important, though she could put no face to it.

—Did you see something down in that well or not? Sally said.

—I'm not sure, Ada said.

—She looks white-eyed, Sally said to Esco.

—It's just a story people tell, Esco said. I've looked in there time and again and never seen a thing myself.

—Yes, said Ada. There was nothing.

But she could not shake the picture from her mind. A wood. A road through it. A clearing. A man, walking. The feeling that she was meant to follow. Or else to wait.

The clock rang out four chimes as flat and wanting in music as striking a pike blade with a hammer.

Ada rose to go, but Sally made her sit. She reached and put the heel of her hand to Ada's cheek.

—You're not hot. Have you eaten today? she said.

—I had something, Ada said.

—Not much I bet, Sally said. You come on with me, I'll give you something to take with you.

Ada followed her inside. The house smelled of dried herbs and strings of peppers that hung in rows down the long central hall, ready to spice the various relishes and sauces and pickles and chutneys that Sally was famous for making. All around the fireplace mantels and doorframes and mirrors were bows of red ribbon, and the newel post in the hall was painted in red and white stripes like a barber pole.

In the kitchen, Sally went to a cupboard and took out a pottery crock of blackberry preserves, the mouth sealed with beeswax. She gave it to Ada and said, This'll be good on your leftover supper biscuits. Ada said her thanks without mentioning her failure as biscuit maker. On the porch, she asked Esco and Sally to stop by if they were out in their buggy and found them-

selves near Black Cove. She walked away, carrying the shawl and the crock of preserves in her arms.

The old footpath crossing the ridge into Black Cove began not five hundred yards up the road from the Swangers' farm, and it climbed steeply away from the river. It first passed through open woods of second-growth oak and hickory and poplar, and then closer to the ridge the timber remained uncut and the trees were immense and became mixed with spruce and hemlock and a few dark balsams. The ground there was a jumble of fallen trees in various stages of decay. Ada climbed without pause, and she found that the rhythm of her walking soon matched up with the tune of Wayfaring Stranger, still chanting itself faintly in her head. Its brave and heartening lines braced her, though she half dreaded to look ahead up the trail for fear a dark shape might step into view.

When she reached the crest of the ridge, she rested, sitting on a rock outcrop which commanded a prospect back into the river valley. Below her she could see the river and the road, and to her right—a fleck of white in the general green—the chapel.

She turned and looked in the other direction, up toward Cold Mountain, pale and grey and distant-looking, then down into Black Cove. Her house and her fields showed no neglect from this distance. They looked crisp and cared for. All compassed round by her woods, her ridges, her creek. With the junglelike rate of growth here, though, she knew that if she were to stay, she would need help; otherwise the fields and yard would soon heal over with weeds and brush and scrub until the house would disappear in a thicket as completely as the bramble-covered palace of Sleeping Beauty. She doubted, though, that any hired man worth having could be found, since anyone fit to work was off warring.

Ada sat and traced the approximate boundaries of her farm, surveying a line with her eyes. When she came back around to her starting point, the land so enclosed seemed such a substan-

tial portion of earth. How it had come to be under her proprietorship still seemed a mystery to her, though she could name every step along the way.

She and her father had come to the mountains six years earlier in hopes of finding relief for the consumption that had slowly worked at Monroe's lungs until he wet a half-dozen handkerchiefs a day with blood. His Charleston doctor, putting all his faith in the powers of cool fresh air and exercise, had recommended a well-known highland resort with a fine dining room and therapeutic mineral hot springs. But Monroe did not relish the idea of a restful quiet place full of the well-to-do and their many afflictions. He instead found a mountain church of his denomination lacking a preacher, reasoning that useful work would be more therapeutic than reeking sulfur water.

They had set out immediately, traveling by train to Spartanburg, the railhead in the upstate. It was a rough town situated hard up against the wall of the mountains, and they had stayed there several days, living in what passed for a hotel, until Monroe could arrange for muleteers to transport their crated belongings across the Blue Ridge to the village of Cold Mountain. During that time Monroe bought a carriage and a horse to draw it, and he was, as always, lucky in the purchase of things. He happened upon a man just rubbing a shine into the final coat of black lacquer on a new and beautifully built cabriolet. In addition, the man had a strong dappled gelding well matched to the carriage. Monroe bought them both without a moment of haggle, counting out money from his wallet into the yellowy and callused hand of the wainwright. It took several moments, but when he was done Monroe had sporty equipage indeed for a country preacher.

Thus outfitted, they went on ahead of their things, traveling first to the little town of Brevard, where there was no hotel, only a boardinghouse. They left from there in the blue light of the

hour before dawn. It was a fine spring morning, and as they passed through the town Monroe had said, I am told we should be to Cold Mountain by suppertime.

The gelding seemed pleased to be on a jaunt. He stepped out smartly, pulling the light rig at a thrilling clip, the shiny spokes of its two high wheels buzzing with speed.

They climbed all through the bright morning. The wagon road was bound tight to left and right by bower and thicket, and it folded back upon itself in an endless succession of switchbacks as it ascended a narrow vale. The blue sky became but a thin cut above the dark slopes. They crossed and recrossed an upper branch of the French Broad and once passed so near a waterfall that the cold spray wet their faces.

Ada had never seen mountains other than the rocky Alps before and was not sure what to make of this strange and vegetal topography, its every cranny and crag home to some leafy plant foreign to the spare and sandy low country. The spreading tops of oak and chestnut and tulip poplar converged to make a canopy that crowded out the sunlight. Close to the ground, azalea and rhododendron ranked up to make an understory thick as a stone wall.

Nor was Ada easy in her mind with this land's pitiful and informal roads. So inferior were these rutted tracks to the broad and sandy pikes of the low country that they seemed more the product of roaming cattle than of man. The road decreased in width at every turning until Ada became convinced that the way would soon disappear altogether, leaving them adrift in a wilderness as trackless and profound as that which leapt up when God first spoke the word *greenwood*.

Monroe, though, was in high glee for a man so recently hemorrhaging. He looked about as if he had been charged, upon penalty of death, with remembering every fold of terrain and every shade of green. Periodically, he startled the horse by suddenly declaiming lines from Wordsworth in a loud voice. When they rounded a bend and stopped before a distant pale vista of

the flat country they had left behind, he hollered, "Earth has not anything to show more fair. Dull would be the soul who could pass by a sight so touching in its majesty."

Later in the afternoon, when the sky had filled with roiling clouds driven by an eastering wind, they paused amid a stand of black balsam where the track topped out at Wagon Road Gap. From there the way ahead plunged alarmingly to follow the fall of waters down a roaring fork of the Pigeon River. Before them they could see the bulk of Cold Mountain reared up better than six thousand feet, its summit hidden by dark clouds and white fog in bands. Between the gap and the mountain was a wild and broken terrain of scarp and gorge. At that lonesome spot Monroe again called upon his favorite poet and cried, "The sick sight and giddy prospect of the raving stream, the unfettered clouds and region of the heavens, tumult and peace, the darkness and the light—were all like workings of one mind, the features of the same face, blossoms upon one tree, characters of the great Apocalypse, the types and symbols of Eternity, of first, and last, and midst, and without end."

Ada had laughed and kissed Monroe's cheek, thinking, I would follow this old man to Liberia if he asked me to do so.

Monroe then eyed the troubled clouds and raised the folded carriage top of painted and waxed canvas, as black and angular on its frame of hinged members as a bat's wing. So new it crackled as he pulled it into place.

He shook the reins, and the sweated gelding pitched forward, happy to be on the easy side of gravity. Soon, though, the road was at such a cant that Monroe had to set the brake to keep the cabriolet from riding up over the horse's haunches.

Rain fell, and then darkness. There was not moonlight nor the prick of lantern light from some welcoming home. The town of Cold Mountain was ahead, but they knew not how far. They drove on into the black, trusting the horse not to fall headlong over some rocky ledge. The lack of even lonesome cabins indi-

cated that they were still a way from the village. Distances, apparently, had been misjudged.

The rain fell aslant, coming at their faces so that the top of the carriage did little good in sheltering them from it. The horse walked head down. They came to turn after turn in the road, every one unmarred by signpost. At each fork, Monroe simply guessed at the route they ought to take.

Late, long after midnight, they came to a dark chapel on a hill above the road and a river. They went in out of the rain and slept stretched out on pews in their sodden clothes.

Morning broke to fog, but its brightness announced that it would burn off quickly. Monroe rose stiffly and walked outside. Ada heard him laugh and then say, Powers that be, I thank you yet again.

She went to him. He stood before the chapel grinning and pointing above the door. She turned and read the sign: Cold Mountain Assembly.

—We have against all odds arrived at home, Monroe had said. At the time, it was a sentiment Ada took with a great deal of skepticism. All of their Charleston friends had expressed the opinion that the mountain region was a heathenish part of creation, outlandish in its many affronts to sensibility, a place of wilderness and gloom and rain where man, woman, and child grew gaunt and brutal, addicted to acts of raw violence with not even a nod in the direction of self-restraint. Only men of gentry affected underdrawers, and women of every station suckled their young, leaving the civilized trade of wet nurse unknown. Ada's informants had claimed the mountaineers to be but one step more advanced in their manner of living than tribes of vagrant savages.

In the weeks that followed their arrival, as she and Monroe visited current and potential members of his congregation, Ada discovered that these people were indeed odd, though not exactly in the ways predicted by Charlestonians. During their visits

they found the people to be touchy and distant, largely unreadable. They often acted as if they had been insulted, though neither Ada nor Monroe could say how. Many homesteads operated as if embattled. Only men would come out onto the porch to meet them as they came visiting, and sometimes Monroe and Ada would be invited in and sometimes not. And often it was worse to be asked in than to be left standing awkwardly out in the yard, for Ada found such visits frightening.

The houses were dark inside, even on a bright day. Those with shutters kept them pulled to. Those with curtains kept them drawn. The houses smelled strangely, though not uncleanly, of cooking and animals and of people who worked. Rifles stood in the corners and hung on pegs above mantels and doors. Monroe would rattle on at great length, introducing himself and explaining his view of the church's mission and talking theology and urging attendance at prayer meetings and services. All the while the men would sit in straight chairs looking at the fire. Many of them went unshod and they stuck their feet out before them with no shame whatsoever. For all you could tell by their bearing, they might have been alone. They looked at the fire and said not a word and moved not one muscle in their faces as response to anything Monroe said. When he pressed them with a direct question they sat and thought about it for a long time, and sometimes they answered in brief vague phrases and more often they just looked sharply at him as if that in itself conveyed all the message they cared to pass. There were hidden people in the houses. Ada could hear them knocking about in other rooms, but they would not come forth. She supposed them to be women, children, and old people. It was as if they found the world beyond their cove so terrible that they might be fouled by any contact with outlanders and that all but kith and kin were best counted as enemy.

After such visits, Ada and Monroe always left at a brisk clip, and as they spun down the road in the cabriolet, he talked of ignorance and devised strategies for its defeat. Ada just felt the

whirl of the wheels, the speed of their retreat, and a vague envy of people who seemed to care nothing at all for the things she and Monroe knew. They had evidently come to entirely different conclusions about life and lived utterly by their own light.

Monroe's greatest debacle as missionary had come later that summer and involved Sally and Esco. A Mies man in the congregation had told Monroe that the Swangers were stunning in their ignorance. Esco, according to Mies, could scarcely read, in fact had never advanced in his understanding of history beyond the earliest doings of the Deity in Genesis. The creation of light was about the last thing he had a firm grasp of. Sally Swanger, Mies had said, was somewhat less informed. They both saw the Bible only as a magic book and used it like a gypsy hand reader. They held it and let it fall open and then stabbed a finger at the page and tried to puzzle out the meaning of the word so indicated. It was deemed oracular, and they acted upon it as instructions straight from God's mind. If God said go, they went. He said abide, they stayed put. He said slay, Esco got the hatchet and went looking for a pullet. They were, despite their ignorance, unavoidably prosperous since their farm occupied a wide piece of cove bottom with dirt so black and rich it would raise sweet potatoes as long as your arm with only the least efforts toward keeping the weeds shaved back. They would make valuable members of the congregation if Monroe could only bring them up-to-date.

So Monroe had gone visiting, Ada at his side. They'd sat together in the parlor, Esco humped forward as Monroe tried to engage him in a discussion of faith. But Esco gave up little of himself and his beliefs. Monroe found no evidence of religion other than a worship of animals and trees and rocks and weather. Esco was some old relic Celt was what Monroe concluded; what few thoughts Esco might have would more than likely be in Gaelic.

Seizing such a unique opportunity, Monroe attempted to explain the high points of true religion. When they got to the holy

trinity Esco had perked up and said, Three into one. Like a turkey foot.

Then in awhile, convinced that Esco had indeed not yet got report of his culture's central narrative, Monroe told the story of Christ from divine birth to bloody crucifixion. He included all the famous details and, while keeping it simple, he summoned all the eloquence he could. When he'd finished, he sat back waiting for a reaction.

Esco said, And you say this took place some time ago?

Monroe said, Two thousand years, if you consider that some time ago.

—Oh, I'd call that a stretch all right, Esco said. He looked at his hands where they hung from the wrists. He flexed the fingers and looked at them critically as if trying the fittings of a new implement. He thought on the story awhile and then said, And what this fellow come down for was to save us?

—Yes, Monroe said.

—From our own bad natures and the like?

—Yes.

—And they still done him like they did? Spiked him up and knifed him and all?

—Yes indeed, Monroe said.

—But you say this story's been passed around some hundred-score years? Esco said.

—Nearly.

—So to say, a long time.

—A very long time.

Esco grinned as if he had solved a puzzle and stood up and slapped Monroe on the shoulder and said, Well, about all we can do is hope it ain't so.

At home that night, Monroe had drawn up plans as to how he might best instruct Esco in proper doctrine and so save him from heathenism. It never entered Monroe's mind that he had been made a butt of humor and that his quest for ignorance had been so apparent from the moment he had entered Esco's gate

as to give grave offense. Nor, of course, did he suppose that—instead of shutting the door in his face or pitching a pan of grey footwash water at him or showing him the bore to his shotgun as some so insulted would have done—Esco, a gentle soul, had simply taken pleasure in giving Monroe great quantities of the ignorance he came seeking.

Esco bragged to no one about what he had done. In fact, he seemed not to care in the least whether or not Monroe ever knew the truth of the matter, which was that he and his wife were dipped Baptists. It was Monroe that spread the tale by way of asking for the names of others so benighted. He found it odd that people took the story as humorous and that people sought him out at the store or on the road and asked him to tell it. They would wait for him to repeat Esco's final line as most men like to do after the recitation of a successful joke. When Monroe failed to do it, some would say the line again themselves, feeling evidently that things would otherwise be left incomplete. This went on until Sally finally took pity and told Monroe that he had been made a jestingstock and why.

Monroe remained low in spirit for days afterward at the ragging he had taken from the settlement at large. He had doubts that he could ever make a place for himself there, until Ada finally said, I think since we've been given a lesson in etiquette, we ought to act in accordance.

After that everything became clearer. They went to the Swangers and apologized and thereafter became friends with them and took meals with them regularly and, apparently to make amends for Esco's prank, the Swangers soon ceased to be Baptists and joined the church.

For that first year, Monroe had kept their Charleston house and they lived in the dank little riverside parsonage that smelled so strongly of mildew in July and August as to burn the nose. Then, when it seemed that the change of climate was working some improvement on Monroe's lungs and the community was finally tolerating him and might someday accept him, he de-

cided to stay indefinitely. He sold the Charleston house and bought the cove from the Black family, who had taken a sudden notion to move to Texas. Monroe liked the picturesque setting, the lay of the land, flat and open at cove bottom, better than twenty acres of it cleared and fenced into fields and pastures. He liked the arc of the wooded hillsides as they swept up, broken by ridge and hollow, to Cold Mountain. Liked the water from the spring, so cold that even in the summer it made your teeth ache and carried the clean neutral taste of the stone it rose from.

And he especially liked the house he had built there, largely because it represented his faith in a future that would include himself for at least a few more years. Monroe drew the plans for the new house with his own hand, supervised the construction. And it turned out well-made in the current mold, tightly covered in whitewashed clapboards outside, dark beadboard walls inside, a deep porch all across the front, attached kitchen extending from the back, a great broad fireplace in the sitting room, and woodstoves in the bedrooms, a rarity in the mountains. The Blacks' log cabin stood a few hundred rods up the hill toward Cold Mountain from the new house, and it became quarters for the hired help.

When Monroe had bought the cove, the place had been a fully operating farm, but Monroe had soon let many parts of it lapse, for he never intended it to be self-sufficient. Nor did it ever need to be if, as he had assumed, the money continued to flow from his Charleston investments in rice and indigo and cotton.

Apparently, however, the money would not continue, as Ada found when she left off surveying her holdings from her perch on the ridge and drew the letter from the book in her pocket and read it. Shortly after the funeral, she had written to Monroe's friend and solicitor in Charleston, informing him of the death and asking for information on her financial position. The letter

was the long-delayed response. It was brittlely phrased, cautious. It discussed as if at arm's length the war, the embargo, the various other expressions of hard times, and their effect on Ada's income, which would be reduced, in fact, to approximately nothing, at least until the war's successful conclusion. Should the war effort be unsuccessful, Ada might realistically expect nothing forevermore. The letter ended with an offer to act as administrator of Monroe's estate since Ada might justifiably feel ill-endowed to perform those duties herself. It was delicately suggested that the task called for judgments and knowledge outside Ada's realm.

She stood and thrust the letter into her pocket and took the trail down into Black Cove. In light of the thought that the present was threat enough and no one knows what horrid things might overtake them in the time ahead, Ada wondered where she might find the courage to search out hope. When she emerged from the big trees of the ridge, she found that the haze had burned or blown away. The sky was clear, and Cold Mountain suddenly looked close enough to reach out and touch. The day was wearing on and the sun was bearing downward and would in two hours tip below the mountains to begin the interminable high-country twilight. A boomer chattered at her from its perch high in a hickory tree as she passed underneath. Shreds of nut shell fell around her.

When she reached the old stone wall that marked the top of the upper pasture, she paused again. It was a lovely spot, one of her favorite corners of the farm. Lichen and moss had grown on the stones so that the wall looked ancient, though it was not. One of the elder Blacks had apparently started it in an attempt to clear the field of stones but had given up after only twenty feet, at which point split rails took over. The wall ran north to south, and on this sunny afternoon its west face was warm with afternoon sun. An apple tree, a golden delicious, grew near it, and a few early ripening apples had fallen into the tall grass. Bees came to the sweet smell of rotting apples and hummed in

the sunshine. The wall did not command a sweeping prospect, just a quiet view of the corner of a woodlot and a blackberry tangle and two big chestnut trees. Ada thought it the most peaceful place she had ever known. She settled herself into the grass at the base of the wall and rolled her shawl into a pillow. She drew the book from her pocket and began reading a chapter titled How Blackbirds Are Taken, and How Blackbirds Fly. She read on and on and forgot herself in the tale of war and outlawry until she eventually fell asleep to the lowering sun and the sound of bees.

She slept a long time and was visited by a strong dream in which she found herself in a train depot amid a crowd of waiting passengers. There was a glass case in the center of the room, and in it stood the bones of a man, much like an anatomy display she had once seen in a museum. As she sat waiting for the train, the case filled with a blue glow, the light rising slowly like twisting up the wick in a lantern globe. Ada saw with horror that the bones were reclothing themselves with flesh, and as the process went on it became clear to her that her father was being reconstructed.

The other passengers drew back in horror to the walls of the room, but Ada, though also terrified, walked to the glass and put her hands to it and waited. Monroe, however, never fully became himself. He remained but an animated corpse, the skin thin as parchment over the bones. His movements were slow yet frenzied, as a man struggling underwater. He put his mouth to the glass and talked with great earnestness and urgency to Ada. His demeanor was that of one telling the most important thing he knew. But Ada, even pressing her ear to the glass, could not hear a thing other than murmuring. Then there was the sound of wind before a storm, and the case was suddenly empty. A conductor came and called the passengers to the train, and it was clear to Ada that its final destination was Charleston in the past, and that if she got on she would arrive at her girlhood, with the clock turned back twenty years. All the passengers boarded, and

they were a jolly band, waving from the windows and smiling. Snatches of song came from some compartments. But Ada stood alone on the siding as the train rolled away.

She awoke to a night sky. The rusty beacon of Mars was just slipping below the line of woodlot trees to the west. That told her it must be past the middle of the night, for she had been marking its early evening position in her notebook. A half-moon stood high in the sky. The night was dry and only a little cool. Ada unrolled the shawl and wrapped it about her. She had, of course, never spent a night in the woods alone, but she found it less frightening than she would have thought, even after her troubling dream. The moon shed a fine blue light on the woods and fields. Cold Mountain was visible only as a faint smudge of darkness across the sky. There was no sound but the call of a bobwhite from the distance. She felt no need to hurry to the house.

Ada pulled the wax seal off the crock of blackberry preserves and dipped two fingers into it and scooped berries into her mouth. The preserves had been made with little sweetening and tasted fresh and sharp. Ada sat for hours and watched the progress of the moon across the sky and ate until the little crock was empty. She thought of her father in the dream and of the dark figure in the well. Though she loved Monroe deeply, she realized she was oddly affected by his appearance in her visions. She did not want him coming for her, nor did she want to follow him too immediately.

Ada sat on long enough to watch the day rise. The first grey light began gathering faintly, and then as the light built the mountains began to form themselves, retaining the dark of night in their bulk. The fog that clung to the peaks lifted and lost the shapes of the mountains and dissipated in the warmth of the morning. In the pasture the forms of trees remained drawn in dew on the grass beneath them. When she stood to walk down to the house, the smell of night still lingered under the two chestnut trees.

At the house, Ada took the lap desk and went to her reading chair. The hallway was in deep gloom but for a patch of the golden light of morning that fell onto the top of the desk where it sat across her legs. The light was sectioned by the muntins of the window sash, and the air it passed through was full of hovering dust motes. Ada put her paper into one of the squares of light and wrote a quick letter thanking the lawyer for his offer but declining it on the grounds that at present she was of the opinion that her qualifications for administering an estate composed of nearly nothing were more than sufficient.

In the hours of her night watch she had gone over and over the possibilities before her. They were few. If she tried to sell out and return to Charleston, the little money she could hope to realize from the farm in such bad times, when buyers would be scarce, could hardly support her for long. She would, after a point, have to attach herself to friends of Monroe's in some mildly disguised parasitic relationship, tutor or music instructor or the like.

That or marry. And the thought of returning to Charleston as some desperate predatory spinster was appalling to her. She could imagine the scenes. Spending much of what money she had on suitable wardrobe and then negotiating matrimony with the kind of aging and ineffectual leftovers of a certain level of Charleston society—one several layers down from the top—when all the men approximately her age were off to war. All she could foresee was eventually finding herself saying to someone that she loved him, when what she would mean was that he happened to have turned up at a particularly needy time. She could not, even under the current duress, push her mind to imagine—beyond a general feeling of press and smother—the marriage act with such a one.

If she returned to Charleston under those humiliating conditions, she could expect little sympathy and much withering commentary, for in the eyes of many she had foolishly squandered the fleeting few years of courtship when young ladies

were elevated to the apex of their culture, and men knelt in deference while all of society stood at attention to watch their progress toward marriage as if the primary moral force of the universe were focused in that direction. At the time, Monroe's friends and acquaintances had found her relative disinterest in the process puzzling.

She had done little to help matters, for in the confines of ladies' parlors following dinner parties where the mated and the mating passed sharp judgment on one another, she was prone to claim she was so dreadfully bored by suitors—all of whom seemed limited in their sphere of interests to business, hunting, and horses—that she felt she ought to have a sign fashioned to read Gentlemen Prohibited hanging from the porch gate. She counted on such pronouncements to evoke a doctrinal response, either from one of the elders in the group or from one of the debutantes eager to ingratiate herself among those who held that the highest expression of married woman was reasonable submission to man's will. Marriage is the end of woman, one of them would say. And Ada would respond, Indeed. There we can agree, at least as long as we do not dwell too long on the meaning of the word located next-to-the-last-but-one from your period. She delighted in the silence that followed as all present counted back to find the piece of diction in question.

As a result of such behavior, it became not an uncommon opinion among their acquaintances to think that Monroe had shaped her into a type of monster, a creature not entirely fit for the society of men and women. There was, therefore, little surprise, though considerable indignation, at Ada's response to two marriage proposals during her nineteenth year: she rejected them out of hand, explaining later that what she found lacking in her suitors was a certain amplitude—of thought, of feeling, of being. That and the fact that both men kept their hair shiny with pomatum, as if to compensate in some visible way for their lack of sparkling wit.

To many of her friends, rejection of a marriage proposal

made by any man of means who was not defective in a clear and demonstrable way was, if not inconceivable, at least inexcusable, and in the year before their move to the mountains, many of her friends had fallen away, finding her too bristly and eccentric.

Even now, return to Charleston was a bitter thought and one that her pride rejected. There was nothing pulling her back there. Certainly not family. She had no relatives closer than her cousin Lucy, no kindly aunts or doting grandparents welcoming her return. And that state of kinlessness too was a bitter thought, considering that all around her the mountain people were bound together in ties of clan so extensive and firm that they could hardly walk a mile along the river road without coming upon a relative.

But still, outsider though she was, this place, the blue mountains, seemed to be holding her where she was. From any direction she came at it, the only conclusion that left her any hope of self-content was this: what she could see around her was all that she could count on. The mountains and a desire to find if she could make a satisfactory life of common things here—together they seemed to offer the promise of a more content and expansive life, though she could in no way picture even its starkest outlines. It was easy enough to say, as Monroe often had, that the path to contentment was to abide by one's own nature and follow its path. Such she believed was clearly true. But if one had not the slightest hint toward finding what one's nature was, then even stepping out on the path became a snaggy matter.

She therefore sat at the window that morning wondering sincerely and with some confusion what her next action should be when she saw a figure come walking up the road. As it neared the house Ada resolved the figure into a girl of sorts, a short one, thin as a chicken neck except across the points of her sharp hipbones, where she was of substantial width. Ada went to the porch and sat, waiting to see what this person might want.

The girl came up to the porch and without asking leave sat in a rocker next to Ada and hooked her heels on the chair rungs.

She started rocking. As a structure, she was stable as a drag sled, low in her center of gravity but knobby and slight in all the extremities. She wore a square-necked dress of coarse homespun cloth, the dusty color of blue that comes from dye made of the inside of ragweed galls.

—Old Lady Swanger said you're in need of help, she said.

Ada examined the girl further. She was a dark thing, corded through the neck and arms. Frail-chested. Her hair was black and coarse as a horse's tail. Broad across the bridge of her nose. Big dark eyes, virtually pupil-less, the whites of them startling in their clarity. She went shoeless, but her feet were clean. The nails to her toes were pale and silver as fish scales.

—Mrs. Swanger is right. I do need help, Ada said, but what I need is in the way of rough work. Plowing, planting, harvesting, woodcutting, and the like. This place has to be made self-sufficient. I believe I need a man-hand for the job.

—Number one, the girl said, if you've got a horse I can plow all day. Number two, Old Lady Swanger told me your straits. Something for you to keep in mind would be that every man worth hiring is off and gone. It's a harsh truth, but that's mostly the way of things, even under favorable conditions.

The girl's name, Ada soon discovered, was Ruby, and though the look of her was not confidence-inspiring, she convincingly depicted herself as capable of any and all farm tasks. Just as importantly, as they talked, Ada found she was enormously cheered by Ruby. Ada's deep impression was that she had a willing heart. And though Ruby had not spent a day of her life in school and could not read a word nor write even her name, Ada thought she saw in her a spark as bright and hard as one struck with steel and flint. And there was this: like Ada, Ruby was a motherless child from the day she was born. They had that to understand each other by, though otherwise they could not have been more alien to each other. In short order, and somewhat to Ada's surprise, they began striking a deal.

Ruby said, I've not ever hired out as hand or servant, and

I've not heard good things told about taking on such a job. But Sally said you needed help, and she was right. What I'm saying is, we have to come to some terms.

This is where we talk about money, Ada thought. Monroe had never consulted her in the matter of hiring, but she was under the impression that the help did not ordinarily lay down conditions for their employment. She said, Right this minute, and possibly for some time to come, money is in short supply.

—Money's not it, Ruby said. Like I said, I'm not exactly looking to hire out. I'm saying if I'm to help you here, it's with both us knowing that everybody empties their own night jar.

Ada started to laugh but then realized this was not meant to be funny. Something on the order of equality, was Ruby's demand. It seemed from Ada's point of view an odd one. But on reflection she decided that since no one else was lined up to help her, and since she had been tossing her own slops all summer, the request was fair enough.

As they talked over the remaining details, the yellow and black rooster walked by the porch and paused to stare at them. He twitched his head and flipped his red comb from one side of his head to the other.

—I despise that bird, Ada said. He tried to flog me.

Ruby said, I'd not keep a flogging rooster.

—Then how might we run it off? Ada said.

Ruby looked at her with a great deal of puzzlement. She rose and stepped off the porch and in one swift motion snatched up the rooster, tucked his body under her left arm, and with her right hand pulled off his head. He struggled under her arm for a minute and then fell still. Ruby threw the head off into a barberry bush by the fence.

—He'll be stringy, so we'd best stew him awhile, Ruby said.

By dinnertime the meat of the rooster was falling from the bone, and gobs of biscuit dough the size of cat heads cooked in the yellow broth.

the color of despair

At another time the scene might have had about it a note of the jaunty. All the elements that composed it suggested the legendary freedom of the open road: the dawn of day, sunlight golden and at a low angle; a cart path bordered on one side by red maples, on the other by a split-rail fence; a tall man in a slouch hat, a knapsack on his back, walking west. But after such wet and miserable nights as he had recently passed, Inman felt like God's most marauded bantling. He stopped and put a boot on the bottom rail of the roadside fence and looked out across the dewy fields. He tried to greet the day with a thankful heart, but in the early pale light his first true vision was of some foul variety of brown flatland viper sliding flabby and turdlike from the roadway into a thick bed of chickweed.

Beyond the fields stood flatwoods. Nothing but trash trees. Jack pine, slash pine, red cedar. Inman hated these planed-off, tangled pinebrakes. All this flat land. Red dirt. Mean towns. He had fought over ground like this from the piedmont to the sea, and it seemed like nothing but the place where all that was foul and sorry had flowed downhill and pooled in the low spots.

Country of swill and sullage, sump of the continent. A miry slough indeed, and he could take little more of it. Out in the woods, cicadas shrilled all around, near and far, a pulsing screech like the sound of many jagged pieces of dry bone twisting against each other. So dense was the noise that it came to seem a vibration conceived inside Inman's head from the jangle of his own troubled mind. A personal affliction, rather than a sensation of the general world shared by all. The wound at his neck felt freshly raw, and it throbbed with every pulse of cicadas. He ran a finger up under the dressing, half expecting to feel a place as deep and red as a gill slit, but instead what he found was a great crusted welt at his collar line.

He calculated that his days of traveling had put little distance between himself and the hospital. His condition had required him to walk more slowly and to rest more often than he would have liked, and he had been able to cover only a few miles at a time, and even that slow pace had been at considerable cost. He was bone tired and at least partially lost, still trying to find a passway bearing directly west toward home. But the country had been one of small farmsteads, all cut up by a welter of interlaced roads, none marked by any signpost to announce it as more likely westering than another. He kept feeling that he had been led farther south than he wanted. And the weather had been bad, hard rain off and on through the period, sudden downpours with thunder and lightning, both day and night. The small clapboard farmhouses had lain close-spaced, one to the other, with cornfields all but run together and nothing but fence rails to mark one man's place from the next. Each farm had two or three vicious hounds set to go off at the merest sound, rushing barkless and low out of the dark shadows of roadside trees to rip at his legs with jaws like scythes. The first night, he had kicked away several attacks and a spotted bitch pierced the hide of his calf as if with a leather punch. After that he had looked for weaponry and found a stout locust limb in a ditch. With some little effort he had beat off the next dog that bit at him, striking at

it with short downward blows like tamping dirt around a new-set post. Through much of that night and the ones thereafter, he had clubbed dogs off with dull percussion to send them scooting back still soundless into the dark. The dogs and the threat of Home Guard out prowling and the gloom of the cloudy nights made for nervous wayfaring.

The night just passed had been the worst. The clouds had broken open and revealed meteors flinging themselves out of an empty point of sky. They had shot in on whizzing trajectories that Inman took to be aimed decidedly himward. Little projectiles flung from on high. Later, a great fireball had come roaring out of the dark, moving slow but aimed to land directly atop Inman. Before it had reached him, though, it simply disappeared like a candle flame pinched out with spittled finger and thumb. The fireball had been close-followed by some stub-winged whooshing nightbird or hog-faced bat, flicking low to Inman's head, causing him to duck and walk stooped for three full strides. Then presently a passing luna moth flashed open its great eye-spotted wings directly in front of Inman's nose, and he had mistaken it for some bizarre green dreamface thrust suddenly at him out of the dark with a message to speak. Inman had yelped and struck out at the air before him with hard blows that hit nothing. Later, he had heard the beat of horses cantering and had climbed a tree and watched as a pack of Guard rumbled by, seeking out just such a one as himself to seize and thrash and return to service. When he had climbed down and begun walking again, every tree stump seemed to take on the shape of a lurker in the dark, and he once pulled his pistol on a scraggly myrtle bush that looked like a big-hatted fatman. Crossing a sunken creek long after midnight, he had reached a finger down into the wet clay bank and daubed on the breast of his jacket two concentric circles with a dot at the center and walked on, marked as the butt of the celestial realm, a night traveler, a fugitive, an outlier. Thinking: this journey will be the axle of my life.

That long night accomplished, his greatest desire now was

to climb over the fence and walk out across that old field into the flatwoods. Den up in the pines and sleep. But having at last reached open country, he needed to move on, so he took his foot off the fence rail and addressed himself anew to his travels.

The sun climbed the sky and turned hot, and all the insect world seemed to find Inman's bodily fluids fascinating. Striped mosquitoes hummed around his ears and bit his back through his shirt. Ticks dropped from trailside brush and attached themselves to him at hairline and pant waist and grew fat. Gnats sought out the water in his eyes. A horsefly followed him for a while, troubling his neck. It was a big black glob of buzzing matter the size of the end joint to his thumb, and he longed to kill it but could not, no matter how he jerked and beat at himself as it landed to bite out gouts of flesh and blood. The blows rang out in the still air. From a distance he would have seemed one of a musical temper experimenting with a new method of percussion, or a loosed bedlamite, at odds with his better nature and striking out flat-palmed with self-loathing.

He stopped and pissed in the dirt. Before he was hardly done, spring azure butterflies alit on it to drink, the color of their wings in the sun like blued metal. They seemed to him things too beautiful to be drinking piss. It was, though, apparently the nature of the place.

In the afternoon, he came to a crossroads settlement. He stopped at the edge of town and surveyed the scene. There was but a store, a few houses, a lean-to where a smith pedaled at a wheel, sharpening the long blade of a scythe. Grinding it wrongly, Inman noted, for the smith was sharpening away from the cutting edge rather than toward, and holding the blade at right angles to the wheel rather than diagonal. There were no other people moving about the town. Inman decided to risk going to the whitewashed store to buy food. He stuck his pistol in the folds of the blanket roll so as to look harmless and not draw attention.

Two men sitting on the porch to the store hardly looked up

as he mounted the steps. One man was hatless, his hair sticking up on one side as if he had just risen from bed and not even run his fingers across his head. He was deeply engaged in cleaning his fingernails with the nipple pick to a rifle musket. All his faculties were so fully brought to bear on the task that the tip of his tongue, grey as the foot of a goose, was stuck out at the corner of his mouth. The other man was studying a newspaper. He wore leavings from a uniform, but the bill to his forage cap had been torn off so that the crown alone topped his head like a grey tarboosh. It was cocked off to the side at a sharp angle, and Inman supposed the man styled himself as a rounder. Propped up against the wall behind the man was a fine Whitworth rifle, an elaborate brass-scoped artifact, with many complex little wheels and screws to adjust for windage and elevation. The hexagonal barrel was plugged with a tompion of maple wood to keep out dirt. Inman had seen but a few Whitworths before. They were favorites of snipers. Imported from England, as were their scarce and expensive paper tube cartridges. At .45 caliber, they were not awesome in power, but they were frightfully accurate at distances up to near a mile. If you could see it and had even a measure of skill in marksmanship, a Whitworth could hit it. Inman wondered how men like these might come by such a fine rifle.

He walked past them into the store, and they still did not look up. Inside by the fire two old men played a game on a barrel top. One man put his hand out on the circle of wood and spread his fingers. The other stabbed at the spaces between the fingers with the point of a pocketknife. Inman watched a minute but could not figure out what the rules might be, nor how score might be kept, nor what might need to occur so that one or the other would be declared the victor.

From the store's meager stock, Inman bought five pounds of cornmeal, a piece of cheese, some dried biscuit, and a big sweet pickle, and then he went out onto the porch. The two men were gone, had left so recently that their rockers were still in motion.

Inman stepped down into the road to go on walking west, eating as he traveled. In front of him a pair of black dogs crossed from one patch of shade to another.

Then, as Inman came to the edge of the town, the two men who had been on the porch came from behind the smithy and stood in the road blocking his way out. The smith stopped pedaling the wheel and stood watching.

—Where you going, son-of-a-bitch? the man with the cap said.

Inman said nothing. He ate the wet pickle in two big bites and stuck the remainder of the cheese and biscuit in the haversack. The nipple-pick man moved off to the side of him. The smith, wearing a heavy leather apron and carrying the scythe, came out of the lean-to and circled around to come at Inman from the other side. They were not big men, not even the smith, who seemed in all ways unsuited to his craft. They looked to be layabouts, drunk maybe, and overconfident, for they appeared to presume, since numbers were in their favor, that they could take him with no more weapon than the scythe.

Inman had begun to reach behind him into the roll of his bedding when the three jumped as one, swarming at him. At once they were fighting him fist and skull. He had not time even to remove his pack and thus brawled encumbered.

Inman fought them backing up. His last wish was for them to mob him over onto the ground, and so he gave way until he was forced against the side of the store.

The smith took a step back and came over his head with the scythe like a man splitting wood. His thinking, apparently, was to cleave Inman down the center, cut him open from collarbone to groin, but it was an awkward blow, made doubly so by the shape of the implement. He missed by a foot and the point of the blade buried itself in the dirt.

Inman jerked the scythe from the smith's hands and used it as it was intended, making long sweeping strokes close to the ground. He went at their feet with it, mowing at them and mak-

ing them drop back before they were cut off at the ankles. It felt natural to him, holding a scythe in his hands again and working with it, though the current effort was different from mowing fodder since his strokes were hard, hoping as he was to strike bone. But even under these unfavorable circumstances he found that all the elements of scything—the way you hold it, the wide-footed way you stand, the heel-down angle of the blade to the plane of the ground—fell into the old pattern and struck him as being a thing he could do to some actual effect.

The men skipped and dodged about to avoid the long blade, but soon they regrouped and swarmed again. Inman went to slash at the shinbones of the smith, but the blade clashed on the stone of the foundation and threw a spray of white sparks and broke off close so that he was left holding but the snath. He fought on with it, though it made a poor cudgel, long and misbalanced and awkwardly curved as it was.

In the end though it was adequate, for he eventually smote the three down to their knees in the dirt of the street so they looked like those of the Romish faith at prayer. Then he kept at it until they all lay prone and quiet, faces down.

He threw the snath off across the road into a patch of ragweed. But as soon as he did it, the smith rolled over and raised up weakly and pulled a small-caliber revolver from under his apron and began drawing a shaky bead on Inman.

Inman said, Shitfire. He palmed the little weapon away and stuck it to the man's head just below an eye and commenced pulling the trigger out of sheer frustration with the willfulness of these sorry offscourings. The caps, though, were damp or otherwise faulty, and the pistol snapped on four chambers before he gave up and beat the man about the head with it and flung it onto the top of the building and walked away.

Outside of town he turned into the woods and walked roadless to elude pursuers. All through the afternoon, the best he could do was to continue westering among pine trunks, thrashing his way through brush, stopping now and again to listen for

anyone following. Sometimes he thought he heard voices in the distance, but they were faint and might have been imagination, as when one sleeps near a river and all night thinks he hears conversation pitched too low for understanding. There was no baying of hounds, and so Inman reckoned that even if the voices were the men from town, he was safe enough, especially with night coming on. For course-setting, Inman had the sun wheeling above him, its light broken by the pine boughs, and he followed as it slid off toward the western edge of the earth.

As Inman walked, he thought of a spell Swimmer had taught him, one of particular potency. It was called To Destroy Life, and the words of it formed themselves over and over in his mind. Swimmer had said that it only worked in Cherokee, not in English, and that there was no consequence in teaching it to Inman. But Inman thought all words had some issue, so he walked and said the spell, aiming it out against the world at large, all his enemies. He repeated it over and over to himself as some people, in fear or hope, will say a single prayer endlessly until it burns itself in their thoughts so that they can work or even carry on a conversation with it still running unimpeded. The words Inman remembered were these:

> Listen. Your path will stretch up toward the Nightland. You will be lonely. You will be like the dog in heat. You will carry dog shit before you in your cupped hands. You will howl like a dog as you walk alone toward the Nightland. You will be smeared with dog shit. It will cling to you. Your black guts will be hanging all about you. They will whip about your feet as you walk. You will be living fitfully. Your soul will fade to blue, the color of despair. Your spirit will wane and dwindle away, never to reappear. Your path lies toward the Nightland. This is your path. There is no other.

Inman carried on this way for some miles, but for all he could tell the words were just flying back to strike him alone.

And then after awhile the sentiments of Swimmer's words brought to mind a sermon of Monroe's, one dense to the point of clotting with quotations from various sages as was Monroe's habit. It had taken for text not some Bible verse but a baffling passage from Emerson, and Inman found in it some similarity to the spell, though all in all he preferred Swimmer's wording. What Inman remembered was this passage, which Monroe had repeated four times at dramatic intervals throughout the sermon: "That which shows God in me, fortifies me. That which shows God out of me, makes me a wart and a wen. There is no longer a necessary reason for my being. Already the long shadows of untimely oblivion creep over me, and I shall decrease forever." Inman thought that had been the best sermon he had ever heard, and Monroe had delivered it on the day Inman first saw Ada.

Inman had attended church expressly for the purpose of viewing her. In the weeks following Ada's arrival in Cold Mountain, Inman had heard much about her before he saw her. She and her father stayed too long green in the country they had taken up, and they soon became a source of great comedy to many households along the river road. For people to sit on the porch and watch Ada and Monroe pass by in the cabriolet or to see Ada on one of her nature walks along the big road was as near to theater as most would come, and she provoked as much discussion as a new production at the Dock Street opera. All agreed that she was pretty enough, but her very choice of Charleston garb or flourish of hairstyle was subject to ridicule. If she were seen holding a stem of beardtongue blossoms to admire their color or stooping to touch the spikes of jimson leaves, some would solemnly call her mazed in the head not to know beardtongue when she saw it, and others would wonder, grinning, was she so wit-scoured as perhaps to eat jimson? Gossip had it that she went about with a notebook and pencil and would stare at a

thing—bird or bush, weed, sunset, mountain—and then scratch at paper awhile as if she were addled enough in her thinking that she might forget what was important to her if she did not mark it down.

So one Sunday morning Inman dressed himself carefully—in a new black suit, white shirt, black tie, black hat—and set out for church to view Ada. It was a time of blackberry winter and a chill rain had fallen without pause for three days, and though the rain had stopped sometime in the night, the morning sun had not yet burned through the clouds, and the slash of sky visible between the ridgelines was dark and low and utterly without feature. The roads were nothing but sucking mud, and so Inman had arrived late and taken a seat at a rear pew. There was already a hymn going. Someone had lit a greenwood fire in the stove. It smoked from around the top plate, and the smoke rose to the ceiling and spread flat against the beadboards and hung there grey like a miniature of the actual sky.

Inman had but the back of her head to find Ada by, yet that took only a moment since her dark hair was done up in a heavy and intricate plait of such recent fashion that it was not then known in the mountains. Below where her hair was twisted up, two faint cords of muscle ran up under the skin on either side of her white neck to hold her head on. Between them a scoop, a shaded hollow of skin. Curls too fine to be worked up into the plait. All through the hymn, Inman's eyes rested there, so that after awhile, even before he saw her face, all he wanted was to press two fingertips against that mystery place.

Monroe began the sermon by commenting on the hymn they had all just mouthed. Its words seemed to look with passionate yearning to a time when they would be immersed in an ocean of love. But Monroe preached that they were misunderstanding the song if they fooled themselves into thinking all creation would someday love them. What it really required was for them to love all creation. That was altogether a more difficult

thing and, to judge by the congregation's reaction, somewhat shocking and distressful.

The remainder of the sermon took the same topic as all others of Monroe's since his arrival in Cold Mountain. Sundays and Wednesdays both, he had talked only of what he thought to be the prime riddle of creation: why was man born to die? It made no sense on the face of it. Over the weeks, he had tried coming at the question from every direction. What the Bible had to say on the matter. How wisemen of many lands and all of known time had reasoned it out. Revelatory metaphors from nature. Monroe tested every hold he could devise to get purchase on it, all without success. After several weeks, grumbling in the congregation made it clear that death troubled him to a greater degree than it did them. Many thought it not the tragedy Monroe did, but saw it rather as a good thing. They were looking forward to the rest. Monroe's thoughts would sit smoother, some had suggested, if he went back to doing what the old dead preacher had done. Mainly condemn sinners and tell Bible tales with entertaining zeal. Baby Moses in the bulrush. Boy David slinging rocks.

Monroe had declined the advice, saying to one elder that such was not his mission. That comment had gotten itself passed all about the community, the general interpretation being that his use of the word *mission* set the congregation in the position of benighted savages. They had, many of them, put up cash money to send missionaries among true savages, folks they pictured in skins of various dim colors living in locales they conceived of as infinitely more remote and heathen than their own, and so the remark did not pass easily.

To wet down the fires that were rising around his ministry, Monroe had therefore begun his sermon on the Sunday in question by explaining how every man and woman had a mission. The word meant no more nor less than a job of work, he said. It was one job of his to think about why man was born to die, and

he was inclined to go on at it with at least the perseverance of a man with a horse to break or a field to clear of stones. And he did go on. At length. Throughout the preachment that morning, Inman sat staring at Ada's neck and listening as Monroe repeated four times the Emerson passage about warts and wens and decreasing forever.

When the service concluded, the men and women left the church by their separate doors. Muddy horses stood asleep in their traces, their rigs and traps behind them mired up to the spokes in mud. The voices of the people awoke them, and one chestnut mare shook her hide with the sound of flapping a dirty carpet. The churchyard was filled with the smell of mud and wet leaves and wet clothes and wet horses. The men lined up to shake hands with Monroe, and then they all milled about the wet churchyard visiting and speculating on whether the rain had quit or was just resting. Some of the elders talked in low voices about the queerness of Monroe's sermon and its lack of Scripture and about how they admired his stubbornness in the face of other people's desires.

The unmarried men wadded up together, standing with their muddy boots and spattered pant cuffs in a circle. Their talk had more of Saturday night to it than Sunday morning, and all of them periodically cut their eyes to where Ada stood at the edge of the graveyard looking altogether foreign and beautiful and utterly awkward. Everyone else wore woolens against the damp chill, but Ada had on an ivory-colored linen dress with lace at the collar and sleeves and hem. She seemed to have chosen it more by the calendar than the weather.

She stood holding her elbows. The older women came to her and said things and then there were knotty pauses and then they went away. Inman noted that every time she was approached, Ada took a step back until she fetched up against the headstone of a man who had fought in the Revolution.

—If I went and told her my name, reckon she'd say ought to

me back? said a Dillard man who had come to church for precisely the same reason Inman had.

—I couldn't say, Inman said.

—You'd not begin to know where to start courting her, Hob Mars said to Dillard. Best leave that to me.

Mars was shortish and big through the chest. He had a fat watch that pooched out his vest pocket and a silver chain that ran to his pant waist and a scrolled fob hanging from the chain.

Dillard said, You think you bore with a mighty big auger.

—I don't think it, I know it, Mars said.

Then another man, one of such slight build and irregular features that he was but a bystander, said, I'd bet a hundred dollars against a half a ginger cake that she's got a husband-elect down in Charleston.

—They can be forgot, Hob said. Many has been before.

Then Hob stared at Inman and surveyed his strict attire. You look like the law, he said. A man courting needs some color about him.

Inman could see that they would all talk the topic round and round until one or another that day might eventually draw up the nerve to go to her and make a fool of himself. Or else they would insult each other until a pair of them would have to meet down the road and fight. So he touched a finger to his brow and said, Boys, and walked away.

He went straight over to Sally Swanger and said, I'd clear an acre of newground for an introduction.

Sally had on a bonnet with a long bill to it so that she had to step back and cock her head to throw the shade off her eyes and look up at Inman. She grinned at him and put her hand up and touched a pinchbeck brooch at her collar and rubbed her fingers across it.

—Notice I'm not even asking who to, she said.

—Now would be the time, Inman said, looking to where Ada stood alone, her back to the people, slightly stooped, peer-

ing in apparent fascination at the inscription on the gravestone. The bottom foot of her dress was wet from the tall gravegrass and the tail of it had sometime dragged in mud.

Mrs. Swanger took Inman's black coat sleeve between finger and thumb and pulled him by such slight harness across the yard to Ada. When his sleeve was let go, he raised the hand to take off his hat; then with the other he raked through his hair all around where it was pressed and banded. He swept the hair back at each temple and rubbed his palm from brow to chin to compose his face. Mrs. Swanger cleared her throat, and Ada turned.

—Miss Monroe, Sally Swanger said, her face bright. Mr. Inman has expressed a deep interest in becoming acquainted. You've met his parents. His people built the chapel, she added by way of reference, before she walked away.

Ada looked Inman directly in the face, and he realized too late that he had not planned what to say. Before he could formulate a phrase, Ada said, Yes?

There was not much patience in her voice, and for some reason Inman found that amusing. He looked off to the side, down toward where the river bent around the hill, and tried to bring down the corners of his mouth. The leaves on trees and rhododendron at the riverbanks were glossed and drooping with the weight of water. The river ran heavy and dark in curves like melted glass where it bowed over hidden rocks and then sank into troughs. Inman held his hat by the crown and for lack of anything to say he looked down into the hole as if, from previous experience, he waited in sincere expectation that something might emerge.

Ada stood a moment looking at his face, and then after a time she looked into the hole of the hat too. Inman caught himself, fearing that the expression on his face was that of a dog sitting at the lip of a groundhog burrow.

He looked at Ada, and she turned up her palms and raised an eyebrow to signify a general question.

—You're free to put your hat back on and say something, she said.

—It's just that you've been the subject of considerable speculation, Inman said.

—Like a novelty, is it, speaking to me?

—No.

—A challenge, then. Perhaps from that circle of dullards there.

—Not at all.

—Well, then, you supply the simile.

—Like grabbing up a chestnut burr, at least thus far.

Ada smiled and nodded. She had not figured him to know the word.

Then she said, Tell me this. A woman earlier commented on the recent weather. She called it sheep-killing weather. I've been wondering, can't get it out of my mind. Did she mean weather appropriate for slaughtering sheep or weather foul enough to kill them itself without assistance, perhaps by drowning or pneumonia?

—The first, Inman said.

—Well, then, I thank you. You've served a useful purpose.

She turned and walked away to her father. Inman watched her touch Monroe's arm and say something to him, and they went to the cabriolet and climbed in and wheeled off, fading down the lane between fencerows thicketed with blossoming blackberry canes.

Eventually, late in the day, Inman emerged from out the foul pinewoods and found himself wandering the banks of a great swollen river. The sun stood just above the low horizon at the far bank, and there was a haze in the air so that everything was cast in a lurid yellow light. The rain had evidently been harder somewhere upstream and had raised the river to its banks and be-

yond, too wide and strong to swim, even had Inman been a good swimmer. So, hoping to find an unguarded bridge or trestle, he walked up the riverbank, following a thin footpath that ran between the grim pine forest to his right and the sorry river to his left.

It was a foul region, planed off flat except where there were raw gullies cut deep in the red clay. Scrubby pines everywhere. Trees of a better make had once stood in their place but had been cut down long ago, the only evidence of them now an occasional hardwood stump as big around as a dinner table. Poison ivy grew in thick beds that stretched as far as Inman could see through the woods. It climbed the pine trees and spread among their limbs. The falling needles caught in the tangled ivy vines and softened the lines of the trunks and limbs and formed heavy new shapes of them until the trees loomed like green and grey beasts risen out of the ground.

The forest looked to be a sick and dangerous place. It recalled to him a time during the fighting down along the coast when a man had shown him a tiny plant, a strange and hairy thing that grew in bogs. It knew to eat meat, and they fed it little pieces of fatback from the end of a splinter. You could hold the tip of a finger to what stood for its mouth and it would snap at you. These flatwoods seemed only a step away from learning the trick on a grander scale.

What Inman wanted was to be out of there, but the river stretched wide before him, a shit-brown clog to his passage. As a liquid, it bore likeness more to molasses as it first thickens in the making than to water. He wished never to become accustomed to this sorry make of waterway. It did not even fit his picture of a river. Where he was from, the word *river* meant rocks and moss and the sound of white water moving fast under the spell of a great deal of collected gravity. Not a river in his whole territory was wider than you could pitch a stick across, and in every one of them you could see bottom wherever you looked.

This broad ditch was a smear on the landscape. But for the

balls of yellow scud collected in drifted foamy heaps upstream of grounded logs, the river was as opaque and unmarked as a sheet of tin painted brown. Foul as the contents of an outhouse pit.

Inman fared on through this territory, criticizing its every feature. How did he ever think this to be his country and worth fighting for? Ignorance alone would account for it. All he could list in his mind worth combat right now was his right to exist unmolested somewhere on the west fork of the Pigeon River drainage basin, up on Cold Mountain near the source of Scapecat Branch.

He thought on homeland, the big timber, the air thin and chill all the year long. Tulip poplars so big through the trunk they put you in mind of locomotives set on end. He thought of getting home and building him a cabin on Cold Mountain so high that not a soul but the nighthawks passing across the clouds in autumn could hear his sad cry. Of living a life so quiet he would not need ears. And if Ada would go with him, there might be the hope, so far off in the distance he did not even really see it, that in time his despair might be honed off to a point so fine and thin that it would be nearly the same as vanishing.

But even though he believed truly that you can think on a thing till it comes real, this last thought never shaped up so, no matter how hard he tried. What hope he had was no brighter than if someone had lit fire to a taper at the mountain's top and left him far away to try setting a course by it.

He walked on and shortly night began to fall and a part of a moon shone through patchy clouds. He came upon a road that ended in the river; beside it, a sign that someone had stuck up at the water's edge read Ferry. $5. Yell Loud.

A stout rope stretched from a thick post across the water and disappeared into it. Toward the far bank, the rope rose from the water again to end at another post. Beyond the landing, Inman saw a house on stilts raised above the highwater mark. A window was lit and smoke came from the chimney.

Inman called out, and in a minute a figure appeared on the

porch and waved and went back in. Soon, though, it reappeared from behind the house dragging a dugout canoe by a line. The boatman got it afloat and mounted it and set out rowing hard upstream in the slower water that flowed near the bank. Still it was a strong current, and he dug with bowed back at the paddle until it looked like he planned to just keep on going. Before he went out of sight, though, he turned and sat up and let the current carry him down, angling to the east bank, working easily, saving effort. Just barely touching the blade to the water to set a course. The dugout was old and the dry wood was sun-bleached, so that the crude and blockish sides of it shone like beaten pewter against the dark water when the moon broke from between clouds.

As the canoe came in toward shore where Inman stood, he saw that it was piloted by no ferryman but an apple-cheeked girl, dark about the head and skin so as to suggest Indian blood back a generation or two. She wore a dress of homespun that in the dim light he took to be yellow. She had big strong hands, and the muscles of her forearms knotted under the skin with every stroke. Her black hair was loose about her shoulders. She whistled a tune as she approached. At the bank she stepped out of the dugout barefooted into the muddy water, pulling the canoe by a line at its bow to beach it. Inman drew a five-dollar note from his pocket and reached it to her. She didn't reach to take it, but only looked at it with some measure of disgust.

—I wouldn't give a thirsty man a dipper of this river water for five dollars, much less paddle you across it, she said.

—The sign says the ferry charge is five.

—This look like a ferryboat to you?

—Is this a ferry crossing or not?

—It is when Daddy's here. He's got a flatboat big enough to carry a team and wagon. He pulls it across on the rope. But with the river up he can't run it. He's gone off hunting, waiting for the water to drop. Until then, I'm charging the utmost somebody's willing to pay, for I've got me a cowhide and I aim to get a saddle

made from it. And when I get me that, I'll start saving for a horse, and when I get one, I'll throw the saddle over it and turn my back to this river and be gone.

—What's the name of this thing? Inman said.

—Why it's nothing but the mighty Cape Fear River is all, the girl said.

—Well, what will you charge me to get over it? Inman said.

—Fifty dollars scrip, the girl said.

—Take twenty?

—Let's go.

Before they could climb into the boat, Inman saw great greasy bubbles rising to the surface thirty feet out from the bank. They shone in the moonlight as they broke, and they moved in a direction counter to the river's flow, going upstream at about the pace of a man walking. The night was windless and still, and there were not other sounds than the water blubbering and the bugs skirling in the pines.

—You see that? Inman said.

—Yeah, the girl said.

—What's making it?

—Hard to say, it being at the bottom of the river.

The water broke as huge and urgent as breath from a drowning cow. Inman and the girl stood and watched as the bubbles gradually climbed the river until the moon was overblown by a bank of clouds and they disappeared in the darkness.

—Could be a catfish rooting along the river bottom to dig up some food, the girl said. They've got a diet would kill a turkey vulture. I seen one the size of a boar hog one time. It was washed up dead on a sandbar. Whiskers on it the size of blacksnakes.

That would be the sort of thing that would grow in this river, Inman figured. Monstrous flabby fish with meat as slack as fatback. He thought of the great contrast between such a creature and the little trout that lived in the upper branches of the Pigeon where the water poured off Cold Mountain. They were seldom

longer than your hand. Bright and firm as shavings from a bar of silver.

Inman tossed his packs in ahead of him and boarded the canoe and settled himself into the prow. The girl got in behind him and dug hard against the water, paddling with a strong and sure hand, keeping a straight course by kicking out at the tail of the stroke rather than constantly switching sides. The splash of the paddle overrode even the insects' squealing.

The girl dug hard at the water to send them a fair piece up the river from the landing, taking advantage of the slower water near the bank. Then she turned about and quit paddling and stuck the blade in the water like a rudder. She angled them out, using the current to drive them toward the river's midpoint. With the moon hidden, the land beyond the riverbank soon disappeared, and they floated blind in a world black as the inside of a cow. In the silence they heard the sound of voices from the eastern landing carrying far across the water. It might have been anybody. Inman doubted the men from the town had enough purpose to follow him so far.

Still, he turned and, whispering, said to the girl, We'd best not be found out. But at that moment he looked up and saw a radius of moon appear from under clouds. It soon stood fully revealed in a little ragged window of sky. The sun-bleached side of the canoe shone out like a beacon on the dark water.

There was a sound like running fingernails across the grain of corduroy and a whacking sound. The crack of gunfire followed.

The Whitworth, Inman thought.

A hole opened up at the back of the canoe at waterline. Brown water streamed in at the alarming rate of a cow pissing. Inman looked ahead to the landing and saw a party of a half-dozen men milling about in the moonlight. Some of them began firing their little pistols, but they had not the carrying power to cover the distance. The man with the rifle, though, had it turned up and was working with the ramrod to tamp in a fresh load. The

only way Inman could figure it, the men must have framed the evening in their minds as a type of coon hunt, as sport; otherwise they would have long since gone back to town.

The ferry girl sized up the situation immediately and threw her weight to rock the canoe hard, tipping it to the gunwales to wet it down and darken it. Inman tore the cuff off his shirt and was plugging the hole when another ball struck the side at waterline and tore off a chunk of wood as big as a hand. The river poured in and soon began filling the bottom of the boat.

—There's nothing else but that we are going to have to get down in the river, the girl said.

Inman first thought she intended them to strike out swimming for shore. Not having come from a country of deep water, though, he doubted his ability to swim that far. Instead, she proposed they get in the water and hold to the canoe, using it for cover. Inman wrapped his packs with his oilcloth and tied the bundle off tight as he could with the loose ends in case the canoe should sink entirely. Then, together, he and the girl threw themselves into the river to let the current take them, bearing them up and away, spinning them off downstream.

Though the surface was smooth as a mirror and looked as if it could move at no greater pace than an ooze, the swollen river boomed along at the speed of a millrace. The dugout, partially filled with water, floated low in the river, just the spade-shaped bow fully above the surface. Inman had swallowed water, and he spit and spit until he could bring up nothing but white foam, trying to clear his mouth of the foul river. Uglier water he had never tasted.

The moon came and went among the clouds, and when there was enough light to aim by, rounds from the Whitworth hit the canoe or struck the water and skipped off stuttering across the surface. Inman and the girl tried to kick with their legs and steer the upturned boat to the western shore, but in its heaviness it seemed to have a mind of its own and would in no way do their bidding. They gave up and let themselves be carried along, just

their faces above water. There was nothing to do but hang on and wait for a bend in the river and hope that the evening would present something to their advantage.

From down in it, the river looked even wider than from the bank. The foul country passing along on either side was vague and ominous in the moonlight. Inman's hope was that it would strike neither mark nor impress on his mental workings, so vile did its contours lie about him.

Even from out in the river he could hear that the bugs squealed among the poison ivy without pause. He was but a little head floating in a great void plane bounded by a dark jungle of venomous plants. Any minute he figured to see the white bewhiskered maw of the monster catfish rise from the water and suck him in. All his life adding up to no more than catfish droppings on the bottom of this swill trough of a river.

He floated along thinking he would like to love the world as it was, and he felt a great deal of accomplishment for the occasions when he did, since the other was so easy. Hate took no effort other than to look about. It was a weakness, he acknowledged, to be of such a mind that all around him had to lie fair for him to call it satisfactory. But there were places he knew where such would generally be the case. Cold Mountain. Scapecat Branch. And right now the first impediment to being there was a hundred yards of river.

After a time, the moon was blinded again by clouds, and they drifted past the landing, and Inman could hear the men talking as clearly as if he stood amid the group. One man, evidently the owner of the Whitworth, said, It was daylight, I could shoot the ears off his head with this thing.

Long moments later the moon again appeared. Inman raised up and looked across the dugout. Way back at the ferry landing, he saw little figures waving their arms and jumping up and down in their rage. They receded, and he could think of many things that he wished could similarly just get smaller and smaller until they disappeared. The main evidence of their exis-

tence was the occasional splash of lead, followed at some interval by the report of the long rifle. Like lightning and thunder, Inman thought. He occupied the time counting the seconds between the slap of a ball and the faint pop. He could not, however, remember the way you were supposed to figure distance from it. Nor did he know if the same principle applied.

The river eventually swept them around a bend and put the landing out of sight. Now that they could safely get to the other side of the canoe they could kick to some effect, and in short order they fetched up on land. That side of the canoe was shot to pieces beyond repair, so they left it wallowing in the shallow water and set out walking upstream.

When they got to the house, Inman gave the girl more money as compensation for the old dugout, and she gave him directions for finding the roads west.

—Some few miles up, this river forks out into the Haw and the Deep. The Deep's the left fork and you'll stay near it for some time, for it runs mainly from the west.

Inman walked on up the river until he reached the forks, and then he went into the brush until he was hid. He dared not light a fire to make corn mush and so ate but a green windfall apple he had picked up out of the road and the cheese and dry biscuit, which now carried a strong foretaste of the Cape Fear. He kicked together a bed of duff deep enough to keep him off the damp ground and stretched out and slept for three hours. He awoke sore and bruised about the face from the fight. Blisters of poison ivy beaded up on his hands and forearms from his flight through the flatwoods. When he put a hand to his neck, he found fresh blood where his wound had cracked open and leaked, from the strain of whipping the three men or from the soaking in the river. He took up his packs and set off again walking.

verbs, all of them tiring

The agreement Ada and Ruby reached on that first morning was this: Ruby would move to the cove and teach Ada how to run a farm. There would be very little money involved in her pay. They would take most of their meals together, but Ruby did not relish the idea of living with anyone else and decided she would move into the old hunting cabin. After they had eaten their first dinner of chicken and dumplings, Ruby went home and was able to wrap everything worth taking in a quilt. She had gathered the ends, slung it over her shoulder, and headed to Black Cove, never looking back.

The two women spent their first days together making an inventory of the place, listing the things that needed doing and their order of urgency. They walked together about the farm, Ruby looking around a lot, evaluating, talking constantly. The most urgent matter, she said, was to get a late-season garden into the ground. Ada followed along, writing it all down in a notebook that heretofore had received only her bits of poetry, her sentiments on life and the large issues of the day. Now she wrote entries such as these:

To be done immediately: Lay out a garden for cool season crops—turnips, onions, cabbage, lettuce, greens.
Cabbage seed, do we have any?
Soon: Patch shingles on barn roof; do we have a maul and froe?
Buy clay crocks for preserving tomatoes and beans.
Pick herbs and make from them worm boluses for the horse.

And on and on. So much to do, for apparently Ruby planned to require every yard of land do its duty.

The hayfields, Ruby said, had not been cut frequently enough, and the grass was in danger of being taken over by spurge and yarrow and ragweed, but it was not too far gone to save. The old cornfield, she declared, had profited from having been left to lie fallow for several years and was now ready for clearing and turning. The outbuildings were in fair shape, but the chicken population was too low. The root cellar in the can house was, in her estimation, a foot too shallow; she feared a bad cold spell might freeze potatoes stored there if they didn't dig it deeper. A martin colony, if they could establish one alongside the garden in gourd houses, would help keep crows away.

Ruby's recommendations extended in all directions, and she never seemed to stop. She had ideas concerning schedules for crop rotation among the various fields. Designs for constructing a tub mill so that once they had a corn crop they could grind their own meal and grits using waterpower from the creek and save having to give the miller his tithe. One evening before she set off in the dark to walk up to the cabin, her last words were, We need us some guineas. I'm not partial to their eggs for frying, but they'll do for baking needs. Even discarding the eggs, guineas are a comfort to have around and useful in a number of ways. They're good watchdogs, and they'll bug out a row of pole beans before you can turn around. All that aside from how pleasant they are to look at walking around the yard.

The next morning her first words were, Pigs. Do you have any loose in the woods?

Ada said, No, we always bought our hams.

—There's a world more to a hog than just the two hams, Ruby said. Take lard for example. We'll need plenty.

Despite the laxity of Monroe's tenure at Black Cove, there was nevertheless much more to work with than Ada had realized. On one of their first walks about the place, Ruby was delighted by the extensive apple orchards. They had been planted and maintained by the Blacks and were only now beginning to show the first marks of inattention. Despite lack of recent pruning, they were thick with maturing fruit.

—Come October, Ruby said, we'll get enough in trade for those apples to make our winter a sight easier than it would be otherwise.

She paused and thought a minute. You don't have a press, do you? she said. When Ada said she thought they might indeed, Ruby whooped in joy.

—Hard cider is worth considerably more in trade than apples, she said. All we'll have to do is make it.

Ruby was pleased too with the tobacco patch. In the spring, Monroe had given the hired man permission to plant a small field of tobacco for his own use. Despite most of a summer of neglect, the plants were surprisingly tall and full-leaved and worm-free, though weeds grew thick in the rows and the plants were badly in need of topping and suckering. Ruby believed the plants had thrived despite disregard because they must have been planted in full accordance with the signs. She calculated that with luck they might get a small crop and said that if they cured the leaves and soaked them in sorghum water and twisted them into plugs, they could trade off tobacco for seed and salt and leavening and other items they could not produce themselves.

Barter was very much on Ada's mind, since she did not understand it and yet found herself suddenly so untethered to the

money economy. In the spirit of partnership and confidence, she had shared with Ruby the details of her shattered finances. When she told Ruby of the little money they had to work with, Ruby said, I've never held a money piece bigger than a dollar in my hand. What Ada came to understand was that though she might be greatly concerned at their lack of cash, Ruby's opinion was that they were about as well off without it. Ruby had always functioned at arm's length from the buying of things and viewed money with a great deal of suspicion even in the best of times, especially when she contrasted it in her mind with the solidity of hunting and gathering, planting and harvesting. At present, matters had pretty much borne out Ruby's darkest opinions. Scrip had gotten so cheapened in its value that it was hard to buy anything with it anyway. On their first trip together into town they had been stunned to have to give fifteen dollars for a pound of soda, five dollars for a paper of triple-ought needles, and ten for a quire of writing paper. Had they been able to afford it, a bolt of cloth would have cost fifty dollars. Ruby pointed out that cloth would cost them not a cent if they had sheep and set about shearing, carding, spinning, winding, dyeing, and weaving the wool into cloth for dresses and underdrawers. All Ada could think was that every step in the process that Ruby had so casually sketched out would be many days of hard work to come up with a few yards of material coarse as sacking. Money made things so much easier.

But even if they had it, shopkeepers really didn't want money since the value of it would likely drop before they could get shut of it. The general feeling was that paper money ought to be spent as soon as possible; otherwise it might easily become worth no more than an equal volume of chaff. Barter was surer. And that Ruby seemed to understand fully. She had a headful of designs as to how they might make Black Cove answer for itself in that regard.

In short order Ruby had devised a plan. She put it to Ada as a choice. The two things she had marked in her inventory of the

place as being valuable and portable and inessential were the cabriolet and the piano. She believed she could trade either one for about all they would need to make it through the winter. Ada weighed them in her mind for two days. At one point she said, It would be a shame to reduce that fine dapple gelding to drawing a plow, and Ruby said, He'll be doing that whichever way you pick. He'll have to work out his feed like anybody else around here.

Ada finally surprised even herself by settling on the piano to part with. Truth be told, though, her hand at the instrument was not particularly fine, and it had been Monroe's choice that she learn to play it to begin with. It had meant so much to him that he had hired a teacher to live with them, a little man named Tip Benson who seldom kept a position for long as he could not refrain from falling in love with his charges. Ada had been no exception. She was fifteen at the time, and one afternoon, as she sat attempting a baffling passage from Bach, Benson had fallen to his knees by the piano bench and pulled her hands from the keys and drawn them to him and pressed their backs to his round cheeks. He was a plump man, no more than twenty-four at the time, with extraordinarily long fingers for one of his squat build. He pressed his pursed red lips to the backs of her hands and kissed them with great ardor. Another girl of Ada's age might have played him to her advantage for a time, but Ada excused herself right then and went straight to Monroe and told him what had passed. Benson had his bags packed and was gone by suppertime. Monroe immediately hired as music tutor an old spinster with clothes that smelled of naphtha and underarms.

Part of Ada's reasoning in choosing the piano for barter was that there would be little room for art in her coming life and what place she had for it could be occupied by drawing. The simple implements of pencil and paper would answer her needs in that regard.

She could see all the good reasons for parting with the

piano. What she was not clear on were the reasons for keeping the cabriolet. There was the fact that it had been Monroe's, but that did not feel like the holding point. She worried that it was the mobility of the thing that held her to it. The promise in its tall wheels that if things got bad enough she could just climb in and ride away. Be like the Blacks before her and take the attitude that there was no burden that couldn't be lightened, no wreckful life that couldn't be set right by heading off down the road.

After Ada made her decision known, Ruby wasted no time. She knew who had excess animals and produce, who would be willing to trade favorably. In this case it was Old Jones up on East Fork she dealt with. His wife had coveted the piano for some time, and knowing that, Ruby traded hard. Jones was finally made to give for it a pied brood sow and a shoat and a hundred pounds of corn grits. And Ruby—thinking how wool was such a useful thing in so many ways, especially with the current high cost of fabric—allowed that it wouldn't hurt to take on a few of the little mountain sheep, not much bigger than a mid-sized breed of dog full grown. So she convinced Jones to throw in a half dozen of them as well. And a wagonload of cabbages. And a ham and ten pounds of bacon from the first hog he killed in November.

Within a matter of days, Ruby had driven the hogs and the little sheep, two of them dark, up into Black Cove. She shooed them onto the slopes of Cold Mountain to fend for themselves through the autumn, fattening on what mast they could find, which would be plenty. Before she let them go she had taken out her knife and marked their left ears with two smooth crops and a slit so that they all fled bloody-headed, squealing and bleating, to the mountain.

Late one afternoon, Old Jones came with a wagon and another old man to get the piano. The two stood in the parlor and looked at it a long time. The other old man said, I'm not so sure

we can lift that thing, and Old Jones said, We've got the advantage of it; we have to. They finally got it into the wagon and roped it in tight, for it hung out past the tailboard.

Ada sat on the porch and watched the piano ride away. It jounced down the road, the unsprung wagon hitting hard on every rut and rock so that the piano played its own alarming and discordant tune in farewell. There was not a lot of regret in Ada's mood, but what she thought about as she watched the wagon go was a party Monroe had given four days before Christmas in the last winter before the war.

The chairs in the parlor had been pushed back against the walls to make room for dancing, and those who could play took turns at the piano, beating out carols and waltzes and sentimental parlor tunes. The dining room table was loaded with tiny ham biscuits, cakes and brown bread and mince pies, and a pot of tea fragrant with orange and cinnamon and clove. Monroe had caused only a minor scandal by serving champagne, there being no Baptists in attendance. All the glass-bowled kerosene lamps were lit, and people marveled over them and their crimped chimney tops like the petals of buds opening, for they were a new thing and had not yet become general. Sally Swanger, though, expressed the fear that they would explode, and she judged the light they cast as too glaring and said tapers and hearth light suited her old eyes better.

Early in the evening people formed like-membered groups and gossiped. Ada sat with the women, but her attention flickered about the room. Six old men drew up chairs near the fire and talked of the looming crisis in Congress and sipped at their flutes and then held them up to the lamplight to study the bubbles. Esco said, It comes to a fight the Federals'll kill us all down. When others in the group violently disagreed, Esco looked into his glass and said, A man made liquor with a bead like this, it'd be judged unsound.

Ada also paid mild heed to the young men, sons of valued members of the congregation. They sat in a back corner of the parlor and talked loudly. Most of them disdained the champagne and drank only somewhat surreptitiously from pocket ticklers full of corn liquor. Hob Mars, who had briefly paid poorly received court to Ada, announced as if speaking to the room at large that he had celebrated the Savior's birth every night for a week. He claimed that from those parties dull enough to have ended before dawn he had lit his way home by pistol fire. He reached and took a drink from another man's flask and then rubbed the back of his hand across his mouth and looked at it and rubbed again. That's got a whang to it, he said loudly and passed the flask back.

Women of mixed ages occupied another corner. Sally Swanger wore a new pair of fine shoes, and she sat awaiting comment on them, her feet out before her like a stiff-legged doll. Another of the older women told a somewhat extended tale of her daughter's poor marriage. At the husband's insistence, the daughter shared a house with a family of hounds who lounged about the kitchen at all times but coon hunts. The woman said she hated to go visit, for there was always dog hair in the gravy. She said her daughter had for several years produced one baby after another so that, contrary to her earlier wildness to be married, the daughter now viewed matrimony in a dim light. She had come to see it as a state summing up to little more than wiping tails. The other women laughed, but Ada felt for a moment as if she could not catch her breath.

Later the groups mixed and some stood around the piano and sang and then some of the younger people danced. Ada took a turn at the keyboard, but her mind hovered above the music. She played a number of waltzes and then left the piano and watched amused as Esco arose and, to no accompaniment other than his own whistling, performed a solitary shuffle step during which his eyes glazed over and his head bobbed like it hung by a string.

As the evening went on, Ada found that she had taken more than one glass of champagne beyond the prudent. Her face felt clammy and her neck was sweating under the ruching at the tall collar of her green velvet dress. Her nose felt as if it had swollen, so much so that she pinched it between thumb and forefinger to check its breadth and then went to the hall mirror, where she was startled to see it looking normal.

Sally Swanger, apparently under the sway of Monroe's champagne as well, had at that moment pulled Ada aside in the hallway and in a whisper said, That Inman boy just got here. I should keep my mouth shut, but you ought to marry him. The two of you'd likely make pretty brown-eyed babies.

Ada had been appalled by the comment and, blushing fiercely, she fled to the kitchen to compose herself.

But there, throwing her thoughts into further disarray, she found Inman alone, sitting in the stove corner. He had arrived late, having ridden through a slow winter rain, and he was warming up and drying out before joining the party. He wore a black suit and sat with his legs crossed, his wet hat suspended from the toe of a dress boot near the hot stove. The palms of his hands were held up to catch the heat of the fire so that he looked like he was pushing something away.

—Oh, my, Ada said. There you are. The ladies are already so pleased to know you're here.

—The old ladies? Inman said.

—Well, everyone. Your arrival has been noted with particular approval by Mrs. Swanger.

This called up a vivid and unplanned image, its theme suggested by Mrs. Swanger's comment, and Ada felt a rushing in her head. She blushed again and quickly added, And by others, no doubt.

—Not feeling qualmish, are you? Inman said, somewhat confused by her behavior.

—No, no. This room is just close.

—You look flushed.

Ada touched her damp face at various points with the backs of her fingers and could not think of a thing to say. She made calipers with her fingers and took the measure of her nose again. She went to the door and opened it for a breath of cool air. The night smelled of wet rotting leaves and was so dark she could not see beyond the drops of water catching the door light as they fell from the porch eve. From the parlor came the simple first notes of Good King Wenceslas, and Ada recognized Monroe's stiff phrasing at the piano. Then from out in the dark, over a great distance, came the high lonesome baying of a grey wolf far off in the mountains.

—That is a forlorn sound, Inman said.

Ada held the door open and waited to hear an answering call, but it never came. Poor thing, she said.

She closed the door and turned to Inman, but when she did the heat of the room and the champagne and the look on Inman's face, which was softer than any contour she had ever seen there, conspired against her and she felt at once faint and giddy. She took a few uncertain steps, and when Inman half stood and reached out a hand to steady her, she took it. And then, by some mechanism she was unable to reconstruct later, she found herself in his lap.

He put his hands to her shoulders a moment and she settled back with her head beneath his chin. Ada remembered thinking that she never wished to leave this place but was not aware that she had said it aloud. What she did remember was that he had seemed as content as she was and had not pressed for more but only moved his hands out to the points of her shoulders and held her there. She remembered the smell of his damp wool suit and a lingering smell of horse and tack.

She might have rested in his lap for half a minute, no more. Then she was up and away, and she remembered turning at the door, her hand on the casing, to look back at him where he sat with a puzzled smile on his face and his hat lying crown down on the floor.

Ada went back to the piano, where she moved Monroe aside and played for quite some time. Inman eventually came and stood, leaning with his shoulder against the doorjamb. He drank from a flute and watched her for a while and then he moved on to talk to Esco, who still sat near the fire. Through the rest of the evening, neither Ada nor Inman mentioned what had taken place in the kitchen. They talked only briefly and awkwardly and Inman left early.

Much later, in the small hours when the party broke up, Ada looked from the parlor window and watched as the young men went down the road, firing their pistols toward the heavens, the muzzle flash lighting them in brief silhouette.

Ada sat awhile after the wagon bearing the piano rounded the bend in the road. Then she lit a lantern and went to the basement, thinking that Monroe might have cellared a case or two of champagne there and that opening a bottle now and again might be pleasant. She found no wine but turned up instead a genuine treasure, one that greatly advanced their efforts toward barter. It was a hundred-pound sack of green coffee beans that Monroe had stored away, sitting there fat and sagging in a corner.

She called Ruby and they immediately filled the roaster and parched a half pound over the fire and ground it and then brewed up the first real coffee either of them had had in over a year. They drank cup after cup and stayed up most of the night, talking nonstop of plans for the future and memories of the past, and at one point Ada retold the entire thrilling plot of *Little Dorrit*, one of the books she had read during the summer. Over the next several days they bartered the coffee by the half pound and by the nogginful to neighbors, keeping back only ten pounds for their own use. When the sack was empty, they had taken in a side of bacon, five bushels of Irish potatoes and four of sweet, a tin of baking powder, eight chickens, various baskets of squash and beans and okra, an old wheel and loom in need of minor re-

pair, six bushels of shell corn, and enough split shakes to reroof the smokehouse. The most valuable trade, though, was the five-pound sack of salt they had gotten, it having become so scarce and dear that some people now dug up their smokehouse floors and boiled and strained the dirt and then boiled it down and strained it again. Over and over until the dirt was gone and the water steamed away, so that in the end they had reclaimed the salt fallen to the ground from the hams of yesteryear.

In such matters of trade and in every other regard, Ruby proved herself a marvel of energy, and she soon imposed a routine on Ada's day. Before dawn Ruby would have walked down from the cabin, fed the horse, milked the cow, and be banging pots and pans in the kitchen, a hot fire going in the stove, yellow corn grits bubbling in a pot, eggs and bacon spitting grease in a black pan. Ada was not accustomed to rising in the grey of morning—in fact, through the summer she had rarely risen before ten—but suddenly there was little choice. If Ada lay abed, Ruby would come roust her out. Ruby figured setting things to working was her job, not waiting on somebody and doing their bidding. On the few occasions when Ada had slipped and given her an order as if to a servant, Ruby had just looked at Ada hard and had then gone on doing what she was doing. What the look said was that Ruby could be gone at a moment's notice like morning fog on a sunny day.

Part of the code for Ruby was that though she did not expect Ada to do the cooking at breakfast, she did expect her, at minimum, to be there to watch its conclusion. So Ada would walk down to the kitchen in her robe and sit in the chair in the warm stove corner and wrap her hands around a cup of coffee. Through the window the day would be starting to take shape, grey and loose in its features. Even on days that would eventually prove to be clear, Ada could seldom make out even the palings of the fence around the kitchen garden through the fog. At some point Ruby would blow out the yellow light of the lamp and the kitchen would go dim and then the light from outside

would rise and fill the room. It seemed a thing of such wonder to Ada, who had not witnessed many dawns.

All during the cooking and the eating, Ruby would talk seamlessly, drawing up hard plans for the coming day that struck Ada as incongruent with its soft vagueness out the window. By the time summer drew toward its conclusion, Ruby seemed to feel the approach of winter as urgently as a bear in autumn, eating all night and half the day to pack on the fat necessary to feed it through hibernation. All Ruby's talk was of exertion. The work it would take to build a momentum of survival to carry them through winter. To Ada, Ruby's monologues seemed composed mainly of verbs, all of them tiring. Plow, plant, hoe, cut, can, feed, kill.

When Ada remarked that at least they could rest when winter came, Ruby said, Oh, when winter comes we'll mend fence and piece quilts and fix what's broke around here, which is a lot.

Simply living had never struck Ada as such a tiresome business. After breakfast was done, they worked constantly. On days when there was not one big thing to do, they did many small ones, choring around as needed. When Monroe was alive, living was little more laborsome than drawing on bank accounts, abstract and distant. Now, with Ruby, all the actual facts and processes connected with food and clothing and shelter were unpleasantly concrete, falling immediately and directly to hand, and every one of them calling for exertion.

Of course, in her previous life Ada had taken little part in the garden Monroe had always paid someone to grow for them, and her mind, in consequence, had latched itself to the product—the food on the table—not the job of getting it there. Ruby disabused her of that practice. The rudeness of eating, of living, that's where Ruby seemed to aim Ada every day that first month. She held Ada's nose to the dirt to see its purpose. She made Ada work when she did not want to, made her dress in rough clothes and grub in the dirt until her nails seemed to her crude as the claws of a beast, made her climb onto the pitched smokehouse

roof and lay shakes even though the green triangle of Cold Mountain seemed to spin about the horizon. Ruby counted her first victory when Ada succeeded in churning cream to butter. Her second victory was when she noted that Ada no longer always put a book in her pocket when she went out to hoe the fields.

Ruby made a point of refusing to tackle all the unpleasant work herself and made Ada hold a struggling chicken down on the chopping block and cleave off its head with a hatchet. When the bleeding headless body staggered about the yard in the time-honored habit of sots, Ruby pointed to it with her ragged sheath knife and said, That's your sustenance there.

The force that Ruby used to drive Ada on was this: somewhere Ada knew that anyone else she might hire would grow weary and walk away and let her fail. Ruby would not let her fail.

The only moments of rest were after the supper dishes had been washed and put away. Then Ada and Ruby sat on the porch and Ada would read aloud in the time remaining before dark. Books and their contents were a great novelty to Ruby, and so Ada had reckoned that the place to begin was near the beginning. After filling Ruby in on who the Greeks were, she had begun reading from Homer. They usually covered fifteen or twenty pages of an evening. Then, when it became too dark to read and the air turned blue and started to congeal with mist, Ada would close the book and solicit stories from Ruby. Over a period of weeks she collected the tale of Ruby's life in pieces.

As Ruby put it, she'd grown up so poor she was forced to cook with no more grease than you would get wiping the frying pan with a meat skin. And she was tired of it. She had never known her mother, and her father had been a notorious local ne'er-do-well and scofflaw called Stobrod Thewes. They lived in a dirt-floored cabin little better than a roofed pen. It was tiny and had about it the air of the temporary. About the only thing distin-

guishing it from a gypsy caravan was its lack of wheels and floor. She had slept on a kind of miniature loft platform, just a shelf, really. She had an old tick for mattress that she stuffed with dried moss. Because there was no ceiling, only the geometrical pattern made by the lapped undersides of the roof shakes, Ruby awoke many a morning with an inch of snow atop her pile of quilts, blown by the wind between the curled edges of the shakes like sifted flour. On such mornings, Ruby found that the great benefit of such a small cabin was that even a fire of twigs warmed it up fast, though the faulty chimney that Stobrod had constructed drew so poorly you could have smoked hams in the place. In all but the foulest weather, she preferred cooking out back under a brush arbor.

Yet, little and plain as it was, the cabin was still more than Stobrod cared to maintain. If not for the inconvenience of his having a daughter, he might happily have taken up dwelling in a hollow tree, for in Ruby's estimation an animal with a memory was about her father's loftiest expression of himself.

Feeding herself was Ruby's to do as soon as she was old enough to be held accountable for it, which in Stobrod's opinion fell close after learning to walk. As an infant, Ruby foraged for food in the woods and up and down the river at charitable farms. Her brightest childhood memory was of walking up the river trail for some of Sally Swanger's white bean soup and on the way home having her nightgown—for several years her usual attire, even in the daytime—get caught on a trailside blackthorn briar. The thorn was long as a cock's spur, and she had been unable to free herself. No one passed that afternoon. Broken clouds blew over and the day faded like a guttering lamp. Night fell and the moon was black, the new moon of May. Ruby was four and spent the night attached to the blackthorn tree.

Those dark hours were a revelation to her, and they never left her. It was chill out in the drifting mists of the riverbank. She remembered shivering and crying for a time, calling out for help. She feared she would be eaten by a wandering panther

down from Cold Mountain. They would carry off a child in a heartbeat, was what she had heard from Stobrod's drinking friends. The way they told it, the mountains were full of creatures hungry for the meat of a child. Bears out foraging. Wolves roaming. Hants aplenty too in the mountains. They would come in many forms, all terrifying, and they would snatch you up and take you to who knew what manner of hell.

She had heard the old Cherokee women talk of cannibal spirits that lived in the rivers and ate the flesh of people, stealing them near daybreak and carrying them down in the water. Children were their favorite food, and when they took one they left in its place a shade, a twin, that moved about and talked but had no real life to it. Seven days later it withered and died.

The night drew together all those threats, and young Ruby thus sat for some time, shivering from the cold and sobbing until she could hardly breathe from the recognition of all the things that seemed ranked up to prey on weakness.

But later she was spoken to by a voice in the dark. Its talk seemed to arise from the rush and splatter of the river noise, but it was no cannibal demon. It seemed some tender force of landscape or sky, an animal sprite, a guardian that took her under its wing and concerned itself with her well-being from that moment on. She remembered every star pattern that passed across the piece of sky visible to her among the tree boughs, and every word spoken directly to her deep core by the calm voice that took her in and comforted and protected her all through the night. She stopped shivering in the thin gown, and her sobbing passed away from her.

The next morning a man fishing set her loose, and she walked home and never spoke a word to Stobrod about it. Nor did he ask where she had been. The voice, though, still echoed in her head, and after that night she became like one born with a caul over one's face, knowing things others never would.

As she got older, she and Stobrod had lived off what Ruby raised on the little bit of their land that diverged far enough

from the vertical for her to plow. For his part, her father spent his time elsewhere, often disappearing for days at a stretch. He'd walk forty miles for a party. At even the rumor of a dance he would head out down the road, toting the fiddle from which he could barely scratch out a handful of standard figures. Ruby might not see him again for days. Lacking that sort of entertainment, Stobrod would go off to the woods. Hunting, he claimed. But he usually provided only an occasional squirrel or groundhog for the stewpot. His ambitions never rose as high as deer, so when rodents were scarce they ate chestnuts and rhubarb and poke and other wild food that Ruby gathered, so it could often be said that a large part of their diet was mast.

Even Stobrod's love of liquor failed to make a farmer of him. Rather than grow corn, he would go out with a tow sack on moonless nights when the ears were ripe and steal corn. From it he distilled a greasy yellow liquor which his fellows claimed was unmatched in rawness and potency.

His one known flirtation with employment had ended in disaster. A man from down the river had hired him to help finish clearing a piece of newground to ready it for spring planting. The big trees had already been felled and lay in great tangles of tree laps piled at the wood's edge. The man wanted Stobrod to help him burn them. They lit a roaring fire and were lopping limbs off the downed trees so they could roll them into the fire when Stobrod suddenly came to the realization that this was more work than he had reckoned on. He turned his shirtsleeves down and headed up the road. The man kept at it alone, working with a log hook to try to roll the tree trunks into the fire. He was standing near the flames when several burning logs shifted and trapped his leg tight down among them. Try as he might, he could not break free, and he hollered for help until his voice gave out. The fire kept moving his way until, rather than be burned up, he took the axe he had used for lopping limbs and hewed away his leg just at the knee. He tied off the bleeding with a strip of his pant leg twisted tight with a stick and then

trimmed a forked limb into a crutch and walked home. He lived, but just.

For years thereafter, Stobrod was wary of walking the road by the man's house, for the peg-legged man had, to Stobrod's bitter disappointment, held a grudge and would sometimes take a shot at him from the porch.

It was not until Ruby was nearly grown that it occurred to her to wonder what kind of woman her mother had been to have married such a man as Stobrod. But by then her mother seemed to have been wiped nearly clean from the slate of his mind, for when Ruby asked what she had been like, Stobrod claimed he had little recollection. I can't even see in my mind whether she was slight or stout, he said.

To the surprise of one and all, in the first days of the war fever, Stobrod had enlisted in the army. He rode off one morning on their old hinny to do battle, and Ruby had heard nothing from him since. Her last remembrance of him was his white shanks shining above his boot tops as he jostled away down the road. She guessed that Stobrod had not warred for long. He had surely died in his first fight, that or deserted forever, for Ruby had heard from a man of his regiment—come home with an arm shot off—that Stobrod was unaccounted for after Sharpsburg.

Whatever his fate, whether he had taken a minié ball to his hinder parts or lit out for the western territories, he had left Ruby high and dry. Without the hinny, she could no longer even plow the sorry fields. All she was able to plant was a little garden that she worked by hand with a single-foot plow and a hoe.

The first year of the war had been hard for her, but at least Stobrod had left his old unrifled musket, figuring he stood a chance of bettering his weaponry if he showed up empty-handed. Ruby had taken the relic piece—more relative to the harquebus than to the current fashion in rifles—and hunted wild turkey and deer through the winter, jerking the venison by the fire like an Indian. Stobrod had taken their only knife, so she sliced up the meat with one she had made from a cast-off section

of a crosscut saw. Her principal tool for the job of bladesmith was the hammer. She heated the saw blade in the fire and scribed a knife shape in the hot metal with a bent horseshoe nail she had picked up out of the road. When the metal cooled, she hammered off the excess from the scribed line and filed burrs from the blade and haft. Again using the hammer, she pounded in rivets made of scrap copper to hold a handle of applewood that she had sawed from a thick limb. She honed the blade keen on a greased river rock. Her handiwork was rough looking, but it cut as good as a bought knife.

Looking back on her life so far, she listed as achievements the fact that by the age of ten, she knew all features of the mountains for twenty-five miles in any direction as intimately as a gardener would his bean rows. And that later, when yet barely a woman, she had whipped men single-handed in encounters she did not wish to detail.

At present, she believed herself to be twenty-one years old, though she did not know for sure because Stobrod had not marked down in his memory either the year of her birth or the day. He could not even recall the season it had been when she arrived. Not that she was planning a birthday party, for celebration had been a lacking feature of her life since survival had such a sharp way of focusing one's attentions elsewhere.

like any other thing, a gift

Late in the night, Inman followed a road of sorts that ran along the banks of the Deep River. It soon dipped into a rocky swale that after a time narrowed and made a gorge. The sky closed up between walls of jumbled rocks and trees until it was only a swath directly above, Milky Way the only light. It was so dark that for a time, down in the cut, he had to feel with his feet for the soft dust of the road to keep his way. The sheen of light on the water was so slight that he could see it only by looking to the side, like detecting faint stars by not peering right at them.

Eventually, traversing a rocky bluff, the road became a narrow notch between the river below a drop-off and a steep bank of broken rock and dirt grown partly over with brush. Inman did not like his position. He feared the Home Guard would be out and about. Horsemen might be upon him before he could find a place to leave the road, and the bank was too broken and steep to climb quietly in the dark. It would be a poor place to make a stand against armed riders. Best to step on out smartly and put this wound in the earth behind him.

Inman broke into a painful little jog trot and kept at it for

some minutes until he saw up ahead a flickery light, which looked to be right in the courseway. He slowed to a walk, and soon he had closed on the light near enough to tell that it was made by a man in a broad-brimmed hat standing in the road, casting a yellow circle around him from a smoky torch of bundled pitchwood splits. Walking quietly, Inman eased closer and stopped alongside a boulder not ten yards away.

The man wore a suit of black clothes, a white shirt. He held a horse by a lead rope tied around its neck. In the light Inman could see that the horse carried a burden, an unformed white thickness across its back like a drooping bundle of linen. As Inman watched, the man sat down in the road and drew his knees up toward his chest with one arm. The elbow of his torch arm rested in the notch between the knees so that his fist stuck out before him and held the fire as steady as if fixed in a sconce. He let his head sink down until the hat brim touched his extended arm. He made a kind of illuminated dark wad in the road.

He's going to fall asleep with that torch blazing, Inman thought. In a minute he'll have his feet on fire.

But the man was not dozing; he was in despair. He looked up toward the horse and let out a moan.

—Lord, Oh, Lord, he cried. We once lived in a land of paradise.

He rocked from side to side on the bones of his ass and said again, Lord, Oh, Lord.

What to do? Inman wondered. Another stone in his passway. Couldn't go back. Couldn't go around. Couldn't stand there like a penned heifer all night. He took out the pistol and held it up to catch what light reached him from the torch and checked his loads.

Inman was about ready to make his move when the man stood and worked the base of the torch around in the dirt until it held upright. He rose and walked to the horse's far side. He began trying to lift the bundle from the horse, which shifted

about nervously and put back its ears, the whites of its eyes visible all along the lower rims.

The man got the bundle off the horse and over his shoulder and came walking from behind the animal in a kind of stagger. Inman could see that what he was lugging was a woman, one limp arm swinging, a cascade of black hair brushing the ground. The man carried her from out the diameter of torchlight so that they became near invisible, but his direction was clearly toward the verge of the drop-off. Inman could hear the man sobbing in the dark as he walked.

Inman ran along the road to the torch and grabbed it up and pitched it softly underhand out toward the sound of crying. What the fire lit when it struck ground was the man standing on the very lip of the bluff with the woman in his arms. He was trying to whirl to see the source of this sudden illumination, but, cumbered as he was, it took some time. With a kind of shuffle, he turned to face Inman.

—Set her down, Inman said.

She dropped in a heap at the man's feet.

—The hell kind of pistol is that? the man said, his eyes fixed on the two big mismatched bores.

—Step away from her, Inman said. Get over here where I can see you.

The man stepped across the body and approached Inman. He held his head tipped down for the hat brim to cut the glare from the torch.

—Best stop right now, Inman said, when the man got close.

—You're a message from God saying no, the man said. He took two steps more and then dropped to his knees in the road and fell forward and hugged Inman about the legs. Inman leveled the pistol at the man's head and put pressure on the trigger until he could feel all the metal parts of its firing mechanism tighten up against each other. But then the man turned his face up, and it caught the light from the torch where it still burned on the ground, and Inman could see that his cheeks were shiny with

tears. So Inman relented as he might have anyway and only struck the man a mid-force blow across the cheekbone with the long barrel of the pistol.

The man sprawled in the road on his back, a shallow cut below his eye. His hat had fallen off and his head was pomaded slick as an apple from the forehead back, and the ends of his yellow hair hung in ringlets about his shoulders. He fingered the cut and looked at the blood.

—I accept the merit of that, he said.

—You merit killing, Inman said. He looked to where the woman lay in a heap at the edge of the bluff. She had not moved. I might still feel the need to do it, Inman said.

—Don't kill me, I'm a man of God, the man said.

—Some say we all are, Inman said.

—A preacher is what I mean, the man said. I'm a preacher.

Inman could think of no response but to blow out air from his nose.

The preacher rose again as far as his knees.

—Is she dead? Inman said.

—No.

—What's the matter with her? Inman said.

—Not much. She's somewhat with child. That and what I gave her.

—What would that be?

—A little packet of powders that I bought off a peddler. He said it would put a man to sleep for four hours. It's been about half that since I dosed her up.

—And you're the daddy?

—Apparently.

—Not married to her, I reckon?

—No.

Inman stepped to the far side of the girl and knelt. He put a hand to her dark head and lifted it. She was breathing with a kind of faint snore, a whistle at the nose. Her face was slack from

being senseless, and the shadows cast from the torch were ugly things, collecting unfavorably in the low spots of her eyes and cheeks. Still, Inman could tell that there might be a beauty to her. He returned her face to the ground and rose from his crouch.

—Put her back on the horse, Inman said. He stepped away, keeping the pistol leveled at the man, who hopped up to his feet, his eyes never leaving the barrel ends. The man hustled over and knelt and struggled to lever the girl off the ground. He rose and staggered to the horse and threw her over. Inman tipped the big pistol up momentarily to catch its profile in the light, thinking how very much he liked the air of urgency and focus it lent to a simple request.

—What now? the man said when he was done. He seemed relieved for someone else to be calling the decisions.

—Hush up, Inman said. He did not know what was next, and his thinking seemed all grainy and sluggish from lack of sleep and hard walking.

—Where did you come from? Inman said.

—There's a town not far off, the man said, gesturing on up the road in the direction Inman was heading.

—Get on out ahead of me and show the way.

Inman picked up the torch and threw it over the ledge. The preacher stood and watched it fall, a diminishing point in the dark.

—Still the Deep River here? Inman said.

—Folks call it that, the preacher said.

They started walking. Inman kept the pistol in his hand and led the horse with the other. The lead rope was thick hemp and the end had been wrapped for some inches in wire to prevent its fraying, and as he grasped the rope he pricked his thumb, drawing blood. Inman walked along sucking at his cut thumb, thinking had he not stumbled upon them, the woman would be a white smear floating on the black river, her skirts belled out

around her and the preacher standing up at the road saying Go down, go down. Inman wondered what the thing to do here would be.

The road soon climbed and crossed a little ridge and left the river behind. It wound through low hills. The moon had risen and Inman could see that the land lay open in great patches where the forest had been burned away to make place for fields. But nothing more toilsome than lighting a fire had been done with it, and so it was a country of black stumps set in runnel-cut clay stretching away bare to a far horizon. The charcoal of the stumps caught the moonlight and glittered. Inman looked about and thought, I could well be on a whole other planet from the place I'm aiming for.

Orion had fully risen and stood at the eastern horizon, and from that Inman made the time to be long past midnight. The great figure of hunter and warrior stood up there like an accusation, like a sign in the sky pointing out your shortfalls. Orion was girded about tight, his weapon ready to strike. Sure of himself as a man can be, if posture is any indication of character. Traveling due west every night and making unfailing good time.

One of the things Inman marked as a comfort was that he could put a name to the brightest star in Orion. He had shared that fact with a Tennessee boy on the night after Fredericksburg. They had sat at the lip of the ditch behind the wall. The night was cold and brittle, and the stars were sharp points of light and the aurora had already flared up and gone out. They had blankets wrapped about them, draped over their heads and shoulders, and their breaths blew out in plumes and hung in the windless air before them like spirits in process of departure.

—It's so cold, you was to lick your gun barrel your tongue'd bind to it, the boy had said.

He held his Enfield up before his face and breathed on the barrel of it and then scratched at the place with a fingernail and raked off frost. He looked at Inman and then did it again. He held the finger up for Inman's inspection and Inman said, I see

it. The boy spit between his feet and then bent to witness if it froze, but the bottom of the ditch was too dark to tell yes or no.

Before them was the battlefield falling away to the town and the river. The land lay bleak as nightmare and seemed to have been recast to fit a new and horrible model, all littered with bodies and churned up by artillery. Hell's newground, one man had called it. To turn his mind from such a place that night, Inman had looked toward Orion and said the name he knew. The Tennessee boy had peered up at the star so indicated and said, How do you know its name is Rigel?

—I read it in a book, Inman said.

—Then that's just a name we give it, the boy said. It ain't God's name.

Inman had thought on the issue a minute and then said, How would you ever come to know God's name for that star?

—You wouldn't, He holds it close, the boy said. It's a thing you'll never know. It's a lesson that sometimes we're meant to settle for ignorance. Right there's what mostly comes of knowledge, the boy said, tipping his chin out at the broken land, apparently not even finding it worthy of sweeping a hand across its contours in sign of dismissal. At the time, Inman had thought the boy a fool and had remained content to know our name for Orion's principal star and to let God keep His a dark secret. But he now wondered if the boy might have had a point about knowledge, or at least some varieties of it.

Inman and the preacher walked in silence for some time, until finally the preacher said, What do you intend doing with me?

—I'm thinking on it, Inman said. How did you get in this fix?

—It is hard to say. None in the settlement suspect a thing even yet. She lives with her grandmother, so old and deaf you must scream to make yourself understood. It was an easy matter for her to slip away at midnight to sport in a hayrick or on a mossy creek bank until the first birds began singing in the hour

before dawn. All through the summer we crept about the night-woods for our meetings.

—Crafty as panthers in the ways of stealth? Is that the picture you're painting?

—Well, yes. After a fashion.

—How did it come to this pass?

—In the normal way. A certain look of eye, bend of voice, brush of hand in passing the chicken when we had dinners on the ground following Sunday services.

—There's a smart distance between that and you with your britches around your ankles in a hayrick.

—Yes.

—Even further to you getting set to pitch her into a gorge like a shoat dead of the hog cholera.

—Well, yes. But it is more tangled than you make it to be. For one thing, there is my position. If we had been found out, I would have been run from the county. Our church is strict. We have churched members for as little as allowing fiddles to be played in their houses. Believe me, I anguished over it through many a night.

—Those would be the rainy nights? When the hayricks and moss banks were too damp.

The preacher walked on.

—There were simpler repairs, Inman said.

—I could not find them.

—Marry her would be one.

—Again, you miss the tangles. I am already betrothed.

—Oh.

—I now believe that when I took to preaching I answered a false call.

—Yes, Inman said. I'd say you're ill suited for that business.

They walked another mile and then before them, on the banks of a river, the same as flowed at the bottom of the gorge, was a kind of town. A collection of wood structures. A clapboard church, whitewashed. A business or two. Houses.

—What I believe we're going to do, Inman said, is put her back in her bed like this night never happened. Have you a kerchief?

—Yes.

—Wad it up and put it in your mouth and lie facedown in the dirt, Inman said. He stripped the wire off the lead rope while the preacher did what he was told. Inman walked up behind the preacher and put a knee in his back and wound the wire around his head a half-dozen turns and then twisted the ends together.

—If you had screamed out, Inman said, people would come running and you could lay this all off on me. There's no way I could tell it to make myself believed here.

They entered the town. At first, dogs barked. But then, recognizing the preacher and familiar with his nighttime rambles, they fell silent.

—Which house? Inman said.

The preacher pointed on down the road and then led the way through the town and out the other side to a little grove of poplars. Set back among the trees was a tiny cottage, just one room, covered over with batten boards and painted white. The preacher looked toward it and nodded. The way the wire stretched back the corners of his mouth made him look all agrin, and the expression ill-consisted with Inman's mood.

—Back up to this little poplar, Inman said. He took the lead rope off the horse and with it tied the preacher by his neck to the tree. Inman took the loose end of rope and drew it over the preacher's shoulder and tied his wrists tight behind him.

—Stand here real quiet and we'll all live through this, Inman said.

He lifted the girl from the horse and adjusted her in his arms to a good balance for carrying. An arm under her waist, another under her soft thigh backs. Her dark head rested on his shoulder and her hair swept across his arm like a breath as he walked. She gave a little moan, like one briefly troubled in regu-

lar sleep by a passing dream. She was such a helpless thing, lying there without even consciousness as defense. Exposed to every danger and guarded only by the rare goodwill of the random world. I ought yet to kill that shitpoke preacher, Inman thought.

He carried her to the house and set her down in a patch of tansy by the stoop. He went onto the porch and looked in a window to a dim room. A fire burned low on the hearth, and an old woman slept on a pallet by the fire. She had lived so long as to have achieved a state of near transparency, her skin the color of parchment, as if, were Inman to snatch her up and hold her in front of the fire, he could read a paper through her. Her mouth was open, snoring. The little bit of light left in the hearth lit up the fact that she had but two pair of teeth remaining. One pair in front on top, the other in front on bottom. The effect was harelike.

Inman tried the door and found it unlatched. He opened it and stuck his head in. He said Hey in a middling voice. The old woman snored on. He clapped his hands twice, but she still did not stir. Safe enough, he decided and walked on in. By the fire was a plate with half a round of corn bread and two pieces of fried pork. Inman took the food and put it in his haversack. There was an empty bedstead at the end of the room away from the fire. The girl's bed, he reckoned. He went to it and threw the covers back and then stepped outside and stood looking at the dark-headed girl. In her pale dress she was just a swatch of light on the black ground.

He lifted her and carried her inside and put her into the bed. He pulled off her shoes and covered her to her chin. Then he thought again and drew the covers down and turned her on her side, for he remembered that a boy of his regiment had passed out drunk on his back and would have smothered in his own spew had someone not taken note and kicked him over. This way she would live to wake in the morning with a pounding head, wondering how she came to be back in her own bed when

the last she could remember was sporting in a hayloft with the preacher.

At that moment, the logs in the fireplace fell from the irons with a crash, shifting into a more favorable relation, and the fire brightened up. The girl's eyes opened and she turned her head and stared straight at Inman. Her face was white in the firelight, her hair a turmoil. She seemed terrified. Confused. Her mouth opened as if to scream, but no sound came out. Inman leaned over and reached out his hand to her and touched her brow and brushed back the hair where it curled at the temples.

—What's your name? he said.

—Laura, the woman said.

—Listen to me, Laura, he said. That preacher does not speak for God. No man does. Go back to sleep and wake up in the morning with me just a strong dream urging you to put him behind you. He means you no good. Set your mind on it.

He touched her eyes with the tips of two fingers as he had seen people do to the dead to close their lids against bad visions. She gentled down under his hand, settling back into sleep.

Inman left her and walked back out to where the preacher stood tied to the tree. At that moment the notion that he should take out his knife and cut the man up had much to recommend it, but instead Inman prowled in his knapsack and took out his pen and ink and paper. He found a place where moonlight came down through the trees. In its blue beam he wrote out the story in brief, putting little headwork and no fine touches to it, merely pressing down what he had learned of the near killing into a paragraph. When he was done he skewered the paper onto a tree branch at head level just beyond the preacher's reach.

The preacher watched him, and when he realized Inman's intent he grew agitated and thrashed about as much as he could while fettered by the neck. He kicked at Inman with his feet, for he guessed at what he had written.

He tried to grunt and squeal through the handkerchief wired to his mouth.

—Testify? Is that what you want? Inman said.

—Ah! the preacher said.

Inman drew out the pistol and set it to the preacher's ear. He pulled back the hammer and flipped down the little lever that directed the firing pin to the lower shotgun barrel. You speak one word above a whisper and you'll be lacking a head, Inman said. He untwisted the wire. The preacher spit out the handkerchief.

—You've ruined my life, he said.

—Don't lay that off on me, Inman said. I wanted no part in this. But I don't want to have to wonder whether in a night or two you'll be back out in that black gorge with her slung over your horse again, Inman said.

—Then shoot me. Just shoot me here and leave me hanging.

—Don't think there's no charm in that offer.

—God damn you to hell for what you're doing to me.

Inman took the wet handkerchief from the ground and forced it into the preacher's mouth and rewired it and strode out. As he walked away he heard fading grunts and moans. Wordless hexes and curses.

Inman walked hard the remainder of the night to put space between himself and that nameless place. When the morning at last lit up at his back like a yellow abscess, he had worked himself into rolling country and he felt worn down to nothing. He had no idea where he was nor did he know that he had accomplished but twelve miles in that long night of walking, for it felt like a hundred.

He stopped and went into the woods and made a bed of ground litter. With his back against a tree he sat and ate the wedge of corn bread and the fatty pork he had taken from the woman's house. For much of the morning he lay on the ground and slept.

Then he found himself awake, gazing at the blue sky

through the pine boughs. He took out his pistol and wiped it with a rag and checked its loads and kept it in his hand for company. What he had come to possess was a LeMat's. And the model Inman held was not one of the early and inferior Belgian models but was stamped Birmingham along the barrel. He had picked it up off the ground and stuck it in his belt right before he took his wound outside Petersburg, and he had managed to hang on to it all through the mess of the field hospital and the train ride south to the capital in the boxcar filled with wounded. It was an oddly configured weapon, somewhat overlarge and of curious proportion, but it was the fiercest sidearm in existence. Its cylinder was big as a fist and held nine .40-caliber rounds. But the dominant feature of it and the thing that marked a strange new direction in pistol style was this: the cylinder turned around a shotgun barrel, a crude and fat thing under the main barrel. Intended as a desperate last chance in close quarters, it fired a single load, either buckshot or a slug so big it would be like shooting leaden duck eggs at your foes. In the hand, despite its size, the LeMat's felt balanced and solid and as of-a-piece as an ingot, and there was a certain amount of serenity associated with simply holding the stout pistol and thinking what it could do in your service.

Inman rubbed at its cylinder and barrel and thought about the fight in the town and the river crossing and the preacher and how he might have done things differently in each case. He wished not to be smirched with the mess of other people. A part of him wanted to hide in the woods far from any road. Be like an owl, move only at dark. Or a ghost. Another part yearned to wear the big pistol openly on his hip and to travel by day under a black flag, respecting all who let him be, fighting all who would seek to fight him, letting rage be his guide against anything that ran counter to his will.

Before the war he had never been much of a one for strife. But once enlisted, fighting had come easy to him. He had decided it was like any other thing, a gift. Like a man who could

whittle birds out of wood. Or one who could pick tunes from a banjo. Or a preacher with the gift of words. You had little to do with it yourself. It was more a matter of how your nerves were strung toward quickness of hand and a steady head so that you did not become witless and vague in battle, your judgment clouded in all kinds of ways, fatal and otherwise. That and having the size to prevail in the close stuff, when it came down to a clench.

In the middle of the afternoon, Inman left his pine bower and tried to cover some distance. After only an hour, though, he found himself nearly bogged down with fatigue. Every step a great effort. Up ahead he saw a pair of figures stopped in the road by a ford, but even from a distance it was clear they were slaves and so he did not even bother slipping off into the woods to hide but kept on walking. One man was trying to drive a red hog that had stopped to roll in the mud. The other carried an armload of bean poles. The drover kicked the hog to no effect, and then he took a pole from the load and struck and prodded the hog until it reluctantly struggled to its feet and waddled along. The men tipped their hats to Inman as they passed and said, Day, Marse.

Inman was so weak feeling he wished momentarily that he were a big red hog and could just lie down and wallow until somebody took a bean pole to him. But he shucked off his boots and waded the ford, and then on the far bank he turned from the road and followed the river downstream, thinking to find a hidden place to cook a sparse meal of corn mush. But the wind shifted, and it carried the scent of real cooking from somewhere farther downriver.

He followed the smell of meat in the air, snuffing his nose and blinking his eyes with his head cocked up like a bear. He soon arrived at a camp in a bend of the river: a wagon, a number of horses, pyramidal tents of grey canvas standing among a grove of birch trees. Inman squatted in the brush and watched the folks go about their campcraft. They were a jumble of people

wearing about every tinge of skin there is. Inman guessed them to be as outlaw and Ishmaelite as himself. Show folk, outliers, a tribe of Irish gypsy horse traders all thrown in together. The horses were hobbled all around, and they grazed in the long grass under the trees. The stock varied from magnificent to near dead. Backlit by the gold light of afternoon, though, they all looked beautiful to Inman, the grace in the deep curve of their down-turned necks, the frail cannon bones so evident through the thin skin above their fetlocks. Inman guessed the traders were hiding them out. So many horses had been killed in the fighting that they were becoming scarce. Prices had swelled beyond belief, but the army had men out rounding up horses, paying nearly nothing for them. A part of Inman wished he had the money to buy a big long-strided gelding. Mount up and canter off and end his life as a footman. But he had not that much money and, too, it is hard to be stealthy when accompanied by a horse. It's a big thing to hide, and uncooperative. So Inman let that dream pass.

Thinking he might find some feeling of kinship with the outcasts, Inman entered the camp holding his empty hands out to his sides. The gypsies took him in with apparent generosity, though he knew they would steal the boots off his feet if they could find advantage to do so. They had an iron pot of dark stew going over a small fire—rabbit, squirrel, a stolen chicken, various pilfered vegetables, chiefly cabbage. Chunks of pumpkin drizzled in molasses roasted over coals in a Dutch oven. A woman in a bright skirt of cloth scraps pieced together like a quilt spooned him up food onto his tin plate and went about frying corn fritters in a pan of lard. The batter popped like distant battle fire when she spooned the grease.

Inman propped against a tree and ate, looking about him at the riffle of water on stones in the river, the yellow leaves of an early turning birch trembling bright in the stir of air, the light falling in beams through the smoke of campfires. A man sitting on a log scratched out jigs and reels from a cigar-box fiddle. Chil-

dren played in the shallow water at the river's edge. Other gypsies worked at the horses. A boy brushed an old mare with a corncob dipped in a bucket of potash and soot to cover her grey hair, and then took a rat-tail file and worked on her teeth. She shed years right before Inman's eyes. A woman snubbed a big bay up to a birch trunk and then twitched it and poured lamp oil on the frog of its hoof and lit fire to it to curb a tendency to lameness. All through the herd, spavins and bots and heaves to be treated or disguised.

Inman had dealt with gypsies before and thought them possessed of a fine honesty in their predatory relationship to the rest of mankind, their bald admission of constantly seeking an opening. But they were benign-seeming in this quiet bend of the river. It was no concern of theirs how the war concluded. Whichever side won, people would still need horses. The contest was no more to them than a temporary hindrance to business.

Inman stayed with the gypsies through the remainder of the day. He took a dip from the stewpot whenever he became hungry. He slept some and listened to the fiddler and watched a woman telling fortunes by reading the pattern of leaves in a cup of herb tea, but he declined her offer to tell his own future for he figured he already had all the discouragement he needed.

Later in the afternoon he watched a dark-haired woman walk among the horses and put a bridle on a dun mare. She was young and wore a man's sweater over a long black skirt and was about as pretty as women get to be. Something in the darkness of her hair or the way she moved or the thinness of her fingers reminded him momentarily of Ada. He sat and stared as she caught up the hems of her long skirt and petticoat and clenched them in her teeth before mounting astride the mare. Her white legs were exposed to the thigh. She rode down the riverbank and crossed at a place deep enough that in the middle the horse lost its footing and swam a stroke or two. It struggled climbing up the far bank, working hard with its haunches. Water streamed

off its back and sides and the woman was wet to the hips. She leaned forward for balance with her face almost resting on the horse's neck. Her hair fell against its black mane so that you could not tell one from the other. When they reached level ground she put her heels to the mare's sides and they galloped away through the open woods. It was to Inman a stirring sight, a happy vision that he was grateful to have been granted.

On toward dusk some little gypsy boys whittled gigs from river-birch limbs and went to a backwater and gigged frogs until they had a basketful. They cut their legs off and strung them on sticks to roast over a fire of hickory coals. While the frog meat was cooking, a man came to Inman with a bottle of Moët he claimed he had taken in trade. The man was not entirely sure what it was that he had, but he knew he wished to sell it for top dollar. So Inman counted out some money and composed himself a plate of supper from the frog legs and part of the wine. He found the two not ill sorted, but when he was done they did not make a real dinner for someone as hungry as he was.

He wandered about the camp looking for other food and eventually made his way to the wagon of show folk. A medicine show. A white man came from where he sat near their tent and talked to Inman and queried him as to his business. The man was thin and tall and had some age on him, for the skin under his eyes was pale and pouched and he wore blacking in his hair. He seemed to run the place. Inman asked if he could buy a meal, and the man said he reckoned so, but that they would not eat until much later for they had to practice their act while there was yet light. Inman was welcome to sit and watch.

In a minute the dark-haired woman he had seen earlier came out of the tent. Inman could not take his eyes off her. He studied her bearing beside the man, trying to guess the forces running between them. He first guessed them to be married and then he guessed not. The two set up a backstop and the woman stood against it and the man threw knives at her so that the blades just missed her and fetched up shivering in the boards.

That seemed to Inman plenty to draw a crowd, but they had as well a big grey-bearded Ethiopian who had a regal bearing and dressed in purple robes and was portrayed to have been in his youth the king of Africa. He played a banjolike thing and could just about make a dead man dance, though his instrument was made of but a gourd and had just one string. As well, the troupe included a little menagerie of Indians of several makes, a Seminole from Florida, a Creek, a Cherokee from Echota, and a Yemassee woman. Their part in shows was to tell jokes and beat drums and dance and chant. The wagon they traveled in was loaded with fancy little colored bottles of medicine, each with its special disease to cure: cancer, consumption, neuralgia, malaria, cachexia, stroke, fit, and seizure.

After dark, they asked Inman to join them for dinner, and they all sat on the ground by the fire and ate great bloody beefsteaks and potatoes pan fried in bacon drippings and wild greens dressed with what drippings the potatoes had not soaked up. The Ethiopian and the Indians joined in the meal as if they were all of a color and equals. They took their turns speaking, and permission to talk was neither sought nor given.

When done, they went and squatted by the water, each scouring his own plate in river sand. Then the white man threw sticks on the coals of the cook fire, building it up with no eye toward thrift of wood until flame stood shoulder high. The show folk passed a bottle around and sat telling Inman stories of their endless travels. The road, they said, was a place apart, a country of its own ruled by no government but natural law, and its one characteristic was freedom. Their stories were of being broke and of sudden windfalls. Card games and horse auctions and the wonderful prevalence of the witless. Various tight spots with the law, disasters narrowly averted, fools bested in trade, wisemen met on the road and their often contradictory wisdom. Townships of gullibility and of particular viciousness. They reminded each other of certain camp places and of meals eaten in them, and they reached consensus that the finest of all was a place

some years in the past where a river of considerable size poured directly from the base of a rock face, and they likewise agreed that they had never eaten better fried chicken than they had cooked in the shadow of that cliff.

After awhile Inman could attend to little but how beautiful the woman looked in the firelight, the way it lit up her hair and the fineness of her skin. And then at some point the white man said a strange thing. He said that someday the world might be ordered so that when a man uses the term *slave* it be only metaphoric.

Sometime deep in the night, Inman took his packsacks and went into the woods beyond camp and spread his bedding within earshot of the gypsy music and the sound of voices. He tried to sleep, but he just tossed about on the ground. He lit a candle stub and poured the remainder of the wine into his tin cup and took his Bartram scroll from his knapsack. He opened the book at random and read and reread the sentence that first fell under his eye. It concerned itself with an unnamed plant similar, as best he could tell, to a rhododendron:

> This shrub grows in copses or little groves, in open, high situations, where trees of large growth are but scatteringly planted; many simple stems arise together from a root or source erect, four, five and six feet high; their limbs or branches, which are produced towards the top of the stems, also stand nearly erect, lightly diverging from the main stems, which are furnished with moderately large ovate pointed intire leaves, of a pale or yellowish green colour; these leaves are of a firm, compact texture, both surfaces smooth and shining, and stand nearly erect upon short petioles; the branches terminate with long, loose panicles or spikes of white flowers, whose segments are five, long and narrow.

Inman occupied himself pleasurably for quite some time with this long sentence. First he read it until each word rested in

his head with a specific weight peculiar to itself, for if he did not, his attention just skittered over phrases so they left no marks. That accomplished, he fixed in his mind the setting, supplying all the missing details of a high open forest: the kinds of trees that would grow there, the birds that would frequent their limbs, the bracken that would grow under them. When he could hold that picture firm and clear, he began constructing the shrub in his mind, forming all its particulars until it arose in his thinking as vivid as he could make it, though it in no way matched any known plant and was in several features quite fantastic.

He blew out his candle and wrapped himself in his bedding and sipped at the last of his wine in preparation for sleep, but his mind turned on the dark-haired woman and on the woman named Laura and the softness of her thigh backs against his arms as he carried her. And then he thought of Ada and of Christmas four years ago, for there had been champagne then too. He leaned his head against the tree bark and took a long draught of the wine and remembered with some particularity the feel of Ada sitting on his lap in the stove corner.

It seemed like another life, another world. He remembered her weight on his legs. The softness of her, and yet the hard angularity of her bones underneath. She had leaned back and rested her head on his shoulder, and her hair smelled of lavender and of herself. Then she sat up and he put his hands to the points of her shoulders and felt the underlayment of muscle and the knobby shoulder joints beneath the skin. He pulled her back to him and wanted to wrap his arms around her and hold her tight, but she blew out air through her pressed lips and stood and pulled at the wrinkles in the skirt of her dress and reached up to smooth back little rings of hair that had sprung loose at her temples. She turned and looked down at him.

—Well, she had said. Well.

Inman had leaned forward, taken her hand and rubbed across its back with his thumb. The fine bones running to the wrist from the knuckles moved beneath the pressure like piano

keys. Then he turned her hand over and smoothed back the fingers when she tried to draw them in and make a fist. He put his lips to her wrist where the slate-blue veins twined. Ada slowly drew her hand away and then stood looking down absently at its palm.

—There's not tidings written on it. Not any we can read, Inman said.

Ada had put her hand down and said, That was unexpected. Then she walked away.

When Inman finally let go the memory and slept, he dreamed a dream as bright as the real day. In it he lay, as he did in the ordinary world, in a forest of hardwoods, their boughs visibly tired from a summer of growing and just weeks away from the color and the fall. Mixed in among the trees were the shrubs he had imagined from his reading of Bartram. They were covered in great hallucinatory blossoms, pentangular in form. In the dream world, fine rain sifted down through the heavy leaves and moved along the ground in curtains so sheer that it did not even wet him through his clothes. Ada appeared among the tree trunks and moved at about the pace of the rain toward him. She wore a white dress and was wound about the shoulders and head in a wrapping of black cloth, but he knew her from her eyes and from the way she walked.

He rose from where he lay on the ground, and though perplexed as to how she came to be there he longed to hold her and went to do it, but three times as he reached his arms to her she fogged through them, vague and flickery and grey. The fourth time, though, she stood firm and substantial and he held her tight. He said, I've been coming for you on a hard road. I'm never letting you go. Never.

She looked at him and took the wrapping from about her head and seemed in the look of her face to agree, though she said not a word.

Inman was roused from sleep by the song of morning birds. The vision of Ada would not loose its grip on his mind, nor did

he wish it to. He arose and there was a heavy dew on the grass and the sun already stood at the treetops. He walked through the woods to the camp, but everyone was gone. The fire where the medicine wagon had been was dead. There was nothing to say the show folk had been real but the big black fire ring and a set of parallel lines cut in the dirt by their wagon wheels. Inman was sorry not to have bid them farewell, but he walked all through the day with some brightening of his spirit from the clear dream he had been awarded in the dark of night.

ashes of roses

One warm afternoon at the brink of fall, Ruby and Ada worked in the lower field, which Ruby had designated as the winter garden. It was the sort of day when joe-pye weed had grown seven feet tall and its autumnal metallic flowerheads suddenly opened and glittered in the sun, looking for all the world like frost early of a morning. They served as reminders of just how rapidly the first real frost was approaching, even though the sun was still hot and the cow still spent the day following the shade of the big hickory tree as it moved across the lower pasture.

Ada and Ruby hoed and pulled weeds among the rows of young cabbages and turnips, collards and onions, the kind of coarse food they would mostly live on for the winter. Some weeks earlier they had prepared the garden carefully, plowing and sweetening the dirt with fireplace ashes and manure from the barn and then harrowing the cloddy ground, Ruby driving the horse while Ada rode the drag to add weight. The harrow was a crude device, knocked together by one of the Blacks from a fork in an oak trunk. Holes had been augered through the green wood of the two spreading ends of the trunk and fitted

with long spikes of cured black locust. As the oak dried, it had tightened hard around the sharpened locust and needed no further attachment. During the work, Ada had sat at the fork, braced with hands and feet as the harrow jounced across the ground, breaking up clumps of plowed dirt and combing it smooth with the tines of locust. She had watched the turned ground passing and had snatched up three partial arrowheads and a flint scraper and one fine complete bird point. When they began planting, Ruby had held out a handful of tiny black seeds. Looks like not much, she said. It takes faith to jump from this to a root cellar filled with turnips some many weeks hence. That and a warm fall, for we started late.

The crops were growing well, largely, Ruby claimed, because they had been planted, at her insistence, in strict accordance with the signs. In Ruby's mind, everything—setting fence posts, making sauerkraut, killing hogs—fell under the rule of the heavens. Cut firewood in the old of the moon, she'd advised, otherwise it won't do much but fry and hiss at you come winter. Next April when the poplar leaves are about the size of a squirrel's ear, we'll plant corn when the signs are in the feet; otherwise the corn will just shank and hang down. November, we'll kill a hog in the growing of the moon, for if we don't the meat will lack grease and pork chops will cup up in the pan.

Monroe would have dismissed such beliefs as superstition, folklore. But Ada, increasingly covetous of Ruby's learning in the ways living things inhabited this particular place, chose to view the signs as metaphoric. They were, as Ada saw them, an expression of stewardship, a means of taking care, a discipline. They provided a ritual of concern for the patterns and tendencies of the material world where it might be seen to intersect with some other world. Ultimately, she decided, the signs were a way of being alert, and under those terms she could honor them.

They worked among the plants for some time that afternoon, and then they heard the sound of wheels, a horse, a metal pail banging against a sideboard with a ring that filled the cove.

A pair of ancient mules and then a wagon rounded the curve of the road and stopped by the fence. The wagon bed was piled full with satchels and boxes to such extent that the people all walked. Ada and Ruby went to the fence and found the group to be made of pilgrims from Tennessee on their way to South Carolina. They had taken a number of wrong turnings along the river, had missed the way to Wagon Road Gap, and were now fetched up at this dead end. The party was composed of three broken women and a half dozen young children. They were tended by a pair of kind slaves, a man and wife, who hovered about the women as close as shadows, even though they might just as easily have cut every throat in the family any night as they slept.

The women said their husbands were off at the fighting, and they were fleeing the Federals in Tennessee, aiming for Camden in South Carolina where one of the women had a sister. They asked leave to sleep in the hayloft, and while they were making up their nests in the hay, Ada and Ruby went to work cooking. Ruby cut the heads off three chickens, for the yard was now so full of chicks they could hardly walk to the springhouse without stepping on one, and the population was such that they could anticipate a sufficiency of capons soon. They cut the chickens up and fried them, cooked pole beans, boiled potatoes and stewed squash. Ruby made a triple recipe of biscuits, and when supper was ready they called in the visitors and sat them at the dining-room table. The slaves had the same fare, but ate out under the pear tree.

The travelers dined hard for quite some time, and when they were done eating, there were but two wings and a thigh left on the chicken platter, and they had gone through more than a pound of butter and a pint pitcher of sorghum. One woman said, My, that was good. It's been two weeks now that we've had little to eat but dry corn bread, without butter or bacon drippings or molasses to wetten it up a little. Choky food.

—How do you come to be on the road? Ada said.

—The Federals rode down on us and robbed even the niggers, the woman said. They took every bit of food we had been able to raise this year. I even saw one man filling his coat pockets with our lard. Dipping it by the handful. Then we were tetotally stripped and searched right down to our very persons by a Federal we were told was a woman in uniform. But it was not. It had an Adam's apple. It took from us every article of jewelry we had hidden. Then they burnt our house down in the rain and rode away. Shortly it was only a chimney standing sentry over a cellar hole full of bitter-smelling black water. We had nothing, but we stayed awhile from lack of will to part from home. On the third day I stood with my least little girl looking down into that hole where was the wreckage of everything we had. She picked up a shard of a broken dinner plate and said, Mama, I expect we'll soon be eating off leaves. Then it was that I knew we had to go.

—That is the way of the Federals, another of the women said. They have come up with a fresh idea in warfare. Make the women and children atone for the deaths of soldiers.

—This is a time that carves the heart down to a bitter nub, the third woman said. You are luckier than you know, hid in this cove.

Ada and Ruby saw the travelers off to bed, and the next morning they cooked nearly all the eggs they had and made a pot of grits and more biscuits. After breakfast, they drew a map of the way to the gap and set them on the next leg of their journey.

That noon, Ruby said she wanted to walk up and check on the apple orchard, so Ada suggested they have their lunch there. They made a picnic of the leftover pieces of last night's fried chicken, a small bowl of potato salad for which Ruby had whipped up the mayonnaise, and some vinegared cucumber slices. They carried the dinner up to the apple orchard in a wooden bucket and ate it under the trees on a quilt spread in the grass.

It was an afternoon of bright haze, the sunlight sourceless

and uniform. Ruby examined the trees and judged solemnly that the apples were making tolerably well. Then, out of the blue, she looked at Ada and said, Point north. She grinned at the long delay as Ada worked out the cardinal directions from her recollection of where the sun set. Such questions were a recent habit Ruby had developed. She seemed to delight in demonstrating how disoriented Ada was in the world. As they walked by the creek one day she had asked, What's the course of that water? Where does it come from and what does it run into? Another day she had said, Name me four plants on that hillside that in a pinch you could eat. How many days to the next new moon? Name two things blooming now and two things fruiting.

Ada did not yet have those answers, but she could feel them coming, and Ruby was her principal text. During the daily rounds of work, Ada had soon noted that Ruby's lore included many impracticalities beyond the raising of crops. The names of useless beings—both animal and vegetable—and the custom of their lives apparently occupied much of Ruby's thinking, for she was constantly pointing out the little creatures that occupy the nooks of the world. Her mind marked every mantis in a stand of ragweed, the corn borers in the little tents they folded out of milkweed leaves, striped and spotted salamanders with their friendly smiling faces under rocks in the creek. Ruby noted little hairy liverish poisonous-looking plants and fungi growing on the damp bark of dying trees, all the larvae and bugs and worms that live alone inside a case of sticks or grit or leaves. Each life with a story behind it. Every little gesture nature made to suggest a mind marking its life as its own caught Ruby's interest.

So as they sat on the blanket, drowsy and full from lunch, Ada told Ruby that she envied her knowledge of how the world runs. Farming, cookery, wild lore. How do you come to know such things? Ada had asked.

Ruby said she had learned what little she knew in the usual way. A lot of it was grandmother knowledge, got from wandering around the settlement talking to any old woman who would talk

back, watching them work and asking questions. Some came from helping Sally Swanger, who knew, Ruby claimed, a great many quiet things such as the names of all plants down to the plainest weed. Partly, though, she claimed she had just puzzled out in her own mind how the world's logic works. It was mostly a matter of being attentive.

—You commence by trying to see what likes what, Ruby said. Which Ada interpreted to mean, Observe and understand the workings of affinity in nature.

Ruby pointed to red splashes of color on the green hillside of the ridge: sumac and dogwood already turning color in advance of other trees. Why would they do that near a month ahead? she said.

—Chance? Ada said.

Ruby made a little sound like spitting a fleck of dirt or a gnat from the tip of her tongue. Her view was that people like to lay off anything they can't fathom as random. She saw it another way. Both sumac and dogwood were full of ripe berries at that time of year. The thing a person had to ask was, What else is happening that might bear on the subject? One thing was, birds moving. They were passing over all day long and all night too. You didn't have to but look up to know that. Enough to make you dizzy at the numbers of them. Then think about standing on a high place like the jump-off rock and looking down on the trees as the birds see them. Then wonder at how green and alike the trees look. One very much resembling another, whether it offers a meal or not. That's all roving birds see. They don't know these woods. They don't know where a particular food tree might live. Ruby's conclusion was, dogwood and sumac maybe turn red to say *eat* to hungry stranger birds.

Ada said, You seem to suppose that a dogwood might have a plan in this.

—Well, maybe they do, Ruby said.

She asked whether Ada had ever looked close up at the particular mess of various birds. Their droppings.

—Hardly, Ada said.

—Don't act so proud about it, Ruby said. In her view that's where the answer to this issue might lie. Every little dogwood can't grow up right where it falls under the big dogwood. Being rooted, they use the birds to move themselves around to more likely ground. Birds eat berries, and the seeds come through whole and unmarred, ready to grow where dropped, already dressed with manure. It was Ruby's opinion that if a person puzzled all this out over time, she might also find a lesson somewhere in it, for much of creation worked by such method and to such ends.

They sat quietly for a while, and then in the warm still air of the afternoon Ruby lay down and dozed on the quilt. Ada was tired too, but she fought off sleep like a child at bedtime. She rose and walked beyond the orchard to the margin of the woods where the tall autumn flowers—goldenrod and ironweed and joe-pye weed—were beginning to bloom yellow and indigo and iron grey. Monarchs and swallowtails worked among the flower heads. Three finches balanced on blackberry canes, the leaves already turned maroon, and then flew away, flaring out low to the ground, their yellow backs flashing between their black wings until they disappeared into a clump of dog hobble and sumac at the transition between field and woods.

Ada stood still and let her eyes go unfocused, and as she did she became aware of the busy movements of myriad tiny creatures vibrating all through the massed flowers, down the stems and clear to the ground. Insects flying, crawling, climbing, eating. Their accumulation of energy was a kind of luminous quiver of life that filled Ada's undirected vision right to the edges.

She stood there, part in a lethargic daze, part watchful, thinking of what the pilgrim woman had said about Ada's great luck. On such a day as this, despite the looming war and all the work she knew the cove required of her, she could not see how she could improve her world. It seemed so fine she doubted it could be done.

That evening after dinner, Ruby and Ada sat on the porch, Ada reading aloud. They were nearly done with Homer. Ruby had grown impatient with Penelope, but she would sit of a long evening and laugh and laugh at the tribulations of Odysseus, all the stones the gods threw in his passway. She held the suspicion, though, that there was more of Stobrod in Odysseus than old Homer was willing to let on, and she found his alibis for stretching out his trip to be suspect in the extreme, an opinion only confirmed by the current passage in which the characters were denned up in a swineherd's hut drinking and telling tales. She concluded that, all in all, not much had altered in the way of things despite the passage of a great volume of time.

When the light began to give out, Ada put down the book. She sat and examined the sky. Something about the color of the light or the smell of night coming on brought to mind a party she had attended on her last trip back to Charleston shortly before Sumter, and she recounted it to Ruby.

It was held at her cousin's house, a grand place situated on a broad bend of the Wando River, and it lasted for three days. For the duration, they all slept only from dawn to noon and lived on little but oysters and champagne and pastry. Each evening there was music and dancing, and then late in the nights, under a moon growing to full, they went out on the slow water in rowing boats. It was a strange time of war fever, and even young men previously considered dull and charmless suddenly acquired an aura of glamour shimmering about them, for they all suspected that shortly many of them would be dead. During those brief days and nights, any man that wished might become somebody's darling.

On the party's final night, Ada had worn a dress of mauve silk, trimmed in lace dyed to match. It was cut close in the waist to suit her slimness. Monroe had bought the entire bolt of cloth from which the dress was made so that no one else might wear

that color. He remarked that it set off her dark hair perfectly and gave her an air of mystery among the more common pinks and pale blues and yellows. That night, a Savannah man—the dashing-looking but largely witless second son of a wealthy indigo merchant—flirted so tirelessly with Ada that finally she agreed to go out on the river with him, though what little she knew of him inclined her to believe he was only a vain fool.

The man's name was Blount. He rowed to the middle of the Wando and drifted. They sat facing each other, Ada with the mauve dress drawn tight around her legs to keep its hem from the tar that caulked the boat's bottom. Neither of them spoke. Blount feathered the oars over and over, letting the water drip from them into the river. He seemed to have something on his mind that accorded well with the sound of the water running off the oars, for he kept on doing it until Ada told him to stop. Blount had brought a pair of flutes and a partial bottle of champagne still cool enough to sweat in the heavy air. He offered Ada a glass, but she declined her portion, so he finished off the bottle and threw it out into the river. The water lay so still that the circles from the splash expanded on and on until they became too distant to see.

Music from the house carried across the water, too faint to identify more precisely than that it was a waltz. In the darkness the low shorelines seemed impossibly far. The normal qualities of the landscape were altered beyond recognition, distilled to strange minimal parts, simple as geometry. Planes and circles and lines. The full moon stood directly overhead, its disc softened by the humidity in the air. The sky glimmered silver, too bright for stars. The wide river was silver as well, only slightly duller. Morning mist already rose from the water, though the dawn was hours away. The only demarcation between river and sky was the line of dark trees at either horizon.

Blount finally spoke out. He talked awhile about himself. He had recently graduated from the university in Columbia and had just begun learning the Charleston portion of the family busi-

ness. But of course he would immediately enlist should war begin, as everyone expected it soon would. He talked with bravado about driving back any force bent on subjugating the Southern states. Ada had heard like sentiments repeated over and over throughout the party and was tired of them.

As Blount continued, though, he apparently became as unconvinced as Ada, for eventually he bogged down in his war talk and fell silent. He stared down into the black bottom of the boat so that Ada could see only the top of his head. Then, under the influence of drink and the strangeness of the night, Blount admitted he was terrified of the fighting that almost certainly lay before him. He was unsure if he would be able to acquit himself in a way that would bring credit. But neither could he see any course of escape that would not be shameful. Further, he had been visited by recurring dreams of horrible death in many forms. One of them, he was certain, would someday claim him.

He had talked looking down, as if addressing his shoe tops, but when he angled his pale face up into the moonlight, Ada noted the shining paths of tears runneling down his cheeks. She realized with an unexpected flush of tenderness that Blount was no warrior but had instead the heart of a shopkeeper. She reached forward and touched his hand where it rested on his knee. She knew that the proper thing to say was that duty and honor demanded brave action in defense of homeland. Women had been uttering like phrases all through the party, but Ada found her throat closed against the words. Lacking them, she could have used a simpler locution, telling him only, Don't worry, or, Be brave. But any such comforting formula seemed at that moment unutterably false to her. So she said nothing and only continued to stroke the back of his hand. She hoped Blount would not think her token of kindness more than it was, since her first impulse, when pressed upon by men, was to draw up and back off. And the rowing boat left little room for retreat. As they drifted along, though, she was relieved to see that Blount was too overwhelmed by fear of the future to think of courting.

They sat that way for some time, until they drifted to the bend of the river. The boat headed straight for the outside of the curve, threatening to ground itself on a sandy bank that shone out as a strip of paleness in the moonlight. Blount composed himself and again took the oars and returned them upstream to the landing.

He walked her to the porch of the brightly lighted house, the interior ablaze with Argand lamps. The silhouettes of dancers passed across the yellow windows, and now the music was distinct enough to identify: first Gungl and then Strauss. Blount stopped at the doorway. He put the ends of two fingers to Ada's chin and tipped her face up and leaned forward to kiss her cheek. It was but a brief and brotherly press of lips. Then he walked away.

Ada now remembered that as she had walked through the house to go upstairs to her room, she had been struck by the figure of a woman's back in a mirror. She stopped and looked. The dress the figure wore was the color called ashes of roses, and Ada stood, held in place by a sharp stitch of envy for the woman's dress and the fine shape of her back and her thick dark hair and the sense of assurance she seemed to evidence in her very posture.

Then Ada took a step forward, and the other woman did too, and Ada realized that it was herself she was admiring, the mirror having caught the reflection of an opposite mirror on the wall behind her. The light of the lamps and the tint of the mirrors had conspired to shift colors, bleaching mauve to rose. She climbed the steps to her room and prepared for bed, but she slept poorly that night, for the music went on until dawn. As she lay awake she thought how odd it had felt to win her own endorsement.

The next day, as the partyers were loading into carriages to be taken back into the city, Ada unexpectedly met Blount on the front steps. He could not meet her eye and he barely spoke, so put out of countenance was he by his performance the night before. Ada thought it to his credit, though, that he had not asked her to keep what had happened secret. She had never seen him

again, but in a letter from her cousin Lucy, Ada learned that Blount had died at Gettysburg. Shot, according to all reports, in the face during the retreat from Cemetery Ridge. He had been walking backward, not wishing to be shot in the back.

At the tale's conclusion, Ruby was not much impressed with Blount's effort toward honor and could only marvel at lives so useless that they required missing sleep and paddling about on a river for pleasure.

—You've missed my point, Ada said.

They sat for a while, watching the light fall away and the details go from the trees on the ridges. Then Ruby rose and said, Time for my night work. It was her habitual way of saying good night. She went off to take a last look at the animals, check the doors on the outbuildings, bank the fire in the kitchen stove.

Meanwhile, the book still in her lap, Ada remained on the porch looking out across the yard and down to the barn. On past the fields to the wooded slopes. Up to the darkening sky. The colors that had reminded her of Charleston were now muted. Everything declining toward stillness. Her thoughts, though, seemed intent on folding back on themselves, for she recalled that she and Monroe had sat thusly on a night just after moving to the cove. These now-familiar elements of landscape had seemed strange to them both. This mountain country was so dark and inclined to the vertical compared with Charleston. Monroe had commented that, like all elements of nature, the features of this magnificent topography were simply tokens of some other world, some deeper life with a whole other existence toward which we ought aim all our yearning. And Ada had then agreed.

But now, as she looked out at the view, she held the opinion that what she saw was no token but was all the life there is. It was a position in most ways contrary to Monroe's; nevertheless, it did

not rule out its own denomination of sharp yearning, though Ada could not entirely set a name to its direction.

Ruby crossed the yard and paused at the gate. She said, The cow needs putting away. Then, without further salute, she went on up the road toward the cabin.

Ada left the porch and walked down past the barn into the pasture. The sun was long gone below the ridgelines, the light falling fast. The mountains stood grey in the dusk, as pale and insubstantial as breath blown on glass. The place seemed inhabited by a great force of loneliness. Even the old-timers talked of the weight that bears down on a person alone in the mountains at that time of day, worse even than full dark on a moonless night, for it is at twilight that the threat of dark makes itself felt most strongly. Ada had sensed that power from the beginning and complained of it. She remembered Monroe had tried to reason that the isolate feeling did not arise from this particular ground, as she claimed. It was nothing unique to her or to the place but was an element of common life. Only a very simple or a very hard mind might not feel it, in the way that some rare constitutions are insensitive to heat or cold. And, as with most things, Monroe had an explanation. He said that in their hearts people feel that long ago God was everywhere all the time; the sense of loneliness is what fills the vacuum when He pulls back one degree more remote.

The air was chill. Dew was in the grass already, and Ada was damp at the hem by the time she got to Waldo, who was lying in the tall grass along the lower fencerow. The cow roused up, stiff in her hip joints, and started to the gate. Ada stepped into the oblong of grass Waldo had flattened. She felt the cow's heat rise from the ground around her legs, and she wanted to lie down there and rest, suddenly unaccountably tired as from an accumulation of the month's work. Instead, she stooped momentarily and worked her hands under the grass and into the dirt that still felt warm as a living thing from the heat of the day and the body of the cow.

An owl hooted from the trees beyond the creek. Ada counted off the rhythm of the five-beat phrase as if scanning a line of poetry: a long, two shorts, two longs. Death bird, people said of the owl, though Ada could see no reason why. The call was so soft and lovely in the slaty light, like a dove's cry but with more substance to it. Waldo bawled at the gate, impatient, needing—as so much did in the cove—the things Ada was learning to do, so she took her hands from the ground and stood.

exile and brute wandering

Inman walked through days of cooling weather, blue skies, and empty roads. His course was necessarily waggling as he sought to avoid pikes and towns, but the way he found through deep country and widely spaced farms seemed safe enough. He met few people and those mainly slaves. The nights were warm and lit by big moons, growing to full and then achieving it and then falling away. There were often hayricks to sleep in so that he could lie back and look at the moon and stars, and he could fancy for a time that he was a footloose vagabond with not a thing to fear in all creation.

The days blended uneventfully together, though he tried to mark something down in his mind from each of them. One day he remembered only as being composed of hard course-setting. There were many road turnings, all of them unmarked by sign-post or blaze so that he had to ask the way over and over. He first came to a house built right in the crotch of two roads, so close that the porch nearly blocked the passway. A tired-looking woman rested spraddle-legged in a straight chair. She chewed on her lower lip, and her eyes seemed focused on some great

and indefinite event at the horizon. Where her skirt dipped at her lap was a pool of shadow.

—Is this the way to Salisbury? Inman said.

The woman sat with her knotty hands in fists on her knees. Intent, apparently, on exercising thrift in gestures, she barely tipped the right thumb in response. It might have been no more than a nervous tic. Not another feature of her moved, but Inman proceeded in the direction suggested.

Later he came on a grey-headed man sitting in the shade of a sweet-gum tree. The man wore a fine vest of yellow silk with no shirt under it, and it was unbuttoned and lay open so that his old dugs hung down like those on a sow hog. His legs stuck out straight before him and he slapped one thigh openhanded as if it were a beloved but misbehaving dog. When he talked, his speech seemed cramped to nothing but vowels.

—Is this the turning to Salisbury? Inman said.

—EEEEE? the man said.

—Salisbury, Inman said. Is this the way?

—AAAAA! the man said with finality.

Inman went on.

Still later he came to a man in a field pulling onions.

—Salisbury? Inman said.

The man spoke not a word but stretched out an arm and pointed the way with an onion.

All Inman remembered of another day's march was the white sky and that sometime during it a crow had died in flight, falling with a puff of dust into the road before him, its black beak open and its grey tongue out as if to taste the dirt, and that later he came upon three farm girls in pale cotton dresses dancing barefoot in the dust of the road. They stopped when they saw him coming and climbed a fence and sat on the top rail with their heels hooked on the second rail and their rusty knees up under their chins. They watched him as he walked by but would not speak when he threw up a hand and said, Hey.

One morning at the end of this time, Inman found himself walking through a wood of young poplar, their leaves already turning to yellow, though the season did not yet call for it. His thinking turned on issues of food. He had been making fair time, but had grown tired of skulking and starving and living off of nothing but corn mush and apples and persimmons and stolen melons. He was thinking how much he would relish some meat and bread. He was weighing that desire against a calculation of the risk he would have to take to get them when he came upon a group of women at a river doing laundry. He stepped into an edge of forest and watched.

The women stood out in water to their calves, slapping the clothes against smooth stones and rinsing and wringing them, then draping them over nearby bushes to dry. Some talked and laughed, and others hummed snatches of song. They had their skirt tails caught up between their legs and tucked into their waistbands to keep them from the water. To Inman they looked like they were wearing the oriental pantaloons of the Zouave regiments, whose soldiers looked so strangely bright and festive scattered dead across a battlefield. The women, not knowing they were being watched, had their skirts hiked up high onto their thighs, and the water running from the clothes sheeted off the pale skin and glistened in the light like oil.

On some other day this would have had its appeal, but Inman's attention rested on the fact that the women had brought their dinners—some in withy baskets and some tied up in cloths. They had left them sitting on the riverbank. He first thought to call out and ask to buy something to eat from them, but he suspected that they would immediately form ranks and take up rocks from the river bottom and drive him away. So he decided to stay hidden.

He worked his way down among the trees and boulders to the riverbank. After sneaking out a hand from behind the shaggy trunk of a big river birch to heft several of the dinners, he took

the heaviest one, leaving much more than fair money in its place, for it seemed especially important at that moment to be generous.

He walked off down the road, swinging the cloth bundle by one of its loose ends, and when he put some distance between himself and the river, he opened the knotted cloth and found three large chunks of poached fish, three boiled potatoes, and a pair of underdone biscuits.

Biscuits with fish? Inman thought. What unseemly cookery. And what a pale meal it made, especially when matched up against the brown feast he had imagined.

He ate it anyway, lunching afoot. A short time later—traveling down a deserted stretch of road, the last of the potatoes two bites from gone—Inman got a feeling like an itch at the back of his head. He paused and looked around. There was a figure in the distance behind him, a man walking fast. Inman finished the potato and stepped out briskly until he came to the first bend in the road. Once he was around it, he went into the woods and took up a good watching position behind a downed tree trunk.

Shortly the walker came around the bend. He went hatless and wore a long grey coat with flapping skirts and carried a lumpish leather knapsack and a walking staff as tall as he was. He strode along, head down, marking his pace with the staff like some mendicant friar from days of yore. As the man drew nearer, it became plain that his face was cut and marked by bruises fading to yellow and green. A split lip was part healed with a dark scab so that he looked like a harelip. Tufts of patchy blond fuzz grew from his white scalp, which was marked here and there by long scabs. So fine was he through the stomach that the top of his britches lapped over like great pleats and was tied with a length of rope. When the walker lifted his blue eyes from looking down at the road beneath his feet, Inman saw immediately that, underneath all the damage, it was the preacher.

Inman raised up from behind the log and said, Hey there.

The preacher stopped and stared. Good God, he said. Just the man I was looking for.

Inman pulled out his knife and held it point down, his arm relaxed. He said, You come to me looking for vengeance, I won't even waste a cartridge. I'll lay you open right here.

—Oh, no. I mean to thank you. You saved me from mortal sin.

—You walked all this way just in hope of saying that?

—No, I'm traveling. A pilgrim like yourself. Though maybe I speak too soon, for all who wander are not pilgrims. At any rate, where are you headed?

Inman looked the preacher over. What happened to your face? he said.

—When I was found as you left me, and when the note was read, a number of the men of the congregation, led by our Deacon Johnston, stripped me and gave me a fair beating. They threw my clothes in the river and cut my hair off with their knives, I think in bafflement over some part of the story of Samson and Delilah. Then they refused even to give me an hour to draw my things together. They held me from behind, and the woman I was to marry came and spit at me and thanked the Almighty that she was not to become a Veasey. I had nothing but my two hands to cover my prides with, and I was told to get out of town or they would hang me naked from the church steeple. It was just as well. I couldn't have lived on there anyway.

—Yes, I imagine not, Inman said. What about the other woman?

—Oh, Laura Foster, Veasey said. They hauled her out to tell what she knew, but she could still hardly put two thoughts together. When it becomes clear what state of motherhood she is in, she will be churched for a time. A year, say. And then she'll be but a subject of gossip. In two or three years more she'll take for husband some old bachelor willing to raise a bastard just as long as a fine-looking woman comes with the deal. She'll wind up all

the better for our relations, and for me having set my mind on putting both her and my betrothed behind me.

—It is still a cloudy matter to me if I did the right thing, letting you live, Inman said.

Without a further word he sheathed his knife and returned to the roadway and made to continue his journey. But the preacher fell in beside him.

—Since you appear to be going west, I'll just walk on with you if you don't mind, he said.

—Thing is, I do, Inman said, thinking it better to go alone than with a fool for comrade.

He made a motion as if to backhand the preacher, but the man did not run or fight or even try to raise his staff to parry. Rather, he hunched his shoulders to take the blow like a cowed dog, and so Inman pulled up and did not strike. He reasoned that lacking the will to drive the man off, he'd just walk on and see what came about.

Veasey drifted along at Inman's elbow, talking seamlessly. He worked under the notion that he had acquired a cohort. His ambition seemed to be to disburden himself of every feature of his prior life by passing it along to Inman. Every misstep he had made—and it was clear he'd made plenty—he sought to share. He was a sorry preacher; that much was apparent even to him.

—I displayed a great poorness at every feature of the job but the pulpitism, he admitted. But there I shined. I've saved more souls than there are fingers to your hands and toes to your feet. But I've foresworn it now and I'm going to the Texes and start fresh.

—Many are.

—There's a place in Judges where it talks about a time when there was no rule in Israel and every man just did what was right in his own eyes. I've heard the same of the Texes. It's a land of freedom.

—That's the tale that's told of it, Inman said. What do you aim to do there, farmer?

—Oh, hardly. I lack aptitude for grubbing in the dirt. As for suitable career, I'm undecided. Short of a clear calling, I might just go and claim me a piece of land the size of a county and run cattle on it until I have me a herd big enough so that you could walk all day across the backs of them without ever putting a foot to ground, Veasey said.

—What are you figuring to use to buy your first bull and cow with?

—This right here.

Veasey pulled from under his coat skirts a great long Colt's Army revolver, which he had appropriated on his way out of town.

—I might train myself to be a pistolero of some note, he said.

—Where did that come from? Inman said.

—Old Johnston's wife knew what had happened and took pity on me. She saw me lurking in the bushes and called out to me to come to the window, and while she went in the bedroom to get me this sorry costume I'm wearing, I espied this pistol on the kitchen table. I reached in through the window and took it and pitched it off in the grass, and then when I was dressed, I picked it up and took it on with me.

He sounded pleased with himself as a boy who had pilfered a cooling pie from a sill.

—That's how the pistoleer idea came to me, he continued. These things give you notions unsought.

He held the Colt's before him, looking into it as if he expected to see his future in the sheen of its cylinder.

That afternoon's march was one of great luck in foraging, for Inman and Veasey had not traveled far when they came upon an abandoned house set back in a grove of oaks. The doors stood open and the windows were broken out and the yard was grown up in mullein and burdock and Indian tobacco. All around the

house were beehives. Some in gums made from sections of the hollow trunks of black-gum trees, holes augered in them and oriented with the points of the compass. Others in straw skeps, grey as old thatch and starting to soften up and cave in at the crowns. Despite neglect, though, bees worked thick in the sunshine, coming and going.

—If we were to rob one of those gums it would be some good eating, Veasey said.

—Go to it, Inman said.

—I take a bee sting hard, Veasey said. I swell up. It wouldn't do for me to get in amongst them.

—But you'd eat the honey if I went to get it, is what you're saying?

—A dish of honey would hit the spot and would give us strength for the road.

Inman could not argue with that point, so he rolled down his shirtsleeves and tucked his pant cuffs into his boots and wrapped his head in his coat, leaving but a fold to sight through. He walked to a gum and slid the roof off and dug out handfuls of honey and comb into his pot until it was heaped over and running down the sides. He moved slowly and deliberately and was stung little.

He and Veasey sat on the edge of the porch, the pot between them, and ate the honey by the spoonful. It was black as coffee, having come from every sort of flower, and it was full of bees' wings and had toughened up from not being robbed in some time. It was nothing if compared to the clear honey from chestnut blossoms that his father had collected from wild bees by lining them to their tree hives as they flew through the woods. But still, Inman and Veasey ate it like it was good. When the honey was nearly gone, Inman lifted out a chunk of the comb and bit off a piece.

—You eating even the comb? Veasey said, a note of disapproval in his voice.

—You say that like there was a rooster in the pot, Inman said. He chewed at the waxy plug.

—It's just that it looks like it would stopper a man up.

—It's good for you. A tonic, Inman said. He took another bite and reached out a piece to Veasey, who ate it without relish.

—I'm still hungry, Veasey said, after the pot was empty.

—That's it unless you can scare up something for us to shoot, Inman said. And we need to be walking, not hunting. This kind of traveling puts a curb on your appetites.

—There's some say that's the way to contentment, get to where there's nothing you crave, where you've lost your appetites. Which is lunacy, Veasey said. Contentment is largely a matter of talking yourself into believing that God will not strike you too hard for leaning in the direction of your hungers. There's few I've seen who benefit from believing that on the Day of Judgment, moon turns to blood. I know I don't wish to give that belief too much credit.

Inman jumped from the porch and set out. They traveled at a fair pace for another hour until the road became but a path that climbed a rolling ridge and then followed the fall of a little twisty stream for a while. The water ran down the hill in a series of white riffles broken now and then by quiet bends and little pools where the land terraced or curved, so that if one were not too careful about the particulars it might be taken for a mountain stream. The damp cove too had the smell of the mountains to Inman's nose. The fragance of galax and rotted leaves, damp dirt. He ventured to say as much.

Veasey put his head back and sniffed. Smells like somebody's ass, he said.

Inman did not even comment. He was tired, and his mind worked at random. His eyes kept to the bright thread of water before them. The path it had found to make its way to lower ground was as coiled as a hog's bowel. He had learned enough of books to think that gravity in its ideal form was supposed to work

in straight lines of force. But looking on the creek as it made its snaky way down the hill, he saw such notions to be just airy thoughts. The creek's turnings marked how all that moves must shape itself to the maze of actual landscape, no matter what its preferences might be.

When it reached flat ground, the creek gentled and became a watercourse little better than a muddy ditch and displayed no further reference that Inman could find to a mountain stream. Veasey stopped and said, Well, look yonder.

There in the creek, which was deep but still narrow enough to step across with scarcely a hop, was a catfish that looked longer than a singletree for an ox team, though much greater in girth. In fact it was stout as a tub. It was ugly in the face with its tiny eyes and pale barbels run out from its mouth and wagging in the current. Its lower jaw was set back to make sucking up bottom trash easier, and its back was greeny black and gritty-looking. Though it was but a runt compared to what Inman had imagined in the depths of the muddy Cape Fear, it nevertheless looked plenty hefty and must have taken a woefully wrong turn somewhere to find itself here in water so narrow it could reverse its direction only if it had a hinge in its middle.

—He would be good eating, Veasey said.

—We lack tackle, Inman pointed out.

—I'd give anything for a pole and a line and a hook baited with a big wad of greasy wheat bread.

—Well, we don't have it, Inman said, disgusted at such custom of flatland fishing. He had no more than moved a foot to walk on when the fish spooked at his shadow on the water and wallowed off upstream.

Veasey followed Inman as he walked away, but he kept turning back and looking up the creek. He made it clear he was sulking. Every hundred yards of progress they made he would say, That was a big fish.

When they had gone only about a half a mile, Veasey stopped and said, There's nothing else but that I've got to have

me that catfish. He turned and set into a jog trot up the trail. Inman followed at a walk. When Veasey got near to where the fish had been, he led them off into the woods and thrashed ahead, circling through them for some time so that when he came back to the water they were well upstream. Inman watched as Veasey began scouting into the woods for downed limbs and dragging them into the stream. He piled them up and jumped on them to pack them down. Eventually he had built a kind of weir, all prickly with limbs.

—What are you up to? Inman said.

—You just wait right here and watch, Veasey said.

Then he circled in the woods again and struck the creek downstream of where he figured the fish to be. He jumped in the creek and walked upstream, kicking the water as he went, and though he did not ever see the fish, he knew he must be driving it before him.

When Veasey neared the weir, Inman could finally see the catfish nosed against the branches trying to find a passage. Veasey pulled off his hat and threw it onto the creek bank. He waded to the fish and bent and dipped his upper half into the water to grapple it out. Fish and man came up thrashing, spilling water off in sheets. Veasey had the fish in a hug about its middle, his hands clenched at its white belly. It fought him with all it had. Its neckless head beat back against his, and the whiskers whipped about his face. Then it bent like a great strong bow, sprung straight, and shot from his arms back into the water.

Veasey stood wheezing for air. His face was marked with long red weals where he had been stung by the whiskers of the fish, and his arms were cut from the spined fins, but he bent and took it up out of the water again and wrestled it to another draw. He tried over and over but failed each time until he and the fish both could hardly move from exhaustion. Veasey climbed wearily from the stream and sat on the bank.

—Could you get down in there and try your hand at it? he asked Inman.

Inman reached to his hip and took out the LeMat's and shot the catfish through the head. It thrashed for a minute and then lay still.

—They God, Veasey said.

They camped there that night. Veasey left the building and tending of the creekside fire to Inman, as well as all the cooking. He apparently knew to do nothing but talk and eat. When Inman cut the fish open, he found among the contents of its stomach the head to a ballpeen hammer and a bluebird that had been swallowed whole. He set them aside on a flat rock. He next peeled the skin off a part of the fish's back and sides and whittled off fillets. Among the stores in Veasey's packsack was a waxed paper parcel of lard. Inman melted it in the pan and rolled pieces of the fish in his own cornmeal and fried them up brown. As they ate, Veasey looked at the rock and speculated on the catfish's diet.

—You reckon it swallowed that hammer entire a long time ago and then the juice in its stomach ate off the handle? he said.

—Might be, Inman said. I've heard stranger things.

But the bluebird was a puzzler. The only satisfactory way Inman could account for it was that a better class of fish, a wondrous trout, say, had risen from the water and taken the bluebird from a low limb of a creekside tree, and then that fine trout had immediately died and the catfish sucked it up whole from the bottom and digested it from the outside in, so all that was left was the bluebird.

They feasted on the fish through the evening, eating until all the meal and lard was gone. Then they just cut chunks of fish and skewered them on green sticks and roasted them bare over fire coals. Veasey talked on and on, and when he tired of relating his own history, he tried to draw out Inman's story. Where his home might be. Where he was heading. Where he had been. But Veasey could get hardly a word in answer. Inman just sat cross-legged and looked into the fire.

—You're about as bad off as Legion, I believe, Veasey finally

said. And he told Inman the story of the man whose wounded spirit Jesus comforted. How Jesus found him naked, fleeing mankind, hiding in the wilderness, gnashing his teeth on tomb rocks, cutting himself with stones. Turned wild by some ill fortune. What few thoughts Legion had just rampant.

—Always, night and day, he was in the mountains and in the tombs, crying and wailing like a dog, Veasey said. And Jesus heard of him and went to him and straightened him right out quicker than a dose of salts running through you. Legion went home a new self.

Inman just sat, and so Veasey said, I know you've run off from the war. That makes us both escapees.

—It doesn't make us both anything together.

—I was not fit for service, Veasey said.

—A fool could see that.

—I mean a doctor said it. I've wondered if I missed much.

—Oh, you missed plenty, Inman said.

—Well, shit. I guessed as much.

—I'll tell you a thing you missed. See how much use a sorry preacher would have been.

What he told Veasey was about the blowup at Petersburg. His regiment had been situated directly beside the South Carolina boys that got exploded by the Federal tunnelers. Inman was in the wattled trenches parching rye to make a pot of what they would call coffee when the ground heaved up along the lines to his right. A column of dirt and men rose into the air and then fell all around. Inman was showered with dirt. A piece of a man's lower leg with the boot still on the foot landed right beside him. A man down the trench from Inman came running through and hollering, Hell has busted!

The men in the trenches to left and right of the hole fell back expecting an attack, but in a little while they realized that the Federals had rushed into the crater and then, amazed at what they had done, just huddled there, confused by that new landscape of pure force.

Right quick Haskell called up his éprouvette mortars and put them just beyond the lip of the crater and had them loaded with a scant ounce and a half of powder, since all they had to do was loft the shells fifty feet to where the Federals milled about like a pen of shoats waiting for the hammer between the eyes. The mortar fire blew many of them to pieces, and when that was done, Inman's regiment led the attack into the crater, and the fighting inside was of a different order from any he had done before. It was war in its most antique form, as if hundreds of men were put into a cave, shoulder to shoulder, and told to kill each other. There was no room for firing and loading muskets, so they mainly used them as clubs. Inman saw one little drummer boy beating a man's head in with an ammunition box. The Federals hardly even bothered to fight back. All underfoot were bodies and pieces of bodies, and so many men had come apart in the blowup and the shelling that the ground was slick and threw a terrible stink from their wet internalments. The raw dirt walls of the crater loomed all around with just a circle of sky above, as if this was all the world there was and fighting was all there was to it. They killed everybody that didn't run away.

—There's the sort of thing you missed, Inman said. You sorry?

Inman spread his bedding and slept, and in the morning they ate carvings off the fish again for breakfast. They roasted up extra chunks to carry along for dinner, but still, when they broke camp, there was more fish left than had been eaten. Three crows waited in the top of a hickory tree.

Late in the afternoon of the following day, clouds gathered up and a wind blew and rain fell hard and steady with no sign of stopping. They walked on into it looking for shelter, Veasey all the while rubbing at the back of his neck and complaining of a piercing headache, a result of Inman having clubbed him to his knees with a wagon hub earlier in the day.

They had gone into a deserted-looking country store to buy food, and no sooner had they walked through the door than Veasey pulled his Colt's and told the shopkeep to empty his till. Inman had taken the first heavy thing that fell to hand—the hub that sat on a shelf by the door—and struck Veasey down. The Colt's went clattering across the wood floor and fetched up against a sack of meal. Veasey knelt on the brink of a swoon, but was taken with a fit of coughing and became thus restored to mindfulness. The shopkeep looked at Veasey and then at Inman and raised an eyebrow and said, The hell?

Inman had quickly made his apologies, picked up the pistol, and grabbed Veasey by the coat collar, lifting him as by a handle. Inman half dragged him out to the stoop and then sat him down on the steps and went back in the store to buy goods. In the interval, though, the man had taken out a shotgun and was squatted behind his counter with it, covering the door.

—Get going, he had said. I've not got thirty cents in silver money here, but I'm killing whoever comes for it.

Inman had held his hands out, palms up.

—He's but a fool, he had said, backing up.

Now, as they walked through the rain, Veasey whined and wished to halt and squat in the drizzle under a pine tree. But Inman, wrapped in his groundsheet, walked on, looking for a likely barn. They found none, but later met a stout old slave woman coming down the road. She had fashioned an enormous rain bonnet in some complicated manner from big flopping catalpa leaves. She went as dry as under an umbrella. Immediately seeing what their state was—a pair of outliers—she told them that lodging lay ahead, run by a man who cared not a whit for the war and would ask no questions.

About a mile on, they found the place, a kind of grim roadside inn and stable. A way station where coaches changed horses and travelers found shelter. The main building was a shambling tavern with a low shed-roofed ell running from the back. It was painted the color of rust and sat under two vast oak trees.

Drovers and their hogs and cattle and geese overnighted there in the days before the war when the turnpikes running to the railhead stock markets were thick with animals. But those times were like a lost paradise, and the sprawly corrals around the place now stood near empty and growing over in ragweed.

Inman and Veasey went to the door and tried it and found it latched, though they could hear voices inside. They knocked and an eye appeared at a crack between boards. The latch lifted and they walked in and found themselves in a dank hole, windowless, with but a fireplace for light and a strong reek of wet clothes and dirty hair. Their eyes were not adjusted to the dark as they moved into the room, but the preacher walked ahead, a grin fixed on his face like he was entering known territory and expected to meet friends. He soon stumbled over an old man sitting on a low stool and knocked him onto the floor. The man on the floor said, They damn, and there were sympathetic mutterings from the dark figures sitting at tables about the room. Inman grabbed Veasey by the shoulder and pulled him around behind him. He righted the overturned chair and helped the old man to his feet.

They walked on into the room and found seats, and when their sight cleared they saw that a recent chimney fire had burnt holes in one end of the roof. The breaches had yet to be patched, and rain fell in all around the hearth about as thick as it did outside so that the wet guests could not profitably stand by the fire to warm and dry themselves. The fireplace was vast, stretching across most of the end of the room and leading one to imagine great blazes of yesteryear. What fire was in it now, though, you could have covered with a saddlecloth.

In a minute a black whore as big as a big man came in from a back room. She carried a bottle in one hand. In the other, five shot glasses. Her thick fingers down in them. Inman could see the red handle of a straight razor thrust into the tangle of hair above her right ear. She wore a leather apron about her stout waist, and her butternut dress was cut low and partially unbut-

toned to display a vast bosom. When she passed before the little fire, every man in the room turned his head to see the outline of her splendid thighs through the thin dress. The dress skirt fell short of full coverage, and so her hard-muscled calves were on complete display. She went barefooted, her feet muddy. Her skin was black as a stove lid and she was fine looking, at least to any man for whom such grand scale had appeal. She paced about the room, pouring drinks, and then came to Inman's table. She set down two glasses and filled them and then pulled up a chair and sat, legs open, skirt hiked. On her inner thigh, Inman could see a pale knife scar running from her knee upward to disappear into the shadow of her bunched skirts.

—Gents, she said, eyeing them to see where advantage might be found. She grinned. Straight white teeth, blue gums. The preacher drained his glass and thrust it out to her, his eyes resting on the cranny between her breasts. She topped up his glass and said, What's your name, honey?

—Veasey, he said. Solomon Veasey. He drank off his second glass of liquor without taking his eyes from the mighty cleft of her chest. He appeared to be trembling, so hard had the feeling of rut fallen upon him.

—Well, Solomon Veasey, she said, what do you have to say for yourself?

—Not much, he said.

—Fair enough. You don't look like much neither, she said. But that don't matter. What would you give to spend some time out back with Big Tildy?

—I'd give a lot, Veasey said. He was as earnest as a man can be.

—But have you got a lot to give is the question, she said.

—Oh, don't you worry about that.

Tildy looked at Inman. You want to come along too? she said.

—You all go on ahead, Inman said.

Before they could leave, though, a man in a filthy leather

jacket and jingly spurs came over from the other side of the room and put a hand on Tildy's shoulder. He had a red wen at his temple and looked to be half drunk. Inman's first impulse was to tally the man's weaponry. A pistol at one hip, sheath knife at the other, a handmade thing like a blackjack hanging from a thong at his belt buckle. The man looked down at Tildy and said, Come over here, big'un. Some of us men want a word with you. He tugged at her shoulder.

—I got business here, she said.

The man looked at Veasey and grinned. He said, This little feller don't have a say in it.

At that Veasey rose and drew his Colt's from under his coat and went about bringing it to bear on the man's belly. But so slow and so obvious was Veasey in making his move that, by the time his pistol barrel reached level, the man had drawn his own pistol. His arm was stretched to its limit and the muzzle sat a finger's length from Veasey's nose.

Veasey's hand wavered uncertainly, and the barrel drooped so that if he had fired he would have but shot the man's foot.

—Put that thing away, Inman said.

Both men cut their eyes in his direction, and when they did, Tildy reached and plucked Veasey's pistol from his hand.

The man looked at Veasey and pursed his lips.

—You a shit-eating dog, he said to Tildy. Then to Veasey he said, She just saved your ass from getting killed, on account of if I shoot you unarmed the law will be on me.

Veasey said to no one in particular, I want my pistol back.

—Time to shut up, Inman said. He spoke to Veasey but did not take his eyes from the man with the wen.

—I'll not do it, the man said.

Inman said nothing.

The man still held the pistol aimed at Veasey's head and seemed not to see a way to bring their contest to a close.

—I expect I'll have to give you a beating with it instead, he said, giving the pistol a little shake in Veasey's face.

—Hey, Inman said.

The man looked, and now the LeMat's was out, lying on its side on the table, Inman's hand resting atop it.

With the forefinger of his free hand Inman signed for the man to step away.

The man stood a long time looking at the LeMat's, and the longer he looked the more calm Inman became. Finally the man holstered his pistol and walked off, muttering as he traversed the room. He drew together his party and went out the door.

—Give me that, Inman said to Tildy. She reached him Veasey's pistol, and he stuck it in his pant waist.

—You're set on getting us both killed, Inman said to Veasey.

—Not likely, Veasey said. It was two on one.

—No, it wasn't. Don't look to me to back you.

—Well, you just did.

—All the same, don't look to me. The next one I might let have you.

Veasey grinned and said, I reckon not. Then he and Tildy rose and left, his arm about what slight indentation she had for waist. Inman moved his chair back against a wall so that he could not be come at from behind. He raised his empty glass to a man in an apron who looked to be a barkeep.

—That's a big fireplace, Inman said to the man when he came with the bottle.

—In the summer we whitewash it and put a bedstead in it. It's the coolest place to sleep you've ever seen, the man said.

—Well, Inman said.

—You taking dinner?

—I will. I've been dining in the woods for some days now.

—Be ready in about two hours, the man said.

As the day wore out, a few other travelers came. A pair of old men on their way to sell a wagonload of produce at the nearby market town. A white-headed peddler pushing a barrow of skillets, spools of ribbon, tin cups, little bottles blown from brown glass containing laudanum and various tinctures of herbs

in alcohol. A few other assorted wanderers. They all ganged up and talked and drank together at a long table. They spoke of the old droving days with great nostalgia. One man said, Oh, I've driv many a beeve through here. Another talked of a great flock of geese and ducks he had escorted down this way one time, and he said that every few days they had to dip the birds' legs in hot tar and then in sand to keep them from wearing the webs off their feet. Every man had tales to tell.

Inman, though, perched alone through the late afternoon on a stool at the dry end of the room, sipping brown liquor that was claimed to be bourbon but lacked all the usual qualities of that drink other than the alcohol. He looked irritably into the pointless fire at the far end of the room. The others glanced at him frequently, a certain amount of worry in their looks. Their faces were mirrors in which Inman could see himself as they evidently did, as a man that might just shoot you.

Inman had paid five dollars Confederate to sleep in the hayloft and five more for supper, which, when it came, was a bowl not more than half full of a dark stew of rabbit and chicken with a wedge of corn bread. Even accounting for the worthlessness of the money, that was still high tariff.

After supper, in the last of twilight, he stood at the stable door under a shake-shingled overhang at the back of the inn. He leaned against a hitching rail and watched the rain fall in heavy drops into the mud of the wagon yard and the road. It came on a cool northerly wind. Two lanterns hung from the rafters. Their light seemed diluted by the water and served little purpose other than to glint off puddles and to cast everything into gloomy contrast. All the highlights and points of things were picked out by the light. Rain dripped steadily off the overhang, and Inman thought of Longstreet's comment at Fredericksburg: Federals falling as steady as rain dripping off an eave. In his mind Inman said, It was nothing like that, no similarity.

The wood of the way station was old, the grain raised, feeling powdery against his palm, even in the damp. In a corral

across the mud road, two wet horses stood in the rain, heads down. Inside the stable, others more fortunate stood in stalls, but they were such horses as will snap at you when you pass by them, and Inman turned and watched as a claybank mare bit a collop of flesh as big as a walnut out of the upper arm of one of the old market-bound men passing through the hall on the way to his room.

After a time of standing and staring with unfocused eyes out into the darkening landscape, Inman decided just to go to bed and rise early and head on. He climbed the ladder into the loft and found that his roommate was already there. It was the white-headed peddler, the other travelers having paid for beds. The man had carried the various satchels and cases from his barrow up into the loft. Inman threw his own packs into a heap under the eaves. He lounged back into a pile of hay just outside the circle of yellow light from the oil lamp that the peddler had brought up from the inn. It hung by its bale from a long nail driven into a roof beam.

Inman watched as the man sat under the wavery light and removed his boots and socks. His feet were blistered at heel and toe in tight bloody bubbles of skin. From a leather case he took a fleam. The lantern light caught the bright steel of the keen instrument and it shone out against the darkness like a barb of dull gold. The man punched at his feet with it until he had opened up the blisters and let the pink fluid run out, pressing with his fingers. He put his boots back on and said, There. He wiped his fingers on his pants and stood and took hobbled steps back and forth across the loft, walking with great tenderness and care.

—There, he said again.

—You've been walking as hard as I have, Inman said.

—I reckon.

The man pulled out a watch from his coat pocket and looked at its face. He tapped it with a knuckle and held it to his ear.

—I'd have thought later, he said. It's but six.

The peddler took the lamp down from its nail and set it on

the floor and joined Inman in the haystack. They sat a minute in silence. The rain beat on the shakes over their heads and reminded them what fine things a tight roof and a stack of dry straw are. The yellow circle of lamplight served to make the vast loft more snug. All the space beyond its radius ended abruptly in blackness, as if the light had scribed the dimensions of a room close around them. They could hear below them the shift of horses in stalls, the outblow of their breath. The drowsy murmur of other people talking.

The peddler dug around in his case again and pulled out a big pewter flask. He unstoppered it and took a long drink. Then he held it out to Inman.

—This is store liquor from Tennessee, he said.

Inman took a pull and it was good, flavors of smoke and leather and other things brown and rich.

Outside, the rain gathered up and wind rose in the darkness and whistled in the shakes. Boards creaked. The light jumped and guttered in the draught. The night was storm-stridden for hours. They drank through boom and flash, sprawled in the straw, telling tales of exile and brute wandering.

Inman found that the man's name was Odell, and by the lamplight Inman could see that he was far from old, though his hair was white as a goose. At most he was just a little farther along in the course of time than Inman.

—I've not had an easy life. Far from it, Odell said. And don't let what I am now stand for what I always was. I was born rich. By rights I ought to be ready to come into a planter's inheritance of cotton and indigo down in south Georgia. A fortune. It could be any time now, for my daddy's old. He could already be dead for all I know, the old shitpike. It would all have been mine. Of land, too much to bother measuring in acres. The borders of it run ten miles across going one way and six going the other. That, and more niggers than you could find useful work for. All mine.

—Why aren't you there? Inman said.

The answer to his question took much of the evening, and when the lantern ran out of oil, the peddler talked out his gloomy tale of careless love into the dark. Odell had been a happy boy. Oldest son. Raised and educated to take over the plantation. The problem was, as a young man of twenty, he had fallen into unseemly love with one of the black housemaids, a slave named Lucinda. As he told it, he loved her far past the point of lunacy, for as everyone knew, just to have loved her at all was a mark of an unsound mind. She was, at the beginning, a woman of twenty-two, an octoroon. Skin not much darker than the color of a tanned deerhide, he said. She was a yellow rose.

To complicate the matter, Odell had not long been married to the daughter of the county's other major planter. So good had been his prospects that he had had the choice of girls from far and near. The one he chose for wife was small and frail, given to spells of nervous fatigue, spent entire afternoons swooned on the fainting couch in the parlor. But she was beautiful in a transparent way, and he had wanted her above all others. After the wedding, though, once he got the heaps of crinolines off her, there seemed to be just about nothing left. She was so slight and wispish. He found little there to keep his mind from wandering.

The whole family lived in the big house—Odell, his new little wife, his parents, his brother, a sister. Odell's duties were light, his father not yet having reached the point where he was ready to let go any of his powers. Not that his father possessed any great mastery of the skills of landownership, for his primary accomplishment in life was successfully affecting a taste for absinthe over whiskey ever since a visit to France as a young man.

With little else to fill his mind, Odell spent much time reading Scott. In the cool months he hunted and in the warm he fished. He developed an interest in horse breeding. He became bored.

Lucinda came into the household as a result of a complicated set of gambling winnings his father accumulated on an autumn bear hunt. As a result of the evening card play, great numbers of hogs, several families of slaves, a saddle horse, a kennelful of bird dogs, a fine English-made shotgun, and Lucinda changed hands. The day she was delivered by her previous owner, she carried nothing but a square of cloth, the ends tied up around all her personal goods so that the bundle was no bigger than a pumpkin.

She was put to work in the kitchen, and that is where Odell first saw her. He walked into the room and fell in love that moment with the brittle blackness of her hair, the fine bones of her hands and feet and ankles, the way her skin stretched tight across her collarbone. She was barefoot, and Odell told Inman that as he stood there looking down at her pretty little feet he wished his wife was dead.

For months afterward, he spent much of his time sitting in a chair in the stove corner drinking coffee and mooning over Lucinda until everyone in the house knew the way things stood. One day his father took him aside and advised settling the matter by taking her into an outbuilding and, as he put it, laying the jemson to her.

Odell was appalled. He was in love, he explained.

His father laughed. I've raised a fool, he said.

The next day Odell's father rented out Lucinda to a family on the far side of the county. They were farmers of small means, unable to buy slaves of their own. They paid Odell's father for her labor and used her for field-work, milking, carrying wood. Whatever needed doing.

Odell fell into despair. He spent many a day lying abed. Or roving around the county, drinking and gambling. Until he discovered that two days a week, the farmer's wife had Lucinda carry eggs into town to sell.

Odell would rise on those mornings, suddenly bright in his mood as a man could be, and announce that he was going out

hunting. He would have a horse saddled, a charged shotgun in a scabbard, a pair of dogs. He would vault onto the horse from the porch and ride for miles at a canter, the dogs loping along, roaming out into the woods to investigate smells with as much glee as if they were actually hunting. He would ride into town, through it, out the other side, and on down the road until he met Lucinda walking barefoot, a basket of eggs on her arm. He would dismount and walk beside her. Take her basket and carry it for her. Would try to find a suitable topic for conversation. Never once in those first months did he try to draw her into the woods. She would beg him to leave her be, for his sake and for her own. At the edge of town he would give her back the basket and take her hand in his, both their heads bent down at parting.

Eventually, of course, Odell did find himself drawing her into the woods and down into a bed of pine straw. After that he began going to her cabin several nights a month. He would hobble his horse in the woods and tie his dogs to a tree. When he entered the clearing in the pinewoods where her cabin stood, she would run to him in a thin nightshirt and he would clasp her to him and then lead her inside to lie with her until just before the dawn of day.

He stayed away from home under various pretexts, chief of which was coon hunting, and soon every slave in the area knew that Odell would pay top dollar for fresh-killed coon. If he could, he would buy one on the way home to prove out his story of night hunting. Otherwise he would return to the house bemoaning his lack of skill in shooting, the greenness of his dogs, the increasing rareness of game.

This went on for a year. Then one night Lucinda informed him that she was pregnant. At this, Odell could bear it no more, and the next day he went to his father, met with him in what was called his study, though all he ever studied there were the big ledgers of the plantation. They stood together by the fireplace. Odell offered to buy Lucinda off of him. He would pay any price named, no dickering. His father sat blinking in amazement. Let

me make sure I'm understanding this, he said. Are you buying this nigger for the fieldwork or the pussy?

Odell struck his father a hard blow to his left ear. The old man fell and then rose and fell again. He bled from his ear hole. Help! he hollered.

Odell spent the next week locked in a canning house, bruised about the head and ribs from the beating he had taken at the hands of his younger brother and his father's foreman. On the second day his father came to the door and spoke through a crack, saying, I've sold that bitch to Mississippi.

Odell flung himself against the door again and again. He bayed through that night like one of his coon dogs and then off and on periodically for the next several days.

When he became too weary to howl, his father unlocked the door. Odell staggered out, blinking, into the light. I believe you have learned your lesson, his father said, and he strode away toward the lower fields, flicking at weed heads and wildflowers with his plaited crop.

Odell walked into the house and packed a satchel of clothes. From the safe box in his father's office he took all the cash he could find—a sizable pouch of gold pieces and a stack of paper bills. He went to his mother's room and took a diamond and ruby brooch, an emerald ring, several strings of pearls. He went and saddled his horse and rode out toward Mississippi.

In the years before the war, he searched the cotton states until he had worn out three horses and exhausted his store of valuables. But he had yet to find Lucinda, and he had never set foot on home ground again.

In a sense, he was still searching. This was the reason that, when it became necessary to make money, he chose a traveling life. His fortunes in business had eventually fallen from tradesman with horse and wagon to tinker pushing a barrow. He had but few more downward steps to go and could picture himself soon dragging some wheelless sledge or travois, that or selling little trinkets from a pack on his back.

When the tale was done, Inman and Odell found they had finished the flask of liquor. Odell went to his packs of goods and brought back two little bottles of patent medicine, mostly grain alcohol. They sat and sipped at it, and after a time Odell said, You've never seen the like of meanness I have. He told of his travels in Mississippi looking for Lucinda, sights that made him fear that she had already passed on into the next world in some horrible and bloody way. And sights that made him fear that she had not. He told of niggers burnt alive. Of them having ears and fingers docked for various misdemeanors. The worst such punishment he came upon was near Natchez. He was going down a lonely road near the river. Off in the woods he heard a turmoil of buzzards, a high wail. He took his shotgun and went investigating, and what he found was a woman in a cage made of bean poles beneath a liveoak. The tree was dusky with buzzards. They roosted on the cage and picked at the woman inside. They had pulled out one of her eyes already and had torn strips of hide from her back and arms.

When she saw Odell out of her one eye she hollered, Shoot me. But Odell fired off both barrels up into the tree. Buzzards hit the ground all about and the rest took lumbering flight. Odell had the sudden fear that the woman was Lucinda. He went to her and broke the cage open with the gun butt and drew her out. He laid her on the ground and gave her water. He had no idea what he intended to do, but before he could decide, the woman vomited blood and died. He looked at her and touched her feet and her collarbone and her hair, but she could not have been Lucinda. She was different-colored and her feet were knotted.

When Odell finished talking he was drunk and sat blotting at his eyes with his shirt cuff.

—It's a feverish world, Inman said, for lack of better comment.

When morning came up grey and foggy, Inman left the

burnt inn and hit the road. Veasey soon followed. He had a thin razor cut under one eye that still wept a trail of blood down his cheek, and he kept wiping at it with his coat sleeve.

—Rough night? Inman said.

—She meant no real harm. This razor scratch came by way of me being too firm in haggling over price for her staying the night. At least my greatest fear went happily unrealized, that she would lay that blade to the limb of my manhood.

—Well, I hope the night was worth it.

—Fully. The fascinations of depraved and unchaste women have been proverbial, and I admit I am a man overly charmed by the peculiarities of the female anatomy. Last night when she drew off that big shift of hers and stood before me, I was sore amazed. Stunned, in fact. It was a sight to mark down for remembrance in old age, one to cheer a mind otherwise falling to despond.

source and root

They had begun walking to town in a chill, mizzling rain. Against it, Ada had worn a long coat of waxed poplin, and Ruby had on an enormous sweater she had knitted of undyed wool with the lanolin left in, her claim being that the oil turned water as well as a mackintosh. The sweater's only failing was that in the damp it broadcast the fragrance of an unshorn ewe. Ada had insisted on carrying umbrellas, but an hour down the road the clouds broke open to sun. So once the trees quit dripping, they carried them furled, Ruby with hers over her shoulder like a woodward huntsman toting a rifle.

The brightening sky was busy with resident birds and with traveler birds moving south ahead of the season: various patterns of duck, geese both grey and white, whistling swan, nighthawk, bluebird, jaybird, quail, lark, kingfisher, Cooper's hawk, red-tailed hawk. All these birds and others Ruby remarked upon during their passage to town, finding a thread of narrative or evidence of character in their minutest customs. Ruby assumed the twitter of birds to be utterance as laden with meaning as human talk and claimed to like especially the time in spring

when the birds come back singing songs to report where they've been and what they've done while she'd stayed right here.

When Ruby and Ada came upon five ravens gathered in council at the edge of a yellow stubblefield, Ruby said, I've heard it claimed that rooks live for many hundreds of years, though how one might test that notion is anybody's guess. When a female cardinal with a sprig of birch in its beak flew by, Ruby was curious. She reckoned it a profoundly confused bird, for why would she carry such a thing if not nest building? But this was not the time of year for it. When they passed a stand of beech trees by the river, Ruby said the river took its name from the great numbers of passenger pigeons that sometimes flocked there to eat the beechnuts, and she said she had eaten many a pigeon in her youth when Stobrod would disappear for days at a time leaving her to fend for herself. They were the easiest game for a child to take. You did not even have to shoot them, just knock them out of trees with sticks and wring their necks before they came to their senses.

When three crows harried a hawk across the sky, Ruby expressed her great respect for the normally reviled crow, finding much worthy of emulation in their outlook on life. She noted with disapproval that many a bird would die rather than eat any but food it relishes. Crows will relish what presents itself. She admired their keenness of wit, lack of pridefulness, love of practical jokes, slyness in a fight. All of these she saw as making up the genius of crow, which was a kind of willed mastery over what she assumed was a natural inclination toward bile and melancholy, as evidenced by its drear plumage.

—We might all take instruction from crow, Ruby said pointedly, for Ada was clearly in something of a mood, the lifting of which lagged considerably behind the fairing sky.

For much of the morning Ada had been so dumb with gloom she might as well have worn a black crepe on her sleeve to announce it to the world. Some of it was attributable to the hard work of the previous week. They had made hay in the neglected

fields, though in the end it was so mixed with ragweed and spurge as to be barely usable. One day they had worked for hours preparing the scythes for cutting. They first needed a file and large whetstone to freshen the nicked and rusting edges of the scythes, which they had found lying reclined across the rafters of the toolshed. Ada could not say one way or the other whether Monroe had owned such implements as file and whetstone. She had her doubts, for the scythes had not been his but were left from the Blacks' tenure in the cove. Together Ada and Ruby had rummaged through the contents of the shed until they found a rat-tail file, its sharp tail end driven into a dusty old cob for handle. But a stone never emerged from the clutter.

—My daddy never had a whetstone either, Ruby said. He'd just spit on a piece of shale and rub his knife on it a pass or two. However sharp it got, that was fine. No great matter of pride to him if it would shave hair on your arm or not. As long as he could saw off a plug of chaw with it, he was happy enough.

In the end they had given up the search and resorted to Stobrod's method, using a smooth flat shale they found near the creek. After much rubbing, the blades were still of only marginal sharpness, but Ada and Ruby went to the field and swung the scythes through the afternoon and then raked the cut grass into windrows, finishing in the last light, well after the sun had set. On the day before the outing, when the hay had dried on the ground, they filled the drag sled over and over with it and unloaded it in the barn. The stubble underfoot stood hard and sharp so they could feel it pushing against their shoe soles. They worked from opposite sides of the rows, alternately forking the hay into the sled. When their rhythm broke apart, the tines of their forks chimed against each other and Ralph, dozing in the traces, would startle and toss his head. The work was hot, though the day had not been particularly so. It was a dusty job, and the chaff hung in their hair and the folds of their clothes and stuck to their sweaty forearms and faces.

When they were done, Ada felt near collapse. Her arms

were mackled red like a measles sufferer from being pricked and scraped with the cut grass ends, and she had a big blood-filled blister in the web of skin between her thumb and forefinger. She had washed up and collapsed in bed before dark, having eaten nothing but a cold biscuit with butter and sugar.

Tired as she was, though, she had found herself over and over rising from true sleep into a foggy hovering state of partial wakefulness, a fretful hybrid of sleep and wake partaking of the worst aspects of each. She felt she was raking and pitching hay all through the night. When she roused enough to open her eyes, she saw the black shadows of tree limbs moving in the block of moonlight cast across the floorboards, and the shapes seemed unaccountably troubling and ominous. Then, sometime in the night, clouds blacked out the moon and rain fell hard and Ada finally fell asleep.

She had awakened to the rainy dawn feeling crippled with muscle ache. Her hands would unclench from their imaginary grip on the hayfork only with effort, and her head throbbed with a general pain. And with a specific one, just above and behind her right eyelid. But she determined that the outing to town would go on as planned, for it was largely a pleasure trip they were taking, though they did need to purchase a few small items. Ruby wanted to replenish their makings for shotgun loads—birdshot, buckshot, and slugs—the cooling weather having put her in a temper to kill wild turkey and deer. For her part, Ada wished to scan the shelves at the back of the stationer's to see if any new books had arrived and to buy a leather-bound journal and a few sketching pencils so she might record some of her efforts toward botanizing. Mainly, though, Ada was feeling thoroughly cove-bound after weeks of work. She yearned so badly to go on a jaunt to town that sore muscles, a black mood, and the morning's unpromising weather had not kept her back. Nor had the unpleasant discovery at the barn that sometime during the previous day's work the horse had stone-bruised the sole of his hoof and was not able to draw the cabriolet.

—I'm going to town if I have to crawl, Ada had said to Ruby's back as Ruby bent in the rain with the horse's muddy hoof in her hands.

So it was a gloomy progress Ada made down the road that morning, despite Ruby's best efforts toward birdlore. They walked past farms set in little valleys and coves, the fields opening up among the wooded hills like rooms in a house. Women and children and old men worked the crops, since every man of age to fight was off warring. The leaves on cornstalks were brown at the tips and edges, and the ears to be left for shell corn still stood on the stalk waiting for sun and frost to dry them out. Pumpkins and winter squash lay bright on the ground between the corn rows. Goldenrod and joe-pye weed and snakeroot blossomed tall along the fence rails, and the leaves on blackberry canes and dogwood were maroon.

In town, Ada and Ruby first walked about the streets looking at the stores, the teams and wagons and the women with their shopping baskets. The day had warmed to the point that Ada carried her waxed coat balled up under an arm. Ruby wore her sweater tied at her waist, and she had yoked her hair back at collar level with a band plaited of horse-tail strands. The air was still hazy. Cold Mountain was a blue smear, a hump on the far ridgeline, made small by the long walk and no more dimensional against the sky than paper pasted on paper.

The county seat was not a town of great refinement. On one side there were four clapboard store buildings in a row, then a hog pen and a mud pit, then two more stores, a church, and a livery. On the other side, three stores, then the courthouse—a cupolaed white frame building set back from the road with a patchy lawn in front—then four more storefronts, two of them brick. After that, the town trailed off into a fenced field of dried cornstalks. The streets were cut deep by narrow wagon wheels. Light glinted off water pooled in the numberless basins made by horse tracks.

Ada and Ruby went to a hardware and bought wadding,

shot, slugs, caps, and powder. At the stationer's, Ada paid more than she could afford for *Adam Bede* in three volumes, six fat charcoal pencils, and an octavo-sized journal of well-made paper that appealed to her because it was small enough to fit in a coat pocket. From a street vendor they bought newspapers—the county paper and the larger one from Asheville. They bought lukewarm root beer from a woman tapping a barrel in a pushcart and drank it down where they stood and handed the woman back her tin cups. For dinner they bought hard cheese and fresh bread and took it down by the river and sat on rocks to eat.

Early in the afternoon they stopped by the house of Mrs. McKennet, a wealthy widow of middle age who had for a season or two taken a keen romantic interest in Monroe and then later, after he failed to see her in the same light, had simply become his friend. It was not the time for tea, but she was so pleased to see Ada that she proposed a greater treat. The summer having been so damp and cool, she still, at that late date, had ice resting in the basement ice pit. It had been cut in great blocks from the lake the previous February and packed in sawdust. And, after swearing them to secrecy, she revealed that she had four barrels of salt and three of sugar stored since long before the war. The extravagance of ice cream was what she had in mind, and she put her handyman—an old grey fellow too feeble for conscription—to chipping ice and cranking the machine. At some time in the past she had made numbers of sugared crepes and twisted them into cones and let them dry, and she served the ice cream in them. Ruby, of course, had never eaten such a thing and she was delighted. After she had licked the last white drop, she reached out her cone to Mrs. McKennet and said, Here's your little horn back.

Their talk turned to the war and its effects, and Mrs. McKennet held opinions exactly in accord with every newspaper editorial Ada had read for four years, which is to say Mrs. McKennet found the fighting glorious and tragic and heroic. Noble beyond all her powers of expression. She told a long and

maudlin story she had read about a recent battle, its obvious fictitiousness apparently lost on her. It was fought—as they all were lately—against dreadful odds. As the battle neared its inevitable conclusion, a dashing young officer was grievously wounded to the chest. He fell back bleeding great gouts of heartblood. A companion stooped and cradled his head to soothe his dying. But as the battle raged around them, the young officer, in the very act of expiring, rose and drew his pistol and added his contribution to the general gunfire. He died erect, with the hammer snapping on empty loads. And there were additional details of somber irony. Found on his person was a letter to his sweetheart, the wording of which foretokened exactly the manner of his death. And further, when the letter was taken by courier to the girl's home, it was discovered that she had died of a strange chest seizure on precisely the day and hour her beloved had passed. During the latter stages of the tale, Ada developed an itch just to either side of her nose. She touched the places discreetly with her fingertips, but then she found that the corners of her mouth would stay down only with great trembling effort.

When Mrs. McKennet finished, Ada looked around at the furniture and carpet and lamps, at a household running effortlessly, at Mrs. McKennet, satisfied and plump in her velvet chair, her hair in tight rolls dangling from the sides of her head. Ada might as well have been in Charleston. And she felt called upon to take up some of her old Charleston demeanor. She said, That is the most preposterous thing I have ever heard. She went further, adding that, contrary to the general view, she found the war to exhibit anything but the fine characteristics of tragedy and nobility. She found it, even at a great distance, brutal and benighted on both sides about equally. Degrading to all.

Her aim was to shock or outrage, but Mrs. McKennet rather seemed amused. She fixed Ada with a half smile and said, You know I have a great affection for you, but you are nevertheless the most naive girl I have yet had the pleasure to encounter.

Ada then fell silent and there was an awkward void that Ruby presently filled by cataloguing the birds she had spied that morning and commenting on the progress of late crops and reporting the amazing fact that Esco Swanger's turnips had grown so big from his black dirt that he could fit but six in a peck basket. But in a minute Mrs. McKennet interrupted her and said, Perhaps you will share your views on the war with us.

Ruby hesitated only a second and then said the war held little interest for her. She had heard stories of the northern country and had come to understand that it was a godless land, or rather a land of only one god, and that was money. The report was that under the rule of such a grabby creed people grew mean and bitter and deranged until, for lack of higher forms of spirit comfort, entire families became morphine-crazed. They had, as well, invented a holiday called Thanksgiving, which Ruby had only recently got news of, but from what she gathered its features to be, she found it to contain the mark of a tainted culture. To be thankful on just the one day.

Later in the afternoon, as Ada and Ruby walked down the main street on the way out of town, they saw a knot of people standing at the side wall of the courthouse with their heads tipped up. They went to see what was happening and found that a prisoner at a second-story window was delivering a talk to the people below. The captive had his hands up gripping the bars, and he had his face thrust as far as it would go between them. The hair his head grew was black and oily and hung down in rat tails below his under jaw. A little tuft of black whiskers sprouted from beneath his bottom lip in the French style. All they could see of his attire before the windowsill cut him off was a shabby uniform jacket buttoned up to the neck.

He talked in the urgent meters of a street preacher, and he had drawn a crowd with the rage in his voice. He had fought hard through the war, he claimed. Had killed many a Federal and had taken a ball to the shoulder at Williamsburg. But he had recently lost faith in the war and he missed his wife. He had not

been drafted but had volunteered for the fighting, and all he did by way of crime was unvolunteer and walk home. Now here he stood jailed. And they might just hang him, war hero though he was.

The captive went on to tell of how the Home Guard had taken him some days previous from a remote cove farm, his father's, on the flank of Balsam Mountain. He had been there with other outliers. The woods were filling up with them, he said. As the lone survivor of the day, it was his duty he believed to narrate all the details from out the barred window of his cell, and Ada and Ruby stayed to hear, though it was a tale of considerable sordor and bloodshed.

It had been coming on toward twilight, and the tops of the mountains were cut off by a grey smother of clouds. Rain had begun falling, so fine and windless it would hardly wet a man out in it all night. It served only to deepen colors, making the dirt of the road redder and the leaves of poplar trees that met overhead greener. The captive and two other outliers and the captive's father had been in the house when they heard horses coming from down below the bend in the road. His father took the shotgun, the only firearm among them, and went out to the road. There not being time to get to the woods, the three others gathered up weapons they had made from farm implements and went to hide in a fodder crib, where they watched the road between the unchinked poles of the wall.

A small party of wordless, ill-accoutered horsemen came traveling around the curve at a slow walk, climbing into the cove. They had apparently been unable to reach consensus on attire. Two great dark men so alike in their features that they might well have been twins rode vaguely uniformed in what could have been leavings scavenged from battlefield dead. A slight white-headed boy wore farm clothes—canvas britches, brown wool shirt, short grey wool jacket. And the other man might have

been taken for a traveling preacher in his long-tailed black suitcoat, pants of moleskin, white shirt with a black cravat at the stand-up collar. Their horses were foul spine-sprung things, malandered about the necks, beshat greenly across the hindquarters, and trailing ropy harls of yellow snot blown from all the orifices of their heads. But the men were well armed with blockish Kerr pistols at their hips, shotguns and rifles in saddle scabbards.

The old man stood awaiting them, and in the grey light and drizzle he appeared to be a kind of specter, some grey being standing astraddle the grassy crest between the wagon tracks. He was dressed in garb of homespun wool, dyed butternut from the pulp of walnut husks. He wore a hat that looked as soft as a sleeping bonnet, and it sat on his head like something melting. His jowls hung in flaps like the flews of a hound, and he held the long gun behind him, run down back of his leg.

—Stop right there, he said, when the horsemen were twenty paces away.

The two big men and the white-headed boy ignored the command and squeezed their mounts with their heels, urging them forward at a slow walk. The preacher-looking man took an angling course, making for the road edge, turning his horse so that its body would hide the short Spencer carbine in its scabbard at his knee. His companions stopped in a group before the old man.

There was quick movement and someone let out a high-pitched scream.

The old man had produced his gun from behind him and had in one swift motion poked it up under the soft of one big man's chin and then pulled it back. It was a fowling piece of antique design. The hammer was cocked, and the bore to it was as big around as a shot glass. A little runnel of blood went down the big man's neck and disappeared into his shirt collar.

The other big man and the white-headed boy sat and looked off across a little bit of cornfield where an old grey stook of last

year's fodder formed a sagging cone at the edge of the woods. They smiled as if they might have been expecting something of modest drollness to appear among the trees.

The old man said, You by the fence. I know who you are. You're Teague. Get over here.

Teague did not move.

The old man said, You not coming?

Teague sat his ground. He had a grin on his face, but his eyes looked like a cold fireplace with the ashes shoveled out.

—These your big niggers? the old man said to Teague.

—I don't know that's what they are, Teague said. But they're not mine. You couldn't give me that pair free.

—Whose then?

—Their own, I reckon, Teague said.

—You get on over here with us, the man said.

—I'll just rest here at the edge of the woods, Teague said.

—You're making me jumpy and I'm fixing to put a load in somebody, the man said.

—You've just got the one barrel, Teague pointed out.

—This gun's right comprehensive when you let fly with it, the man said. He took several steps backward until he judged the three men before him were all compassed by the wide shot pattern the big gun threw. Then he said, Get down off them horses and stand in a bunch.

Everyone but Teague dismounted. The horses stood with their reins dragging the ground, their ears forward like they were enjoying themselves. The man with the wound, Byron by name, put his fingers to it and looked at the blood and then wiped his hands on his loose shirt tail. The other one, name of Ayron, held his head cocked up to the side, and a pink tip of tongue showed at his mouth, so carefully was he now attending to every detail of the current scene. The white-headed boy rubbed his blue eyes and pulled in several directions at his clothing as if he had just woken up from sleeping in them. Then he stood and examined with great fascination the nail to his left

index finger. It was near as long as the finger itself, the way some people will grow them for cutting butter and dipping lard and other such tasks.

The old man stood with the shotgun covering the three of them and surveyed their various armature.

—What do them niggers use their long cavalry sabers for? Hold meat over a fire to roast? he asked Teague.

There was a long moment of silence and then the old man said, What are you up here after?

—You know, Teague said. Catch up outliers.

—They're all gone, the old man said. Long since. Laying out in the woods where they'll be hard to find. Or passed on over the mountains to cross the lines and oath allegiance.

—Oh, Teague said. If I take your point, we best just go back to town then. Is that what you're saying?

—Save us all trouble if you do, the man said.

—You don't watch out, we're liable to hang your old ass too, Teague said. They were gone, you wouldn't be meeting us in the road armed.

At that moment the white-headed boy fell prone in the dirt and yelled out, King of kings!

The first instant that the old man's attention collected on the boy, Ayron lunged with a grace unexpected in one of so much size and struck the man a clubbing blow to the head with his left fist. He followed that with a slap to the hand, knocking the shotgun away. The old man fell on his back, his hat in the dirt beside him. Ayron stepped over and picked up the shotgun and beat the old man with it until the stock broke off and then he beat him with just the barrel. After a time the man lay still in the road. He was somewhat conscious but had a puzzled look in his eyes. Something ran from one ear that had all the features of red-eye gravy.

Byron spit at the ground and wiped away the blood on his head, and then he drew his saber and put the point of it under

the old man's lapped chin and pressed until he caused a runnel of blood equal to his own.

—Hold meat over a fire, he said.

—Leave him be, Ayron said. There's no harm left in him.

Both men, despite their size, had little keen voices, pitched high as birdsong.

Byron took the sword from the man's chin, but then, before anyone could make out his intentions, he took the haft in both hands, and in a motion that looked no more effortful than plunging the dasher into a butter churn, he skewered the old man through the stomach.

Byron stepped away with his hands held out open to either side. There was nothing to see of the sword blade, just the scrolled guard and wire-wrapped grip sticking from beneath the old man's chest. He tried to rise but only his head and knees came up, for he was spiked to the ground.

Byron looked at Teague and said, You want me to finish him?

—Just let him fight it out with his Maker, said Teague.

The boy rose from where he still lay on the ground and went and stood over the man and gawped at him.

—He's ready for death, the boy said. His lamp is burning and he waits for the bridegroom.

They all laughed except for the old man and Teague. Teague said, Shut up, Birch. Let's move.

They mounted to ride to the house, and as they did the old man breathed his last and died with a wail. In passing, Byron leaned low from his saddle, agile as a trick rider in a tent show, and drew out the saber and wiped it on the mane of his horse before returning it to its scabbard.

Byron went to the gate and kicked it open to break the latch, and they rode through it and right up to the porch.

—Come on out, Teague called. There was a note of the festive to his voice.

When no one appeared, Teague looked at Byron and Ayron and tipped his chin at the front door.

The two dismounted and looped their reins around porch posts and set about making circuits of the house in opposite directions, pistols drawn. They moved as a partnership of wolves will hunt, in wordless coordination of effort toward a shared purpose. They were naturally quick and their movements were easy and fluent, despite their being so bulky. But in a clench was where their main advantage was, for between the two of them they looked to be about able to dismember a man with their hands.

After they had orbited the empty house three times they burst through the front and back doors at the same instant. In a minute they came out, Ayron with a fistful of tapers paired by their wicks and Byron carrying part of a ham, which he held by the shank of its white bone like a chicken leg. They put them in panniers on the horses. Then without word or gesture of command or even suggestion, Teague and Birch climbed down to earth from their mounts and they all walked to the barn, where they threw open the doors to the stalls. They found but one old mule inside. They trod about among the hay in the loft and ran their sabers into the deepest piles and then they came out and turned their attention to the fodder crib, but as they approached it, the door sprung open and the three outliers broke to run.

The men were hindered in their escape, for they carried improvised weapons that had the look of artifacts from a yet darker age—a sharpened plow point swinging at the end of a chain, an old spade beaten and filed into the semblance of a spear, a pine-knot cudgel spiked at its head with horseshoe nails.

Teague let the men run a ways and then he put the carbine to his shoulder and shot down the two frontrunners, who fell with a great clatter of weaponry. The last man, the captive, stopped and raised his hands and faced them. Teague looked at him a minute. The man went bootless that day, and he dug his toes at the dirt as if looking for a better hold. Teague licked his

thumb and wiped it on the fore sight of his Spencer and raised the carbine and fit bead to notch. The man stood there motionless. He kept his grip on the spiked cudgel so that he stood with it raised over his head as savages are depicted in bookplates.

Teague lowered the carbine and put the butt of it on the ground and held it loose in one hand by the barrel.

—Throw that stick down, or I'm sending these two over to pull you apart, he said.

The captive looked at the two big men and then dropped the pine knot at his feet.

—Good, Teague said. Now just stand there.

The men all walked over to the captive, and Ayron grabbed him by the neck and snatched him up like a pup by the scruff. They then turned their attention toward the two men on the ground. One was dead and had hardly bled enough to stain his clothes. The other had taken a bullet to the bowels. He yet lived, but barely. He was propped up on his elbows and had pulled his britches and drawers down about his knees. He probed his wound with a pair of fingers and then looked at them and hollered, I'm kill't.

The Guard came and stood around him but when they smelled the tang in the air they backed off. The captive squirmed like he wanted to go to his downed friend and Ayron hit him at the side of the head, three flat blows with the meat of his fist heel. Birch took out a black twist of chaw and gripped one end between his teeth and took his knife and sawed it off at his lips and put the remainder in his pocket. When he spit he scuffed dirt with his boot toe over the amber spot as if fastidious about marking the ground, heedful of leaving sign.

The shot man lay back flat and blinked at the sky and seemed baffled by it. His mouth formed words but he made no sound beyond the clickings of a dry mouth. Then his eyes closed and for some time he might have been thought dead except that at wide intervals he worked his fingers. He bled beyond all reason. The grass around him was matted red and his clothes hung

heavy and slick like oilcloth. Even in the dim light it looked bright. Then the blood quit coming and he opened his eyes again without any effort toward focus.

They guessed he had died.

Birch offered to go spit juice in his eye to see would he blink, but Teague said, We don't need to test him. He's passed.

—This'uns preceded you in death like your old daddy, Birch said to the captive.

The man said nothing and Teague said, Birch, hush, and get me something to tie his hands and then we'll lead him back to town on the end of a line.

The boy went to the horses and came back with a coil of rope. But when Teague bent to tie his hands, the captive lost his mind. There was no accounting for his actions other than that he would rather die than be bound. He kicked out in fright, fetching Teague a glancing blow to the thigh. So Teague and the big men fought him and the man was so wild that for a time it was unclear who would prevail. He struck at them with every limb he had and butted with his head as well. He screamed the whole time, a high warbling scream that near to unnerved them all. But finally they threw him to the ground and lashed his wrists and ankles together. Even then he bucked and strained and reached with his head until he bit Teague on the hand, drawing blood. Teague wiped his hand on a coattail and looked at it.

—I'd rather take a hog bite than a man, he said.

He sent Birch back to the house for a straight chair and then they all worked at tying the man into it, binding him down with his arms to his sides and looping rope about his neck until he could do little but wiggle his fingers and twist his head about in the way turtles will do when flipped onto their backs.

—There, Teague said. Like to see him bite me now.

—Berserk, Birch said. I've read about it. It's a word for a thing people can go.

They paused and squatted and caught their breaths, and the man strained against the ropes until his neck bled and then he

fell quiet. Byron and Ayron rested with their forearms on their massy thighs. Teague sucked at his wound and then took out a kerchief and brushed the dirt from his black coat and wiped at the toe marks the man had left on the thigh of his pale pants. Birch held up his left hand and saw that in the struggle he had torn his long fingernail halfway across. He took out his knife and pared it away, cursing all the while at his loss.

Ayron said, We could take that little drag sled there and set him up in it and ride him into town harnessed to that chair.

—Could, Teague said. But I'm leaning right now toward carrying him up to the barn loft and roping his neck to a rafter and shoving him out the hay door.

—You can't hang a man a-sitting, Birch said.

—Can't? Teague said. I'd like to know why not? Hell, I've seen it done.

—Well, still, it'd look better if we brought somebody in now and then, Birch said.

The men stood and conferred and they evidently saw the reason in Birch's thinking, for they gathered around the chair and lifted it and carried it to the sled. They tied the chair to the sled and harnessed it to the mule and set off for town, the man's head jouncing for he had no will to even hold it level.

—This world won't stand long, the captive hollered in conclusion to his tale. God won't let it stand this way long.

By the time he was done talking, the sun had fallen well to the west, and Ada and Ruby turned from the courthouse and started walking home. They were both grim and initially wordless, and then later along the way they discussed the captive's story. Ada wanted to cast it as exaggeration, but Ruby's conclusion was that it ought to be viewed as truth since it sorted so well with the capabilities of men. Then they argued generally for a mile or two as to whether the world might better be viewed as such a place of threat and fear that the only consonant attitude

one could maintain was gloom, or whether one should strive for light and cheer even though a dark-fisted hand seemed poised ready to strike at any moment.

When they reached the west fork of the Pigeon and turned up the river road, the light was growing thin and a shadow already draped itself over the knob called Big Stomp, cast by the larger mountains of the Blue Ridge. The water looked black and cold, and the smell of river hung in the air, about equal parts mineral and vegetable. Though the river had fallen some since morning, it was still up from the last night's rain, and the rocks out in it were wet and dark where trees from either bank nearly met in the middle and kept the watercourse shaded all day.

They had not walked far above the fork when Ruby stopped and squared her body to the water, sighting on something in it as if to take range. She sank down in her knees just a notch, like a fighter lowering his center of gravity to compose himself for attack. She said, Well, look there. That's not a common sight.

Off in the river stood a great blue heron. It was a tall bird to begin with, but something about the angle from which they viewed it and the cast of low sun made it seem even taller. It looked high as a man in the slant light with its long shadow blown out across the water. Its legs and the tips of its wings were black as the river. The beak of it was black on top and yellow underneath, and the light shone off it with muted sheen as from satin or chipped flint. The heron stared down into the water with fierce concentration. At wide intervals it took delicate slow steps, lifting a foot from out the water and pausing, as if waiting for it to quit dripping, and then placing it back on the river bottom in a new spot apparently chosen only after deep reflection.

Ruby said, He's looking for a frog or a fish.

But his staring so heedfully into the water reminded Ada of Narcissus, and to further their continuing studies of the Greeks, she told Ruby a brief version of the tale.

—That bird's not thinking about himself at all, Ruby said, when Ada had finished the story. Look at that beak on him. Stab

wounds; that's his main nature. He's thinking about what other thing he can stab and eat.

They stepped slowly toward the river edge and the heron turned to look at them with some interest. He made tiny precise adjustments of his narrow head as if having trouble sighting around his blade of beak. His eyes seemed to Ada to be searching for her merits and coming up short.

—What are you doing up here? she said aloud to the heron. But she knew by the look of him that his nature was anchorite and mystic. Like all of his kind, he was a solitary pilgrim, strange in his ways and governed by no policy or creed common to flocking birds. Ada wondered that herons could tolerate each other close enough to breed. She had seen a scant number in her life, and those so lonesome as to make the heart sting on their behalf. Exile birds. Everywhere they were seemed far from home.

The heron walked toward them to the river edge and stood on a welt of mud. He was not ten feet away. He tipped his head a notch off level, raised a black leg, scales as big as fingernails, the foot held just off the ground. Ada stared down at the strange footprint in the mud. When she looked up, the bird was staring at her as at someone met long ago, dimly registered in memory.

Then the heron slowly opened its wings. The process was carried out as if it were a matter of hinges and levers, cranks and pulleys. All the long bones under feathers and skin were much in evidence. When it was done the wings were so broad that Ada could not imagine how it would get out among the trees. The bird took a step toward Ada, lifted itself from the ground, and with only a slow beat or two of the immense wings soared just above her head and up and away through the forest canopy. Ada felt the sweep of wings, the stir of air, a cold blue shadow across the ground, across the skin of her face. She wheeled and watched until the heron was gone into the sky. She threw up a hand like waving 'bye to visiting kin. What would that be? she wondered. A blessing? A warning beacon? Picket of the spirit world?

Ada took out her new journal and whittled one of the charcoal pencils to a point with her penknife. She made a quick, loose-lined memory sketch of the heron as it had stood in the mud. When she was done she was dissatisfied with the curve of the neck and the angle of the beak, but she had the legs and the ruff of feathers at his crop and the look in his eye just right. Across the bottom of the page in her runic hand she wrote *Blue heron/Forks of the Pigeon/9 October 1864.* She looked up at the sky and then said to Ruby, What time would you guess it to be?

Ruby cocked an eye to the west and said, A little after five, and Ada wrote down *five o'clock* and closed the journal.

As they walked on up the river they talked of the bird, and Ruby revealed what she felt to be her snaggy relationship with herons. Stobrod, she said, had often during her childhood disclaimed her, saying she had no man-father. Her mother, during her pregnancy with Ruby—when drunk and embittered and wishing to get a rise out of him—had often charged that Stobrod had no part in the baby and that its cause was a tall blue heron. She claimed it had lit at the creek one morning and, after spending the forenoon spearing crawfish, had come into the yard where she was breaking apart a crust of old corn bread and scattering it on the ground for the chickens. The tale Ruby's mother told, as recounted by Stobrod, was that the heron strode up on its long back-hinged legs and looked her eye to eye. She claimed, Stobrod said, that the look was unmistakable, not open to but one interpretation. She turned and ran, but the heron chased her into the house, where, as she hunkered on hands and knees trying to squeeze under the bedstead to hide, the heron came upon her from behind. She described what ensued as like a flogging of dreadful scope.

—He told me that story a hundred times, Ruby said. I mostly know it to be one of his lies, but I still can't look on one of those birds without wondering.

Ada did not know what to say. The light under the trees by the river had fallen to gold and the leaves on beech and poplar

shivered in a small wind. Ruby stopped and put on her sweater and Ada shook the wrinkles out of the coat and draped it over her shoulders like a cloak. They walked on, and at the ford of the river they met a young woman carrying a baby wrapped in a checked tablecloth slung over her shoulder. She skipped barefoot across the stepping stones as graceful as a deer running and said not a word nor even met their eyes when she passed, though the baby stared at them expressionless from eyes as brown as acorn caps set in his head. Soon after the ford, small birds flew from an apple tree standing alone in an old field. They flew close to the ground and entered the woods. The setting sun was in Ruby's eyes so that she could only make a guess at their kind, but for weather purposes it did not matter. The thing their pattern of flying told was more rain.

Yet farther up the road, near a hole in the river where people were sometimes dipped in baptism, a cloud of martins erupted out of a maple tree nearing the peak of its color. The sun's bottom limb was just touching the ridge and the sky was the color of hammered pewter. The martins flew from the tree as one body, still in the shape of the round maple they had filled. Then they banked into the wind, slipped sideways in the moving air on extended wings for two heartbeats, so that Ada viewed them in thin profile and saw much silver space between the individual birds. Immediately, as if on signal, they swept into a steep climb and the fullness of their wings turned toward her and closed the bright gaps between the birds so that the flock looked like the black image of the red maple projected into the sky. The bird shadows across the long field grass beyond the road flickered.

Twilight rose up around Ada and Ruby as if the dark from the river were seeping skyward. Ruby's fanciful heron story of source and root reminded Ada of a story Monroe had told not long before his death. It concerned the manner in which he had wooed her mother, and to pass the darkening miles upriver, Ada recounted it in some detail to Ruby.

Ada had known that Monroe and her mother had married relatively late in life, he at forty-five, she at thirty-six. And Ada knew their time together had been brief. But she did not know the circumstances of their courtship and marriage, assuming it an alliance of calm friendship, the sort of tie she had seen formed numerous times between peculiar old bachelors and aging spinsters. She supposed herself to be a product of some sad miscalculation.

That is until one afternoon in the winter before Monroe's death. A wet snow had fallen all day, the large flakes melting as they struck the ground. Ada and Monroe sat by the fire through the long afternoon, Ada reading to him from a new book, *The Conduct of Life*. Monroe had for many years followed Mr. Emerson's every published utterance with keen interest, and that day he thought Emerson, as always, even in old age, perhaps one degree more extreme in his spiritual views than was called for.

As the day drew to a close outside the windows, Ada put the book aside. Monroe looked tired, grey, his eyes sunken. He sat studying the fire, which had settled into its ashes and burned slowly, with scarce flame. Eventually he said, I have never told you how I came to marry your mother.

—No, Ada said.

—It is a thing that keeps coming into my mind of late. I don't know why. You've never known that I met your mother when she was barely sixteen and I twenty-five.

—No, Ada said.

—Oh, yes. The first time I saw her I thought she was the loveliest thing I'd ever seen. It was February. A grey day, chill, with a faint damp breeze blowing from off the ocean. I was out riding. I had then recently bought a great Hanoverian gelding. Seventeen hands if an inch. A bloodstone chestnut. He was just the slightest bit cow-hocked, but not enough to matter. His can-

ter was a thing of wonder, like floating. I had ridden him some way out of Charleston, north along the Ashley, past Middleton. Then over and down to Hanahan on my way back home. It was a long ride. The horse was lathered despite the coolness of the air, and I was hungry and anxious for supper. It was just this time of day. Grey night. We were at the first point where you could with confidence say we had left the country and entered the city.

We came to a house, one that could be described as neither modest nor grand. It had a broad porch with old palmettos at either end. It was too near the road for my tastes. Its windows were dark, and it had a water trough in the yard. Thinking no one home, I stopped and dismounted to water my horse. From the porch a woman's voice came, saying, You might ask leave first.

She had apparently been sitting alone on a bench beneath the windows. I took off my hat and said, I beg your pardon. She stepped out from the shadow of the porch and walked down the steps and stopped on the bottom one. She wore a winter dress of grey wool, a black shawl about her shoulders. Hair the color of a crow's wing. She had been brushing it, for it was down nearly to the small of her back, and she held a brush with a tortoiseshell handle. Her face was pale as marble. There was not a thing about her that was not either black, white, or a shade between the two.

Despite her harsh attire, I was totally disarmed. I have never seen the match to her. There is not a word for how beautiful she looked to me. All I could say was, Again, miss, I beg your pardon. I mounted and rode away, flustered, my thoughts all in a churn. Some time that night, after I had taken dinner and gone to bed, it came to me. That was the woman I was meant to marry.

The next day I set about courting her, and I went at it just as hard and as carefully as a man can. First I collected information. I found that her name was Claire Dechutes. Her father, a Frenchman, made a living trading back and forth with his home

country, importing wine and exporting rice. He was a man of comfort, if not of great means. I arranged a meeting with him at his warehouse near a dock on the Cooper. A dank and gloomy place that smelled of the river. It was filled with wooden crates of claret, both fine and cheap, and tow sacks of our rice. We were introduced by my friend Aswell, who had done business with Dechutes in the past. Dechutes, your grandfather, was a short man, and heavy. Portly would be the term. More French in his ways than I care for, if you take my meaning. Neither you nor your mother shared any observable characteristic with him.

I made my intentions clear from the start: I wished to marry his daughter and sought his approval and assistance. I offered to provide him with references, financial statements, anything that might convince him of my desirability as a son-in-law. I could see his mind working. He tugged at his cravat. Rolled his eyes. He went off to the side and conferred with Aswell for a time. When he returned, he reached out his hand and said, May I offer any assistance within my power.

His only sticking point was this: he wished Claire not to marry before her eighteenth birthday. I agreed. Two years seemed not too long to wait, and a fair request on his part. Within a few days he took me home to dinner as his guest. My introduction to your mother was at his hand. I could see in her eyes that she knew me from the night in the yard, but she said not a word of it. I believed from the beginning that my feeling toward her was returned.

We courted for months, through the spring and summer and into the autumn. We met at balls to which I arranged her invitation. I rode north to the Dechutes house over and over on the Hanoverian gelding. Claire and I sat on the bench on the broad porch night after night through the humid summer and talked of every subject dear to our hearts. Days when I could not ride out, we posted letters which crossed paths somewhere on Meeting Street. In the late fall, I had a ring made. It was a blue diamond, a stone as big as the end of your little finger. It was set in a band

of white filigreed gold. I made up my mind to present it to her one evening in late November as a surprise.

On the chosen date, I rode the Hanoverian out north in the dusk, the ring nestling in a pouch of velvet in my waistcoat pocket. It was a night with a chill in the air, brisk and wintery, at least in Charleston terms. A night alike in its every feature to the one on which we had first met.

By the time I reached the Dechutes house, the sky was fully dark. But the house was lighted, every window ablaze in welcome. The sound of a piano, Bach, faintly reached me from inside. I sat in the road a moment, thinking the night to be the culmination of the previous seasons' effort. All my heart's desire within easy reach.

Then I heard the low murmur of voices from the porch. Saw movement. Claire's profile leaned forward, her black silhouette framed in the yellow light of the window. There was no mistaking it for anyone else's. From the other side of the window leaned another face, a man's. They met and kissed, a long kiss and a passionate one from what I could tell. Their faces parted, and her hand reached to his face and guided it back again. My stomach clenched. And my hands. I longed to step to the porch and shout my outrage and thrash someone. But the humiliating role of the betrayed suitor was not one I relished playing.

Without another thought I put spurs to the horse and sped off north at a feverish pace. We went for miles and miles. That tall horse stretching out long in its gallop. It was like riding in a dream, hurling through a dark world at a rate more akin to winged flight than riding horseback. We passed through dense flats of turkey oak and slash pine and yaupon, through open barrens of wire grass and saw grass, until finally, in a place where wax myrtle thickets hemmed in the road to left and right, the horse slowed and walked, blowing hard, head down.

I had no clear idea where I was. I had not kept up with the turnings of the roads or even the fine points of the compass bearing we had been following. Generally north was all I knew,

for we had not plunged into either the Ashley or the Cooper and drowned. In the scant light of a partial moon, the sweated chestnut gelding looked black as ebony, and as glossy. Other than act fully the wildman and set a course west to lose myself for life in the trackless territories of Texas, there was little to do but turn and head home. As I fixed to do so, however, I saw that ahead of me the sky was lighted up yellow over the wax myrtles as by a bonfire. Other features of creation seemed as inflamed as I was. The fire provided, I reasoned, an interim direction.

I made toward its light, and in a turn or two of the road came upon a church afire. Its roof and steeple were ablaze, but the body of the building was yet untouched. I left the horse and walked to the church and entered the door and walked down the aisle. I took the ring pouch from my pocket and placed it on the altar and then stood there in the smoke and the garish light. Pieces of roof began falling about me flaming. I am the groom waiting at the altar; I will burn myself down, I thought.

Just then a man burst through the doors. His clothes were twisted on him and he carried a quart liquor bottle with but an inch left glowing amber at the bottom. He said, What are you doing here? Get out.

Pride, I guess, made me say, I happened by. I came in to see if I could be of help.

—Well, get out, he said.

I left the church with him, and we determined to try to save it, though he was drunk and I was half out of my mind. From a creek nearby, we carried what water we could in his liquor bottle. We'd squat by the creek waiting for the bottle to glug full through its narrow neck and then together we would walk to the church and throw the water on the fire a quart at a time, not so much in hope of putting it out as to be able to say, if asked, that we tried. When dawn came, the man and I stood with sooty faces looking at a round black circle on the land.

—Well, that's that. Everything's burned but the hinges and the doorknobs, the man said.

—Yes, I said.

—We did what we could.

—Without a doubt.

—There's not a man that could lay blame on us for lack of effort.

—No. Not a man, I said

He shook the last drops of water out of his liquor bottle onto the singed grass at the edge of the fire ring and put it in his coat pocket and walked on up the road. I went to the horse and mounted and rode back into Charleston.

A week later I booked passage on a ship bound for England, and for the next year I did little but roam about examining old churches and old paintings. When I returned, I found that your mother had married the man I had seen her with on the porch. He was a Frenchman, an associate of her father's, a broker of wines. She had gone with him to live in France. It was like a door closed.

I had always been drawn to matters of the spirit, and so I withdrew from my duties in the family business and went into ministry with both resignation and glee. I have never for a moment regretted that decision.

Nineteen years passed, and one spring day I discovered that Claire had returned from France alone. Her husband had died. It had been a childless marriage, and not entirely a pleasant one if gossip was to be believed. Bitter, in fact. The little Frenchman had lived up to my most selfish dreams.

Within days of hearing this news I returned to the warehouse on the Cooper and met again with Dechutes. He was now an old man, great of waist and flabby at the jowls, and I had a widow's peak and had grown grey at the temples. The look he gave me would serve perfectly as illustration of the word *supercilious*. He said, How might I help you? in a tone that some previous time might have led to seconds and pistols.

I said, We are going to go at this thing again, and this time I intend to see that it sticks.

That autumn, your mother and I married, and for two years I was as happy as a man can be. And I think I made her happy as well. Her previous husband, the little Frenchman, had been unsatisfactory in every regard. He blamed her for the lack of children and grew sour and harsh. I made it my business to reimburse her for every slight, every meanness.

The months when we knew you were to come seemed a strange blessing for a pair such as we were: old and marred by the past. When Claire died in childbirth, I could not hardly think that God would be so short with us. I could do little for weeks. Kind neighbors found a wet nurse for you and I took to my bed. When I rose again, it was with the determination that my life was now at your service.

When her father's story was done, Ada had stood and walked behind his chair and stroked his hair back from his brow and kissed him on the crown of his head. She knew not what to say. She was so taken aback by this tale of her creation. She could not at that moment easily frame herself anew, not as some staid erratum but as the product of passion extended against great odds.

By the time Ada's story was done, full dark had almost fallen and a hazy moon stood above a bank of clouds to the east. The dark shape of a high bird passed across the face of the moon. Then another, and then more and more in fleet chords. Some night-flying race of grebe or snipe maybe, in passage south. The stars as yet were not out, but to the west two planets, bright beacons in the indigo sky, neared setting behind a trailing flange of Cold Mountain.

—The blue one, that brighter one, is Venus, Ada said, as she and Ruby turned up the road to Black Cove.

to live like a gamecock

Midday, Inman and Veasey came upon a new-sawn tree, a fair-sized hickory, felled parallel to the track they walked. Beside it lay a long crosscut saw, its blade oiled and entirely free of rust, all the intricate teeth of its cutting edge bright from recent sharpening.

—Lookee there, Veasey said. An abandoned saw. Somebody would give me a pretty penny for that.

He went to pick it up, and Inman said, The woodcutters have just gone to get their dinners. They're shortly coming back to buck and split this hickory.

—I don't know any such thing, other than there's a saw by the road and I found it.

Veasey picked it up and balanced the length of it across his shoulder and walked on. At every step the wood handles at either end bounced and the big blade hummed and sproinged like the music of a Jew's harp.

—I'll sell this off to the first man we meet, he said.

—You seem mighty free and easy with the property of

others. I'd like to have heard how you squared that up with gospel in your sermons, Inman said.

—Make no mistake about it, on the issue of property God is none too particular. His respect for it is not great, a prejudice He demonstrates at every turn. Note especially the way He uses fire and flood. Have you ever seen a pattern of justice in their application?

—No. Not that you'd notice.

—Exactly. All I can say is that a man who aims to model himself on the Deity can't put too much thinking into who a particular saw belongs to. Such things distract you from the grand view.

—The grand view? Inman said. He looked at the preacher's scabby pate, the thin cut under his eye from the big whore, and the mark still there from the pistol stroke Inman had given him by the Deep River. You're a one to be talking of the grand view with the whippings you've taken, he said. Every one of them just, at that.

—I'm not saying I didn't need whipping, Veasey said. And many a better man has taken a worse one. But I don't aim to take another lightly.

That thought turned Veasey's mind to matters of defense, and he said, Let me see that mighty pistol of yours.

—No, Inman said.

—Come on. I won't hurt it.

—No.

—All I was thinking was that it would be just the armature for a pistoleer.

—Too big and heavy, Inman said. You need a Navy pistol. A Colt's or a Starr. It's the right heft for drawing out fast.

—I'd at least like mine back.

—I plan to hold it until we part ways, Inman said.

—That might come unexpected, Veasey said. And then I'd be left weaponless.

—And the world a better place for it.

They presently walked under an enormous honey locust tree that leaned over the road. Lacking better victuals, they stooped and filled their pockets with its long rusty pods. They journeyed on, splitting the pods with their thumbnails and eating out the sweet white pulp by scraping it against their teeth. After a time, they spied a man standing off below the road, seemingly in deep contemplation over the scene before him, the chief feature of which was a great black bull, dead in the fork of a creek. The man saw them passing by and hailed them, asking if two such sports might come down from the road and give a hand. Inman climbed down. Veasey set his saw by the roadside and followed.

They stood beside the man and looked at the swollen bull, branch water lapping against its belly, flies in clouds about its mouth and ass. They all had their arms crossed, eyes downcast, the posture of workers faced with a job they don't want to have to do.

The man was not precisely old, but he was working his way there. Thick through the barrel as virile males of most mammal species from ape to horse will get in their late maturity. He wore a hat, a black wool relic with a sugar-loaf crown. Though the day was not much cold, he had tied the broad brim down around his ears with a piece of sisal until it fit about his head like a bonnet. Great bushy burnsides furzed out to his jawbone, and he peered from under the brim's shadow with dark eyes, the lids swollen and hooded as a raptor's. He had a little round mouth that reminded Inman of the blowhole on an enormous snouted fish he had seen during a brief spell of fighting along the coast back near the war's start.

Propped against a nearby tree was a single-barreled ten-gauge shotgun. The barrel looked to have been sawed off somewhat short to throw a pattern wider than was either common or practical. The job had been done with insufficient tools, for the muzzle was ragged and not entirely square to the barrel, as if cut on the bias.

—How do you aim to get it out? Veasey said.

The man paused before answering and formed pincers with thumb and forefinger and then went investigating under his pants for some minute creature troubling his groin. He pulled out his pincers and held them close to his eyes and seemed to crack something between his thick yellow nails. His hands were large and the skin of them had a chalky scurf to it.

The bull, he explained, had wandered off days earlier and died of some unknown disorder. The branch, he said, was their water source, and its normal neutral flavor had taken on a certain tart rankness that had sent him walking up its banks looking for the reason. He had a length of rope with him, and he reckoned they might all work together and snatch the bull from the water.

Inman regarded the man and Veasey. And then he looked at the humped mass of the bull. It would take at least a team of draft horses to drag that bull out, he judged.

—We could try to pull it, he said. But that's a big bull. We might better think of some other way.

The man ignored him and tied on to the bull's neck and they all took hold of the rope and heaved. The carcass moved not an inch.

—Levers, the man said. We can lever him out if we can find poles.

—We don't have to find them; we can cut poles to suit, Veasey said. I've got a good saw, which you might want to buy off me when we're done. He ran up the bank to get the crosscut. He was excited as a boy getting to do a job with men for the first time.

Inman thought the idea a poor one, and so he sat on a downed log and watched with amusement as the two men set to work with great and misplaced enthusiasm. They reminded him of army engineers and their minions setting to build a bridge or the like, their eagerness all out of proportion to the actual worth of the thing they were working at, and the end result would be a

whole lot of effort on a job that generally struck Inman as better off left undone.

As Inman watched, Veasey and the man cut three stout poles. In short order they were up to their shanks in the water and had thrown big rocks in place to act as fulcrums. They worked in concert, trying to roll the bull over, but could get it to do little more than wiggle flabbily as they strained against the poles. Inman joined them, and this time it did move. Problem was, even with the pole ends pulled all the way down into the water, they could achieve only about a foot of lift. Then they would tire and let up on the poles, and the bull would fall back with a splash.

—I know, Veasey said. We can lever it up and then shove rocks under it with our feet to hold it. Then we lever it again from there with a higher fulcrum and add more rocks. We do it over and over and by and by we get it rolled.

Inman eyed the distance from the bull to dry ground.

—We roll it over once and it will still be in the water, he said.

—Roll it twice, then, Veasey said.

—That will get it to the bank, Inman said, but it will still rot and run into the water.

—Roll it thrice, Veasey said. He was consumed in all his parts by the wonder of the lever and the manly work of engineering.

Inman could picture them there until dark jacking up the bull and chocking it with rocks and jacking again. Hour upon hour of good walking time or good resting time passing away.

Inman went to the stream bank where Veasey had left the saw. He picked it up and returned to the bull and set the edge of the blade to its neck.

—Somebody get on the other end, he said.

Veasey looked sorely disappointed, but the man took the far handle, and in a few pulls they had the head off. Then, soon after, a section of chest with the forelegs attached. The next cut separated hindquarters from belly. It opened up with a great

flush of organs and dark fluid and a release of gas. Veasey watched and then bent and vomited into the water. A spume of honey-locust pulp floated away downstream.

The man looked over and cackled as if a rare joke had been passed. Weak in the stomach, he said.

—He's a pulpiteer, Inman said. This is some distance from his chosen work.

When they were done with the sawing, the branch was strewn with bull parts, which they soon dragged out and left far aground. Still the water ran red and it put Inman in mind of the creek at Sharpsburg.

—I'd not drink that water for a few days yet, Inman said.

—No, the man said. I reckon not.

The man and Inman rinsed their hands and forearms in the clear water upstream.

—Come eat supper with us, the man said. And we've a hayloft that's good for sleeping.

—Only if you'll take that saw off our hands, Inman said to the man.

—I expect two dollars federal. Fifty in state scrip, Veasey said, perking up.

—Take it on, Inman said. No fee.

The man picked up the saw and balanced the midpoint across his shoulder, and with his free hand he took up the marred shotgun. Inman and Veasey went with him, walking on down the road, which followed the stream course. The man seemed lightened in his mood by having removed the bull from his drinking water, jocular in fact. They had not walked far when he stopped and put a finger to his nose and winked. He went to a big oak with a hollow in its trunk at about eye level. He ran his arm up in the hole and drew out a stoppered brown bottle.

—I've a number of these secreted around for when I might feel the need, he said.

They sat against the trunk of the tree and passed the bottle among them. The man said his name was Junior, and he set off

on a tale of his young manhood, of his days traveling the cockfighting circuits. He told of one particular cock, a big dominicker that lived for nothing but to fight and tread hens. Of how it whipped everything thrown against it for months. Of epic struggles, spectacular victories in which the dominicker, looking to be facing certain defeat, would fly into the rafters of the barn the fight was held in and roost there until all the spectators jeered. Then, when the jeering reached its zenith, it would drop like a hammer on the opposing bird, leaving a bright pile of blood and feathers in the dirt.

Junior told also of how the women flung themselves at him in his travels with about the vigor of the dominicker falling on his foe. One in particular that came to his mind was a married woman whose husband had invited him to stay with them for a few days between fights. She set her sights on him, rubbing against him at every chance. One day when the husband was off plowing she had gone out to dip water from the well. When she bent over to catch the bucket, Junior said he came up behind her and threw her skirts over her back. The way he told it, she was drawerless under the skirts, and he said she tipped her hind end up and stood on her toes. He had her right there, bent over the pit of the well. It lasted about as long as it took her to wind up a bucket of water, he said. When he was done he went on down the road with his rooster under his arm. He led Inman and Veasey to believe that there had been a great number of such wonderful days in his earlier life. I had my nose in the butter many a time, he said.

Veasey thought this a fine story, for the liquor had run to his head, his stomach being empty. He whooped at its conclusion and jabbered on about how that was the life for a man.

—To live like a gamecock, that is my target, he said in a wistful voice.

Junior agreed that the roving life had been a fine one for him, and said that his troubles all began when he settled down and took a wife, for it came to pass that three years after the

wedding she bore him a negro baby. And further, she refused to name the father, denying Junior his just revenge. He set about instead to divorce her, but the judge had declined to grant one on the grounds that Junior knew she was a slut when he married her.

She had later brought her two sisters to live with them, and they had proved her equals in harlotry, for one had borne twin boys of somewhat indeterminate race, and though they were now several years old—he could not put an exact figure to it—they had been raised with no more guidance than a pair of feral hogs, and neither the mother nor anyone else in the household had yet taken the trouble to name them, making reference to them singularly only by hooking a thumb in the direction of the intended boy and saying, That'un.

Junior claimed that the sum of his marital experience had caused him to believe that he should have married a thirteen-year old and raised her to suit himself. As it was, he claimed to lie awake many a night thinking that every moment till his death would be gloom and that his only recourse would be to cut all their throats in their sleep and then put the shotgun to his own head or take to the woods and eventually be hunted down by dogs and treed and shot like a coon.

This put something of a damper on Veasey's glee, and in a moment Junior returned the bottle to its place and took up the saw again. He led them down the road a bend or two to his house, which sat off below the road in a damp swale. It was a large structure, batten-sided and in such poor repair that an end of it had fallen off the stacks of flat river stones that served for foundation. As a result, it stood tipped up as if it were in the process of diving into the earth.

The yard was littered with pyramidal gamecock dwellings made from unpeeled sticks tied together with honeysuckle vines. Inside, bright birds glared out the slots with cold shiny eyes that saw the whole world as little other than opportunity for an adversary. Thin white smoke rose from the chimney, and a

black pillar of smoke swelled skyward from some other source behind the house.

As they left the road to descend into Junior's bottomland, a three-legged, patchy-haired dog of the terrier kind clamored out from under the porch and ran low to the ground and completely soundless on a trajectory straight to Inman, who had learned to heed a silent dog more than a barking dog. Before it got to him, Inman kicked and caught it under the chin with a boot toe. The dog collapsed and lay motionless in the dirt.

Inman looked to Junior and said, What was I to do?

—All are not thieves that dogs bark at, Veasey said.

Junior just stood and looked.

The dog eventually rose shakily onto its tripod and in a series of vague tacking maneuvers made its way back under the porch.

—I'm glad he's not dead, Inman said.

—I don't give a shit one way or the other, Junior said.

They walked on down to the house and into the kitchen and dining room. Junior immediately went to a pie safe and took out another bottle and three tin cups. The floor to the place was ramplike in its tilt, and when Inman went to sit in a straight chair at the table, he had to clench to the floor as best he could with his feet to keep from skidding with gravity to the low wall. In the chimney corner was a bedstead, and Inman could see that they had not even tried to shim it level but had only made the modest effort of turning it so that the head was to the high side.

There were pictures cut from books and newspapers hanging on the walls, but some were hung parallel to the cocked-up floor, some to a more abstract line that might have been arrived at with a spirit level. There was a fire smoldering in the fireplace, and a Dutch oven sitting in the coals putting out a smell of rank meat cooking. The hearth was at such a rake that the smoke in its rise banked off the sidewall before finding the way up the chimney.

With all one's expectations of the world's plumb line so

thrown off, even pouring a dram of liquor from the bottle into a cup became a puzzler, and when Inman went to do it, he missed the glass entirely and wet his shoe tops before he found the proper range and lead. When he had succeeded in filling the glass, he took a drink and reached to set the cup on the dinner table and noted that little bumpers sawn from birch limbs had been nailed around each place at the table so that the plates and cups would not slide off the low side.

Veasey walked around supping from his cup and looking at the place, trudging uphill and down. Then an idea struck him.

—We could rig levers under the down end and soon set this thing right, he said.

Levers seemed to have come to occupy the foreground of his thinking, as if he had discovered a machine that could be applied to all the puzzles that might be thrown at a person. Stick a lever under anything wrong and make it sit right and square to the world.

—I reckon we could lever it, Junior said. But it's been this way so long, we've got the hang of it now. It would seem queer to live in a place without a grade to it.

They drank on awhile, the liquor going fast to Inman's head, for he had eaten nothing but the pods since last evening's sparse supper. It hit Veasey's empty stomach harder, and he sat with his head cocked oddly, looking down into his cup.

Shortly a girl of eight or ten walked in the front door. She was a slight child, thin at ankle and shoulder bone. Her skin was the color of heavy cream, her hair brown, falling below her shoulders in crisp ringlets. Inman had seldom seen a prettier child.

—Your mama here? Junior said.

—Yep, the girl said.

—Where's she at? Junior said.

—Out back. Was a minute ago.

Veasey looked up from his cup and examined the child. He

said to Junior, Why, I've seen white children darker complected than that. What would you make her to be, octoroon or less?

—Octoroon or quadroon, makes no difference. She's a niggaroon is all I can see, Junior said.

Veasey suddenly stood and wove his way to the bed. He lay down and passed out.

—What's your name? Inman asked the girl.

—Lula, she said.

—No, it ain't, Junior said. He turned to the girl and glared. Say what it is, he said.

—Mama says it's Lula, the girl said.

—Well, it ain't. That's just the kind of cathouse name your mama would come up with. But I do the naming here. Your name is Chastity.

—Either makes a fine name, I'd say, Inman said.

—No, said Junior. My name throws the other one into the shade, for mine commemorates what a whore her mama is.

He drank off what was left in his cup and said, Come on. Without looking to see if Inman followed, he led Inman out onto the front porch and sat in a rocker.

Inman walked out into the yard and cast back his head to look at the sky. It was coming on evening and the light was thin and slanting, and a portion of moon and the beacon of Venus stood in the eastern sky. The air was dry and there was a chill in it and Inman took a deep pull into his lungs and the smell and feel of it brought a thought to his mind: fall's right now on me. What the air told was that the wheel of the year had turned yet another notch.

—Lila, Junior called.

In a minute a young woman came wandering around the corner of the house and sat on the porch steps directly between Inman and Junior. She drew her knees up high and examined Inman with a critical eye. She was a towheaded, ample-haunched thing in a cotton dress so thin and bleached from

washing that a man could very nearly see the texture of her skin through its parchment-colored fabric. The dress had once been a print of little flowers in files but they had faded out till what was left looked more like characters, faint scribble from one of the vertical languages.

The girl was, in all her lines, circular, and the lower halves of her pale thighs were on full display where the dress hem fell back against the steps. Her eyes were the pale color of harebell blossoms. She went about with her head not combed. Her feet were bare and briar scratched, and there was something about her that spoke of oddity so much that Inman found himself clearing his mind by adding up muddy toes on one of her round feet to check if the mystic five would indeed be the sum. Junior drew a cob pipe with a clay stem from his pocket. And with it a great wizened pouch of tobacco. He filled the pipe and thrust it into the hole of his mouth. He dangled the pouch for Inman to examine.

—Bull sack, he said. A man can't make a better pouch than God did. Such things are a test from God to see if we will make do with what He provides or if we will shun dominion and seek improvement by our own weak devices.

Then he addressed the girl. Light, he said.

She arose with a certain amount of disturbance and gaping of her dress skirt and went into the house and returned with a lit shuck. She bent over to fit the shuck to the pipe, and as she did she presented her hind end to Inman. The thin dress gathered in the cleft of her buttocks and sheathed it over so tight that he could see the cupped space in the muscle at the sides of her clenched ass and the twin dimples atop the place where her spine met her hipbones. All her underlying structure lay revealed before him, and Inman felt face-to-face with an alien visage, though not an entirely unfriendly one.

But then the girl twisted and squealed out like a rabbit at the end of an owl's stoop, and Inman could see Junior's pincered fingers retreating from the vicinity of her bosom.

—Junior, goddammit, she said.

Lila returned to her seat on the steps and sat with a forearm pressed tight against her breast and Junior smoked awhile, and then Lila moved her arm and there was a tiny spot of black blood soaked up into the cloth of the front of her dress.

Junior said, Get these bitches to feed you. I've got a mare to check on down in the lower pasture.

He arose and went to the edge of the porch and dug in his britches and then pissed in a thick arc onto a snowball bush. He shook himself off, repacked, and walked out into the yard and on down the dimming road still smoking and singing a tune around the pipe stem. The words of it that Inman heard were: God gave Noah the rainbow sign, not no water but the fire next time.

Inman followed Lila around the house. Outbuildings—smokehouse, can house, springhouse, henhouse, corncrib—bordered a space of packed earth like a courtyard. In the center of it was a fire of great logs. It flicked up high as Lila's head and threw sparks higher yet. The night was collecting itself and shading black at the edge of trees beyond the weedy gardens of corn and picked-over beans in the middle distance. Nearby stood a kitchen garden enclosed by pales, limp dead crows stuck to the sharpened ends in various stages of rot. The yellow firelight reached out into the dark and threw crisp shadows against the walls of the unpainted buildings. The dome of sky directly overhead, though, was yet silvery and unmarked by stars.

—Hey, Lila called.

From the smokehouse came two pale females, the obvious sistern of Lila, for they resembled her in sufficient particulars so that they might have been triplets. And then from the springhouse a pair of dark-headed boy-children emerged. They all gathered about the fire and Lila said, Supper done?

Nobody said anything, and one of the sisters stuck a rusty forefinger into the loop at the neck of a stoppered earthenware jug and lifted it from the ground near the fire. She balanced it on the crook of her arm and took a deep and resonant swig. She

passed it along and when it got to Inman he expected some foul homebrew, but the flavor of it matched up with no known liquor. It tasted like rich earth and something else, some potent extract blended from tree fungus and animal gland with medicinal properties known to few. The jug went around a number of times.

One of the sisters backed up to the fire and hiked up the tail of her dress and bent over and thrust out her scut to it and stared at Inman with a look of glazed pleasure in her blue eyes. Her breasts hung round and pendulous as if to crack open her thin bodice. He wondered what sort of house of sluts he had stumbled into.

The third sister stood a minute, cupping a hand to her groin and looking off across the cornfield, and then she went into the smokehouse and came back with a wood-tined rake. She raked in the ashes at the edges of the fire and began turning up charred bundles of corn husks. The pair of boys seemed momentarily engaged. They looked on, and one of them walked over to the pile and said, Doughboy dough, in a flat voice.

Otherwise the children appeared to Inman stunned. They were hollow-eyed and they moved about in the firelight of the courtyard hantlike and wordless. They paced about the glaring yard in what seemed to be designs repeated over and over, rubbed into the earth with the shuffle of their footsteps. When Inman spoke to them they neither answered nor flickered an eye in his direction to even acknowledge the sound of his voice, and he began to assume that what the boy had spoken at the fire comprised their collective word hoard.

The sisters began breaking open the husk bundles, and steam rose from them in the cool air. When they were done they had six loaves of dark bread, each shaped to depict a big-headed homunculus, even down to the detail of swollen organs rising up along the bellies of the figures. The girls cast the husks into the fire and they flared up and burned away in a breath.

—We knowed you'd come, Lila said.

The two sisters gave a loaf to each of the boys. They tore at them and thrust pieces as big as their fists into their mouths. When they were done eating they began again treading the faint pathways they had worn in the dirt. Inman watched them, trying to make out what forms they were shaping with their walking. Here might be a sign he ought not miss. But after a time he gave it up. He could make no sense of the marks on the ground.

The two girls took the remaining four loaves and went into the house. Lila came and stood next to Inman. She put a hand onto his shoulder and said, Big man like you.

He could not see what response was called for here. Finally he took off his haversack, with his money and the LeMat's in it, and set it on the ground at his feet. The night had risen up to all but full dark now, and he could see off on a hillside that there seemed to be a yellow light moving wavery and inconclusive through the trees, one moment haloed and diffuse, the next a hard bright point. So odd did the light appear that Inman wondered if it emanated from no outside source but was an effect of some misfunction in his thinking.

—What is that? Inman said.

Lila followed the light a moment and said, That's nothing. It's little tonight. Sometimes it's big as an extra moon. What it is, up on that hill one time when I was a girl, Junior killed a man and his dog. Cleaved off their two heads with a froe and set them each by each up on a hickory stump. We all went and looked. The man's face was turned almost nigger black, and he had a funny look in its eyes. Ever since then, some nights there's that light moving across the hill. You could go up there right now and not see a thing, but maybe something would rub up against you like an old dry heifer hide.

—Why did he kill the man? Inman asked.

—He never said. He's got a temper on him. And he's quick to strike out. He shot his own mama dead. Way he tells it, she had her apron wrapped about her and he took her for a swan.

—I've not noticed a surplus of swans in this country.

—They's few.

The light on the hill had sharpened off to blue and picked up speed, flickering among the trees. And then it was gone.

—What do you think that light is? Inman said.

—Godamighty Hisself says clear as day in the Bible that the dead don't have a idea in their heads. Every thought flies from them. So it's not that headless man. I believe it's like people say, sometimes specter dogs carry lanterns on their heads. But I could be wrong. The old folks say there used to be a sight more ghosts than now.

Lila looked at him a fair length of time. She rubbed her hand on his forearm. I believe you traveling under a black flag, she said.

I'm under no colors, he said.

One of the sisters came to the back stoop and said, Come eat. Inman carried the haversack to the porch and Lila reached and took the straps of his pack over his shoulders and down his arms and set it beside the sack. Inman looked down at it and thought, That would be a mistake, but he could not order his thoughts farther.

As Lila and her sister turned to walk into the house, he took the haversack and thrust it elbow deep into a space between sticks of cordwood stacked on the porch. He followed the girls into the house, which now seemed unaccountably larger than it had earlier. They led him down a ramplike hallway of unpainted plank walls, and he felt that his feet were about to slide out from under him. In the dark the place seemed a vast warren, cut up mazy into many tiny rooms with doors on each wall. The rooms fed into each other in ways that defied logic, but eventually Inman and Lila made their way into the canted main room, where places were set at the bumpered table. Veasey slept on like the dead in the chimney corner.

A lamp was smoking on the table, and its feeble light moved across the surfaces of wall and floor and tablecloth like shadows on the stones of a creek bottom. Lila sat Inman at the head of

the table and tied a checked napkin around his neck. A loaf from the ashes was wrapped in another napkin in the center of the table.

One of the sisters brought a platter from the hearth, atop it a massive joint of meat swimming in lucent grease. Inman could not say just what creature it came from. It seemed too big for hog but too pale for cow. It was a ball-and-socket arrangement, clods of meat at either bone end. White threads of tendon and ligament wove through the meat. The girl set the platter in front of him, chocking it level with the bowl of an upturned cooking spoon. There was only a rust-spotted knife at his place. He picked it up and looked at Lila.

—We've nary meat fork, she said.

Inman gripped the bone with his left hand and carved and carved, but never made scarce a mark on the pith of the joint.

All three girls now had gathered about the table to gauge his progress. Together they cast a breedy scent like that arising from dank beds of galax, and it overpowered even the reek of the strange meat. Lila eased over next to Inman and rubbed the soft of her belly against his shoulder and then she shifted up on the balls of her feet and he could feel the bewhiskered notch of her legs scratch at his skin through the thin dress.

—You a fine-looking thing, she said. Bet you draw the women like dog hair draws lightning.

One of the sisters gazed at Inman and said, I wish he'd hug me till I grunt.

Lila said, This is mine. All that's left for you is just to look at him and then to go to wishing in one hand and shitting in the other and see which one gets full first.

Inman felt a kind of weary numbness. He was still sawing on the joint but his arms felt heavy. The burning wick of the lantern seemed to be casting out strange rays into the dim of the room. Inman thought back on the jug and wondered what fashion of drunk he was.

Lila took his greasy left hand from its grip on the bone and

ran it up under her skirt and rested it high on her thigh so that he could feel that she had on no drawers.

—Get on out, she said to the sisters, and they walked to the hall. One of them turned at the door and said, You just like the preacher says. You church founded on peter.

Lila shoved the meat platter to the high end of the table with a thumb, knocking it off the spoon and slopping out grey gravy, which ran downhill and dripped from the table end. Lila shifted and rolled until she was sitting on the table before Inman, her legs astraddle him, her bare feet resting on the arms of his chair. She pulled her skirt back to a bunch at her waist and leaned back on her elbows and said, How about that? What does that favor?

Not a thing other than itself, Inman thought. But his mind would not shape words, for he felt as inert as one behexed. His glossy handprint remained on her pale thigh, and beyond that, the gaping aperture. It seemed extraordinarily fascinating though it was but a mere slot in flesh.

—Get you some, she said, and she shrugged her shoulders out of the dress top and breasts came spilling out, pale nipples as big around as the mouth of a pint jar. Lila leaned forward and pulled Inman's head into the rift between her breasts.

At that moment the door burst open and Junior stood with a smoking lantern in one hand and the ten-gauge in the other.

—The hell's going on? he said.

Inman sat back in his chair and watched as Junior leveled the shotgun at him and cocked the pointy hammer that looked as long as a mule's ear. The raw hole at the end of the short barrel was black and enormous. It would throw a shot pattern covering most of the wall. Lila rolled off the table and began yanking in various directions at her dress until she was largely covered again.

This would be one sorry shithole to die in, Inman thought.

There was a long pause and Junior stood sucking on an eye-

tooth and studying deep on something, and then he said, What you about to learn is they ain't no balm in Gilead.

Inman sat at the table looking at the bore to Junior's shotgun and thought, There would be a thing to do here. A right action to take. But he could not arrive at it. He felt fixed as stone. His hands lay in front of him on the tablecloth and he stared at them and thought uselessly, They're starting to look like my father's, though not long ago they didn't.

Junior said, The only way I can reason this out to my satisfaction is that we've got a marrying coming. That or a killing, one.

Lila said, Goody.

—Wait, Inman said.

—Wait? Junior said. It's too late to wait.

He looked over to where Veasey lay asleep in the chimney corner. Go wake him up, he said to Lila.

—Wait, Inman said again, but he could not formulate a sentence beyond that point. His thoughts would not serve his purpose. They refused to achieve order or proportion, and he wondered again what had been in the jug by the yard fire.

Lila went and bent over Veasey and shook him. He woke with breasts in his face, grinning as if he had passed on to a new world. Until he saw the shotgun bore.

—Now you go get them other ones, Junior said to Lila. He walked over to her and slapped her hard across the face. She put a hand to the rising red mark and left the room.

—They's one other thing, Junior said to Inman. Get up.

Inman stood but he felt that he frabbled on his feet. Junior moved around, keeping Inman covered, and took Veasey by the coat collar and stood him up and walked him slowly across the room. Veasey was yanked up onto the balls of his feet so he walked like a man sneaking up on something. When he had them paired, Junior prodded Inman in the ass with the jagged shotgun barrel.

—Take a look out yonder at what I fetched, Junior said.

Inman moved as one would under water, effortfully and slow, out to the front porch. Up at the road he could see faint movement in the dark, shapes and masses only. He heard the expelled breath of a horse. A man's cough. The tick of a hoof on stone. A light was struck and a lantern flared. Then another, and yet one more, until in the glaring yellowy light Inman could make out a band of Home Guard. Behind them, afoot, a tangle of men, shackled and downcast, shading off into the murk.

—You're not the first one I've snared in here, Junior said to Inman. I get five dollars a head for every outlier I turn over.

One of the horsemen called out, We going or what?

But an hour later they had still not gone. They had tied Inman and Veasey onto a string of prisoners and shoved them all against the wall of the smokehouse. None of the tied men had said a word. They moved to the wall with barely more animation than a parade of cadavers. All shuffle-footed and vague, blank-eyed, so tired from the manner of their recent living—as soldier, fugitive, captive—that they leaned back and immediately fell into openmouthed sleep without twitch or snort. Inman and Veasey, though, sat wakeful as the night progressed. At intervals they wrenched against the windings of rope at their hands, hoping for any sign of give.

The Guard built up the fire until it stood as high as the eaves of the house and threw glare and shade against the walls of the buildings. The light of it blanked out the true stars and sparks flew up in a column and then disappeared into the dark, a vision which suggested to Inman that the stars had drawn together in congress and agreed to flee, to shed light on some more cordial world. Off on the hillside, the beacon of the ghost dog shone orange as a pumpkin and skittered about among the trees. Inman turned and stared at the fire. Dark figures passed back and forth before it, and after a time one of the guards brought out a fiddle and plinked at the strings to quiz the instrument for tune. Satisfied, he pulled on the bow and struck up a simple droning fig-

ure of notes, which soon revealed itself to be circular in logic. The pattern came around again and again at close intervals and seemed equally suited to dancing or—if repeated long enough—to throwing a man into a daze. The guardsmen, silhouetted against the fire, pitched back from the hips and pulled at the contents of various jugs and stoups. Then they danced about the fire, and sometimes they could be seen paired up with Lila or one of the sisters, rubbing in various shadowy tableaus of rut.

—There is not great variance between this place and a damn jenny barn, Veasey said. Other than they've not charged anybody anything yet.

Those men not immediately occupied with Lila or the sisters danced alone. They went round and round, jerking in a buck-and-wing, bent at the waist, stepping with high knees, their faces alternately staring down at their feet on the ground and bending back to speculate on the blanked heavens. Now and again, possessed by the music, one would squeal out as if wounded.

They danced until they all had to stop and blow and then Junior, apparently far gone in drink, tried to organize a wedding between Inman and Lila.

—I went in the house, and that tall one was just getting into the shortrows with Lila, Junior said. We ought to wed them.

—You're not no preacher, the Guard captain said.

—That little shaved-off one is, Junior said, looking at Veasey.

—Goddamn, the captain said. He don't much look like it.

—Will you witness? Junior said.

—If that will get us on the road, the man said.

They got Inman and Veasey from the smokehouse and untied them and walked them at gunpoint to the fire. The three girls stood waiting, the pair of dark-headed boys with them. The Guard off to the side spectating, their shadows jittery and huge against the walls of the house.

—Get over there, Junior said. Inman took a step toward

Lila, but then a thought that had been trying to come into his mind finally arrived. He said, But she's already married.

—By the law she is. Not in my mind or God's eyes, Junior said. Get on over.

Inman went will-less to stand alongside Lila.

—Oh, boy, she said.

Her hair was newly bound up in a snoodlike wad at her neck. Her cheeks had been daubed with face paint, but under it the left side of her face was still flushed with the mark of Junior's hand. She held clutched against her belly a bunch of goldenrod and ironweed pulled from the fencerow of the cornfield. She described little delighted circles in the dirt with her toes. Junior and Veasey stood to the side, the shotgun pressed to the base of Veasey's spine.

—I'll say what needs to be said and you just say Uh-huh, Junior said to Veasey.

Junior untied the string at his chin and removed his hat and set it on the ground at his feet. His head was covered with a faint smear of coarse hair spread thin across his pate, a stand of hair more suited to be growing on a man's ass. He struck a formal pose with the shotgun cradled in his arms and commenced a rawk-voiced prothalamion. It vaguely took the form of song, modal and dark, and the dire jig of its tune grated on the ear. The theme of its lyric, the best Inman could decipher it, was death and its inevitability and the unpleasant consequences of life. The pair of boy-children tapped their feet as if they knew the main rhythm of the song and approved of it.

When he was done singing, Junior began the talking portion of the ceremony. The words *bound* and *death* and *sickness* were featured prominently. Inman looked off to the hillside, and the ghost light was moving again through the trees. Inman wished it would just come on and carry him away.

When the wedding was over, Lila threw the flowers into the fire and hugged Inman tight. Pressed one full thigh up between his legs. She looked him in the eye and said, Bye, bye.

One of the Home Guard stepped behind him and clapped a Colt's pistol to his temple and said, Figure that. One minute a bride, and the next, if I pull this trigger, she'll put a smile on her face and scoop her husband's harns off the ground into a napkin.

I do not understand you people, Inman said, and they retied him and Veasey to the string of men and marched them off down the road east.

For several days Inman walked tied at the wrists to the end of a long rope with fifteen other men so that they went strung together like tailed colts. Veasey was tied directly before Inman, and he slogged along with his head down, stunned at his misfortune. When the line started or stopped he was yanked forward and his bound hands flew up before his face like a man in sudden need of prayer. Some of the men farther up the line were old greybeards, others little more than boys, all of them accused of being deserters or sympathizers. Most of them were country people in homespun. Inman gathered they were all prison bound. That or to be sent back fighting. Some men periodically called out to the Guard, shouting excuses and declaring to be altogether other men from what they were accused of being. Innocence was their claim. Others muttered out threats, saying were their hands not tied and had they an axe, they would cleave the guardsmen down from crown to groin, dividing them into equal bleeding parts onto which they would piss before walking away to find home. Others sobbed and begged to be freed, calling upon some imagined force of kindness resident in men's hearts to advance their interests.

Like the vast bulk of people, the captives would pass from the earth without hardly making any mark more lasting than plowing a furrow. You could bury them and knife their names onto an oak plank and stand it up in the dirt, and not one thing—not their acts of meanness or kindness or cowardice or courage, not their fears or hopes, not the features of their faces—would

be remembered even as long as it would take the gouged characters in the plank to weather away. They walked therefore bent, as if bearing the burden of lives lived beyond recollection.

Inman hated being sutured up to the others, hated going unarmed, hated most moving retrograde to his desires. Every step east he trod was bitter as backsliding. The miles passed, and hope of home began fleeing from him. When the sun rose full in his face he spit at it, having no other way of striking out.

The prisoners walked all that day and for several days following with hardly a word spoken among them. To entertain himself one afternoon, a guardsman rode down the line and with the barrel to his shotgun knocked every man's hat onto the ground and any man who bent to pick up his hat was beat with the stock end of the gun. They walked on leaving fifteen black hats lying in the road as spoor of their passage.

For food they were given nothing, and for drink they had but what water they could bend and scoop a cupped hand of whenever the road forded a creek. The old men of the party grew especially weak from such short rations, and when they could no longer walk, even when prodded by rifle barrels, they were fed a gruel made of buttermilk with old corn bread crumbed up in it. When their heads cleared they marched on.

The men had got in such a scrape, each of them, in the usual way, one damn event treading on the heels of another until they were in a place they never expected to be and could see no way clear of. Inman's thoughts turned constantly on such matters. And other than to be set free, there was nothing he longed for more than to see Junior's blood running.

Some days the Guard drove the prisoners all day and they slept at night. Some days they would sleep and arise at sundown and set out walking and keep at it all night. But after each march, where they arrived was much of a sameness with where they had been: pinewoods so dense at their crowns that the sun would never shine on the ground. For all the variance in landscape Inman could see, he might have been moving through the

dark at about the strange and sluggish pace of a man in a dream who runs away from what he fears but, try as he might, makes little headway against it.

And, too, he hurt from the hard traveling. He felt weak and dizzy. Hungry as well. The wound at his neck throbbed with his heartbeat, and he thought it might break open and start spitting things out as it had at the hospital. The lens to a field glass, a corkscrew, a bloody little Psalter.

He watched all the westward miles he had accomplished start coming unspooled in a tangle under his feet. After some days of walking, they stopped at nightfall and the prisoners were left tied, without food or water. The Guard, as on the previous nights, made no provision for their sleeping, neither giving them blankets nor striking fire. In their exhaustion the roped men piled up like a dog pack to sleep on the bare red ground.

Inman had read books where prisoners in castlekeeps scratch marks on sticks or rocks to track the passage of days, but he had not even the means to do that, though he could see how useful it would be because he had already started to doubt his mental calendar. No further accounting needed to be kept, though, for deep in the night the prisoners were rousted from thin sleep by one of the guards. He shined a lantern in their faces and told them to stand. The other half-dozen guards stood in a loose group. Some of them were smoking pipes and they held their rifle muskets butt down on the ground. One of them who acted in the role of leader said, We had us a talk and decided that you pack of shit are just wasting our time.

At that the Guard raised their rifles.

A captive boy, not much over twelve, fell to his knees and commenced crying. An old man, grey headed, said, You can't mean to kill us all here.

One of the guards lowered his weapon and looked to the leader and said, I didn't sign on to kill grandpaws and little boys.

The leader said to him, Cock back to fire or get down there with them.

Inman looked off into the dark pinewoods. The view from my last resting place, he said within himself.

Then the firing started with a volley. Men and boys began falling all around. Veasey stepped forward as far as the rope would allow and shouted amid the firing. He said, It is not too late to put away this meanness. Then he was shot through a number of times.

The ball that hit Inman had already passed through Veasey's shoulder and as a result did not strike with full briskness. It took Inman in the side of the head at his hairline and ran along his skull between hide and bone, routing a shallow groove there as it passed. It exited behind his ear. He fell as if struck by a lathing hatchet, but consciousness did not leave him entirely. He could not move, not so much as to blink an eye, nor did he wish to. The world moved on about him and he observed it, though he felt not a part of it. It seemed to scorn understanding. People died all around him and fell all bound together.

When the firing was done, the Guard stood as if unclear as to what the next step might be. One of them seemed taken by some fit or spell, and he danced about and sang Cotton Eye Joe and capered until another man hit him at the base of his spine with the stock of his musket. Finally one said, We'd best get them under ground.

They went about the job poorly, just digging out a shallow bed and strewing the men in and covering them over with dirt about to the depth that one would plant potatoes. When done, they mounted up and rode away.

Inman had fallen with his face in the crook of his arm and he had breathing space, though the covering of dirt over him was so thin and loose that he might have lain there and starved before he smothered. He rested, drifting in and out of muddled wakefulness. The smell of the dirt pulled at him and drew him down and he could not find the force to raise himself from it. Dying there seemed easier than not.

But before the dawn of day, feral hogs descended from the

woods, drawn by the tang in the air. They plowed at the ground with their snouts and dug out arms and feet and heads, and soon Inman found himself uprooted, staring eye to eye, forlorn and hostile and baffled, into the long face of a great tushed boar.

—Yaah, Inman said.

The boar shied off a few feet and stopped and looked back at him dumbfounded, his little eyes blinking. Inman prised his length out of the ground. To rise and bloom again, that became his wish. When Inman worked his way upright once more, the boar lost interest and went back to grubbing at the ground.

Inman cast back his head to the sky and found it did not look right. There were stars in it, but he could not reason out even one known constellation in the moonless sky. It looked as if someone had taken a stick and stirred it up so that no sense remained, just a smattering of light cast patternless on the general dark.

As head wounds will do, his had bled all out of proportion to its actual direness. Blood covered his face and dirt had gummed to it, so that his visage was ocher in color and appeared like a clay sculpture illustrating some earlier phase of mankind when facial features were yet provisional. He found the two holes in his scalp and probed them with his fingers and found them numb and beginning to clot shut. He wiped at himself to little effect with the tail of his shirt. He commenced pulling on the rope at his hands, bent his back to it, and in a minute Veasey emerged from the ground like a big hooked bass pulled up from a muddy lake. Veasey's face was locked in an expression of numb bewilderment. His eyes were open and dirt clung to the wet of them.

Looking on him, Inman could find no great sorrow at his death, but neither could he find this an example of justice working its way around to show proof that the wrong a man does flies back at him. Inman had seen so much death it had come to seem a random thing entirely. He could not even make a start at reckoning up how many deaths he had witnessed of late. It would

number, no doubt, in the thousands. Accomplished in every custom you could imagine, and some you couldn't come up with if you thought at it for days. He had grown so used to seeing death, walking among the dead, sleeping among them, numbering himself calmly as among the near-dead, that it seemed no longer dark and mysterious. He feared his heart had been touched by the fire so often he might never make a civilian again.

Inman cast about until he came up with a sharp stone, and he sat until sunrise rubbing his bound wrists against it. When he finally freed himself, he looked again at Veasey. One eyelid now drooped near closed. Inman wished to commit some kind gesture toward him, but lacking even a shovel for burial, all he could think to do was roll Veasey over, facedown.

Inman put the dawn to his back and set out walking west. All that morning he felt stunned and wrenched. His head ached in accordance with the beat of his pulse and felt as if his skull was about to fall into a great number of pieces at his feet. From a fencerow he gathered a wad of the feathery leaves of yarrow and tied it to his head with the stripped stem of the plant. The power of yarrow is to draw out pain, which to an extent it did. The leaves waggled in time with his tired walk, and he spent the morning watching the shadows of them move before him down the road.

By noon he stood at a crossroads, his mind cloudy, unable to settle on one of the three choices laid out on the ground before him. He had only sense to rule out the way he had come. He looked to the sky for orientation, but the sun stood straight up. It could fall any which way. He put his hand to the ridged-up skin at his head, felt the crusty blood under his hairline, thinking, I'll soon be naught but scar. The red Petersburg welt at his neck began to hurt as if in sympathy with its new brethren. All his upper parts felt like some great raw ulcer. He decided to sit in the pine litter at roadside and wait for some sign or token to mark one of the passways before him as preferable to the others.

After a time during which he lapsed in and out of wakeful-

ness, he saw a yellow slave coming down the road driving a mismatched team of steers, one red and one white. They dragged a sled loaded with fresh barrels and a great number of small dark melons stacked neat as cordwood. The man caught sight of Inman and whoa'd up the steers.

—They Lord God amighty, he said. You look like a dirt man.

He reached into the sled and knocked with his fist at two or three melons before selecting one and tossing it underhand to Inman. Inman cracked it open against the edge of a stone. The ragged meat in the halves was pink and firm and cloven by dark seeds, and he plunged his head down into first one and then the other like a hungry dog.

When he arose from them, they were naught but thin hulls and his beard dripped pink juice onto the dirt of the road. Inman stared down for some time onto the pattern the drops made to see if it held significance in the direction of augury, for he knew he needed aid, no matter from what strange fount it arose. The drops in the dust, though, offered no ready sign, neither pictograph nor totem, no matter from what angle he viewed them. The invisible world, he declared to himself, had abandoned him as a gypsy soul to wander singular, without guide or chart, through a broken world composed of little but impediment.

Inman quit his study of the ground and looked up and said his thanks for the melon. The yellow man was a wiry fellow, slim in all his parts but corded with muscle in the neck and the forearms where he had the sleeves of his grey wool shirt turned back to the elbow. His canvas britches had been made for a taller man and were rolled up into deep cuffs above his bare feet.

—Get on this sled and come with me, he said.

Inman rode a ways sitting on the tailboard, his back against a bright barrel, fragrant of fresh-split white oak. He tried to sleep but could not, and he stared down as in a trance at the drag trails of the wide ash runners, watching them fall away down the dusty road, paired lines that seemed to offer some lesson as they drew

nearer and nearer to each other the more distant they got. He pulled off the yarrow headdress and dropped it piece by piece into the space between the runner trails.

When the yellow man neared the farm where he was owned, he had Inman crawl into one of the barrels, and then he took him on in and unloaded the sled in the barn hall. He hid Inman in the hay under the loft eaves, and Inman rested there in the fodder for some days, and once again he lost track of the count. He spent the time sleeping and being fed by the slaves on corn pone fried in lard, sharp greens, roasted chines of pork rich and crackling with charred fat.

When his legs felt able to bear weight again, Inman prepared to fare forth once more. His clothes had been boiled clean, and his head was some improved and covered with an old black hat stained dark about the brow band with slave sweat. There was a half-moon in the sky, and Inman stood at the barn door bidding the yellow man farewell.

—I need to be going, Inman said. I've got a little business down this way, and then I've got to get home.

—You listen, the yellow man said. A band of Federals broke out of Salisbury prison last week, and the roads are running thick with patrols riding day and night looking for them. You try to go through there, they'll sure catch you up, you're not careful. Probably catch you even if you are.

—What would be best to do?

—Where you headed?

—West.

—Cut north. Go toward Wilkes. Taking that heading, there's Moravians and Quakers all the way that will help. Hit the bottom of the Blue Ridge and then cut south again following the foothills. Or go on into the mountains and follow the ridges back down to your course. But, they say it's cold and rough back in there.

—That's where I'm from, Inman said.

The yellow man gave him cornmeal twisted up in paper and

tied with twine, a strip of salt pork, and some pieces of roast pork. Then he worked for some time scratching out a map in ink on a piece of paper, and when it was done it was a work of art. All detailed with little houses and odd-shaped barns and crooked trees with faces in their trunks and limbs like arms and hair. A fancy compass rose in one corner. And there were notes in a precise script to say who could be trusted and who could not. Gradually things got vague and far apart until in the west all was white but for interlinked arcs the man had drawn to suggest the shapes of mountains.

—That's as far as I've been, he said. Just right there to the edge.

—You can read and write? Inman said.

—Got a crazy man for a master. That law don't mean a thing to him.

Inman reached in his pockets for money to give the man. He thought to draw out a generous amount, but he found his pockets empty and remembered that what money he had left was in the haversack hidden in Junior's woodpile.

—I wish I had something to pay you with, Inman said.

—I might not have took it anyway, the man said.

Several nights later Inman stood in front of the slanted house. It sat toadlike down in its swale, and the windows were all black. He softly called the three-legged dog from out its den and offered it a piece of pork bone that he had carried in his pocket wrapped in sycamore leaves. The dog came sniffing, soundless. It snatched the bone and then disappeared under the front porch.

Inman followed the dog down to the house and circled around to the rear. The big fire was but a cold black pock on the ground. He went to the back porch. His knapsack still lay there in a pile. He looked through it, and everything was there but for Veasey's Colt pistol. He thrust his arm into the woodstack and

seized the haversack and felt the butt of the LeMat's through the fabric. He drew it forth and it was like a tonic to feel the weight of the pistol in his hand, the balance and the sound when he pulled back the hammer.

A rind of light shone under the smokehouse door and Inman went and cracked the door and looked inside. Junior stood rubbing salt on a ham. A bayonet was stobbed into the dirt floor, and its muzzle socket held a taper as neatly as a silver candlestick. The floor of the smokehouse was so packed and greasy that the flame cast glints off it. Junior bent over the ham. He had his hat on and his face was dark in the shade of its brim. Inman opened the door fully and stood in the light. Junior raised up his face and looked at him but seemed not to recognize him. Inman stepped to Junior and struck him across the ear with the barrel of the LeMat's and then clubbed at him with the butt until he lay flat on his back. There was no movement out of him but for the bright flow of blood which ran from his nose and cuts to his head and the corners of his eyes. It gathered and pooled on the black earth of the smokehouse floor.

Inman stopped and squatted and rested his forearms on his knees to catch his breath. He twisted the candle out of its socket and felt the roughness of it where roaches had been eating at the tallow. He held the light to Junior's face. What lay before him was indeed a horrid thing, and yet Inman feared that the minds of all men share the same nature with little true variance. He blew out the candle and then turned and walked outside. There was a wedge of grey light at the east horizon where the moon was fixing to rise. On the hill the ghost light was weak, fluttery in its movement. It faded off and vanished, though so slowly that you could not have said exactly when.

Inman walked all that night circling north through a heavily peopled country, window lights shining everywhere, dogs barking. And the yellow man was right; horsemen passed over and over in the dark, but Inman could hear them coming in time to step into the bushes. When morning came there was fog, so, not

having to worry about a little smoke, he lit a fire in the woods and boiled two strips of salt pork and poured meal into the water and made a mess of corn mush. He laid up all that day in a thicket, sleeping some and fretting some. There were crows in the limbs above him, three of them, and they were harrying a rat snake they had discovered up in the tree. They sat on the limbs above the snake and gabbled at it, and now and again one flew close by and feinted at it with glinting bill. The snake made the customary vicious displays of its kind, erecting itself and hooding out its neck and hissing and striking as if it were deadly. But all its efforts were met with hilarity and ridicule by the crows, and the snake soon departed. The crows stayed on through much of the afternoon, celebrating their victory. Inman watched them anytime his eyes were open, observing closely their deportment and method of expression. And when his eyes were closed, he dreamed he lived in a kind of world where if a man wished it he could think himself into crow form, so that, though filled with dark error, he still had power either to fly from enemies or laugh them away. Then, after awhile of passing time in such wise, Inman watched night fall, and it seemed to him as if the crows had swelled out to blacken everything.

in place of the truth

The morning sky was featureless, a color like that made on paper from a thin wash of lampblack. Ralph stood stopped in the field, head down, blowing. He was harnessed to a sled load of locust fence rails, and they were heavy as a similar amount of stones. He seemed not to care to draw them one pace farther toward the edge of the creek along which Ruby intended to lay out the snake for a new pasture fence. Ada held the plaited carriage whip, and she popped Ralph's back a time or two with the frizzled end of it to no effect.

—He's a carriage horse, she said to Ruby.

Ruby said, He's a horse.

She went to Ralph's head and took his chin in her hand and looked him in the eye. He put back his ears and showed her a rim of white at the tops of his eyeballs.

Ruby pressed her lips to the velvet nose of the horse and then backed off an inch and opened her mouth wide and blew out a deep slow breath into its flanged nostrils. The dispatch sent by such a gesture, she believed, concerned an understanding between them. What it said was that she and Ralph were of like

minds on the issue at hand. You settled horses' thinking that way. They took it as a message to let down from their usual state of high nerves. You could calm white-eyed horses with such a companionable breath.

Ruby breathed again and then took Ralph by a handful of mane above his withers and pulled. He stepped out, pulling the sled, and when they got to the creek Ruby loosed him from his harness. She set him to grazing on clover that grew at the edge of the tree shade, and then she and Ada worked at laying out a zagging line of locust down the creek bank. When they got the time, they would lay three more lapped courses atop the snake to make the fence.

Ada had noticed that it was not always Ruby's way to start a job and finish it all at one time. She worked at things as they came up, taking them in order of urgency. If nothing was particularly urgent, Ruby did whatever could be done in the time at hand. Putting down the first row of fence rails was chosen that morning because it could be done in the hour or so before Ruby went off to trade with Esco: apples for cabbages and turnips.

For the job of handling the heavy rails, Ada wore a pair of leather work gloves, but they had been made rough side to, and so when she was done her fingertips were about as raw as if she had gone bare-handed. She sat on the sled and felt for blisters and then rubbed her hands in the creek and dried them on her skirt.

They led the horse back to the barn and unharnessed him and started to bridle him in preparation for Ruby's trading trip. But Ruby stopped and stood looking at an old trap hanging from a peg on the barn wall. It was sized for beaver and groundhogs and like-bodied animals. Something the Blacks had left when they pulled out for Texas. Its jaws were nearly fused shut, and it had been there so long that rust streaks stained the siding below it.

—That's exactly the thing we need, she said. Might as well set it before I go.

They were concerned over the corncrib. A little bit of corn

had been missing each morning for days. After Ruby noticed the shortage, she had fitted the door with a hasp and lock and worked on the chinking where it had dried up and fallen away. But the next morning she found a new hole gouged out in the fresh mud between the crib logs. It was a space plenty big enough for a hand or a squirrel, and maybe big enough for a small coon or possum or groundhog. She had daubed mud into the hole twice, only to find it open again the next morning. Not much corn was stolen at a time, just barely enough to notice, but if the loss kept on it would soon amount to something worth worrying about.

So Ada and Ruby worked over the trap, scrubbing the rust with a wire brush and greasing its joints with lard. When they were done Ruby put her foot to it and sprung open the jaws. Then she touched the trip plate with a stick and the thing snapped shut so hard it jumped off the ground. They carried it to the crib and nestled it in among the corn just within reach of the hole. Ruby hammered the spike at the end of its chain as deep as it would go into the packed dirt of the floor. In case the pilferage was from man rather than beast, Ada urged wrapping the teeth of the trap with strips of sacking, which Ruby did, judging the padding carefully so as not to err too much in the direction of kindness.

When done, Ruby bridled Ralph and slung two big sacks of apples over his withers. She mounted and rode off bareback, and at the road she stopped and hollered to Ada to make herself useful by putting up a scarecrow in the winter garden. Then she touched her heels to the horse and trotted away.

It was with some relief that Ada watched Ruby round the bend. She now had the entire midday stretching before her with no more required than the pleasant and somehow childlike task of making a big doll.

A band of crows had been working in the winter garden, picking at the young plants in a sort of bored way, but even so, without some discouragement they would soon pick it clean.

One crow had feathers missing from both trailing wing edges, identical square notches. It seemed to be the chief of the crows and was always the first to fly from field or limb. The rest were but followers. Notchwing was more vocal than the others and said every kind of crow word there was, from the sound of a dry hinge to the gabble of a duck being killed by a fox. Ada had been tracking its doings for weeks, and Ruby had once got so ill at it that she let off a precious barrel of shot in its direction, though at too great a range to do any good. So Ada took pleasure in imagining that her scarecrow would be a thing that Notchwing would have to include in its thinking.

With mixed feelings she said aloud, I am living a life now where I keep account of the doings of particular birds.

She went to the house. Upstairs she opened a trunk and took out an old pair of riding breeches and a maroon wool shirt of Monroe's. His beaver hat and a bright throat scarf. From them she might craft a fine and stylish scarecrow. But as she stood looking down at the folded clothes in her hands, all she could imagine was every day walking out and seeing the effigy of Monroe standing in the field. From the porch at dusk it would be a dark figure watching. Her fear was that it would loom larger and more troubling in her mind than it would in the crows'.

Ada put the clothes back in the trunk and went to her room and riffled through drawers and wardrobes, and finally she decided on the mauve dress that she had worn the last night of the party on the Wando River. And she took out a French-made straw hat Monroe had bought her fifteen years earlier on their tour of Europe and now frizzing apart at the brim edge. Ruby, she knew, would object to the dress, not on grounds of sentiment but because the material could be put to better use. Cut up, it could make pillow covers, quilt tops, antimacassars for chairbacks, any number of useful things. Ada, though, decided that if it was silk that was wanted, she had a number of other gowns that could as easily be put into service. This was the one she wanted to see standing in a field through rain and shine.

She carried the dress outside and then wired together a rood of bean poles as armature and planted it out in the center of the garden, beating it firm into the dirt with a hand sledge. She topped it with a head made by stuffing the end of a worn-out pillowcase with leaves and straw and daubing a grinning face on it with paint she stirred up from chimney soot and lamp oil. She put the dress over the poles and fleshed out the bodice with straw and gave the figure the straw hat for millinery. From the end of one arm she hung a small tin pail with a rust hole in its bottom. She went to the fencerow and broke off stems of goldenrod and aster and filled the pail with them.

When she was done Ada backed off and examined her work. The figure stood staring off toward Cold Mountain, as if during a leisurely walk gathering flowers for a table arrangement she had been struck momentarily still by the beauty of the scene before her. The full skirts of the lavender dress swayed in the breeze, and all Ada could think was that after a year of weather it would become bleached to the color of an old shuck. Ada herself wore a fading print dress and a straw bonnet. She wondered if an observer standing off on Jonas Ridge and looking down into the cove would choose right if asked to pick the scarecrow from the two figures standing in the field.

She washed her hands at the basin on the kitchen porch and fixed herself a dinner of a few umber shavings from Esco's ham, cold biscuits left from breakfast, and a wedge of baked pumpkin from supper the evening before. She took her journal and her plate and went to the table under the pear tree. When she was done eating, she paged through the journal—past the sketch of the heron, studies of dogwood berries, clusters of sumac fruit, a pair of water striders—until she reached the first blank page, and on it she sketched the scarecrow and above it the notched wings of the crow. She wrote down the date, and an approximation of the time, and then the current phase of the moon. At the bottom of the page she put down the names of the flowers in the

scarecrow's bucket, and in an unused corner of the page she sketched a detail of aster blossom.

Shortly after Ada was done, Ruby came walking up the road. She led the horse, six lumpy sacks of cabbages paired up and slung across his back. That was two sacks more than was fair, but Ruby had not been so proud as to deny Esco the impulse toward generosity. Ada went to the road. Ruby walked to her and stopped and reached in a skirt pocket and took out a letter.

—Here you go, she said. I stopped at the mill. In her tone was the conviction that any message conveyed other than by voice, face-to-face, was likely to be unwelcome. The letter was creased and wrinkled, dirty as an old work glove. It had been wet at some point in its journey and had dried puckered and stained. It lacked return address, but Ada knew the hand in which her own name was written. She pocketed the letter, not wanting to read it under Ruby's scrutiny.

Together they unloaded the sacks beside the smokehouse, and while Ruby put the horse away Ada went to the kitchen and made another plate the like of her own dinner. Then Ruby ate, talking all the while of cabbages and the many things they would make from them, which to Ada seemed few indeed—kraut, fried cabbage, boiled cabbage, stuffed cabbage, slaw.

When Ruby had eaten they went to the sacks. One they held back for making into sauerkraut when the signs came around right for it again. Do it otherwise and it might rot in the crocks. The rest they buried for the winter. It was to Ada an odd and troubling job, digging the gravelike trench behind the smokehouse and lining it with straw and heaping the pale heads in and covering them with more straw and then dirt. When they were done mounding up the dirt, Ruby marked the place with a plank, beating at it with the heel of her shovel until it stood like a tombstone.

—There, Ruby said. That might save us having to scratch around in the snow come January.

All Ada could think was how grim it would be on some cloudy midwinter afternoon—wind blowing, bare trees heaving, the ground covered in a grey crust of old snow—to come out and dig into that barrow pit for a mere cabbage.

Late that afternoon they sat on the stone steps, Ada behind Ruby and a riser above her. Ruby leaned against Ada's shins and knees like they were the ladder to a chairback. Watching the sun fall. The blue shadow of Jonas Ridge advancing across the creek and then the pasture. Barn swallows in jittery and reckless flight. Ada stroked Ruby's dark hair with an English-made brush of boar bristles. She worked until the hair was sleek and had the sheen of a new gunbarrel. She ran her fingers through it, parting it into seven sections, and each cord had its own heft and resistance in her hands. She spaced them across Ruby's shoulders and studied them.

Ada and Ruby were having a hair contest. It had been Ada's idea, suggested to her from watching Ruby absentmindedly plait Ralph's tail in intricate patterns. Ruby would stand behind him, her thoughts elsewhere, eyes unfocused, fingers moving apparently without effort through the long tail hair. It seemed to assist in her thinking. And it would about put Ralph to sleep. He would stand with one hind hoof tipped and his eyelids flickering. Afterward, though, he went about with his backquarters slightly tucked under him, nervous and embarrassed-looking, until one or the other of them went and undid his tail and brushed it out.

Ruby seemed so enviably dreamy during the making of the plaits that Ada imagined her as a lonely and abandoned child wandering the countryside to braid the tails of old solitary plow horses out of need for proximity to something live and warm. To touch it in a way both intimate and distant, not to lay a hand directly to its life but to the beautiful and bloodless extrusion of it. In such spirit, Ada had proposed they vie to see who could compose the most intricate or beautiful or outlandish plait of the other's hair. It would make the competition all the more interesting that neither would know what had been done with her

own hair—only what she had done with the other's—until they went inside and stood with paired mirrors to examine the backs of their heads. The loser was to perform all the night work while the winner rocked on the porch and watched the sky darken and counted the stars as they appeared.

Ada's hair had already been finished. Ruby had worked for some time, pulling and twisting until it was yanked back tight at Ada's temples. She could feel its pull at her eye corners. She started to pat the back of her head, but Ruby reached and slapped her hand away to prevent any foreknowledge as to how the competition stood.

Ada took the three tresses at the center of Ruby's back and made a simple pigtail. That was the easy part. With the remaining pieces she planned to build a complex overbraid, lapping and weaving in a herringbone pattern like a favorite raffia basket of hers. She took up two of the side pieces and began lacing them up.

Four crows, Notchwing in the lead, drifted down into the cove and then flared when they saw the new scarecrow. They flew away squealing like shot pigs.

Ruby called it a favorable comment on Ada's construction.

—That hat in particular's a fine touch, she said.

—It came from France, Ada said,

—France? Ruby said. We've got hats here. A man up East Fork weaves straw hats and will swap them for butter and eggs. Hatter in town makes beaver and wool but generally wants money.

This business of carrying hats halfway around the world to sell made no sense to her. It marked a lack of seriousness in a person that they could think about such matters. There was not one thing in a place like France or New York or Charleston that Ruby wanted. And little she even needed that she couldn't make or grow or find on Cold Mountain. She held a deep distrust of travel, whether to Europe or anywhere else. Her view was that a world properly put together would yield inhabitants so suited to

their lives in their assigned place that they would have neither need nor wish to travel. No stagecoach or railway or steamship would be required; all such vehicles would sit idle. Folks would, out of utter contentment, choose to stay home since the failure to do so was patently the root of many ills, current and historic. In such a stable world as she envisioned, some might live many happy years hearing the bay of a distant neighbor's dog and yet never venture out far enough from their own fields to see whether the yawp was from hound or setter, plain or pied.

Ada did not bother arguing, for she figured that her life was moving toward a place where travel and imported hats would figure small. The braid was finished, and she looked on it with disappointment. As with all her efforts toward art, it did not match up with her imagining of it. She thought it looked like a hemp lanyard twisted together by a mad or drunken sailor.

Ada and Ruby stood up from the steps and took turns touching each other's braids to smooth down stray hairs and tuck in loose pieces. They went to Ada's bedroom and backed up to the large mirror over the commode table and took a silver hand mirror and paired up the images. Ada's plait was simple and tight, and when she put her fingers to it she thought it felt like touching a chestnut limb. You could work all day and it would not spring loose.

When it came Ruby's turn, she took a long time looking. She had never seen the back of her head before. She put her hand to her hair and touched it flat-palmed, patting it over and over. She declared it perfect and would hear of nothing but that Ada be judged victor.

They went back to the porch and Ruby went on into the yard, ready to get on with the night work. But she stopped and stood looking around and then up at the sky. She touched the hair at her neck and at the crown of her head. Out from under the shade of the porch she could see that there was yet light enough to read a few pages from *Midsummer Night's Dream*, and she said as much. So they sat back on the steps and Ada

read, glossing as she went, and when she got to a line of Robin's—where he says, "Like horse, hound, hog, bear, fire, at every turn"—Ruby was immensely amused and said the words over and over as if they held a great deal of meaning and delight just in themselves.

The light soon fell too grey to read. A pair of bobwhites called their identical three-word messages back and forth from the field to the woods. Ruby rose and said, I better get on.

—Check our trap, Ada said.

—No point. You don't catch anything by day, Ruby said, before walking away.

Ada closed the book and plucked a boxwood leaf as page marker. She took Inman's letter from her skirt pocket and tipped the face of it to the west to gather what light remained there. She had read the utterly vague announcement of his wound and his planned return five times that afternoon. She could make no more of it after the fifth reading than she had from the first, which was that Inman seemed to have reached some firm conclusion about the state of feeling existing between them, though Ada could not herself put a name to how she thought things stood. She had not seen him in almost four years, and it had been more than four months since she had last heard from him. Just a brief dashed note from Petersburg, its tone impersonal as something one would write to a distant relation, though that was not unusual, for early on Inman had asked that they never speculate on what might happen between them after the war. Nobody could say how things would be then, and imagining the various possibilities—either pleasant or grim—only cast a shadow over his thoughts. Their correspondence through the war had been irregular. Flurries of letters, and then stretches of silence. This last stretch, though, was a long one even by their standards.

The letter Ada now held was without date, nor did it contain any mention of recent events or even weather by which it could be dated. It could have been written the week past, or it might

be three months old. The letter's battered condition argued for a date nearer the latter, but there was no way to know. And she was unclear about his coming home. Did he mean now or at the end of the war? If he meant now, there was no telling whether he was long overdue to return or just setting out on his journey. Ada thought of the story she and Ruby had heard the captive tell from the barred window of the courthouse. She feared every county would have its Teague.

She squinted at the paper. Inman's hand being somewhat cramped and minute, all Ada could make clear in the dark was this brief paragraph:

> Should you still possess the likeness I sent four years ago, I ask you, please, do not look at it. I currently bear it no resemblance in either form or spirit.

Ada of course went immediately to her bedroom and lit a lamp and opened drawers until she found the portrait. She had put it away because she never thought it looked much like him to begin with. When it arrived, she showed it to Monroe, who held a dim view toward photography and had never been photographed and never intended to be, though he had twice in his younger years sat for painters. He had examined Inman's countenance with some interest and then snapped the case shut. He went to the shelves and pulled out a volume and read from Emerson on the experience of being daguerreotyped, saying these words: "And in your zeal not to blur the image, did you keep every finger in its place with such energy that your hands became clenched as for fight or despair, and in your resolution to keep your face still, did you feel every moment more rigid; the brows contracted into a Tartarean frown, and the eyes fixed as they are fixed in a fit, in madness, or in death?"

And though that was not precisely the effect of Inman's picture, Ada had been forced to admit that it was not far off the

mark either. So she had put it away in order not to have her memory of Inman blurred by it.

Such little mechanical portraits as Ada now held in her hand were not rare. She had seen any number of them. Nearly every family in the settlement with a son or husband off fighting had one, even if only cased in tin. Displayed on mantel or table with the Bible, a taper, sprigs of galax, so that the effect was altarlike. In sixty-one, any soldier with a dollar and seventy-five cents could have his aspect recorded in the form of ambrotype, tintype, calotype, or daguerreotype. In those early days of war, Ada had found most of the ones she had seen comic. Later she found them depressing in their depictions of men now dead. One after the other, they had sat bristling with weaponry before the portraitist for the long exposure. They held pistols crossed at their breasts or bayoneted rifles at their sides. Shiny new bowie knives brandished for the camera. Forage caps set at swank angles on their heads. Farm boys more bright in their moods than on hog-killing days. Their costumes were various. Men wore every kind of thing to fight in, from clothes you might put on for plowing to actual uniforms, to garbs of such immense ridiculousness that even in peacetime someone might take a shot at you for wearing them.

Inman's portrait differed from most in that he had spent more money on the case than was usual. It was a beautiful little filigreed silver thing and Ada rubbed it, front and back, against the skirt at her hip to polish away the dusty tarnish. She opened it and held it to the lamp. The image was like oil on water. She had to tip it in her hand, making fine adjustments to get the light to make sense of it.

Inman's regiment had been casual about uniform, having agreed with their captain that nothing in the killing of Federals required an alteration of one's ordinary attire. In accordance with that belief, Inman wore a loosely constructed tweed jacket, collarless shirt, and soft slouch hat, the brim of which drooped to his brow. He had then affected a little pointed goatee and appeared less a soldier than a gentleman vagabond. He had a Colt's

Navy at his hip, but his jacket covered all but the grip of it. He did not touch it. His hands were open, resting on the tops of his legs. He had tried to fix his eyes on a spot some twenty degrees to the side of the lens, but sometime during the exposure he had moved them and they were blurred and strange. His expression was intent and stern so that he seemed to be staring hard at nothing identifiable, interested in something other than the camera or the act of portraiture or indeed even in the viewer's opinion of him in this static form.

Saying he no longer matched that image didn't tell Ada much. It didn't in any regard capture her recollection of him on the last day she saw him before he left, and that could not have been more than a matter of weeks before the picture was made. He had come by the house to say goodbye. He was, at the time, still living in a room at the county seat but would be leaving in two days, three at the most. Monroe had been reading by the fire in the parlor and had not bothered to come out to speak. Ada and Inman had walked together down to the creek. Ada could not remember a thing of Inman's attire but his slouch hat—the same as in the picture—and that his boots were newly made. It was a damp, chill morning following a day of rain, and the sky was still half filled with high thin clouds. The cow pasture by the creek was turning pale green with new shoots rising through the grey stubble of the previous year. It was sodden from the rain so that the two had to pick their way through it to keep from miring shin-deep. Along the creek and up the hillside, blossoms on redbud and dogwood shone out against the grey trees, their limbs frosted green with the first thin edges of leaf growth.

They walked down the creek bank beyond the pasture and then stopped in a mixed stand of oak and tulip trees. As they talked, Inman seemed alternately cheerful and solemn, and at one point he took off his hat, which Ada understood to be in preparation for a kiss. He reached out to pluck away a pale green

dogwood petal that was tangled in her hair and then his hand dropped to caress her shoulder and to draw her to him, but in doing so he brushed an onyx-and-pearl brooch at her collar. The pin snapped open and the brooch fell, bouncing off a rock and into the creek.

Inman put his hat back on and splashed in the water and scrabbled about the mossy rocks for some time until he came up with the brooch. He repinned it to her collar, but it was wet and his hands were wet and her dress was smeared dark at the neck. He stepped back from her. His pant cuffs dripped. He raised one of his new boots and let the water fall off of it. He seemed saddened that the tender moment had been lost and he could find no way to bring it back.

Ada found herself wondering, What if he is killed? But she could not, of course, voice the thought. She did not have to, though, for Inman at that instant said, If I am shot to death, in five years you'll hardly remember my name.

She had not been sure if he was teasing or testing her or simply saying what he thought was the truth.

—You know it's not that way, she said.

In her heart, though, she wondered, Is anything remembered forever?

Inman looked off and seemed to be made shy by what he had said.

—Look there, he said. He tipped his head back to take in Cold Mountain, where all was yet wintery and drab as a slate shingle. Inman stood looking up at the mountain and told her a story about it. He had heard it as a child from an old Cherokee woman who had successfully hidden from the army when they scoured the mountains, gathering the Indians in preparation for driving them out on the Trail of Tears. The woman had frightened him. She claimed to be a hundred and thirty-five years old and to remember a time before any white man had yet come to this territory. She spoke in a voice that conveyed all her disgust with the time between then and now. Her face was seamed and

gnarled. One eye entirely lacked color and was set in her head as slick and white as a boiled bird egg with the shell off. Her face was tattooed with two snakes, their bodies stretching in wavery lines to where their tails coiled into the hair at her temples. Their heads were opposite each other at the corners of her mouth so that when she spoke the snakes opened their mouths too, and seemed to share in telling the tale. It was about a village called Kanuga that many years ago stood at the fork of the Pigeon River. It is long since gone and no trace remains other than potsherds that people sometimes find, looking for stickbait at the river edge.

One day a man looking like any other man came into this Kanuga. He appeared to be an outlander, but the people greeted him and fed him. That was their custom toward any with an open hand. As he ate, they asked him if he came from far away in the western settlements.

—No, he said. I live in a town nearby. We are all, in fact, relatives of yours.

They were puzzled. Any kinsmen living nearby would be known.

—What town is it that you come from? they asked.

—Oh, you have never seen it, he said, even though it is just there. And he pointed south in the direction of Datsunalasgunyi, which the snake woman said was the name they had for Cold Mountain and did not signify either cold or mountain at all but something else entirely.

—There is no village up there, the people said.

—Oh, yes, the stranger said. The Shining Rocks are the gateposts to our country.

—But I have been to the Shining Rocks many times and have seen no such country, said one. And others agreed, for they knew the place he spoke of well.

—You must fast, the stranger said; otherwise we see you but you do not see us. Our land is not altogether like yours. Here is constant fighting, sickness, foes wherever you turn. And soon a

stronger enemy than you have yet faced will come and take your country away from you and leave you exiles. But there we have peace. And though we die as all men do and must struggle for our food, we need not think of danger. Our minds are not filled with fear. We do not endlessly contend with each other. I come to invite you to live with us. Your place is ready. There is room for all of you. But if you are to come, everyone must first go into the town house and fast seven days and never leave during that time and never raise the war cry. When that is done, climb to the Shining Rocks and they will open as a door and you may enter our country and live with us.

Having said this, the stranger went away. The people watched him go and then began arguing the merits of his invitation. Some thought he was a savior and some thought a liar. At length, though, they decided to accept. They went into the town house, and for seven days they all remained there fasting, drinking only a sip or two of water each day. All but one man, who slipped away every night when the others were asleep. He went to his house and ate smoked deer meat and then returned before dawn.

On the morning of the seventh day the people began climbing Datsunalasgunyi toward the Shining Rocks. They arrived just at sunset. The rocks were white as a snowdrift, and when the people stood before them, a cave opened like a door, and it ran to the heart of the mountain. But inside was light rather than dark. In the distance, inside the mountain, they could see an open country. A river. Rich bottomland. Broad fields of corn. A valley town, the houses in long rows, a town house atop a pyramidal mount, people in the square-ground dancing. The faint sound of drums.

Then there was thunder. Great claps and peals that seemed to be drawing near. The sky turned black and lightning fell around the people outside the cave. They all trembled, but only the man who had eaten the deer meat lost his senses from fear. He ran to the mouth of the cave and shouted the war cry, and

when he did the lightning ceased and the thunder began to fade into the distance and soon it was gone, moving off to the west. The people turned to watch it go. When they looked back to the rocks, they saw no cave but only the solid face of white rock, shining in the last light of the sun.

They went back to Kanuga, walking down the dark path as if in mourning, and every mind was fixed on the vision they had seen within the mountain. Soon, what the stranger had fore-visioned came about. Their land was taken from them, and they were driven away into exile, except for the few who fought and hid among the crags, living frightened and hunted like animals.

When Inman was finished Ada did not know what to say, so she said, Well, that was certainly folkloric.

She immediately regretted it, for the story evidently meant something to Inman, though she was not entirely sure what.

He looked at her and started to say something and then he stopped and looked at the creek. In a minute he said, That old woman looked older than God and she cried tears out of her white eyeball when she told the story.

—But you don't take it for the truth? Ada said.

—I take it that she could have been living in a better world, but she ended up fugitive, hiding in the balsams.

Neither knew what to say further, and so Inman said, I need to get on. He took Ada's hand and just brushed his lips to the back of it and turned it loose.

When not twenty feet gone, though, he looked back over his shoulder and saw her just turning to walk to the house. Too soon. She had not even waited for him to round the first bend in the road.

Ada caught herself and stopped and looked at him. She threw up a hand in a wave and then realized that he was still too near for that to be a suitable gesture, so she drew her hand up awkwardly and tucked a stray bit of hair back into the heavy bun at her neck as if that had been her first intent.

Inman stopped and turned to face her and said, You can walk on home. You don't have to stand watch on my going.

—I know I don't, Ada said.

—You don't want to, is my point.

—It would serve no purpose that I can see, she said.

—Some men might be made to feel better for it.

—Not you, Ada said, trying with little success to achieve a tone of lightness.

—Not me, Inman said, as if testing the idea to see if it stood plumb and level to the visible world.

In a moment, he took his hat off and held it down by his leg. He ran his other hand through his hair and then put one finger to his brow and saluted her.

—No, I guess, not me, he said. I'll see you when I see you.

They walked away, this time without looking back.

That night, though, Ada felt not so cavalier about the war and about Inman's going to it. It was a gloomy evening, ushered in by a brief rain before sunset. Immediately after dinner, Monroe went to his study and closed the door to work for hours on the week's sermon. Ada sat alone in the parlor with one taper lit. She read from the latest number of the *North American Review*, and when that failed to engage her she riffled through Monroe's old issues of the *Dial* and *Southern Literary Messenger*. Then she sat and pecked at the piano for a time. When she stopped there was just the faint sound of the creek, a drip now and then from the eaves, a peeper that soon fell quiet, the house settling. Occasionally the muffled sound of Monroe's voice as he tried a newly composed phrase aloud for cadence. In Charleston at this time of night there would be waves beating on bulkheads, palmetto leaves rattling in the wind. The iron hoops of carriage wheels rumbling, and the hooves of horses tocking like great clocks keeping erratic time. Voices of promenaders and the brush of their shoe leather on gaslit street cobbles. In this mountain cove, though, Ada could hear her ears ring from lack of

other report. It was so mum she began to think she felt it as an ache behind her brow bones. And the dark outside the windowpanes was as total as would have been achieved by painting the glass black.

Her thoughts tossed about in such void. A number of things about the morning bothered her. Not among them was that she had shed no tears. Nor that she had left unsaid the things many thousands of women, married and unmarried, said as men left, all of which boiled down to the sentiment that they would await the man's return forever.

What did bother her was Inman's question. How might she react to news of his death? She did not know, though the prospect of it loomed darker in her mind that evening than she would have thought. And she worried that she had rudely dismissed Inman's story, had not summoned the wit at the time to see that it had not been about an old woman but about his own fears and desires.

All in all, she suspected that her performance had been glib. Or flinty and pinched. None of which she really wished to be. True, those manners had their uses. They excelled in causing people to take half a step back and give one breathing room. But she had fallen into them out of habit, and at the wrong time, and she regretted it. She feared that without some act of atonement they would take hold and harden within her and that one day she would find herself clenched tight as a dogwood bud in January.

She had slept poorly that night, tossing in her damp and chilly bed. Later she struck fire to wick and tried to read awhile at *Bleak House*, but she could not adjust her mind to it. She blew out the light and lay twisted in her covers. She wished she had a draught of opium. Sometime long after midnight she took the easement of maiden, spinster, widow. As a girl she had spent her thirteenth year troubled by the belief that she alone had discovered such an act, or perhaps that she alone was capable of it due to some malformation or unique baseness. So it had been a considerable relief when her cousin Lucy, older by some months,

had set her straight on the matter of lone love. Lucy's shocking view was that, as habits go, it approached tobacco chewing and snuff dipping and pipe smoking in degree of commonness, which was to say it might as well be considered universal. Ada had proclaimed such opinion to be utterly base and cynical. But Lucy did not budge in her view and remained blithe to the point of frivolity about a thing Ada held to be a dark mystery arising from desperation so great that one must surely go through the next day with a visible stain across one's countenance. Neither Lucy's views nor the intervening years had greatly changed Ada's feelings on the matter.

On that fretful night, the pictures flowing into her mind unbidden and dreamlike were of Inman. And because her knowledge of anatomy was to a degree hypothetical—founded only on various animals and boy-babies and the amazing statues of Italy—the images that appeared to her most clearly were of his fingers and wrists and forearms. All else was speculative and therefore shadowy and without true form. Afterward, she lay wakeful until near dawn, still filled with yearning and hopelessness.

But she awoke the next day clearheaded and bright, and with firm resolve to set right her errors. The day was cloudless and warmer, and Ada told Monroe she wanted to go out for a drive, knowing full well where they ended up anytime he held the reins. He had the hired man harness Ralph to the cabriolet, and in an hour they wheeled into town. They went to the livery, where the horse was taken from between the thills and put in a stall and given a half measure of grain.

Out on the street, Monroe patted at the various pockets to his pants and waistcoat and topcoat until he found his money purse. He picked out a little twenty-dollar gold piece and handed it to Ada with no more thought than if it were a nickel. He suggested she buy something nice in the way of clothes and books and then meet back at the livery in two hours. She knew he was setting out to find a friend of his, an old doctor, and that they would talk about writers and painters and the like, and that

in the process he would drink either one tiny glass of Scotch whisky or one large glass of claret, and that he would be exactly fifteen minutes late in meeting her.

She went straight to the stationer's and without browsing bought sheet music for a number of recent tunes by Stephen Foster, a songster about whom she and Monroe held violently differing opinions. As for books, the first thing that fell to hand was a three-volume Trollope, near cubic in its mass. She had no particular desire to read it, but it was there. She had the purchases wrapped in paper and sent to the livery. Then she went to a mercantile and quickly bought a scarf, a pair of buff leather gloves, ankle boots the color of doeskin. These too she had wrapped and sent on ahead. She went out on the street, consulted the time, and found that she had successfully spent considerably less than an hour in shopping.

Knowing what she did was more than unseemly, she turned down the lane between the law office and the smithy. She climbed the open board steps to the covered landing before Inman's door and knocked.

He'd been blacking a boot and still had his left hand thrust up in it when he opened the door. A rag in the other where he kept his grip on the knob. One foot with but a sock and the other shod but its boot yet unpolished. He wore no jacket, and his shirtsleeves were turned back nearly to the elbow. His head was bare.

Inman's face was a display of total wonderment as he looked on Ada, materialized in the least likely place either of them could have imagined. He seemed not to know what words to say, only that those which would invite her in were not among the possibles. He held up a forefinger to signify a brief period of time, a moment. Then he closed the door, leaving her standing there.

What Ada had seen of the room through the opened door was disheartening. It was tiny with but one small window high on the far wall, and that with a prospect only on the clapboards

and the shakes of the store across the alley. For furnishing, the room had a narrow iron bedstead, a chest of drawers with a washbasin atop it, a straight chair and writing table, some books in stacks. It was a cell. All in all more fit, she thought, for a monk than for someone she might class as beau.

True to Inman's signal, the door soon reopened. He had turned down his shirt cuffs and put on a jacket and a hat. Both boots were on, though one was dirty brown and the other black as a greased stove lid. And he had gathered his thoughts somewhat.

—I'm sorry, he said. I was taken by surprise.

—I hope not an unpleasant one.

—A happy one, he said, though nothing about his expression supported such sentiment.

Inman came out on the landing and leaned back against the railing, his arms crossed at his chest. Out in the sun, his hat cast a shadow on his face so that all above his mouth was dim. There was a long silence. He looked back at the door. He had left it open, and Ada guessed he wished he'd closed it but could not now decide which was worse, the awkwardness of taking the two strides to do it, or the sharp intimacy suggested by the yawning doorway and the narrow bedstead.

She said, I wanted to tell you I thought things concluded badly yesterday. Not at all as I wished them to. Not in a satisfying way.

Inman's mouth tightened like a cord had been pulled in him. He said, I don't believe I take your meaning. I was headed upriver to say my goodbyes to Esco and Sally. When I came to the road up Black Cove, I thought I might as well say one to you too. And I did. It was, as best I could tell, satisfactory.

Ada lacked experience in having her apologies rejected, and her first thought was to turn and walk down the steps and put Inman forever behind her. But what she said was, We might never speak again, and I don't plan to leave that comment standing in place of the truth. You're not owning up to it, but you

came with expectations and they were not realized. Largely because I behaved contrary to my heart. I'm sorry for that. And I would do it differently if given a chance to go back and revise.

—That's not a thing any of us are granted. To go back. Wipe away what later doesn't suit us and make it the way we wish it. You just go on.

Inman still stood with his arms crossed, and Ada reached and touched where his shirt cuff came out from his coat sleeve. She held the cuff between finger and thumb and pulled until she unlocked his arms. She touched the back of his hand, tracing with one finger the curving course of a vein from knuckle to wrist. Then she took his wrist and squeezed it hard, and the feel of him in her hand made her wonder what the rest of him would be like.

Neither of them, for a moment, could look the other in the face. Then Inman pulled his hand away and took his hat off and spun it by the brim into the air. He caught it and flipped his wrist and sent it skimming through the door to land inside where it would. They both smiled, and Inman put one hand to Ada's waist and the other to the back of her head. Her hair was in a loose upsweep, held with a clasp, and it was the cold nacre that Inman's fingers touched as he tipped her head to him for the kiss that had eluded them the day before.

Ada had on about all the clothes women of her station then wore, and so her body was all cased up underneath many lapped and pleated yards of dead fabric. His hand at her waist touched the whalebones of corset stays, and when she took a step back and looked at him, the bones creaked against each other as she moved and breathed. She guessed she felt to him like a terrapin shut up inside its hull, giving little evidence that a distinct living thing, warm and in its skin, lay inside.

They walked together down the steps, and the door as they passed it stood like a promise between them. Near the mouth to the lane, Ada turned and put her forefinger to Inman's collar button to stop him.

—Here is far enough, she said. Go on back. As you said, I'll see you when I see you.

—But I hope that's soon.

—We both do, then.

That day they had thought the most suitable units of time to measure Inman's absence would be mere months. The war, though, turned out to be a longer experience than either had counted on.

the doing of it

Inman followed the yellow man's artful map through what the locals called hill country. Nights were cool and leaves were beginning to color. After he had walked for the better part of a week, he advanced to the bare white places at the map's far margin, and he could see the Blue Ridge hanging like a drift of smoke across the sky ahead. It took him three more nights to pass through a foul place called Happy Valley, a long broad swath of cropland and pastureland at the foot of the mountains. There was too much open ground to feel good about walking by day, and by night there was pistol fire and torchlight, the roads so full of dark riders that Inman spent as much time hiding in ditches and haystacks as walking. He reckoned the riders were Home Guard, all drunk as coon hunters greeting the dawn. Out searching for the Federals broken free from the Salisbury jail. Quick to trip a trigger.

At wide intervals in the valley stood big houses with white columns. They were ringed around with scattered hovels so that the valley land seemed cut up into fiefdoms. Inman looked at the lights in the big houses at night and knew he had been fight-

ing battles for such men as lived in them, and it made him sick. He just wanted to get on into the thinly settled regions of the mountains, where he hoped people would offer less impediment. So as soon as he could, Inman forsook the dangerous roads of the valley country and took to a narrow cart track that aimed northward and climbed a ridge and fell into a deep river gorge and then rose hard toward the crest of the Blue Ridge. Inman climbed part of one day and all of the next and there was still a wall of mountain reared up before him, the track rising tack and tack endlessly. It soon lifted him into a later stage of autumn, for in the heights the season was already far along, and there were as many leaves on the ground as in the trees.

Late in the afternoon, cold rain began falling, and Inman walked with little enthusiasm through the close of day into dark. Sometime well past the middle of the night, nearly given out, wet as an otter, he stumbled upon a big chestnut tree with a hollow at its base, the bark healed around it like thick lips. He crawled inside and though there was not room to find a position more comfortable than a squat, he was at least in the dry. He sat for a long time listening to the rain fall. He rolled up dead leaves into tight cylinders between thumb and forefinger, then flicked them out into the dark. Lodged there in the tree, he began to feel himself to be a sodden wraith askulk in the night, some gnome or underbridge troll. An outcast, resentful and ready to lash out from spite at any passerby. Later he dozed in and out, waiting for morning, and then eventually he fell fast asleep wedged tight into the heart of the chestnut.

He dreamed his dream of Fredericksburg, and then sometime shortly after dawn he awoke shivering and in a sour mood. He felt as if things were not as he had left them. He tried to rise from the mouth of the tree but found that all the lower reaches of his body had gone dead. He scrabbled out from the tree, pulling himself along with his arms. For all the feeling in his legs, he might have been sawed off from the waist down. It was as if nothing were there, himself in the process of becoming some

mere figment, fading from the ground up, as if the journey ahead were to be continued in the form of a veil or mist. A tissue.

The idea had its appeal. A traveling shade.

Inman stretched out on the wet ground litter and looked up through the tree limbs and their dripping leaves. The clouds were thick and grey. Blue patches of fog, fine and pale as powder, moved through the overstory of chestnut limbs and oak limbs clutching bright autumn leaves. A grouse drummed off in the woods, a deep violent sound like the beat of Inman's own heart in the moment before it shattered within his chest. He cocked his head up off the ground and listened, thinking that if this was his last day on earth he might at least be alert. But in a moment, wingbeats burst and spluttered and faded off into the woods. Inman looked down his length, and it was with mixed feelings that he found himself mostly there. He tried to wiggle his feet, and they answered the call. He rubbed his face hard with his palms and pulled his twisted clothes into place. He was wet to the skin.

He crawled to fetch his sacks from the tree and sat back against it and uncapped his water flask and took a long pull. All the food he had left in his haversack was a cup of cornmeal, so he drew together sticks to make a fire for cooking mush. He lit the tinder and blew on it until little silver orbs danced all across his vision, but the fire only flared up once and threw considerable smoke and then went out altogether.

—I'll just get up and walk on and on, Inman said, to anything that might be listening.

After he said it, though, he just sat there for a long time.

I am stronger every minute, he thought to himself. But when he sought supporting evidence, he could find none.

Inman climbed up from the wet ground and stood, wavery as a toper. He walked awhile and then, involuntarily, he bent over. His middle was wrenched with dry heaves so strong he feared some necessary part of himself might be fetched up. The wound at his neck and the newer ones at his head burned and

throbbed in conspiracy against him. He sat awhile on a rock, and then got up and walked all morning through the dim woods. The track was ill used, so coiled and knotted he could not say what its general tendency was. It aimed nowhere certain but up. The brush and bracken grew thick in the footway, and the ground seemed to be healing over, so that in some near future the way would not even remain as scar. For several miles it mostly wound its way through a forest of immense hemlocks, and the fog lay among them so thick that their green boughs were hidden. Only the black trunks were visible, rising into the low sky like old menhirs stood up by a forgotten race to memorialize the darkest events of their history.

Inman had not caught sight of a single mark of human being other than the path through this wilderness. No one to puzzle out his locale from. He felt fuddled and wayless, and the track gyred higher and higher. He still moved one foot before the other, but little more. And even this he did with no confidence that it advanced him one jot toward any mark he wished to hit.

Near midday he rounded a bend and came up on a pinched-off little scrag of a person hunkered down under a big hemlock. There was not much but its head and shoulders showing above a bed of tall bracken burnt by frost, each brown fern tip adangle with a bright drop of collected fog. From the person's posture, Inman's first thought was that he had interrupted some old coot in mid-shit. But when he drew closer he saw that it was a little old woman, squatting to bait the sweek stick of a bird trap with a suet gob. Not coot but crone, then.

Inman stopped and said, Hey, mam.

The little woman looked up briefly but waved not a hand. She stayed hunkered down, adjusting the trap in great detail, blissful-looking at her task. When she was done, she stood and walked around and around the trap, examining it until there was a perfect circle beat into the ferns. She was quite old, that much was clear, but aside from the wrinkles and wattles, her cheek skin glowed pink and fine as a girl's. She wore a man's felt hat,

and the white hair hanging below it was thin and hung to her shoulders. Her clothes—voluminous skirt and blouse both—were made of soft tanned hides, and they looked to have been cut to pattern with a clasp knife and stitched up in haste. She had a greasy cotton apron tied around her middle, the butt of a small-caliber pistol sticking out from the sash of it. Her boots appeared cobbled by a newcomer to the trade and curled up like sledge runners at the toes. Propped against a big tulip tree stood a long-barreled fowling piece, remnant from a previous century.

Inman regarded the woman a breath or two and said, You'll not catch quail one in that snare if they smell people all around it.

—I don't throw much scent, the woman said.

—Suit yourself, Inman said. What I'm wondering is whether this road goes somewhere or if it just closes down shortly.

—It turns to nothing but a foot trail in a mile or two, but it goes on and on as far as I know.

—Westward?

—Generally west. It follows the ridges. Southwest would be more accurate. Old trade trail from Indian days.

—Obliged, Inman said. He hooked a thumb under a pack strap, making ready to walk on. But rain began falling from the low sky, wide-spaced drops and heavy, falling like lead from a shot tower.

The woman held out a cupped hand and watched the water pool in it. Then she looked at Inman. There were no dressings on his wounds, and she studied him and said, Them look like bullet holes.

Inman had nothing to say to that.

—You look faint, she said. White.

—I'm fine, Inman said.

The woman looked at him more. You seem like you could eat something, she said.

—If you could fry me an egg I'd pay, Inman said.

—What? she said.

—I wondered if I might pay you to fry me a few eggs, Inman said.

—Sell you a meal? she said. Reckon not. I'm not that bad off yet. But might be I'd give you a meal. I got no eggs, though. Can't tolerate living around a chicken. No spirit to a chicken at all.

—Is your place nigh?

—Not a mile off, and you'd blithen my day if you'd take shelter and dinner at my camp.

—Then I'd be a fool to say no.

Inman followed the woman, noting that she stepped with inturned toes, a style of walking often said to be favored by Indians, though Inman had known many a Cherokee, Swimmer among them, who walked splay-footed as mergansers. They climbed to a bend and from there they walked on great slabs of rock. It seemed to Inman that they were at the lip of a cliff, for the smell of the thin air spoke of considerable height, though the fog closed off all visual check of loftiness. The rain tailed off into a thin drizzle, and then turned to hard pellets of snow that rattled against the stones. They stopped to watch it fall, but it lasted only a minute and then the fog started lifting, moving fast, sheets of fog sweeping on an updraft. Blue patches of sky opened above him, and Inman craned his head back to look at them. He reckoned it was going to be a day of just every kind of weather.

Then he looked back down and felt a rush of vertigo as the lower world was suddenly revealed between his boot toes. He was indeed at the lip of a cliff, and he took one step back. A river gorge—apparently the one he had climbed out of—stretched blue and purple beneath him, and he suspected he could spit and nearly hit where he'd walked the day before yesterday. The country around was high, broken. Inman looked about and was startled to see a great knobby mountain forming up out of the fog to the west, looming into the sky. The sun broke through a slot in the clouds, and a great band of Jacob's ladder suddenly hung in the air like a gauze curtain between Inman and the blue

mountain. On its north flank was a figuration of rocks, the profile of an immense bearded man reclining across the horizon.

—Has that mountain got a name? he said.

—Tanawha, the woman said. The Indians called it that.

Inman looked at the big grandfather mountain and then he looked beyond it to the lesser mountains as they faded off into the southwest horizon, bathed in faint smoky haze. Waves of mountains. For all the evidence the eye told, they were endless. The grey overlapping humps of the farthest peaks distinguished themselves only as slightly darker values of the pale grey air. The shapes and their ghostly appearance spoke to Inman in a way he could not clearly interpret. They graded off like the tapering of pain from the neck wound as it healed.

The woman swept an arm to where he was looking, gesturing toward two keen barbs on a distant edge of horizon.

—Table Rock, she said. Hawk's Bill. They say Indians built fires on them of a night and you could see them for a hundred miles around. She rose and started walking. The camp is just up here, she said.

They soon left the main way and entered a narrow and heavily treed cut in the mountain, a dark pocket of cove, odorous with plant rot and soggy earth. A little rill of water cut through it. The trees grew stunted and gnarled and bearded with lichen, and they all leaned hard in the same direction. Inman could imagine the place in February with a howling downhill wind driving snow sideways among the bare trees. When they came to the woman's camp, Inman saw it to be a construction that had evidently begun life nomadic but had taken root. It was a little rust-colored caravan standing in a clearing among the canted trees. The shakes of its arched roof were spotted with black mildew, green moss, grey lichen. Three ravens walked about on the roof and picked at something in the cracks. Vines of bindweed twined in the spokes of the tall wheels. The sides of the caravan were painted up with garish scenes and portraits and crude lettered epigraphs and slogans, and under the eaves hung

bunches of drying herbs, strings of red peppers, various wizened roots. There was a thin line of smoke coming from a pipe out of the roof.

The woman stopped and hollered, Hey there.

At her call, the ravens flew away cawing, and little delicate two-toned goats came from out the woods and around the side of the caravan. They were suddenly all about, two dozen or more. They walked up to inspect Inman and peered at him with upstretched necks, their slotted yellow eyes bright and smart. Inman wondered how a goat could look so much more curious and witful than a sheep when they were in many features alike. The goats clustered about him, shifting position. They shouldered one another, bleated, jingled the bells about their necks. Some in the rear rose to put their little hooves onto the backs of those before them so as to get a better view.

The woman kept on walking and Inman tried to follow her, but one big he-goat backed up a step or two, shoving lesser goats aside. The goat rared onto his back legs and fell forward, butting Inman in the thigh. He was weak from the hard walking of the past days, and his head was awhirl from lack of food, and so the goat butt drove him to his knees and then onto his back in the ground litter. The billy was colored black and brown and had long chin whiskers worn pointed in the fashion of Satan. He came and stood over Inman as if to examine his handiwork. The dizziness in Inman's head and the pain in his head swelled until he feared he might pass into a swoon. But he gathered himself and sat and pulled off his hat and slapped the goat across the face to back it off. Then he rose tottering to his feet and got his bearings. He reached out and slapped the goat again.

The woman had not even stopped in her walking, and she had disappeared around the side of the caravan. Inman and the billy and a number of the other goats followed her. He found her squatted under a lean-to roofed with pine boughs, putting kindling on the banked coals of her cook fire. When she had a blaze going, Inman went to it and put out his hands to warm. The

woman threw larger chunks of hickory on the fire and then she picked up a white enameled basin and walked some distance away and sat on the ground. A little spotted brown-and-white goat came to her and she stroked it and scratched below its neck until it folded its legs and lay down. The animal's long neck was stretched forward. The old woman scratched it close under its jaw and stroked its ears. Inman thought it a peaceful scene. He watched as she continued to scratch with her left hand and reach with her right into an apron pocket. With one motion she pulled out a short-bladed knife and cut deep into the artery below the jawline and shoved the white basin underneath to catch the leap of bright blood. The animal jerked once, then lay trembling as she continued to scratch the fur and fondle the ears. The basin filled slowly. The goat and the woman stared intently off toward the distance as if waiting for a signal.

As the goat finished its dying, Inman inspected the caravan and its markings. A border of little blue people shapes, hand in hand, danced across the bottom. Above that, in no particular order, were various portraits, some unfinished, apparently abandoned part way through. One face, its features screwed up in anguish, was labeled Job. Below that was writing in black script letters, and what it said was partially covered by a stretched goat hide, so Inman could see only a fragment, which read, At odds with his Maker. Another picture was of a man down on his hands and knees, his head cocked up to look toward a white orb above him. Sun? Moon? What? A blank look on the man's face. Beneath him the question, Are you among the lost? One of the partial faces was merely a smear of paint with eyes. Its caption was, Our personal lives are brief indeed.

Inman turned from the pictures and watched the woman work. She split the little goat from breastbone to asshole and let the bowels fall in the basin with the blood. Then she shucked the goat out of its skin, and it looked strange and long-necked and goggle-eyed. She cut it into parts. The tenderest pieces she coated with a dry rub of herbs, ground peppers, salt, a little

sugar. These she skewered on green twigs and set to roast. The other pieces she put into an iron pot with water, onions, an entire bulb of garlic, five dried red peppers, leaves of sage, and summer savory scrubbed between her palms. The pot had little legs, and she took a stick and scraped coals under it for slow cooking.

—In a little bit I'll put us some white beans in there and by dinnertime we'll have some good eating, she said.

Later, the fog gathered up again and rain dripped on the roof of the caravan. Inman sat by the tiny stove in the dim cramped quarters. The place smelled of herbs and roots, earth, woodsmoke. He had entered it through the back door and passed into what amounted to a corridor, a narrow walkway three paces long between a cabinet and table on one side, a narrow sleeping pallet on the other. You came out into a place like a room, though it compassed no more space than two grave plots. There was a little iron stove shoved tight into one corner, and the body of it was not much bigger than a lard bucket. The walls behind were sheathed with roofing tin to keep them from catching afire. The woman had two little grease lamps lit, cracked teacups filled with lard, twisted bits of rag dipped down in them for wicks. They smoked as they burned and smelled faintly of goat.

The table was piled high with paperwork, its surface a shamble of books, mostly flapped open and layered facedown one on the other, page edges foxy from the damp. Scattered about and pinned to the walls were spidery pen-and-ink sketches of plants and animals, some colored with thin washes of mute tones, each with a great deal of tiny writing around the margins, as if stories of many particulars were required to explain the spare images. Bundles of dried herbs and roots hung on strings from the ceiling, and various brown peltry of small animals lay in stacks among the books and on the floor. The wings of a nighthawk, the dark feathers spread as in flight, rested atop the highest book

pile. Thin smoke from the smoldering sprucewood fire rose through cracks in the stove door and then hung in a layer against the lath of the roof and the arched ribs of the joists.

Inman watched the woman cook. She was frying flatbread from cornmeal batter in a skillet over the one stove lid. She dipped out batter into sputtering lard and cooked piece after piece. When she had a tall stack in a plate, she folded a flap of the bread around a piece of roast goat and handed it to Inman. The bread was shiny with lard and the meat was deep reddish brown from the fire and the rub of spices.

—Thank you, Inman said.

He ate so fast that the woman just handed him a plate of meat and bread and let him fold his own. While he ate, she swapped the skillet for a pot and began making cheese from goat milk. She stirred the thickening milk, and when it was ready she separated it through a sieve of twisted willow withes, letting the whey run into a tin pot. The remaining curds she tapped out into a small oaken keeler. While she worked, Inman kept having to move his feet to keep them out of her way. They had little to say to each other, for she was busy and Inman was eating with great concentration. When she was done, she handed him a pottery beaker of warm whey the color of dishwater.

—When you got up this morning did you think before sunset you'd see cheese made? she said.

Inman thought about the question. He had long since decided there was little usefulness in speculating much on what a day will bring. It led a person to the equal errors of being either dreadful or hopeful. Neither, in his experience, served to ease your mind. But he did have to allow that cheese had not factored into this day's dawn thoughts.

The woman sat in a chair by the stove and took her shoes off. She opened the stove door and lit a briar pipe with a broomstraw. Her bare feet and the shanks of her legs sticking out to the fire were yellow and scaled like the lower parts of a chicken. She took her hat off and raked at her hair with her fingers, and it was

so thin you could see through to pink scalp whatever sight line you chose.

—You fresh from killing men in Petersburg? she said.

—Well, there's the other side to that. Seems like men have been doing their best to kill me for quite some time.

—You run off or what?

Inman pulled out his collar and showed the angry weal at his neck. Wounded and furloughed, he said.

—Airy papers to show that?

—I lost them.

—Oh, I'd wager you did, she said. She drew on her pipe and cocked her feet back on their heels so that her smutched soles took the full benefit of the fire. Inman ate the last of the bread and washed it down with a drink of the goat whey. It tasted about as he had figured it would.

—I'm out of cheese is why I'm making more, she said. Otherwise I'd offer you some right now.

—You just live in this thing all the time? Inman said.

—Got no place else. And I like to be able to move on. I don't want to stay in a place any longer than it suits me.

Inman looked at the caravan, its smallness, and the hard, narrow sleeping pallet. He thought about the vines in the wheel spokes and said, How long have you been camped here?

The woman held out her hands palm side to and looked down at her fingers and Inman thought she was about to count up years by tapping thumb to digits, but instead she turned her hands over and looked at their backs. The skin was wrinkled, crosshatched with fine lines dense as deep shadow in a steel engraving. The woman went to the narrow cabinet and opened the doors, which swung on leather hinges. She shuffled among shelves of leather-bound journals until she came upon the one sought, and then she stood and paged through it at great length.

—It would make twenty-five years if this is sixty-three, she eventually said.

—It's sixty-four, Inman said.

—Twenty-six, then.

—You've lived here twenty-six years?

The woman peered again into the journal and said, Twenty-seven come next April.

—Lord God, Inman said, looking again at the narrow pallet.

The woman set the journal, binding up, atop a pile of books on the table. I could leave any time, she said. Harness up the goats and break the wheels out of the ground and travel on. Used to be the goats drew me around as suited my fancy. I journeyed all over the world. As far north as Richmond. All the way south nearly to Charleston, and everywhere in between.

—Never married, I don't guess?

The woman pursed up her lips and worked her nose like smelling clabber. Yes, I was, she said. Might yet be, though I reckon he's long since dead. I was a little ignorant girl, and he was old. Three wives had already died on him. But he had a nice farm, and my folks next thing to sold me to him. There was a boy I had my eye on. Yellow hair. I see his smile yet about once a year in my dreams. Walked me home from a dance one time and kissed me at every turning of the road. But they put me under that old man instead. He didn't treat me like much more than a field hand. He'd buried the other three wives up on a hill under a sycamore tree, and he'd go up there sometimes by himself and sit. You've seen these old men—sixty-five, seventy—and they've gone through about five wives. Killed them from work and babies and meanness. I woke up one night laying in bed next to him and knew that's all I was: fourth in a row of five headstones. I got right up and rode out before dawn on his best horse and traded it a week later for this cart and eight goats. By now there's not enough greats to say how far these goats are distant from the first batch. And the cart's like what they say about a hundred-year-old axe, it's not had but two new heads and four new handles.

—And been on your own since? Inman said.

—Every day. What I soon learned was that a body can mainly live off goats, their milk and cheese. And their meat in

times of year when they start increasing to more than I need. I pull whatever wild green is in season. Trap birds. There's a world of food growing volunteer if you know where to look. And there's a little town about a half day's walk north. I go barter off cheese for taters, meal, lard, and the like. Brew simples from plants and sell them. Medicine. Tinctures. Salve. Conjure warts.

—A root doctor then, Inman said.

—That, and I make a few brownies now and then selling tracts.

—Tracts on what?

—There's ones on sin and salvation, she said. I sell a right smart of those. And there's one on proper diet. Says a man ought to forsake flesh and eat bread of Graham flour and root crops mostly. Another one on head knobs and how to read what they might say about a person.

She reached out to finger Inman's scalp, but he twisted his head away and said, I'll buy the one on food. When I get hungry I can just read it. He pulled from his pocket a wad of various scrip.

—I take nothing but specie, she said. Three cent.

Inman jingled around in his pockets until he came up with it.

The woman stepped to a cabinet and took down a yellow pamphlet and handed it to him.

—It says on the front it will change your life if you follow it, she said. But I'm making no claims.

Inman looked through the pamphlet. It was poorly printed on coarse grey paper. There were headings like The Potato: Food of the Gods. The Collard: Tonic for the Spirit. Graham Flour: Pathway to the More Abundant Life.

That last phrase caught Inman's eye. He said it aloud. Pathway to the More Abundant Life.

—It's what many seek, the woman said. But I'm not sure a sack of flour will set your foot on it.

—Yes, Inman said. Abundance did seem, in his experience, to be an elusive thing. Unless you counted plenty of hardship.

There was ample of that. But abundance of something a man might want was a different matter.

—Scarcity's much more the general bearing of life, is the way I see it, the woman said.

—Yes, Inman said.

The woman leaned to the stove and knocked the last of the fire out of her pipe and put it to her mouth and blew through it until it nearly whistled. She drew a tobacco pouch from an apron pocket and refilled the pipe, tamping the tobacco down hard with a callused thumb. She lit a straw in the stove and held it to the pipe and drew until it was going to her satisfaction.

—How do you come to have that big red wound and them two little new ones? she said.

—I took the neck wound out by Globe Tavern last summer.

—A dramshop knifing?

—A battle. Below Petersburg.

—Federals shot you, then?

—They were making to take the Weldon rail line and we aimed to stop them. We went at it all that afternoon, fighting in pine thickets, broom grass, old fields, all sorts of a place. Awful flat scrubby country. It was hot and we sweated so bad we could reach down and roll lather off our pant legs with our hands.

—You've thought a number of times, I guess, that if the ball had struck a thumb's width different you'd be dead? It near to took your head off as it is.

—Yes.

—It looks like it could bust open yet.

—It feels about like it could.

—And the new ones, how'd you come by them?

—The usual way. Got shot, Inman said.

—Federals?

—No. The other bunch.

The woman waved her hand through the tobacco smoke like she couldn't be troubled with the confusing details of his wounds. She said, Well, these new ones're not as bad. When

they heal up, the hair'll cover them and it'll be just you and your sweetheart to know. She'll feel a little welt when she runs her fingers through your hair. What I want to know is, was it worth it, all that fighting for the big man's nigger?

—That's not the way I saw it.

—What's the other way? she said. I've traveled a fair bit in those low counties. Nigger-owning makes the rich man proud and ugly and it makes the poor man mean. It's a curse laid on the land. We've lit a fire and now it's burning us down. God is going to liberate niggers, and fighting to prevent it is against God. Did you own any?

—No. Not hardly anybody I knew did.

—Then what stirred you up enough for fighting and dying?

—Four years ago I maybe could have told you. Now I don't know. I've had all of it I want, though.

—That's lacking some as an answer.

—I reckon many of us fought to drive off invaders. One man I knew had been north to the big cities, and he said it was every feature of such places that we were fighting to prevent. All I know is anyone thinking the Federals are willing to die to set loose slaves has got an overly merciful view of mankind.

—With all those fine reasons for fighting, thing I want to know is why did you run off?

—Furloughed.

—Yes, she said, and she reared back and cackled as if a joke had been cracked. Man on furlough, she said. Nary papers, though. Had them stole off him.

—Lost them.

She stopped laughing and looked at Inman. She said, Listen here, I lack all affiliation. I don't care no more than spitting in that fire that you've run off.

And to make her point she spat a dark gob of matter, arcing it expertly into the open stove door. She looked back at Inman and said, It's dangerous for you, is all.

He looked her in the eyes and was surprised to find that they

were wells of kindness despite all her hard talk. Not a soul he had met in some time drew him out as this goatwoman did, and so he told her what was in his heart. The shame he felt now to think of his zeal in sixty-one to go off and fight the downtrodden mill workers of the Federal army, men so ignorant it took many lessons to convince them to load their cartridges ball foremost. These were the foes, so numberless that not even their own government put much value to them. They just ran them at you for years on end, and there seemed no shortage. You could kill them down until you grew heartsick and they would still keep ranking up to march southward.

Then he told her how this very morning he had found a late-bearing bush of huckleberries, dusty blue on their sunward faces, still green on their shady back halves. How he had picked and eaten them for breakfast and watched as a cloud of passenger pigeons darked out the sun momentarily as they passed over, going to wherever they wintered in the remote south. At least that much remained unchanged, he had thought, berries ripening and birds flying. He said he had seen not much other than change for four years, and he guessed the promise of it was part of what made up the war frenzy in the early days. The powerful draw of new faces, new places, new lives. And new laws whereunder you might kill all you wanted and not be jailed, but rather be decorated. Men talked of war as if they committed it to preserve what they had and what they believed. But Inman now guessed it was boredom with the repetition of the daily rounds that had made them take up weapons. The endless arc of the sun, wheel of seasons. War took a man out of that circle of regular life and made a season of its own, not much dependent on anything else. He had not been immune to its pull. But sooner or later you get awful tired and just plain sick of watching people killing one another for every kind of reason at all, using whatever implements fall to hand. So that morning he had looked at the berries and the birds and had felt cheered by them, happy they had

waited for him to come to his senses, even though he feared himself deeply at variance with such elements of the harmonious.

The woman thought about what he had said, and then she waved her pipe stem at his head and neck. Them hurting bad still? she said.

—They seem not to want to quit.

—Looks like it. Red as a damn winesap. But I can do something for you there. That's within my realm of power.

She got up and went to the cabinet and took out a basketful of withered poppies and set about making laudanum. She picked out the poppy heads one by one, pierced the capsules with a sewing needle and then dropped them into a small glazed crock and set it near the stove for the opium to sweat out.

—Before long this will be about right. I'll take and add me a little corn liquor and sugar to it. Makes it go down better. Let it sit and it gets thick. It's good for any kind of pain—sore joints, headaches, any hurt. If you can't sleep, just have a drink of it and stretch out in the bed and pretty soon you'll know no more.

She went back to the cabinet and took out a little narrow-mouth crock and ran a finger down in it. She daubed at Inman's neck and at his head wounds with what looked like black axle grease but smelled of bitter herbs and roots. He jerked when her finger first touched his wounds.

—That's just pain, she said. It goes eventually. And when it's gone, there's no lasting memory. Not the worst of it, anyway. It fades. Our minds aren't made to hold on to the particulars of pain the way we do bliss. It's a gift God gives us, a sign of His care for us.

Inman first thought to argue and then he thought he'd keep silent and let her think what she wished if it gave her comfort, no matter how filled with error her logic. But then his mouth just started working and he said, I wouldn't want to puzzle too long about the why of pain nor the frame of mind somebody would be in to make up a thing like it to begin with.

The old woman looked at the fire in the stove door, and then she looked at her forefinger, greasy from the medicine. She rubbed her thumb over it three times rapidly, and then she twisted it in her apron hem to wipe it off. She dismissed her hand from her thoughts and it fell to rest at her side. She said, You get to be my age, just recollecting pleasures long ago is pain enough.

She stoppered the salve crock with a cob and put it in Inman's coat pocket. Take it with you, she said. Keep it rubbed on thick until it's gone, but keep your collar off it. It don't wash out. Then she reached into a wide goat-hide purse and pulled out a handful of great lozenges made of rolled and bound herbs, like fat little sections of cheroot. She heaped them into Inman's hand.

—Swallow one of these a day. Starting now.

Inman put them in his pocket, saving one. He put it in his mouth and tried to swallow. It seemed to swell. A great soggy bolus like a chaw of tobacco. It would not go down, and it threw off a taste like old socks. Inman's eyes watered. He gagged and grabbed for his beaker of whey and drank it down.

Sometime in the evening they ate the stew of white beans and the pieces of the little goat. They sat side by side under the brush arbor and listened to the faint rain come down in the woods. Inman ate three bowlsful and then they both had little earthen cups of laudanum and fed the fire and talked. To Inman's surprise, he found himself telling about Ada. He described her character and her person item by item and said the verdict he had come to at the hospital was that he loved her and wished to marry her, though he realized marriage implied some faith in a theoretical future, a projection of paired lines running forward through time, drawing nearer and nearer to one another until they became one line. It was a doctrine he could not entirely credit. Nor was he at all sure Ada would find his offer welcome, not from a man galled in body and mind as he had become. He concluded by saying that though Ada was somewhat thistleish in comportment, she was, by his way of thinking,

very beautiful. Her eyes were down-turned and set slightly asymmetrically in her head, and it gave her always a sad expression which in his view only served to point up her beauty.

The woman looked as if she thought Inman spoke the greatest foolishness she had ever heard. She pointed her pipe stem at him and said, You listen. Marrying a woman for her beauty makes no more sense than eating a bird for its singing. But it's a common mistake nonetheless.

They sat for a while without talking, just sipping the laudanum. It was sweet and had thickened up so that it was not much runnier than sorghum, nor much clearer. It tasted some like metheglin, though without the taste of honey, and it clung to the cup with such determination that Inman found himself licking it out. The rain came down harder and a few drops made their way through the thatching of the arbor and hissed in the fire. It was a lonesome sound, the rain and the fire and nothing else. Inman tried to picture himself living similarly hermetic in just such a stark and lonesome refuge on Cold Mountain. Build a cabin on a misty frag of rock and go for months without seeing another of his kind. A life just as pure and apart as the goatwoman's seemed to be. It was a powerful vision, and yet in his mind he saw himself hating every minute of it, his days poisoned by lonesomeness and longing.

—It must get cold in winter up here, Inman said.

—Cold enough. In the chillest months I keep the fire hot and the blankets deep, and my biggest concern is that my ink and watercolors not freeze while I work at the desk. There are days so cold I sit with a cup of water between my legs to warm it. And still when I daub a wet brush in color, the bristles freeze before I can touch the tip to paper.

—What is it you do in those books? Inman said.

—I make a record, the woman said. Draw pictures and write.

—About what?

—Everything. The goats. Plants. Weather. I keep track of

what everything's up to. It can take up all your time just marking down what happens. Miss a day and you get behind and might never catch back up.

—How did you learn to write and read and draw? Inman asked.

—Same way you did. Somebody taught me.

—And you've spent your life this way?

—So far I have. I'm not dead yet.

—Do you not get lonesome living here? Inman said.

—Now and again, maybe. But there's plenty of work and the doing of it keeps me from worrying too much.

—What if you get sick up here by yourself? Inman said.

—I've got my herbs.

—And if you die?

The woman said that living with such great scope of privacy had some disadvantages. She knew she could not expect help under any circumstances, nor did she much want to live past the point where she could fend for herself, though she calculated that date still to be writ on a fairly distant calendar. Knowing she was likely to die alone and lie unburied did not trouble her a whit. When she felt death coming, she planned to stretch out at the top of the rock cliff and let the ravens peck her apart and carry her away.

—It's that or worms, she said. Of the two I'd as soon have ravens carry me off on their black wings.

The rain began falling harder yet, dripping fast through the roofing of the arbor. They called the evening concluded, and Inman crawled under the caravan and rolled up in his blankets and slept. When he woke a day had passed and night was again coming on. A raven sat perched on a spoke looking at him. Inman got up and daubed his wounds with the salve and ate his herb medicines and took another draught of laudanum and liquor. The woman fixed him more of the bean and goat stew, and while he ate they sat together on the caravan steps. The woman told a long and maundering tale of a goat-trading mis-

sion she had made down as far as the capital city once. She had sold a half dozen goats to a man. Had the money in her hand when she remembered that she wanted to take the bells back with her. The man declined, saying the deal was completed. She said the bells had never been part of the deal, but he called the dogs on her and ran her off. Late that night she had gone back with a knife and cut the leather collars and gotten the bells and had, as she put it, walked out through the streets of the capital just a-cussing.

Inman felt very foggy throughout the story, for he could feel the medicines working in him, but when she was done he reached over and patted the back of her etched and spotted hand and said, The heroine of the goat bells.

Inman slept again. When he awoke it was dark and no longer raining, but cold. The goats had crowded around him to get warm and their smell was so sharp as to about make his eyes water. He had no idea if it was the same dark he had fallen asleep to or whether a day had intervened. Light from a grease lamp fell in threads through cracks in the caravan floor, and so Inman crawled out and stood in the wet leaves on the ground. There was a sherd of moon partway up the eastern sky, and the stars all stood in their expected places and looked chill and brittle. At the ridge above the cove, an enormous pike of bare rock stood black against the sky like a picket watching for any siege the heavens might throw down. The strong urge to walk came over Inman. He went and knocked at the door and waited for the old woman to let him in, but there was no answer. Inman opened the door and stepped inside and found the place empty. He looked about the desk at the papers. He picked up a journal and opened it to a drawing of goats. They had eyes and feet on them like people, and the sentences of the entry below were hard to parse, but they seemed to contrast the behavior of certain goats on cold days to their behavior on hot. Inman leafed through farther and found pictures of plants and then more pictures of goats in every imaginable attitude, all done in a mute

and limited palette, as if she painted with clothes dye. Inman read the stories that went with the pictures, and they told of what the goats ate and how they acted toward each other and what moods seized them from day to day. It seemed to Inman that the woman's aim was to list in every detail the habits of their culture.

This would be one way to live, Inman thought, a hermit among the clouds. The contentious world but a fading memory. Mind turned only toward God's finer productions. But the more he studied the journal, the more he wondered how it must be for the woman to count back through the decades, figuring how many years had passed since some event in her youth—the romance with the yellow-haired farmboy she had wanted to marry instead of the old man, an autumn day of particular glory, a dance that evening after the harvest, later out on the porch an amber moon rising over the trees, kissing the boy with her lips parted while inside fiddlers played a piece of ancient music to which she had attached an unreasonable enthusiasm. So many years gone between then and now that even the bare number would seem unutterably sad even without some sweet attendant memory.

Inman looked about and found there was not a scrap of mirror in the caravan, and he therefore assumed the woman must go about her grooming by feel. Did she even know her own recent countenance? Long hair as pale and fine as cobwebs, hide sagged and puckered and folded about her eyes and jowls, brindled across her brow, bristles growing from her ears. Only her cheeks pink, the discs in her eyes still bright and blue. If you held a glass up to her would she wrench back in surprise and fright at the relic looking out, her mind still grasping a picture of herself in an incarnation some decades previous? A person might get to such a state of mind, living so remote.

Inman waited a long time for the goatwoman to come back. Dawn rose, and he blew out the lamp and broke some sticks to put in the little stove. He wanted to get on, but he did not wish

to leave without thanking her. She did not return until the morning was far advanced. She walked through the door with a brace of rabbits hanging limp from her grip on their hind legs.

—I need to be going, Inman said. I just wanted to see if I could pay you for the food and medicine.

—You could try, the woman said. But I wouldn't take it.

—Well, thank you, Inman said.

—Look here, the woman said. If I had a boy, I'd tell him the same as I'm telling you. Watch yourself.

—I will, Inman said.

He turned to walk out of the caravan, but she stopped him. She said, Here, take this with you, and she handed him a square of paper on which was drawn in great detail the globular blue-purple berry cluster of the carrion flower plant in autumn.

freewill savages

At the first gesture of dawn, Ruby was up and out, on her way down to the house to fire up the stove and put on a pot of grits and fry up a few eggs. It was barely light enough to see, and the air was thick with the fog that pooled for an hour or two along the bottom of Black Cove on most mornings in all seasons but winter. But as she neared the house she could make out a man in a dark suit of clothes standing by the corncrib. She walked straight to the kitchen porch and went inside and took the shotgun from where it rested, charged, in the crotch of two forked limbs nailed over the doorframe. She pulled back both hammers and walked briskly toward the crib.

The man wore a big grey slouch hat pulled low on his brow, and his head was tipped down. He was leaned with his shoulder to the crib wall, one leg crossed over the other and cocked up on its toe. Casual as a traveler propped against a roadside tree waiting for a stage to come by, whiling away the time absorbed in his own thoughts.

Ruby could see, even in the poor light, that the man was dressed in clothes of the finest material and making. And his

boots, though somewhat scuffed, were more fit for a squire than a corn thief. Only one thing argued against the man's being utterly relaxed in his current posture. His right arm was entirely inside the hole in the chinking of the crib.

Ruby walked right up to him, the shotgun held at a low angle but nevertheless aimed at about his knees. She was ready to dress him down good for corn thieving, but when she neared the man he tipped his head back to get the hat brim out of his line of sight. He looked at Ruby and grinned and said, They hell fire.

—So you're not dead? Ruby said.

—Not yet, said Stobrod. Set your daddy loose.

Ruby propped the shotgun against the side of the crib and unlocked the door and went inside. She unstaked the trap from the dirt floor and pried open the jaws from around Stobrod's hand and walked back outside. Despite the padding, after he had withdrawn his arm from out the hole in the chinking, Stobrod stood and dripped blood from a cut to his wrist where the skin was thin over the bones. His forearm was bruised blue all around it. He rubbed it with his good hand. He took out a kerchief of fine linen and removed his hat and wiped at his forehead and neck.

—Long night a-standing here trapped, he said.

—No doubt, Ruby said. She looked him over. He had changed some. He seemed such an old man, standing there before her. His hair half gone from his head, whiskers grizzled. He had not filled out any, though. He was still just a little withy man. A quilting frame had more flesh to it.

—How old are you now? she said.

He stood moving his mouth a little as he tried to do the figures in his mind.

—Maybe forty-five, he said eventually.

—Forty-five, Ruby said.

—About.

—You don't look it.

—Thankee.

—I meant the other way.

—Oh.

—Anybody else, Ruby said, I'd ask why you been dipping our corn when you don't look hurting for money. But I know you better than that. You're going around getting a little here and a little there to run a batch of liquor. And you took that suit off somebody or won it in a card game.

—Something like.

—You've run off from the fighting, no doubt.

—I was owed a furlough, being a hero as I was.

—You?

—Every battle I was in, I led the charge, Stobrod said.

—I've heard it told that the officers like to run the greatest shitheels to the fore, said Ruby. They get shut of them quicker that way.

Then, before Stobrod could answer, she said, You come on with me. She picked up the shotgun and went to the house. She told him to sit on the porch steps and wait. Inside, she lit the fire and put on a pot to make coffee. She mixed biscuit dough and rattled about putting breakfast together. Biscuits, grits, and eggs. A few strips of fried side meat.

Ada came down and sat in her chair by the window and drank coffee, glum as usual in the early morning.

—We finally caught something in that trap, Ruby said.

—It's about time. What was it?

—My daddy. He's out on the porch now, Ruby said. She was stirring a pan of white gravy made from the drippings of the side meat.

—Pardon?

—Stobrod. He's made it home from the war. But alive or dead, he's of little matter to me. A plate of breakfast and then we'll send him on his way.

Ada rose and looked out the door at Stobrod's thin back where he sat humped up on the bottom step. He held his left hand out before him, and he hummed to himself, and the fingers

were working, tapping against the heel of his hand like a man doing sums.

—You might have asked him in, Ada said when she had returned to her chair.

—He can wait out there.

When breakfast was cooked, Ruby carried his plate to the table under the pear tree. She and Ada took their breakfast in the dining room, and they could see from the window that Stobrod ate quickly and with urgency, his hat brim bobbing in time with his chewing. He stopped just short of picking up his plate and licking the last skim of grease from it.

—He could have eaten in here, Ada said.

—That's where I draw the line, Ruby said.

She went outside to collect his plate.

—Have you got somewhere to go? Ruby said to Stobrod.

Stobrod told her that he did indeed have a home and a society of sorts, for he had fallen in with a collection of heavily armed outliers. They lived in a deep cave of the mountain like freewill savages. All they wished to do was hunt and eat and lay up all night drunk, making music.

—Well, I guess that suits you, Ruby said. Your aim in life always was to dance all night with a bottle in your hand. Now I've fed you. You can get on out of here. We've got nothing else for you. You go dipping our corn again, I might put a barrel of shot into you, and I don't load salt.

She flapped her hands at him as if shooing cattle, and he walked off at a saunter, hands in his pockets, taking a course toward Cold Mountain.

The day that followed was warm and brilliant and dry. There had been nothing but one faint morning rain so far that month, and the leaves that had fallen and those yet on the trees were crisp as cold cracklings. They rattled aloft in the breeze and underfoot as Ruby and Ada walked down to the barn to see how the tobacco

was drying. The broad leaves had been tied together at their stem ends and they hung in rows upside down from poles strung underneath the shelter of the barn's cantilevered ends. There was something human and female and ominous in their flared hanging shapes, the bunched leaves fanning out like old yellowed cotton skirts. Ruby walked among them, touching the leaves, rubbing them between her fingers. She pronounced everything in fine order, owing to the favorably dry weather and to the care with which the tobacco was planted and harvested in accord with the signs. They would soon be able to soak it in molasses water and twist it into plugs and use it for trade.

Ruby then proposed that they take a rest in the hayloft, a fine place for a sit-down, she said. She climbed the ladder and sat spraddle-legged in the wide hay door and dangled her feet into the open space below in a way that no other grown woman Ada knew would have done.

Ada at first hesitated to join her. She sat in the hay with her legs under her and her skirts composed. Ruby looked at her with some amusement, as if to say, I can do this because I never have been proper, and you can do it because you have recently quit being so. Ada went and sat at the hay door too. They lounged and chewed on pieces of hay and swung their legs like boys. The big door framed the view uphill to the house and beyond, across the upper fields, to Cold Mountain, which looked close and sharp-edged in the dry air, all mottled with the colors of autumn. The house looked pert, unsmudged white. A feather of blue smoke rose straight up from the black kitchen pipe. Then a breeze swept down the cove and swirled it away.

—You say you want to get to know the running of this land, Ruby said.

—Yes, Ada said.

Ruby rose and knelt behind Ada and cupped her hands over Ada's eyes.

—Listen, Ruby said. Her hands were warm and rough over Ada's face. They smelled of hay, tobacco leaves, flour, and some-

thing deeper, a clean animal smell. Ada felt their thin bones against her fluttering eyes.

—What do you hear? Ruby said.

Ada heard the sound of wind in the trees, the dry rattle of their late leaves. She said as much.

—Trees, Ruby said contemptuously, as if she had expected just such a foolish answer. Just general trees is all? You've got a long way to go.

She removed her hands and took her seat again and said nothing more on the topic, leaving Ada to conclude that what she meant was that this is a particular world. Until Ada could listen and at the bare minimum tell the sound of poplar from oak at this time of year when it is easiest to do, she had not even started to know the place.

Late that afternoon, despite the warmth, the light fell brittle and blue and announced clearly in its slant that the year was circling toward its close. This was surely one of the last of the warm dry days, and in its honor Ada and Ruby decided to take supper outdoors at the table under the pear tree. They roasted a venison tenderloin that Esco had brought by. Fried a skillet of potatoes and onions, and drizzled bacon drippings over some late lettuce to wilt it. They had brushed the brown leaves from the table and were just setting places for the two of them when Stobrod appeared from out the woods. He carried a tow sack, and he came and took a seat at the table as if he carried an invitation in his coat pocket.

—You say the word, I'll run him off again, Ruby said to Ada.

Ada said, We have plenty.

During the meal Ruby refused to speak, and Stobrod engaged Ada in talk of the war. He wished it would end so he could come down off the mountain but feared that it would drag on and that hard times would bear down upon everyone. Ada heard herself agree, but as she looked about her cove in the blue falling light, hard times seemed far away.

When supper was done, Stobrod took his sack off the

ground and drew from it a fiddle and set it across his knees. It was of novel design, for where the scroll would normally be was instead the whittled head of a great serpent curled back against the neck, detailed right down to the scales and the slit pupils of the eyes. It was clear Stobrod was proud as could be of it, and he had a right, for though the fiddle was far from perfect, he had fashioned it himself during the months of living fugitive. His previous instrument had been stolen from him during his trip home, and so, lacking a model, he had shaped the new one from memory of a fiddle's proportions, and it therefore looked like a rare artifact from some primitive period of instrument-making.

He turned it front and back so they could admire its faces, and he told them the story of its creation. He had spent weeks tramping the ridges to cut spruce and maple and boxwood, and when they were cured he sat for hours on end knifing out fiddle parts. He cut forms and clamps of his own devising. Boiled the wood of the side pieces soft and shaped them so that when they cooled and dried they set to the forms in smooth curves that would not come unsprung. He carved the tailpiece and bridge and fingerboard freehand. Boiled down deer hooves for glue. Augered out holes for the tuning pegs, pieced it all together, and let it dry. Then, he set the sound post with aid of a wire, dyed the boxwood fingerboard dark with the juice of poke berries, and sat for hours carving the viper's head curled over against its body. Finally, he stole a little tin of varnish from a man's toolshed in the dark of night and put the finish on it. Then he strung it up and tuned it. Even went out one night and trimmed a horse's tail to hair his bow.

He then looked upon his work and thought, I've almost got my music now, for he had but one job left, the killing of a snake. For some time, he had speculated that putting the tailpiece to a rattlesnake inside the instrument would work a vast improvement on the sound, would give it a sizz and knell like no other. The greater the number of rattles the better, was his thinking on the matter. He described it along the lines of a quest. The musi-

cal improvement he was seeking would come as likely from the mystic discipline of getting the rattles as from their actual function within the fiddle.

To that end, he had roamed Cold Mountain. He knew that in the first cool days of autumn the snakes were moving in anticipation of winter, looking for dens. He killed a number of fair-sized rattlers, but once he had them dead, their little tails seemed pitifully insufficient. Finally, after climbing high, up where the black balsams grow, he ran upon a great old timber rattler, laid out on a flat slate to sun. It was not enormous in length, for they do not get terribly long, but it was stouter through the body than the fat part of a man's arm. The markings on its back had all run together until it was black as a blacksnake, almost. It had grown a set of rattles as long as Stobrod's index finger. In telling this to Ada he held out the finger and then with the thumbnail of the other hand he marked off a place right at the third knuckle. He said, They was that long. And he snicked the nail repeatedly across the dry skin.

Stobrod had walked up near the stone and said to the snake, Hey, I aim to take them rattles. The big snake had a head like a fist, and it raised it up off the stone and evaluated Stobrod through slitted yellow eyes. It shifted into a part coil, declaring it would rather fight than move. The snake quivered its tail a moment, warming up. Then it went to rattling with a screech so dreadful as to make one's thinking seize up in all its units.

Stobrod took a step back as he was intended by nature to do. But he wanted those rattles. He drew out his pocketknife and cut a forked stick about four feet long and went back to the snake, which had not moved and seemed to relish the prospect of a contest. Stobrod stood about arm's length outside what he judged the striking range to be. The snake perked up, raised its head farther from the ground. Stobrod urged it to strike.

Whooh! he said, shaking the stick in its face.

The snake rattled on, unfazed.

Waah! Stobrod said, poking at it with the fork. The rattling

diminished a bit in volume and pitch as the snake shifted its coils. Then it fell silent, as if from boredom.

The snake clearly required an offering of more substance. Stobrod eased forward, then crouched. He put the knife between his teeth and held the split sapling in his right hand, poised on high. He waved his left hand fast, well within striking distance of the snake. It lunged, parallel to the ground. Its jaws unhinged, fangs down. The pink of its mouth looked big as the palm of an opened hand. It missed.

Stobrod jabbed with the sapling and trapped the head against the rock. Moving fast he set his foot to the back of the snake's head. He grabbed the thrashing tail. Drew his knife from his mouth. Cut the rattles off clean, right at the buttons. Jumped back the way a cat will do when startled. The snake writhed, collected itself again into striking stance. It tried to rattle, though it had now but a bleeding stub.

—Live on if you care to, Stobrod had said, and he walked away shaking the rattles. He believed that from then on, every note he bowed would have a new voice. In it somewhere underneath would be the dire keen of snake warning.

After he had finished telling Ruby and Ada of the fiddle's creation, Stobrod sat and looked at it as if it were a thing of wonder. He took the fiddle up and held it before them as an exhibit, part of a demonstration intended to show that he was now another man in some regards than the one that went off to fight. Something about the war had made him and his music a whole different thing, he claimed.

Ruby remained a skeptic. She said, Before the war you never showed more interest in fiddling than would be required to get a free drink for playing at a dance.

—Some say I now fiddle like a man wild with fever, Stobrod said in his own defense.

The revision in him had come unexpected, he said. It happened near Richmond in the month of January 1862. The army he was with had set up winter quarters. One day a man had

come into camp asking for a fiddler and was sent to Stobrod. The man said that his daughter, a girl of fifteen, had, in kindling the morning fire, done as she often did and poured coal oil down onto the fresh kindling. This morning, though, it had hit live coals and gone off in her face a moment after she had set the stove lid back into its place. The circle of cast iron had been blown with great force into her head, and the beam of fire that had come out of the opening had charred her flesh near to the bone. She was dying. That was certain. But she had come to consciousness after an hour or two, and when asked what might ease her passing, she answered that fiddle music would do fine.

Stobrod took up his instrument and followed the man to his house, an hour's walk away. In the bedroom he found the family sitting around the perimeter of the room. The burned girl was propped up on pillows. Her hair was in patches and her face looked like a skinned coon. The pillowcase was damp around her head where her raw hide had oozed. There was a deep gash above her ear where the stove lid had struck. The wound had stopped bleeding but had not even turned brown yet. She looked Stobrod up and down and the whites of her eyes were startling against the rawness of her skin. Play me something, she said.

Stobrod sat in a straight chair at the bedside and began tuning. He twiddled so long at the pegs that the girl said, You best get to it if you aim to play me out.

Stobrod took a turn at Peas in the Pot, and then at Sally Ann, and so on through his entire repertoire of six tunes. They were all dance figures, and even Stobrod knew them to be in poor keeping with the occasion, so he did his best to slow them down, but they refused to be somber, no matter how sluggish the tempo. When he was done the girl had not yet died.

—Play me another, she said.

—I don't know no more, Stobrod said.

—That's pitiful, the girl said. What kind of a fiddler are you?

—Bum and shoddy, he said.

That brought a quick smile to the girl's face, but the pain of

it showed in her eyes and brought the corners of her mouth down quick.

—Make me up a tune then, she said.

Stobrod marveled at such a strange request. It had never entered his mind to give composition a try.

—I don't believe I could, he said.

—Why not? Have you never tackled it before?

—No.

—Best go to it, she said. Time's short.

He sat thinking for a minute. He plucked the strings and retuned. He set the fiddle to his neck and struck the bow to it and was himself surprised by the sounds that issued. The melody he spun out was slow and halting, and it found its mood mainly through drones and double stops. He could not have put a name to it, but the tune was in the frightening and awful Phrygian mode, and when the girl's mother heard it she burst into tears and ran from her chair out into the hall.

When he was done the girl looked at Stobrod and said, Now that was fine.

—It wasn't neither, he said modestly.

—Was, the girl said. She turned her face away and her breathing grew wheezy and wet.

The girl's father came to Stobrod and took him by the elbow and led him down to the kitchen. He sat him at the table and poured Stobrod a cup of milk and went back up the steps. By the time the cup was empty, the man had returned.

—She's gone, he said. He took a Federal dollar from his pocket and pressed it into Stobrod's hand. You eased her way some up there, he said.

Stobrod put the dollar in his shirt pocket and left. Time and again during the walk back to camp he stopped and looked at his fiddle as if for the first time. He had never before thought of trying to improve his playing, but now it seemed worthwhile to go at every tune as if all within earshot had been recently set afire.

The music he had made up for the girl was a thing he had

played every day since. He never tired of it and, in fact, believed the tune to be so inexhaustible that he could play it every day for the rest of his life, learning something new each time. His fingers had stopped the strings and his arm had drawn the bow in the shape of the tune so many times by now that he no longer thought about the playing. The notes just happened effortlessly. The tune had become a thing unto itself, a habit that served to give order and meaning to a day's end, as some might pray and others double-check the latch on the door and yet others take a drink when night has fallen.

From that day of the burning on, music came more and more into his mind. The war just didn't engage him anymore. He became casual in his attendance. And he was little missed. He came to prefer spending as much of his time as he could manage in the dim regions of Richmond's taverns, rank places that smelled of unwashed bodies, spilled liquor, cheap perfume, and unemptied chamber pots. In truth, he had throughout the war spent as much time as he could afford in such places, but the difference now was that his main interest became the musical niggers that often played for the customers. Many a night Stobrod wandered from place to place until he found a fellow working at a stringed instrument with authority, some genius of the guitar or banjo. Then he'd take out his fiddle and play until dawn, and every time he did, he learned something new.

He first spent his attention on matters of tuning and fingering and phrasing. Then he began listening to the words of the songs the niggers sang, admiring how they chanted out every desire and fear in their lives as clear and proud as could be. And he soon had a growing feeling that he was learning things about himself that had never sifted into his thinking before. One thing he discovered with a great deal of astonishment was that music held more for him than just pleasure. There was meat to it. The grouping of sounds, their forms in the air as they rang out and faded, said something comforting to him about the rule of creation. What the music said was that there is a right way for things

to be ordered so that life might not always be just tangle and drift but have a shape, an aim. It was a powerful argument against the notion that things just happen. By now he knew nine hundred fiddle tunes, some hundred of them being his own compositions.

Ruby expressed doubt at the figure, pointing out that his two hands of fingers had always served his entire need for numerals in all other features of life.

—He's never had enough of anything to have to count past ten, she said.

—Nine hundred tunes, Stobrod said.

—Well, play one, Ruby said.

Stobrod sat and thought a minute, and then he ran his thumb down the strings and twisted a peg and tried them again and twisted other pegs until he had achieved an exotic tuning with the E string run down about three frets so that it matched up with the third note on the A string.

—I've never stopped to name this one, he said. But I reckon you could call it Green-Eyed Girl.

When he set the bow to the new fiddle, the tone was startling in its clarity, sharp and pure, and the redundancy in the tuning led to curious and dissonant harmonic effects. The tune was slow and modal, but demanding in its rhythm and of considerable range. More than that, its melody constantly pressed upon you the somber notion that it was a passing thing, here and gone, unfixable. Yearning was its main theme.

Ada and Ruby watched amazed as Stobrod spun out the music. He had apparently, at least for this forlorn piece, forsaken the short choppy bow strokes of all known fiddlers and was long-bowing notes of great sweetness and stridency. It was music the like of which Ruby had never heard. Nor, for that matter, had Ada. His playing was easy as a man drawing breath, yet with utter conviction in its centrality to a life worth claiming.

When Stobrod finished and took the fiddle from under his grey-stubbled chin, there was a long silence in which the voices

of peepers down by the creek sounded exceptionally sad and hopeful in the face of the coming winter. He looked at Ruby as if prepared for harsh evaluation. Ada looked at her too, and the expression on Ruby's face said it would take more than a tale and a fiddle tune to soften her heart toward him. She did not address him but turned to Ada and said, Might queer that this far on in life he's finally found the only tool he's ever shown any skill at working. A man so sorry he got his nickname from being beat half to death with a stob after he was caught stealing a ham.

To Ada, though, it seemed akin to miracle that Stobrod, of all people, should offer himself up as proof positive that no matter what a waste one has made of one's life, it is ever possible to find some path to redemption, however partial.

bride bed full of blood

Inman wandered the mountains for days, lost and befogged through a stretch of wretched weather. It seemed to rain from about the new moon to the full, though with the sky blanked out who could tell, unless you thought to keep count of days starting when the first drop fell. Inman had not seen sun, moon, or stars for at least a week and would not have been surprised to find that for the entire time he had walked in circles or in geometric figures more complex but equally directionless. To keep his course straight, he tried picking out points directly ahead of him, a certain tree or rock, to make for. He kept on at this until the thought occurred to him that the points he picked might all link up to make a big circle, and there seemed little to recommend walking in big ones to walking in little. So he went blindly through the fog, taking whatever tack he felt at that moment to be west, and tried to make himself content with just motion.

He had used the goatwoman's medicine until it was gone, and in short order the wounds at his head had become little puckered scars and the place at his neck was a hard silver slash. The pain settled into a distant noise, like living by a river, one

that he figured he could listen to indefinitely. But his thoughts had not healed with like speed.

His haversack became empty of food. At first he hunted, but the high balsam woods seemed abandoned by game. Then he tried grabbling for crawfish to boil, but found that he worked for hours to catch enough to fill the crown of his hat, and then after eating them he felt he had gained little by it. He stripped the bark off an elm sapling and chewed it and then ate the cap to a ruby-colored bolete as big across as a frying pan. Fifteen minutes later he was again ravenous. He soon fell simply to drinking creek water out of cupped hands and pulling wild cress from stream margins.

He found himself one afternoon crawling on the mossy ground of the creekside, grazing at the water edge like a beast of the wild, his head wet to the ears, the sharp taste of cress in his mouth and no idea whatsoever in his mind. He looked down into a pool and caught sight of his visage looking up at him, wavery and sinister, and he immediately frabbled his fingers in the water to break up the image for he had no desire to look upon himself.

God, if I could sprout wings and fly, he thought. I would be gone from this place, my great wings bearing me up and out, long feathers hissing in the wind. The world would unfurl below me like a bright picture on a scroll of paper and there would be nothing holding me to ground. The watercourses and hills passing under me effortless and simple. And me just rising and rising till I was but a dark speck on the clear sky. Gone on elsewhere. To live among the tree limbs and cliff rocks. Elements of humanity might come now and again like emissaries to draw me back to the society of people. Unsuccessful every time. Fly off to some high ridge and perch, observing the bright light of common day.

He sat up and listened for a while to the talk of the creek on the round stones, the rain in the down leaves. A wet crow descended to a chestnut limb and tried to shake the water out of its feathers and then sat hunched and ill looking. Inman rose erect

and went on bipedal, as was his fate, until he struck a little-used track.

Sometime the next day Inman began to feel that he was being followed. He wheeled around and saw a little hog-eyed man dressed in faded overalls and a black suitcoat walking noiseless right up behind him. He could nearly have reached out and throttled the man by the neck.

—Who the hell are you? Inman said.

The man skipped off into the trees, ducking behind a big tulip poplar. Inman walked over to the poplar and looked behind it. Nothing.

He walked on, looking back behind him over and over. He'd spin, trying to catch the shadowy follower unawares, and sometimes the man would be there, hanging back in the trees. He's finding my direction and then he'll be off to tell the Guard, Inman thought. He pulled out the LeMat's and waved it about.

—I'll shoot you dead, Inman hollered to the woods. Just watch me. I'll do it and not think twice. I'll blow a hole in your belly you could run a dog through.

The hog-eyed man hung back but followed on, flitting through the trees.

Finally, as Inman rounded a bend in the road, the man stepped out from behind a rock ahead of him.

—What the hell do you want? Inman said.

The little man put two fingers to his mouth and held them there a moment, and Inman recognized the gesture as one of the signs of the Red String Band or the Heroes of America, he could not remember which. A volunteer worker in the hospital had passed along information about such sympathizers with the Federal cause. They were all as bad as Masons for making up secret signals. Inman gave the countersignal of running one finger by his right eye.

The little man smiled and said, These are gloomy times. Inman knew this to be another code. The correct response would be to say, Yes, but we expect better. Then the man would

say Why? And Inman would say, Because we look for the cord of our deliverance.

What Inman said instead was, You can just stop right there. I'm not HOA or anything else. I've got no allegiances in that direction or in much of any other.

—You an outlier?

—I would be if I was in a place fit for lying out.

—Comes right down to cases, I'm about as unaffiliated as you are. My boy got shot to death at Sharpsburg and I've not give a pinch of shit for neither side since.

—I attended the fight at Sharpsburg, Inman said.

The man stuck out his hand and said, Potts.

Inman shook his hand and said his own name.

—What was Sharpsburg like? Potts said.

—About like 'em all, but bigger than common. First they threw bombs among us and we among them. Then there was the charging and the shooting, grapeshot and musketball. Lots of boys died.

They stood for a time examining the nearby forest, and then Potts said, You look worn to a nub.

—Food's been scarce and I've been walking hard as I can, which has been slow.

—I'd give you something to eat if I had any handy, but I don't. They's a good gal down the road three or four mile that will feed you and ask no questions.

Rain fell slantwise and stinging on the wind. Inman wrapped himself in his ground cloth and walked on without slackening his pace. He looked cowled and robed as a pilgrim from days of yore, a dark monk out awander for the good of his soul, seeking remedy in walking from being fouled by contact with the world. Rain dripped off his nose and into his beard.

Within the hour he reached the house Potts had described, a lonesome little one-room cabin of squared-off timbers set above the road at the mouth to a dank cove. The windows were greased paper. Thin brown smoke rose from the mud-and-stick

chimney and then whipped away on the wind. A hog shifted about in a pen up the hill. Roosting boxes for chickens in the corner between the house and chimney. Inman stepped up to the gate in the fence and yelled out his presence.

The rain had become mixed with spitting ice. His two face cheeks felt pinched together such that they seemed to touch on the inside of his empty mouth. While he waited he regarded a spicebush just on the other side of the fence, ice beginning to cling to the red berries. He yelled out again and a young woman, a girl really, cracked the door and stuck her brown head out and then pulled it back in again. He heard the clack of a latch to secure the door. Afraid with good cause, Inman thought.

He called out once more, this time adding that Potts had sent him for a meal. The door opened and the girl stepped out onto the porch.

—Why didn't you say so? she said.

She was a pretty thing, little and slim and tight-skinned. She was brown-headed and wore a cotton print dress which ill sorted with the bitter weather. Inman slipped the length of chain off the nail on the gatepost and walked up to the porch, unwrapping himself as he went. He shook the ground cloth out and draped it along the porch edge to drip. He took off the knapsack and haversack and set them on the porch in the dry. He stood there in the falling ice waiting.

—Well, come on up, she said.

—I'll pay for what I eat, Inman said. He stepped onto the porch next to the woman.

—I'm hard up but not that far gone that I have to take money for what little I can offer. There's a pone of corn bread and some beans is all.

She turned and walked into the house. Inman followed. The room was dark, lit by just the fire and the little brown light that came through the paper windows and fell on the scrubbed plank floor, but he could see that though it was bare as a barn the room

was clean. There was sparse furniture. A table, a pair of chairs, a cupboard, a rope bed.

Other than a quilt on the bed there was not a mark of ornament in the place. Not a picture of a loved one or of Jesus or even an illustration cut from a magazine on the wall, as if herein great strictures toward graven images held sway. Nor was there even a little figurine on the mantel or bow of ribbon tied to the hearth broom. The quilt alone stood as garnish to the eye. It was pieced together into no named pattern native to this country, not star flower or flying bird or churn dasher or poplar leaf, but was some entirely made-up bestiary or zodiac of half-visionary creatures. Its colors were the dim tones of red and green and yellow that can be drawn from bark and flower and nut hull. Otherwise there was not a speck of color but brown elsewhere in the cabin, except for the raw-skinned face of a recent baby that lay swaddled up tight in a cradle crafted rudely from pine sticks, the bark still on.

As he looked about the room, Inman was suddenly aware of his filth. In this clean, closed space he found that his clothes threw a powerful reek from the gathered sweat of his long walking. His boots and pant legs were caked muddy to the shins, and he left tracks as he stepped. He considered taking the boots off but feared that his socks would stink like rotted meat. It had been some time since he had last gone unshod. The cabin was not an old one and still held a faint crisp smell of dressed timbers, chestnut and hickory, and Inman felt marked and at odds with their bouquet.

The woman pulled one of the chairs to the side of the fire and gestured for him to sit. In a minute a faint steam had begun to rise around him from his sodden clothes, and little puddles of muddy water had dripped from his cuffs onto the floorboards. He looked down at his feet and noted that a half circle of puncheon was scuffed and worn pale around the front of the hearth the way a dog on a rope will beat down the dirt at the perimeter of its range.

The pot of pinto beans swung by its bail on an iron rod to the side of the fire. A fresh round of corn bread rested in a Dutch oven on the hearth. The woman served him up a plate heaped high with beans and bread and a big peeled onion. She set a pail of spring water and a dipper down next to him.

—You can eat at the table or here. Its warmer here, she said.

Inman took the plate and a knife and spoon into his lap and fell to eating. A part of him wished to be polite, but it was overcome by some dog organ deep in his brain, and so he ate loudly and in gulps, pausing to chew only when absolutely necessary. He forewent slicing the onion and ate on it like an apple. He spooned the hot beans into his mouth and gnawed the wedges of greasy bread at such a rate that he alarmed even himself. The liquor of the beans dripped off his beard and onto the front of his filthy shirt. His breath came short and whistled in his nose from lack of regular breathing.

With some effort he slowed down his chewing. He drank a dipperful of the cold spring water. The woman had pulled the chair to the other side of the hearth and sat watching him as one would a boar feeding on carrion, that is to say with a certain measure of fascinated disgust.

—I'm sorry. I've not taken actual food in days. Just wild cress and creek water, he said.

—It's no need to be sorry, she said, in such an even tone that Inman could not interpret whether in that last word she had meant to absolve or admonish.

Inman looked at her closely for the first time. She was indeed just a pale slim girl here alone in this dark hollow where the sun never would shine bright for long. Her life so bare that she lacked buttons, for he noted that the top of her dress was held to with a long briar from a cockspur bush.

—How old are you? Inman said.

—Eighteen, she said.

—Name's Inman. Yours?

—Sara.

—How do you come to be here all alone?

—My man, John, went off for the fighting. He died awhile back. They killed him up in Virginia. He never saw his baby, and it's just us two now.

Inman sat silent for a minute, thinking that every man that died in that war on either side might just as soon have put a pistol against the soft of his palate and blown out the back of his head for all the meaning it had.

—Have you got any help here? he said.

—Not a lick.

—How do you make it?

—I take a push plow and do what I can to lay me out a little patch of corn and a kitchen garden around the side of the hill apiece, though neither one didn't make much this year. I've got a tub mill to grind up the corn in. And there's a few chickens for the eggs. We had us a cow but the raiders came over the mountain and took it off back in the summer and burnt down what little shed of a barn there was and robbed the bee gums and took a hatchet and broke open a bluetick hound we had right out there on the porch to scare me. That big hog in the pen is mostly it for the winter. I've got to slaughter it soon and I dread it, because I've never killed hogs on my own yet.

—You'll need help, Inman said. She seemed such a slight thing to be butchering hogs.

—Needing and getting don't seem likely to match up anytime soon. All my family's dead now, and there's no neighbors around here I can ask but Potts, and he's no help at all when it comes to work. What needs doing is mine to do.

She would be old in five years from such a load, and recognizing this Inman wished he had not set foot in this house, wished he had kept walking even if it meant falling by the wayside never to rise again. He saw with sorrow that hers was a life he could step right into and keep working at hard from tonight

till death. If he allowed himself to ponder it for a minute he saw all the world hanging over the girl like the deadfall to a trap, ready to drop and crush.

It was near dark outside now and the room was murky as a bear den except for the wedge of yellow light cast by the fire. The girl's legs were stretched out before her to the heat. She had on a thick pair of grey men's socks turned down at the ankles and her dress hem had risen so that he could see shining in the firelight fine gold hairs lying flat and soft against the skin at the sides of her narrow calves. So disordered was his mind from the past days' fasting that he thought to stroke it like the neck of a nervous horse one would seek to calm, for he could see etched in every angle of her body all the lineaments of despair.

—I could help, Inman discovered himself to be saying. It's some early, but this would pass for hog-killing weather.

—I couldn't ask it.

—You didn't ask it. I offered.

—I'd have to trade you something. I could clean and mend those clothes of yours. It's not like they don't need it. That big rent in the coat could use a wedge sewed over it. Meanwhile, you could put on clothes my man left. He was about as long as you are.

Inman bent and ate some more from the plate in his lap, and shortly he mopped up the last juice with a crust of corn bread and finished it off. Without asking, Sara spooned him up another pile of beans and forked out a wedge of bread. The baby commenced crying. While he worked on the second plate of food she went back into the dim of the room and unbuttoned her dress near to the waist and nursed the baby sitting sideways on the bed to Inman.

He wished not to look but could nevertheless see the round side of her breast, full and luminous white in the grainy light. In awhile she pulled the baby off and a point of firelight caught on the end of her wet nipple.

When she returned to the hearth she carried a stack of

folded clothes with a clean pair of good boots standing atop them. He handed her the empty plate and she put the clothes and boots in his lap.

—You can go out on the porch and put these on. And use this.

She handed him water in a basin made from the bottom of a gourd, a chunk of grey soap, and a rag.

He stepped out into the night. There was a washboard at the end of the porch, and on the post above the board hung a little round mirror of polished metal going to rust. Young John's shaving place. Fine ice still rattled on the dry leaves clinging yet to the black oaks, but at the open end of the hollow he could see breaking clouds scudding across the face of the moon behind them. Inman thought about the dog the raiders had killed on the porch, the girl watching. He stripped off in the cold, and the clothes he removed were like skinned pelts, wet and heavy and limp. He did not look in the mirror but scrubbed hard at himself with the soap and rag. He poured the remainder of the gourd water over his head and then he dressed. The dead man's clothes were a fair fit, soft and thin from much washing, and the boots fit like they were cut to his feet, though all in all he felt he had donned the husk of another life. When he reentered the cabin he felt as a ghost must, occupying the shape of the past to little effect. Sara had lit a tallow dip and was at the table washing dishes in a basin. The air around the light seemed thick. All the bright objects close to it appeared haloed. Everything in the shadows beyond it was extinguished completely, as if never to reappear. The curve of the girl's back as she bent over the table seemed to Inman a shape not to be duplicated in all the time stretched out before him. A thing to fix in mind and hold, so that should he become an old man the memory might be useful, not a remedy against time but nevertheless a consolation.

He sat again at the chair by the hearth. Soon the girl joined him, and they sat quiet, staring into the red fire. She looked up at him, her face an unreadable lovely blank.

—If I had a barn you could sleep there, she said. But I don't now.

—The corncrib will do fine.

She looked back into the fire as if to dismiss him, and Inman walked out onto the porch again and collected his packs and his sodden bedding and walked behind the house to the crib. The clouds were breaking in earnest and the near landscape was gathering and starting to form up under the light of the revealed moon. The air was chilling off toward a hard freeze. Inman climbed into the crib and burrowed up with his blankets as best he could into the cobs. Up the cove an owl called out a number of times, the calls descending the scale. The hog stirred and snuffled and then fell silent.

Inman figured it to be a bleak and knobby night of sleep coming on, but all-in-all favorable in contrast to stretching out on the bare ground. Bars of blue moonlight came in between the crib slats, and Inman could see to take the LeMat's from the haversack and check its ten loads and rub it down with the tail of the dead husband's shirt and set it to half cock. He took out his knife and stropped its edge against the clean leather of a boot sole, and then he rolled up in the blankets to sleep.

But he had slept little before he was wakened by footsteps in the leaves. He reached and set his hand on the pistol, moving slowly so as not to rattle the cobs. The steps stopped a dozen feet from the crib.

—Come inside please, Sara said. And she turned and walked away.

Inman clambered out and stood and slid the pistol inside the waist of the pants and cast back his head to survey the narrow slot of sky. Orion was fully risen and seemed to bestride the close ridgelines at either side of the cove with the sure demeanor of one who knows his own mind and follows it. Inman walked on back to the house, and as he approached it he saw that the paper windows glowed like a Japanese lantern. Inside he found that the girl had fed the fire with hickory logs and it

blazed high and the room was as bright and warm as it would ever be.

She was in bed and had taken the plait out of her hair and it spread thick across her shoulders and shone in the light. Inman walked to the hearth and set the pistol up on a little shelf that served for mantel. The crib was drawn up near the fire and the baby slept facedown so that all that could be seen was a pale fuzzed orb arising from covers.

—You look like an outlaw with that big pistol, she said.

—I'm not sure there's a thing I am right now that you could set a name to.

—If I was to ask you to do something, would you do it?

Inman considered that he should frame an answer here on the order of Maybe, or If I can, or some like provisional phrase. What he said was, Yes.

—If I was to ask you to come over here and lay in bed with me but not do a thing else, could you do it?

Inman looked at her there and wondered what she saw looking back. Some dread shape filling the clothes of her husband? A visitation of spirit half desired, half feared? His eyes rested on the quilt over her. Its squares depicted blocky beasts, big-eyed and little-legged, awkward but heraldic. They seemed patched together out of partial remembrances of dream animals. Their shoulders humped with muscle, feet bristling with spikes, howling mouths stretched wide and filled with long teeth.

—Could you? she said.

—Yes.

—I believed you could or I'd never have asked.

He went to the bed and drew off the boots and climbed under the quilts fully clothed and lay under the covers flat on his back. The tick over the rope was filled with fresh straw and smelled dry and autumnal and sweet, and underlying that was the smell of the girl herself, like a stand of wet laurels after their blooms have fallen to the ground.

They both kept as still as if a charged and cocked shotgun

rested there between them. And then in a few minutes Inman heard her crying great dry sobs.

—I'll go if that would be better, he said.

—Hush.

She cried on awhile and then stopped and sat up and wiped her eyes on the quilt corner and began talking about her husband. She required of Inman only that he bear witness to her tale. Every time he went to speak she said, Hush. There was nothing about her story remarkable other than that it was her life. She told the manner in which she and John had met and fallen in love. The building of this cabin and her working like a man beside him, felling the trees and raising the dressed logs and chinking the gaps. The happy life they had planned in this lost place which to Inman seemed so unlikely of sustenance. The hardness of the past four years, John's death, the shortness of food. The only bright spot was John's brief furlough, a time of great happiness which produced the baby sleeping by the fire. Without her, Sara said, there'd be nothing holding me to earth.

The final thing she said was, That will be a good hog out there. It fed on chestnut mast mainly, and I brought it in from the woods and gave it corn for the past two weeks so the lard will render out clear. It's so fat its eyes have about swole shut.

When she was done talking, she reached out and touched the scar at Inman's collar line, first with just her fingertips and then with her whole palm. She rested her hand there a moment and then she took it away. She rolled over with her back to him and soon her breathing became deep and regular. He figured she had found some calm just in telling to another person what a lonely thin edge of life she occupied, where one hog could act as stopple to a demijohn of woes.

Worn as he was, Inman could not rest. While Sara slept he lay looking up, watching the light of the fire diminish on the underside of the roof as the logs burned away. A woman had not touched a hand to him with any degree of tenderness in so long that he had come to see himself as another kind of creature alto-

gether from what he had been. It was his lot to bear the penalty of the unredeemed, that tenderness be forevermore denied him and that his life be marked down a dark mistake. And in his troubled mind and constant sorrow he did not even think it possible to reach a hand to Sara's hip and pull her to him and hold her close till daylight.

What little sleep he did get was troubled by dreams that emanated from the quilt top. The beasts of it chased after him in a dark wood, and there was not place one for sanctuary no matter where he turned. All the world of that dark realm gathered dire and intent against lone him, and everything about it was grey and black, but for teeth and claws as white as the moon.

When Inman awoke it was to Sara shaking his shoulder and saying urgently, Get up and get out.

It was just grey dawn and the cabin was freezing cold and there was the faint sound of horses on the road leading up to the house.

—Get, Sara said. Whether it's Home Guard or raiders, we're both better off if you're not here.

She ran to the back door and opened it. Inman jerked on the boots and took the LeMat's from the mantel and rushed out. He went at a dead run to the line of trees and brush beyond the spring. He plunged in and then, hidden from sight, he worked his way around until he found a thick stand of twisted laurel situated to give him a view of the front of the house. He crawled up in the darkness pooled under the laurel and sighted through a fork in a trunk to hide his face. The ground was frozen to a crunchy grit under him.

He could see Sara run barefoot across the frosted ground in her nightgown to the hog pen. She dropped the poles of the pen gate from their stanchions and tried to coax the hog out, but it would not rise. She walked into the muddy pen and kicked at the hog, and her feet when she raised them were black with mud

and hog shit where she had broken through the frozen crust to the muck. The hog rose and began to walk, but it was so immense and low slung that it could hardly step over the gate poles on the ground. It had just left the pen and begun to gain some momentum with Sara driving it toward the woods when there was a call from down at the road.

—Stop right there.

Blue jackets. Inman saw three of them on sorry horses. They dismounted and came through the front gate. Two of them carried Springfield rifles in the crooks of their left arms. The muzzles were aimed half at the ground but the men's fingers were inside the trigger guards. The other man held a Navy revolver pointed up as if he aimed to shoot down a high bird, but his eyes were aimed straight at Sara.

The man with the pistol went to her and told her to sit on the ground and she did. The hog reclined on the ground beside her. The two with rifles climbed onto the porch and entered the house, one covering the other as he opened the door and stepped in. They were inside awhile and all that time the man with the pistol stood over Sara without looking at her or speaking to her. From the house came sounds of clash and breakage. When the two inside reappeared, one of them carried the baby by a fold in its swaddling as one would carry a satchel. It cried out and Sara half rose to go to it and the man with the pistol shoved her back to the frozen ground.

The three Federals convened in the yard, but Inman could not make out what they were saying over the sound of the baby and of Sara pleading with them to give her the child. He could hear their accents though, flat and quick as hammer blows, and they brought up in him the urge to strike back hard. He was, however, beyond reliable range for the LeMat's, and even if he were not, he could think of no plan of attack that would result in anything but death for Sara and the baby and himself.

Then he could hear that they were asking her about money,

where she had it hidden. That's their nourishment, Inman thought. Sara said what could only have been the truth, that all she had of worldly goods was the little they could see. They asked again and again and then they led her to the porch and Pistol held her hands behind her while one of the riflemen went to the horses and took straps that looked to be pieces of old plow line from a canvas saddlebag. Pistol tied her to a post with the straps and then just pointed a finger at the baby. One of the men unswaddled the baby and set it out on the frozen ground. Inman could hear the man with the pistol say, We have all day, and then he could hear Sara scream.

The men sat on the porch edge and dangled their feet and talked among themselves. They made cigarettes and smoked them to spittled nubs. The two underlings went to the horses and came back with sabers, and they went about the yard prodding into the cold ground hoping to hit treasure. They went about it for some time. The baby screaming and Sara pleading. Then the one with the pistol arose from his seat on the porch edge and walked to Sara and stuck the barrel of the pistol to the fork of her legs and said, You really don't have shit, do you? The other two came and stood close by, watching.

Inman began moving back through the woods to put the house between him and the porch so that when he came at them he could at least shoot one as he came around the corner before they saw him. It was a poor plan, but it was all he had, given the open ground he had to cross to get at them. He had no thought other than that he and the woman and the baby would likely all be killed, but he could see no other way out of this.

Before he moved far, though, the men stepped away from Sara. Inman stopped and watched, hoping for some advantageous realignment of forces. Pistol went to his horse and got a length of rope and walked over to the hog and tied it on to its neck. One of the riflemen unhitched Sara from the post and the other went to the baby and hoisted it by an arm and thrust it out

to her. They began chasing about the yard gathering up chickens. They caught three hens and tied their legs with twine and hung them upside down behind their saddles.

Sara held the baby to her. When she saw Pistol leading the hog off she yelled out, That hog's all I've got. You take it and you might as well knock both of us in the head and kill us now, for it will all come out the same. But the men mounted up and headed back down the road, Pistol leading the hog, which trotted along effortfully at the end of the rope. They turned a curve and were gone.

Inman ran down to the porch and looked up to Sara. He said, Warm your baby up and then build you a fire just as high as your head and put on a cauldron of water to boil. And then he jogged off down the road.

He trailed the Federals, sticking to the margins of the woods and wondering what it was he intended to do. All he could hope was that something would present itself.

They did not go long, about two or three miles, until they pulled off the road into a swale at the mouth to a ragged little cove. They went up it a ways and tied the hog to a locust sapling and set about building a fire close up to a rock ledge near a swift creek. Inman reckoned their aim was to camp there for the night and eat until they were full, even if that meant cutting the hams off the hog. Inman circled through the woods until he was above them at the top of the ledge. He hid in the rocks and watched them wring the necks of two of the chickens and pluck and gut them and put them on spits of green limbs above the fire.

They sat with their backs to the rock and watched the chickens cook. Inman could hear that they were talking of home and it came out that the two were from Philadelphia and the one with the pistol was from New York City. They spoke of how they missed home and how they wished they were there, and Inman wished they were there too, for he was not anxious to do what he was about to try to do.

He moved a fair way along the top of the ledge, going quiet

and slow, until it declined into the common level of the ground. Near the edge of the rock outcropping he found a shallow cave and stuck his head in to find that it went only ten feet deep into the rock. It had long ago sheltered coon hunters or the like, for there was an old black fire ring at the mouth. The cave had also sheltered other men even earlier on. Their sign was scribbled on the walls of the cave, odd angular marks from some lost pattern of writing. None alive now could look on it and tell alpha from zed. Other marks depicted beasts long departed from this earth or never here, mere figment residents of brainpans long since empty as an old gourd.

Inman left the cave and kept circling the ledge until he could approach the encampment walking downhill along the stream through the gorge. Just out of eyesight of the men, he found a big hemlock with low-growing limbs, and he climbed up about ten feet into it and stood tall on the limb right up against the dark trunk like he had seen long-eared owls do when they're laying up in the daytime and seeking to stay hid. Three times he gobbled out the call of a wild turkey and then he waited.

He could hear the men talking, but he could not tell what they were saying. In just a minute Pistol came easing along with the Navy revolver out in front of him. He walked right under the tree and stopped. Inman was looking down on his hat crown. Pistol stuck his revolver under his armpit and took the hat off and ran his hand through his hair. He was going bald at the back of his head. There was a white spot of scalp the size of a poker chip and Inman took aim at it.

He said, Hey.

Pistol looked up and Inman shot down on him at such an angle that he missed the bald spot. The bullet entered at the shoulder near the neck and erupted from the stomach in a bright outpouring that resembled violent vomiting. The man fell to the ground as if the bones in his legs had suddenly liquified. He tried to pull himself along the ground with his arms, but earth seemed to elude his grasp. He rolled and looked above

him to see what make of predator had fallen on him with such weight. When their eyes met, Inman put two fingers to his hat brim in greeting, and then the man died in an attitude of deep confusion.

—Did you hit it? one of the riflemen called out from down the hill.

After that it was fairly simple. Inman descended from the tree and retraced his steps, making a quick flanking movement back up and around the long rock outcropping so that this time he approached the camp coming up the creek. He stopped at a thicket of rhododendron and waited.

The two riflemen by the fire called out to the dead man over and over, and Inman discovered that his name had been Eben. The men eventually gave up calling and took up their Springfields and headed upstream to find him. Inman followed them, screened by trees, until they came upon Eben. They stood for a time at a distance from the partially disassembled body and talked over what they ought to do. In their voices it was clear that their true wish was to forget what lay before them and turn and go home. But they decided to do what Inman knew they would, go on upstream looking for the killer, which they could not imagine as having done other than fled.

Inman followed behind, stalking them up the cove. They moved along among the big tight-spaced trees near the creek bank, fearful of straying far from it lest they lose their way. They were city boys wary of woods and thoughtful in the face of the killing they assumed they were getting ready to do. This was to them a trackless wilderness, and they entered it with great timidity, yet to Inman they seemed like men walking up a thoroughfare. They made show of looking for sign of the killer's passage, but anything short of a big deep footprint in mud was lost on them.

Inman drew nearer and nearer to them, and when he shot them with the LeMat's, he was so near he might have reached out and touched them at their collars with his hand. The first

one took a bullet near the point where his spine met his skull and the ball carried away most of his forehead on its path out. He fell, needless to say, in a heap. The other, Inman caught half turning, at about the armpit. Mortal damage was not done, much to Inman's dismay. The man fell to his knees, gripping his rifle before him.

—If you'd stayed home this would not have come to pass, Inman said. The man tried to swing the long Springfield around to bear on Inman, but Inman shot out the man's chest at such close range that the muzzle flash set his jacket breast on fire.

The Philadelphians had fallen not far above the cave, so Inman dragged them into it and sat them up together. He went back and got the Springfields and propped them against the wall beside the men, and then he walked down the gorge. Under the hemlock he found that the remaining hen had gotten free and had its head immersed in the broken open belly of Eben the New Yorker. It pecked at the colorful flesh pulp of his exploded guts.

Inman fished in the man's pockets for cigarette makings and then squatted on the ground and watched the hen work. He rolled a cigarette and smoked it down and rubbed out the fire of it on a boot heel. He was reminded of a sacred song usually done counterpoint, but he hummed a little of it to himself and thought the words. They were these:

The fear of the grave is removed forever.
When I die I'll live again.
My soul will rejoice by the crystal river.
When I die I'll live again.
Hallelujah I'll live again.

Inman decided to view what was before him in this context: next to the field in front of the sunken road at Fredericksburg or the accumulated mess at the bottom of the crater, this was near nothing. At either place he had probably killed any number of men more satisfactory in all their attributes than this

Eben. Nevertheless, he figured this might be a story he would never tell.

He rose and grabbed the chicken by the feet and pulled it from out the New Yorker and took it over to the creek and sloshed it in the water until it was white again. He tied its feet with a piece of the Federals' twine and set it on the ground. It twisted its head about and regarded the world through its black eyes with what struck Inman as a new level of interest and enthusiasm.

He dragged the New Yorker by his feet to the cave and sat him up inside with his companions. The cave was little enough that the men sat almost in a circle. They looked stunned and perplexed, and in their demeanor they seemed like drunks about to play a hand of cards. From the expressions on their faces, death seemed to have settled in on them much like melancholy, a sinking of the spirits. Inman took a stick of charcoal from the old fire at the cave mouth and sketched on the cave wall depictions of Sara's quilt beasts that had pursued him through the dream world of the night before. In all their angularity they reminded him of how frail the human body is against all that is sharp and hard. His pictures fit in like near kin with the antique scratchings already put there by Cherokee or whatever kind of person came before them.

Inman returned to the clearing and checked the horses and saw that they had army brands, which saddened him. He untacked them and made three trips to the cave, hauling the Federals' gear to rest with them, all but for one haversack. Into it he placed the two cooked chickens. He led the horses up the cove far beyond the cave and then shot them in the heads. It was not a happy thing to do, but marked as they were there was no other way that would not threaten to fly back at him or Sara. At the camp again, he put the live chicken into the haversack with the cooked chickens and slung it over his shoulder. He untied the hog and pulled at its rope, and then he left that place behind him.

When he returned to the cabin, Sara had a strong fire going in the yard. Over it, a black cauldron of water boiled up a cloud of steam into the crisp air. She had washed his clothes and they were spread on bushes to dry. Inman tipped back his head to the sun and saw that it was yet morning though it did not seem possible to him that it could still be such.

They made an early lunch of the cooked chickens and set to work. Within two hours the hog—killed, scalded, and scraped of its hair—was hanging pale from a big tree limb by a gambrel stick run through the tendons of its hind feet. Its various organs and fluids steamed in tubs on the ground. The girl was working at a lard tub. She held up a sheet of caul fat and looked through it as if it were a lace shawl, and then she wadded it up and put it in the tub for rendering. Inman partitioned up the carcass with a hatchet. He chopped down on both sides of the spine until the hog fell into two sides of meat, which he then further divided along the joints into the natural categories of pork.

They worked into near dark, rendering all the fat into lard, washing out the intestines for chittlings, grinding and canning the trimmings and scraps into sausage, salting down the hams and middling meat, soaking the blood out of the head to ready it for making souse.

They washed up and went inside, and Sara began on supper while Inman snacked on a plate of cracklings that she had intended to add to the corn bread. Since they wouldn't keep, she cooked up a kind of stew of the liver and lights, spiced with much onion and hot pepper. They ate and then stopped and rested. Then they ate again.

After dinner Sara said, I believe you'd look some better if you shaved down.

—If you've a razor I'll give it a try, Inman said.

She went to the trunk and dug around and came back with a razor and a heavy strop of oiled leather. She set them in Inman's lap.

—That was John's too, she said.

She dipped enough water for a shave out of the water piggin into a black pot and set it to heat over the fire. When the water started steaming she poured it into the small gourd basin. She lit a candle in a tin holder, and Inman carried all of it out and spread it on the washboard at the end of the porch.

Inman stropped the razor and wet his beard. He held the razor up and took note of a brown smear of blood on the cuff of John's shirt. Man or hog, one. He looked in the metal mirror, put the razor's edge to his face, and went to work in the flickery light of the candle flame.

He had not gone beardless since the second year of the war, and he was mixed in his feelings about seeing what he looked like after all that time. He scraped at the hair until the razor dulled and then he restropped. He did not like looking on himself long enough for shaving, was one reason why he quit. That and the hardness of keeping track of a razor and making hot water during the past two years. Going bearded seemed one less thing to have to fail at.

The job at hand took some time, but eventually his face was bared. The mirror had gone to rust in scattered brown patches, and as Inman regarded himself in it, his pale face appeared scabbed over with crusty wounds. The eyes that looked back had a slit and sideling quality that he did not remember. A pinched and hollow cast to the features that was more than just food hunger.

What's looking out from there now is all different from her boy-husband, Inman thought. Some killer visage lodged in the place where once young John looked out. What would be the reaction if you sat by a fire in winter and looked up to a black window and saw that face staring back? he wondered. What seizure or spasm would it set off?

It was to Inman's credit, though, that he tried to believe such a face was not him in any true way and that it could in time be altered for the better.

When he went back in, Sara smiled at him and said, You look part human now.

They sat and looked at the fire and Sara rocked the baby in her arms. It had a croupy cough. Inman figured there was little reason to expect it to come out the other side of winter alive. It fretted in Sara's arms and would not sleep and so she sang it a song.

She sang as if shamed by her own sounds, by the way her life voiced itself aloud. As she began, it seemed that a blockage had set up in her throat. And so the chant that escaped her did so with much effort. The force of air from her chest needed somewhere to go, but finding the jaw set firm and jutted and the mouth clenched against music, it took the far way out and reached expression in high nasal tones that hurt to hear in their loneliness.

The singing carried shrill into the twilight and its tones spoke of despair, resentment, an undertone of panic. Her singing against such resistance seemed to Inman about the bravest thing he had ever witnessed. It was like watching a bitter fight carried to a costly draw. The sound of her was that of a woman of the previous century living on in the present, that old and weary. Sara was such a child to sound that way. Had she been an old woman who long ago in her youth sang beautifully, one might have said that she had learned to use the diminished nature of her voice to maximum effect, that it was a lesson in how to live with damage, how to make peace with it and use it for what it can do. But she was not an old woman. The effect was eerie, troubling. You'd have thought the baby would cry out in distress to hear its mother in such a state, but it did not. It fell asleep in her arms as to a lullaby.

The words to the song, though, were no lullaby. They linked up to make a horrible story, a murder ballad called Fair Margaret and Sweet William. It was an old song, but Inman had not heard it before. The lines were these:

I dreamed that my bower was full of red swine,
And my bride bed full of blood.

When that one was done she started in on Wayfaring Stranger, at first just humming it and tapping her foot. When she eventually pitched in singing, it bore little kin to music but was more like some pinched declamation of spirit sickness, a squeal of barren lonesomeness as pure and undiluted as the pain following a sharp blow to the nose. When she finished, there was a long silence broken only by the sound of an owl calling in the dark woods, fit conclusion to songs so burdened with themes of death and solitude and carrying more than a hint of the specter world.

Sara's offering of such music might have seemed to give no hope of consolation, either to the baby or, especially, to Inman. How unlikely that such a severe gift might yield a reduction of sadness when it was itself so bleak. Yet such proved to be the case, for though they talked but little the rest of the evening, they sat side by side in front of the fire, tired from the business of living, content and resting and happy, and later they again lay in bed together.

The next morning before he set out onto the road, Inman ate the brains of the hog, parboiled and scrambled up with an egg from the hen that had been eating on the raider from New York.

a satisfied mind

Ada and Ruby spent much of the autumn working with apples. Apples had come in heavy and had to be picked, peeled, sliced, and juiced: pleasant clean work, out among the trees handling the fruit. The sky for much of the time was cloudless blue, the air dry. The light, even at midday, brittle and raking, so that by angle alone it told of the year's waning. In the mornings they went carrying ladders when the dew still stood in the orchard grass. They'd climb among the tree limbs to fill sacks with apples, the ladders swaying as the limbs they were propped against gave under their weight. When all the sacks were full, they would bring the horse and sled to the orchard, haul them in, empty them and begin again.

It was work that was just moderately tiring and, unlike the haying, produced only a peaceful still picture in Ada's mind as she lay in bed at night: a red or yellow apple hanging from a drooping limb, behind it deep blue sky, her hand palm up, reaching out to the apple but not touching it.

For a long time Ada and Ruby ate apples at every meal, fried and stewed and pied and sauced. They dried rings of them into

little scraps of apple leather, which they stored in cloth bags and hung from the ceiling in the kitchen. One day they built a fire in the yard and made a black kettle of apple butter so big that when they stood over it and stirred the apple mash with spurtles, the scene put Ada in mind of the witches in *Macbeth* working at their brew. The apple butter had come out thick, the color of old harness from spice and brown sugar, and they sealed enough of it in crocks to eat on for a year. They pressed cider from rusty culls and fallen apples, and they fed the pomace to the hogs, for Ruby said it would make the meat sweet.

The cider had hardened up enough by now to be worth something, and for that reason Ruby went out one afternoon on a trading mission. She had heard that an Adams man down the river had killed a beef, and she had gone off with two jugs of cider to see how much meat they might bring. She left Ada with two tasks. Burn the brush that had resulted from their earlier clearing a portion of the neglected lower field. And, using the method Ruby had taught her, split the six rounds of an old black-oak log they had discovered already cut into lengths out in the tall grass at the field edge. It would be a good initiation into timber work, for they would soon need to go up on the mountain and cut a hickory or an oak, limb it, and let the horse drag it home with a J-grab to be sectioned and split. Ada had wondered if they had the strength for such work, but Ruby argued in detail that it did not necessarily require pure power. Just pacing, patience, rhythm. Pull the saw and release. Wait for the one at the other end of the saw to draw it away and then pull again. Avoid binding up. The main thing, Ruby said, was not to get ahead of yourself. Go at a rhythm that could be sustained on and on. Do just as much as you could do and still be able to get up and do again tomorrow. No more, and no less.

Ada watched Ruby go down the road and decided to split the logs first and enjoy the fire in the cool of afternoon. She walked from the garden to the toolshed and got a maul and a wedge and carried them to the lower field and stamped out a cir-

cle in the waist-high grass around the oak logs to make working room. The logs lay on their sides and were better than two feet across the cut ends. The wood was grey, for they had been lying forgotten since the tree was felled two or three years earlier by the hired man. Ruby had warned that the dry logs would not want to split easily as when fresh and wet.

Ada upended the big cylinders of wood, feeling the way they clung to the ground, and when she got them upright she found shiny black stag beetles the size of her thumb burrowing in the rotting bark. She went at the job as Ruby had shown her, first examining the cut end for a likely crack, then working it with the wedge. Moving slow, not straining, just lifting the seven-pound maul and letting it fall so that weight and gravity and the magic of angle combined to disassemble the log. She liked driving the wedge in halfway and then stopping to listen for the ripped-cloth sound of the crack as it kept opening for several seconds after the last blow. The work was calm despite all the pounding. The stubborn coherence of the wood and the weight of the maul imposed a slow rhythm to the task. In not much over an hour Ada had split everything but one difficult section where big limbs had once attached to the trunk and confused the grain. From each section she had split eight good-sized pieces of firewood and she reckoned there were forty pieces lying in a jumble on the ground ready to be hauled to the house and burned. She felt a great sense of accomplishment until she realized that the wood would only serve for four, maybe five, days of fire. She started to calculate the approximate number of pieces they would need for the whole winter, but she soon stopped for the figure would be dauntingly high.

Ada's dress was soaked through across the shoulders and back with sweat, and her hair was wet against her neck. So she went to the house and drank two dippers of water from the spring and took off her hat and poured two more over her hair and then twisted the water out of it. She wet her face and rubbed it with her hands and then dried it on her dress sleeve.

She went in and got her lap desk and notebook and came out to sit in the sun on the porch edge until she dried.

Ada dipped her pen in ink and started a letter to her cousin Lucy in Charleston. For a time there was hardly a sound but the scritch of nib on paper as she wrote.

> I suspect, were we to meet on Market Street, you would not know me; nor, upon seeing the current want of delicacy in my aspect and costume, would you much care to.
>
> I'm at the moment sitting on my back stoop writing this across my knees, my dress an old print shirtwaist soaked through with perspiration from splitting oak logs, and I have been wearing a straw chapeau coming apart at brim and crown so that it bristles every bit as much as the haystacks we long ago lodged in to await the conclusion of rainstorms (do you remember?). The fingers gripping the pen are dark as stirrup leathers, stained from shucking walnuts out of their stinking, pulpy husks, and the nail of the forefinger is ragged as a hackerd and wants filing. The silver bracelet with the dogwood blossoms cut in it stands out in bright contrast to the dark skin of my wrist. It is a day so autumnal that to write anything about it would be to engage in elegy. I am resting and waiting for the dress to dry before I turn my attention to burning a brush pile.
>
> I cannot begin to recount all such rough work that I have done in the time since Father died. It has changed me. It is amazing the physical alterations that can transpire in but a few months of labor. I am brown as a penny from being outdoors all day, and I am growing somewhat ropy through the wrists and forearms. In the glass I see a somewhat firmer face than previously, hollower under the cheekbones. And a new expression, I think, has sometimes come to occupy it. Working in the fields, there are brief times when I go totally without

thought. Not one idea crosses my mind, though my senses are alert to all around me. Should a crow fly over, I mark it in all its details, but I do not seek analogy for its blackness. I know it is a type of nothing, not metaphoric. A thing unto itself without comparison. I believe those moments to be the root of my new mien. You would not know it on me for I suspect it is somehow akin to contentment.

She scanned back over the letter and thought it odd and somewhat deceitful that she had not mentioned Ruby, leaving the impression that she was alone. Thinking to rectify the matter later, she put the letter unfinished inside the desk lid. She collected a pitchfork, some matches, a shawl, the third volume of *Adam Bede*, and a little straight chair with the legs sawn off short and carried them down to the brush pile.

She and Ruby had worked with scythes and brush hooks and bow saws most of a day the previous month and had let the cut brush fall where it would. The mix of blackberry canes, tall grass, good-sized jack pines, and sumac had sunned for several weeks spread on the ground and was now fairly dry. Ada worked awhile with the fork to draw the brush together, and when she was done the pile was big as the corncrib and the air was full of the sere odor of cut and withered foliage. She kicked up some duff and some doty sticks at the edge of the pile and set it afire. While it caught and burned she pulled the short chair into range of its warmth and sat to read *Adam Bede*, but the book did not go well. She could not keep her mind on it for she had to rise often to head off outrunners of flame that strayed across the stubble of the field. She beat them out with the back of the fork. And then, when the fire burned down flat, she had to draw the pile together and heap it high again, each time with a narrower diameter, and as the afternoon grew old the pile stood tall and conical in the field, flames rising from it like a miniature of a spewing volcano she had seen pictured in a book on South America.

So she had work as an excuse for not focusing her thoughts on the page. But, too, she had long since grown impatient with Adam and Hetty and the rest and would have quit the book but for the fact that she had paid so much for it. She wished all the people of the story to be more expansive, not so cramped by circumstance. What they needed was more scope, greater range. Go to the Indes, she directed them. Or to the Andes.

She marked her place with a yarrow stem and closed the book and set it in her lap. She wondered if literature might lose some of its interest when she reached an age or state of mind where her life was set on such a sure course that the things she read might stop seeming so powerfully like alternate directions for her being.

A bull thistle stood beside her. She remembered working around it with the scythe out of admiration for the fist-sized purple bloom, but it was now dry and silver white. She reached out and began picking apart the head. Her thinking was that since every tiny place in the world seemed to make a home for some creature, she would discover who the thistle dwellers might be. Soon down blew about in the breeze and caught in her smoky clothes and hair. She found but one fierce little crablike thing no bigger than a pinhead living solitary inside the dried blossom. It clutched to a thread of down with some of its hind legs and waved a minute pair of pincers before it in a way intended to be menacing. With a puff she blew away the luminous thistledown and nameless creature and watched as they caught an updraft and soared until they disappeared skyward as the souls of the dead are claimed to do.

When she had first lit the fire and begun reading, the light had been bright and even and the sky graded rather too evenly from horizon to zenith, white to blue, in the way Ada associated with landscape paintings of less than the highest quality. But now the seal of evening was on the wooded hillsides and on the pastures. The sky broke into bands and whorls of muted color until the entire west was like the marbled endpapers of her jour-

nal. Canada geese—V'd and honking—flew over southward, looking for a place to stay the night. A breeze blew up and flapped the skirts of the scarecrow out in the garden.

Waldo had gone to the gate by the barn. She was waiting and would soon bawl to have her bag stripped, so Ada left her chair and put the cow in her stall and milked. The air was still and damp, cooling with the fall of day, and when the cow turned her head to look back at the milking, her breath fogged and smelled like wet grass. Ada pulled at the teats and watched the milk come out listening for the change in pitch as the pail filled, first a high sizzle against the side and bottom, then a lower drizzle. The skin of her fingers was dark against the pink teat skin.

After Ada put the milk in the springhouse she returned to the field, where the fire still burned slowly, falling into ash. It would have been safe to leave it for the night, though Ada did not wish to. She wanted Ruby to come walking up the road and find her sooty, standing sentry over the afternoon's work.

The air had a cold edge to it, and Ada drew her shawl around her. She reckoned it only a matter of days before the evenings would become too chill to sit out at sunset, even wrapped in a blanket. There was dew in the grass, and she stooped and took *Adam Bede* from where she had dropped it and wiped its faces against her skirts. She went and stirred the fire with the fork and it threw sparks into the sky. At the edge of the field, she collected downed hickory limbs and dry jack pine and pitched them on the fire and it soon blazed up and heated a wider circle of air. Ada pulled her chair close and put her hands out to warm. She looked at the lines of mountain ridges, the variety in their darkness as they faded into the distance. She studied the sky to see when it would fall deep enough toward indigo that the beacons of two planets, Venus and another—which she reckoned must be Jupiter or Saturn—might first shine forth low in the west in preparation for the dizzy wheel and spin of the night sky.

This evening she marked where the sun dove to the horizon,

for over the weeks she had made a practice of noting its setting point on the ridge. She had watched it march southward as the days snuffed out earlier and earlier. Were she to decide fully to live here in Black Cove unto death, she believed she would erect towers on the ridge marking the south and north points of the sun's annual swing. She owned the entire span of ridge where the sun set through the year, and that was a thing to savor. One had then just to mark the points in December and June when the sun wrenched itself from its course and doubled back for another set of seasons. Though upon reflection, she decided a tower was not entirely needed. Only clear some trees to notch the ridge at the turning point. It would be a great pleasure year after year to watch with anticipation as the sun drew nigh to the notch and then on a specified day fell into it and then rose out of it and retraced its path. Over time, watching that happen again and again might make the years seem not such an awful linear progress but instead a looping and a return. Keeping track of such a thing would place a person, would be a way of saying, You are here, in this one station, now. It would be an answer to the question, Where am I?

Ada sat by the fire long after sunset waiting for Ruby. Venus and Saturn had shone out bright to the west and then fallen to the horizon and the full moon had risen, when Ada heard a stirring in the woods. Footsteps in leaves. Low voices. By instinct she took the pitchfork from where it stood in the dirt and moved out of the firelight and watched. Forms moved at the edge of the field and Ada backed farther into the dark and held the fork before her with the five sharp tines aimed toward the sounds of movement. Then she heard her name.

—Hey, Miss Ada Monroe, a voice called softly.

Both names were pronounced in the ways that her father had hated. He had never tired of setting people right on the matter: Broad initial A in Ada; accented second syllable in Monroe, he would say. But over the summer, Ada had given up trying to enforce her name against everyone's natural leaning, and she

was learning to be the Ada Monroe that the voice called. Long A, heavy Mon.

—Who is it? she said.

—Us.

Stobrod and a comrade walked out to be lit by the fire. Stobrod carried his fiddle and bow cradled in the crook of his left arm. The other man held a rough-cast banjo by the neck, poking it out before him as a man at a border crossing might present papers in validation of identity. Both of them squinted against the glare.

—Miss Monroe, Stobrod called again. It's just us.

Ada walked nearer to them, billing a hand over her brow to block the light.

—Ruby is not here, she said.

—We're just generally visiting, Stobrod said. If you don't mind the company.

He and the other man put down their instruments and Stobrod sat on the ground right beside her chair. Ada pulled it a comfortable distance from him and sat too.

—Get us some more wood to liven up the fire, Stobrod said to the banjo man.

Wordless, the man went into the dark edge of woods, and Ada could hear him picking up limbs and breaking them into burning lengths. Stobrod dug around beneath his coat and pulled out a pint pocket tickler full of brown liquor. The glass was dulled almost opaque with scratches and fingerprints. He unstoppered it and passed the mouth of it beneath his nose. He held the glass to the fire and looked at the light through the whiskey and then drank a delicate sip. He made a little whispery two-note whistle, high to low.

—Too good for me, but I'll drink it anyway, he said.

He took a long pull and then worked the stopper back in with his thumb and put the bottle away.

—We haven't seen you in some time, Ada said. Have you been well?

—Fair, he said. Living on the mountain like an outlaw is no lark.

Ada was put in mind of the story she'd heard the captive tell through the jail bars. She began recounting it to Stobrod as warning of what might lie in wait for outliers, but he knew it already. It had passed about the county several times, first as news and then as yarn and later as legend.

—That Teague bunch is killers, Stobrod said. Especially so when they've got numbers in their favor.

The wood gatherer came back into the light and threw some broken limbs on the fire and then made several trips into the trees for more wood, which he piled for later. When he was done he sat on the ground beside Stobrod. The man said not a word nor looked at Ada, but angled himself away from the fire so he could keep his eyes on Stobrod.

—Who's your companion? Ada asked.

—He's a Swanger boy, or a Pangle. Sometimes he says one, sometimes the other. Neither bunch will claim him, for he's simpleminded, but he's got the look of a Pangle to me.

The man had a big round head which sat unbalanced on him like God was being witty about making the insides of it so small. Though he was nearly thirty according to Stobrod, people still called him a boy because his thoughts would not wrap around the least puzzle. To him, the world had no order of succession, no causation, no precedent. Everything he saw was new-minted, and thus every day was a parade of wonders.

He was a fat soft thing, broad-assed, as if he had been raised on a diet of meal and fatback. He had titties like a sow that pushed out his shirtfront and flapped when he walked. His pants were tucked into his boots and bloused out above them, and his tiny feet were hardly big enough to bear up his weight. His hair was the next thing to white and his skin was greyish, so that overall he gave the impression of a china plate filled with biscuit and sawmill gravy. He had no talent in the world but his recently discovered ability to play the banjo, unless one counted as talent

the fact that he was gentle and kind and looked on everything that passed before him with soft wide eyes.

Stobrod described how they had hooked up, and while he did the boy paid not the least attention, did not seem to know or care that he was the topic of discussion. Pangle had been raised somewhat casually, was the way Stobrod told it. The general feeling was that he held no value, for he could not think right nor could he be pressed into labor. Work him too hard and he'd sit down. Whip him and he'd take it without a flinch and still not move. He had, therefore, been set loose in early manhood and had spent the time since wandering Cold Mountain. He came to know its every slit and chink. Ate what presented itself, with little discrimination between grubs and venison. Paid little heed to time of day, and during the brighter moon phases went largely nocturnal. In summer he slept on the beds of fragrant duff beneath hemlock and balsam except in rains of some duration, when he sheltered under rock ledges. In winter he took instruction from toad and groundhog and bear: he denned up in a cave, scarcely moving during the cold months.

When, with some surprise, Pangle discovered the outliers had taken up residence in his cave, he settled himself among them. He particularly attached himself to Stobrod out of being lovesick for fiddle music. Stobrod was to him a man of deep lore, a wizard, a revelator. When Stobrod struck bow to fiddle strings, the Pangle boy sometimes tried to sing along, but he had a voice like blowing a duck call. After the others shouted him silent, he would get up and stomp out a dance of great mystery, ancient Celtic jerk and spasm such as might have been performed after any number of defeats in battle against Roman and Jute, Saxon and Angle and Brit. The boy would fling around until he blossomed out in sweat beads, and then he would flop down on the floury tamped cave ground and follow the fiddling, his nose describing the music patterns in air like a man watching a fly hover.

Stobrod would get a figure of notes going and it would come round again and again and after a time it would work a spell on

Pangle's mind. Pangle liked that feeling he got from Stobrod's playing and became a fool for the fiddle and for the fiddler. He began following Stobrod about, always with the devotion of a spaniel awaiting food. At night in the outliers' cave on the mountain, he would lie awake until Stobrod fell asleep and then he would crawl up and lie pressed against his bowed back. Stobrod would awake at dawn and beat the boy away to a comfortable distance with his hat. The boy would then sit by the fire on his hams and gaze at Stobrod as if at any minute a miracle might happen.

Stobrod had come upon Pangle's banjo one day on a raid, a term the cave dwellers used to lend dignity to their recent habit of robbing any wealthy farmer against whom one of their number held a vague grudge. Some slight ten years ago would serve as pretext. A man had cantered by and splashed you when you stood afoot in the muddy roadway, had brushed past you and bumped your arm coming out of a store without a word of apology, had hired you for a job of work and shorted you on pay or had given orders to you in a tone that could be glossed to mean you were less than he. Any snub, slur, or taunt, however old, would do. Times might never be better configured to settle up.

They'd descended on a Walker man's house. He was one of the county's few gentry, a leading slaveholder, and that fell afoul of the cave society, their general opinion having lately swung round to blame the owners of niggers for the war and its related troubles. As well, Walker had long been a high-handed bastard with all he considered his lessers, which in his estimation included most everybody. Punishment, the cavers had decided, was in order.

They had come down on the farm at nightfall and tied Walker and his wife to the stair rails and taken turns slapping Walker about the face. They had gone through the outbuildings and collected all the food they could easily find—hams and middle meat, quantities of crocked goods, sacks of meal and corn

grits. From the house they took a mahogany table, silver flatware and candlesticks, beeswax candles, a painted picture of General Washington off the dining room wall, English china, Tennessee store liquor. They had since decorated the cave up with the plunder. Washington propped in a niche of the wall, candles in silver holders. Table set with Wedgwood and silver, though many of them had eaten all their lives from table service made entirely of gourd and horn.

In some way, though, Stobrod's imagination had not been fully engaged by the Walker raid, and Pangle's banjo had been the whole of his looting. He had taken it from a peg in Walker's toolshed. It was somewhat ugly, lacking as it did the expected symmetry in its round parts, but the head was of cat skin and the strings of gut, and it had a fine mellow tone. And he had slapped Walker's face only once in payment for a time long ago when he had overheard Walker call him a fool as he sat drunk on a log by the road trying in vain to scratch music out of a fiddle. I've now got mastery of a fiddle, Stobrod had said after he popped Walker's already red cheek. In retrospect, he had decided the Walker raid worried him. For the first time in his life he considered the possibility that his actions might be called to account.

Back at the cave, Stobrod had given the banjo to the Pangle boy and showed him what little he knew of its working: how to twist the pegs to make a few tunings, how to frail it with thumb and forefinger, sometimes strumming, sometimes grabbing at the strings like a barred owl grabbing at a rabbit. The boy, apparently out of stunning natural talent and a heartfelt desire to provide fitting accompaniment to Stobrod's fiddle, had shown little more difficulty in discovering how to play it than one would in learning to beat a drum.

He and Pangle had done not much since the raid but make music. For drink they had Walker's good liquor, and they ate nothing besides stolen jellies. They slept only when they were too drunk to play, and they had not traveled to the cave mouth

frequently enough even to keep track of when day and night occurred. As a result, however, the Pangle boy now knew Stobrod's entire repertoire and they had become a duo.

When Ruby finally returned, she carried only a small bloody brisket wrapped in paper and one jug of cider, for Adams was willing to part with considerably less beef than she had hoped. Ruby stood and looked at her father and the boy and didn't say a word. Her eyes were black in her head, and during her walk her hair had come loose from its tie and spread across her shoulders. She wore a dark green and cream paneled wool skirt, her grey sweater, and a grey felt man's hat with a tiny cardinal feather in the satin band. She held the paper bundle in her upturned hand and made little up-and-down weighing motions.

—Not hardly four pounds, she said. She set it and the jug on the ground and went to the house and came back carrying four small glasses and a cup of salt, sugar, black pepper, and red pepper all mixed together. She opened the paper and rubbed the mixture on the meat to case it, and then she buried it in the ashes of the fire and sat on the ground beside Ada. The skirt was long since dingy and would be none the worse for her sitting in the dirt.

While the meat cooked, they all sipped at the cider, and then Stobrod took out his fiddle, shook it to hear the rattles inside, and then put it to his chin, bowed a note, and twisted a peg. When he did the boy sat up and grabbed his instrument and frailed off a series of chiming phrases. Stobrod set off on a minor key tune that was yet somehow sprightly.

When he was finished Ada said, The plaintive fiddle.

Ruby looked at her funny.

—My father called it that, always ironically, Ada explained. She went on to say that unlike the common run of preachers—who oppose fiddle music as a sin and see the instrument itself as

the devil's box—Monroe despised it on aesthetic grounds. His critique was that all fiddle tunes sound just alike and all have strange names.

—That's what I like about them, Stobrod said. He tuned some more and then said, This is one of mine. I call it Drunk Neggar. It was a careening tune, loopy and syncopated, with little work for the left hand but the bow arm working as frantic as a man fighting off a deer fly from around his head.

Stobrod ran through a number more of his compositions. Altogether, they were an odd music. Harshly rhythmic but unsuited, many of them, for dancing, which was the only purpose to which Ruby had ever heard the fiddle addressed. Ada and Ruby sat together and listened, and as they did Ruby took Ada's hand and held it and absently removed Ada's silver bracelet and slipped it over her own hand and then after a time returned it to its place.

Stobrod changed tunings and called out the names of the pieces before playing them, and gradually Ada and Ruby began to suspect that what they heard collectively formed a sort of autobiography of his war years. Among the tunes were these: Touching the Elephant, Musket Stock Was My Pillow, Ramrod, Six Nights Drunk, Tavern Fight, Don't Sell It Give It Away, Razor Cut, Ladies of Richmond, Farewell General Lee.

To conclude the series he played one he called Stone Was My Bedstead, a tune made up largely of scraping sounds, chiefly of middling tempo, rhythms of approach and retreat, a great deal of suspense in the relations among its measures. There was no lyric other than a moment when Stobrod threw back his head and chanted the title three times. The Pangle boy had sense enough to add only subtle little runs and fills, muting the banjo's ring by just softly touching the strings with the meatiest part of thumb and forefinger.

Coarse as the song was, Ada found herself moved by it. More so, she believed, than at any opera she had attended from

Dock Street to Milan because Stobrod delivered it with such utter faith in its substance, in its ability to lead one toward a better life, one in which a satisfied mind might one day be attainable. Ada wished there were a way to capture what she was hearing in the way an ambrotype captures images, so it could be held in reserve for the benefit of a future whose residents might again need access to what it stood for.

As the tune drew toward a close, Stobrod jacked back his head so that he seemed to be reviewing the stars, but his eyes were shut. The butt of the fiddle pressed against his heart and the bow worked in jerky, stuttering little strokes. His mouth flew open at the ultimate moment, but he did not hoot or squeal as Ada expected. Instead, he smiled a deep long smile of silent delight.

He stopped and held the bow in the air at the place where the last upstroke ended and opened his eyes and looked at the others in the firelight to see what effect his playing had. At that moment, his was a saint's blithesome face, loose and half a-smile with the generosity of his gift and with a becoming neutrality toward his own abilities, as if he had long since cheerfully submitted to knowing that however well he rendered a piece, he could always imagine doing better. If all the world had a like countenance, war would be only bitter memory.

—He's done you some good there, Pangle said to Ada. And then he seemed appalled at having spoken directly to her and ducked his head and then looked off into the woods.

—We'll do one last one, Stobrod said.

He and Pangle put down their instruments and took off their hats in signification that the next song would be holy. A gospel. Stobrod led off singing and Pangle followed him. Stobrod had trained the boy's natural gabble into a strained high tenor, and so Pangle chattered partial repetitions of Stobrod's phrases in a style that might, under a whole other system of thinking, have been viewed as comic. Their voices mostly fought against each other until the chorus came around, and then they matched up and found a deep place of concord. The song was

about how dark our lives are, how cold and stormy, how void of understanding, and at the end death. That was all. The song ended somewhat incomplete and blockaded, for contrary to every expectation of the genre, there was no shining path limned out at the last minute to lead one onward with hope. It seemed short one crucial verse. But the chorus harmonies were close and brotherlike, sweet enough in themselves to make partial headway against the song's otherwise gloom.

They put their hats back on and Stobrod held out his glass. Ruby poured him a dram of the cider and stopped and then he touched the back of her hand with a forefinger. Ada, watching, thought it a tender gesture until she realized it was but to urge the pouring of an extra measure.

After Mars had risen red from behind Jonas Ridge and the fire had burned down to a bed of coals, Ruby pronounced the meat done and dug it from the ashes with the pitchfork. The spices had formed a crust around the brisket, and Ruby put it on a stump butt and sliced it thin across the grain with her knife. The inside was pink and running with juice. They ate it with their fingers without benefit of plates and there was nothing else to the dinner. When they finished they pulled dry sedge grass from the field edge and scrubbed their hands clean.

Stobrod then buttoned the top button of his shirt and grabbed his lapels and pulled at them alternately to square his jacket on him. He took off his hat and wiped the two sprigs of hair back from his temples with his palms and put the hat back on.

Ruby watched and then said to no one in particular, He's about to need somebody to do something for him.

Stobrod said, I want to talk to you is all. To ask you something.

—Well? she said.

—Thing is, I need caring for, Stobrod said.

—Has your liquor give out?

—Of that, there's aplenty. What it is, he said, is I'm scared.

His fear, he explained, was that the raiding was going to

bring the law down on them. A leader had arisen from the outliers—the bearskin man. He was a talker and had given them a common creed: that their fighting in the war had not been pure as they once thought. It had been tainted because they had fought witless for the big man's ownership of his nigger, the human weakness of hatred driving them on. They were a company of former fools, but they had seen the light. They talked about it all the time, gathered about the fire in seminar. All subsequent warring, they agreed, would be for no other interests but their own. They would not be taken easy and sent back to the armies.

—He's wanting us all to take a blood oath to die like dogs, Stobrod said. With our teeth in someone's throat. But I didn't quit one army to sign on with another.

What Stobrod had decided was that he and Pangle would before long pull out, seek other shelter. Leave the warrior band. What he needed was a promise of food, a dry barn loft in bad weather, and maybe now and then a little money, at least until the fighting was over and he could come out free.

—Eat roots, Ruby said. Drink muddy water. Sleep in a hollow log.

—Have you not got more feeling than that for your daddy? Stobrod said.

—I'm just offering instruction in woodcraft. It comes from experience. I've dined on many a root when you were off roundering. Slept in worse places than hollow logs.

—You know I did my best toward you. Times was hard.

—Not hard as now. And don't go telling you did your best. You didn't do a thing at all other than what suited you. And I'll not stand you letting on we're much to each other. I never was anything to you. You came and went and I could have been there or not when you got back. It didn't much matter one way or the other. If I had died on the mountain, you might have wondered a week or two would I show up. Like one coon dog of a many-numbered pack missing when the horn blows and dawn comes.

Just that much regret and no more. So don't expect me to go jumping now when you call.

—But I'm an old man, Stobrod said.

—You told me you're not yet fifty.

—I feel old.

—So do I, for what that's worth. And there's this. If what's told about Teague is counted as even half true, we have plenty to worry about harboring you. This is not my place. It's not my say. But if it was, I'd say no.

They both looked to Ada. She sat with her shawl about her and her hands caught up in the skirts between her knees to keep warm. She could see in their faces that they looked to her as arbiter, maybe for reasons of landownership or education or culture. And though she did have a certain dominion over the immediate land, she found herself uncomfortable in the role of master. All she could think was that Ruby's father had come back from something like the dead, and that it was a second chance which few are granted.

She said, There is the view that he is your father and that at some point it becomes your duty to take care of him.

—Amen, Stobrod said.

Ruby shook her head. We've got two differing ideas of father then, she said. I'll tell you something about it from my view. I don't know how old I was except that I was still cutting teeth. He took off stilling.

She turned to Stobrod and said, Do you even remember? You and Poozler and Cold Mountain? That strike a chord?

—I remember, Stobrod said.

—Well, tell your part of it, Ruby said.

So Stobrod told his story. He and a partner had taken the notion of making liquor for profit, and they went off and lived in bark lean-tos on the mountain. Ruby had seemed to him on her own sufficient, so he had left her for three months when she was not yet eight. He and Poozler were not craftsmen of the liquor trade. They ran quick little batches that would hardly fill a

teapot, and they found it was too much bother putting washed fire coals in the singlings to filter it, and so nearly every run dripped out either cloudy green or cloudy yellow. But it was strong. They'd not temper it down past about three quarters straight alcohol. It differed only in minor particulars from the usquebaugh and poteen of their Celt forebears. Many customers, though, found it overly exhilarating to the bowels. Business withered away and they made no money, for after they had poured off what they required for their own needs, the remainder of the liquor was only enough to trade for the next batch of makings. Stobrod had stayed until the poor economy of the venture and the cold weather of November drove him off the mountain.

When he finished Ruby told her part, what she had done during those months while he was gone. She foraged for wild food. Grubbed for roots, caught fish in traps she twisted together out of willow boughs, took birds in snares of similar make. She ate whatever bird she caught with little discrimination other than to avoid fish eaters when possible and carrion eaters always. Learned only by trial and error what of their internalments were to be eaten and what not. One memorable week she had been luckless in her trapping and ate only chestnuts and hickory nuts ground into meal and baked to a crumbly pone on a piece of fireside slate. One day out gathering nuts, Ruby had come upon the still. Stobrod was sleeping under a lean-to and his partner said, He just lays up in bed all day. Only thing that tells you he's not dead is now and then he works his toes. She'd have gladly, at that moment and at several since, have swapped her lot with any wolf child. In Ruby's opinion, Romulus and Remus that Ada had read her about were lucky boys, for they at least had a fierce guardian.

Despite such hard and lonesome times, though, Ruby did in fairness have to say this for Stobrod: he had never laid a hand to her in anger. She could not remember ever being struck. Then

again, he had never even patted her head or put his hand to her cheek in a moment of kindness.

She looked at Ada and said, There. Square that with your notion of duty.

Before Ada could formulate a complete thought or even just say Oh, my, Ruby rose and stalked off into the darkness.

Stobrod said nothing, and Pangle said softly, as if to himself, She's got her drawers in a wad now.

Sometime later, having sent Stobrod and Pangle away with only vague hopes of compromise, Ada walked up the path to the outhouse. The night was turning much colder, and she guessed there would be frost by dawn. The moon, full and high, threw such light that every tree limb cast a blue shadow. Had Ada wished, she could have pulled *Adam Bede* from her pocket and opened it to the moon and read. Only the brightest stars shone out against the grey sky. Surveying them, Ada noted Orion climbing in the east, and then she saw that the moon was missing a part. A thin scoop was cut from out it. Eclipse was what it was.

She went back in the house and got three quilts and Monroe's spyglass. It was Italian and pretty to look at, with much scrollwork cut into the brass, though not so fine in its optics as those the Germans made. She went to the shed and got a campaign chair, wondering as she drew one from the stack of four if it was the chair in which Monroe had died. She unfolded it in the front yard and wrapped up close in the quilts and stretched out with her face tipped up to the heavens. She looked through the glass, twisting it into focus. The moon snapped sharp in her eye, the shadowed edge copper but still clearly visible. One crater at the top with a mountain at its center.

Ada watched the progress of the shadow as it marched across the bright face, and even when the eclipse was complete, the moon was still slightly visible, the color of an old cent

brownie and to all appearances just about that big. With the moon all but gone, the Milky Way shone out, a river of light across the sky, a band like blown road dust. Ada ran the glass across it and stopped and peered into the deep of it. Through the glass the stars multiplied into tangled thickets of light and seemed to go on and on until she began to feel that she lay poised and exposed at the edge of a gorge. As if she were looking down, not up, hanging at the bottom limb of her planet's radius. For a moment she spun into the kind of vertigo she had felt at Esco's well lip, as if she might become unstuck and fall helpless into those thorns of light.

She opened her other eye and put aside the spyglass. The dark walls of Black Cove rose up and held her fixed in a cup of land, and she lay content and watched the sky as the moon gradually emerged from the earth's shadow. She thought about the refrain of a tune Stobrod had sung that night, a ragged love song. Its ultimate line was: Come back to me is my request. Stobrod could not have uttered it with more conviction had it been one of the profounder lines of *Endymion*. Ada had to admit that, at least now and again, just saying what your heart felt, straight and simple and unguarded, could be more useful than four thousand lines of John Keats. She had never been able to do it in her whole life, but she thought she would like to learn how.

She went in the house and got her lap desk and a candle lantern and came back to the chair. She inked her pen and then sat and stared at the paper until her nib dried out. Every phrase she thought of seemed nothing but pose and irony. She wiped the pen clean on a blotter and dipped again and wrote, Come back to me is my request. She signed her name and folded the paper and addressed it to the hospital in the capital. She wrapped up tight in the quilts and soon she was asleep and frost fell on her and the outer quilt became crisp with rime.

a vow to bear

Inman walked through mountain country and kept to trails and saw few people. He measured out distance in portions of a day. A full day's walk. Half a day. Less than half a day. Anything shorter than that was just a little piece down the road. Miles and hours became concepts he disdained since he had not the means to measure either.

He was held back in his travels after he came upon a little-sized woman sitting humped up on a fence rail crying for her dead girl. The woman's bonnet hood shaded her face so all Inman could see was black but the tip of her nose. When she turned her face up to Inman, though, the tears dripping from her jawbones sparkled in the morning light. She held her mouth slitted open in anguish so that in Inman's mind it resembled the sputcheon to a sword scabbard. The sun was not up good yet and she was about to have to bury her child wound up in an old quilt, for she had no idea of how to make a box.

Inman offered his help and spent the day in her backyard, knocking together a little casket from boards pulled off an ancient curing house. They smelled of hog fat and hickory smoke,

and the inside faces of the boards were black and glossy from many years of making hams. From time to time the woman came to the back door to check his progress and each time she said, My girl's bowels was loose as stove ash for two weeks before she died.

When Inman was done with the carpentry he layered the bottom of the box with dry pine needles. He went into the house and got the girl, who lay on a downstairs bed, cased in the quilt. He lifted her, and she was a hard, tight bundle like a pod or gall. He carried her through the back door and the mother sat at the kitchen table and looked at him out of blank eyes. He unwrapped the quilt and set the girl on the coffin lid and tried not to let his mind dwell on her pinched grey cheeks and keen nose. He cut the quilt with his knife and tacked it into the casket for lining, and then he lifted up the girl and settled her in the box and picked up the hammer and went to the door.

—I'd better nail it to, he said.

The woman came out and kissed the girl on each caved cheek and on her forehead, then she sat on the porch edge and watched Inman hammer the lid tight.

They buried her on a nearby knoll where lay four old graves, marked with scratched flats of river shale. The first three were infants, birth dates lacking a month of being a year apart. Death dates falling mere days after birth. The fourth grave was the mother, and Inman noted she had died on the birth date of the last child. He did quick sums in his head and saw that she lived only to twenty. Inman dug the hole for the new grave at the end of the little row of stones, and when he was done he said, Do you want to say something?

—No, the woman said. Every word in me would come out bitter.

By the time Inman refilled the hole, dark was coming on. He and the woman went back to the house.

She said, I ought to feed you, but I haven't got it in me to even light a fire, much less cook a meal.

She went inside and came back with provisions. Two little cloth bundles, one of corn grits and the other of flour. A chunk of lard tied in paper dark with grease, a brown piece of smoke-cured hog neckbone, some parched corn, about a cup of soup beans twisted in a square of paper, a leek and a turnip and three carrots, a bar of lye soap. Inman took them and thanked the woman and turned to walk away. But before he reached the fence gate the woman called to him.

—I can't ever look back on this day with a still mind if I let you go without cooking for you, she said.

Inman kindled up a fire, and the woman sat on a low hearth-stool and fried him a great beefsteak from a neighbor's heifer that had mired in a slough and died before anyone noticed it missing. The woman filled a brown crockery plate with yellow corn grits cooked thin so they ran to the edges. The steak cupped up in the frying like a hand held out for change, and she put it atop the grits with the cupped side down and then mounted a pair of fried eggs atop the dome of meat. As final garnish she scooped a plug of butter as big as a squirrel's head onto the eggs.

When she set it on the table in front of Inman, he looked down on the plate and nearly cried as he watched the butter melt across the egg yolks and the whites and the brown meat and the yellow grits until the whole plate glistered in the taper light. He sat with knife and fork fisted up before him, but he could not eat. The food seemed to require some special thanks to be returned, and he could not find the words. Outside in the dark a bobwhite called and waited for an answer and then called again, and a small wind rose and there was a momentary rain that rattled the leaves and the roof shakes and then it stopped.

—This meal needs blessing, Inman said.

—Say one, then, the woman said.

Inman thought a minute and said, I can't call one up.

—For what I am about to receive, I am thankful. That's one, she said.

Inman said her words, trying them on for fit. Then he said, You don't know how long it's been.

As he ate, the woman took a picture from a shelf and studied it.

—We had our likeness made one time, she said. Man traveling in a wagon with all his picture tackle. I'm the one survivor now.

She wiped the dust from it on her sleeve and then reached out the little framed artifact for Inman to admire.

Inman took it and tipped it to the candle. A daguerreotype. There was a father, the woman some years younger, an old granny, six children ranging from boys old enough to wear brimmed hats to bonneted babies. All the members wore black and sat with hunched shoulders and all looked either suspicious or stunned, as if report of their deaths had just reached them.

—I'm sorry, Inman said.

When he was finished eating, the woman sent him on his way. He walked into the dark until new star patterns arose, and then he made a fireless bivouac alongside a thin creek. He tramped out a sleeping place in the tall dead grass and rolled up in his blanket and slept hard.

Then, for several wet days following, he walked as long as he could and slept in the haunts of birds. One night he found lodging in a log pigeonnier and the birds ignored him except when he rolled over, and then they all stirred and made watery gurgling sounds and settled back in. The next night he slept on the dry square of ground under a steepled dovecote, a structure suggestive of a temple devoted to a tiny null god. He had to sleep balled up, for if he stretched out, either his feet or his head would catch the drip from the steep hip roof. Another night he slept in an abandoned chicken house, and he spread his ground cloth over the floor, which was thick with chalky old chicken shit that gritted under him when he moved and smelled like the dusty remainders of ancient deadmen. When he woke sometime long before dawn and could not get back to sleep, he dug in his pack and found a stub of candle and lit it. He unrolled the Bartram

and held it to the yellow light and riffled through the pages until his eyes fell on a passage that caught his attention. It was this:

> The mountainous wilderness which I had lately traversed appeared regularly undulated as the great ocean after a tempest; the undulations gradually depressing, yet perfectly regular, as the squama of fish, or imbrications of tile on a roof: the nearest ground to me of a perfect full green; next more glaucous; and lastly almost blue as the ether with which the most distant curve of the horizon seemed to be blended. My imagination thus wholly engaged in the contemplation of this magnificent landscape, infinitely varied, and without bound, I was almost insensible or regardless of the charming objects more within my reach.

A picture of the land Bartram detailed leapt dimensional into Inman's mind. Mountains and valleys on and on forever. A gnarled and taliped and snaggy landscape where man might be seen as an afterthought. Inman had many times looked across the view Bartram described. It was the border country stretching endlessly north and west from the slope of Cold Mountain. Inman knew it well. He had walked its contours in detail, had felt all its seasons and registered its colors and smelled its smells. Bartram was only a traveler and knew but the one season of his visit and the weather that happened to fall in a matter of days. But to Inman's mind the land stood not as he'd seen it and known it for all his life, but as Bartram had summed it up. The peaks now stood higher, the vales deeper than they did in truth. Inman imagined the fading rows of ridges standing pale and tall as cloudbanks, and he built the contours of them and he colored them, each a shade paler and bluer until, when he had finally reached the invented ridgeline where it faded into sky, he was asleep.

The next day found Inman angling down to the southwest,

footslogging an old cart path through the mountains. A brisk day with all the leaves dead and on the ground. He was not even aware of what county he was in. Bloody Madison, perhaps. He came to a sign and on one side it read TOBO55M and on the other TOAV65M. All he could figure was that it would be a fair walk to whatever towns were meant.

He rounded a bend and came to a small pool, a kind of spring, the rocks around it green with sphagnum. The spring bottom was covered with rotting oak and poplar leaves and the water was amber like a weak steeping of them, a tea. Inman bent to dip his canteen. Wind blew up and he heard a strange tock and click, a sound like an attempt at music using only dry sticks as instruments. He looked off into the poolside woods toward the sound and discovered an odd sight. Inman found himself viewing a trio of hanging skeletons swaying in the breeze and tapping into each other.

The canteen glugged full. Inman stood and stoppered it and walked to the bones. They hung in a row from the lower limb of a big hemlock. Not even hung with rope, just plaited strips of bark from hickory saplings. The pelvis and leg bones of one had fallen to the ground and lay in a heap, with the toes of one foot sticking up. On one of the complete skeletons, the plaits had stretched so much that the man's toes reached the ground. Inman swept the leaves away, thinking to find a tamped patch in the dirt where the man had danced around and packed the earth in his dying. His hair had fallen off the skull and lay among the leaves about his toe bones. Blond. All the bones so white, teeth in the slack jaws yellow. Inman ran his hand down the arm bones of the man that had half fallen away. They had a grain to them. The bones of legs and feet in a pile as kindling for a fire. He couldn't cut himself down, Inman thought, but if he'll be patient, it will happen.

Some days later, Inman climbed all morning not really knowing where he was. Mists moved ahead of him like deer through the trees. And then for the afternoon he walked a ridgeline trail that rolled between balsam highlands and little gladed gaps where stood beech groves and the tail ends of cove hardwoods as they reached the highest places where they could live. As he walked he began to suspect that he knew roughly where he was. It was an old passway, that much was clear. He passed a rock cairn that the Cherokee in times long past were in the habit of building along the way to signify something, though whether way marker or memorial or holy place was now unknowable. Inman picked up a fresh rock and dropped it on the pile in passing as commemoration of some old upward yearning.

Late in the day he found himself on a rocky scarp bordered by heath bald, a thick tangle of waist-high azalea and laurel and myrtle growing right to the bare rock of the ledge. The trail emptied onto it as if travelers had made a custom of stopping to admire the view. Then the way reentered the forest through a faint passage in the azalea not forty feet from where he had emerged.

The sun was falling, and Inman reckoned he would again make a bivouac without benefit of fire or water. In the space near the edge of the scarp, he scraped together what little duff there was to soften a sleeping place. He ate parched corn from his palm and stretched out in his bedding to sleep, wishing there were a bigger moon in the sky to light the prospect before him.

He was awakened at first grey dawn by the sound of walking in the heath. He sat up and set the LeMat's on full cock and leveled it at the sound. In a minute a black sow bear poked her head through the leaves not twenty feet from where Inman sat. She stood, tan muzzle up, neck stretched long, sniffing the breeze and blinking her little eyes.

She did not like what she smelled. She shuffled forward and grunted. A single cub not much bigger than a man's head

climbed a little way up the trunk of a young Fraser fir behind her. Inman knew that with her poor sight she could smell him but not see him in the faint light. She was in fact so near that even with his man's poor nose he could take her scent. Wet dog and something deeper.

The bear twice whoofed out air from nose and mouth and moved forward tentatively. Inman shifted about and stood, and the bear pricked up her ears. She blinked and stretched her neck again and sniffed and moved another step forward.

Inman set the pistol down on his bedding, for he had taken upon himself a vow to bear, never again to shoot one, though he had killed and eaten many in his youth and knew that he had still in him a strong liking for the flavor of bear grease. The decision came as a result of a series of dreams he had over the period of a week in the muddy trenches of Petersburg. In the first of the dreams he had started as a man. He was sick and drank tea from bearberry leaves as tonic, and gradually he became transformed into a black bear. During the nights the bear visions rode him, Inman roamed the green dream mountains alone and four-legged, avoiding all of his own kind and of other kinds. He rooted in the ground for pale grubs and tore at bee trees for honey and ate huckleberries by the bushful and was happy and strong. In that manner of life, he thought, there might be a lesson in how to wage peace and heal the wounds of war into white scars.

In the final dream, though, he was shot by hunters after a long chase. He was strung from a tree by a rope about his neck and skinned, and he watched the process as from above. His dripping red carcass was as he knew an actual bear's to be after skinning: that is to say, manlike, thinner than one would expect, the structure of paws beneath the fur long like a man's hand. With that killing, the dreams had run their course, and he awoke that last morning feeling bear was an animal of particular import to him, one he might observe and learn from, and that it would

be on the order of a sin for him to kill one no matter what the expense, for there was something in bear that spoke to him of hope.

Still, he did not much favor his current position, backed up against the brow of the rocky ledge, the heath knotted up before him, and the sow nervous with a cub born out of season. In his favor was this: he knew a bear was much more likely to run than attack, that she might at most make a false charge, rushing forward fifteen feet or so, bouncing as she came on her front legs and snorting out air. The purpose would be to scare him off, not to hurt him. But he had nowhere to run. He wanted her to know where he was, so he spoke to her, saying, I've no aim to trouble you. I'll walk on from here and never be back. I'm just asking for clear passage. He spoke calm and straight and he wanted his voice to carry respect.

The bear sniffed more. She shifted from foot to foot, rocked from side to side. Inman slowly rolled up his bedding and slipped on his sacks.

—I'll be going, he said.

He moved two steps and the bear false-charged.

Inman could figure in his mind as it happened that none of the measurements would work out. Like a problem of carpentry where none of the dimensions match up. He had only three feet to back up. She had all the momentum of her bulk and only ten feet ahead of her before the lip of the cliff.

Inman took a step to the side and the bear rushed by him and plunged over the high ledge that she never saw in the gloom. He could smell her strong as she went by. Wet dog, black dirt.

He looked over and saw her break open on the rocks far below like a great red blossom in the dawn light. Black pelt scraps littering the rocks.

Shit, he thought. Even my best intentions come to naught, and hope itself is but an obstacle.

The cub in the fir bawled out in its anguish. It was not even yet a weanling and would wither and die without a mother. It

would wail away for days until it starved or was eaten by wolf or panther.

Inman walked to the tree and looked into the little bear's face. It blinked its black eyes at him and opened its mouth and cried like a human baby.

To his credit, Inman could imagine reaching up and grabbing the cub by the scruff of its neck and saying, We're kin. Then taking his knapsack off and thrusting the cub in with only its head sticking out. Then putting the pack back on and walking away, the bear looking about from this new perspective as bright-eyed as a papoose. Give it to Ada as a pet. Or if she turned him away, he might raise it to be a part-tame bear, and when full grown it might stop by his hermit cabin on Cold Mountain now and again for company. Bring its wife and children so that in years to come Inman could have an animal family if no other. That would be one way this dead bear calamity might be rectified.

What Inman did, though, was all he could do. He picked up the LeMat's and shot the cub in the head and watched it pause as its grip on the tree failed and it fell to ground.

So as not to waste the meat, Inman built a fire and skinned out the cub and cut it in pieces and parboiled it. He laid the black pelt out on a rock and it was no bigger than a coon's. While the bear cooked he sat and waited at the scarp as morning came on. The mists broke and he could see mountains and rivers ranked to the earth's far verge. Shadows slid down the slopes of the nearest line of ridges, falling into the valley as if draining into a vast pool of dark under the ground. Rags of cloud hung in the valleys below Inman's feet, but in all that vista there was not a rooftop or plume of smoke or cleared field to mark a place where man had settled. You could look out across that folded landscape and every sense you had told only that this was all the world there was.

The wind sweeping up the mountain carried away the smell of the bear boiling and left only the odor of wet stone. Inman

could see west for scores of miles. Crest and scarp and crag, stacked and grey, to the long horizon. Cataloochee, the Cherokee word was. Meaning waves of mountains in fading rows. And this day the waves could hardly be differed from the raw winter sky. Both were barred and marbled with the same shades of grey only, so the outlook stretched high and low like a great slab of streaked meat. Inman himself could not have been better dressed to conceal himself amid this world, for all he wore was grey and black and dirty white.

Bleak as the scene was, though, there was growing joy in Inman's heart. He was nearing home; he could feel it in the touch of thin air on skin, in his longing to see the leap of hearth smoke from the houses of people he had known all his life. People he would not be called upon to hate or fear. He rose and took a wide stance on the rock and stood and pinched down his eyes to sharpen the view across the vast prospect to one far mountain. It stood apart from the sky only as the stroke of a poorly inked pen, a line thin and quick and gestural. But the shape slowly grew plain and unmistakable. It was to Cold Mountain he looked. He had achieved a vista of what for him was homeland.

As he studied on it, he recognized the line of every far ridge and valley to be more than remembered. They seemed long ago scribed indelible on his corneas with a sharp instrument. He looked out at this highland and knew the names of places and things. He said them aloud: Little Beartail Ridge, Wagon Road Gap, Ripshin, Hunger Creek, Clawhammer Knob, Rocky Face. Not a mountain or watercourse lacked denomination. Not bird or bush anonymous. His place.

He rocked his head from side to side, and it felt balanced anew on his neck stem. He entertained the notion that he stood unfamiliarly plumb to the horizon. For a moment it seemed thinkable that he might not always feel cored out. Surely off in that knotty country there was room for a man to vanish. He could walk and the wind would blow the yellow leaves across his

footsteps and he would be hid and safe from the wolfish gaze of the world at large.

Inman sat and admired his country until the bear pieces were cooked, and then he dredged them in flour and fried them up in the last lard from the twisted paper the woman had given him days before. He ate sitting at the cliff top. He had not eaten bear of such youth before, and though the meat was less black and greasy than that of older bear, it still tasted nevertheless like sin. He tried to name which of the deadly seven might apply, and when he failed he decided to append an eighth, regret.

naught and grief

If the lobe of mountain they climbed had a name, Stobrod did not know it. He and his two companions walked humped up, their down-turned faces clenched against the cold, hat brims raked near to their noses, hands pulled up into coat sleeves. Their shadows blew out long before them so that they trod on their resemblances. The woods passed unremarked around them. Bare sticks of buckeye, silver bell, tulip tree, and basswood waved in the breeze. Many wet millennia of leaves underfoot muted their steps.

The Pangle boy trod close upon Stobrod's heels. The third figure followed six paces back. Stobrod carried his fiddle in its sack clamped under his arm, and Pangle had his banjo thonged neck down over his shoulder. The third man had no music device but toted all the party's meager goods in a knapsack. He had enshrouded himself in a moth-riddled butternut blanket that trailed on the ground, dragging a wake in the leaves.

Their bowels were all a-clamor from the previous night's supper, which they'd made from a doe they'd found dead on the ground, frozen to it. In their meat hunger, they'd chosen to

ignore signs of how long the thing had been there or how it might have died. They'd built a smoky little fire of wet poplar and cooked up its haunch until it was not much more than thawed out. They ate it in some quantity, and now they regretted it. They did not talk. Now and again one of them flared off into a laurel thicket and caught back up later.

No wind hissed nor bird called. The only sound fine needles falling when they passed beneath stands of hemlock. Vestiges of dawn yet fanned out ocher in the east, and thin clouds scudded fast across the brittle sun. The twined dark limbs of hardwoods stood etched against the weak light. For some time there was no color to anything earthly other than somber tones of brown and grey. Then they passed an icy rock ledge and saw growing on it some flabby yellow sect of wort or lichen, so bright it hurt the eyes. Pangle reached out and broke off a scalloped leathern flap and ate it speculatively and with great attentiveness. He neither spit it out nor pulled off more, so his judgment on the taste was hard to call. Afterward, though, he walked along bright in his perceptions, alert for other such gifts the world might give.

In time they ascended to a piece of flat ground where three passways came together: the one they had arrived by falling, two yet fainter climbing on. The greater of the forks had begun life as a buffalo trail and then an Indian path, and it remained still too tight in its passage between trees to make even a wagon road. Hunters had camped here and left a well-used fire ring and had cut trees for firewood and the woods were thin some fifty paces back from where the ways Y'd off. An immense poplar, though, stood in the forks of the rising tracks. It had not been spared cutting out of any homage to its beauty or its girth or its age. There was just not a crosscut saw in any near settlement long enough to span it. Its trunk was big around as a corncrib where it entered the ground.

Stobrod, thinking he dimly remembered the place, stopped to survey it, and when he did Pangle trod on his boot heel. Stobrod's foot came out entire, and he stood sock-footed on frozen

leaf mold. He turned and put a hard finger to the boy's breastbone and pushed him a step away and then stooped and put his fiddle sack on the ground and reshod himself.

The men stood together blowing from the climb and looking at the two paths ahead of them. Their breaths hovered about them as if in concern, and then the vague shapes lost interest and vanished. There was a creek tumbling somewhere nearby within earshot, and it provided all the sound there was to the place.

—It's cold, the third man said.

Stobrod looked at him and then cleared his throat and spit in commentary on the bleakness of the scene and the depthlessness of the observation.

Pangle reached a hand out of his sleeve and turned it palm up to the elements and then fisted it and drew it back in as a turtle its head.

—Ah, God, shrivel you cullions up in you belly, he said.

—What I mean, the third man said.

They had acquired the man at the outlier's cave. He had not offered a name nor did Stobrod care to know it. He was a Georgia boy of no more than seventeen years, black-headed, brown-skinned, little fine wisps of chin whiskers, but smooth-cheeked as a maid. Some Cherokee blood, or maybe Creek. Like everybody else, he had a war tale. He and his cousin had been pitiful little conscriptees, and they had been put into the troops in sixty-three. They had fought out a year of war in the same regiment, though there was not much they could contribute since their rifle muskets stood higher than their hat crowns. They'd slept every night under the same blanket, and they had deserted together. Their reasoning was that no war lasts forever, and though man was born to die, it would be foolish to do so on the eve of peace. So they left. But the walk home was long and confusing, and they had not reckoned on quite so much landscape passing under their feet. It had taken them three months to reach Cold Mountain, and they did not even know what state it was in.

They'd become profoundly lost, and the cousin had died in a grim cove, feverish and wracked with coughs from some wet lung disorder.

The boy had been found by one of the cavers some days later, wandering aimless. He had been given over to Stobrod and Pangle, who were setting off to found their own community of two somewhere up near the Shining Rocks. Even though Georgia was a state Stobrod held in low regard, he had agreed to point it out to the boy when they reached a height where they had a great southern vista.

First, however, they had descended from the cave to a hiding place for food, telling the boy along the way about Ada and how she had eventually led Ruby toward benevolence. Ruby had laid down conditions for her charity, though. She and Ada were themselves working on tight margins for the winter and could give only a little, not enough for the two men to live on entirely. And she thought it risky for Stobrod and Pangle to visit. She did not want to see so much as their shadows about the farm again. The food would have to be left somewhere safe and hidden, and she had suggested a place up along the ridge that she had discovered in her rambles as a child. A round flat stone marked from rim to rim with all manner of odd scripture. And further, she did not want to be tied down to any schedule. She'd take food there when she felt like it and not take it when she didn't. It was up to Stobrod to check.

When the men had gotten to the place, Stobrod cast his eyes about and then knelt and felt around with his hands under the leaves. Then he started raking with the edge of his boot and soon he had uncovered a round flat stone set in the ground. It was about the size of the mouth of a washtub, and the markings showed not any feature of the Cherokee style. They were too abrupt and strict in the angles of their characters, which jittered across the stone as a spider on a skillet. It might have come from some race prior to man. Under the edge of the rock they found a tin box of cornmeal, some dried apples twisted up in a piece of

newspaper, a few shavings of side meat, an earthen crock of pickled beans. These they had added to their own provisions of liquor and smoking tobacco and chewing tobacco.

—Reckon which trail we want? the Georgia boy now said to Stobrod. The blanket bumped out where his elbow gestured toward the trail forks and made folds to the ground like drapery in carved stone.

Stobrod looked as directed, but he was not at all sure where they were nor which way they were going. He just knew higher, more remote. It was a big mountain. Walk a circuit around what might rightly be called the base of it and you'd walk not far short of a hundred mile. There's a right smart of range encompassed therein, even if it were flat as a plat map rather than rared up into the sky and folded into every kind of cove and hollow and vale. As well, Stobrod's previous experience of Cold Mountain had been, whenever possible, as a drunk. So in his mind, the trails tangled together and could lead anywhither.

Pangle watched Stobrod's confused study of the landscape. And then finally, with a halting preamble of apology for knowing more that his mentor, he said he knew exactly where he was and knew that the right-hand fork soon grew faint but worked its way on and on across the mountain, leading farther than he had ever cared to follow, going wherever it was the Indians went. The left fork was broader at first but just wandered around and petered out shortly near a dank pool of water.

—We'll cook us a meal and head on, then, Stobrod said.

The men drew together wood and struck a reluctant blaze in the old black ring of stones. They put some cornmeal mush to boiling in creek water, supposing that its blandness might settle their moiled stomachs. They pulled up sitting logs and lit clay pipes and puffed and crowded as near to the faint flames as they could without setting their clothes and their boot soles afire. They passed the liquor bottle and took long swigs. The keen

weather had seeped into their bones and jelled their marrow hard as cold lard. They sat quiet waiting for the warmth of fire and liquor to loosen them up.

After a time, Stobrod became deeply engaged in probing his knife blade into the crock of pickled beans he held before him. He nibbled one bean at a time from the end of the knife and between each one wiped the vinegar off the blade against his pant leg. Pangle ate a little withered ring of dried apple, first rubbing it out flat between his palms and holding it up to his eye as if its core hole served as spyglass to give new perspective on the things of the world. The Georgia boy sat humped forward, hands to the fire. His blanket was cowled over his head, and it left his visage all shadowed but for the firelight striking off his black eyes. He put a hand to his belly and stiffened up as if someone had run a pointed stick through his vitals.

—If I'd known I'd have the scours this bad I'd not have eat one mouthful of that venison, he said.

He stood and walked slowly and with some delicacy off into the rhododendron thicket beyond the clearing. Stobrod watched him go.

—I feel sorry for that boy, he said. He's wishing he'd never left home, but he's not even got sense to know what kind of vile state he's from. If I had a brother in jail and one in Georgia, I'd try to bust the one out of Georgia first.

—I never been so far as Georgia, Pangle said.

—I went just the one time, Stobrod said. Not but a little piece into it. Just until I could see what poor stuff it was made of, and then I turned back.

The fire flared up from a puff of wind, and the men put their hands out to warm. Stobrod dozed off. His head nodded until his chin was at his chest. When it jerked back up, he was looking at mounted men in the trail, just cresting the brow of the hill. A little bunch of sorry-looking scouts led by a dandyman and a slight boy. But the men had sabers and pistols and rifles, several of which were pointed at Stobrod. The Guard rode bundled in

heavy coats and wrapped in blankets and the horses steamed in the cold air and puffed out plumes from their pooched nostrils. There was a skin of ice in the roadway, and when they stepped forward their hooves gritted in it like pestle against mortar.

The Guard came on up the trail and into the clearing until they loomed over the men and threw their shadows on them. Stobrod made to rise and Teague said, Sit still. He sat loose in the saddle and he held a short-barreled Spencer carbine with the in-curved butt plate of it fit against the swell of his thigh. He had on wool gloves, the thumb and forefinger cut off the right hand so he could pull back a hammer and trip a trigger unhindered. Plaited reins held finely between the covered finger and thumb of his other hand. He studied the pair of men before him for some time. Their skin was grey and their eyes looked raw as holes burnt in a quilt top. The fat boy's hair stood in greasy brown peaks like meringue on one side of his head and lay matted to the skull on the other. The skin of Stobrod's balding pate was grainy and dull, slack-looking over the bone, altogether lacking in the tight sheen common to the hairless. His face looked to have collapsed all around the point of his nose so that he resembled a funnel.

Teague said, I'm not even going to ask if you've got papers. I've heard every falsehood there is to tell in that regard. We're after a bunch of outliers said to live in a cave. They've been robbing folks. If a man knew where that cave bores into the mountain, it might be in his favor to tell it.

—I don't exactly know, Stobrod said. His voice was real quick and bright, though inside he was gloomy, figuring that within a month he would be back in bloody Virginia working a ramrod into a musket. I'd say if I did, he said. I've just heard talk of such a thing. Some say it's way over on the backside of the mountain, close on Bearpen Branch or Shining Creek or some like place.

Pangle looked funny at Stobrod. Puzzlement dark on his face as a shadow.

—What's your word on this? Teague said to Pangle.

The boy sat with his torso canted back, his weight settled on the platform of his wide hipbones. A hand shaded his eyes from the hazed sun that stood behind the shoulders of the horsemen grouped before him. He peered from his little-sized eyes in some confusion. He wondered how best to answer the question that had been put to him. All manner of thoughts crossing his soft face.

—Why that's not even close to it, Pangle finally said, looking to Stobrod. It's this side. You know. Over on Big Stomp. Not three mile up Nick Creek. You get where it turkey-foots out and there's a stand of hickory trees growing up on the right-hand slope. A sight of squirrels works the ground under them in the fall. Squirrels thick on the ground. You can kill them with rocks. You climb straight up a ways through them hickories to a rock fall, and then at the top of it there you are. There's a hollow in the clift there big as a great barn loft.

—Much obliged, Teague said. He turned to two big dark horsemen and twisted up a slight shade of meaning with one corner of his mouth. He put his weight in his stirrups and his leathers squeaked and he swung a leg over and dismounted.

The other men followed.

—We'll join you at your fire if you don't mind, Teague said to Stobrod. Take some breakfast with you. Cook and eat. And then in a little bit we'll hear you boys pick some. See if you're any account.

They built up the fire and sat around it as if they were all fellowmen. The Guard had a great quantity of sausage tied up in casings, and when they pulled it out of their saddlebags it was frozen hard and coiled like the bowels of something. They had to cut it in cooking pieces with a little hand axe. They put the cut pieces on flat stones at the edge of the fire to thaw enough to run sharpened sticks through them and hold them out to roast.

The fire was soon tall flame and red coal and a bed of white ash, and it threw enough heat that Pangle unbuttoned his jacket and then his shirt and put out a strip of his pale chest and belly

to it and became all at ease. He had no sense that there was anything to the moment but warmth and comradeship and the smell of food cooking. He studied his banjo a minute, seeming to admire its form and the rightness of its materials as if he had never seen it before. As though he liked studying its geometry nearly as much as he did playing it. Soon his eyes fogged over and closed and he sat slumped, all the weight of him collapsed through his trunk onto the broad base of his ass, so that the front of him was a cascade of white flesh rolls. He was a sculpture carved in the medium of lard.

—Gone from the world, Stobrod said. Wore out.

Teague took a bottle of liquor from his coat pocket and held it out to Stobrod.

—Not too early for you, is it? he said.

—I commenced some time ago, Stobrod said. When you've not slept but a snatch or two in days it's hard to say what's too early.

He took the offered bottle and drew the cork and tipped it to his mouth, and though it was only of mediocre quality he was polite in his estimation of it. He smacked his lips and blew out his breath and nodded at the taste.

—Why have you not slept? Teague said.

Stobrod explained that they had been picking music and gambling for a few days and nights with some sharps, though he neglected to say that it had been at the outliers' cave. Cards, chicken fights, dog fights, dice. Any contest they could think up to lay bets on. Big gamblers hot to wager. Some in such a fever they would win the hat off your head and then oddman for your hair. Lacking anything more striking, they'd put money on which of a gathering of birds would fly off a limb first. Stobrod bragged that he had broken even, which in such company was a thing to marvel at.

Teague put the knuckles of his fingers together and made a motion like thumbing cards off a deck.

—Sportsmen, he said.

The sausages swelled, oozed fat, squealed faintly in their casings, made spitting sounds when they dripped in the coals. Eventually they were brown. All the men but Pangle, who yet slept, ate them off the points of the cooking sticks. And when they had eaten until the meat was gone, Teague looked at the fiddle and banjo and said, Can you play those things?

—Some, Stobrod said.

—Pick me something then, Teague said.

Stobrod did not much want to. He was tired. And he figured his audience had no thought of music, lacked entirely what was needed to love it. But he took up his fiddle anyway and just brushed the dry skin of his palm across the strings and knew from their whisper what keys to twist.

—What do you want to hear? he said.

—No matter. You call it.

Stobrod reached over and prodded Pangle in the shoulder. The boy came to, his little eyes just slitted. With evident effort he pulled his thoughts together so that they trained up to some purpose.

—They want to hear us pick a tune, Stobrod said.

Pangle said nothing, but worked his finger joints awhile in the heat of the fire. He picked up his banjo and twiddled with the pegs and then, without waiting for Stobrod, began knocking out a few notes to Backstep Cindy. As he picked, the rolled fat of his front jiggled in time with the frailing, but when he got to where the tune was ready to come around again, the notes scrambled all together and he bogged down and halted.

—That'un's come to naught and grief, he said to Stobrod. If you was to pitch in we might get somewhere.

Stobrod bowed a note or two from Cindy, and then some other notes, seeming at random, unrelated. He went over them and over them, and it began to be clear that they made no sense. But he suddenly gathered them up and worked a variation on them, and then another yet more precise, and they unexpectedly fell together into a tune. He found the pattern he was seeking,

and he followed the trail of notes where they led, finding the way of their logic, which was brisk, brittle, effortless as laughing. He played the run of it a time or two until Pangle had his chord changes down and had spun off a series of quick answering notes, bright and harsh. Then they set off together to see what sort of thing they had composed.

Though in form it was neither jig nor reel, it was yet right for dancing. Their stomachs, however, were still in such a rage that neither of them could have shuffled out a step. Pangle, nevertheless, had one foot patting ground on the offbeat and his head was nodding and his eyes were loose-closed so that there was but a trembling rim of white showing between the lashes. Stobrod played a run of notes and then lowered the fiddle from under his bristled neck so that the butt of it rested against his chest. He beat out the rhythm on the strings with his bow. Pangle caught on and did the same with his flattened hand against the groundhog hide of the banjo head, and momentarily there was a sense that the instruments they played were just elaborations on the drum. To the thumping, Stobrod put back his head and sang out a lyric he was making up at the moment. It had to do with women whose bellies were hard as the necks of mules. Such women, the song proclaimed, were cruel beyond the generality of their sex.

When he was done singing, they played one more round and then stopped. They consulted and twisted the pegs again to make the dead man's tuning, and they then set in playing a piece slightly reminiscent of Bonaparte's Retreat, which some name General Washington's tune. This was softer, more meditative, yet nevertheless grim as death. When the minor key drifted in it was like shadows under trees, and the piece called up something of dark woods, lantern light. It was awful old music in one of the ancient modalities, music that sums up a culture and is the true expression of its inner life.

Birch said, Jesus wept. The fit's took them now.

None of the Guard had ever heard fiddle and banjo played

together in that tuning, nor had they heard playing of such strength and rhythm applied to musical themes so direful and elegiac. Pangle's use of the thumb on the fifth string and dropping to the second was an especial thing of arrogant wonder. It was like ringing a dinner bell, yet solemn. His other two fingers worked in a mere hard, groping style, but one honed to brutish perfection. Stobrod's fingers on the fiddle neck found patterns that seemed set firm as the laws of nature. There was a deliberation, a study, to their clamping of the strings that was wholly absent from the reckless bowing of the right hand. What lyric Stobrod sang recounted a dream—his or some fictive speaker's—said to have been dreamed on a bed of hemlocks and containing a rich vision of lost love, the passage of awful time, a girl wearing a mantle of green. The words without music would have seemed hardly fuller in detail than a telegraphic message, but together they made a complete world.

When the song fell closed, Birch said to Teague, Good God, these is holy men. Their mind turns on matters kept secret from the likes of you and me.

Teague sucked on a tooth and looked off in the distance as if trying to remember something. He stood and squared his coat lapels and twisted at his pant waist until he had his britches adjusted to his satisfaction. He took his Spencer's from the ground and brought the muzzle of it to bear on the space between Stobrod and Pangle. He had the forestock of it resting across the back of his left wrist and the hand drooped down calm.

—Stand up against that big poplar, he said, looking at Stobrod. And take that boy with you.

For lack of a better idea, Stobrod went and stood at the tree. It rose near a hundred feet straight and clear and monolithic above him before there was a limb. Even then there were but two, the size of regular trees themselves, rising in curves like the arms of a candelabra. The crown of the tree had broken off sometime in the previous century, and the mossy stout cylinder of it lay remnant on the ground nearby, slowly melting into the

dirt, so soft with rot that you could have kicked it apart like an old dung pile and watched the hister beetles scuttle away.

Stobrod held the fiddle before him in the crook of his arm. The bow hung from a finger and twitched slightly, in time with his heartbeat. Pangle stood beside him, and theirs was the proud and nervous pose men struck when having ambrotypes made at the start of the war, though instead of rifle musket and Colt pistol and bowie knife, Stobrod and Pangle held fiddle and banjo before them as defining implements.

Pangle put his free arm around Stobrod's shoulders as schoolboy companions once did. The Guard raised their rifles and Pangle grinned at them. There was not a bit of irony or bravado in the smile. It was merely friendly.

—I can't shoot a man grinning at me, one of the men said, half lowering his rifle.

—Quit grinning, Teague said to Pangle.

Pangle twisted his mouth up and worked to straighten it, but then it twitched and went back into a grin.

—There is nothing funny here, Teague said. Not a thing. Compose yourself to die.

Pangle wiped both hands down his face from hairline to chin. He pulled down the corners of his mouth with his pair of thumbs and when he let them go they sprung back up on him so that his face broke open in smile like a blossom.

—Take your hat off, Teague said.

Pangle took his hat off and, still grinning, held it two-handed at waist level by the brim. He turned it around and around as if in demonstration of how the world turns.

—Hold it over your face, Teague said.

Pangle raised the hat and put it over his face, and when he did the Guard tripped the triggers and wood chips flew from the great poplar trunk where balls struck after passing through the meat of the two men.

black bark in winter

—And when they finished up jerking their trigger fingers, the horses all jumped and spooked and the head man went to cussing them and took his hat off and went and slapped them all in their faces with it. They didn't cover them or even go stand over them to say words except that one of them said that what had passed might fairly be called a shootout since shots had been fired. Then one of them laughed and one of them went and made water in the fire and they mounted up and rode off. I don't know what kind of place this is that I'm in, where people do one another that way.

The Georgia boy's bearing was of a man in the near aftermath of fright. He was yet excited, and there was urgency in his desire to express a tale he believed to be thrilling yet truthful.

—I seen it all done, he said. Seen it all.

—Then why were you not killed or taken, if you were close enough to witness? Ada said.

The boy thought about it. He looked off to the side and he raked his hair off his brow with splayed fingers and then flipped at the gate latch with his thumb. He stood on the road side of the

yard fence, Ada and Ruby on the other. They talked over the gate palings, and they could smell the woodsmoke in his damp sweated clothes, his wet unwashed hair.

—Heard it done, anyways, he answered. Heard what I didn't see, would be more as it was. I'd stepped into the woods, back a piece into the laurels. Of a necessity, like.

—Yes, Ada said.

—For the privacy, so to say.

—We took your meaning, Ruby said. What's the upshot of all this?

—It's what I'm trying to tell you. That I left them a-laying there bloody and dead in a heap under a big poplar. And then I run all the way here. I remembered where the fiddler said you lived. I went to that picture rock where we stopped yesterday for food. And I run down from there till I found the house.

—How long? Ruby said.

The boy looked around and examined the flat grey clouds and the blue ridgelines as if trying to get his bearings. But he could not call in which quarter west lay, nor did the sky give much assistance in saying what the hour might be, for it held no bright spots, only the few colors of an old axehead.

—It's three, Ada informed him. Two-thirty at the earliest.

—Three? the boy said, as if mildly surprised. He looked down and examined the beaten ground at the threshold to the yard. He pressed his lips together and worked his mouth. He was counting back. He reached up and gripped two of the palings in his fists. He blew out air between his lips in a way as not quite to make a whistle.

—Seven hours, he finally said. Six or seven, I'd say.

—And you running all the way? Ruby said.

—Some of it running, he said. I was scared. It's hard to recollect, but I run till I give out. Then I run some and walked some. First one and then the other.

—We'll need you to guide us back there, Ada said.

But the boy did not wish to go back up on the mountain and

would, he claimed, rather be shot where he stood than visit it again. He'd seen all of it he cared to see. Every companion he'd had there was now dead in its woods. He wanted to be home, was his only desire. And by his way of keeping tally, the news he had brought ought of its own to be worth some food and another blanket and a thing or two else he might need on the journey.

—Many another man would have left the two lie where they fell and not care that the wolves would soon strip them to bone, he said. And he told the women he reckoned wolves had already gotten to his dead cousin. Without digging implements the best he had been able to do by way of burial was to set the body under the lip of a little waterfall in the creek. There had been a dry place there beneath an undercut ledge where the water spilled over and made a curtain, so it was like a chamber between earth and water. He told how he sat his cousin up cross-legged against a rock and said some words over the still face to the effect that there was this world and one more and in that next one they might meet again. He said he walked away, and then he looked back and the sun was shining through the mist of the waterfall and striking rainbows out of it. So, no. He had no intention of setting foot back on that mountain.

—Cold Mountain stands right in the way of where you want to be, Ruby said, but do as you please. We've got no need for you. I know about where you're talking of, and we can lead the horse and not lack much of making it in five hours, walking every step of the way. We'll feed you, though. It's not like we've not been feeding every other stray that wanders through.

Ruby opened the gate and let the boy into the yard. He went and sat on the front steps between the big boxwoods and rubbed his hands together and breathed on them. Ruby stayed at the gate. She reached up and rested a hand on a bare twisted bough of the crabapple tree and stood looking out into the road.

Ada stepped to her side and looked at the side of her face. In Ada's experience, what women did at such times of loss was to

weep and embrace each other and speak words of comfort and faith. And though she did not entirely trust those formulas anymore, she was ready to offer any of them to Ruby that might do her good. Ada did in fact reach out and touch the dark hair gathered up and bound with a hide strip at Ruby's neck.

Ruby, though, seemed not to welcome even that small comfort. She twisted her head away. She was not crying or balling up her apron hem in her hands, or in any other visible way fretting over the news of Stobrod's death. She just rested her hand on the crabapple limb and looked out into the road. She expressed but one concern aloud. Were they burying the men on the mountain or bringing them to Black Cove and resting them in the little graveyard among the Blacks? There were reasons for and against either way. But since Stobrod and the Blacks had not cared for each other in life, she thought it, all in all, better to keep them separate in death.

—We need to know now, for it comes to a matter of what we pack, Ruby said. Shovels and the like.

Ada was somewhat confused about not bringing the men back. It sounded so informal, like burying a dog.

—We cannot just go up there and dig a hole and put them in it and come home, she said.

—How would that differ from what we'd do if we hauled them down here? Ruby said. It was me, I'd about rather rest on the mountain than anywhere else you could name.

Put that way, Ada could find no argument. She needed to go into the house to make dinner for the boy, but before she did she reached out and hugged Ruby for her own comfort if nothing else. Ada realized it was the first time they had embraced, and Ruby stood with her arms to her sides and was just a hard knot of a person in Ada's arms.

In the kitchen Ada made a plate of cold leftovers from their dinner—fried apples, corn bread, some dried lima beans that had cooked overlong to mush. The beans had congealed in the

pot as they cooled and had a color and consistency that reminded her of pâté. And so on a whim she unmolded the beans from the pot and cut two slices.

When she went outside and handed the boy the plate he studied the beans for some time. The look on his face said he believed he had found yet more evidence of the kind of place he was in.

—That's beans, Ada said.

The boy looked at them again and then forked off a tiny bite to test her word.

—We don't eat them thataway atall where I'm from, he said.

While the boy sat on the steps and ate, Ruby sat a step above him and talked him out a map of the long way around Cold Mountain. Ada sat in a porch rocker and watched them, two short dark people of such resemblance they might be taken for brother and sister. Ruby told the boy how to stick to the high ridges and avoid the main ways along creek valleys where people would be. Described all the landmarks he would need to make his way up Cold Spring Knob, then to Double Spring Gap and on to Bearpen Gap, Horsebone Gap, Beech Gap. From there head downhill, and at any fork of trail or creek, bear to the southwest. By such route the boy's flat and sorry home lay no more than two weeks distant.

—Go by dark and sleep by day and don't strike a light, Ruby said. Reckon even if you don't run all the way you'll be there for Christmas. They say you know Georgia when you come to it, for it's nothing but red dirt and rough roads.

Ruby dismissed him from her attention and turned to Ada and started planning their journey. The timing worked out poorly. It was Ruby's reasoning that with the days approaching the shortest of the year, one way or the other, either going or coming, they'd spend a night in the woods. It did not much matter which, was her thinking. They might as well get on. So she and Ada left the boy mopping his plate with a heel of corn bread and went in the house and banked up the fire and quickly threw

together a camping kit to Ruby's specification. Bedding, cookware, food, candles, a tin box of lucifer matches and the sandpaper needed to ignite them, a dry bundle of fatwood kindling, a coil of rope, a hand axe, shotgun with powder and shot and wadding, grain for the horse, a mattock and spade. They heaped the gear in paired hemp sacks and tied the necks together and threw them over Ralph's back like rude lumpish panniers.

Ruby looked about at the sky for any marks of cloud or air or light that might foreshow the weather, and what they told was snow and gathering cold.

She said, Have you got any britches in the house?

—Trousers? Ada said.

—Woolen or canvas, either one. Two pair.

—Of my father's, yes.

—We need to go put them on, Ruby said.

—Men's trousers? Ada said.

—You wear what you want, but I don't relish the feel of a winter wind blowing up my dress tail. And who's up there to see?

They found two pairs of heavy wool hunting trousers, one pair black and the other grey. They dressed in long underwear and then drew the trousers on and cuffed up the bottoms and cinched the waists in with belts so that the extra material gathered like big pleats. They put on wool shirts and sweaters, and Ruby noted Monroe's broad-brimmed hats and said they would keep the snow from their faces, so they took two down from the shelf and put them on as well. Had the circumstances been happier, Ada thought, this would have been like the hair contest, a game of dress-up against which they might wager to see who could accouter herself most convincing as a man. Take lamp soot and draw mustaches and burnsides on their faces, carry around unlit cigars and mimic the silly gestures men used in smoking them. Instead they hardly spoke as they dressed, and they both were filled with dread toward the next pair of days.

Before they left, they rubbed beeswax into their boots and opened the door to the henhouse and likewise the door to the

cow's stall and they heaped down hay on the floor. Ruby reckoned Waldo would be bawling to have her bag stripped by the time they got back. They gave the boy food and bedding and told him to sleep in the hayloft until dark made it safe for him to travel. When they went off leading the horse, the boy still sat between the boxwoods, and he waved to them like a host bidding visitors farewell.

Toward evening, snow fell through fog in the woods. Ada and Ruby walked in dim light under fir trees, and they were but vague dark shapes moving through a place that lacked all color other than gradations of gloom. The nearest trees looked very much like genuine trees, but those only slightly farther away were but a suggestion of trees as in a quick sketch, a casual gesture toward the form of trees. All of it seemed to Ada as if there were no such thing as landscape and that she wandered along in a cloud, with what little she could know an arm's length away. All else shrouded from understanding. It made Ralph nervous, and the horse went bowing his neck to left and right and working his ears back and forth to catch sounds of threat.

They had climbed for a long time under the thick canopy of dark hemlock. Then they crossed a low ridge and descended into a creek valley. They had long since left what to Ada was familiar territory. The footing was soft from layers of dropped needles, and snow fell through the treetops as dry as sifted meal and swirled about the ground in patterns of arcs and loops. It seemed not to want to lie down.

After a time they crossed a black creek, stepping with care on the dry backs of humped stones. Ada looked at the way the creek was seizing up with a thin rim of bright ice along its banks and around rocks and fallen trees and nubbles of moss, anything that hindered the flow. In the center of the creek, though, the fast water ripped along as always.

Where it ran shallower and slower, then, were the places

prone to freezing. Monroe would have made a lesson of such a thing, Ada thought. He would have said what the match of that creek's parts would be in a person's life, what God intended it to be the type of. All God's works but elaborate analogy. Every bright image in the visible world only a shadow of a divine thing, so that earth and heaven, low and high, strangely agreed in form and meaning because they were in fact congruent.

Monroe had a book wherein you could look up the types. The rose—its thorns and its blossom—a type of the difficult and dangerous path to spiritual awakening. The baby—come wailing to the world in pain and blood—a type of our miserable earthly lives, so consumed with violence. The crow—its blackness, its outlaw nature, its tendency to feast on carrion—a type of the dark forces that wait to overtake man's soul.

So Ada quite naturally thought the stream and the ice might offer a weapon of the spirit. Or, perhaps, a warning. But she refused to believe that a book could say just how it should be construed or to what use it might be put. Whatever a book said would lack something essential and be as useless by itself as the gudgeon to a door hinge with no pintle.

On the stream's far bank the horse stopped and shook its hide until the pots rattled in their sacks, and then he stretched his neck and breathed soft and long out into the world in hope of some assuring companion breath in return. Ada cupped her hand to his velvet muzzle. He put his tongue out and she took it between thumb and forefinger and waggled it gently and then they went on.

For a time they kept to the creekside as it tumbled from the mountain, but then the trail turned up a faint branch and entered a forest of hardwoods where there were yet twisted scraps of leaves clinging to the oak trees. They were old tired oaks and had globes of mistletoe in their branches. Snow fell harder and began to stick to the ground and the trail became a faint sunken line through the woods, an easy thing to miss as night came on. What path there was held not even the cupped tracks of hogs. It

seemed some abandoned Indian trail, long unwalked, linking a set of points that no longer existed.

They walked on well past nightfall, the snow still coming down. The clouds were thick and hid the waxing moon. Nevertheless there was light in the snow where it stood gathered up under the black tree trunks.

Shelter was Ada's first thought, and at every rock ledge she said, There's a place we could sleep. But Ruby said she knew a better place, or at least thought she remembered a place nearby, and they walked on.

In time, they came to a tumble of great flat rocks. Ruby cast about until she found what she was looking for: three that had fallen upon each other so as to form a lean-to, a sort of accidental dolmen with flat straight walls, a capstone fitted tight and angled back so as to shed water, leaving underneath a room no bigger than a cock loft, but enough to sit up and shift around in. As architecture, its shape reminded Ada of the symbol for pi. Inside, the floor was thick with dry leaves. Spring water rose from the ground not twenty yards away. All set around with chestnut and oak trees that had never been cut since the day of creation. It made as fine a camp as anyone could ever expect to find, and Ruby said that though she had not visited the place in years, it was exactly as she remembered from having spent many a night there as a child out foraging for food.

Ruby put Ada to gathering armloads of the dryest limbs she could find, and within half an hour they had a warm blaze going at the mouth of the shelter. A pot of water boiling for tea. When it was done steeping, they sat and drank it, ate a few dried biscuits and some dried apples. The rings were from apples so small as to be little more than a bite apiece but their sharp taste bound together all the best features of the past warm season.

They did not talk much while they ate, other than for Ada to say that the Georgia boy did not seem like much of a one as far as men went. Ruby said she found him not particularly worse than the general order of men, which is to say that he would

greatly benefit from having someone's foot in his back every waking minute.

When they were done eating, Ruby brushed away the leaves of the shelter floor with the heel of her hand and scooped out dirt and sifted it through her fingers and held out a palm to the firelight for Ada to see. Fragments of charcoal and splinters of flint. Ancient fire and partial arrow points flawed and discarded. Flakes of old hope however slight.

Neither of them said anything, but Ada picked through the flint splinters and kept the point nearest completion and found comfort that people in some dim other time had done as they were doing, had found shelter in the rock pile and eaten a meal and slept.

The snow hissed as it fell and the temperature was dropping fast, but the fire soon heated the stones, and when Ada and Ruby wrapped themselves in blankets and burrowed in among the dry leaves and heaped more leaves atop the quilts, they were warm as lying in a bed at home. This would do, Ada thought, as she lay there. The abandoned trail through mountains and rivers. Not a soul around. The stone shelter warm and dry and strange as an elfin lodge. Though others might view it as an utterly bare haven, it matched her needs so much that she could just move in and live there.

The fire threw patterns of light and shadow on the pitched roof stone, and Ada found that if she watched long enough the fire would form the shapes of things in the world. A bird. A bear. A snake. A fox. Or perhaps it was a wolf. The fire seemed to have no interests other than animals.

The pictures put Ada in mind of a song, one of Stobrod's. It had particularly stuck in her mind. She had noted it for the oddity of its lyric and for Stobrod's singing, which had been of an intensity that Ada could only assume represented deep personal expression. It took as subject the imagined behavior of its speaker, what he would do had he the power to become one of a variety of brute creature. A lizard in the spring—hear his darling

sing. A bird with wings to fly—go back to his darling weep and moan till he dies. A mole in the ground—root a mountain down.

Ada worried over the song. The animals seemed wonderful and horrible in their desires, especially the mole, a little powerless hermit blind thing propelled by lonesomeness and resentment to bring the world falling around him. More wonderful and horrible still was the human voice speaking the song's words, wishing away its humanity to ease the pain inflicted by lost love, love betrayed, love left unexpressed, wasted love.

Ada could hear in Ruby's breathing that she was yet awake, and so she said, Do you remember that song of your father's about the mole in the ground?

Ruby said that she did, and Ada asked if Ruby thought Stobrod had written the song. Ruby said there were many songs that you could not say anybody in particular made by himself. A song went around from fiddler to fiddler and each one added something and took something away so that in time the song became a different thing from what it had been, barely recognizable in either tune or lyric. But you could not say the song had been improved, for as was true of all human effort, there was never advancement. Everything added meant something lost, and about as often as not the thing lost was preferable to the thing gained, so that over time we'd be lucky if we just broke even. Any thought otherwise was empty pride.

Ada lay and watched the fire shadows and listened to the sound of snow in the leaves and soon drifted off and slept a dreamless sleep, not even waking when Ruby rose to toss more wood on the fire. When Ada awoke it was first light, and she could see that the snow had slackened in its falling but had not stopped. It lay anklebone deep on the ground. Neither Ruby nor Ada was eager to get on with the day that stretched before them. They sat with the blankets around their shoulders, and Ruby blew up the coals and stoked the fire. She fried a piece of side meat and forked it out of its grease and put it on a flat rock. Then she added water to the grease and cooked a pot of grits and took

the side meat from the rock and crumbled it into the pot and stirred it into the grits. In the smaller pot Ada made tea, and as they sipped Ruby told how when she first had tea, supplied by Mrs. Swanger, she admired it so much that she gave Stobrod a handful of it tied in a square of cloth as he went off on a coon hunt. The next time she saw him some weeks later she had asked him how he liked it. Stobrod had said it was no better than fair and that he didn't find it preferable to any other kind of greens. Ruby came to find out he had cooked it up with a strip of fatback and eaten it like cresses.

When they reached the trail fork, they found the Pangle boy lying alone, face up beneath the poplar. He was covered with a mantle of snow. It lay slumped over him, thinner than on the ground nearby, and it was clear how the snow had first melted about him and then had not. Ruby brushed away the snow to look at his face, and when she did she found him still smiling, though with a look of confusion in his eyes, which might have been just the look of death. Ruby cupped her hand to his fat cheek and then touched him with her fingertips on his brow, as if to stamp him with the badge of a like outcast.

Ada turned from him and began kicking at the snow with her boot toe. And when she did she turned up pieces of broken banjo. Then the broken fiddlestick, the frog piece dangling from horsehair. She kicked around more, looking for the fiddle, but she did not find it. No fiddle and no Stobrod.

—Where is he? Ada said.

—There's not anybody from Georgia can tell more than half the truth, Ruby said. Dead or alive, they took him with them.

They decided to bury Pangle on a little shelf of land up above the trail near a chestnut tree. The ground dug easily and they hardly needed the mattock, for only a thin rind of ground was frozen and under that the topsoil was black and loose and went down and down. They took turns with the shovel, and soon

they were hot in their coats and they took them off and hung them on tree limbs. Then they were too cold, but it was better to be cold than to wet your clothes with sweat. By the time they started hitting significant rocks they had quite a hole, though it was still two feet shallower than the six which Ada thought to be the rule of graves. But it would do, Ruby said.

They went to Pangle and each took a leg and dragged him through the snow to the grave and slid him in. They had no box, nor even a spare blanket to shroud him with, so Ada spread her kerchief over his face before they began shoveling the dirt. By the time they had covered him to where only one boot toe was left showing, Ada was weeping, though she had seen the boy but once in life, and that by firelight, and all the words that had passed between them had been him saying Stobrod's playing had done her good.

Ada remembered her thoughts when they had buried winter cabbages, how she had made it metaphoric. But she found this burial to be an entirely different matter. Beyond the bare fact of holes in the ground, there was no similarity at all between the two.

When they had filled the grave above level, they had more dirt left, which Ruby noted and attributed to the time of the month, the growing of the moon toward full. Dig a grave a week into the wane and you'd have a swale when you were done. They mounded the moon's extra dirt over Pangle and packed it with the back of the spade. Then Ada took her clasp knife and stripped bark from a hickory sapling and sought out a black locust and lopped two of its limbs with the hand axe and lashed them together with the hickory withes to form up a cross. She stood it in the soft ground at Pangle's head, and though she did not say words aloud over him, she made some in her mind. She'd heard Ruby say locust had such will to live that you could split fence posts from the wood of its trunk and they'd sometimes take root in the postholes and grow. Such was Ada's hope for her

own construction, that someday a tall locust would stand to mark Pangle's place, and that every year into the next century it would tell in brief a tale like Persephone's. Black bark in winter, white blossoms in spring.

Their hands were dirty. Ruby just cupped up snow and rubbed it between her palms and shook off the dirty water. But Ada went through the woods to the creek and knelt and washed her hands and then dashed icy water in her face. She stood and shook her head and looked about. Her eyes fell on a low rock ledge beyond the creek. It made an overhang, a shelter. The brown of the dirt stood out dark against the snow. Under the rock lip sat Stobrod, though it took a minute for Ada to make him out since his clothes matched up with the dark of the exposed earth. He was still, eyes closed, and he sat with his legs crossed, his head to the side and his hands composed around the fiddle in his lap. A little wind rose up and rattled the few oak leaves and shook snow from bare limbs. It fell in Ada's hair and onto the creek face, where it melted as it struck.

—Ruby, Ada called. Ruby, I need you here.

They stood over him and his face was the hue of the snow and he looked so meager in his parts. Such a little man. He had lost a great deal of blood through the wounds and had spit up yet more, and he was stained all down his shirtfront. Ruby took the fiddle from his lap and handed it to Ada, and the snake rattles shifted dryly inside it. When Ruby undid his buttons, the blood in his shirt was black and stiff. His chest was frail and white. Ruby put her ear to it and pulled away and then listened again.

—He's yet living, she said.

She pulled apart his clothes and turned him about to survey the damage and found he'd been hit three times. Through his bow hand where he held it before him. Through the meat of his ham nigh to the hipbone. And—the most serious—through the nipple to his chest. That ball had broken a rib and scored the top of his lung and lodged in his back muscles above the shoulder

blade. There was a blue lump under his skin the size of a crab-apple. In the moving of him he did not break consciousness or even moan in pain.

Ruby drew together kindling and whittled off shavings from a pine branch and struck fire from the matches. When the fire was going, she held the blade of the homemade knife in the flames. She cut into Stobrod's back and he still made no sound nor fluttered his eyes. There was just a bare rindle of blood from the cut, as if he had not enough left for the new wound to do more than sweat a few red drops. Ruby put her finger into his back and inquired around with it and then she hooked the ball out. She reached and put it into Ada's hand and it was like a gobbet of raw meat.

—Go rinse that off, Ruby said. He'll want it someday.

Ada went to the creek and held her hand in the water and let the current run through her caged fingers. When she drew it out and looked at it, the lead was clean and grey. In passing through Stobrod it had been pressed into a shape like a mushroom, the cap fluted and split and misgrown. The stem end, though, was intact, cut with three precise rings during its manufacture to take best advantage of a barrel's rifling.

Ada went back to the ledge and set the bullet beside the fiddle. Ruby had Stobrod wrapped in blankets and the fire was burning knee high.

—You stay and boil me some water, Ruby said to Ada.

Ada watched her wander off through the woods, the shovel over her shoulder and her head down, looking for healing roots which she could know only from their dried stalks and husks poking up from the snow. Ada arranged stones around the fire for pot rest and went to the horse and got a pot from the sacks. She dipped it full of creek water and put it on the stones to heat. She sat and looked at Stobrod, and he lay like a dead man. There was no sign to show he lived other than a slight movement of his jacket front when he breathed. Ada wondered about his hun-

dreds of tunes. Where were they now and where might they go if he died.

When Ruby returned an hour later, she had her pockets full of any root she could find that might be remotely useful—mullein, yarrow, burdock, ginseng. But she had not found goldenseal, which was the thing she needed most. The herb had been scarce of late. Hard to find. She worried that people were proving themselves not worthy of healing and that goldenseal had departed in disgust. She packed a mash of mullein and yarrow root and burdock into Stobrod's wounds and bound them with strips cut from a blanket. She brewed tea from the mullein and ginseng and dribbled it into his mouth, but his throat seemed clenched shut and she could not tell if any went down or not.

After awhile she said, It's too far home. He'll not make it there alive. It might be days before he can travel, and I'd not be surprised if there was more snow coming. We need better shelter than this.

—Back to the rock lodge? Ada said.

—We wouldn't all fit. Not and have room to cook and work over him. There's a place I know. If it's there yet.

They left Stobrod where he lay while they cut long poles to make shafts for a drag sledge. They tied the poles together with rope and lashed more across for web sling and harnessed the rig to the horse. They carried Stobrod across the creek in the blankets and put him on, but when they headed up the left trail fork with him dragging behind the horse and bumping on every rock and root, they could see that their thoughts had been wrong and that the jarring would tear him apart at his wounds. So they pulled the sledge to pieces, coiled the rope, and draped Stobrod over the horse and went on slowly.

The sky was flat and grey and it hovered over their heads so close it seemed they could reach up and touch it. For a brief while, snow again emerged out of it, blown on a cutting wind. First it came in great flakes like goosedown, then faint and dry as

ashes. When the snow stopped, fog welled up thick around them, and the only thing clear was that the day was falling away.

They walked for some time without speaking except when Ruby would say, Here, and then they would turn at a fork. Ada did not know which way they went, for she had long since lost certainty of the cardinal points.

When they stopped to rest, the horse stood head down, tired and miserable, exhausted from the load he was carrying and the altitude. Ada and Ruby brushed the snow off a log and sat. They could not see a thing in the fog but the nearest trees. The feel of the air, though, suggested that they were on a ridge and that there was much open air and gravity around them. Ada huddled inside her coat, trying not to think of going through another day of this or of where they might spend the night, just the next mile. Stobrod lay draped over the horse exactly where Ada and Ruby had placed him.

While they sat, two peregrines came bursting out of the fog. They flew into the shifting wind, their wings making short choppy strokes for purchase against the difficult air. They flared so close that Ada could hear the hiss of wind through the feathers. Stobrod awoke and raised his head momentarily as the birds passed and then he stared after them vaguely as they faded back in the fog. A line of blood ran to his chin from his mouth corner, thin as a razor cut.

—Pigeon hawk, he said, as if putting a name to the birds might help him regain his footing.

He started struggling and it seemed he wanted to square himself on the horse to ride, and so Ruby helped him. But when she let go he fell forward until his head rested on the withers. His eyes were closed and his arms stretched past his head to grip the mane with both hands. His legs swung limp below Ralph's round belly. Ruby wiped his mouth with her coat sleeve and they went on.

For most of an hour they descended a steep hillside and then Ada thought they were cupped in a valley, though she could

not see far enough in any direction to verify the feeling. They crossed a marshy place and on either side of the trail huckleberry bushes grew head high. At the bottom of the valley they passed a pool of still black water. It came up out of the fog as if a hole had opened in the world. Old dead ribbons of taupe bunchgrass ringed it, and ice scalloped all around its verge like a camera iris closing. Three black ducks floated motionless in the pool's center, their heads tucked against their breasts. Were she writing a book of types, Ada thought, that would do for fear.

The fog was thinning some. They climbed again, just a low ridge with hemlocks growing on its spine and many were blown down with their root plates standing revealed in the air like a dissection. They descended through the trees and into a stand of chestnuts. They were moving toward a stream which they could hear but not see. It was rough walking. There was not really a trail at all, just enough space between the trees and the ragged brush and low scrub to make way for passage. When they came off the ridge toward a pinched creek bottom, the light had not changed, though the day felt all but spent.

Ada began to make out rectangular shapes through the trees. Huts. Cabins. A tiny Cherokee village, a ghost town, its people long since driven out onto the Trail of Tears and banished to a barren land. Except for one rotted relic from the age of wattle and daub, the cabins were made of chestnut logs, peeled and notched and lapped. Roofed with shingles and curls of chestnut bark. A big white oak had fallen across one hut, but the rest were largely intact after three decades alone, and such was the power of chestnut timber against damp that they might remain so for a hundred years more before melting into the ground. Grey lichen grew on the cabin logs and dried stalks of horseweed and pigweed and fleabane rose from the snow in the doorways. There was not flat ground for raising much in the way of crops, so it might have been a seasonal hunting camp. Or refuge wherein a handful of carnivore outcasts had lived, nearly anchoritic. All in all, only a half-dozen little windowless cells.

They were set at uneven intervals down the bank of the creek, which was deep and strong and black, its way broken by great smooth boulders with green moss grown on their faces.

In Ada's fatigue, she thought it a matter of great importance to know, without asking, on which bank of the creek the cabins stood. North, south, east, west. It would go a way toward ordering her mind congruent with where she was. Ruby always seemed to know the compass points and to find them significant, not just when giving directions but even in telling a story and indicating where an event had happened. West bank of the Little East Fork, east bank of the West Fork, that sort of thing. What was required to speak that language was a picture held in the mind of the land one occupied. Ada knew the ridges and coves and drainages were the frame of it, the skeleton. You learned them and where they stood in relation to each other, and then you filled in the details working from those known marks. General to particular. Everything had a name. To live fully in a place all your life, you kept aiming smaller and smaller in attention to detail.

Ada had only just begun to form such a picture, and she looked to the sky for help in finding direction. But it offered none, for the sky lay so close it seemed she might hit her head on it. And there were no other hints to follow. In this lush climate, moss grew on whatever side of a tree it cared to. North meant nothing to moss here. So Ada knew only that, as far as she was concerned, the village could stand on any bank of the creek whatsoever. No direction could be ruled out.

The cabins they passed among seemed solemn in their abandonment, cramped by the watercourse and the overhanging brow of the cloudy mountain. Some of its people might yet be living, and Ada wondered how often they remembered this lonesome place, now still as a held breath. Whatever word they had called it would soon be numbered among the names of things which have not been passed down to us and are exiled from our memories. She doubted that its people, even in the last days,

had ever looked ahead and imagined loss so total and so soon. They had not foreseen a near time when theirs would be another world filled with other people whose mouths would speak other words, whose sleep would be eased or troubled with other dreams, whose prayers would be offered up to other gods.

Ruby picked the best of the cabins, and they stopped before it. They took Stobrod off the horse and made him a nest on the ground of the tarpaulin and blankets, and then they went into the hut's one windowless room. The door was made of hewn planks and had swung on leather hinges, long since broken. It lay on the floor. All that could be done to close it was to prop it in its hole. The packed dirt floor was littered with blown leaves, and they swept it with a pine bough. There was a drystone hearth, a mud-and-stick chimney. Ruby put her head in and looked up and saw daylight. But it had apparently never drawn well, and the chestnut-log roof beams were dark and shiny with years of accumulated smoke. Beneath the odor of dust, the house was still infused with the rich smell of a thousand old campfires. There was a wooden sleeping platform along one wall, a layer of grey straw still on it. They carried Stobrod in and rested him there.

While Ruby built up a fire in the hearth, Ada went out and cut a long straight limb and trimmed it sharp with the hatchet and hammered it into the ground and staked out the horse under a cedar. But he was wet and shivering. He stood with his head down and his winter coat was pressed in dark curls to his skin from snowmelt. Ada looked at him and at the sky and judged the cold by the sting of her cheeks. Ralph might be dead on the ground by morning.

She loosed him from the stake and tried to lead him into one of the huts, but he did not want to duck his head to go through the door. She pulled at the lead rope and he lowered his hind end and backed away, pulling her until she fell forward into the snow. She got up and found a stick as big around as her wrist and she got behind the horse and hit him again and again with all the

strength she had left in her, which was not an awful lot. Finally he plunged into that black door hole as if into death.

Once inside, though, Ralph was immediately content, for the hut hardly differed in dimensions or materials from a barn stall. Within minutes he had relaxed. He shook out his hide and spraddled his legs and pissed a long and satisfying piss. Ada fed him grain out of the cook pot and then took the pot and rinsed it in the creek.

It was almost dark and Ada stood and looked at the final sheen of light on the water. She was tired and cold and scared. This seemed like the lonesomest place on earth. She dreaded night and the moment when the campcraft was all done and she would have to wrap herself in a blanket and lie in the dark on the cold dirt floor of the ghost cabin to wait for morning. She was so tired her legs felt burnt out from under her, but she believed she could get through this if she did one thing at a time and thought of the remaining things left to be done as sequential, not cumulative.

She went inside and found that Ruby had cooked a supper like to their breakfast. But when Ada put the first spoon of the greasy grits to her mouth, they would not go down. Her stomach knotted up. She stood and went out and vomited in the snow, though about all she had left in her to bring up was black bile. Then she rubbed her mouth with snow and went inside and ate again until her bowl was empty. She sat with it in her lap, exhausted in stunned silence before the hearth.

She had forgotten to drink water for most of the day. That and the cold, the walking and the work of burying and healing had turned her mind strange so that her only wish was to seek happier visions in the fire coals. She looked and looked but found none in either the liquid shapes of flame or the geometric scorings charred in the sides of the fire logs. But the burning wood made squeaking sounds like footsteps tramping in dry snow and even Ada knew what that betokened. More ready to fall.

footsteps in the snow

When he reached the place where three ways came together there was barely enough light left behind the western clouds for Inman to study signs on the ground for the story they told. The snow was marked by tracks coming up to the flat ground at the fork and then going on up the rising left-hand trail. There was black blood on the ground beneath a big poplar where killing had been done. The snow all about was churned up by the walking of people and horses. There had been a recent fire in a ring of stones beyond the poplar, and the ashes were cold but still held the smell of pork fat. Footsteps and a drag trail led to a cross of sticks standing at the head of a raw dig. Inman squatted and looked at it, thinking this: if there is a world beyond the grave as hymns claim, such a hole makes a grim lonesome portal to it.

He was somewhat puzzled. There ought to have been two burials. And though Inman had seen men laid one atop another to save shovel work, he reckoned that was not the case here. He rose and went back to studying the signs, and he followed them across the creek to the rock ledge and thereunder he found

more blood on the ground and the still-warm coals of a little fire. A pile of sodden roots where they had been cast on the ground with their cooking water. He picked up pieces of root and rubbed them in his hand and smelled them, and he could tell ginseng and mullein.

He set them on a rock and went to the creek and dipped up a handful of water to drink. A salamander, wildly spotted in colors and patterns unique to that one creek, moved among the stones. Inman lifted it out and held it cupped in his hand and looked at the salamander's face. The way its mouth curved around its head shaped a smile of such great serenity as to cause Inman envy and distress. Living hid under a creek rock would be about the only way to achieve such countenance, Inman thought. He returned the salamander to its place and walked back and stood in the crotch of the trail and looked off where the tracks led. He could see hardly ten feet ahead before they faded in the dark that was settling fast. He figured Ada might recede before him forever and leave him a lone pilgrim going on and on.

The clouds hung low and thick. There would be no moon and the night would soon be black as the inside of a cold stove. He put back his head and sniffed the air and it smelled like snow. It was a matter of which was worse, to lose the track in the night or to have it covered over.

Of the two, the dark was certain and nigh, and so Inman went back to the ledge and sat and watched the last light fall away. He listened to the creek and tried to make up a story to fit the signs, one that would explain the single grave and why the two women had gone on across the mountain instead of following their own tracks home.

But it was hard to reason things out in the state he was in. Part from choice and part from necessity, Inman was fasting and his senses would not row up properly. He had not eaten bite one in the days since he had cooked the bear cub. The creek had the sound of voices in the rush of its water and the clicking of its bed stones against one another, and he thought they might tell him

what had taken place there if he listened hard enough. But the voices shifted and blurred and the words had no meaning to him, try as he might to make them out. Then he reckoned he was not hearing voices at all, just words forming up in his head, and even then he could not make sense of them. He was too empty for sense.

His sacks held no food but for a few walnuts he had picked up off the ground two days previous at a place where a cabin had burned. There was nothing left of it but a cone of sooty dirt where the clay chimney had stood and a good-sized walnut tree beyond where the front of the house would have been. There had been yet walnuts on the ground under it. The black shells lay inside little nests in the grass where the grass had grown long around the husks and the husks had rotted away. Inman had put what nuts he could find in his haversack, but had never got around to eating them, for the more he thought the more he reckoned that the work it would take to break them open would overbalance the sustenance he would get from them, each one holding no more meat than would be around the end joint of your forefinger. Yet he didn't throw them out, for he worried that if you put all of life to such a test it would not seem worth living. And, too, he found the sound of them comforting as he walked. They rattled against each other with the dry tock of old bones hanging in trees.

He looked at the bitter roots on the rock where he had laid them. He first thought to nibble at them, but then he picked them up and threw them into the creek. He took a walnut out of his sack and threw it in the creek too, and it made the valved sound of a scared frog plunging in water. He left the other nuts in his sack, though he intended to eat nothing until he found Ada. If she would not have him he would go on to the heights and see if the portals at the Shining Rocks would open to him as the woman with the snake tattoos had suggested they would to one with a fasting heart, empty in all his faculties. Inman could think of no reason to hold back. He doubted there was a man in

the world emptier than he at that moment. He would walk right out of this world and keep on going into that happy valley she had described.

Inman broke up limbs and kindled a strong fire on the coals of the earlier fire. He rolled two large stones into it to heat. For a long time he lay wrapped in his blankets with his feet to the fire and thought about that pair of tracks leading away.

When he had started the day he had not thought that by dark he would be lying on the cold ground again. Once home, he assumed he would differ from his recent self in every regard, in his design of living, his views on life, and even in the way he walked and stood. And that morning he had thought certainly by nightfall to have declared himself to Ada and to have gotten some response. Yea, nay, or maybe. He had played out the scene in his mind many days as he walked and as he lay waiting for sleep in every bare camp along the way. He would come walking up the road into Black Cove, and he would be weary looking. What he had been through would show in his face and in his frame, but only so much as to suggest heroism. He would be bathed and in a clean suit. Ada would step out the door onto the porch without knowing he was coming, just going about her doings. She would be dressed in her fine clothes. She would see him and know him in every feature. She would run to him, lifting her skirts above her ankle boots as she came down the steps. She would rush across the yard and through the gate in a flurry of petticoats, and before the gate had even clapped shut they would be holding each other in the roadway. He had seen it in his mind over and over until it came to seem that there was no other way it could happen except that he be killed getting home.

Such an imagined scene of homecoming had been the hope in his heart when he had come walking up the Black Cove road before noon. He had done his part to make it so, for he arrived weary but clean, having on the day previous—aware that he

looked rougher than the lowest muleteer—stopped at a creek to bathe and to wash his clothes. It had been chill weather for such work, but he built a fire of dry logs until the flames stood shoulder high. He heated pot after pot of water almost to boiling and unfolded his soap from its brown paper wrapping, dark and greasy from the tallow. He poured the water on the clothes and rubbed them with the soap and twisted them and battled them on stones and then rinsed them in the creek. He had spread the clothes on bushes near the fire to dry and then he started in on himself. The soap was brown and gritty and had a great deal of lye in it so that it would about take off hide. He had washed himself with water as hot as he could stand and scrubbed with the soap until his skin felt raw. Then he touched his face and hair. He had just about raised a new beard since shaving at the girl's cabin, and his hair was half wild about his head. He had no razor, and so the beard would have to stand. And he reckoned himself a poor barber even had he scissors and a glass. With nothing but a sheath knife and a still pool at the creek edge, he could not expect to improve his haircut any. The best he could do was to heat more water, soap and rinse his hair, comb it out with his fingers and try to shape it to his head so that it would not stand up and look alarming.

When he had finished washing, he sat through the remainder of the chill day squatting naked but clean under his blankets. He slept naked, wrapped in his blankets while his clothes dried over the fire. Where he had camped, the snow but came spitting out of the sky awhile and then stopped. When he dressed in the morning, the clothes at least smelled of lye soap and creek water and chestnut smoke rather than sweat.

He had then made his way to Black Cove over trails, taking care not to strike the road until he was but a bend or two below the house. When he came to it there was smoke from the chimney but no other sign of life. The little snow in the yard lay unmarked. He opened the gate and went to the door and knocked. No one came, and he knocked again. He went around back,

where he found the tracks of a man's boots in the snow between the house and the privy. A frozen nightgown hung stiff from the clothesline. Chickens in the henhouse fluttered and clucked and then settled down. He went to the back door and knocked hard, and in a minute an upstairs window flew open and a black-haired boy stuck his head out and asked him who the hell he was and what the hell he meant making such a racket.

In time, Inman got the Georgia boy to come to the door and let him in. They sat by the fire and Inman heard the tale of the killings. The boy had worked over the story in his mind and refined it until it had taken on all the earmarks of a great gun battle during which the boy had fought his way clear but Stobrod and Pangle had been captured and killed. And in this latest version, Stobrod's final tune had been of his own composition and it arose out of the full knowledge of immediate death. Stobrod had titled it Fiddler's Farewell and it was the saddest song that had ever been made and had drawn tears from the eyes of all present, even his executioners. But the boy was not a musician and could not reproduce the tune, not even to whistle it accurately and so it was unfortunately lost forever. He had run all the way to tell the women the story, and they had, in appreciation, insisted he spend as many days eating and resting in the house as it took him to recover from the ague he had acquired on his desperate flight down the mountain. It was a strange and possibly fatal affliction, with few external marks.

Inman had put a number of questions to the boy but found he did not know who Monroe was nor where he might be and could offer no help in identifying Ada's female companion other than that he thought her to be the fiddler's daughter. The boy had given the best directions he could, and Inman set out once more walking.

Thus it was he found himself sleeping again on the ground. His mind was all tangled. He lay by the fire and thoughts came and

went and he had no control over them. Inman was afraid he was falling apart at a bad time. Then he wondered when a good time might be. He couldn't think of one. He tried to force the raggedness from his breathing and make it come steady. The assumption he worked from was that mastery of his thoughts might follow mastery of his lungs, but he could not even make his chest rise and fall at his bidding and so his breath and his mind went where they would in juddering fashion.

He thought Ada might save him from his troubles and redeem him from the past four years and that there would be time ahead for her to do it in. He suspected you could work yourself some good in calming your mind by thinking forward to what great pleasure it would be to hold your grandchild on your knee. But to believe such an event might actually happen required deep faith in right order. How would you go about getting it when it was in such short supply? A dark voice came in Inman's mind and said no matter how much you might yearn for it and pray for it, you would never get it. You could be too far ruined. Fear and hate riddling out your core like heartworms. At such time, faith and hope were not to the point. You were ready for your hole in the ground. There were many preachers the like of Veasey who swore they could save the souls of the awfulest kinds of sinner. They offered salvation to killers and thieves and adulterers and even those gnawed by despair. But Inman's dark voice figured such braggart claims to be lies. Those men could not even save their own selves from living bad lives. The false hope they offered was poisonous as any venom. All the resurrection any man might expect was Veasey's, to be dragged dead from the grave at rope's end.

There was fact in what the dark voice said. You could become so lost in bitterness and anger that you could not find your way back. No map nor guidebook for such journey. One part of Inman knew that. But he knew too that there were footsteps in the snow and that if he awoke one more day he would follow them to wherever they led as long as he could put one foot in front of the other.

The fire began to die out, and he rolled the hot stones onto the ground and stretched out next to them and fell asleep. When the cold wakened him before dawn, he was curled around the bigger of them as if it were his sweetheart.

At first light he set out, and to the eye there was not hardly a trail at all, just a felt vacancy that drew him forward. Were it not for tracing the tracks in the old snow, Inman could not have kept to the way. He had lost confidence in his sense of direction, since during the past months he had been lost in every kind of place where parallel fences did not hem him in from going wrong. The clouds lowered. Then a little wind fell downslope, carrying on it snow too dry and fine to be called flakes. It came so hard one minute as to sting the cheeks, and then it stopped the next. Inman looked at the cupped tracks and they held the new snow like blown grit.

He came to a black pool set round as a jar lid on the ground. Ice had rimmed it and a lone drake rode the water at its center and it did not care enough even to turn its head to look at Inman. It seemed to look at nothing. Inman reckoned the drake's world was constricting about it and that it would float there until the ice clenched at the webbing of its feet. Then, flap as it might, it would be pulled down to death. Inman first thought to shoot it and change its fate at least in minor detail, but if he did he would have to go wading to get it for he abhorred killing an animal and not eating it. And if he got it he would be left in a quandary over his fast. So he left the duck to struggle it out with its Maker and went on.

When the trail turned uphill, snow started falling again. This time it was real snow in flakes like thistledown, falling slantwise so thick it made Inman dizzy with its movement. The tracks began fading off like twilight as the snow filled them. He walked fast, climbing to a ridge, and when the tracks started to disappear he broke into a run. He ran and ran downhill through dark hemlocks. He watched the tracks fill and their edges blur. No matter how fast he ran, the footprints disappeared before him

until they were faint, like scars from old wounds. Then like watermarks through paper held to window light. Then the snow lay even all around, unmarked.

The flakes still fell hard and Inman could not even feel the way the trail went, but he ran on until finally he stopped in a place where the hemlocks stood black around him and made a world undifferentiated, with no compass degree preferable to another and with not a sound but snow falling on snow, and he reckoned if he lay down it would cover him and when it melted it would wash the tears from his eyes and, in time, the eyes from his head and the skin from his skull.

Ada and Ruby slept until Stobrod began coughing wet racking coughs. Ada had bedded down in her clothes and she awoke with the odd sensation of britches twisted about her legs. The hut was cold and dim and the fire had burned down to a smolder. The light from outside was odd and upthrown and spoke of snow. Ruby went to Stobrod. He had a line of fresh blood running from his mouth corner to his collar. His eyes opened but he did not appear to know her. She put her hand to his brow and looked at Ada and said, He's burning up. Ruby went to the corners of the hut and pulled down spiderwebs until she had a ball of them in her hands; then she dug through her pouch of roots and took out two and said, Get some water and I'll make up a fresh poultice to dab on that borehole in his chest. She went and threw wood on the coals and bent to blow up the fire.

Ada gathered her hair and put on her hat to keep it up. She took the pot to the spring and dipped it full of water and took it to the horse. He drank it dry with a great sound of suction. She refilled the pot at the creek and started back. The snow fell hard out of a dull low sky and it whited her coat sleeve where she held out her arm carrying the pot. A wind blew up and flapped her collar against her face.

When she had nearly reached the hut, something, a slight

movement, drew her eye upslope toward where she had entered the village the afternoon before. There, picking their way through the snow, went a flock of wild turkeys, ten or twelve of them among the bare trees of the hillside. A big male, colored pale grey as a dove, led them. He would take a step or two and then stop and probe in the snow with his bill and then move on. When the turkeys walked uphill they pitched forward, their backs nearly horizontal to the ground. Their walking looked effortful, like old men harnessed to loads with tumplines. They were slim-bodied birds, long, not at all configured like yard turkeys.

Ada moved slowly until she had put the hut between herself and the birds. She went in and set the pot down by the fire. Stobrod lay quiet. His eyes were closed and his face ashy yellow, the color of cold lard. Ruby rose from where she sat beside him and busied herself setting the water to boil and readying the herb roots.

—There are turkeys on the hillside, Ada said to Ruby as she bent over her work, peeling and mincing the roots.

Ruby looked up. I could do to grease my chin with a turkey leg, she said. That shotgun's charged, both barrels. Go kill us one.

—I've never fired a gun, Ada said.

—It's about as easy a thing as there is. Pull back the hammers, point it, fit the bead in the notch, trip either trigger, and don't shut your eyes when you do it. If you miss, pull the other trigger. Clamp the gun butt hard to your shoulder, or it might break your collarbone when it kicks. Move slow, for wild turkeys have the gift to disappear on you. If you can't get at least twenty steps near to them, don't waste a load.

Ruby began mashing the root pieces against a stone with the flat of the knife blade. But Ada did not move, and Ruby looked up again. She saw the uncertainty on Ada's face.

Ruby said, Quit puzzling over it. The worst you can do is fail to kill a turkey and there's not a hunter in the world hasn't done that. Go on.

Ada climbed the slope with great care and deliberation. She could see the turkeys moving through the stand of chestnuts ahead of her and above her. They walked in the direction the falling snow was slanting on the wind. They were traversing the slope and seemed in no hurry. When the grey male found something to eat, they would bunch up and pick at it on the ground and then move ahead.

Ada knew Ruby to be wrong in saying the worst one could do was miss. Everyone in the community had heard the story of the war widow from down the river. The winter previous, the woman had climbed a tree into a deer stand and had dropped her gun and it discharged when it hit the ground so that, in effect, she shot herself out of the tree. She was lucky to have lived to be ridiculed for it. The woman had broken a leg in the fall and never walked straight thereafter, and she had two buckshot scars in her cheek like pox marks.

Thinking such worrying thoughts of poor huntsmanship and its consequences, Ada made troubled progress up the slope. The shotgun felt long and misbalanced before her and seemed to quiver in her hands. She tried to circle around into the turkeys' path and wait for them, but they shifted directions and went more directly up. She followed them for some time, climbing when they climbed and stopping when they stopped. As she walked she tried to be quiet and still in her movements. She set each foot down slowly, letting the snow muffle her steps, and she was glad she wore britches, for trying to be stealthy in long skirts and their underlying petticoats would be impossible, like walking through the woods flapping a bed quilt around.

Even with all her care, Ada feared that the birds would do as Ruby claimed and vanish. She did not take her eyes off them and was patient and eventually she closed to about the distance Ruby had specified. The turkeys stopped and swiveled their heads to look around. She stood still and they did not see her. They pecked in the snow for food. Ada guessed that was about as clear a shot as she was likely to get, so she raised the gun slowly and

sighted on the trailing birds. She fired, and to her amazement a pair fell. The others took off flying low in a turmoil, and in their fright they flew downhill right at her. For a second, two hundred pounds of birds tore through the air about her head.

They went to cover in a laurel brake, and Ada stood and remembered to breathe. She thought back and could find no memory of a kick, though her shoulder felt numb. She did know—even though she had never used a firearm of any type in her life and had just the one discharge to tell her—that the shotgun's action was vague, that the trigger pull was long and had a crackle to it and that it was a matter of some uncertainty where along its travel you would find the point of tension and release. She looked down at the scrollwork of the gun, the motif of vines and leaves and the elaborate hammers which carried out that theme. She let the second one down slowly from where it stood at alert.

When Ada reached the fallen birds, she found a hen and a young cock. Their feathers had the hue and glint of metal, and one scaly grey foot of the hen was still clenching and unclenching in the snow.

Inman heard a shot at no great distance from where he stood. He pulled back the main hammer of the LeMat's to full cock and went forward. He came out from under the dense hemlock shade into a chestnut grove which sloped off toward a bold creek tumbling somewhere below. The light was low and grainy and snow was falling in the chestnuts and had frosted their limbs. He walked down into them and there was a gap in the way they grew so that the black trunks stood rowed on either side and the white fringe of limbs met overhead to shape a tunnel. Underneath was the suggestion of a lane, though no road had ever run there. The snow blew hard and smeared details. Though Inman could see clearly but three trees ahead through the blur, it seemed that at the end of the lane was a vague circle of light fringed around

with snowy limbs. He held the pistol loose in his hand, its muzzles aimed nowhere in particular other than forward. His finger made contact with the trigger so that all the metal parts linking it with the hammer touched and tightened like a spark running through from one to the other.

He walked ahead, and soon a figure bloomed out of the light before him, a black silhouette arched over by tree limbs. It stood straddle-legged at the end of the chestnut tunnel and when it saw him it brought to bear on him a long gun. The place was so quiet Inman could hear the click of metal as a hammer was thumbed back.

A hunter, Inman guessed. He called out, saying, I'm lost. And besides, we don't know enough about one another to start killing one another yet.

He stepped forward slowly. First he could see the turkeys laid each by each on the ground. Then he saw Ada's fine face atop some strange trousered figure, like a mannish boy.

—Ada Monroe? Inman said. Ada?

She did not answer but just looked at him.

He was to the point that he figured, based upon experience, that his senses were not a thing to put much stock in. He believed his thought life might have gone astray so that it had no more direction to it than a litter of blind puppies in a box lid. What he saw might be some trick of light working on a disordered mind, bad spirits come upon him in form to befuddle. People saw things in the woods, even those with full bellies and steady minds. Lights moving where no lights could be, the forms of those long dead walking through the trees and speaking words in lost voices, trickster spirits in the shape of your deepest desire leading you on and on to die mazed in some laurel hell. Inman racked back the little secondary shot-shell hammer of the LeMat's.

Ada, hearing her name spoken, was confused. She let the muzzles to the shotgun droop some inches from where they had been aimed at his chest. She examined him and did not know

him. He appeared to be a beggar in cast-off clothes, rags thrown over a rood of sticks. His face was drawn and hollow-cheeked above the stubbled beard, and he stared at her out of strange black eyes shining deep in their sockets under the shadow of his hat brim.

They stood wary, about the number of paces apart specified for duelists. Not clasping heart to heart as Inman had imagined, but armed against each other, weapons glinting hard light into the space between them.

Inman studied Ada for trickery from within himself or from the spirit world. Her face was firmer than he remembered, harder. But the more he saw the more he believed it to be truly her, despite the unlooked-for costume. So, having in the past taken up arms thoughtless to the consequences, he decided now to put them away the same. He let down his hammer and brushed back his jacket and stuck the pistol under his belt. He looked her in the eyes and knew it was her and was overcome by love like a ringing in his soul.

He did not know what to say, so he said what his dream in the gypsy camp had told him. I've been coming to you on a hard road and I'm not letting you go.

But something in him would not let him step forward to embrace her. It was not only the shotgun keeping him back. Dying was not the point. He could not step forward. He held out his empty hands palms up at his sides.

Ada still did not know him. He seemed to her some madman awander in the storm, knapsack on his back, snow in his beard and on his hat brim, speaking wild and tender words to whatever appeared before him, rock and tree and rill. Likely as not to cut somebody's throat, would be Ruby's estimation. Ada raised the shotgun again so it would break him open if she but pulled the trigger.

—I do not know you, she said.

Inman heard the words and they seemed just. Entirely warranted, and in some way expected. He thought, Four years gone

warring, but back now on home ground and I'm no better than a rank stranger here. A wandering pilgrim in my own place. Such is the price I'll pay for the past four years. Firearms standing between me and everything I want.

—I believe I have made a mistake, he said.

He turned to walk away. Go on up to the Shining Rocks and see would they have him. If not, take up Veasey's quest and walk to Texas or parts even more ungoverned, if such existed. But there was no trail to follow. Ahead of him just trees and snow and his own steps filling fast.

He turned back to her and held out his empty hands again and said, If I knew where to go I'd go there.

It might have been timbre of voice, angle of profile. Something. Length of bone in his forearm, shape of knucklebones under the skin of his hands. But suddenly Ada knew him, or thought she did. She lowered the shotgun to where it would but cut him off at the knees. She said his name and he said yes.

Then Ada had only to look at his drawn face to see not a madman but Inman. He was blasted and ravaged, worn ragged and weary and thin, but he was nevertheless Inman. Hunger's seal on his brow, like a shadow over him. Yearning for food, warmth, kindness. In the hollows of his eyes she could see that the depredations of the long war and the hard road home had left his mind scoured and his heart jailed within the bars of his ribs. Tears started in her eyes, but she blinked once and they were gone. She lowered the muzzles toward the ground and put her hammer to rest.

—You come with me, she said.

She paired the turkeys' feet for handles and grabbed them up breast to breast, and when she did their wings opened and their heads flopped and their long necks twined as if in strange inverted love. She walked off carrying the gun balanced over her shoulder, stock behind, the barrel held loosely in her upraised left hand. Inman followed and he was so tired he did not even think to offer to take some of her load.

They came curving down the slope through the chestnuts and before long they could see the creek and its mossy boulders and the village far below them, smoke rising from the chimney of Ruby's hut. The smell of the smoke rose through the woods.

As they walked, Ada talked to Inman in the voice she had heard Ruby use to speak to the horse when it was nervous. The words did not much matter. You could say anything. Speculate in the most common way on the weather or recite lines from *The Ancient Mariner*, it was all the same. All that was needed was a calming tone, the easement of a companion voice.

Ada therefore talked of the first thing that came to mind. She counted off the features of the current scene they inhabited. Herself in dark huntsman's clothes returning with game down wooded hills, the hutments of a village below with smoke rising, blue mountains all around.

—It lacks but fire on the ground and a few people to make it Hunters in the Snow, Ada said. And she talked on seamlessly, recollecting her viewing of that painting years ago with Monroe during their European travels. He had disliked its every feature, finding it too plain, too muted in its colors, lacking any reference to a world other than this. No Italian would have any interest in painting such a thing, had been Monroe's view. Ada, though, had been drawn to it and she had circled around it for a time but ultimately lacked courage to say how she felt, since her reasons for liking it were, point-for-point, identical to those Monroe used as support for his disapproval.

Inman was too cloudy in his thinking to follow anything she said other than that she spoke of Monroe as if he were dead and that she seemed to have a clear destination in mind and that some note in her voice said, Right this minute I know more than you do, and what I know is everything might well be fine.

the far side of trouble

The hut was hot and bright from the leaping fire at the hearth, and with the door shut there was little sign to say if it was morning or night outside. Ruby had made coffee. Ada and Inman sat drinking it, so close to the fireside that the melted snow in their coats steamed around them. Nobody said much of anything and the place seemed tiny with four people in it. Ruby hardly acknowledged Inman's existence other than to dip a bowl of grits and set it on the ground beside him for breakfast.

Stobrod rose into partial consciousness and moved his head from side to side. He opened his eyes, and they had a look of confusion and hurt in them. Then he lay still again.

—He doesn't know where he is, Ada said.

—How could he? Ruby said.

Stobrod, his eyes closed, said to no one in particular, There was so much music back then.

He put his head down and lapsed into sleep again. Ruby went and stood over him and stripped back her sleeve and put her wrist to his brow.

—Clammy, she said. That can be good or bad.

Inman looked at the bowl of grits and could not decide whether to take it up or not. He set the coffee cup beside it. He tried to think what the next thing ought to be. But overwearied and warm from the fire, he could not keep his eyes open. His head bobbed and came back up, and then he had to work to bring his eyes into focus. There were so many things he wanted, but the first thing he needed was sleep.

—That one looks played out, Ruby said.

Ada folded a blanket and made him a pallet on the floor. She led him to it and tried to help him with his boot laces and with his coat, but he would have none of it. He stretched out and fell asleep fully clothed.

Ada and Ruby stoked the fire and left the two men bedded down. While Inman and Stobrod slept, the snow fell and fell, and the women spent a cold and almost wordless hour collecting wood and cleaning out another of the cabins and cutting fir boughs to close up a small breach in the old bark shingles. In this one there were dead bugs all about the floor, dried-up blistered things. They crunched and popped underfoot. Hut-dweller bugs of some antique make. Ada swept them out the door with a cedar limb.

In the floor clutter she found an old wooden beaker. Or a bowl, more like. Its shape was somewhat indeterminate. It had a wide crack where the wood had dried, and the crack was patched with beeswax, cured brittle and hard. She looked at the grain and thought, Dogwood. She pictured in her mind the making of the thing and the use and then the patching of it, and she decided the bowl might stand as marker for much that was lost.

There was a little niche in the wall of the cabin, a shelf cut in the wood, and she set the bowl there as people in other parts of the world might feature icons or little carved animal totems.

When the hut was clean and the roof patched, they propped the door in place and built a hot fire in the hearth with any kind of wood they could find in the snow. While it burned they made a deep bed of lapped hemlock boughs and they spread it over

with a quilt. Then they plucked and cleaned the birds, heaping the bowels into a big curl of bark peeled off a downed chestnut trunk. Ada threw bark and all behind a tree down the creek, and it made an ugly pink and grey pile in the snow.

Later, when the fire had burned down to a bed of coals, they put on green hickory limbs to smoke. They ran the turkey carcasses through with sharpened sticks and roasted them all day over a slow fire, watching the skins turn to umber. The hut was warm and dim, and it smelled of hickory smoke and turkey. When the wind blew, snow sifted through the patched place in the roof and fell about them and melted. For a long time they sat close to the fire together and neither of them spoke, and they hardly moved other than for Ruby on occasion to go out and throw more wood on the men's fire and to put her wrist to Stobrod's brow.

When dark had begun settling in, Ruby sat by the fire, square to the world, her knees apart and her hands upon her knees. She had a blanket wrapped around her and it stretched taut and flat as a bedsheet across her lap. She worked at a hickory twig with her knife until she had whittled it to a sharp point. She poked irritably at the turkeys with the stick until clear juice ran from under the stippled skin and fell spitting and sizzling in the coals.

—What? Ada said.

Ruby said, I was watching you in there this morning with him and I've been thinking ever since.

—About him? Ada asked.

—You.

—What about me?

—I've been trying to know what you're thinking. But I can't come to it. So I'll just say out plain what's on my mind. It's that we can do without him. You might think we can't, but we can. We're just starting. I've got a vision in my mind of how that cove needs to be. And I know what needs doing to get there. The crops and animals. Land and buildings. It will take a long time.

But I know how to get there. War or peace, there's not a thing we can't do ourselves. You don't need him.

Ada looked at the fire. She patted the back of Ruby's hand where it rested and then Ada picked it up off Ruby's knee and rubbed the palm of it hard with her thumb until she could feel the cords under the skin. She took off one of her rings and put it on Ruby's hand and tipped it down to the firelight to look at it. A big emerald set in white gold with smaller rubies around it. A Christmas gift some years ago from Monroe. Ada made motions to leave the ring where she had put it, but Ruby took it off and twisted it roughly back on Ada's finger.

—You don't need him, Ruby said.

—I know I don't need him, Ada said. But I think I want him.

—Well that's a whole different thing.

Ada paused, not knowing what to say further but thinking furiously. Things that in her previous life were unimaginable suddenly seemed possible, and then they seemed necessary. She thought that Inman had been alone too long, an outlier. Without the comfort of a human touch, a loving hand laid soft and warm on shoulder, back, leg. And herself the same as well.

—What I'm certain I don't want, she finally said aloud, is to find myself someday in a new century, an old bitter woman looking back, wishing that right now I'd had more nerve.

It was after dark when Inman awoke. The fire lay in its ashes and shed but a dim glow into the hut. There was no way to tell how far the night had progressed. And for a while he misremembered even where he was. It had been so long since he had slept in the same place twice that he had to lie still and try to reconstruct in his mind a sequence of days that would put him in a known bed. He sat up and broke sticks and threw them on the coals and blew on them until new flames blazed up and cast shadows on the walls. Only then was he able to say for sure what point of geography he occupied.

Inman heard a sound of breath being drawn, a wet rattle. He twisted around and saw Stobrod on his bunk, his eyes open and black and shining in the light. Inman tried to remember who the man was. He had been told but could not recollect.

Stobrod worked his mouth and it made clicking sounds. He looked at Inman and said, Ary water?

Inman looked around and saw neither pail nor jug. He rose and rubbed his hands on his face and through his hair.

—I'll get you a drink, he said.

He went to his packsacks and took out his water bottle and shook it and found it empty. He put the pistol in his haversack and put the strap over his shoulder.

—I'll be back directly, he said.

He moved the door from the passway. Outside was black night and snow came blowing in.

Inman turned and said, Where did they go?

Stobrod lay with his eyes closed. He made no effort toward reply other than two slight jerks of the forefinger and middle finger of one hand that lay outside his blanket.

Inman stepped out and propped the door back in place and stood and waited for his eyes to come to terms with the dark. There was the smell of cold and snow in the air like sheared metal. And the conflicting odors of woodsmoke and wet creek stones. When he could see enough to walk, Inman made his way down to the water. The snow he walked through lay shank high on the ground. The creek looked black and bottomless and might as well have been running in a deep vein that cut to the world's core. He squatted and put the bottle in to fill, and the water against his hand and wrist felt warmer than the air.

When he started back he could see firelight glowing yellow from gaps in the chinking of the hut where he had slept. And also from another hut farther down the creek. He smelled meat cooking and was suddenly overtaken by a mighty hunger.

Inman went back inside and raised Stobrod up and dribbled

water in his mouth. Then Stobrod propped himself on his elbows, and with Inman holding the bottle he drank until he choked and coughed, and then he drank some more. He held his head up, his mouth open, his neck stretched. His gullet worked to swallow. That attitude and the way his hair stood up and his whiskers bristled and the blind look in his eyes put Inman in mind of a new-hatched nestling, the same frail horrifying appetite to live.

He had seen it before, and he had seen its opposite, the will to die. Men took wounds different ways. Inman had seen so many men shot in recent years that it seemed as normal to be shot as not. A natural condition of the world. He'd seen men shot in every part of the body there was to shoot. And he had seen every result of being shot that there was to have, from immediate death to screaming agony to one man at Malvern Hill who had stood with blood dripping from his shattered right hand and laughed a great booming laugh, knowing that he would not die but would thereafter be unable to pull a trigger.

Inman could not tell what Stobrod's fate might be, neither from the look in his face nor from the condition of his wound, which, upon inspection, Inman found to be dry and packed with spiderweb and root shavings. Stobrod was hot to the touch, but Inman had long since quit trying to forecast whether shot men would die or not. In his experience, great wounds sometimes healed, small sometimes festered. Any wound might heal on the skin side but keep on burrowing inward to a man's core until it ate him up. The why of it, like much in life, offered little access to logic.

Inman built the fire to a blaze, and when the hut was bright and warm he left Stobrod asleep and went outside. He trod in his own tracks to the creek again and cupped up water in his hand and dashed it in his face. He pulled a twig off a beech limb and frazzled the end of it with his thumbnail and brushed his teeth. Then he walked down to the other lighted hut. He stood

outside and listened but could hear no voices. The smell of roasted turkey filled the air.

Inman said, Hello?

He waited and there was no response and he said it again. Then he knocked on the door. Ruby edged it open about a hand wide and looked out.

—Oh, she said, as if she might have been expecting somebody else.

—I woke up, he said. I don't know how long I was asleep. That man back there wanted water and I gave him some.

—You've slept twelve hours or better, Ruby said. She slid the door out of the way to let him in.

Ada sat cross-legged on the ground before the fire, and as Inman entered she looked up at him. The yellow light was on her face, and her dark hair was loose on her shoulders. Inman thought her about as handsome a sight as men are allowed to see, and he was momentarily taken aback by it. She looked so beautiful to him it made his cheekbones hurt. He pressed a knuckle beneath his eye. He did not know what to do with himself. No previous formula of etiquette seemed to apply, other than to take off his hat. There was little ceremony to stand on in an Indian hut in a snowstorm, at least none that he was privy to. He thought he might just as well go and sit beside her.

But before he had any more than made up his mind and set his haversack in the corner, she rose and stepped close in front of him and did a thing he knew he would never forget. She reached behind him and put one palm on the small of his back. The other she pressed against his stomach just above his pant waist.

—You feel so thin between my hands, she said.

Inman could think of no response that he would not later regret as inadequate.

Ada took her hands away and said, When did you last eat?

Inman counted back. Three days, he said. Or four. Four, I think.

—Well, then, you'll be hungry enough not to worry about the details of cookery.

Ruby had already torn the meat off the bones of one bird and had its carcass boiling in the big pot over the fire to make broth for Stobrod. So Ada sat Inman down by the hearth and handed him a plate of the pulled turkey to start nibbling on. Ruby knelt and tended the pot with great concentration. She skimmed the grey foam off the water with a spurtle she had whittled that afternoon out of a poplar limb for lack of the dogwood she needed to do the job right. She flung the foam in the fire, where it hissed away.

While Inman ate the chunks of turkey, Ada worked at composing a real supper. She put dried apple rings in water, and while they soaked she fried wedges of leftover grits in grease from a strip of fatback. When the grits were crisp and brown at the edges, she took them out and put the apples in the pan and stirred them around. She cooked cross-legged for a time, leaning forward to tend the food. Then she turned sideways and stretched one leg out straight before her and kept the other bent. Inman watched with great interest. He had not yet gotten used to her in britches, and he found the poses they allowed her to take stirring in their freedom.

The meal Ada arrived at was rich and brown, flavored with woodsmoke and pork fat, and it was just the kind of food called for by the upcoming solstice of winter, food that offered consolation against short days and long nights. Inman fell to eating it like the starving man he was, but then he stopped and said, Are you not having any?

—We dined some time ago, Ada said.

Inman ate without talking. Before he was finished, Ruby judged that the turkey carcass had given the creek water about all it had to give in the way of sustenance. She dipped out enough to half fill the smaller pot. The broth had the life of the wild bird in it and was rich and cloudy, the color of nutmeats toasted in a dry pan.

—I'll see if I can get him to take some of this, she said.

She took the pot by its bail and went to the door. She stopped before she went out and said, It's time to change the packing on that wound, and I'm going to sit with him some. So to say, I might be gone awhile.

After Ruby left, the hut seemed smaller, its walls pressing in. Neither of them could think of anything much to say. Momentarily, all the old strictures against a young woman and man being left alone in a house came rolling in and made them awkward. Ada told herself that Charleston, with its cadres of ancient aunts enforcing elaborate rituals of chaperonage, was perhaps some made-up place, with only a tangent relation to the world she now lived in, like Arcady or the Isle of Prospero.

Inman, to fill the silence, began commenting favorably on the food, as if he were at a Sunday dinner. But he had hardly begun praising the turkey when he stopped and felt foolish. Then, immediately, longing of so many kinds welled up in him that he was afraid it would all come spilling out in a frightening mess of words if he didn't shut his mouth and find some better direction for his thoughts.

He rose and went to his sack and pulled out the Bartram and showed it to Ada as if it were evidence of something. It was scrolled up and tied with a bow knot of dirty string and had been wet and dry and wet again for months now and looked grimy and ancient enough to contain the aggregate knowledge of a lost civilization. He told her how it had helped sustain him on his journey, how he had read it many a night by the firelight of a lonesome bivouac. Ada was unfamiliar with it, and Inman described it to her as a book concerned with this very part of the world and with everything that was important in it. He shared with her his view that the book stood nigh to holiness and was of such richness that one might dip into it at random and read only one sentence and yet be sure of finding instruction and delight.

To prove his point, he pulled the end of the bow and let the limp coverless book flap open. He put his finger to a sentence

which, as usual, began with the climbing of a mountain and went on for much of a page, and as he read it aloud he could not wait to reach its period for all it seemed to be about was sex, and it caused his voice to crack and threatened to flush his face. It was this:

> Having gained its summit, we enjoyed a most enchanting view; a vast expanse of green meadows and strawberry fields; a meandering river gliding through, saluting in its various turnings the swelling, green, turfy knolls, embellished with parterres of flowers and fruitful strawberry beds; flocks of turkies strolling about them; herds of deer prancing in the meads or bounding over the hills; companies of young, innocent Cherokee virgins, some busy gathering the rich fragrant fruit, others having already filled their baskets, lay reclined under the shade of floriferous and fragrant native bowers of Magnolia, Azalea, Philadelphus, perfumed Calycanthus, sweet Yellow Jessamine and cerulean Glycine frutescens, disclosing their beauties to the fluttering breeze, and bathing their limbs in the cool fleeting streams; whilst other parties, more gay and libertine, were yet collecting strawberries, or wantonly chasing their companions, tantalising them, staining their lips and cheeks with the rich fruit.

When he had finished he sat silent.

Ada said, Is it all like that?

—Not hardly any of it, Inman said.

What he wanted to do was recline on the hemlock bed with Ada beside him and hold her close, as Bartram apparently yearned to lie with the virgins under their bowers. But what Inman did was scroll up the book and set it in the niche of the wall with an old wooden cup. He began collecting the cookware. He stood with it stacked and shifting in his arms.

—I'll go scour these out, he said.

He went to the door and looked back. Ada sat without mov-

ing, staring into the coals. Inman went on down to the water, and he squatted and scrubbed each piece with sand dredged from the bed of the black creek. The snowfall had not eased up a jot. It came straight down hard, and even the boulders in the creek had tall topknots of snow standing on them. Inman blew out clouds of breath through the flakes and tried to think what to do. It would take more than twelve hours' sleep and one big supper to set him right, but at least now he could row his thoughts up again. What he knew he most wanted was to disburden himself of solitude. He had become too proud of walking singular, of his oneness, his loneness.

His stomach and back still held the press of Ada's palms. And as he squatted there in the dark of Cold Mountain, that loving touch seemed like the key to life on earth. Whatever words were in him that needed saying, they ranked as nothing to that laying on of hands.

Inman reentered the cabin with his mind set on going to Ada and putting one hand to her neck and one to her waist and pulling her to him and thereby making all his wishes clear. But when he put the door in its place, the warmth of the fire struck him and his fingers knotted up. They were raw from the sand, stiff from the cold water, frozen in attitudes like the pincers of blue crabs he had seen on his tour of duty along the coast. Nightmare creatures who waved ragged weapons toward all the world, even their own kind. He looked down at the plates and flatware, the pot and frying pan, and he saw they still had a white film of congealed grease on them. So his efforts had been wasted, and he might as well have stayed inside and put the cook pieces facedown in the coals to burn clean.

Ada looked up at him and he watched her take two breaths and then she looked away. He could guess from the set of her face that it had taken all the nerve she could draw up to touch him as she had, to take him between her hands. She could not previously have done a thing so intimate. He knew that. She had made her way to a place where an entirely other order prevailed

from what she had always known. But he had been the one who penned those words in August, and now the burden was on him to find a way to say what he had to say.

Inman set his load down and went to her. He sat behind her and rubbed his palms against each other and then against his thighs. He folded his arms and hugged his hands under them and held them tight against his sides. Then he reached around her and spread his hands to the fire and pressed the insides of his wrists and forearms against her shoulders.

—Did you write me letters while I was in the hospital? he said.

—Several, she said. Two during the summer and a brief note in the fall. But I did not know you were there until you were gone. So the first two letters went to Virginia.

—They didn't find me there, he said. Tell me what they were about.

Ada gave summaries, though not precisely of the letters as they had been. She described them as they would be could she revise them from her current perspective. It was an opportunity life seldom offers, to rewrite even a shard of the past, and so she made the most of it. In amended form, the letters were more satisfactory to both of them than would have been the originals. More revealing in the details of her life, more passionate in sensibility, more certain and direct in expression. Altogether more. The note, though, she left unspoken.

—I wish I'd gotten them, Inman said when she was done. He started to add that they'd have eased some bad days, but he did not want to talk about the hospital right that moment.

He held his hands to the warm hearth and counted back the winters it had lain dark and cold. He said, Twenty-six years since a fire was kindled here.

It gave them a topic. They sat for a while easy together and talked as people do in the ruins of the past, having the unavoidable feeling that we are a short time here, a long time gone. They imagined the last fire that had burned in the hearth, and

they cast the players they imagined sitting before it. A Cherokee family. Mother, father, children, an old grannywoman. They gave them personalities unique to each one, tragic or comic as fit the tale they were telling. Inman made one of the boys to be much like Swimmer, strange and mystic. It satisfied them to invent lives for the imagined family that were more whole by instinct than any they themselves could ever achieve with hard effort. In their story of the family, Ada and Inman gave them premonitions of the end of their world. And though it is true that every age considers the world to be in a precarious state, at the very edge of dark, nevertheless Ada and Inman doubted if at any foretime in history the sense of an ending was as justified as it had been then. Those people's fears had been fully realized. The wider world had found them, even hidden here, and had fallen on them with all its weight.

When they finished, they sat quiet for a while and felt the uneasy feel of occupying space wherein other lives have unfolded and then disappeared.

After awhile Inman told her how all the way home all he could think was hoping she would have him, would marry him. He had kept it in his mind, and it rose up in his dreams. But now, he said, he couldn't ask her to bind herself to him. Not to one disordered as he knew himself to be.

—I'm ruined beyond repair, is what I fear, he said. And if so, in time we'd both be wretched and bitter.

Ada shifted and turned and looked at him over her shoulder. He had unbuttoned his collar in the warmth, and there was the white wound at his neck. Others in the look of his face and in his eyes, which would not quite meet hers.

She turned back around. What she thought was that cures of all sorts exist in the natural world. Its every nook and cranny apparently lay filled with physic and restorative to bind up rents from the outside. Even the most hidden root or web served some use. And there was spirit rising from within to knit sturdy scar over the backsides of wounds. Either way, though, you had

to work at it, and they'd both fail you if you doubted them too much. She had gathered that from Ruby, at least.

Finally, without looking at him, she said, I know people can be mended. Not all, and some more immediately than others. But some can be. I don't see why not you.

—Why not me? Inman said, as if to test the thought.

He took his hands from where he held them to warm at the fire and touched his fingertips to his face to see if they were still cold as the nub ends of icicles. He found them unexpectedly warm. They felt not at all like the parts of a weapon. He reached to Ada's dark hair, which lay loose on her back, and he gathered it into a thick bunch in his hand. He lifted it with one hand, and with the fingertips of the other he brushed the hollow of her neck between the cords that ran down into her shoulders, the fine curls of hair. He leaned forward and touched his lips to the hollow of her neck. He let the hair fall back into place and he kissed her on the crown of her head and took in the remembered smell of her hair. He leaned back and pulled her against him, her waist into his stomach, her shoulders into his chest.

She fit her head under his chin, and he could feel her weight settle into him. He held her tight and words spilled out of him without prior composition. And this time he made no effort to clamp his jaw and pinch them off. He told her about the first time he had looked on the back of her neck as she sat in the church pew. Of the feeling that had never let go of him since. He talked to her of the great waste of years between then and now. A long time gone. And it was pointless, he said, to think how those years could have been put to better use, for he could hardly have put them to worse. There was no recovering them now. You could grieve endlessly for the loss of time and for the damage done therein. For the dead, and for your own lost self. But what the wisdom of the ages says is that we do well not to grieve on and on. And those old ones knew a thing or two and had some truth to tell, Inman said, for you can grieve your heart out and in the end you are still where you were. All your grief

hasn't changed a thing. What you have lost will not be returned to you. It will always be lost. You're left with only your scars to mark the void. All you can choose to do is go on or not. But if you go on, it's knowing you carry your scars with you. Nevertheless, over all those wasted years, he had held in his mind the wish to kiss her there at the back of her neck, and now he had done it. There was a redemption of some kind, he believed, in such complete fulfillment of a desire so long deferred.

Ada did not remember that Sunday in much particularity, one out of many. There was nothing she could add to his recollection of the day to make it into a shared memory. But she knew that what Inman had done in his talking was to reimburse her in his own way for the touch she had given him when he entered the cabin. She reached back and swept the hair from her shoulders and up from her neck and she held it with her wrist against the back of her head. She tipped her head slightly forward.

—Do that once more, she said.

But before Inman could act, there was a sound at the door. By the time Ruby had it out of its frame and stuck her head in, Ada was sitting up again and her hair was down on her shoulders. Ruby regarded the two, their awkwardness and the oddity of him sitting behind her.

—You want me to go back out and cough? she said.

Nobody said anything. Ruby closed the door and put the pot on the floor. She brushed the snow off her coat and beat her hat against her leg.

—His fever's down some right now, Ruby said. But that's not saying much. It goes up and down.

Ruby looked at Inman. She said, I cut some boughs and made up a more proper bed than just a pallet of blankets. She paused and then added, Somebody can make use of it, I reckon.

Ada picked up a stick of wood and poked at the fire and then set the stick in to burn. You go on, she said to Inman. I know you're tired.

Tired as he was, though, Inman had a hard time getting to

sleep. Stobrod snored and muttered snatches of the chorus to an idiotic fiddle tune, which—as best Inman could tell—was no more than this: The higher up the monkey climbed, the greater he showed his ya-ta-dada-la-ta-di-da. Inman had heard men say all kinds of things when they were submerged in the dark of a profound wound, everything from prayers to curses. But this took the prize for foolery.

In the intervals of silence, Inman tried to decide which part of the evening he might dwell on most pleasurably. Ada's hand on his stomach or her request just before Ruby opened the door. He was still trying to decide when he drifted off.

Ada lay a long time awake too. Thinking any number of thoughts. That Inman looked so much older than four years ought to account for, so thin and grim and held within himself. And she thought momentarily that she ought to worry about losing her beauty, about having become brown and stringy and rough. And then she thought that you went on living one day after another, and in time you were somebody else, your previous self only like a close relative, a sister or brother, with whom you shared a past. But a different person, a separate life. Certainly neither she nor Inman were the people they had been the last time they were together. And she believed maybe she liked them both better now.

Ruby flounced in her bed and rolled over and settled down and then turned again. She sat up and puffed in frustration. I can't get to sleep, she said. And I know you're awake over there thinking love thoughts.

—I'm awake, Ada said.

—What's keeping me from sleeping is I'm thinking about what I'll do with him if he lives, Ruby said.

—With Inman? Ada said, confused.

—With Pap. A wound like that will be slow healing. And knowing him, he'll lay extra long a-bed. I can't figure what I'll do with him.

—We'll take him home and care for him is what, Ada said. Hurt as he is, nobody will come looking for him. Not anytime soon. And this war has to end someday.

—I'm obliged, Ruby said.

—You've never been obliged to anybody before, Ada said. I don't care to be the first. Just thank you will do.

—That too, Ruby said.

She was quiet awhile and then she said, Many a night when I was little, alone in that cabin, I wished I could take that fiddle of his up to the jump-off and pitch it and let the wind fly it away. In my mind I'd just watch it go till it was just a speck, and then I'd think about the sweet sound it would make breaking to pieces on the river rocks way down below.

The next day dawned grey and colder yet. The snow no longer spilled hard out of the sky in fat flakes; it came down soft and fine like ground cornmeal falling from between millstones. They all slept late, and Inman took breakfast in the women's hut, turkey broth with shreds of turkey in it.

Then, later in the morning, Ada and Inman fed and watered the horse and went hunting together. They hoped to kill more birds or, if they were extremely lucky, a deer. They walked up the hill and found nothing moving in the woods, nor even animal tracks marking the deep snow. They climbed up through the chestnuts and into the firs and onto the ridge. They followed its spine where it curved. There was still no game but a few chattering boomers high in the fir boughs. Even if you could hit one, it would make but a mouthful of grey meat, so they did not waste a shot.

They came eventually to a flat rock cropped out at a ledge, and Inman brushed the snow off it and they sat cross-legged facing each other, knees to knees, with the ground cloth Inman had in his pack tented over them, resting on the crowns of their heads. What light came through the weave of it was brown and

dim. Inman took the walnuts out of the sack and cracked them open with a stone the size of his fist, and they picked out the meats and ate them. When they were done, he put his hands on Ada's shoulders and leaned forward and touched his forehead to hers. For a while only the sounds of the snow striking the ground cloth broke the silence, but after a time Ada began talking.

She wanted to tell how she had come to be what she was. They were different people now. He needed to know that. She told of Monroe's death, the look on his face in the rain and the wet dogwood petals. She told Inman about deciding not to return to Charleston, about the summer, and all about Ruby. About weather and animals and plants and the things that she was starting to know. All the ways life takes shape. You could build your own life on the observation of it. She still missed Monroe more than she could say, and she told Inman many wonderful things about him. But she told as well one terrible thing: that he had tried to keep her a child and that, with little resistance from her, he had largely succeeded.

—And there's something you need to know about Ruby, Ada said. Whatever comes to pass between you and me, I want her to stay in Black Cove as long as she cares to. If she never leaves I will be glad, and if she does I'll mourn her absence.

—Could she learn to put up with me around is the question, Inman said.

—I think she can, Ada said. If you understand that she is not a servant nor a hired hand. She is my friend. She does not take orders, and she does not empty night jars other than her own.

They left the rock and hunted on, going netherward into a damp swale rich with the odor of places where galax grows, descending through scattered clumps of twisted laurel to a thin creek. They walked around a blown-down hemlock stretched across the woods floor. The plate of roots stood as high in the air as the gable end of a house, and clenched in the roots many feet above the ground were stones larger than whiskey barrels.

Down in that hollow, Ada found a stand of goldenseal, the crowfoot leaves withered but identifiable where they stuck through the thinner snow on the lee side of a poplar so big through the trunk it would have taken five people holding hands in a circle to go around it.

—Ruby needs goldenseal for her father, Ada said.

She knelt at the tree and grubbed at the plants with her hands. Inman stood and watched. The scene was a plain one. Just a woman on her knees digging in the ground, a tall man standing and looking about, waiting. If not for the store cloth of their coats, it could have been any place in time at all. So few markers to show any particular epoch. Ada knocked the dirt from the pale roots and put them in her pocket.

It was in standing that she spotted the arrow in the poplar. Ada's eyes nearly skimmed right over it, marking it as a broken twig, for a part of the shaft remained, though not the fletching. The wood was half rotted away, but still bound to the head with tight windings of sinew. Grey flint point, chipped in smooth scoops. As perfect in symmetry of shape as a handmade thing can be. It lay buried more than an inch into the tree, some of that from the growing of the tree around it in a welted scar. But enough remained exposed to see that the head was broad and long. Not a little bird point. Ada aimed a finger at it to draw Inman's attention.

—Deer arrow, Inman said. Or man killer.

He wet a thumb tip on his tongue and ran it across the revealed portion of the cutting edge like one checking the hone on a pocketknife.

—It would cut meat yet, he said.

During the late-summer plowing and harrowing, Ada and Ruby had unburied any number of bird points and scrapers, but this seemed somehow different to her, as if yet partially alive because of its placement. Ada backed up and regarded it in perspective. Summing up much, it was yet such a little thing. A

missed shot a hundred years back. Maybe more. Long ago. Or not long if one took the right view. Ada stepped to the tree and put a finger on the end of the shaft and wiggled it. Firm.

It would have been possible to frame the arrow as some relic, a piece of another world, and Ada did something like that. She saw it as an object already numbered among the things that were.

But it did not seem entirely so to Inman. He said, Someone went hungry. Then wondered, Was the missing due to want of skill? Desperation? Shift of wind? Bad light?

—You mark this spot in your mind, he said to Ada.

And Inman went on to recommend that they revisit it throughout their lives to check the advancement of rot along the arrow shaft, the growth of the green poplar wood around the flint point. He described a future scene, he and Ada bent, grey as ash, bringing children to the tree in some metallic future world, the dominant features of which he could not even imagine. By then the shaft would be gone. Fallen away. And the poplar would be yet stouter, grown round to envelop the stone entirely. Nothing visible but a lobed scar in bark.

Inman could not imagine whose they would be, but the children will stand entranced and watch as the two old people cut into the soft poplar with knives and dig out a dipperful of new wood, and then, suddenly, the children will see the flint blade as if it had been conjured up. A little piece of art with a clear purpose is how Inman pictured it. And though Ada could not fully envision that distant time, she could imagine the amazement on little faces.

—Indians, Ada said, caught up in Inman's story. The old couple will just say, Indians.

They returned to the village that afternoon without game. All they had to show for the outing was the goldenseal and firewood. They dragged the wood behind them and it carved bands and lines in the snow. Big limbs from a chestnut and smaller ones

from a cedar. They found Ruby sitting by Stobrod. He was to some extent awake and seemed to know Ruby and Ada, but he was frightened of Inman.

—Who's that big dark man? he said.

Inman went and squatted at Stobrod's side so as not to loom over him. He said, I gave you water. I'm not after you.

Stobrod said, Well.

Ruby wet a cloth and swabbed at his face and he struggled against it like a child. She mashed pieces of the goldenseal and packed it into the wounds and she brewed other pieces into tea and made Stobrod drink it. When she was done he fell immediately asleep.

Ada looked at Inman, the tiredness in his face. She said, I believe you ought to go do the same.

—Just don't let me sleep past dark, Inman said. He went out, and while the door was open Ada and Ruby could see snow behind him, streaking the air in its falling. They could hear the sounds of him breaking limbs, and in a minute the door opened again. He set an armload of chestnut wood down just inside and then he left. They built the fire up and sat together for a long time with their backs against the cabin wall, a blanket around them.

Ada said, Tell me what we'll do next, when warm weather comes. What things to put the place in order?

Ruby took up a stick and drew out a map in the dirt, Black Cove. She put in the road and the house and the barn, scratched up areas to show current fields, woodlots, the orchard. Then she talked, and her vision was one of plenty and how to get there. Trade for a team of mules. Reclaim the old fields from ragweed and sumac. Establish new vegetable gardens. Break a little more newground. Grow enough corn and wheat to suit their needs for bread. Enlarge the orchard. Build a proper can house and apple house. Years and years of work. But they would one day see the fields standing high in summer with crops. Chickens pecking in the yard, cows grazing in the pasture, pigs foraging on the hillside mast. So many that they could have two bunches: bacon pigs, thin

of leg and long of side; and ham pigs, close-coupled and stout, with their bellies swinging against the ground. Hams and bacon sides hanging thick in the smokehouse; a skillet good and greasy all the time on the stove top. Apples heaped in the apple house, jar after jar of vegetables rowed on shelves in the can house. Plenty.

—It will be a sight to see, Ada said.

Ruby rubbed her map away with her palm. They sat quiet, and after a while Ruby slumped and leaned her shoulder into Ada's and dozed off, tired from the effort of imagination. Ada sat and watched the fire and listened to its pop and hiss, and later the brittle fall of its embers. She smelled the sweet woodsmoke and thought that it would be a measure of one's success at attending to the details of the world if one could identify trees by the scent of their smoke. It would be a skill one might happily aspire to master. There were many worse things to know. Things that did damage to others and eventually to oneself.

When Ruby awoke, it was late in the afternoon, almost dark. She sat up and blinked her eyes and rubbed her face and yawned. She went to check on Stobrod. She touched his face and forehead, pulled back the covers and looked at his wound.

—His fever's back up, she said. Night will be the crisis, I believe. He'll stay or go, but tonight will be the deciding of it. I'd better not leave him.

Ada came over and put her wrist to Stobrod's forehead. She could feel no difference from earlier tests. She looked at Ruby, but Ruby would not look back.

—I wouldn't feel right leaving him tonight, Ruby said.

It was dark when Ada walked down the creek to the other hut. The snow fell in fine flakes. What lay on the ground was so deep she had to walk awkwardly, stepping high-kneed, even though she trod in earlier footsteps. The snow held whatever light came through the clouds so that the earth seemed lit evenly from within, luminous as a mica lantern. She opened the door quietly and entered. Inman lay asleep, and he did not stir. The

fire had burned low. Before it, Ada saw that his things were laid out to dry like objects displayed in a museum, as if each one needed space around it to reveal its true meaning and be properly valued. His clothing, his boots, his hat, rucksack, haversack, cook gear, sheath knife, and the great ugly pistol with its attendant parts: ramrod and cap tin and nipple pick and cartridges, and the wadding, powder, and buckshot for the shotgun barrel. To be complete as a display, it needed but the Bartram taken down from its niche and laid alongside the pistol. A white printed card to label what one saw: The Outlier, His Kit.

Ada took off her coat and put three cedar limbs on the fire and blew on the coals. Then she went to Inman and knelt beside him. He lay with his face to the wall. The bed of hemlock boughs smelled sharp and clean with the needles crushed under him. She touched his brow, smoothed back his hair, ran her fingertips across his eyelids, cheekbones, nose, lips, stubbled chin. She drew back the blanket and found that he had his shirt off, and she pressed her palm to the side of his neck, the tight new scar of his wound. She ran her hand to his shoulder top and gripped him tight and held him there.

He woke slowly. He shifted in the bed and turned and looked at her and seemed to understand her intent, but then, apparently without willing it, his eyes closed and he slept again.

The world was such an incredibly lonely place, and to lie down beside him, skin to skin, seemed the only cure. The wish to do it swept through Ada's mind. Then, like leaves stirring in the wind, something akin to panic shivered within her. But she put it away from her and stood and started undoing the waist button and long strange row of fly buttons on her britches.

She discovered them to be a garment you cannot remove gracefully. The first leg came off fine, but then in switching her weight from one foot to the other she lost her balance and had to crow-hop twice to get it back. She looked toward Inman and found his eyes were open, watching her. She felt foolish and wished she were in the dark instead of standing before the low

yellow flames of the smoky cedar fire. Or that she were wearing a gown which she could let fall in a smooth cascade around her. A pool at her feet which she could step away from. But here she stood with Monroe's britches still clenched around one leg.

—Turn your back, she said.

—Not for every gold dollar in the Federal treasury, Inman said.

She turned away from him, nervous and awkward. Then when she was undressed she held her clothes before her and half turned toward him.

Inman sat up with the blanket around his waist. He had been living like a dead man and this was life before him, an offering within his reach. He leaned forward and pulled the clothes from her hands and drew her to him. He put the flats of his palms on her thigh fronts, and then he moved his hands up her flanks and rested his forearms on her hipbones and touched his fingertips to the swale at the small of her back. He moved his fingers up and touched one by one the knobs of her backbone. He touched the insides of her arms, ran his hands down her sides until they rested on the flare of her hips. He bowed his forehead to the soft of her stomach. Then he kissed her there and she smelled like hickory smoke. He pulled her against him and held her and held her. She put a hand to the back of his neck and pulled him harder, and then she pressed her white arms around him as if forever.

With the snow piling up outside, the warm dry cabin hidden in its fold of the mountain felt like a safe haven indeed, though it had not been such for the people who had lived there. Soldiers had found them and made the cabin trailhead to a path of exile, loss, and death. But for a while that night, it was a place that held within its walls no pain nor even a vague memory collection of pain.

Later, Ada and Inman lay woven together on their bed of hemlock boughs. The old cabin was nearly dark, and the cedar limbs

smoked in the hearth and the hot resin smelled as if someone had walked through swinging a censer. The fire popped. Snow hissed and sighed as it fell. And they did what lovers often do when they think the future stretches out endless before them as bright as on the noon of creation day: they talked ceaselessly of the past, as if each must be caught up on the other's previous doings before they can move forward paired.

They talked through most of the night, as if charged by law with recounting in the greatest of detail their childhoods, their youths. And they both painted them as idylls. Even the brutal muggy heat of Charleston summers took on an element of drama in Ada's telling. When Inman reached the war years, though, he accounted for them in only the weak detail of a newspaper account—the names of the generals who had commanded him, the large movements of troops, the failure and success of various strategies, the frequent force of blind luck in determining which side prevailed. What he wanted Ada to know was that you could tell such things on and on and yet no more get to the full truth of the war than you could get to the full truth of an old sow bear's life by following her sign through the woods. A claw mark on a bee tree and a great pone of greasy scat shot through with yellow berry seeds told only two brief and possibly misleading installments in the big black mystery of the bear itself. No man, not even if you went all the way up to Lee, could accurately describe more than one blunt forehand of the bear—its hooked black claws, the plump cracked pads, the coarse and shiny hair cupping down over the paw ends. Inman figured he himself might only know something as fleeting as the smell of her breath. No one could know the entirety any more than we can know the life of any animal, for they each inhabit a world that is their own and not ours.

All Inman would reveal of a personal nature were little stories like the time during winter camp of sixty-two when the mud-and-stick chimney of his hut caught fire, and the bark-and-moss roof fell burning onto him and his sleeping mates, and they

ran whooping and laughing out into the cold in their underdrawers and watched it burn and threw snowballs at each other, and then when the fire died down they fed it with fence rails to keep warm through the night.

Ada asked him if he had ever seen the great celebrated warriors. The allegedly godlike Lee, grim Jackson, gaudy Stuart, stolid Longstreet. Or the lesser lights. Tragic Pelham, pathetic Pickett.

Inman had seen all except Pelham, but he told Ada he had nothing to say about them, neither the living ones nor the dead. Nor did he care to comment upon the Federal leaders, though he had seen some from a distance and knew the rest by their acts. He wished to live a life where little interest could be found in one gang of despots launching attacks upon another. Nor did he want to enumerate further the acts he himself had committed, for he wanted someday, in a time when people weren't dying so much, to judge himself by another measure.

—Then tell me of your long journey home, Ada said.

Inman thought about it, but then he let himself imagine he had at last come out on the far side of trouble and had no wish to revisit it, so he told only how along the way he watched the nights of the moon and counted them out to twenty-eight and then started over, how he watched Orion climb higher up the slope of sky night by night, and how he had tried to walk with no hope and no fear but had failed miserably, for he had done both. But how on the best days of walking he achieved some success in matching his thoughts to the weather, dark or bright, so as to attune with what freak of God's mind sent cloud or shine.

Then he added, I met a number of folks on the way. There was a goatwoman that fed me, and she claimed it's a sign of God's mercy that He won't let us remember the reddest details of pain. He knows the parts we can't bear and won't let our minds render them again. In time, from disuse, they pale away. At least such was her thinking. God lays the unbearable on you and then takes some back.

Ada begged to differ with a part of the goatwoman's thoughts. She said, I think you have to give Him some help in forgetting. You have to work at not trying to call such thoughts up, for if you call hard enough they'll come.

When they had momentarily exhausted the past, they turned to the future. They talked of all kinds of prospective things. In Virginia, Inman had seen a sawmill, portable and water powered. Even in the mountains, clapboard houses were overtaking log, so he thought that such a sawmill would be a fine thing to have. He could haul it to a man's land and set it up and saw out the material for a house from the man's own timber. There would be an economy in that, and a satisfaction for the man as well, for he could sit in his completed house and delight in all its parts coming right from his own land. Inman could take payment in cash, or lacking that he could be paid in timber, which he could then mill and sell. He could borrow money from his family to buy the equipment. It was not a bad plan. Many a man had got rich on less.

And there were other plans. They would order books on many topics: agriculture, art, botany, travel. They would take up musical instruments, fiddle and guitar or perhaps the mandolin. Should Stobrod live, he could teach them. And Inman aspired to learn Greek. That would be quite a thing to know. With it, he could continue the efforts of Balis. He told her the story of the man in the hospital, his lost leg and the sheaf of papers he had left behind him at his sad passing. It's not without sense they call it a dead language, Inman said in conclusion.

They talked on, and time was what they discussed. They detailed an imaginary marriage, the years passing happy and peaceful. Black Cove put in order to Ruby's specifications. Ada described the plans in detail, and all Inman wished to amend was the absence of goats, for he would like to keep a few. They agreed they neither gave two hoots now as to how marriages were normally conducted. They would do as they pleased and run their lives by the roll of the seasons. In autumn the apple

trees would be bright and heavy with apples and they would hunt birds together, since Ada had proved so successful with the turkeys. They would not hunt with the gaudy Italian piece of Monroe's but with fine simple shotguns they would order from England. In summer they would catch trout with tackle from the same sporting country. They would grow old together measuring time by the life spans of a succession of speckled bird dogs. At some point, well past midlife, they might take up painting and get little tin fieldboxes of watercolors, likewise from England. Go on country walks, and when they saw a scene that pleased them, stop and dip cups of water from a creek and form the lines and tints on paper for future reference. Contest with each other to see which might more successfully render the scene. They could picture ships navigating the treacherous North Atlantic for some decades to bring them fine implements of diversion. Oh, the things they would do.

They were both at such an age that they stood on a cusp. They could think in one part of their minds that their whole lives stretched out before them without boundary or limit. At the same time another part guessed that youth was about over for them and what lay ahead was another country entirely, wherein the possibilities narrowed down moment by moment.

spirits of crows, dancing

By the morning of the third day in the village the clouds broke open to clear sky, bright sun. The snow began to melt. It dropped in wads from the bent limbs of trees, and all day there was the sound of water running under the snow on the ground. That evening the moon rose full from behind the ridge, and its light fell so bright as to throw crisp shadows of tree trunks and tree limbs on the snow. The pearly night seemed not day's opposite but a new variant of it, a deputation.

Ada and Inman lay under covers for some time twined and talking, the fire low and the door to their hut open, letting a brilliant trapezoid of cold moonlight project onto their bed. They composed a plan for themselves, and it took much of the night to talk out. The shape of light moved across the floor and its angles changed, and at some point Inman put the door back in its place and stoked the fire. The plan, despite the length of time it took to form, was simple and in no way unique to them. Many other pairs of lovers in those last days reached identical conclusions, for there were but three courses to pick from, each dangerous and in its own way bitter.

The logic they followed was simple. The war was as good as lost and could not go on many more months. It might end in spring and it might not. But by no act of imagination could it be pictured as continuing past late summer. The choices were these. Inman could return to the army. Short-handed as they were, he would be received with open arms and then immediately be put back in the muddy trenches of Petersburg, where he would try to keep his head down and hope for an early end. Or he could stay hidden in the mountains or in Black Cove as an outlier and be hunted like bear, wolf, catamount. Or he could cross the mountains north and put himself in the hands of the Federals, the very bastards who had spent four years shooting at him. They would make him sign his name to their oath of allegiance, but then he could wait out the fighting and come home.

They tried to devise other plans, but they just spun out illusions. Inman told Ada of Veasey's dream of Texas, the wildness and freedom and opportunity of it. They could get a second horse, a camping kit, set out riding west. And if Texas proved bleak there was the Colorado territory. Wyoming. The great Columbia River territory. But the war was out there too. If they had money, they could sail to some far off sunny place, to Spain or Italy. But they had no money and there was the blockade. As a last resort, they could fast for the prescribed number of days and wait for the portals of the Shining Rocks to open and welcome them into the land of peace.

Finally, they acknowledged that there were limits to things. Those original bitter three were all the choices the war allowed. Inman rejected the first as unacceptable. And Ada vetoed the second as, in her estimation, the most dangerous. So by default it was the third they settled on. Over the Blue Ridge. Three days or four of steady walking, keeping to wilderness trails, and then he would cross the state line. Put up his hands and bow his head and say he'd been whipped. Salute their striped banner which he'd fought all he could. Learn from the faces of the enemy that, contrary to the teachings of various religions, the man that whips

generally feels better than the man that takes the whipping, no matter who's in the wrong of the matter.

—But this too, Ada said to him. It's often believed by preachers and old women that being beaten breeds compassion. And they're right. It can. But it also breeds hardness. There's to some degree a choice.

In the end, what they both vowed to keep their minds on was the homecoming some months hence. They would go forward from there into whatever new world the war left behind. Make their part of it match the vision of the future they'd talked out to each other during the two nights previous.

On the fourth day in the village, patches of brown leaves and black dirt began to open up in clearings, and mixed flocks of nuthatches and titmice came to them and pecked at something on the uncovered ground. That day Stobrod could sit unassisted and talk so as to make partial sense, which Ruby said was about all you could expect of him, even in the brightest bloom of health. His wounds were clean and odorless and showed signs of soon beginning to knit up. And he could eat solid food, though all they had left was a little bit of grits and five squirrels that Ruby had shot and gutted and skinned. She had skewered them on sticks and roasted them with the heads on over chestnut coals, and that evening Ruby and Stobrod and Inman ate theirs like you would an ear of corn. Ada sat a minute and examined her portion. The front teeth were yellow and long. She was not accustomed to eating things with the teeth still in them. Stobrod watched her and said, That head'll twist right off, if it's bothering you.

By the dawning of the fifth day, the snow was better than halfway gone. There were needles thick on the banks of snow that remained under the hemlock trees, and the bark on the trunks was streaked wet and black from the melt. High clouds

had blown in after two days of sun, and Stobrod proclaimed himself ready to travel.

—Six hours home, Ruby said. Seven at most. That's accounting for the poor footing and stopping some to rest.

Ada assumed they would all go as a party, but Inman would not hear of it.

—The woods feel so empty sometimes, and then so full others. You two can go where you want without being bothered. It's us they'd want, he said, flicking a thumb at Stobrod. No sense putting everybody in danger.

He would hear of nothing but that Ruby and Ada walk on ahead. He would come behind shortly with Stobrod astride the horse. Wait in the woods until dark. The next morning, if the weather looked promising, he would set out to surrender. They would keep Stobrod home and hidden, and if the war had not ended by the time he healed, they'd send him across the mountains to join Inman.

Stobrod had no opinion on the matter, but Ruby judged there was sense in what Inman said, so that is what they did. The women started out afoot, and Inman stood and watched them climb the slope. When Ada disappeared into the trees, it was like a part of the richness of the world had gone with her. He had been alone in the world and empty for so long. But she filled him full, and so he believed everything that had been taken out of him might have been for a purpose. To clear space for something better.

He waited awhile and then loaded Stobrod on the horse and followed. Stobrod sometimes rode with his chin bouncing on his sternum and sometimes he sat with his head up and his eyes bright. They passed the round pool, and it was frozen over and the ice was unmarked by a drake or even the carcass of one. It had drowned and sunk to the muddy bottom or flown away. There was no telling which, though Inman pictured it flapping and struggling and then rising into the sky, trailing shards of the ice that had clutched at the taut yellow webs of its feet.

When they came to the forking of the trail, Stobrod looked at the great poplar and the bright blazes of sapwood where the bullets had chipped away the bark. Son-of-a-bitching big tree, he said.

They passed by Pangle's grave, and it lay in the shade on the north slope, and the snow still covered it almost up to the lashed joint of Ada's locust cross. Inman just pointed, and Stobrod looked as they passed. He told about Pangle crawling up to sleep at his back in the cave. The boy wanting nothing but warmth and music. Then Stobrod said, If God was to set out killing every man on earth in order of their demerits, that boy would bring up the hind end of the line.

They wayed on for some miles, dark clouds hovering over them, the pathway rough and steep. They came to a place where laurel thickets rowed the trail on either side and arched over like the roof to a tunnel. Galax thick on the ground, the leaves shiny and maroon. The laurel leaves were clenched in tubes from the cold.

They came out of the tunnel into a little clearing, and they walked on and then they heard sounds behind them. They turned, and there were horsemen moving out to fill the trail.

—Good God, Stobrod said.

Teague said, That's a hard man to kill. Resembles death warmed over, though.

Stobrod looked at the scouts and found them somewhat reconfigured. Teague and the boy he kept at his side remained. They had lost a man or two and gained a man or two in the days since they had shot him. Stobrod recognized a face from the outlier cave, white trash. And the Guard had gained, as well, a pair of mismatched dogs. Droop-eared bloodhound. Wire-beard wolfhound. The dogs sat slouched and casual. Then without prompt from anyone but herself, the wolfhound rose and began sidling toward Inman and Stobrod.

Teague sat astride his horse, the reins loose in his left hand. The other hand he used to monkey with the hammer to his

Spencer carbine, as if uncertain whether pulling it full back were called for.

—We're obliged to you and the boy for setting us onto that cave. Nice dry place to sit out the snow.

The wolfhound cut back and circled, not moving fast, coming at an angle. She would not make eye contact, but everything she did moved her closer.

Inman looked around to gauge the contours of the land to see how it lay for fighting, and he recognized himself back in the familiar terrain of violence. He wanted a stone wall, but there was not one. He studied the Guard and he knew them by the look in their eyes. There was no sense talking with such men. Language would change nothing, no more than gabbling empty sounds into the air. No sense waiting.

He leaned toward Stobrod and made motions to check the halter and lead rope. In a whisper he said, Hold on.

He hit the horse hard on its rump with his left fist, and he pulled out his pistol with his right. In a single curve of motion he shot the wolfhound that was coming toward him and then he shot one of the men. There was not hardly time between the two reports to blink your eyes. The hound and the man fell likestricken, and they moved but little where they fell. Stobrod went bucking off down the trail like a man breaking a three-year-old to saddle. He was gone in the trees.

There was a moment of stillness, and then there was a great deal of motion. The horses all jumped and stepped in place with their hind ends gathered under them. They had no common direction, but they wanted badly to go somewhere other than here. The bloodhound ran among their legs and riled them further, and then he was kicked in the head and went down yelping.

The riders sawed at the reins to hold the horses back. The empty horse the man had been shot off of looked around for guidance, but finding none, it broke to run blindly. It had not gone three strides, though, before it stepped on its dragging

reins and went stumbling into the other horses, and they all went to squealing and spinning, and the riders just tried to hold on.

Inman charged straight at the disordered party of scouts. There was no cover worth the name, just thin trees. No wall to get behind. No direction to go but forward, no time but now. No hope to do anything but run into their midst and try to kill them all.

In full stride, he shot one rider from the saddle. That left but three, and one of them looked already to be in retreat, or his horse had bolted. It went off capering sideways, uphill into a stand of hickory trees.

The two remaining riders were bunched together, and their horses jumped again at the sound of new gunfire and then one of the horses was down and squealing and scrabbling in the dirt to get its hind legs back under it. Its rider was grabbing at his own leg, squeezing it to find the damage where the horse had fallen on him. When he touched a ragged end of bare bone broken through skin and pantleg, he hollered in anguish, and some of it was just sounds and some of it was words, and those were prayers to God and harsh comments about what a heavy thing a horse is. He hollered so loud as to about smother the sound of his horse squealing.

The other horse wheeled out of control. It spun in a tight circle with its neck bent around and its feet bunched under it. Teague yanked at the reins one-handed and held aloft the carbine in the other. He had lost a stirrup, and there was daylight between him and his saddle. He was about to come off, and he fired an involuntary shot into the air. The horse jumped again like you had run a hot poker through it. It wheeled even faster.

Inman ran into the still place around which the horse spun. He reached up and yanked the Spencer from Teague's hand and let it drop to the ground. He and Teague locked eyes, and Teague reached with his free hand to his belt and pulled a long knife and hollered, I'll black my knife blade with your blood.

Inman cocked back the shotshell hammer of the LeMat's and fired. The big pistol about leapt out of his hand, like it was

trying to get away. The charge took Teague in the chest and opened him up. He went tumbling on the ground and lay in a heap, and his horse hopped off a few steps and stood with its eye whites showing and its ears pinned to its head.

Inman turned and looked at the howling man. Now he was howling curses at Inman and scrabbling toward his pistol, which lay in a mess of slush. Inman reached down and picked the Spencer up by the barrel end. He swung it one-handed and took the man in the side of the head with the flat of the butt stock, and the man quit howling. Inman picked up the man's pistol and stuck it in his pant waist.

The downed horse was on its legs again. It was grey and in the low light it looked like the ghost of a horse. It went and stood alongside the other riderless horses, and they all seemed too stunned to flee. They whickered back and forth, seeking any signs that could be interpreted as a comfort to them.

Inman looked around for the last rider. He expected the man to be long gone, but he found him off in the thickest part of the stand of hickory trees, some fifty paces distant. Far enough to make a pistol shot somewhat open to doubt. There was snow still under the trees and a mist rose from it and also from the horse's wet coat, and two puffs of breath rose from its muzzle. The horse was a skewbald mare, and she patterned up so well with the snow and the trees and the patches of open ground that she appeared to be melting into them. Behind the hickories, a steep broken pitch of rock.

The rider tried to jockey the horse to keep a tree between him and Inman, but he was only partly successful at it. In the times when he was exposed, he revealed himself to be but a boy. Inman could see that he had lost his hat. His head was white. He looked to have German or Dutch blood in him. Maybe Irish or some inbred product of Cornwall. No matter. He was now American all through, white skin, white hair, and a killer. But he looked as if his first shave lay still ahead of him, and Inman hoped not to have to shoot a boy.

—Come on out of there, Inman said, pitching his voice loud enough to be heard.

Nothing.

The boy stayed behind the tree. All that showed was the rump and the head of the horse bisected by the hickory. The horse stepped a pace forward and then the boy reined her back.

—Come on, Inman said. I'm not asking again. Put down what arms you've got and you can ride on home.

—Naw sir, the boy said. Here's fine.

—Not with me, Inman said. Not fine at all. I'll just shoot your horse. That'll flush you out.

—Shoot her then, the boy said. She ain't mine.

—Damn it, Inman said. I'm looking for a way not to kill you. We can do this so that twenty years on, we might run into one another in town and take a drink together and remember this dark time and shake our heads over it.

—Not and me throw down my pistol we can't, the boy said. Have you shoot me anyway.

—I'm not one of you-all and that's not the way I do. But I'll kill you before I walk down this mountain worrying every step that you're behind a rock drawing a bead on my head.

—Oh, I'd be laying for you, the boy said. I'd be laying.

—Well, that about says it, Inman said. You'll have to come through me to get out of there.

Inman went and picked up the Spencer and checked the tube magazine in the butt stock and found it empty. A spent brass cartridge in the chamber. He threw it down and looked to the cylinder of the LeMat's. Six loads left out of the nine, and the shot barrel fired. He took a paper cartridge from his pocket and bit the end off it and let the powder run into the big barrel. Then he pushed the paper of shot into the barrel and rammed it home with the little ramrod and fitted a brass cap to the nipple. He stood square to the world and waited.

—You're going to have to come out from behind that tree sometime, he said.

In a minute the horse stepped forward. The boy tried to break through the woods and circle back to the trail. Inman ran to cut him off. It was just a man on a mount and one afoot chasing each other in the woods. They used the trees and the lay of the ground, and they went jockeying back and forth, trying to find a clear shot but also trying not to get too close.

The mare was confused and had her own wants, first of which was to go stand shoulder to shoulder with the other frightened horses. Taking the bit in her teeth, she flared off from where the boy was trying to guide her with the reins, and she ran straight at Inman. When she was near to him, she half bucked and then brushed the boy against a hickory trunk and raked him from the saddle. With the bit loose in her mouth, she brayed like a mule and cantered off and went to the other horses and they touched noses and quivered.

The boy lay in the snow where he had fallen. Then he half sat and fiddled with the caps and the hammer to his pistol.

—Put that thing down, Inman said. He had the shot hammer back and the bore leveled at the boy.

The boy looked at him and his blue eyes were empty as a round of ice frozen on a bucket top. He looked white in the face and even whiter in crescents under his eyes. He was a little wormy blond thing, his hair cropped close as if he had recently been battling headlice. Face blank.

Nothing about the boy moved but his hand, and it moved quicker than you could see.

Inman suddenly lay on the ground.

The boy sat and looked at him and then looked at the pistol in his hand and said, They God. As if he had not reckoned at all on it functioning as it had.

Ada heard the gunshots in the distance, dry and thin as sticks breaking. She did not say anything to Ruby. She just turned and ran. Her hat flew off her head and she kept on running and left

it on the ground like a shadow behind her. She met Stobrod and he held Ralph's mane in a death grip, though the horse had slowed to a trot.

—Back there, Stobrod said. He kept on going.

When she reached the place, the boy had already gathered up the horses and gone. She went to the men on the ground and looked at them, and then she found Inman apart from them. She sat and held him in her lap. He tried to talk, but she hushed him. He drifted in and out and dreamed a bright dream of a home. It had a coldwater spring rising out of rock, black dirt fields, old trees. In his dream the year seemed to be happening all at one time, all the seasons blending together. Apple trees hanging heavy with fruit but yet unaccountably blossoming, ice rimming the spring, okra plants blooming yellow and maroon, maple leaves red as October, corn tops tasseling, a stuffed chair pulled up to the glowing parlor hearth, pumpkins shining in the fields, laurels blooming on the hillsides, ditch banks full of orange jewelweed, white blossoms on dogwood, purple on redbud. Everything coming around at once. And there were white oaks, and a great number of crows, or at least the spirits of crows, dancing and singing in the upper limbs. There was something he wanted to say.

An observer situated up on the brow of the ridge would have looked down on a still, distant tableau in the winter woods. A creek, remnants of snow. A wooded glade, secluded from the generality of mankind. A pair of lovers. The man reclined with his head in the woman's lap. She, looking down into his eyes, smoothing back the hair from his brow. He, reaching an arm awkwardly around to hold her at the soft part of her hip. Both touching each other with great intimacy. A scene of such quiet and peace that the observer on the ridge could avouch to it later in such a way as might lead those of glad temperaments to imagine some conceivable history where long decades of happy union stretched before the two on the ground.

epilogue

October of 1874

Even after all this time and three children together, Ada still found them clasping each other at the oddest moments. In the barn loft after knocking down the mud-cup nests of swallows. Behind the smokehouse after stoking a fire with wet cobs and hickory limbs. Earlier this day, it had been out in the potato field while breaking up the ground with big grubbing hoes. They had stood awkward and wide-footed in the furrows, each embracing with one arm, gripping the hoes with their free hands.

Ada first thought to make some wry comment. Do I need to cough? But then she noted the hoe handles. The angles at which they descended to the dirt suggested levers that worked the secret engines of earth. She just went on about her business and let them be.

The boy had never gone back to Georgia and had become a man in Black Cove, and not a half-bad one at that. Ruby had seen to it. She had kept at him the two years he had been a hand, and she did not let up when he became her husband. A foot in the back when that was needed, a hug otherwise. It worked out to about equal measures. His name was Reid. Their babies had

been born eighteen months apart, all boys, with full scalps of black hair and shiny brown eyes like little chestnuts set in their heads. They were growing into stout short things with pink cheeks and ready smiles, and Ruby worked them hard and played them hard. Despite the age difference, when they rolled around in the yard below the boxwoods, they looked alike as a litter of puppies.

Now, late in the afternoon, the three boys squatted around a firepit behind the house. Four small chickens barbecuing over coals on the ground, the boys quarreling with each other over whose turn it was to swab them with a sauce of vinegar and hot peppers.

Ada stood under the pear tree watching them, as she spread a cloth and rowed eight plates nearly lip to lip on the small table. She had thus far missed but one year since the war of having a last picnic there before cold weather set in. And that had been three years ago, an October unlike all others, heavy skies and rain throughout the month except for one day when it had spit snow.

Ada had tried to love all the year equally, with no discrimination against the greyness of winter, its smell of rotted leaves underfoot, the stillness in the woods and fields. Nevertheless, she could not get over loving autumn best, and she could not entirely overcome the sentimentality of finding poignancy in the fall of leaves, of seeing it as the conclusion to the year and therefore metaphoric, though she knew the seasons came around and around and had neither inauguration nor epilogue.

October of 1874 was shaping up, to her delight, just as fine as the month can be in the mountains. It had been dry and warm and clear for weeks, and the leaves had progressed in their change to the point that poplar was yellow and maple was red, but oak was still green. Cold Mountain was a mottle of color rising behind the house. It changed day by day, and if you watched closely you could follow the color as it overtook the green and came down the mountain and spread into the cove like a wave breaking over you slowly.

Shortly, with an hour of daylight left, Ruby came out from the kitchen. At her side, a tall slender girl of nine. Both of them carrying baskets. Potato salad, corn, corn bread, string beans. Reid took the chickens from the coals, and Ruby and the girl spread the food on the table. Stobrod came up from the barn where he had been milking. He set the pail on the ground by the table and the children dipped their cups full. They all took their places.

Later, with twilight settling into the cove, they built up the fire and Stobrod took out his fiddle and played some variant he had made of Bonnie George Campbell, speeding it up and overlaying a dance jig. The children all ran around the fire and yelled. They were not dancing but just running to the music, and the girl waved a burning stick and made cursive shapes in the dim air with the yellow ember at its tip until Ada told her to stop it.

The girl said, But Mama, and Ada shook her head. The girl came and kissed her cheek and danced away and threw the stick into the flames.

Stobrod played the simple figure of the tune around and around until the children were flushed and damp. When he stopped, they collapsed on the ground by the fire. Stobrod took his fiddle down from his chin. He wanted to sing a gospel, and the fiddle was after all the devil's box and universally prohibited from such songs. Nevertheless, he held it preciously, cradled against his chest, the bow depending from a crooked finger. He sang Angel Band, a new tune. The girl sang behind him on the chorus, her voice clear and high and strong. Bear me away on your snowy wings.

Stobrod put the fiddle away, and the children begged for a story. Ada took a book from her apron and tipped it toward the firelight and read. Baucis and Philemon. She turned the pages with slight difficulty because she had lost the end of her right index finger four years previous on the day after winter solstice.

She had been up on the ridge alone cutting trees in the spot where she had marked the sun setting the day before from the porch. The log chain had kinked, and she had been trying to work loose the disordered links when the horse started forward in the traces and pinched off the fingertip clean as snapping a tomato sucker. Ruby poulticed it, and though it took the better part of a year, it healed so neatly you would think that was the way the ends of people's fingers were meant to look.

When Ada reached the story's conclusion, and the old lovers after long years together in peace and harmony had turned to oak and linden, it was full dark. The night was growing cool, and Ada put the book away. A crescent moon stood close upon Venus in the sky. The children were sleepy, and morning would dawn as early and demanding as always. Time to go inside and cover up the coals and pull in the latch string.

acknowledgments

I would like to offer thanks to several people for their support during the writing of *Cold Mountain*. I am happily in their debt. My father, Charles O. Frazier, preserved the family stories and shared them with me. He set me on Inman's trail, and his detailed knowledge of western North Carolina history and culture was helpful throughout. Kaye Gibbons was generous with her advice and encouragement; she took my writing seriously before I did and offered a model of hard work and commitment. W. F. and Dora Beal provided me with a wonderful writer's retreat in the North Carolina mountains, where much of the book was written; the long view from the porch is the book's presiding spirit. Leigh Feldman prodded me along when I bogged down and helped me find the story's direction. Elisabeth Schmitz's thoughtful, sensitive, and enthusiastic editing significantly improved its final shape.

A number of books were helpful in developing the cultural and historical background for the novel, these in particular: Robert Cantwell, *Bluegrass Breakdown: The Making of the Old Southern Sound* (1984); Richard Chase, *Jack Tales* (1943) and *Grandfather Tales* (1948); Walter Clark, *Histories of the Several Regiments and Battalions from North Carolina in the Great War* (1901); Daniel Ellis, *Thrilling Adventures* (1867); J. V. Hadley, *Seven Months a Prisoner* (1898); Horace Kephart, *Our Southern Highlanders* (1913); W. K. McNeil, *Appalachian Images in Folk and Popular Culture* (1995); James Mooney, *Myths of the Cherokee* (1900) and *Sacred Formulas of the Cherokees* (1891); Philip Shaw Paludin, *Victims* (1981); William R. Trotter, *Bushwhackers: The Civil War in North Carolina*, Vol. II, *The Mountains* (1988).

Finally, I would like to offer apologies for the great liberties I have taken with W. P. Inman's life and with the geography surrounding Cold Mountain (6030 feet).